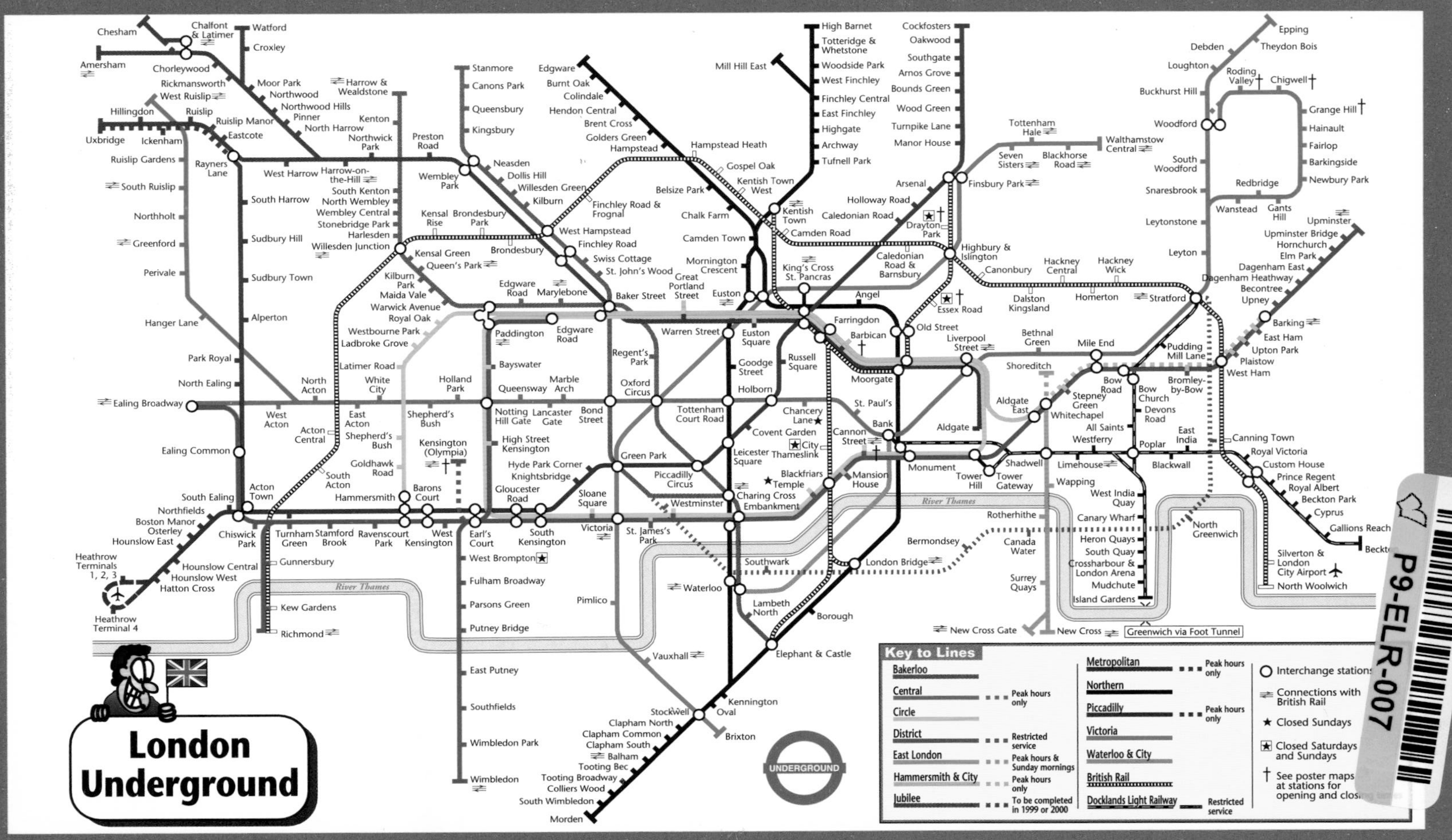

London Underground
Key to Lines
Bakerloo
Central
Peak hours only
Circle
District
Restricted service
East London
Peak hours & Sunday mornings
Hammersmith & City
Peak hours only
Jubilee
To be completed in 1999 or 2000
Metropolitan
Peak hours only
Northern
Piccadilly
Peak hours only
Victoria
Waterloo & City
British Rail
Docklands Light Railway
Restricted service
Interchange stations
Connections with British Rail
Closed Sundays
Closed Saturdays and Sundays
See poster maps at stations for opening and closing
UNDERGROUND
River Thames
Greenwich via Foot Tunnel
Chesham
Chalfont & Latimer
Watford
Croxley
Amersham
Chorleywood
Rickmansworth
Moor Park
Northwood
Northwood Hills
Pinner
North Harrow
West Ruislip
Hillingdon
Ruislip
Ruislip Manor
Eastcote
Uxbridge
Ickenham
Ruislip Gardens
Rayners Lane
South Ruislip
Northolt
Greenford
Perivale
Hanger Lane
Park Royal
North Ealing
Ealing Broadway
Ealing Common
South Ealing
Northfields
Boston Manor
Osterley
Hounslow East
Hounslow Central
Hounslow West
Hatton Cross
Heathrow Terminals 1, 2, 3
Heathrow Terminal 4
West Harrow
South Harrow
Sudbury Hill
Sudbury Town
Alperton
Harrow & Wealdstone
Kenton
Northwick Park
Harrow-on-the-Hill
South Kenton
North Wembley
Wembley Central
Stonebridge Park
Harlesden
Willesden Junction
Preston Road
Wembley Park
Stanmore
Canons Park
Queensbury
Kingsbury
Neasden
Dollis Hill
Willesden Green
Kilburn
Edgware
Burnt Oak
Colindale
Hendon Central
Brent Cross
Golders Green
Hampstead
Hampstead Heath
Gospel Oak
Kentish Town West
Belsize Park
Chalk Farm
Camden Town
Finchley Road & Frognal
West Hampstead
Finchley Road
Swiss Cottage
St. John's Wood
Kensal Rise
Brondesbury Park
Brondesbury
Kensal Green
Queen's Park
Kilburn Park
Maida Vale
Warwick Avenue
Royal Oak
Westbourne Park
Ladbroke Grove
Latimer Road
White City
North Acton
West Acton
East Acton
Acton Central
Shepherd's Bush
South Acton
Goldhawk Road
Acton Town
Chiswick Park
Turnham Green
Stamford Brook
Ravenscourt Park
Hammersmith
Gunnersbury
Kew Gardens
Richmond
Holland Park
Kensington (Olympia)
Barons Court
West Kensington
Earl's Court
West Brompton
Fulham Broadway
Parsons Green
Putney Bridge
East Putney
Southfields
Wimbledon Park
Wimbledon
Edgware Road
Marylebone
Baker Street
Paddington
Bayswater
Queensway
Notting Hill Gate
Lancaster Gate
Marble Arch
Bond Street
High Street Kensington
Hyde Park Corner
Knightsbridge
Gloucester Road
South Kensington
Sloane Square
Victoria
St. James's Park
Westminster
Pimlico
Vauxhall
Regent's Park
Oxford Circus
Green Park
Piccadilly Circus
Great Portland Street
Mornington Crescent
Euston
Warren Street
Euston Square
Goodge Street
Tottenham Court Road
Leicester Square
Covent Garden
Charing Cross
Embankment
Temple
Blackfriars
City Thameslink
Holborn
Chancery Lane
Russell Square
King's Cross St. Pancras
Kentish Town
Camden Road
Caledonian Road
Holloway Road
Drayton Park
Arsenal
Caledonian Road & Barnsbury
Highbury & Islington
Canonbury
Angel
Farringdon
Barbican
Moorgate
Old Street
Essex Road
Liverpool Street
St. Paul's
Bank
Cannon Street
Mansion House
Monument
Aldgate
Aldgate East
Tower Hill
Tower Gateway
Waterloo
Southwark
Lambeth North
Borough
Elephant & Castle
London Bridge
Kennington
Oval
Stockwell
Brixton
Clapham North
Clapham Common
Clapham South
Balham
Tooting Bec
Tooting Broadway
Colliers Wood
South Wimbledon
Morden
Mill Hill East
High Barnet
Totteridge & Whetstone
Woodside Park
West Finchley
Finchley Central
East Finchley
Highgate
Archway
Tufnell Park
Cockfosters
Oakwood
Southgate
Arnos Grove
Bounds Green
Wood Green
Turnpike Lane
Manor House
Finsbury Park
Seven Sisters
Tottenham Hale
Blackhorse Road
Walthamstow Central
Dalston Kingsland
Hackney Central
Hackney Wick
Homerton
Stratford
Bethnal Green
Mile End
Shoreditch
Whitechapel
Stepney Green
Bow Road
Bow Church
Devons Road
Bromley-by-Bow
Pudding Mill Lane
All Saints
Westferry
Poplar
East India
Blackwall
Shadwell
Limehouse
Wapping
Rotherhithe
Canada Water
Surrey Quays
New Cross Gate
New Cross
Bermondsey
West India Quay
Canary Wharf
Heron Quays
South Quay
Crossharbour & London Arena
Mudchute
Island Gardens
North Greenwich
Canning Town
Royal Victoria
Custom House
Prince Regent
Royal Albert
Beckton Park
Cyprus
Gallions Reach
Beckton
Silverton & London City Airport
North Woolwich
West Ham
Plaistow
Upton Park
East Ham
Barking
Upney
Becontree
Dagenham Heathway
Dagenham East
Elm Park
Hornchurch
Upminster Bridge
Upminster
Leyton
Leytonstone
Wanstead
Redbridge
Gants Hill
Snaresbrook
South Woodford
Woodford
Buckhurst Hill
Loughton
Debden
Theydon Bois
Epping
Roding Valley
Chigwell
Grange Hill
Hainault
Fairlop
Barkingside
Newbury Park

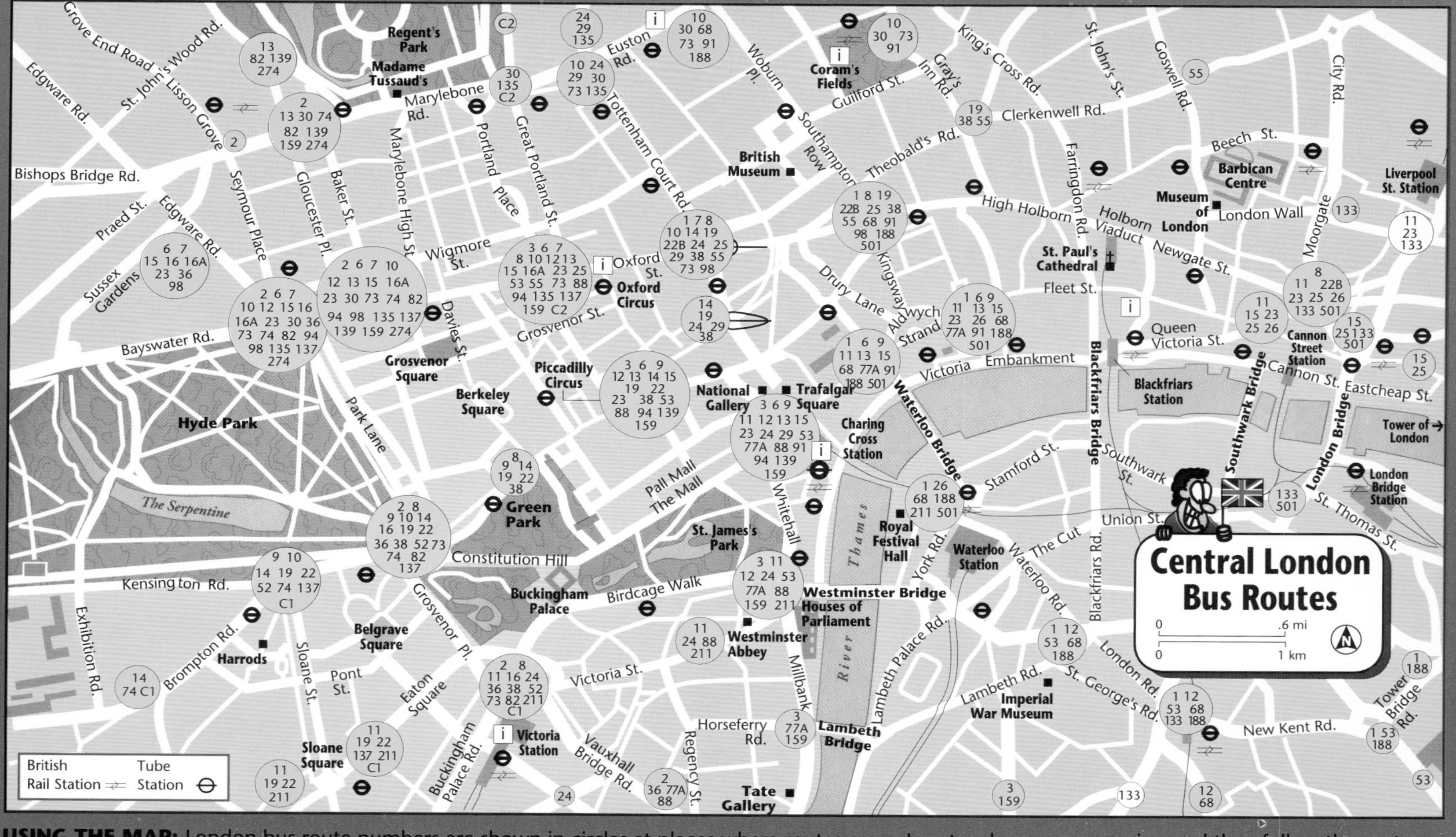

USING THE MAP: London bus route numbers are shown in circles at places where routes cross. Locate where you are going and then follow the route circles back toward your starting point. This will show if and where you need to change buses and the bus route number or numbers for your trip.

London

by Donald Olson

Macmillan Travel Alpha Books
Divisions of Macmillan Reference USA
A Pearson Education Company
1633 Broadway, New York NY 10019-6785

ISBN 0-02-862899-3
ISSN 1520-5614

Editor: Suzanne Roe Jannetta
Production Editor: Lori Cates
Digital Cartography by Raffaele De Gennaro
Illustrations by Kevin Spear
Page Layout: Eric Brinkman, Melissa Auciello-Brogan, Laura Goetz, Sean Monkhouse, and Linda Quigley

Manufactured in the United States of America

Contents

Part 1 What You Need to Know Before You Go 1

1 How to Get Started 2

Information, Please . . . 2
- Tourist Offices: At Your Service . . . 2
- Surfing the Net . . . 3
- Hitting the Books . . . 4

When Should I Go? . . . 4
- Weather (or Not) . . . 5
- Happy Holidays . . . 7
- Without Reservations . . . 7

London Calendar of Events . . . 8

We Are Family: Tips on Traveling with the Kids . . . 11
- Kid-Friendly Sleeps & Eats . . . 11
- The Family That Plans Together . . . 12
- The Long Haul . . . 12
- Parents' Night Out, Kids' Night In . . . 13

Travel Advice for the Senior Set . . . 13
- What . . . No Elevator? . . . 14
- Senior Safety: No Problem . . . 15

Access London: Tips for Travelers with Disabilities . . . 15
- Where to Go for Information & Advice . . . 15
- Escorted Tours . . . 16
- Wheelchair Accessibility in London . . . 17
- Accessible Places to Stay & Dine . . . 18
- Accessing the Sights . . . 18
- Some Other Things to Consider . . . 18

Out & About: Travel Tips for Gays & Lesbians . . . 18
- Lesbigay Resources . . . 19
- Gay Media in London . . . 19

2 Money Matters 20

Making Sense of Pounds & Pence . . . 20

Should I Carry Traveler's Checks? . . . 21

Can I Use My ATM Card in London? . . . 22

Paying with Plastic . . . 23

How Much Money Can I Bring into the U.K.? . . . 24

How Do I Change Dollars to Pounds? . . . 24

Stop, Thief! What If My Money Is Stolen? . . . 25

So, What's This Trip Gonna Cost Me? . . . 26
- Budgeting Basics . . . 27
- Lodging . . . 27
- Transportation . . . 28

Dining 28
Attractions 28
Shopping & Entertainment 28
Drat the VAT 29
What If I'm Worried I Can't Afford It? 29
Budget Worksheet: You Can Afford This Trip 31

3 How Will I Get There? 32
Travel Agent: Friend or Foe? 32
Should I Join an Escorted Tour or Travel on My Own? 34
Before You Sign on the Dotted Line 34
The Pros & Cons of Package Tours 35
Picking the Package That's Right for You 35
Let's Make a Deal: Sample Airline Package Prices 36
Taking Flight: Finding the Best Airfare 37
Consolidators: What Are They & What Can They Do for Me? 38
Surfing the Web to Fly the Skies 38
Does It Matter Which Airport I Fly Into? 39
The Friendlier Skies: Making Your Flight More Pleasant 40
Beating Jet Lag 41
Fare Game—Choosing an Airline 41
Schedule & Flight Information Worksheets 42

4 Tying Up the Loose Ends 46
Passport, Please 47
How Do I Apply for a Passport? 47
When Should I Apply for a Passport? 49
What If I'm Traveling with the Kids? 49
Anything Else I Should Know? 49
What If I (Gulp) Lose My Passport? 50
What About Visas & Health Certificates? 50
I DO Declare! Getting Through Customs 50
Do I Need to Rent a Car in London? 50
Driving on the Left, Passing on the Right 51
Travel Insurance: What Is It & Do I Need It? 52
Aaaachooo! What If I Get Sick Away from Home? 53
Mad Cows & Englishmen 54
I'll Take Two on the Aisle: Making Reservations & Getting Tickets Ahead of Time 54
The Show Must Go On 55
How Do I Find Out What's Playing Where? 55
Pack It Up, I'll Take It 56
What to Bring 56
And How to Pack It 57
It's Not Heavy, It's My Carry-on 58

London Unplugged: Electronics *Not* to Bring 58
Your Last-Minute Checklist: Did You Turn Off the Iron? 59

Part 2 Finding the Hotel That's Right for You 61

5 Pillow Talk: The Lowdown on the London Hotel Scene 62
Location, Location, Location 63
The West End 63
Central London Beyond the West End 68
The Price Is Right 70
What's in It for Me? What You Get for Your Money 71
Taxing Matters 73
What Kind of Place Is Right for You? 73
The ABCs of B&Bs 73
Hotels, Schmotels 74
Gimme the Best Room in the Joint 74
Where Else Can I Look for a Place to Stay? 75
Hotel Strategies for Families Traveling with Kids 75
What If I Didn't Plan Ahead? 76

6 London Hotels from A to Z 77
Quick Picks—London's Hotels at a Glance 78
Hotel Index by Location 78
Hotel Index by Price 79
My Favorite London Hotels 82
Help! I'm So Confused! 106
Hotel Preferences Worksheet 108

Part 3 Learning Your Way Around London 111

7 Getting Your Bearings 112
You've Just Arrived—Now What? 112
If You Arrive at Heathrow 114
If You Arrive at Gatwick 117
If You Arrive at Another Airport 117
Which Way to the Tower? Orienting Yourself in London 118
How to Tell Your Bloomsbury from Your Marylebone: London's Neighborhoods in Brief 119
Where It All Began: The City of London 119
Everywhere You Want to Be: The West End 'Hoods 119
Wait, There's More: Central London Beyond the West End 123
Culturesville: The South Bank 125

Street Smarts: Where to Get Information & Guidance After You Reach London 125

8 **Getting Around London** **127**

Traveling by Tube: The London Underground 128

You've Got a Ticket to Ride 129

The Ins & Outs of Travelcards 129

Double the Fun, Double the Headache: Getting Around by Bus 130

Fare Game 131

In the Wee Hours: Night Buses 131

Home, James, and Don't Spare the Horsepower: London by Taxi 132

Pounding the Pavement 132

Part 4 London's Best Restaurants **134**

9 **The Lowdown on the London Dining Scene** **135**

The Leaders of the Pack 135

Cuisine, Cuisine 136

Location, Location, Location 137

The Price Is Right 137

Eating More for Less 137

Pub Grub 138

Wine Bars 138

Cafes 139

Check, Please 139

At What Time Do We Dine, Dear? 139

Top Hat & Tails? Dressing to Dine 139

10 **London Restaurants A to Z** **141**

Quick Picks: London's Restaurants at a Glance 142

Restaurant Index by Location 142

Restaurant Index by Price 144

Restaurant Index by Cuisine 145

My Favorite London Restaurants 150

11 **Light Bites & Munchies** **176**

Museum Cafes & Restaurants 176

Between the Bread: London Sandwich Bars 177

Fish & Chips 177

Consuming Consumers: Department Store Restaurants 178

Tea for Two, Please: Tearooms & Patisseries 179

Traditional Afternoon Teas 180

Meat Pies & Jellied Eels: Yum, Yum! 181

Pasta on the Run 181

Ice-Cream Parlors 181

Where to Have a Picnic 182

Part 5 Ready, Set, Go! Exploring London **183**

12 Should I Just Take a Guided Tour? **184**
Who, Me? Take a Guided Tour? .184
By Bus, Boat, or Pavement: Which London Tour Is Right for Me? .185
Where Am I? Orientation Tours .185
River Dance: Thames Cruises .187
Walkie-Talkies: Walking Tours of London .188
London Garden Tours .189

13 London's Top Sights from A to Z **190**
Quick Picks—London's Top Attractions at a Glance .191
Index by Location .191
Index by Type of Attraction .194
The Top Sights .195
Worksheet: Your Must-See Attractions .213

14 More Fun Stuff to Do **214**
London for the History Buff .215
London for the Art Lover .218
London for the Bookish .219
More Museums of All Shapes, Sorts & Sizes .220
London for the Young (& the Young at Heart) .222
Dungeons Without Dragons .224
Shakespeare Sights .225
Shipshape London .226
A Fabulous View .227
Where to See How the Other Half Lived .227
Where to Stop & Smell the Roses .228
A Quaint Village Just a Tube Ride Away .229
More Royal Castles & Palaces .230
Greenwich: The Center of Time .231

15 Charge It! A Shopper's Guide to London **234**
Shopping Hours .235
Taxing Matters .235
How to Claim Your VAT Refund .236
I Need a Drugstore! .237
How to Save a Bundle: The London Sales .237
On the Way Home: Duty-Free Airport Shopping .237
Getting Your Stuff Through Customs .238
The Biggies: London Department Stores .239
London's Prime Shopping Grounds .240

16 Battle Plans for Seeing the Sights—Eight Great Itineraries **253**
Itinerary 1—Trafalgar Square, the National Gallery, St. James's Park & Buckingham Palace .254

Itinerary 2—Green Park, Buckingham Palace, Pall Mall, Trafalgar Square, the National Gallery & Soho 256
Itinerary 3—Piccadilly Circus, Trafalgar Square, the National Gallery, the National Portrait Gallery & Covent Garden 258
Itinerary 4—The British Museum, Oxford Street, Hyde Park & Harrods 259
Itinerary 5—The Tower of London, Tower Bridge, Southwark & St. Paul's Cathedral 261
Itinerary 6—Tate Gallery, Houses of Parliament, Westminster Abbey & the South Bank 263
Itinerary 7—Westminster Abbey, Houses of Parliament, Cabinet War Rooms, Whitehall, Downing Street, Horse Guards & Trafalgar Square 265
Itinerary 8—South Kensington Museums, Kensington Gardens & Kensington Palace 266

17 Designing Your Own Itinerary **268**
Back to the Drawing Board—Your Top Attractions 268
Budgeting Your Time 271
Am I Staying in the Right Place? 272
Getting All Your Ducks in a Row 274
Fill-Ins 274
Sketching Out Your Itineraries 275
Planning Your Nighttime Right 281

Part 6 On the Town: Nightlife & Entertainment **283**

18 The Play's the Thing: The London Theatre Scene **284**
The Play May Be the Thing . . . but What's Playing? 285
How Do I Book a Theatre Seat? 285
  Ticket Agencies 285
  How Do I Reserve a Seat Before I Arrive? 286
The Big Hits: London's West End 287
Beyond the West End 290
On the Fringe 291
Seeing the Stars Under the Stars 291
My God, They've Put Me in the Stalls! 292
Theatre Etiquette 292
So, What Should I Wear? 292
Should I Have Dinner Before or After the Show? 292
  When to Eat 292
  Where to Eat 293
  What to Eat 293

19 The Performing Arts **294**
Finding Out What's On 294
Getting Your Tickets 295
Grand Opera 295

Mozart, Mahler & Mussourgsky 296
The Major Minors: Churches with Concert Programs 297
Music Under the Stars 297
A Bit of Everything 298
On Your Toes: Other Dance Venues 298
Humongous Rock Concerts 298
Forget the Live Stuff—I Want to Go to the Movies 299

20 Hitting the Clubs, Pubs & Bars 300
Pub Crawling 300
Hot Spots for Cool Jazz 301
Nothing but the Blues 304
Where to Shake 'n' Sweat to Live Music 305
Where to Go-Go to Disco 305
A Meal & a Song 306
Where to Go If You're Feeling Folksy 306
Where to Go for a Classy Cocktail 307
Into the Wee Hours 307
Where to Go for a Laugh 307
Where Life Is a Cabaret 308
Gaming Clubs 308
Gay Clubs & Discos 308

Part 7 Day Trips from London 309

21 Can I *Really* Get There & Back in a Day? Yes You Can! 310
Bath: Hot Water & Cool Georgian Splendor 312
Oxford: You Don't Need a Degree to Enjoy It 314
Stratford-upon-Avon: In the Footsteps of the Bard 319
Salisbury & Stonehenge: Gothic Splendor & Prehistoric Mysteries 324

Appendices

A London from A to Z—Facts at Your Fingertips 328

B Toll-Free Phone Numbers & Web Sites for Airlines & Hotels 334

Index 335

Maps

London Accommodation Overview 64

West End Hotels 80

Westminster & Victoria Hotels 83

Hotels from Knightsbridge to Earl's Court 84

Marylebone, Paddington, Bayswater & Notting Hill Hotels 88

England 113

London Neighborhoods 120

Restaurants in & Around the City 143

West End Restaurants & Light Bites 146

Westminster & Victoria Restaurants & Light Bites . .149

Restaurants & Light Bites from Knightsbridge to Earl's Court 152

Restaurants & Light Bites from Marylebone to Notting Hill 156

London's Top Sights 192

St. Paul's Cathedral 206

Tower of London 209

Westminster Abbey 212

More London Attractions 216

Hampstead 231

West End Shopping 242

Shopping in Knightsbridge & Chelsea 250

Itinerary 1—Trafalgar Square, the National Gallery, St. James's Park & Buckingham Palace 255

Itinerary 2—Green Park, Buckingham Palace, Pall Mall, Trafalgar Square, the National Gallery & Soho 257

Itinerary 3—Piccadilly Circus, Trafalgar Square, the National Gallery, the National Portrait Gallery & Covent Garden 258

Itinerary 4—The British Museum, Oxford Street, Hyde Park & Harrods 260

Itinerary 5—The Tower of London, Tower Bridge, Southwark & St. Paul's Cathedral 262

Itinerary 6—Tate Gallery, Houses of Parliament, Westminster Abbey & the South Bank 264

Itinerary 7—Westminster Abbey, Houses of Parliament, Cabinet War Rooms, Whitehall, Downing Street, Horse Guards & Trafalgar Square 266

Itinerary 8—South Kensington Museums, Kensington Gardens & Kensington Palace 267

Central London Theatres 289

London Clubs, Pubs & Bars 302

Side Trips from London 311

Bath .313

Oxford 315

Stratford-upon-Avon 321

About the Author

Donald Olson is a novelist, playwright, and travel writer. His last novel, *The Confessions of Aubrey Beardsley,* was published in the U.K. by Bantam Press and his play, *Beardsley,* was produced in London. His travel stories have appeared in the *New York Times, Travel & Leisure,* and many other national publications. He has also written guidebooks on Berlin and Oregon. His new novel, *Queer Corners,* will be published by Bridgecity books in June 1999. London is one of his all-time favorite cities.

An Invitation to the Reader

In researching this book, we discovered many wonderful places—hotels, restaurants, shops, and more. We're sure you'll find others. Please tell us about them, so we can share the information with your fellow travelers in upcoming editions. If you were disappointed with a recommendation, we'd love to know that, too. Please write to:

Donald Olson
The Complete Idiot's Travel Guide to London
Macmillan Travel
1633 Broadway
New York, NY 10019

An Additional Note

Please be advised that travel information is subject to change at any time—and this is especially true of prices. We therefore suggest that you write or call ahead for confirmation when making your travel plans. The authors, editors, and publisher cannot be held responsible for the experiences of readers while traveling. Your safety is important to us, however, so we encourage you to stay alert and be aware of your surroundings. Keep a close eye on cameras, purses, and wallets, all favorite targets of thieves and pickpockets.

Introduction

Let's face it: London could make anyone feel like an idiot, and that goes double for first-time visitors. It's in a foreign country (albeit one where they speak your language), it requires a transatlantic flight, it uses a different currency, and it's huge. Relax! *The Complete Idiot's Travel Guide to London* will boost your London street smarts by several IQ points. It's clear, easy to read, and easy to use.

Part 1 covers the fundamentals: what you need to know before you go. You'll find answers to those endless questions you've been asking yourself—when should I go, how will I get there, should I take an escorted tour, how do I deal with the currency, and what do things cost? Everything from passports to packing is covered.

Part 2 is dedicated to London's hotel scene. I give you the rundown on Central London neighborhoods and the attractions and kinds of hotels you'll find in them. My recommended hotels are listed alphabetically, with special indexes to help you zoom in on price and location.

Part 3 is about orientation and finding your way around the city. I tell you how to get into London from the airport and what transportation options are available to you once you're there.

Part 4 is all about eating. I discuss the different kinds of food you'll encounter and the types of restaurants you'll find. My recommended restaurant list is augmented by special indexes that help you choose what's right in terms of price, location, and cuisine.

Part 5 is about having fun. I tell you about the myriad guided tour possibilities, from sightseeing by bus to special walking tours. Included in this section are all of London's major attractions and scores of its lesser-known tourist delights, with easy-to-follow directions, opening hours, and admission prices. The shopping chapter covers everything from huge department stores to small specialty shops. You'll find worksheets to help you plan your own itinerary, as well as eight suggested itineraries that allow you to get out and explore on your own.

Part 6 is devoted to nightlife and entertainment. I discuss London's theatre, music, and performing arts scenes and tell you how to get tickets. There's also a chapter on pubs, discos, and music clubs.

Part 7 takes you beyond London with four fascinating day trips.

Extras

This book has several special features that you won't find in other guidebooks and that will help you make better use of the information provided and do it faster.

As mentioned above, **indexes** cross reference the information in ways that let you see at a glance what your options are in a particular subcategory—Italian restaurants, downtown hotels, hotels for people with disabilities, and so on.

We've also sectioned off little tidbits of useful information in **sidebars,** which come in five types:

Extra! Extra!

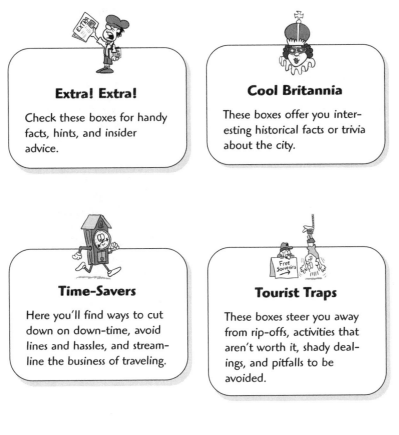

Check these boxes for handy facts, hints, and insider advice.

Cool Britannia

These boxes offer you interesting historical facts or trivia about the city.

Time-Savers

Here you'll find ways to cut down on down-time, avoid lines and hassles, and streamline the business of traveling.

Tourist Traps

These boxes steer you away from rip-offs, activities that aren't worth it, shady dealings, and pitfalls to be avoided.

Dollars & Sense

Here you'll find tips on saving money and cutting corners to make your enjoyable trip affordable.

Sometimes the best way to fix something in your mind is to write it down, and with that in mind we've provided **worksheets** to help you concretize your thinking and make your decisions. (Underlining or highlighting as you read along isn't a bad idea, either.)

Kids A "**kid-friendly" icon** is used throughout the book to identify those activities, attractions, and establishments that are especially suited to people traveling with children.

The **appendixes** at the back of the book list important numbers and addresses covering every aspect of your trip, from reservations to emergencies.

Reader Alert:
London's Phone Numbers Are Changing

The London telephone city codes (area codes) will change as of June 1999. One code, 020, will replace the existing 0171 and 0181 codes. The new code, 020, will be followed by an eight-digit number beginning with either a 7 or an 8 (7 for a number that had a 0171 code, 8 for a number that had a 0181 code). When calling London from the United States, dial 011 (international code), 44 (Britain's country code) and 20 (dropping the initial zero from city code), and then the eight-digit local number. If you're calling within the United Kingdom but not in London, use 020 followed by the new eight-digit number. If you're calling within London, simply leave off the code and dial only the eight-digit number.

Part 1

What You Need to Know Before You Go

"I'm going to London." Gives you a thrill just to think about it, right? The capital of the United Kingdom is one of the world's top destinations, visited year-round by millions of visitors from all corners of the globe. Once you actually arrive, you'll be making your way through one of the most historic, cultured, and exciting cities on earth. There's every reason to feel a tingle of anticipation.

But for all its historic panache, time-honored traditions, quaint corners, and associations with royal pomp and ceremony, London is very much a modern European city (maybe I should say "half-European," since the Brits continue to resist full incorporation with the European Union). It's a rich blend of the very old and the very new. And it's big, in both size and population, with more than nine million residents in the megalopolis known as Greater London.

For first-timers, especially those not accustomed to big-city life, London can be a challenge. It's not laid out on a grid. The crowds and traffic can be intimidating. When crossing the street, you have to look left instead of right. The currency is different. None of these differences is a major obstacle, however. If anything, they should add to the pleasure of your trip, because they're reminders that you are, after all, in a different country (albeit one where you speak the same language as the natives). With a bit of planning and some useful information under your belt, you'll find that visiting London is easier than you thought. It might be far from where you live, but for many people a trip to London is like going home.

Chapter 1

How to Get Started

In This Chapter

- What you need to find out
- Where to go for information
- Thinking ahead
- When to go
- Who do you think you are? (Evaluating your special needs and interests)

Information, Please

The more you know about London before you hop the pond (cross the Atlantic, that is), the more rewarding your trip will be. Your visit begins long before you set foot on a plane; it begins when you start to accumulate travel facts. In addition to this guide, many sources of information are available to help you learn more about this fascinating city before you go—from tourist authority brochures to Internet sites.

Tourist Offices: At Your Service

For general information about London, contact an office of the **British Tourist Authority (BTA).** It has many free brochures (with maps) that can help you plan your London trip. Just keep in mind that the material is promotional and the glossy ads are paid for. Take everything the ads promise with a grain of salt, and compare your data with the information in this book.

In the U.S. The main BTA office is at 551 Fifth Ave., Suite 701, **New York,** NY 10176-0799 (☎ **800/462-2748;** fax 212/986-1188). There's a branch office at 625 N. Michigan Ave., Suite 1510, **Chicago,** IL 60611-1977. There's no phone number for the Chicago office; all requests for information go through the toll-free number listed for New York.

In Canada 111 Avenue Rd., Suite 450, **Toronto,** Ontario M5R 3J8 (☎ **800/847-4885**).

In Australia University Centre, 8th floor, 210 Clarence St., **Sydney** NSW 2000 (☎ **02/267-4555;** fax 02/267-4442).

In New Zealand Suite 305, Dilworth Building, Queen and Customs streets, Auckland 1 (☎ **09/303-1446;** fax 09/377-6965).

Surfing the Net

The Web is one of the best places to find information on London. With a click of the mouse, you can pull up everything from the latest news emanating from No. 10 Downing St. to current opera and concert schedules. You can even book tickets for a West End show. If you're not hooked up to the Internet, your local library will probably have computers you can access. Try these Web sites for starters:

- **www.visitbritain.com** The Web page for the **British Tourist Authority** is an excellent resource for visitors to London and the U.K. in general.
- **www.timeout.co.uk** ***Time Out*** is an indispensable weekly listings magazine that gives you the lowdown on London's cultural events, entertainment, restaurants, and nightlife. (After you arrive, pick up a copy at any newsagent.)
- **www.guardian.co.uk** The ***Daily Guardian,*** London's left-of-center daily newspaper, provides up-to-the minute online news coverage on what's going on in the city.

Cool Britannia

Things came to a head for the scandal-ridden House of Windsor after Princess Diana's death, when national polls showed that the British public viewed the monarchy as aloof, out of touch, and something of a waste of taxpayers' money. The queen was so shocked at the findings (so out of touch), that in February 1998, she decided to hire a Washington-style spin doctor to boost the family's sagging ratings. If you want more history, information, and trivia about the Windsors (really the Saxe-Coburg-Gothas; they wisely changed their German name at the onset of World War I) and the British monarchy in general, check out the official Monarchy Web site at www.royal.gov.uk.

- **www.the-times.co.uk** ***The Times*** and ***The Sunday Times,*** the most traditional of London's papers, are good sources for general news and culture.
- **www.ft.com** The London ***Financial Times*** keeps you abreast of top stories, arts events, and financial news.

Hitting the Books

Most bookstores with travel sections have at least one or two titles pertaining to London. Many have an entire shelf, because London is one of the world's most-visited cities. Here are a few books that might be useful for your trip:

- ***Frommer's London*** is a comprehensive guide to the city. It has extensive hotel, restaurant, shopping, and entertainment coverage; delves into London's neighborhoods; and gives details on all the sites of interest.
- ***Frommer's London from $75 a Day*** is a time-honored Bible for budget-minded travelers who want to visit London but don't want to spend a fortune doing do.
- ***Frommer's Irreverent Guide to London*** is an entertaining guide for sophisticated travelers who want the basic lowdown without a lot of added verbiage.
- ***Frommer's Memorable Walks in London*** is an excellent resource for those who want to explore the city in depth and on foot. Each walking tour provides clear, easy-to-follow directions and describes important sights along the way.
- ***Frommer's Born to Shop London*** is a must for travelers eager to cruise London with a credit card. It covers everything from top department stores to tiny boutiques and will help you find the best, brightest, most unique, and most quintessentially English goods.

When Should I Go?

London is one of those cities that doesn't really have a high or low tourist season. It's popular year-round. So popular, in fact, that according to the latest figures from the British Tourist Authority, nearly 12½ *million* tourists from around the globe visited London in 1996; more than two million of them were from the United States.

When you're planning a London trip, consider your personal preferences and priorities. If you're on a tight budget, getting the lowest possible airfare might be your biggest concern. That means you probably won't be traveling in the high summer season. Likewise, if you can't bear crowds, summer is not a good time to visit London. These considerations should not deter you. London's "off-season" is in many ways an even better time to visit. There are fewer tourists and more things going on culturally.

Most visitors converge on the city from **late April to mid-October.** During those peak-season months, the lines (*queues,* in Britspeak) for major attractions like the Tower of London and Madame Tussaud's can be interminably long, airfares are most expensive, centrally located hotels are often difficult to come by, and you might bump into your next-door neighbor from Poughkeepsie. If "good weather" (or "potentially better weather," I should say) and outdoor activities are high on your priority list, you'll want to plan your trip for the summer. From mid-May to mid-August, London's parks and gardens are at their greenest, and walking can be a pleasure instead of a soaked, shivering endurance test.

London's **off-season** is November 1 to December 12 and December 25 to March 14. At these times, airplane flights are cheaper and hotel prices can drop by as much as 20%. If you arrive after the Christmas holidays, you can also take advantage of London's famous post-Christmas sales (more on this in chapter 15, "Charge It! A Shopper's Guide to London"). Don't let the term "off-season" put you off, because this is in many ways a better time to visit—especially if you're an indoors-oriented culture vulture. Not only can you still visit all the great museums and historic sights, but you'll actually have a bit of elbow room around you. The cultural scene is in full swing, so you'll be able to see plays, go to the opera, and attend concerts. Winter travelers should keep in mind, however, that the city virtually shuts down on December 25 and 26 and New Year's Day, and darkness sets in as early as 4:30pm.

Dollars & Sense

London's **off-season** is November 1 to December 12 and December 25 to March 14. At these times, airfares are cheaper and hotel prices can drop by as much as 20%. If you arrive after the Christmas holidays, you can also take advantage of London's famous post-Christmas sales (more on this in chapter 15).

Weather (or Not)

It's hard to predict just what the weather will be like in London in any given season: It's what you might call "changeable." Remember that England is an island, and its weather patterns are determined by the seas surrounding it and its northern location. In general, however, the climate is fairly mild year-round, rarely dipping below freezing or rising above 80°F (at least for extended periods).

It can be drizzly, it can be muggy, it can be hot, it can be clammy, and it can be glorious. For the daily **London weather report,** you can call ☎ **900/WEATHER** (U.S. only) or check the Web sites for the newspapers listed above.

Spring London is famed for its beautiful parks and gardens. The city is at its green, blooming best in the spring, particularly **April** and **May.** Springtime is when you'll find the gardens and countryside at their peak of lushness. The Chelsea Flower Show, that quintessential London spring event, takes place in May.

Cool Britannia

One thing to keep in mind if you visit London in the winter months is that the British generally keep their thermostats set about 10° lower than Americans. Rather than turn up the heat, they don their woollies. You should do the same—or be prepared for a chronic case of goose pimples.

Summer London has a temperate climate, but occasional summer heat waves can drive the mercury up into the 80s and 90s. **July** and **August,** in particular, can be warm and muggy. A hot spell, exacerbated by London's soot and (unleaded) gas and diesel fumes, can turn the most affable travelers cranky. Keep in mind, too, that most budget-class hotels and many business establishments don't have air-conditioning. Statistically, July and August are also the months of highest rainfall. But when the summer weather is fine, it's very fine indeed, and the city moves outdoors to take advantage of it. There are outdoor theatres, concerts, and festivals to be enjoyed. Summer evenings in London are long and often cool, even if the day has been hot.

Fall The golden glow of autumn casts a lovely spell over London. Falling leaves skitter down the streets and through the squares, there's a crispness in the air, and the setting sun (when you can see it) gives the old stone buildings and church spires a mellow patina. **September** and **October** are wonderful months to visit London, because there are fewer tourists and the city's cultural calendar springs to life. Yes, autumn may bring rain (every season may do that in London), but you're just as likely to encounter what Americans call "Indian summer."

Winter Londoners love to be cozy, and there's no better time for coziness than winter. It might be gray and wet for weeks on end, and by mid-winter it gets dark in the late afternoon. But nothing stops—in fact, everything gets busier. Why? Because this is "the season." Everyone's social calendar is packed, the arts (theatre, opera, concerts) are in full swing, the stores decorate and prepare for Christmas, and Londoners have their city to themselves—sort of (there's another peak London tourist season from about mid-December to Christmas).

London's Average Temperatures (°F) & Rainfall (in.)

	Jan	Feb	Mar	Apr	May	June	July	Aug	Sept	Oct	Nov	Dec
Temp.	40	40	44	49	55	61	64	64	59	52	46	42
Rainfall	2.1	1.6	1.5	1.5	1.8	1.8	2.2	2.3	1.9	2.2	2.5	1.9

Happy Holidays

Americans might be unfamiliar with some British holidays, particularly the spring and summer **bank holidays** (the last Monday in May and August), when everyone takes off for a long weekend. Most banks and many shops, museums, historic houses, and other places of interest are closed then, and public transport services are reduced. The same holds true on other major British holidays: **Christmas, Boxing Day** (the first weekday after Christmas, when Christmas gifts are given to service workers), **New Year's Day, Good Friday, Easter Monday,** and **May Day** (the first Monday in May). The London crowds swell during **school holidays:** mid-July to early September, 3 weeks at Christmas and Easter, and 1 week in mid-October and mid-February (when are those kids ever in school?).

Without Reservations

Given the volume of annual visitors, it's not wise to arrive in London at any time of year without hotel reservations. But if you are planning your trip **between April and mid-October,** and especially if you want to be in London at the **millennium,** it is *essential* that you plan ahead. Agencies in London can help you find a hotel room or B&B during peak tourist season if you turn up in the city without reservations (see chapter 5, "Pillow Talk: The Lowdown on the London Hotel Scene"). However, the queues are usually long, and you never know quite what you'll get or where it will be (you might end up commuting into central London from one of the outlying districts).

London Calling

Let's really talk about getting started—how to make a phone call to London or the United Kingdom from the U.S. First you dial **011,** followed by the **country code** for the U.K., which is **44.** After that, you dial the **city code.** London has two city codes (given for every number in this guide): **0171** covers Central London, and **0181** covers the outlying districts. When calling London from outside the U.K., drop the initial zero from the city code. So dial 171 or 181 then the number you want to call. Keep in mind that London is 5 hours ahead of New York (add another hour for each time zone moving west). *Note: The city codes for London will change as of June 1999. See the "Reader Alert" on page xiv.*

If you want to eat at one of the city's top restaurants or see one of the hottest-ticket West End shows, you might consider reserving that ahead as well. You can find planning information in chapter 4, "Tying up the Loose Ends."

London Calendar of Events

London is brimming with festivals and special events of all kinds, some of them harking back to centuries past. For recorded information on weekly London events, call the London Tourist Board's 24-hour **Visitorcall** at ☎ **0839/123-456** when you arrive. Calls cost 49 pence (about 80¢) per minute and aren't accessible from outside the U.K. You can also call the numbers listed after each event below, but they are all London or U.K. numbers. Better yet, call the British Tourist Authority and ask for information on specific events or request a copy of their free ***London Planner*** brochure; the various BTA phone numbers are listed above.

January

➤ **The London Parade** features marching bands, floats, and the Lord Mayor of Westminster traipsing in a procession from Parliament Square to Berkeley Square. Call ☎ **0181/566-8586** for more details. January 1, noon to 3pm.

March

➤ **St. Patrick's Day** is a big to-do in London, which has the third-largest Irish population after New York and Dublin. No parades, but you'll see lots of general merriment. March 17.

➤ **The Oxford and Cambridge Boat Race,** between Putney Bridge and Mortlake Bridge. Rowing eights from the two famous universities compete for the Beefeater Cup. A good viewing spot is the Hammersmith Mall. The first Saturday in April (but check local press for the exact date).

➤ **London Marathon.** First held in 1981, the London Marathon has become one of the most popular sporting events in London. In 1998 an estimated 30,000 runners took part, men and women, champion athletes and first-timers. The 26.2-mile race begins in Greenwich, winds its way past the Tower of London and along the Thames, and finishes in The Mall in front of Buckingham Palace, one of the best viewing spots. Call ☎ **0171/620-4117** for more information, or write London Marathon, Box 1234, London SE1 8RZ. Mid-April.

May

➤ **Chelsea Flower Show,** Swan Walk, on the grounds of the Chelsea Royal Hospital. One of London's most famous spring events, the flower show draws tens of thousands of visitors from around the world. It's a good idea to order tickets in advance; you can order them from the New York office of **Keith Prowse** (☎ **800/669-8687** or 212/398-1430; tickets@keithprowse.com). Call ☎ **0171/834-4333** for more information. Late May.

➤ **Football Association FA Cup Final,** Wembley Stadium. Remember that "football" in the U.K. is soccer, and that tickets are difficult to obtain given the sport's popularity. Contact Box Office, Wembley Stadium Ltd., Wembley HA9 ODW; ☎ **0181/902-0902.** Mid-May.

June

- **Trooping the Colour.** June 4 is the Queen's official birthday, but her official birthday parade usually takes place in mid-June. The Queen's Horse Guards celebrate "Ma'am's" birthday in Whitehall with an equestrian display full of pomp and ceremony. For free tickets, send a self-addressed stamped envelope from January 1 to February 28 to Ticket Office, Headquarters, Household Division, Chelsea Barracks, London SW1H 8RF; ☎ **0171/414-2279.** Mid-June.
- **Wimbledon Lawn Tennis Championships.** The world's top tennis players whack their rackets at Wimbledon Stadium. Getting a ticket to this prestigious sporting event is complicated. From August 1 to December 31, you can apply to enter the public lottery for next year's tickets by sending a self-addressed stamped envelope to **All England Lawn Tennis Club,** P.O. Box 98, Church Road, Wimbledon, London SW19 5AE. For more information, call ☎ **0181/944-1066** or 0181/946-2244 (recorded information) or visit the Web site at www.Wimbledon.com. Late June to early July.
- **City of London Festival.** The festival presents a series of classical concerts, poetry readings, and theatre in historic churches and buildings, including St. Paul's Cathedral and the Tower of London. Call ☎ **0171/638-8891** for the box office or 0171/377-0540 for more information. Mid-June to mid-July.
- **Royal Academy Summer Exhibition.** This juried exhibition presents more than 1,000 works of art by living artists from all over the U.K. Royal Academy, Piccadilly W1 (☎ **0171/439-7438**). Early June to mid-August.
- **Kenwood Lakeside Concerts.** Kenwood, a lovely estate at the top of Hampstead Heath, is the host of a summer season of Saturday night open-air concerts. Call ☎ **0171-973-3427** for more information. Late June to early September.

July

- **The Proms.** A much-loved standing-room-only event, the BBC Henry Wood Promenade Concerts is a 2-month series of classical and popular concerts at the Royal Albert Hall. Call ☎ **0171/589-8212** for more information. July and August.
- **Royal Tournament,** Earl's Court Exhibition Centre, Warwick Road. Two weeks of pageants in which the British armed forces display their athletic skills and military prowess. For more information, call ☎ **0171/244-0244.** July 21 through August 2; dates may vary from year to year.

August

- **Buckingham Palace** opens to the public. See chapter 13, "London's Top Sights from A to Z," for details. August and September.

- **Summer Rites,** Brockwell Park in South London. This is a gay-oriented festival with bars, funfair, and live performances. Call ☎ **0171/737-2183** for details. August 1.
- **Notting Hill Carnival.** Steel bands, dancing, and Caribbean fun take over in the streets of Notting Hill (Portobello Road, Ladbroke Grove, All Saints Road). Call ☎ **0181/964-0544** for more information. Held over Bank Holiday weekend in August.

September

- **Thames Festival** is a celebration of the mighty river, with giant illuminated floats. Call ☎ **0171/401-3610** for more information. Mid-September.
- **Chelsea Antiques Fair** draws antiques lovers to Chelsea Old Town Hall for 10 days. Call ☎ **01444/482-514** for more information. Mid-September (also held in mid-March).

October

- **Pearly Harvest Festival,** St. Martin-in-the-Fields, Trafalgar Square. This celebration dedicated to the Cockneys features Pearly kings and queens prancing about in their eccentric spangled finery and playing ukuleles. (No, I'm not making this up.) Call ☎ **0171/930-0089** to get more information. First Sunday in October.

November

- **Guy Fawkes Night.** Bonfires and fireworks commemorate Guy Fawkes' failure to blow up Parliament in 1605. Events include the Lord Mayor's Show, in which the new Lord Mayor of London goes on a grand procession through the city from Guildhall to the Royal Courts of Justice in his 18th-century gilded coach; a carnival in Paternoster Square; and fireworks on the Thames. Call ☎ **0171/971-0026** for more information. November 5.
- **State Opening of Parliament.** The Queen sets out from Buckingham Palace in her coach for Westminster, where she reads the government's program for the coming year. (This event is televised.) Call ☎ **0171/219-4272** to find out more. First week in November.
- **London Film Festival.** Although based at the National Film Theatre on the South Bank, the festival presents screenings all over town during most of November. Call ☎ **0171/815-1323** in November for recorded daily updates on what's showing where.

December

- **Christmas lights** go on in Oxford Street, Regent Street, Covent Garden, and Bond Street.
- **Lighting ceremony** of the Christmas tree in Trafalgar Square (the first week of December), which is also the site of **New Year's Eve celebrations.**

We Are Family: Tips on Traveling with the Kids

You'll still see nannies pushing prams and watching their privileged wards in London's parks. But you'll also see plenty of London mums and dads out for a day with the kids. There's no reason why you shouldn't bring your children with you on your trip to London, too. Just bear in mind that London is a huge city, and the crowds can be intimidating (or fascinating) to youngsters. The following resources are useful for family trip planning:

- **About Family Travel,** 424 Bridge St., Ashland, OR 97520 (☎ **800/826-7165** or 541/488-3074; fax 541/488-3067; aft@about-family-travel.com; www.about-family-travel.com), is a travel agency and tour-planning service for families with children. It can tailor a tour specifically for families traveling to London, including airfares, hotels, transportation, theatre tickets, where to go, what to see, and even where to rent a stroller.
- ***Family Travel Times,*** published quarterly by TWYCH (Travel With Your Children), offers a call-in service for subscribers. You can order a subscription ($40 a year) by mail from TWYCH, 40 Fifth Ave., New York, NY 10011 (☎ **212/477-5524;** fax 212/477-5173); or request its information packet, including a sample newsletter, for $2.

Kid-Friendly Sleeps & Eats

Assuming that you reserve in advance and let them know you're traveling with children, most hotels will be happy to accommodate you and your flock. You might require an extra cot or have to share a larger room, but such requests are not out of the ordinary. People with children travel to London every day of the year. In smaller B&Bs, you might run into difficulties, like cramped rooms and shared toilet facilities; ask questions before you reserve. Be sure to look out for the special "Kids" icon in chapter 6 to find hotels that are particularly family friendly.

London has plenty of fast-food American-style places. Your kids will recognize them all: Burger King, McDonald's, Kentucky Fried Chicken. Younger teens will probably want to check out the Hard Rock Cafe in Mayfair or the scene at the Pepsi Trocadero in Piccadilly Circus (see chapter 10), where you'll find theme restaurants such as Planet Hollywood and the Rainforest Cafe.

Extra! Extra!

Kids Look for this icon as you flip through this book. I've used it to highlight those hotels, restaurants, and attractions that are particularly family friendly. Zeroing in on these listings will help you plan your trip more quickly and easily.

Eating out in swankier places is more problematic because the menus are not always geared to the taste buds of younger Americans, and the prices can be exorbitant. Eating at a restaurant with a pretheatre fixed-price menu (usually served from about 6pm to 7pm is one way to keep costs down. London might also be the time and place to introduce your kids to some delicious and exotic cuisine they perhaps haven't tried before: Indian, Chinese, and Japanese, to name just three. In chapters 10 and 11, you'll find a list of restaurants that are particularly family friendly. If the weather is fine, you might also want to consider a picnic in Kensington Gardens—a perennial favorite with children—or Hyde Park (see "Where to Have a Picnic" in chapter 11 for more picnic suggestions).

The Family That Plans Together . . .

Kids can have a great time in London, and if they know about some of the special things in store for them, they'll be as excited about the trip as you are. Before you leave, sit down with your children and plan out a family strategy. Go over the list of sights and activities in chapters 13 and 14. Let them choose a few of the things they'd like to see and do, in order of preference, and make a similar list of your own. You might want to let older children do some London research on the Internet. Then, together, plot out a day-by-day schedule that strikes a balance between your desires and those of your offspring.

You can whet children's appetite for adventure by telling them how you'll be traveling around London in the Underground or taking a boat trip down the Thames. Incite their curiosity about historic sites like the Tower of London or H.M.S. *Cutty Sark*. In short, get their imaginations involved. If all else fails, promise them a meal at the Hard Rock Cafe. Let your younger children read *Peter Pan* and then tell them about his statue in Kensington Gardens.

But don't overschedule, or you'll exhaust yourself and your young ones. Some kid and adult activities can easily overlap. You might want to spend one afternoon in Kensington Gardens: After everyone visits Kensington Palace, the kids can blow off steam in the park. The truth of the matter is that many kid-oriented activities in London are just as interesting for parents. From the dinosaur exhibit in the Natural History Museum to the animatronic robots re-creating historic scenes in Madame Tussaud's, you and your kids will have plenty to look forward to.

The Long Haul

Unless you're flying on the Concorde, the shortest international trip to London (from New York) is about 6 hours; if you're traveling from Australia, air time might be 25 hours. This is a lot of time for kids to sit buckled into a seat. Some of the time can be spent watching one (or more) movies offered by the airlines. But you should also come prepared with some extra diversions: games, puzzles, and books. Request a special menu for children at least 1 day in advance. If baby food is required, bring your own and ask a flight attendant to warm it to the right temperature. Dealing with jet lag can be hard on adults but even harder for the little ones. Don't schedule too much for your first day in London. Get everyone comfortably settled, and take it from there.

Parents' Night Out, Kids' Night In

You're longing to see that hot new play—but what to do with the kids? First, ask your hotel whether it can recommend a local baby-sitting service. Most of the hotels marked with a "Kids" icon in chapter 6 will arrange for baby-sitting. London also has several respected and trustworthy baby-sitting agencies that provide registered nurses, carefully screened mothers, and trained nannies as sitters. The daytime rate at **Childminders** (☎ **0171/935-3000** or 0171/935-2049) is £5.50 ($9) per hour; night rates are £3.70 to £4.70 ($6 to $7.50). There's a 4-hour minimum, and hotel guests pay a £5 ($8) booking fee each time they use a sitter. You must also pay reasonable transportation costs.

Other agencies to try are **Nanny Service** (☎ **0171/935-3515**), the quaintly named **Universal Aunts** (☎ **0171/738-8937**), and **Baby-Sitters Unlimited** (☎ **0181/892-8888**).

Parents who are planning a big night out in London—so big that they won't be returning until the wee hours—have an unusual option for their small ones. **Pippa Pop-ins,** 430 Fulham Rd., SW6 1DU (☎ **0171/385-2458;** fax 0171/385-5706), is a fully licensed children's hotel where you can safely park the little ones for an overnight stay in a lovely, toy-filled nursery staffed by experienced caregivers. The charge for a weekend overnight, including dinner and breakfast, is £50 ($83) per child, plus a registration fee of £15 to £30 ($25 to $50) per child. Baby-sitting is available at £7 ($12) per hour before 11:30pm, and they'll care for your child for the day for a fee of £45 ($74).

Travel Advice for the Senior Set

People over the age of 60 are traveling more than ever before. And why not? Being a senior citizen entitles you to some terrific travel bargains. In most cities, London included, people over the age of 60 often get reduced admission at theatres, museums, and other attractions. Carrying identification with proof of age can pay off in all these situations. *Note:* In London and the U.K., you might find that some discounts are available only to members of a British association; public transportation reductions, for instance, are available only to U.K. residents with British Pension books. But always ask, even if the reduction is not posted.

If you're not a member of **AARP (American Association of Retired Persons),** 601 E St. NW, Washington, DC 20049 (☎ **202/434-AARP**), do yourself a favor and join. You'll get discounts on car rentals and hotels. The association offers $8 yearly ($20 for 3 years) memberships that include discounts of 12% to 25% on Virgin Atlantic flights to London from eight U.S. cities.

National Council of Senior Citizens, 8403 Colesville Rd., Suite 1200, Silver Spring, MD 20910 (☎ **301/578-8800**), is a nonprofit organization offering memberships ($12 a couple) that include a subscription to the council's bimonthly magazine and discounts on hotels, car rentals, and purchases at pharmacies.

Dollars & Sense

Most of the major **airlines**—including American, United, Continental, US Airways, and TWA—offer discount programs for senior travelers. Be sure to ask whenever you book a flight. The discounts are usually about 10% on select fares. Special promotional fares are not discounted.

Elderhostel, 75 Federal St., Boston, MA 02110-1941 (☎ **617/426-8056**), has a variety of university-based educational programs in London and throughout England for those 55 and older. These are great, value-packed, hassle-free ways to learn while you travel. Cost includes airfare, accommodations, meals, tuition, tips, gratuities, and insurance. And you'll be glad to know that there are no grades. One popular London offering, called "Inside the Parliament," is a course that covers the history, settings, culture, and procedures of the oldest Parliamentary democracy in the world. The cost for this course, from New York, is about $3,000.

SAGA International Holidays, 222 Berkeley St., Boston, MA 02116 (☎ **800/343-0273**), has inclusive tours for those 50 and older. Though their tours cover places outside of London (such as Cornwall), you can get a pre- or post-tour London extension.

Grand Circle Travel, 347 Congress St., Suite 3A, Boston, MA 02210 (☎ **800/221-2610** or 617/350-7500; fax 617/350-6206), is another agency that has escorted tours for mature travelers. Write to them for their publication ***101 Tips for the Mature Traveler.***

Literally hundreds of other travel agencies specialize in vacations for seniors. But beware: Many are of the tour-bus variety, with free trips thrown in for those who organize groups of 20 or more. Seniors seeking more independent travel should probably consult a regular travel agent.

The Mature Traveler, a monthly 12-page newsletter on senior-citizen travel, is a valuable resource. It is available by subscription ($30 a year) from GEM Publishing Group, Box 50400, Reno, NV 89513-0400. GEM also publishes ***The Book of Deals,*** a collection of more than 1,000 senior discounts on airlines, lodging, tours, and attractions around the country; it's available for $9.95 by calling ☎ **800/460-6676.**

What . . . No Elevator?

If you're a senior who's fit as a fiddle, London won't present any particular problems for you. But if you're moving more slowly and have trouble with stairs, please be aware that not all hotels—particularly less-expensive B&Bs—have elevators. The steep staircases in some places are a test for anyone with luggage. When you're reserving a hotel, ask whether there is an elevator—or "lift," as they're called in England.

Senior Safety: No Problem

One nice thing about London, though—it might be crowded, but people are generally polite and courteous. You might be jostled on a major street (even this is unlikely), but the British are very orderly when it comes to standing in lines and respecting one's personal space. There's no need to be overly concerned about crime. Yes, it does occur, but with far less frequency than in many other major cities.

Access London: Tips for Travelers with Disabilities

A disability shouldn't stop anybody from traveling. There are more options and resources out there than ever before. More good news is that London is much more accessible for travelers in wheelchairs than it used to be. Many hotels and restaurants are happy to accommodate people with disabilities. All the top sights in chapter 13 and many of the attractions in chapter 14 are wheelchair accessible (it's a good idea to call first to make arrangements and get specific directions to special entrances and elevators). Theatres and performing arts venues are often wheelchair accessible as well.

But the U.K. doesn't yet have a federal program like the Americans with Disabilities Act—though by 2002, some form of legislation might be in place. So if you have any kind of disability, a trip to this huge metropolis is going to require some intensive planning.

In addition to consulting the resources and publications listed below, be sure to discuss with your **travel agent** means of travel that will accommodate your physical needs (train, plane, tour group); special accommodations or services you might require (transportation within the airport, help with a wheelchair, special seating, special meals); and what special assistance you can expect from your transportation company, hotel, tour group, and so on.

Where to Go for Information & Advice

The **British Tourist Authority** (for U.S. addresses, see above) publishes a free brochure called ***Britain for People with Disabilities.*** BritRail's **British Travel Shop,** 1500 Broadway, New York, NY 10036 (mailing address) or 551 Fifth Ave., 7th floor, New York, NY 10176 (for visits in person only), offers several useful publications, including ***A.A. Guide for the Disabled Traveller.*** Call ☎ **800/677-8585** or 212/575-2667. The best and most comprehensive London guide for travelers with disabilities or anyone with a mobility problem is ***Access in London,*** available at many London bookstores for £7.95 ($13). It provides full access information for all the major sites, hotels, and modes of transportation.

A World of Options, a 658-page book of resources for travelers with disabilities, covers everything from biking trips to scuba outfitters. It costs $45 and is available from **Mobility International USA,** P.O. Box 10767, Eugene, OR, 97440 (☎ **541/343-1284,** voice and TDD; miusa@igc.apc.org; www.miusa.org). For more personal assistance, call the **Travel Information Service** at ☎ **215/456-9603** or 215/456-9602 (for TTY). Another good resource is ***How To Travel (A Guidebook for Persons with a***

Disability), by Fred Rosen, Science & Humanities Press, P.O. Box 7151, Chesterfield, MO 63006-7151 (☎ **314/394-4950**).

Access to Travel Magazine, P.O. Box 43, 29 Bartlett Lane, Delmar, NY 12054-1105 (☎ **518/439-4146;** fax 518/439-9004), covers sites and provides practical information for travelers with disabilities. ***Air Transportation of Handicapped Persons,*** a free booklet published by the U.S. Department of Transportation, is available by writing to Free Advisory Circular No. 12032, Distribution Unit, Department of Transportation, Publications Division, M-4332, Washington, DC 20590.

Other Resources in the U.S. **Travel Information Service** (☎ **215/456-9603;** TTY 215/456-9602), a referral service of the Moss Rehab Hospital in Philadelphia, provides travel assistance to telephone callers only. Check out its Web site at www.mossresourcenet.org.

Society for the Advancement of Travel for the Handicapped, 347 Fifth Ave., Suite 610, New York, NY 10016 (☎ **212/447-7284;** fax 212/725-8253; sathtravel@aol.com), is a membership organization with names and addresses of tour operators specializing in travel for people with disabilities. You can call to subscribe to its magazine, *Open World,* or obtain more information at its Web site (www.sath.org).

Vision-impaired travelers should contact the **American Foundation for the Blind,** 11 Penn Plaza, Suite 300, New York, NY 10001 (☎ **800/232-5463**), for information on traveling with Seeing-Eye dogs; it also issues ID cards to those who are legally blind.

Other Resources in London & the U.K. For information and advice on suitable accommodations, transport, and other facilities, contact **Holiday Care Service,** 2nd Floor, Imperial Buildings, Victoria Road, Horley RH6 7PZ, U.K. (☎ **01293/774-535;** TDD 01293/776-943; fax 01293/784-647).

Tripscope, The Courtyard, Evelyn Road, London W4 5JI (☎ **0181/994-9294**), provides travel and transportation information and advice, including tips on airport facilities.

RADAR (Royal Association for Disability and Rehabilitation), 12 City Forum, 250 City Rd., London EC14 8AF (☎ **0171/250-3222;** fax 0171/250-0212), publishes information for travelers with disabilities in Britain.

Artsline (☎ **0171/388-2227**) provides advice on the accessibility of London arts and entertainment events. The **Society of London Theatres,** Bedford Chambers, The Piazza, Covent Garden, London WC2E 8HQ, UK, has a free guide called ***The Disabled Guide to London's Theatres.***

Escorted Tours

Travelers with disabilities might want to consider joining a tour that caters specifically to them. One of the best operators is **Flying Wheels Travel,** 143 West Bridge (P.O. Box 382), Owatonna, MN 55060 (☎ **800/525-6790**), which offers various escorted tours and cruises, as well as private tours in minivans with lifts. Here are some other reliable tour operators for travelers with disabilities who are going to London:

➤ **Accessible Journeys** (☎ **800/846-4537;** fax 610/521-6959; sales@disabilitytravel.com; www.disabilitytravel.com); tours include Britain and London in a minibus or motor coach.

➤ **Access Tours** (☎ **800/533-5343;** fax 914/241-1700); individual customized travel and tours.

➤ **The Guided Tour** (☎ **800/783-5841;** fax 215/635-2637; gtour400@aol.com) has 1- and 2-week guided tours for individuals; there is one staff member for every three travelers.

➤ **Roll Around Britain** (☎ **215/969-0542;** fax 215/969-9251; 105066.2062@compuserve.com) provides specialty travel and tours for small groups or families traveling with a person in a wheelchair.

Wheelchair Accessibility in London

London is an old city, and although its streets and sidewalks are generally kept in good repair, you won't find many modern curb cuts. Public transportation is going to be a concern, but some stations of the London Underground have elevators and ramps. Public buses are not wheelchair accessible. The old black London cabs are roomy enough for wheelchairs. **London Transport's Unit for Disabled Passengers,** 172 Buckingham Palace Rd., SW1 W9TN (☎ **0171/918-3312;** TDD 0171/918-3015; fax 0171/918-3876), publishes a free brochure called ***Access to the Underground.*** It also provides information on wheelchair-accessible "minibus" service (called **Stationlink**) between all the major BritRail stations and Victoria Coach Station in Central London, and it has Braille maps.

Extra! Extra!

Many of the major car-rental companies now offer hand-controlled cars for drivers with disabilities. **Avis** (☎ **800/331-1084**) can provide such a vehicle in London, but drivers need to bring their own disability parking stickers. **Kenning** (☎ **800/227-8990**), another London rental service with hand-controlled cars, supplies parking stickers for those with disabilities. In both cases, you should rent the cars before you leave home.

The **Airbus** (☎ **0181/400-6655**) services from Heathrow Airport to Central London have been converted to take two wheelchair passengers on each bus.

Trains throughout the U.K. now have wide doors, grab rails, and provisions for wheelchairs. For more information, or to obtain a copy of the leaflet ***Rail***

Travel for Disabled Passengers, contact The Project Manager (Disability), British Rail, Euston House, Eversholt Street, London NW1 1DZ (☎ **0171/922-6984**).

Wheelchair Travel, 1 Johnston Green, Guildford, Surrey GU2 6XS, England (☎ **1483/237-772;** fax 1483/237-772; info@wheelchairtravel.co.uk; www.wheelchair-travel.co.uk), is an independent transport service for travelers with disabilities arriving in London. It has self-drive cars and minibuses, and can provide wheelchairs. Driver guides are also available on request. You will need to bring your own stickers and permits for disabilities.

Accessible Places to Stay & Dine

Some hotels and restaurants provide wheelchair ramps, but not all. Most of the less-expensive B&Bs and older hotels do not have elevators, or the elevator is too small for a wheelchair. London bathrooms are often hard to manage if you have a disability. Ask about this when you reserve, or use a travel agency that specializes in travel for people with disabilities. In the hotel descriptions in chapter 6, I've noted those hotels that are equipped in one way or another for visitors in wheelchairs.

Accessing the Sights

All London's better-known museums and sightseeing attractions (listed in chapter 13) are accessible, but in some cases, visiting them requires going to a different entrance or calling ahead for special help and directions. Persons with disabilities are often entitled to special discounts at sightseeing and entertainment venues. These discounts are called **concessions** (often shortened to "concs") in Britain.

Some Other Things to Consider

Before you go, talk to your **physician** about your general physical condition, medical equipment you should take on the trip, and how to get medical assistance when you are away from home. Carry all **prescription medicines** in their original bottles with the contents clearly marked, along with a letter from your doctor. It is advisable to list the generic names of any prescription drugs, in case you need to replace or refill your prescription during your visit. Pack necessary medications in your hand luggage in case your checked luggage is lost or stolen.

If you're in a **wheelchair,** have a maintenance check in advance of the trip and take some basic tools and extra parts if necessary. If you don't use a wheelchair but have trouble walking or become easily tired, consider renting a wheelchair to take with you as checked baggage.

Out & About: Travel Tips for Gays & Lesbians

London has always been a popular travel destination for gays and lesbians (unless, that is, they were fleeing to the Continent to escape prosecution, a sad state of affairs that ended only in 1967). These days, with a more tolerant government at the helm, gay pride is busting out all over the place. The city government has actually spent money to promote gay tourism. There are gay theatres, gay shops, more than 100 gay pubs, famous gay discos, and gay community groups of all sorts.

Old Compton Street in Soho is the heart of London's Gay Village, filled with dozens of gay pubs, restaurants, and upscale bar-cafes. The **Earl's Court** area, long a gay bastion, has several gay and lesbian hotels and restaurants. Check the box in chapter 6, "Best Gay or Gay-Friendly Hotels," for some of the best choices.

Lesbigay Resources

To help plan your London trip, you might want to check out the following Web sites; all of them are specifically geared toward gay and lesbian travelers to London and the U.K.

- www.pinkpassport.com
- www.demon.co.uk/world/ukgay/
- www.gaytravel.co.uk
- www.gayguide.co.uk
- *Gay London Guide,* a listing of current gay venues, can be accessed at www.gaylondonguide.co.uk.

London's Lesbian and Gay Switchboard (☎ **0171/837-7324**) also has a Web site (accessed on Yahoo) at www.llgs.org.uk/.

The newest and most useful travel guide is ***Frommer's Gay & Lesbian Europe,*** available at most bookstores and at A Different Light Bookstore in New York, 151 W. 19th St. (☎ **800/343-4002**), or San Francisco, 489 Castro St., San Francisco, CA 94114 (☎ **415/431-0891;** www.adlbooks.com).

Gay Media in London

Several gay magazines are available in gay pubs, clubs, bars, and cafes and are useful for their listings and news coverage. The most popular are *Boyz, Pink Paper,* and *QX* (Queer Xtra; www.qxmag.co.uk). *Gay Times* (www.gaytimes.co.uk) is a high-quality monthly news-oriented magazine available at most newsagents. ***Time Out,*** indispensable for its city-wide listings (including gay listings), appears at newsagents on Wednesday.

Chapter 2

Money Matters

In This Chapter

- How to make sense of pounds and pence
- Traveling with cash, credit cards, traveler's checks (or all three)
- How and where to change your dollars into pounds once you arrive
- What things cost in London
- The lowdown on taxes and tipping
- Strategies for cutting costs and a can't-miss budget worksheet

If there's one thing that first-time travelers to foreign destinations really worry about, it's money. Conversion rates, where to change one currency into another, what things cost, whether to use traveler's checks or credit cards, how ATMs work—there's a seemingly endless list of money matters to consider. And you have to contend with them because you'll be spending money every day of your trip, often in ways that you don't at home. London's currency is different, I'll grant you that. But it's certainly not incomprehensible. In this chapter, you'll learn the basics of British pounds and pence.

Making Sense of Pounds & Pence

Britain's unit of currency is the **pound sterling (£).** Every pound is divided into **100 pence (p).** Coins come in denominations of 1p, 2p, 5p, 10p, 20p, 50p, £1, and £2. Notes are available in £5, £10, £20, and £50 denominations. The notes are larger than U.S. dollars and don't always fit easily in American wallets.

The **exchange rate** fluctuates every day. In general, $1 U.S. = £0.67 (or £1 = $1.65 U.S.). These are approximate figures, but they're what I've used for all prices in this guide (rounded to the nearest dollar). Check with your bank or in the newspaper to find out what the current rate is.

Simple Currency Conversions

U.S.	U.K.	U.K.	U.S.
$1	67p	£1	$1.65
$5	£3.35	£2	$3.30
$10	£6.70	£5	$8.25
$20	£13.40	£10	$16.50
$50	£33.50	£20	$33.00
$100	£67.00	£50	$82.50

Should I Carry Traveler's Checks?

Traveler's checks are something of a throwback to the days when people used to write personal checks all the time instead of going to the ATM. In those days, travelers couldn't be sure of finding a place that would cash a check for them on vacation. Because traveler's checks could be replaced if lost or stolen, they were a sound alternative to filling your wallet with cash at the beginning of a trip.

These days, traveler's checks are less necessary because most European cities, including London, have 24-hour ATMs linked to a national network that most likely includes your bank at home (see "Can I Use My ATM Card in London?" below). Relying on ATM cards and credit cards is much cheaper and easier than relying on traveler's checks. You'll get a better exchange rate using ATMs and credit cards, you'll avoid paying commission for cashing traveler's checks, and you won't have to deal with the hassle of showing your passport every time you want to cash a check.

One compelling reason still exists, though, to bring along some traveler's checks: **insurance.** They're theft-proof; unlike hard currency, if you lose your traveler's checks, you can get replacements at no charge (be sure to keep a list of the check

Extra! Extra!

You might have heard that a single European currency, called the **euro,** is about to go into effect in Europe. Eleven countries will adopt the euro on January 1, 1999, but contentious Britain has opted out from switching over just yet. Even if you are traveling on from London to other countries in the European Union, you don't have to worry about dealing with the euro. The changeover in 1999 is basically between financial institutions and businesses. The various national currencies will not switch over to euros until sometime in 2002.

numbers in a safe place, separate from the checks themselves; otherwise, you can't get reimbursed). If you rely solely on your ATM and credit cards and your wallet gets stolen, a handful of traveler's checks in your money belt can save the day.

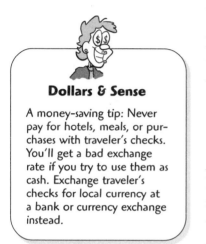

You can get traveler's checks at almost any U.S. bank. **American Express** offers checks in denominations of $10, $20, $50, $100, $500, and $1,000. You'll pay a service charge ranging from 1% to 4%, though AAA members can obtain checks without a fee at most AAA offices. You can also get American Express traveler's checks over the phone by calling ☎ **800/221-7282;** Amex gold and platinum cardholders who call this number are exempt from the 1% fee.

Dollars & Sense

A money-saving tip: Never pay for hotels, meals, or purchases with traveler's checks. You'll get a bad exchange rate if you try to use them as cash. Exchange traveler's checks for local currency at a bank or currency exchange instead.

Visa also offers traveler's checks, available at Citibank locations across the country and at several other banks. The service charge ranges between 1.5% and 2%; checks come in denominations of $20, $50, $100, $500, and $1,000. **MasterCard** also offers traveler's checks. Call ☎ **800/223-9920** for a location near you.

Your traveler's checks will be in dollars. After you arrive in London, you'll have to convert them into pounds and pence.

Can I Use My ATM Card in London?

Yes. A decade ago in Europe, your bank card was just so much more useless plastic. These days you can saunter up to an ATM in virtually any city (and most small towns) and get local cash out the same as you would at home. ATMs offer a fast, easy, and cheap way to exchange money. You get to take advantage of the bank's bulk exchange rate, which is better than any rate you'll get on the street. You can withdraw only as much cash as you need every couple of days, so that you don't feel insecure carrying around a huge wad of cash. (Note, however, that many banks impose a fee ranging from 50¢ to $3 every time you use the ATM in a different city. Your own bank may also charge you a fee for using ATMs from other banks.)

You'll find 24-hour ATMs all over London—outside banks, in large supermarkets, and even in some Underground (subway) stations. **Cirrus** (☎ **800/424-7787** or 800/4CIRRUS; www.mastercard.com/atm) and **Plus** (www.visa.com/atms) are the two most popular networks; check the back of your ATM card to see which network your bank belongs to. The toll-free number and Web sites give you specific locations of ATMs where you can withdraw money while on vacation. (Plus also has a toll-free ATM locator number, ☎ **800/843-7587,** but it locates only ATMs in the U.S.) You will need a four-digit PIN (personal identification number) to use your ATM in

London; if you have a six- or eight-digit PIN, you will need to have a new PIN assigned.

You can also use ATMs to get **credit card cash advances,** but you'll need a PIN suitable for overseas use. Make certain that you have your PIN before you arrive in London. Check with your bank or credit card company for details. If you've forgotten your PIN or didn't even know you had one, call the phone number on the back of your credit card and ask the bank to send it to you. It usually takes 5 to 7 business days, although some banks will do it over the phone if you tell them your mother's maiden name or some other security clearance. Keep in mind, however, that when you get a cash advance on your credit card from an ATM, interest usually starts accruing immediately (and you won't receive frequent-flyer miles on an airline credit card).

Dollars & Sense

If you go to withdraw cash from an ATM and you get a weird message saying your card isn't valid for international transactions, most likely the bank just can't make the phone connection to check it (occasionally this epidemic can be citywide). Don't panic. Try another ATM or wait until the next day.

Paying with Plastic

Credit cards are invaluable when traveling. They are a safe way to carry money and provide a convenient record of all your travel expenses when you arrive home. **Visa, MasterCard, American Express,** and **Diners Club** are all widely accepted in London. A Eurocard or Access sign displayed at an establishment means that it accepts MasterCard.

On my trips, I have come to rely more and more on credit cards to pay for hotels, restaurants, theatre and concert tickets, and many other purchases. This isn't because I'm a chargeaholic; it's just much easier than carrying around a wad of pound notes or stopping to cash traveler's checks or use an ATM every other day. Credit card purchases are usually translated from pounds to dollars at a favorable rate and show up on your monthly statement, so it's easier to keep track of expenditures.

Many travelers use credit cards because they can get **cash advances** at any bank or from an ATM (see "Can I Use My ATM Card in London?" above), although you'll start paying interest on the advance the moment you receive the cash, and you won't receive frequent-flyer miles on an airline credit card.

Extra! Extra!

British retailers now have the option to charge more for goods and services bought by credit card, although they're obliged to display a clear indication that differentiated pricing applies.

How Much Money Can I Bring into the U.K.?

There are no exchange controls in Britain, so you can bring as much cash and as many traveler's checks into the country as you want. It's always better to arrive with too much rather than too little, because upon arrival you might be asked by the immigration authorities just how much money you have with you. To enter the U.K., visitors must have sufficient means (cash, traveler's checks, credit cards) to maintain and accommodate themselves and any dependents without recourse to public funds. That includes holding a valid return ticket to your own country or next destination.

How Do I Change Dollars to Pounds?

Changing money (cash or traveler's checks) into a foreign currency makes many people apprehensive, particularly if they've never done it before. But it's really a fairly simple operation. Just remember that **every time you exchange money, you will need to show your passport.**

Dollars & Sense

All **Bureaux de Change** and other money-changing establishments in the U.K. are required to clearly display exchange rates and full details of any fees and rates of commission with equal prominence. Rates must be displayed at or near the entrance to the premises. Rates do fluctuate from place to place, so it sometimes pays to shop around.

Beware of Bureaux de Change that offer good exchange rates but charge a heavy commission fee (up to 8%!). You will find such places in many major tourist sections of London (some are open 24 hours a day). Some **hotels** also cash traveler's checks, but their commissions are often considerably higher than at banks or independent Bureaux de Change. Before you exchange your money, always check to see what the exchange rate is, how much commission will be charged, and whether any additional fees apply.

If you want some pounds in hand when you arrive, you can exchange currency before you leave home at many banks and at foreign exchange services at international airports. Otherwise, when you arrive, you can easily exchange cash (dollars or foreign currency) or traveler's checks at the major London **airports,** at any branch of a major **bank,** at all major **rail** and **Underground stations** in Central London, at a **post office,** or at an **American Express** or **Thomas Cook** office. Currency exchange services, called **Bureaux de Change,** are generally open from 8am to 9pm. Banks are generally open weekdays from 9:30am to 4:30pm, but a few open earlier. Some banks are open all day on Saturday (usually based in busy shopping centers), and some are now open on Sundays for a few hours; they're all closed on public holidays. Be aware that the commission charge varies from place to place. At the post office, it's 1% of the total transaction—one of the lowest rates available. At banks and Bureaux de Change, the commission rate can fluctuate from 2% to 8%.

Reputable London banks and Bureaux de Change will exchange money at a competitive rate, but they do charge a **commission** (typically 1% to 3% of the total transaction) and a small fee on top of that. Some currency exchange services now guarantee you the same exchange rate when you return pounds for dollars (keep your receipt if this service is offered).

Dollars & Sense

You can avoid paying a commission fee for cashing traveler's checks if you use American Express traveler's checks and cash them at the American Express office, 6 Haymarket, SW1 (☎ **0171/930-4411;** Tube Piccadilly). The Amex foreign exchange bureau is open Monday through Friday from 9am to 5:30pm, Saturday from 9am to 6pm, and Sunday from 10am to 5pm. Amex has other foreign exchange offices in heavily visited areas throughout Central London: 78 Brompton Rd., Knightsbridge SW3 (☎ **0171/584-3431**); 84 Kensington High St., Kensington W8 (☎ **0171/795-8703**); 51 Great Russell St., Bloomsbury WC1 (☎ **0171/404-8700**); and 1 Savoy Court, The Strand WC2 (☎ **0171/240-1521**).

Stop, Thief! What If My Money Is Stolen?

Almost every credit card company has an emergency 800 number you can call if your wallet or purse is stolen. The company might be able to wire you a cash advance off your credit card immediately, and in many places, it can get you an emergency credit card in a day or two. The issuing bank's 800 number is usually on the back of your credit card. (But that doesn't help you much if the card was stolen, does it? It's a good idea to jot down your credit card's emergency 800 number and keep it in a safe place). **Visa's** U.S. emergency number is ☎ **800/847-2911;** if you're in London, you can call the U.K. toll-free number (☎ **0800/89-1725**). **Mastercard's** U.S. emergency number is ☎ **800/307-7309;** in the United Kingdom, call ☎ **0800/96-4767. American Express** cardholders and traveler's check holders should call ☎ **800/221-7282** in the U.S. for all money emergencies; the toll-free U.K. number is ☎ **0800/521-313.** Amex card or traveler's check holders can also report a stolen card or get replacement traveler's checks at the Amex office in London (see appendix A, "London from A to Z—Facts at Your

Fingertips"). **MasterCard** holders should call ☎ **800/307-7309** in the U.S.; the 24-hour toll-free number from London is ☎ **0800/96-4767.**

If you opt to carry traveler's checks, be sure to keep a record of their serial numbers so that you can handle just such an emergency.

Odds are that if your wallet is gone, you've seen the last of it, and the police aren't likely to recover it for you. However, after you realize that it's gone and you cancel your credit cards, it is still worth a call to inform the police. You might need the police report number for credit-card or insurance purposes later.

Dollars & Sense

Write down the **identification number of each traveler's check** as you cash or use it. When you're in your hotel room each night, take out your master list of numbers and cross off the ones used. If the balance of checks gets stolen at some point, you need to be able to report exactly which checks are gone in order to get them replaced. The check issuer will tell you where to pick up the new checks.

So, What's This Trip Gonna Cost Me?

Okay, now it's time for a financial reality check. Before the alarm bells go off, remember that clear-eyed budgeting at this stage can help to allay any pre-trip anxiety about traveling to London.

Here's an important statistic to consider: U.S. visitors to London spend an average of £638 ($1,053) per visit. This breaks down to about £70 ($115) per day per person on a 9-day trip (the average amount of time spent in London by American tourists). The $115 per day average includes accommodations, but in most cases, this is the result of booking an air-hotel package tour through the airlines (see chapter 3 for more information on airline package tours). In other words, the average daily rate will be considerably higher if you book your own flight and hotel.

Even if you book a package tour and charge most of your large purchases while in London, you'll still need pounds in hand to pay for transportation, museums, special tours, snacks, and whatever else strikes your fancy (although some packages include transportation passes and one or two sightseeing tours). I recommend that you have a minimum of £50 ($82.50) *per person* with you every day for spending money. This is assuming that you pay for hotels, restaurants, and other large purchases with credit cards.

What Things Cost in London

Transportation from airport to Central London	
From Heathrow Airport by Underground	$6.00
From Gatwick Airport by train	$15.00
One-way Underground fare within Central London	$2.25
Double room at The Savoy Hotel (very expensive)	$485–$525
Double room at Hazlitt's (expensive)	$280
Double room with breakfast at the Cranley (moderate)	$206–$275
Double room at Hotel 167 B&B (inexpensive)	$141–$155
Double room at Aston's Budget Studios (self-catering)	$117
Meal for one at Oxo Tower, excluding wine (expensive)	$80
Set-price dinner for one at Rules, excluding wine (moderate)	$28
Dinner for one at The Oratory, excluding wine (inexpensive)	$20
Pizza at Gourmet Pizza Company (inexpensive)	$10
Pub meal for one at Museum Tavern (inexpensive)	$12.50
Afternoon tea for one at The Savoy (expensive)	$32.25
Pint of beer at a pub	$3.50
Coffee and cake at Pâtisserie Valerie (inexpensive)	$10
Admission to the Tower of London (adult/child)	$13.50/$9
Admission to Madame Tussaud's (adult/child)	$14.50/$9.50
Theatre ticket	$25–$95

Budgeting Basics

Budgeting for your London vacation isn't difficult, but keeping a firm eye on costs while you are there is another matter. Using the **worksheet at the end of this chapter** will help you get an approximate idea of how much your trip will cost. A good way to get a handle on all costs is to start the tally from the moment you leave home. Walk yourself mentally through the trip. Begin with transportation to your nearest airport, then add flight costs (see "Taking Flight: How to Get the Best Airfare" in chapter 3 for tips on how to fly to London for less), the price of getting from the London airport to your hotel, the hotel rate per day, meals (exclude breakfast if it's included in the hotel rate), public transportation costs, admission prices to museums, and theatre or entertainment expenses. After you do all that, add another 15% to 20% for good measure.

Lodging

In London, accommodation expenses are going to take the largest bite out of your budget. On the other hand, many mid-range London hotels and all B&Bs include breakfast as part of the room rate. Rates vary considerably from B&B to B&B, so it's difficult to give an "average" rate. But if you're using the recommendations in this guide, the rate for a B&B will *generally* fall somewhere between $90 and $150. A moderate hotel costs anywhere from $150 to $225. And an expensive hotel ranges in price from $225 to $300. After that, you hit the stratosphere of $300+.

What Are All Those Dollar Signs, Anyway?

In certain places in this book (for example, in the hotel and restaurant listings), you'll see from one to three dollar signs next to each item. These symbols are neither decorative nor arbitrary; they're keyed to a scale at the beginning of the chapter and help you tell at a glance what particular price bracket that item falls into. For example, a hotel prefaced by $$ costs from $150 to $225, and one marked with $$$ costs from $225 to $300.

Transportation

Here's some good news: You won't need to rent a car in London, which will save you a bundle. The London Underground (called "the Tube") is fast, convenient, and easy to use. Special reduced-price transportation passes (see chapter 8) make getting around the city relatively inexpensive.

Dining

The food in England used to be the butt of many a joke, but in recent years London has emerged as one of the great food capitals of the world, and eating at the top restaurants is going to cost you. There are countless pubs and restaurants where you can dine cheaply and well, however. In addition, many of the best London restaurants offer special fixed-price meals, which can be a real bargain. If you eat lunch and dinner at the moderately priced restaurants recommended in chapter 10, you can expect to pay anywhere from $30 to $70 total per person per day, not including wine. This assumes that breakfast is included in your room rate.

Attractions

Your budget for entrance fees and admissions depends, of course, on what you want to see. Refer to chapter 13 and make a list of your must-sees. Some of the top sites, like the British Museum and the National Gallery, are free. Some of the other museums, particularly those in South Kensington, offer free admission after 4:30pm (this means, however, that you have only an hour for your visit). It's not always a good idea to cut costs when it comes to sightseeing, though. After all, the sights are what you came all this way to see. Sure, it costs $16 to get into the Tower of London, but would you really want to miss out on seeing the crown jewels housed there?

Shopping & Entertainment

These two areas represent flexible parts of your budget. You don't have to buy anything at all, and you can hit the sack right after dinner instead of heading out to a play or pub. You know yourself and your habits. Flip through the shopping discussion in chapter 15 and the nightlife options in part 6, and see what strikes your fancy (and budget accordingly). Keep in mind that a pint in a pub will set you back about $3.50, and a theatre ticket can go for anywhere between $25 and $95.

Drat the VAT

Britain's version of a national sales tax is called the **value-added tax (VAT).** Brace yourself: It amounts to 17.5%. (This explains in part why London prices are often so high.) VAT is added to the total price of consumer goods (the price on the tag already includes it) and hotel and restaurant bills. If you're not a resident of the European Union, you can get your VAT refunded on purchases made in the U.K. (this doesn't include hotels and restaurants). See chapter 15 for details.

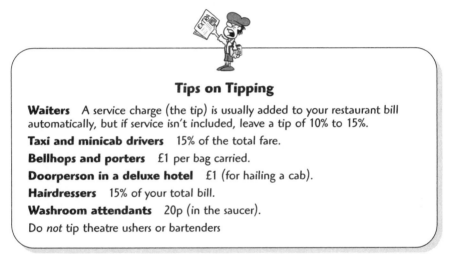

Tips on Tipping

Waiters A service charge (the tip) is usually added to your restaurant bill automatically, but if service isn't included, leave a tip of 10% to 15%.

Taxi and minicab drivers 15% of the total fare.

Bellhops and porters £1 per bag carried.

Doorperson in a deluxe hotel £1 (for hailing a cab).

Hairdressers 15% of your total bill.

Washroom attendants 20p (in the saucer).

Do *not* tip theatre ushers or bartenders

What If I'm Worried I Can't Afford It?

This is a fear everyone but millionaires, people on expense accounts, and the royals have. You might think that going to London will be prohibitively expensive because it's "in Europe" and involves a transatlantic flight. But because London is such a popular destination, you can often find bargain airfares that in some cases are cheaper than flying within the U.S. When you add everything up, a trip to London is actually comparable in cost to a trip to New York, San Francisco, or Los Angeles.

Dollars & Sense sidebars appear throughout the book to give you tips on reducing costs. Here are some additional cost-cutting strategies:

- **Go in the off-season.** If you can travel at non-peak times (October through mid-December or January through March), you'll find hotel prices that can be as much as 20% lower than they are during peak months.

- **Travel on off days of the week.** Airfares vary depending on the day of the week. If you can travel on a Tuesday, Wednesday, or Thursday, you might find cheaper flights to London. When you inquire about airfares, ask whether you can get a cheaper rate by flying on a different day.
- **Try a package tour.** For popular destinations like London, you can book airfare, a hotel, ground transportation, and even some sightseeing just by making one call to a travel agent or packager for a lot less than if you tried to put the trip together yourself. (See "The Pros & Cons of Package Tours" in chapter 3 for specific suggestions on airlines to call.)
- **Reserve a hotel room with a kitchen and do your own cooking.** In London, this kind of room is called a "self-catering unit." It might not feel like as much of a vacation if you still have to do your own cooking and dishes, but you'll save money by not eating in restaurants two or three times a day. Even if you only make breakfast and an occasional bag lunch in the kitchen, you'll still save in the long run. And you'll never be shocked by a hefty room service bill.
- **Always ask for discount rates.** Membership in AAA, frequent-flyer plans, trade unions, AARP, or other groups might qualify you for discounted rates on plane tickets, hotel rooms, and even meals. Ask about everything; you could be pleasantly surprised.
- **Ask whether your kids can stay in your room with you.** A room with two double beds usually doesn't cost any more than one with a queen-size bed. And many hotels won't charge you the additional person rate if the additional person is pint-sized and related to you. Even if you have to pay a few pounds extra for a rollaway bed, you'll save hundreds of dollars by not taking two rooms.
- **Try expensive restaurants at lunch instead of dinner.** Lunch tabs are usually a fraction of what dinner would cost at most top restaurants, and the menu often boasts many of the same specialties. Also look for fixed-price menus offered by more and more London restaurants.
- **Walk a lot.** London is large, but it's an eminently walkable city, and a good pair of walking shoes can save you a lot of money in taxis and other local transportation. And as a bonus, you'll get to know the city more intimately and explore it at a slower pace.
- **Skip the souvenirs.** Your photographs and your memories should be the best mementos of your trip. If you're worried about money, you can do without the T-shirts, key chains, tea mugs, and other "royal" trinkets.

Budget Worksheet: You Can Afford This Trip

Expense	Amount
Airfare (× no. of people traveling)	
Car rental (if applicable). I don't recommend renting a car in London.	
Lodging (× no. of nights)	
Parking (× no. of nights). Applicable only if you rent a car, which I don't recommend. (Did I say that already?)	
Breakfast (× no. of nights) *Note: May be included in your room rate.*	
Lunch (× no. of nights)	
Dinner (× no. of nights)	
Baby-sitting	
Attractions (admission charges to museums, tours, theatres, nightclubs)	
Transportation (cabs, Underground, buses)	
Souvenirs (T-shirts, postcards, that antique commode you just gotta have)	
Tips (Think 15% of your cab fare plus about £1/$1.65 per bag every time a bellhop moves your luggage.) Service is automatically added on in most London restaurants.	
Don't forget the cost of getting to/from the airport in your home town, plus long-term parking (× no. of nights)	
Grand Total	

Chapter 3

How Will I Get There?

In This Chapter

- How useful is a travel agent?
- Should you travel on your own or take an escorted tour?
- Is a package tour the way to go?
- London's airports
- Worksheets to help you schedule your flight

Travel Agent: Friend or Foe?

Any travel agent can help you find a bargain airfare, hotel, or rental car. A good travel agent will stop you from ruining your vacation by trying to save a few dollars. The best travel agents can tell you how much time you should budget in a destination, find a cheap flight that doesn't require you to change planes in Atlanta and Chicago, get you a better hotel room for about the same price, and even give you recommendations on restaurants.

The best way to find a good travel agent is the same way you find a good plumber or mechanic or doctor—by word of mouth. Make sure that you pick an agent who knows London. It's also a good idea to check out any prospective agent with your local Better Business Bureau.

Dollars & Sense

Travel agents work on commission. The good news is that *you* don't pay the commission—the airlines, accommodations, and tour companies do. The bad news is that unscrupulous travel agents will try to persuade you to book the vacations that let them snap up the most money in commissions.

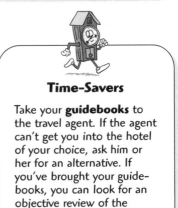

Time-Savers

Take your **guidebooks** to the travel agent. If the agent can't get you into the hotel of your choice, ask him or her for an alternative. If you've brought your guidebooks, you can look for an objective review of the agent's suggestion right then and there.

To make sure that you get the most out of your travel agent, do a little homework. Read about your destination (you've already made a sound decision by buying this book), and pick out some accommodations and attractions you think you'll like. If necessary, get a more comprehensive travel guide like *Frommer's London* or *Frommer's London from $75 a Day*. If you have access to the Internet, check prices on the Web in advance (see "Taking Flight: Finding the Best Airfare" later in this chapter) so that you can do a little prodding. Then take your guidebook and Web information to the travel agent and ask him or her to make the arrangements for you. Because they have access to more resources than even the most complete Web travel site, travel agents should be able to get you a better price than you could get by yourself. And they can issue your tickets and vouchers right there. If they can't get you into the hotel of your choice, they can recommend an alternative, and you can look for an objective review in your guidebook right then and there.

Extra! Extra!

In the past 2 years, some airlines and resorts have begun limiting or eliminating travel agent commissions altogether. The immediate result has been that travel agents don't bother booking these services unless the customer specifically requests them. Some travel industry analysts predict that if other airlines and accommodations throughout the industry cut out these commissions, travel agents might have to start charging customers for their services. When that day arrives, the best agents should prove even harder to find.

Should I Join an Escorted Tour or Travel on My Own?

When you travel, do you like to let a tour-bus driver worry about traffic while you sit in comfort and listen to the guide explain everything you see? Or do you prefer hopping on a subway and following your nose, even if you don't catch all the highlights? Do you like to have lots of events planned for each day, or would you rather improvise as you go along? The answers to these questions will determine whether you should choose the guided tour or travel à la carte.

Some people love escorted tours. You spend less time getting from one place to the next, all the details are taken care of, and you're told what to expect at each attraction. You know your costs up front, and there aren't many surprises. Escorted tours can take you to the maximum number of sights in the minimum amount of time with the least amount of hassle.

Other people need more freedom and spontaneity—they can't stand guided tours. They prefer to discover a destination by themselves and don't mind getting caught in a thunderstorm without an umbrella or finding that a recommended restaurant is no longer in business. That's just the adventure of travel.

There are dozens of companies that offer escorted tours to London. Many of them cater to specific interests, such as the theatre or historic sites, while others are more general. Your best bet is to check with a travel agent or to scan the travel section in your local paper. **American Express** offers escorted tours, and so do many of the airlines.

Before You Sign on the Dotted Line . . .

If you do choose an escorted tour, ask a few simple questions before you buy:

- **What is the cancellation policy?** Do I have to put down a deposit? Can they cancel the trip if they don't get enough people? How late can I cancel if I am unable to go? When do I pay? Do I get a refund if I cancel? If *they* cancel?
- **How jam-packed is the schedule?** Do they try to fit 25 hours into a 24-hour day, or is there ample time for relaxing or shopping? If you don't enjoy getting up at 7am every day and returning to your hotel at 6pm or 7pm, certain escorted tours might not be for you.
- **How big is the group?** The smaller the group, the more flexible it will be and the less time you'll spend waiting for people to get on and off the bus. Tour operators might be evasive about this because they might not know the exact size of the group until everybody has made their reservations, but they should be able to give you a rough estimate. Some tours have a minimum group size and might cancel the tour if they don't book enough people.
- **What is included?** Don't assume anything. You might have to pay to get yourself to and from the airport. Or a box lunch might be included

in an excursion but drinks are extra. Or beer might be included but wine isn't. How much choice do you have? Can you opt out of certain activities, or does the bus leave once a day, with no exceptions? Are all your meals planned? Can you choose your entree at dinner, or does everybody get the same chicken cutlet?

Dollars & Sense

If you choose an escorted tour, think strongly about purchasing **travel insurance,** especially if the tour operator asks you to pay up front. But don't buy insurance from the tour operator! If they don't fulfill their obligation to provide you with the vacation you've paid for, there's no reason to think they'll fulfill their insurance obligations either. Get travel insurance through an independent agency. See "Travel Insurance: What Is It & Do I Need It?" in chapter 4.

The Pros & Cons of Package Tours

First off: Package tours are *not* the same thing as escorted tours. They are simply a way of buying your airfare and accommodations at the same time. Independent types who would never dream of joining an escorted tour might be wise to consider a package tour. For popular destinations like London, package tours are really the smart way to go because they can save you a *ton* of money.

In many cases, a package that includes airfare, a hotel, and transportation to and from the airport will cost you less than just the hotel alone if you booked it yourself. That's because packages are sold in bulk to tour operators, who resell them to the public.

Packages vary considerably. Some packages offer a better class of hotels than others. Some offer the same hotels for lower prices. Some offer flights on scheduled airlines, while others book charters. In some packages, your choices of accommodations and travel days may be limited. Some packages let you choose between escorted vacations and independent vacations; others allow you to add on just a few excursions or escorted day trips (also at prices lower than if you booked them yourself) without booking an entirely escorted tour.

Each destination usually has one or two packagers that are better than the rest because they buy in even bigger bulk. The time you spend shopping around will be well rewarded.

Picking the Package That's Right for You

The best place to start looking for package tours is the travel section of your local Sunday newspaper. Also check the ads in the back of national travel magazines like *Travel & Leisure, National Geographic Traveler,* and *Condé Nast Traveler.* **Liberty Travel** (many locations; check your local directory—there is no central 800 number) is one of the biggest packagers in the Northeast and usually boasts a full-page ad in Sunday papers. You won't get much in the way of service, but you will get a good deal. **American Express Vacations** (☎ **800/241-1700**) is another option.

Another good resource is the airlines themselves, which often package their flights together with accommodations. When you pick the airline, you can choose one that has frequent service to your hometown and the one on which you accumulate frequent-flyer miles. Although disreputable packagers are uncommon, they do exist. By buying your package through the airline, however, you can be pretty sure that the company will still be in business when your departure date arrives. Among the London airline packages, your options include **American Airlines Vacations** (☎ 800/321-2121), **British Airways Holidays** (☎ 800/AIRWAYS), **Continental Airlines Vacations** (☎ 800/634-5555), **Delta Dream Vacations** (☎ 800/872-7786), **Northwest Airlines Vacations** (☎ 800/447-4747), **Trans World Airlines Getaway Vacations** (☎ 800/438-2929), **United Airlines** (☎ 800/328-6877), and **Virgin Atlantic Vacations** (☎ 888/937-8474).

The biggest hotel chains also offer packages. If you already know where you want to stay, call the hotel itself and ask whether it can offer land/air packages. Large hotel groups with properties in London include **Forte and Le Meridien Hotels & Resorts** (☎ 800/225-5843), **Hyatt** (☎ 800/228-3336), **Hilton International** (☎ 800/HILTONS), **Intercontinental Hotels & Resorts** (☎ 800/327-0200), **ITT Sheraton** (☎ 800/325-3535), and **Thistle Hotels Worldwide** (☎ 800/847-4358).

The Highs & Lows of Airline Packages

During London's **peak season** (late April to mid-October), airfares are higher than during the **off-season** (November 1 to December 12 and December 25 to March 14). The same applies for some—but not all—air-hotel packages. If you're planning a package tour (always a bargain, no matter what time of year you travel), make certain that you check the rates carefully. Some package rates are good all year, but others charge more or less depending on the season. Package rates also vary according to the type of hotel you stay in.

Let's Make a Deal: Sample Airline Package Prices

Please note that the following airline package prices are per person, based on double occupancy. Single supplements are available for persons traveling solo, but they increase the price considerably. The packages listed below do not include airport taxes and surcharges, which typically amount to about

$80. All hotels have private baths or showers, and breakfast is included. Some package prices are good all year, but many are seasonal. Rates also vary according to the class of hotel you choose to stay in. The following packages were available at press time; they may or may not be available when you travel, but they should give you an idea of what's typically offered.

British Airways' Taste of London packages range from $619 to $1,159 for 4 days/3 nights and $769 to $1,719 for 7 days/6 nights. Prices include airfare, transportation to your hotel from Heathrow or Gatwick, hotel accommodations, and an open-top bus tour. Treasures of London, a 7-day/6-night package for $899 to $1,399, includes a 7-day Travelcard for the bus and Underground and a more comprehensive sightseeing tour. BA also offers London Family Vacations, with a special reduced-price ticket for museums and a theatre ticket or sightseeing tour; prices start at $739 per adult and $349 per child for 4 days/3 nights.

TWA's London Theatre Week package, from $1,099 to $1,599 (depending on the season and hotel choice), includes airfare, a motor-coach tour of London, 5 nights in a hotel, two West End shows, and a 3-day Travelcard for the Underground and buses in Central London.

Delta's City Stay Vacations packages include airfare and hotel accommodations. There's a 3-night minimum, and the price depends on the season in which you travel and the kind of hotel you stay in. Package prices range from $619 to $1,239; you can add extra nights for $60 to $150 a night.

Continental Airlines offers one of the best deals going. The airline's London City Stay package includes round-trip airfare and 5 nights in a hotel for $669 to $769, depending on the city of departure. Many add-ons are available, including tours and theatre tickets.

Taking Flight: Finding the Best Airfare

Airfares are capitalism at its purest. Passengers in the same cabin on an airplane rarely pay the same fare. Instead, they pay what the market will bear.

Business travelers who need the flexibility to purchase their tickets at the last minute, need to change their itinerary at a moment's notice, or want to get home before the weekend pay the premium rate—known as the **full fare.** Passengers who can book their ticket well in advance, who don't mind staying over Saturday night, or who are willing to travel on a Tuesday, Wednesday, or Thursday pay the least—usually a fraction of the full fare.

The airlines also periodically hold sales, in which they lower the prices on their most popular routes. These fares have advance-purchase requirements and date-of-travel restrictions, but you can't beat the price: usually no more than $400 for a transatlantic flight (from the East Coast). Keep your eyes open for these sales as you are planning your vacation, and then pounce on them. The sales tend to take place during seasons of low travel volume. You'll almost never see a sale around the peak summer vacation months of July and August.

Extra! Extra

After you start researching airfares to London, use the handy **worksheets** at the end of this chapter to record flight information and quoted fares. This will make it easier to locate a specific flight and fare again when you're ready to buy your ticket.

Consolidators: What Are They & What Can They Do for Me?

Consolidators, also known as **bucket shops,** are a good place to check for the lowest fares. Consolidators act as wholesalers: They buy up blocks of unused seats directly from the airlines and resell the seats to the public at cut rates. Their prices are much better than the fares you could get yourself—usually 10% to 30% lower than the published rates—and are often even lower than what your travel agent can get you. You see consolidators' ads in the small boxes at the bottom of the page in your Sunday travel section. Some of the most reliable consolidators include **1-800-FLY-4-LESS** and **1-800-FLY-CHEAP.** Another good choice, **Council Travel** (☎ **800/226-8624**), caters especially to young travelers, but its bargain-basement prices are available to people of all ages.

Surfing the Web to Fly the Skies

Another way to find the cheapest fare is by using the Internet to do your searching for you. After all, that's what computers do best—search through millions of pieces of data and return information in rank order. The number of virtual travel agents on the Internet has increased exponentially in recent years. Agencies now compete the way locksmiths do in the Yellow Pages for the first alphabetical listing. At this writing, 007Travel, 1st Choice Travel, and 1Travel.com all precede A Plus Travel in an alphabetical listing of online travel agents.

There are too many companies now to mention, but a few of the more well-respected ones are **Travelocity** (**www.travelocity.com**), **Microsoft Expedia Travel** (**www.expedia.msn.com**), and **Yahoo! Travel** (**http://travel.yahoo.com/destinations**). Each has its own little quirks (Travelocity, for example, requires you to register with them), but they all provide variations of the same service. Just enter the dates you want to fly and the cities you want to visit, and the computer looks for the lowest fares. The Yahoo! site has a feature called Fare Beater, which checks flights on other airlines or at different times or dates in hopes of finding an even cheaper fare. Expedia's site e-mails you the best airfare deal once a week if you so choose. Travelocity uses the SABRE computer reservations system that most travel agents use and has a Last Minute Deals database that advertises really cheap fares for those who can get away at a moment's notice.

Great last-minute deals are also available directly from the airlines through free e-mail services. Each week, the participating airlines send you a list of discounted flights, usually leaving the upcoming Friday or Saturday and returning the following Monday or Tuesday (or Wednesday for international flights). Some of the airlines also offer deals on car rentals and accommodations in cities where discounted airfares are offered. You can sign up for all the major airlines at once by logging on to **Epicurious Travel** (http://travel.epicurious.com/travel/c_planning/02_airfares/email/signup.html), or by going to each individual airline's Web site (see below).

You can also check out airline Web sites for details on any special deals or packages they are offering. The following Web sites are available for airlines flying into London:

- American Airlines: www.americanair.com
- British Airways: www.british-airways.com
- Continental Airlines: www.flycontinental.com
- Delta Air Lines: www.delta-air.com
- Icelandair: www.icelandair.is
- Northwest Airlines: www.nwa.com
- TWA: www.twa.com
- United Airlines: www.ual.com
- Virgin Atlantic Airways: www.virgin.com

Does It Matter Which Airport I Fly Into?

Four airports serve regularly scheduled flights to the London metropolitan area, and a fifth charter airport is less frequently used. Where you arrive depends on the city you're flying from and the airline you're using. If you're on a regularly scheduled international flight from the U.S., you'll arrive at Heathrow or Gatwick. If you're on a flight from the Continent, you might be landing at Stansted or London City Airport. It's unlikely that you'll be arriving at Luton, London's fifth airport: It's much smaller than the others and is used mostly for charter flights from the Continent. Public transportation service into Central London is available from all five of these airports. (See chapter 7, "Getting Your Bearings," for specific information on getting into London from the airports.)

Heathrow, the main international airport, is about 15 miles west of Central London. It is served by Air New Zealand, American Airlines, British Airways, Continental, Delta, Icelandair, United, and Virgin Atlantic. You can get into London on the Underground (subway) in about a half hour for £3.30 ($5.50). There's also a new **FastTrain** service between Heathrow and Paddington rail station for £5 ($8.25) and an **Airbus** that offers bus service to Victoria and Euston stations for £6 ($10).

Gatwick is a smaller airport about 25 miles south of London. It is served by American Airlines, American Trans Air, British Airways, Delta, Continental, Northwest Airlines, Icelandair, Trans World Airlines, and Virgin Atlantic.

Gatwick Express trains will take you from the airport to Victoria Station in Central London in about a half hour for £8.90 ($15).

Stansted, about 50 miles northeast of London, is used for national and European flights. The **Stansted Express Train** to Liverpool Street Station takes 40 minutes and costs £11 ($18).

London City Airport, only 6 miles east of Central London, services European destinations. A bus charges £3 ($5) to take you from the airport to Liverpool Street Station.

Luton Airport, 28 miles northwest of London, services mostly charter flights; trains from the airport will take you to King's Cross Station for £8.10 ($14).

The Friendlier Skies: Making Your Flight More Pleasant

Flight times vary, of course, depending on your point of departure. Here are the approximate flight times from various U.S. cities to London: from New York, 6 hours; from Boston, 6½ hours; from Washington, D.C., 7 hours; from Chicago, 8 hours; from Atlanta, 8 hours; from Los Angeles, 10½ hours; and from Seattle, 9½ hours.

The seats in the front row of each airplane cabin, called the **bulkhead seats,** usually have the most legroom. They have some drawbacks, however. Because there's no seat in front of you, there's no place to put your carry-on luggage, except in the overhead bin. The front row also might not be the best place to see the in-flight movie. And lately, airlines have started putting passengers with young children in the bulkhead row so that the kids can sleep on the floor. This is terrific if you have kids but a nightmare if you have a headache.

If you have **special dietary needs,** be sure to order a special meal. Most airlines offer vegetarian meals, macrobiotic meals, kosher meals, meals for the lactose intolerant, and several other meals in a large variety of categories. Ask when you make your reservation whether the airline can accommodate your dietary restrictions. Some people without any special dietary needs order special meals anyway because they are made to order, unlike the mass-produced dinners served to the rest of the passengers.

Emergency exit row seats also have extra legroom. They are assigned at the airport, usually on a first-come, first-served basis. Ask when you check in whether you can be seated in one of these rows. In the unlikely event of an emergency, you'll be expected to open the emergency exit door and help direct traffic.

Wear comfortable clothes. The days of getting dressed up in a coat and tie to ride on an airplane went out with Nehru jackets and poodle skirts. And dress in layers; the supposedly controlled climate in airplane cabins is anything but predictable. You'll be glad to have a sweater or jacket that you can put on or take off as the temperature on board dictates.

Bring some toiletries on long flights. Airplane cabins are notoriously dry places. Take a travel-size bottle of moisturizer or lotion to refresh your face and hands at the end of the flight. If you're taking an overnight flight, don't forget to pack a toothbrush to combat that feeling upon waking that you've been sucking on your seat cushion for 6 hours. If you wear contact lenses, take them out before you get on board and wear glasses instead. Or at least bring eyedrops.

Extra! Extra!

If you're flying with kids, don't forget chewing gum to help relieve ear-pressure problems, a deck of cards or favorite toys to keep them entertained, extra bottles or pacifiers, diapers, and so on.

Beating Jet Lag

Jet lag is usually a problem for passengers flying to London. It might be a 6-hour flight (from New York), but you're moving through 6 hours of time changes, so when you arrive at 1am *your* time, it's 7am *London* time. The best advice is to get acclimated to local time as quickly as possible. Don't keep looking at your watch and saying, "It's 9am here but 3am in New York." Think local time. Stay up as long as you can the first day, and then try to wake up at a normal time the second day. Drink plenty of water both days, as well as on the plane, to avoid dehydration. Try to eat at normal local London time. On your first day, especially if you arrive in the mid-morning or early afternoon, don't try to take in too many sights. Choose one or two that are relatively undemanding and give yourself time to adjust to your new surroundings.

Fare Game—Choosing an Airline

Arranging and booking a flight is a complicated business—that's why a whole industry has grown up to handle it for you. If you're searching around for a deal, though, it helps to leave a trail of breadcrumbs through the maze so that you can easily find your way to your destination and back. You can use the worksheets on the following pages to do just that.

There's a chance that you won't be able to get a direct flight, especially if you're looking to save money, so I've included space for you to map out any connections you'll have to make. If a connection is involved in the fares you're quoted, make sure to ask how much of a layover you'll have between flights. Nobody likes hanging around the airport for 8 to 10 hours. Be sure to mark the layover times in the appropriate spot on the worksheet so that you can compare them easily when you go back over everything to make a decision.

1 Schedule & Flight Information Worksheets

Travel Agency: ____________________ **Phone #:** ________________

Agent's Name: ______________________ **Quoted Fare:** ____________

Departure Schedule & Flight Information

Airline: ________________________ Airport: ______________________

Flight #: _________________ Date: ____________ Time: ________ am/pm

Arrives in __________________________________ Time: ________ am/pm

Connecting Flight (if any)

Amount of time between flights: _________ hours/mins.

Airline:___________________ Flight #:__________ Time: ________ am/pm

Arrives in __________________________________ Time: ________ am/pm

Return Trip Schedule & Flight Information

Airline:__________________________ Airport: ______________________

Flight #: _________________ Date: ____________ Time: ________ am/pm

Arrives in __________________________________ Time: ________ am/pm

Connecting Flight (if any)

Amount of time between flights: _________ hours/mins.

Airline:___________________ Flight #:__________ Time: ________ am/pm

Arrives in __________________________________ Time: ________ am/pm

2 Schedule & Flight Information Worksheets

Travel Agency: ____________________ **Phone #:** ________________

Agent's Name: ______________________ **Quoted Fare:** ____________

Departure Schedule & Flight Information

Airline: ________________________ **Airport:** ______________________

Flight #: ________________ Date: ___________ Time: ________ am/pm

Arrives in __________________________________ Time: ________ am/pm

Connecting Flight (if any)

Amount of time between flights: _________ hours/mins.

Airline:__________________ Flight #:__________ Time: ________ am/pm

Arrives in __________________________________ Time: ________ am/pm

Return Trip Schedule & Flight Information

Airline:_________________________ **Airport:** ______________________

Flight #: ________________ Date: ___________ Time: ________ am/pm

Arrives in __________________________________ Time: ________ am/pm

Connecting Flight (if any)

Amount of time between flights: _________ hours/mins.

Airline:__________________ Flight #:__________ Time: ________ am/pm

Arrives in __________________________________ Time: ________ am/pm

3 Schedule & Flight Information Worksheets

Travel Agency: ____________________ **Phone #:** ________________

Agent's Name: ______________________ **Quoted Fare:** ____________

Departure Schedule & Flight Information

Airline: _______________________ **Airport:** ______________________

Flight #: _________________ Date: ____________ Time: _________ am/pm

Arrives in __________________________________ Time: _________ am/pm

Connecting Flight (if any)

Amount of time between flights: _________ hours/mins.

Airline:___________________ Flight #:__________ Time: _________ am/pm

Arrives in __________________________________ Time: _________ am/pm

Return Trip Schedule & Flight Information

Airline:_________________________ **Airport:** ______________________

Flight #: _________________ Date: ____________ Time: _________ am/pm

Arrives in __________________________________ Time: _________ am/pm

Connecting Flight (if any)

Amount of time between flights: _________ hours/mins.

Airline:___________________ Flight #:__________ Time: _________ am/pm

Arrives in __________________________________ Time: _________ am/pm

Schedule & Flight Information Worksheets

Travel Agency: ____________________ **Phone #:** ________________

Agent's Name: ______________________ **Quoted Fare:** _____________

Departure Schedule & Flight Information

Airline: ________________________ **Airport:** ______________________

Flight #: _________________ Date: ____________ Time: ________ am/pm

Arrives in __________________________________ Time: ________ am/pm

Connecting Flight (if any)

Amount of time between flights: _________ hours/mins.

Airline:__________________ Flight #:__________ Time: ________ am/pm

Arrives in __________________________________ Time: ________ am/pm

Return Trip Schedule & Flight Information

Airline:__________________________ **Airport:** ______________________

Flight #: _________________ Date: ____________ Time: ________ am/pm

Arrives in __________________________________ Time: ________ am/pm

Connecting Flight (if any)

Amount of time between flights: _________ hours/mins.

Airline:__________________ Flight #:__________ Time: ________ am/pm

Arrives in __________________________________ Time: ________ am/pm

Chapter 4

Tying Up the Loose Ends

In This Chapter

- The fine print of travel: passports, customs, insurance, and other boring but important subjects
- Health concerns: hospitals, emergencies, and whether it's safe to drink the water and eat the beef
- Planning: making reservations for the things you just can't miss
- The fine art of packing light: what to take and what not to take
- The lowdown on electronics and adapters, from hair dryers to laptops

The trip is planned. You're primed and ready to go. Now you have to start thinking about packing. But before you do that, you have to take care of at least one other essential detail: obtaining a passport. And maybe you're wondering about customs regulations, or what you'll do if you get sick, or whether it's a good idea to buy trip insurance, or whether you need to reserve in advance for that West End musical you're longing to see, or whether you know the proper way to curtsy should you meet the queen (well, you probably won't have to worry about that one)? My goal in this chapter is to anticipate and answer all those little nagging questions that might pop up as your vacation date approaches. I'll also give you some tips on to how to pack light (if you're already heading to the attic for your steamer trunk, boy, do we have to talk).

I grew up with the Boy Scout's motto: Be Prepared. I want you to be prepared, too. But I also want you to remember that you're not going to some totally alien culture where you have to pack laundry detergent and a washboard because you're afraid you won't find a Laundromat. You're going to London, old chap, the highly civilized capital of the United Kingdom, where they do have Laundromats—and every other convenience you can think of.

Passport, Please

The only legal form of identification recognized around the world is a valid passport. You cannot cross an international border without it. Besides clothing, it is the only item you absolutely must have in order to travel. Getting a passport is easy, but it takes some time to complete the process.

Extra! Extra!

The **U.S. State Department's Bureau of Consular Affairs** maintains a Web site (travel.state.gov) that gives you more than you ever wanted to know about passports (including a downloadable application), customs, and other aspects of travel in which the government has a say.

How Do I Apply for a Passport?

If you're applying for a first-time passport and you are 13 years of age or older, you need to apply in person at one of the following locations:

- One of the 13 passport offices located throughout the United States—in Boston, Chicago, Honolulu, Houston, Los Angeles, Miami, New Orleans, New York City, Philadelphia, San Francisco, Seattle, Stamford (CT), and Washington, D.C.
- A federal, state, or probate court.
- A major post office. (Not all accept applications; call the number in the following paragraph to find the ones that do.)

You will need to fill out a passport application. If you are applying for your first passport, you need form **DSP-11.** If you are renewing your passport, you need form **DSP-82.** You can obtain the appropriate application from the locations listed above or by mail from Passport Services, Office of Correspondence, Department of State, 1111 19th St. NW, Washington, DC 20522-1705. You can also download the appropriate application off the Internet; go to the **U.S. State Department's Bureau of Consular Affairs'** Web site (**travel.state.gov**).

Time-Savers

Why wait in long lines at passport offices when you can accomplish the same thing at a **post office or clerk of court's office?** Bring your documents and a check or money order for the appropriate amount. In larger cities, a special passport window is usually located in the post office.

You'll need to bring the following when you go to apply for your passport:

- **Your completed passport application.** You can fill out this form in advance to save time. However, ***do not* sign** the application until you present it in person at the passport agency, post office, or court.
- **Proof of U.S. citizenship.** Bring an old passport if you're renewing; otherwise, bring a certified copy of your birth certificate with a registrar's seal, a report of your birth abroad, or your naturalized citizenship documents.
- **Proof of identity.** Among the accepted documents are a valid driver's license, a state or military ID, a student ID (if you are currently enrolled), an old passport, or a naturalization certificate.
- **Two identical 2-inch × 2-inch photographs with a white or off-white background.** You can get these taken at just about any corner photo shop; these places have a special camera to make them identical. You cannot use the strip photos from one of those photo vending machines. Expect to pay up to $12.50 for these photos.
- **Application fee.** For people over the age of 15, a passport costs $60 ($45 plus a $15 handling fee); for those 15 and under, it costs $40 total.

Time-Savers

When you get your **passport photos** taken, get six to eight total made up. You'll need them to apply for student and teacher identification cards, and kids will need one in London to apply for a Travelcard—a money-saving transportation pass (see "The Ins & Outs of Travelcards" in chapter 8).

When Should I Apply for a Passport?

Apply for your passport at least a month, preferably two, before you plan to leave on your trip. The processing takes an average of 3 weeks, but it can run longer in busy periods (especially in the spring). For people over the age of 15, a passport is valid for 10 years; for those 15 and under, it's valid for 5 years.

Need your passport in a hurry (to take advantage of that incredibly low airline fare to London)? To **expedite your passport** (in which case you'll get it in 5 business days), visit an agency directly (or go through the court or post office and have them send the application via overnight mail). You'll pay an additional $35 fee. For more information, and to find your regional passport office, call the **National Passport Information Center** (☎ **900/225-5674**) or get on the Web site (**travel.state.gov**).

Time-Savers

If you're 18 or older and **renewing a passport** that was issued no more than 12 years ago, you don't have to apply in person—you can do it all by mail. Include your expired passport, pink renewal form DSP-82, and a check or money order for $40 (no extra processing fee). Send it (registered, just to be safe) to one of the agencies listed on the back of the application form. Allow at least a month to 6 weeks for your application to be processed and your new passport to be sent to you.

What If I'm Traveling with the Kids?

Everyone who's going with you to London will have to be accounted for upon arrival. Children 14 to 18 years of age must apply for their passports in person (just like you). They will need the same application and documents listed above. Parents or guardians of children under 13 can obtain passports for them by presenting two photos of each child. Children's passports are valid for 5 years, as opposed to 10 years for adults.

Anything Else I Should Know?

Once you reach the U.K., you will show your passport at the Customs and Immigration area when you arrive at your London airport. After your passport is stamped, you can remain in the U.K. as a tourist for up to 3 months.

Keep your passport with you at all times. The only times to give it up are at the bank or currency exchange when you're converting traveler's checks or foreign currency. You'll also need to present your passport to the hotel clerk when you check in; after examining your passport, the clerk will return it to you. If you're not going to need your passport for currency exchange, ask whether the hotel has a safe where you can keep it locked up.

What If I (Gulp) Lose My Passport?

If you lose your passport in London, go *directly* to the nearest consulate or high commission office (do no pass Go, do not collect $200). Bring all forms of identification you have, and they'll get started on generating you a new passport. For the addresses of consulates and high commissions, see appendix A, "London from A to Z—Facts at Your Fingertips."

What About Visas & Health Certificates?

No **visa** is required if you are going to stay in the U.K. for less than 3 months. The U.S. Department of State's Bureau of Consular Affairs operates a phone line for current visa information: ☎ **202/663-1225** (Monday through Friday from 8:30am to 4pm). Or you can check its Web site (travel.state.gov).

You do not need an **International Certificate of Vaccination** to enter the U.K. The country is notoriously concerned about rabies, but that doesn't apply to you—only your pet (which will be quarantined upon arrival; this applies to Seeing-Eye dogs as well).

I DO Declare! Getting Through Customs

For visitors entering England, goods fall into two basic categories: purchases made in a non-European Union (EU) country (or bought tax-free within the EU) and purchases on which tax was paid in the European Union. In the first category, limits on imports by individuals 17 and older include 200 cigarettes, 50 cigars, or 250 grams (8.8 oz.) of loose tobacco; 2 liters (2.1 qt.) of still table wine, 1 liter of liquor with an alcohol content of more than 22% or 2 liters of liquor with an alcohol content of less than 22%; and 2 fluid ounces of perfume.

Limits are much higher in the second category, because tax has already been paid: 800 cigarettes, 200 cigarettes and 1 kilogram (2.2 lb.) of loose tobacco, 90 liters (23.8 gal.) of wine, 10 liters (2.6 gal.) of liquor with an alcohol content of more than 22%, 110 liters (29.1 gal.) of beer, and unlimited amounts of perfume.

See chapter 15, "Charge It! A Shopper's Guide to London," for duty-free shopping and limits on what you can and cannot bring home.

Do I Need to Rent a Car in London?

No! I'm really adamant on this subject. Having a car in London is far more of a hassle than a help. Maneuvering through London's congested and complicated maze of streets can be an endurance test even for Londoners. Doing so while driving on the left-hand side of the road can turn even the best American driver into a gibbering nut case. Parking is difficult to find and expensive (street meters cost £1/$1.65) for 20 minutes). Gas (*petrol* in Britspeak) is prohibitive. Public transportation—especially the Underground (subway)—will get you everywhere you want to go at a fraction of the cost.

Do yourself a favor: Forget about renting a car. Even if you're planning excursions outside of London, the trains are a better option. But if you *must* have a car, read on.

Driving on the Left, Passing on the Right

Although the car-rental market in Britain is highly competitive, it's still going to cost you more to rent a car in the U.K. than it would at home. Unless, that is, you can find a special promotional offer from an airline or car-rental agency. Before you even consider renting a car, ask yourself whether you'd be comfortable driving a car with a steering wheel on the right-hand side of the vehicle while shifting with your left hand (you can get an automatic, but it will cost considerably more). You will be driving on the left side of the street and passing on the right. You'll be confronted by roundabouts (circular traffic exchanges with streets leading into them), narrow streets that suddenly become one-ways, and extremely aggressive drivers. Can you handle all that and still have a good time? Let me say it again: Public transportation in London is far more convenient and economical. It will get you where you want to go without an added headache.

Most U.K. car-rental agencies will accept your U.S. driver's license. In most cases, you must be at least 23 years old (21 in some instances), no older than 70, and have had your U.S. license for more than a year.

You can often get a discount on the rate if you reserve 48 hours in advance through the toll-free reservations offices. Weekly rentals are almost always less expensive than daily rates. And the rate, of course, depends on the size of the vehicle.

When you're making your reservation, ask whether the quoted price includes the 17.5% VAT and unlimited mileage. Then find out whether *personal accident insurance* (PAI), *collision-damage waiver* (CDW), and any other insurance options are included. If these options are not included, which is usually the case, be sure to ask what they cost. It's a good idea when driving in any foreign country (or anywhere, for that matter) to have as much coverage as possible.

Dollars & Sense

Collision-damage waivers and other types of insurance coverage are sometimes offered free of charge by **credit-card companies** if you use that card to pay for the rental. If you are planning to rent a car, check directly with your credit-card company to see what is covered, or you might end up paying for coverage you already have. It's important, however, to find out exactly what kind of coverage your credit-card company provides; it could be that you're covered for collision but not liability. You don't want to find out *after* you've been involved in an accident that you don't have the coverage you thought you did.

You can reserve a car for use in London or the U.K. while still in the U.S. through **Avis** (☎ 800/331-1084; www.avis.com), **British Airways** (☎ 800/AIRWAYS; www.british-airways.com), **Budget Rent-a-Car** (☎ 800/472-3325; www.budgetrentacar.com), **Hertz** (☎ 800/654-3001; www.hertz.com), **Kemwel Holiday Autos** (☎ 800/678-0678; www.kemwel.com), and **Auto Europe** (☎ 800/223-5555; www.autoeurope.com).

Watch Out for Pedestrians!

You should know about one essential rule if you're driving in London or anywhere in the U.K.: Pedestrian crossings are marked by striped lines (zebra crossings) on the road; flashing lights near the curb indicate that drivers must stop and yield the right of way if a pedestrian has stepped out into the zebra crossing to cross the street.

Several airlines offer **fly/drive packages** that include airfare and a rental car for self-driving tours. These can be good bargains if you're planning to explore the countryside outside of London. You plan your own itinerary for a certain number of days. Automobiles are picked up and dropped off at the airport. Airlines offering fly/drive packages include **American Airlines** (☎ 800/433-7300; www.americanair.com), **British Airways** (☎ 800/AIRWAYS; www.british-airways.com), **Continental Airlines** (☎ 800/231-0856; www.flycontinental.com), **Delta Air Lines** (☎ 800/241-4141; www.delta-air.com), and **United** (☎ 800/538-2929; www.ual.com). The rates for these packages depend on the size of the car and the time you will be using it.

Travel Insurance: What Is It & Do I Need It?

There are three kinds of travel insurance: **trip cancellation, medical, and lost luggage.** Trip cancellation insurance is a good idea if you have paid a large portion of your vacation expenses up front.

But the other two types of insurance don't make sense for most travelers. Your existing health insurance should cover you if you get sick while on vacation (although if you belong to an HMO, you should check to see whether you are fully covered while in the U.K.). And your homeowner's or renter's insurance should cover stolen luggage if you have off-premises theft coverage. Check your existing policies before you buy any additional coverage. The airlines are responsible for $1,250 on domestic flights and $635 per bag (with a maximum of two bags) on international flights if they lose your luggage. If you plan to carry anything more valuable than that, keep it in your carry-on bag.

Some credit cards (American Express and certain gold and platinum Visa and MasterCards, for example) offer automatic flight insurance against death or dismemberment in case of an airplane crash.

If you still feel that you need more insurance, try one of the companies listed below. But don't pay for more insurance than you need. If you need only trip-cancellation insurance, for example, don't purchase coverage for lost or stolen property. Trip-cancellation insurance costs approximately 6% to 8% of the total value of your vacation. Some of the reputable issuers of travel insurance follow:

- **Access America,** 6600 W. Broad St., Richmond, VA 23230 (☎ **800/284-8300**).
- **Mutual of Omaha,** Mutual of Omaha Plaza, Omaha, NE 68175 (☎ **800/228-9792**).
- **Travel Guard International,** 1145 Clark St., Stevens Point, WI 54481 (☎ **800/826-1300**).
- **Travel Insured International, Inc.,** P.O. Box 280568, East Hartford, CT 06128 (☎ **800/243-3174**).

Aaaachooo! What If I Get Sick Away from Home?

It can be hard to find a doctor you trust when you're away from home. And getting sick could ruin your vacation. Bring all your medications with you, as well as a prescription for more if you worry that you'll run out. If you have health insurance, be sure to carry your identification card in your wallet. Bring an extra pair of contact lenses in case you lose one. And don't forget the Pepto-Bismol for common travelers' ailments like upset stomach or diarrhea, which sometimes accompany jet lag.

If you have a chronic illness, talk to your doctor before taking the trip. For such conditions as epilepsy, diabetes, or a heart condition, wear a **Medic Alert identification tag,** which immediately alerts any doctor to your condition and gives him or her access to your medical records through Medic Alert's 24-hour hot line. A worldwide toll-free emergency response number is on the tag, so if you become ill in London, you'll know exactly whom to call. Membership is $35, plus a $15 annual fee. Contact the Medic Alert Foundation, P.O. Box 1009, Turlock, CA 95381-1009 (☎ **800/825-3785**). If you worry about getting sick away from home, purchase medical insurance (see the section on travel insurance above); it will cover you more completely than your existing health insurance.

If you do get sick, ask the concierge at your hotel to recommend a local doctor—even his or her own doctor, if necessary. If you can't locate a doctor, try contacting your embassy or consulate (see appendix A for addresses and phone numbers); or dial ☎ **999** (no coins required)—the number for police and medical emergencies. If the situation is life-threatening, go to the emergency or accident department at the local hospital. Under the U.K.'s national healthcare system, you are eligible only for free *emergency* care. If you are admitted to a hospital (even from an accident and emergency department) as an in-patient, you are required to pay unless you are a U.K. resident or resident of the European Economic Area. This holds true for follow-up care as well. For the names, addresses, and phone numbers of hospitals offering 24-hour emergency care, see "Hospitals" in appendix A.

Extra! Extra!

If you do end up paying for healthcare, especially if you have to be admitted to a London hospital for any reason, most **health insurance plans and HMOs** will cover at least part of out-of-country hospital visits and procedures. Most make you pay the bills up front at the time of care, however, and give you a refund after you return and file all the paperwork. Members of **Blue Cross/Blue Shield** can use their cards at select hospitals in most major cities worldwide just as they would at home, which means lower out-of-pocket costs. They have five facilities in the London area alone. Call ☎ **800/810-BLUE** or visit the Web site **www.bluecares.com/blue/bluecard/wwn** for a list of participating hospitals.

Extra! Extra!

You can obtain a list of English doctors before leaving home from the **International Association of Medical Assistance to Travelers** (IAMAT). The address in the U.S. is 417 Center St., Lewiston, NY 14092 (☎ **716/754-4883**); in Canada, it's at 40 Regal Rd., Guelph, Ontario N1K 1B5 (☎ **519/754-4883**).

Mad Cows & Englishmen

You don't have to worry about drinking tap water in London, but what about eating British beef? You might remember reading about "mad-cow disease," which garnered international headlines in 1997. This was a national health crisis, and the British government wasn't exactly prompt in dealing with it—in part because British beef is an important part of the economy. The mad-cow crisis changed the beef-eating habits of many U.K. residents and visitors, but nationalistic types pooh-poohed it as hysteria. Today the crisis has abated, and nearly everyone will tell you it's once again safe to eat British beef. But I'm not going to be the one to tell you to do so. There is still plenty of beef to be had in London restaurants; if you want to be careful, make certain that you know where it came from (often it's from France).

I'll Take Two on the Aisle: Making Reservations & Getting Tickets Ahead of Time

If your time in London is limited and there are plays, concerts, or restaurants you don't want to miss, it might be worth your while to book them in advance. Having said that, I can also tell you that you can generally get into all but a handful of restaurants on fairly short notice. It's important to book, but you can do so when you arrive. Otherwise, you'll have to call (or fax) the restaurant directly (phone numbers are listed for restaurants in chapters 10 and 11) or ask the concierge at your hotel to make the reservation for you. For a list of hot restaurants in London that require advance booking, see chapter 9, "The Lowdown on the London Dining Scene."

The Show Must Go On

Even if a major West End show is officially sold out, your chances of getting a seat are often good if you go directly to the box office. Every London theatre has a row (or more) of house seats kept until the last possible moment. Those seats, and any returns, generally go on sale the day of the performance—sometimes in the morning, sometimes an hour before.

If there's something you absolutely can't miss, you can book (and pay an additional commission) before you leave by contacting the following:

➤ **www.keithprowse.com**

The New York office of **Keith Prowse** (☎ **800/669-8687** or 212/398-1430; tickets@keithprowse.com), a London-based ticket agency, handles West End shows, the English National Opera, pop concerts, and events like the Chelsea Flower Show and the British Open. After the agency receives payment, it sends you a voucher that you can exchange for tickets at the box office.

➤ **www.albemarle-london.com**

The respected **Albemarle booking agency** (74 Mortimer St., London, W1N 8HL; ☎ **017/637 9041;** fax 0171/631-0375; sales@albemarle-london.com) maintains a definitive **UK Theatre Web** site with listings of all current West End shows, opera, ballet, and rock and pop concerts. If you see something you like, you can book it via e-mail. Their prices include a booking fee of 22% plus tax. They sell the best seats to most shows for £44.10 ($73); the face value of the ticket is £35 ($58). If there's time, they'll mail tickets worldwide; otherwise, you can pick up the tickets at the theatre or have them delivered to your hotel.

How Do I Find Out What's Playing Where?

The following Web sites are useful for finding out what's going on in London:

➤ **www.timeout.co.uk**

You'll find the most comprehensive online theatre, music, dance, and other event listings in *Time Out.* You can browse through and find everything that's currently playing.

➤ **www.telegraph.co.uk**

Electronic Telegraph, the online version of *The Daily Telegraph,* reviews theatre and other performance events in its "Arts & Books" section.

➤ **www.the-times.co.uk**

In the Internet edition of London's *The Times* and *The Sunday Times,* look under "Arts" and "Culture" for reviews and listings of West End shows and other events.

➤ **www.thisislondon.co.uk**

The online version of the *Evening Standard* newspaper has listings of current theatre and music events.

➤ **www.royalopera.org**

The Royal Opera's Web site provides a summary of its opera and ballet season.

To get more information on booking ahead for special London events, such as the Chelsea Flower Show or Wimbledon, check the numbers listed in the "London Calendar of Events" section in chapter 1.

Pack It Up, I'll Take It

Lugging around too much luggage is a drag on your time, your energy, and your arms. Before you start packing, think realistically about what you'll need for the length of time you'll be gone. And think practically. A sauce stain on a white silk dress or white dress shirt will render it unwearable. In general, think *layers*. Think *nonwhite*. And unless you're going to London in the height of summer (perhaps even then), think *45° to 60° and often damp*.

There's a very good reason why the English favor wools: They're warm, they're practical, and they hold their shape even after a drenching downpour. Keep in mind that many hotels have contraptions called *trouser presses* in the rooms. These get out the wrinkles and save you the hassle of toting along a travel iron. And remember, you're going to be in one of the great shopping cities of the world. If there's any essential item you've forgotten, you can buy it in London.

What to Bring

Start your packing by taking everything you think you'll need and laying it out on the bed. Then get rid of half of it.

I don't say this because the airlines won't let you take it all (they will, with some limits), but because you don't want to get a hernia from lugging half your house around with you. Negotiating your way to and from the airport and to your hotel can be difficult enough; if you're staying in a B&B without an elevator, lugging a heavy load of suitcases up and down narrow London stairways can be taxing, to say the least.

Some essentials: comfortable walking shoes, a camera, a versatile (that is, dark-colored) sweater, a jacket (preferably one with a hood), a belt, toiletries, medications (pack these in your carry-on bag so that you'll have them if the airline loses your luggage), and something to sleep in (London thermostats are often set at about 10° lower than in the U.S.). Unless you'll be attending a board meeting, a funeral, or one of the city's finest restaurants, you probably won't need a suit or a fancy dress. You'll get much more use out of a pair of jeans or khakis and a comfortable sweater. (See the packing list below for other essential advice.) On the other hand, if you arrive at an exclusive hotel like The Savoy wearing a jogging suit and sneakers, you'll feel out of place from the word go.

London can be drizzly at any time of the year, so packing a collapsible umbrella (or *brolly,* as the Brits call them) is always a wise idea. You can forego this if you have a waterproof jacket with a hood. If you're traveling to London in the late fall or winter, a lined raincoat and a heavy sweater or two will be put to good use, as will a pair of gloves and a scarf.

At the end of this chapter is a handy **packing checklist** that will make getting your act together and taking it on the road a snap.

Cool Britannia

According to 18th-century writer Dr. Samuel Johnson, "When two Englishmen meet, their first talk is of the **weather.**" Things haven't changed much since then. The unpredictability of the English climate has led to another sound British maxim: "There is no such thing as bad weather, there's only inappropriate clothing."

And How to Pack It

When choosing your suitcase, think about the kind of traveling you'll be doing. If you'll be doing a lot of walking with your luggage on hard floors, then a bag with wheels makes sense. If you'll be carrying your luggage over uneven roads or up and down stairs, wheels won't help much. A fold-over garment bag will help keep dressy clothes wrinkle-free but can be a nuisance if you'll be packing and unpacking a lot. Hard-sided luggage protects breakable items better but weighs more than soft-sided bags.

When packing, start with the biggest, hardest items (usually shoes), then fit smaller items in and around them. Pack breakable items between several layers of clothes, or keep them in your carry-on bag. Put things that could leak, like shampoos and colognes, in sealed plastic bags. Lock your suitcase with small padlocks (available at most luggage stores, if your bag doesn't already have them), and put an identification tag on the outside as well as a slip of paper with your name, home address, and destination on the inside.

It's Not Heavy, It's My Carry-on

You're allowed **two pieces** of carry-on luggage, both of which must fit in the overhead compartment or beneath the seat in front of you. Each airline has its own **dimension limits** for carry-ons, but they usually average around 60 inches total (10 × 14 × 36 inches). Your carry-on should contain a book, any breakable items you don't want to put in your suitcase, a snack in case you don't like the airline food, any medications you're taking with you, and any vital documents you don't want to lose with your luggage (like your return tickets, passport, wallet, and so on). It's a wise idea to have one of your carry-ons be a backpack or shoulder bag that can double as an all-purpose carry-along bag while you're in London. You'll be traipsing around with guidebooks, maps, and a camera—all of which can fit in your bag.

Tourist Trap

Make sure that the identification tag on your luggage has a flap or tab to **conceal your address.** Some criminals peruse visible luggage tags at the airport, collecting the addresses of people leaving on vacation.

London Unplugged: Electronics *Not* to Bring

When personal cassette players first came out, I made the mistake of taking one with me on a trip. The battery-operated cassette player itself wasn't so bad, but the dozen tapes I thought I just had to have to keep me happy turned out to be a pain in the you-know-what. To make matters worse, after I arrived at my destination, the last thing I wanted was to tune myself *out* of what was going on around me. I wanted to tune myself into where I was. That, after all, is the experience of traveling. I say this because we now live in an age when we think we have to tote along every new electronic toy or gadget. Trust me, doing so will not add anything to your trip—in fact, it will detract from it.

Some electronic items might be necessary—a **laptop computer,** for instance, if you have to work while you're on vacation. Other than that? Most hotels in London now have hair dryers in the rooms or at the front desk if you need one. Video games for the kids? These will only prevent them from soaking up the sights and sounds of a new place. My advice? ***Leave all the electronics at home.*** When are you really going to have time to listen to a CD on your portable CD player? In the plane you can listen to music on their headphones. On the streets you'll be too preoccupied and too busy reminding yourself to look left, instead of right, to get much pleasure out of your favorite tape or CD. Plus, electronic gear takes up too much valuable space in your luggage.

Still determined to lug around half of a Radio Shack? Here's what you need to know. American current runs 110V, 60 cycles. The standard voltage throughout Britain is 240v AC, 50 cycles. Translation: You can't plug an

Your Last-Minute Checklist: Did You Turn Off the Iron?

There are plenty of housekeeping details you need to take care of before you leave. Although most are fairly obvious, they are easy to overlook in the excitement of getting ready for a trip. It's best not to leave a house unattended; try at least to have a neighbor look in on your house from time to time to pick up the mail, feed the cats, water the plants, and generally make the place appear less abandoned. For longer trips, consider getting a full-time house-sitter. Here are other household details you need to handle before you leave:

- ☐ Put a hold on your mail and newspaper deliveries or arrange for a neighbor to pick them up for you. Nothing screams "We're not home" louder than a pile of newspapers on your doorstep.
- ☐ Get someone to look after your pets (or kennel them) and water the plants.
- ☐ Empty/defrost the refrigerator.
- ☐ Reconfirm your plane's seat reservations and hotel bookings.
- ☐ Put several lights in the house on timers (dining room at dinner time, TV room during prime time, and so on).
- ☐ Have a neighbor start your car once a week or so.
- ☐ Lock all windows and doors (don't forget the basement and garage).
- ☐ Arrange for a friend or car service to take you to the airport (in the end, this method is cheaper and better than leaving your car in the airport garage).
- ☐ Call the airline to double-check that your flight is on time.
- ☐ Get to the airport *at least* 2 hours before your flight.
- ☐ Sit back on the plane, take a deep breath, and tell yourself: "I'm on my way to London!" Cheerio! Have a blast. Send me a postcard.

American appliance into a British outlet without frying your appliance and/or blowing a fuse. You need a **currency converter** or **transformer** to bring the voltage down and the cycles up. Two-pronged American plugs will not fit into the square, three-pronged British wall sockets. You need a square, three-pronged **adapter** and/or converter when using appliances in Britain. Plug adapters and converters are available at most travel, luggage, electronics, and hardware stores. Some plug adapters are also currency converters, but not all.

Travel-sized versions of hair dryers, irons, shavers, and so on come in "dual-voltage," which means they have built-in converters (usually you have to turn a switch to go back and forth). Most contemporary **laptop computers** automatically sense the current and adapt accordingly (check the operating manual, bottom of the machine, or with the manufacturer first to make sure you won't burn the thing out). If you're still in doubt, call the **Franzus**

Corporation (☎ **203/723-6664**) for a copy of its "Foreign Electricity Is No Deep Dark Secret" pamphlet (complete, of course, with a convenient order form for adapters and converters).

If you insist on lugging your own **hair dryer** or electric shaver to London, make sure that it is dual-voltage or that you carry along a converter. Hotels black out on a regular basis when an American plugs in his 110V hair dryer and the appliance explodes in an impressive shower of sparks or melts in his hands. Hoteliers and other guests will not be amused, and neither will you.

For shaving, I'd stick with a straight-edge razor unless you have a battery-operated **electric shaver;** that way, you won't have to bother with voltage problems. However, most hotels have a special plug for low-wattage shavers—and shavers *only.*

Part 2

Finding the Hotel That's Right for You

Many travelers don't care where they stay, as long as it's cheap. The reasoning is, "I'm only going to be in a hotel room to sleep." That's true, as far as it goes, but having stayed in my share of dumps, I also know that a hotel room can color your mood and turn a potentially memorable vacation into something unnecessarily dreary. Some of this has to do with age and expectations. Young travelers are more resilient (and generally have less money to spend). Older travelers like a few creature comforts.

The choice is up to you. Do you want to wake up in a dark room on an air shaft, a place that makes you want to bolt outdoors as quickly as possible and not return until you absolutely have to? Or do you want to stay in a place where you can comfortably relax and put your feet up between forays into London? Or do you want to treat yourself to marble bathrooms, luxurious surroundings, and 24-hour room service? (We all want that—the question is, can you afford it?)

London accommodations come in all shapes, sizes, and prices. Nothing is going to be as inexpensive as that Motel 6 on the freeway back home, but there are good budget hotels and plenty of B&Bs that won't cost you an arm and a leg. There are wonderful small hotels full of charm and character, unique boutique hotels, large chain hotels, and several ultra-luxurious places known the world over.

Chapter 5

Pillow Talk: The Lowdown on the London Hotel Scene

In This Chapter

- How to choose a neighborhood
- How to get the most hotel for your money
- The kinds of hotels you'll find in London
- What to do if you arrive without a hotel reservation

Finding an inexpensive hotel room in London can be difficult, but it's certainly not impossible. You just have to adjust your idea of what "inexpensive" means. London contains an abundance of clean, well-run B&Bs and hotels where you can rest your weary head for less than $150 a night and enjoy a solid English breakfast in the morning. Moderately priced hotels—those in the $150 to $225 range—are somewhat harder to find. There's no lack of expensive ($225 to $300) and very expensive ($300 to $400) hotels. And if money is no object, you can check into one of London's many exclusive hotels, where rooms *start* at an expletive-deleted $400 a night—without breakfast. Self-catering accommodations with kitchens are also available and are sometimes better for families and those on a tight budget.

Whatever your hotel or accommodation choice in London, I remind you again that it's **important to book ahead,** especially if you're planning your trip between mid-April and early October. Hotel rooms in the inexpensive to moderate price range are the first ones to be snapped up by visitors, but space can be tight everywhere if there is a trade show or convention.

A hotel reservation is never considered confirmed unless the hotel receives partial or full payment (this varies from hotel to hotel). You can generally reserve immediately with a credit card; otherwise, you will have to send payment by mail (generally an international money order).

London Calling

Many hotels in London don't have toll-free numbers, so here's what you do to make a phone call to London or the United Kingdom from the U.S. First you dial **011,** then the **country code** for the U.K., which is **44.** After that, you dial the **city code.** London has two city codes (given for every number in this guide): **0171** and **0181**, but if you're calling from outside the U.K., drop the initial zero. Then dial the number itself. Keep in mind that London is 5 hours ahead of New York (add another hour for each time zone moving west). *Note: The city codes for London will change as of June 1999. See "Reader Alert" on page xiv.*

Location, Location, Location

Central London, considered the city center, is divided into three areas: the city, the West End, and West London (or Central London beyond the West End). Below are brief descriptions of the Central London neighborhoods where the hotels recommended in chapter 6 are located. Not all of Central London is covered here, because it's unlikely you'll be staying in the city (which has many tourist sites but few hotels) or Holborn (the legal heart of London).

For a more complete description of Central London, see chapter 7, "Getting Your Bearings." Crime is less prevalent in London than in other major cities, and all the neighborhoods below are safe areas.

The West End

Covent Garden & The Strand Covent Garden is home of the Royal Opera House and the revamped Covent Garden Market, one of the hippest and most popular gathering spots in London. It's chock-a-block with shops, restaurants, and pubs. The Fielding, one of London's best budget hotels, and the Covent Garden Hotel, a luxurious "boutique" hotel created from an old hospital, are both here. Covent Garden and Leicester Square tube stops provide the closest access, but you can easily walk to anywhere in the West End or neighboring Soho.

South of Covent Garden is **The Strand,** a major street flanked with theatres, shops, restaurants, and hotels (The Savoy being the most famous), but architecturally it's far less distinctive than the area around Covent Garden.

If you stay here: You'll be in the heart of the West End, close to theatres and entertainment; it's busy all day long and far into the night, so noise could be a problem (although noise won't be a problem at either of the two hotels I recommend in this area in chapter 6).

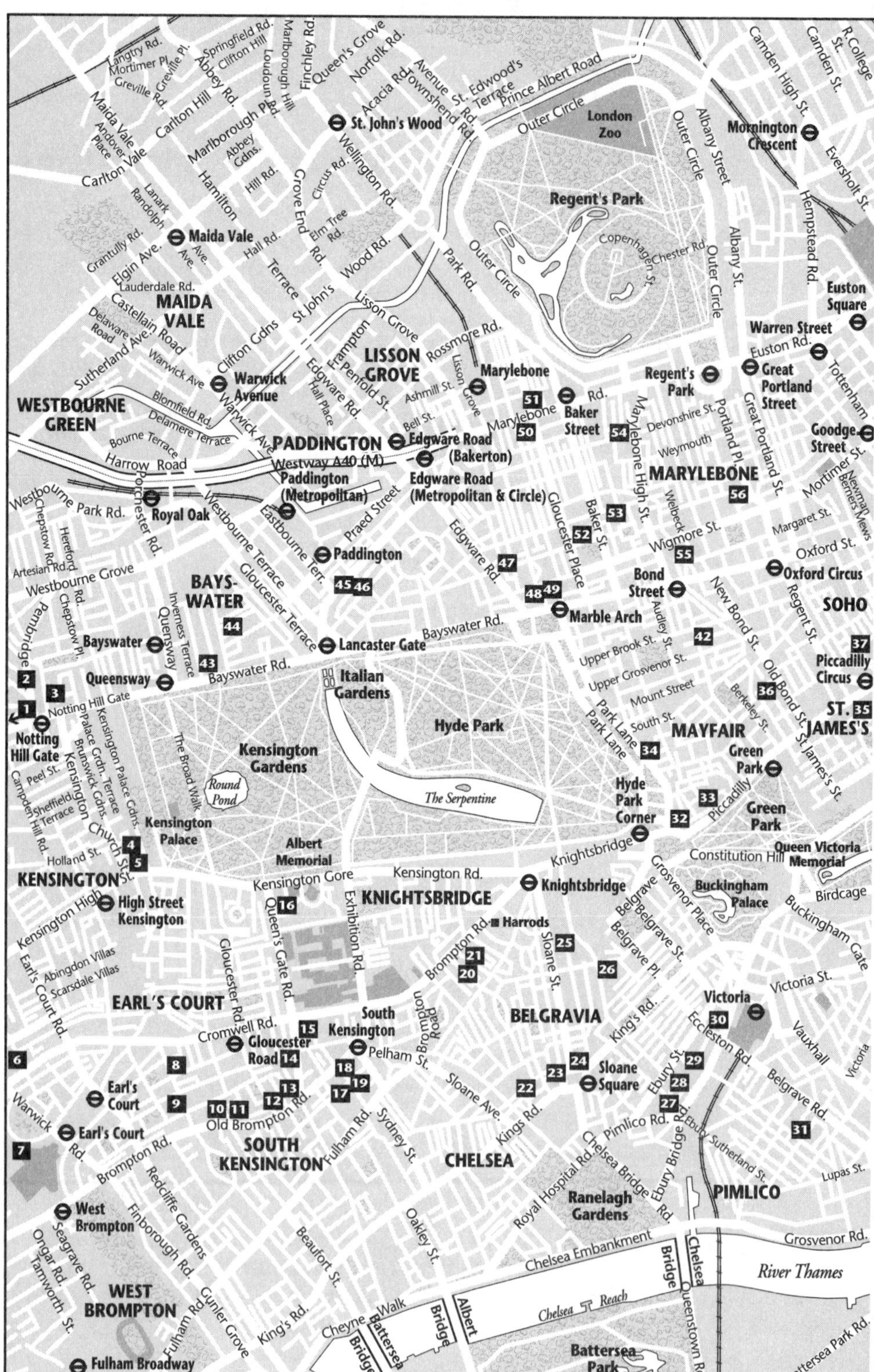

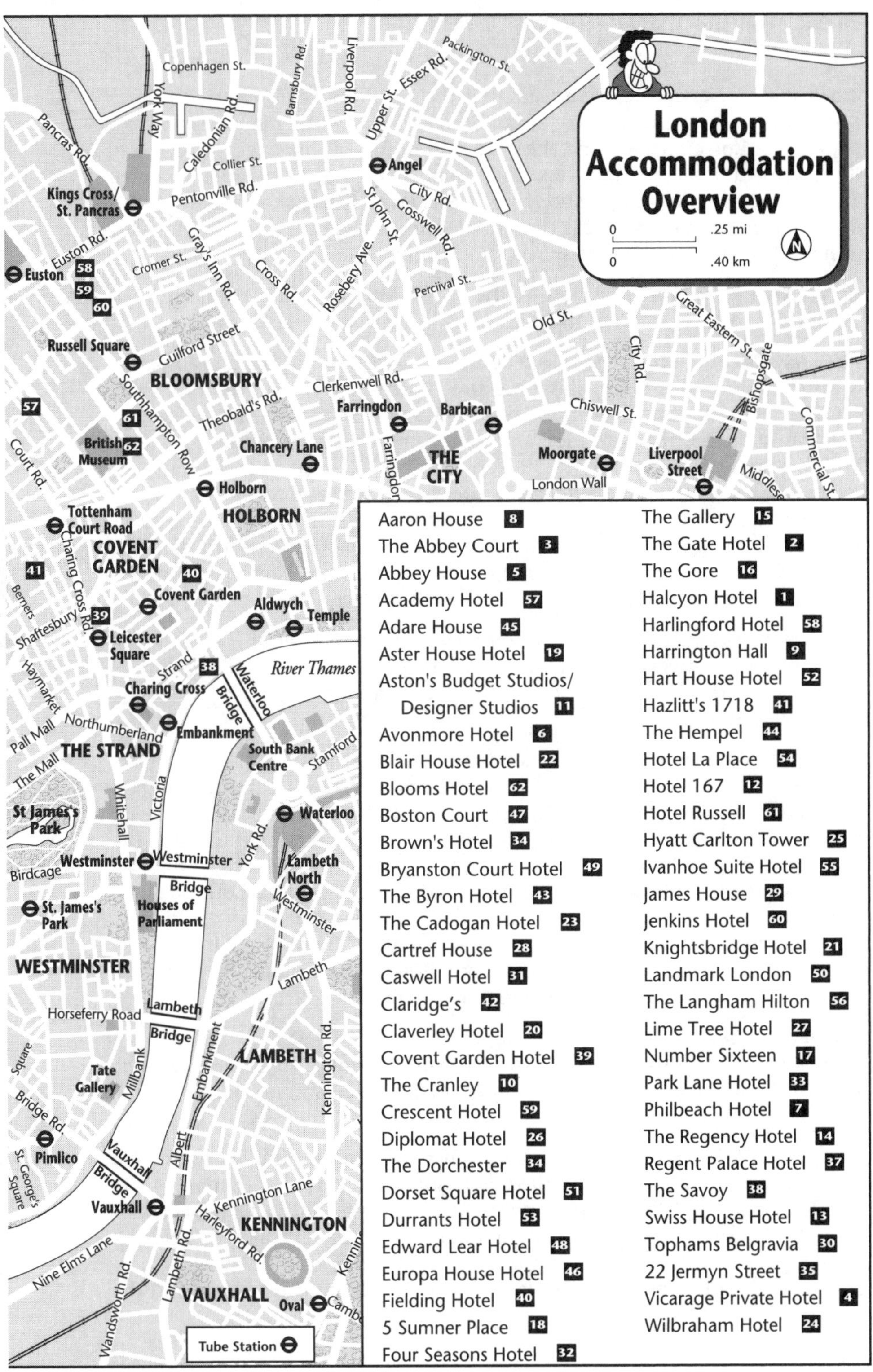
London Accommodation Overview
0 .25 mi
0 .40 km
N
Copenhagen St.
York Way
Caledonian Rd.
Barnsbury Rd.
Liverpool Rd.
Upper St.
Essex Rd.
Packington St.
Pancras Rd.
Collier St.
Angel
Pentonville Rd.
Kings Cross/ St. Pancras
City Rd.
St John St.
Goswell Rd.
Euston Rd.
Cromer St.
Gray's Inn Rd.
Cross Rd.
Rosebery Ave.
Percival St.
Euston
Russell Square
Guilford Street
BLOOMSBURY
Old St.
Great Eastern St.
City Rd.
Bishopsgate
Commercial St.
Southampton Row
Theobald's Rd.
Clerkenwell Rd.
Farringdon
Barbican
Chiswell St.
British Museum
Chancery Lane
Farringdon
THE CITY
Moorgate
London Wall
Liverpool Street
Middlesex
Court Rd.
Holborn
HOLBORN
Tottenham Court Road
Charing Cross Rd.
COVENT GARDEN
Covent Garden
Berners
Shaftesbury
Leicester Square
Aldwych
Temple
Haymarket
Strand
Charing Cross
River Thames
Waterloo Bridge
Pall Mall
Northumberland
Embankment
South Bank Centre
Stamford
The Mall
THE STRAND
St James's Park
Whitehall
Victoria
Waterloo
York Rd.
Birdcage
Westminster
Westminster Bridge
Lambeth North
St. James's Park
Houses of Parliament
Westminster
WESTMINSTER
Lambeth
Horseferry Road
Lambeth Bridge
Square
Tate Gallery
Millbank
Embankment
LAMBETH
Kennington Rd.
Bridge Rd.
Pimlico
Albert
Vauxhall Bridge
St. George's Square
Vauxhall
Kennington Lane
Harleyford Rd.
KENNINGTON
Nine Elms Lane
Wandsworth Rd.
Lambeth Rd.
VAUXHALL
Oval
Tube Station
Aaron House 8
The Abbey Court 3
Abbey House 5
Academy Hotel 57
Adare House 45
Aster House Hotel 19
Aston's Budget Studios/ Designer Studios 11
Avonmore Hotel 6
Blair House Hotel 22
Blooms Hotel 62
Boston Court 47
Brown's Hotel 34
Bryanston Court Hotel 49
The Byron Hotel 43
The Cadogan Hotel 23
Cartref House 28
Caswell Hotel 31
Claridge's 42
Claverley Hotel 20
Covent Garden Hotel 39
The Cranley 10
Crescent Hotel 59
Diplomat Hotel 26
The Dorchester 34
Dorset Square Hotel 51
Durrants Hotel 53
Edward Lear Hotel 48
Europa House Hotel 46
Fielding Hotel 40
5 Sumner Place 18
Four Seasons Hotel 32
The Gallery 15
The Gate Hotel 2
The Gore 16
Halcyon Hotel 1
Harlingford Hotel 58
Harrington Hall 9
Hart House Hotel 52
Hazlitt's 1718 41
The Hempel 44
Hotel La Place 54
Hotel 167 12
Hotel Russell 61
Hyatt Carlton Tower 25
Ivanhoe Suite Hotel 55
James House 29
Jenkins Hotel 60
Knightsbridge Hotel 21
Landmark London 50
The Langham Hilton 56
Lime Tree Hotel 27
Number Sixteen 17
Park Lane Hotel 33
Philbeach Hotel 7
The Regency Hotel 14
Regent Palace Hotel 37
The Savoy 38
Swiss House Hotel 13
Tophams Belgravia 30
22 Jermyn Street 35
Vicarage Private Hotel 4
Wilbraham Hotel 24

Bloomsbury North of Covent Garden is the Bloomsbury district, with the British Museum, the University of London, and many other colleges and bookstores. Russell Square and the streets around it are lined with hotels and B&Bs favored by budget travelers. Tottenham Court Road and Goodge Street are Bloomsbury's two major shopping streets and, with Russell Square, the main Underground stops. This centrally located area tends to be quiet and rather staid, but there are many restaurants and pubs.

If you stay here: You'll be close to the British Museum and within walking distance of the West End; at night the area is less active.

Piccadilly Circus, Leicester Square & Charing Cross Central London's major theatre, entertainment, and shopping streets are found to the west of Covent Garden. Piccadilly Circus is one of the world's best-known tourist meccas, full of megastores, glitzy arcades, and touristy restaurants. Commercial West End theatres and first-run movie palaces lie on or adjacent to Shaftesbury Avenue and Leicester Square. Charing Cross Road is famed for its bookstores and booksellers. There are some older tourist hotels in this busy area, but the streets tend to be crowded, noisy, and rather anonymous. Transportation is easy, however, with tube stations at Piccadilly Circus, Leicester Square, and Charing Cross Road, which is also a major rail station.

If you stay here: You'll be in the commercial heart of London, close to major shopping streets and entertainment; be prepared for lots of street action, day and night. On weekends, this area can become somewhat boisterous and rowdy.

Soho The warren of densely packed streets east of Leicester Square is Soho. It has always been known for its restaurants and clubs, but it had a rather seedy air until about a decade ago when gentrification took over big time. Soho remains a major tourist hub for shopping, eating, and nightclubbing. It has also become London's Gay Village, with dozens of gay pubs, restaurants, and upscale cafe-bars found around Old Compton Street. London's Chinatown is centered around Gerrard Street. Soho isn't particularly known for its hotel accommodations, but there are a few, including Hazlitt's 1718, one of London's oldest and most charming hotels. The closest tube stops are Leicester Square, Covent Garden, and Tottenham Court Road.

If you stay here: Soho is a nightclub, restaurant, and cafe mecca, with a few seedy porn shops thrown in. Theatres and entertainment are minutes away. The streets can be confusing, and they're often packed and noisy late into the night.

Westminster & Victoria Westminster has been the seat of British government since 1050, when Edward the Confessor moved his court here. Trafalgar Square, a famous gathering point for tourists (and pigeons) across from the National Gallery and the National Portrait Gallery, marks its northern periphery. From there, the Westminster area extends south, running beside the Thames and east of St. James's Park to Westminster Abbey and the Houses of Parliament.

Dollars & Sense

If you're looking for an **inexpensive to moderate hotel or B&B,** try Bayswater, Earl's Court, Notting Hill, Paddington, or Westminster/Victoria.

If you want to spend a few more pounds on **a moderate to expensive hotel or B&B,** try Bloomsbury, Chelsea, Covent Garden, Marylebone, Soho, or South Kensington.

If you want to go all out on a **luxury hotel,** head to Belgravia, Knightsbridge, Mayfair, or The Strand.

The Victoria area around massive **Victoria Station** is a good spot to track down convenient B&Bs and hotels, especially on Ebury Street. Victoria Station is one of London's major transportation hubs—a nucleus for the Underground, BritRail, and Victoria Coach Station.

If you stay here: Hotels along Ebury Street are plentiful and won't break the piggy bank. Although public transportation options are great, you might feel slightly out of the loop in this area, especially at night.

St. James's There are lots of tony hotels in St. James's. Named after the Court of St. James's, this posh neighborhood—which begins at Piccadilly Circus and moves southwest to include Pall Mall, the Mall, St. James's Park, and Green Park—is often called Royal London. The Queen herself lives here, at Buckingham Palace. It might be the most convenient area in the West End, because it includes the American Express office on the Haymarket and such upscale shopping emporiums as Fortnum & Mason (where the Queen buys her groceries) on Regent Street.

If you stay here: You'll be near the seats of royal power and privilege and some great shopping, as well as two lovely parks; but you'll pay top dollar (or pound, I should say) for the choice location.

Mayfair Luxury hotels are clustered along the quiet streets of Mayfair, an area filled with elegant Georgian town houses and exclusive shops. It's considered the most fashionable section of London. There are no major tourist attractions. The American Embassy is located at Grosvenor (pronounced *Grove-nur)* Square, and according to song legend, a nightingale once sang in Berkeley (pronounced *Bark-lee)* Square. You can access Mayfair to the north by the Bond Street or Marble Arch Underground stations, and to the south by Hyde Park Corner or Green Park stations.

If you stay here: You'll be in a lovely place—if you can afford it. Most of the hotels are luxury establishments and are extremely expensive. You'll have to go elsewhere for your fun.

Marylebone Marylebone (pronounced *Mar-lee-bone),* which includes Regent's Park (home of the London Zoo), is north of Bloomsbury and Mayfair. Here you'll find that perennial tourist favorite, Madame Tussaud's. Baker Street continues to draw Sherlock Holmes aficionados. There are some lovely squares, such as Portman Place, laid out by Robert Adam in the late 18th century, but later development robbed Marylebone of much of its village character.

If you stay here: You'll find plenty of hotels and restaurants, as well as a huge park that's great for kids. This neighborhood is less convenient, however—especially at night, if you are going to be spending much of your time at the West End theatres. The area is more business oriented and less residential, so the side streets are generally deserted after 8pm.

Central London Beyond the West End

Knightsbridge Knightsbridge, a fashionable and fashion-conscious area south of Hyde Park and west of Green Park, is famed for its shopping. Harrods, one of the world's great department stores, is located here. Chic, expensive boutiques and upscale restaurants are found along Beauchamp (pronounced *Beech-am)* Place. The area has some super-expensive high-rise and boutique hotels and a few midrange hotels.

If you stay here: The hotels are generally in the expensive-plus category, and although the area is an upscale-shopper's dream, there is surprisingly little nightlife for ordinary folks. On the other hand, you're close to Hyde Park.

Extra! Extra!

If you want to stay in a **large tourist hotel,** you'll find the most options in Piccadilly Circus and The Strand.

Belgravia Belgravia, extending south of Knightsbridge to the river, has been a residential quarter for London aristocrats since Queen Victoria's time. It rivals Mayfair for poshness and wealth, and like Mayfair, it doesn't have any major museums or tourist attractions. The hotels here tend to be on the upper end of the price scale.

If you stay here: Be prepared for steep prices and empty streets at night.

Chelsea Flanking the river to the southwest of Belgravia is the lovely Chelsea district, full of expensively charming town houses and quiet mews (former stables converted into residences). Upper crusts (including the late Princess Diana) who lived and/or shopped around Sloane Square, Chelsea's northern boundary, were called the Sloane Rangers in the 1980s. In the 19th century, Chelsea was the preferred place of residence for artistic and literary luminaries. The lovely 17th-century Chelsea Physic Garden is located on the grounds of the Chelsea Royal Hospital, which also plays host to the annual Chelsea Flower Show. Trendy King's Road, Chelsea's major shopping (and traffic) artery, has been in the forefront of contemporary London street fashion since the 1960s.

If you stay here: The area is charming, but public transportation by the Underground (tube) to/from here is a royal pain in the you-know-what, so getting to the West End can be time-consuming. King's Road is a lively shopping street, but it closes down after 6pm.

Kensington & Holland Park The Royal Borough of Kensington lies west of Kensington Gardens, one of London's most beautiful parks. In the park itself is Kensington Palace, once the home of Princess Diana and still lived in by Princess Margaret and other royals. Two major shopping streets traverse Kensington: Kensington High Street to the south and Kensington Church Street to the east. Nearby Holland Park, another tony neighborhood, has an open-air theatre and is a lovely place for a quiet stroll. The hotels here generally are converted Victorian town houses.

If you stay here: Proximity to Kensington Gardens and Holland Park and the abundance of shopping make this area great during the daytime. At night the residential nature of the neighborhood takes over, so you might feel a bit lonely—plus you'll have to allot extra time for getting to and from the West End.

Best Neighborhoods for Museum Mavens

For proximity to museums, check out the hotel and B&B choices in South Kensington, Bloomsbury, and Westminster.

South Kensington South Kensington, a busy residential neighborhood south of Kensington Gardens, is prime hotel and restaurant territory. Popular with European and American travelers, its streets and squares are lined with solid, frequently identical Victorian terrace houses, many of them converted into B&Bs and small hotels. Gloucester Road tube station provides easy access into the rest of London and is a stop on the Piccadilly Line from Heathrow Airport. South Kensington is the other major tube station in the area. South Ken is frequently referred to as Museumland because the Natural History Museum, the Victoria and Albert Museum, and the Science Museum are all located here. So is Royal Albert Hall, a landmark concert hall. Kensington Gardens is never more than a few minutes' walk from anywhere in South Ken. All in all, this is one of the best areas to stay in.

If you stay here: This area offers an abundance of reasonably priced hotels and B&Bs, major museums located practically on your doorstep, and lots of restaurants. The one potential problem—and it's not a great one—is that you'll need to allot some extra time for traveling by Underground to the West End.

Out & About

London's best selection of **gay hotels and B&Bs** is located in Earl's Court.

Earl's Court South of Kensington (and west of South Kensington) is Earl's Court, sometimes called Kangaroo Court for the preponderance of

Australians who favor its budget hotels and non-swank pubs and restaurants. Earl's Court is a bit tattered in places, but it's being gentrified, and for cheap rooms and eats, it still can't be beat. Visitors pour into the major exhibitions held at the Earl's Court Exhibition Centre. For decades the neighborhood has been home to a sizable gay community, and although much of the action has moved to Soho, Earl's Court still has several gay pubs, restaurants, and hotels. Earl's Court is the area's primary tube station.

If you stay here: The area is noted for its inexpensive lodging, but it isn't the prettiest part of town by any stretch; in places, it's down-at-the-heels. Also, at night you might feel that you're far from the glittering center of London—and in fact, you are.

Paddington & Bayswater The Paddington area, north of Kensington Gardens and Hyde Park, has Paddington Station as its focal point. Norfolk Square and Sussex Gardens are crammed with inexpensive B&Bs. Quaint Paddington isn't; it's busy rather than lively. There are no major tourist sites here.

Bayswater, south of Paddington Station, is another area to look for B&Bs. Most are found in Victorian terrace houses around large squares. Like Paddington, Bayswater has no major tourist sites, but it's close to Hyde Park. Tube stations are Paddington, Bayswater, Queensway, Lancaster Gate, and Marble Arch.

If you stay here: Budget hotels are plentiful, but Paddington and Bayswater are not very distinguished and certainly not inspiring. You won't end up spending a great deal of your precious time in either area, except to sleep.

Notting Hill The Notting Hill area, with busy Bayswater Road to the north and Kensington to the west, has become a hot spot in recent years, particularly the neighborhood of Notting Hill Gate. People used to avoid it, but now it draws visitors to restaurants and clubs. Portobello Road is the site of one of London's most famous street markets. The nicer parts of Notting Hill are filled with small, late-Victorian houses and mansions sitting on quiet, leafy streets. The tube station is Notting Hill Gate.

If you stay here: Although it's on its way to gentrification, some visitors (especially older ones) might find this area less than desirable because it's still a bit tatty and run-down around the corners. You're close to popular Portobello Market, but you probably won't spend more than a few hours there; getting to and from the West End at night requires extra time.

The Price Is Right

The **rack rate** is the maximum rate a hotel charges for a room. It's the rate you'd get if you walked in off the street and asked for a room for the night. You sometimes see the rate printed on the fire/emergency exit diagrams posted on the back of your door.

Hotels are happy to charge you the rack rate, but you don't have to pay it! Hardly anybody does. Perhaps the best way to avoid paying the rack rate is surprisingly simple: Just ask for a cheaper or discounted rate. You might be pleasantly surprised. This does not generally apply to smaller hotels and B&Bs, where prices are really not negotiable. Some of them might offer special rates for longer stays, however.

In all but the smallest accommodations, the rate you pay for a room depends on many factors, not the least of which is how you make your reservation. A **travel agent** might be able to negotiate a better price with certain hotels than you could get yourself. (That's because the hotel gives the agent a discount in exchange for steering his or her business toward that hotel.) Reserving a room through the hotel's **800 number** might also result in a lower rate than if you called the hotel directly. On the other hand, the person at the central reservations number might not know about discount rates at specific locations. Local franchises might offer a special group rate for a wedding or family reunion, for example, but they might neglect to tell the central booking line. Your best bet is to call both the local number and the 800 number and see which one gives you a better deal. I know this takes time and costs money, but it could save you a bundle in the long run. (Smaller and less expensive B&Bs and hotels generally don't have an 800 number, so you'll have to call, fax, or e-mail the establishment directly.)

But the best rates of all will probably be with an **air/hotel package** (see "The Pros & Cons of Package Tours" in chapter 3). With these packages, which are sometimes astonishingly cheap, you have to choose a hotel that is part of the package. Package hotels tend to be large chains, and your selection is limited, but you could save hundreds of dollars.

Dollars & Sense

Room rates also change as occupancy rates rise and fall. If a hotel is close to full, it is less likely to extend discount rates; if it's close to empty, it might be willing to negotiate. Business hotels are most crowded on weekdays and usually offer discounted rates for weekend stays. Be sure to mention membership in **AAA, AARP, frequent-flyer programs,** and any other **corporate rewards program** when you make your hotel reservation. This won't work with budget hotels and small B&Bs, but you never know when it might be worth a few dollars off your room rate in larger hotels.

What's in It for Me? What You Get for Your Money

Every recommended hotel has one or more dollar signs ($) next to it to help you hone in on your price limit. These $ symbols are based on the rack rate (no discounts). (*Note:* Dollar signs reflect the average of a hotel's high- and low-end rack rates.) Room prices are subject to change without notice, so even the rates quoted in this book may be different than the actual rate you receive when you make your reservation. Don't be surprised if the rate you are offered is lower than the rack rates listed here; likewise, don't be too alarmed if the price has crept up slightly.

$ ($150 and under) This category covers many B&Bs and some small hotels. You'll get breakfast. The room will have a washbasin and perhaps a built-in shower, but you might have to share a bathroom. Expect small rooms and a basic no-frills approach to decorating. You'll probably have to carry your own bags, and there might not be an elevator. Don't expect air-conditioning.

$$ ($150–$225) The B&Bs and hotels in this price range will generally show a bit more flair, but the rooms could still be on the small side. Most will include breakfast. Again, your room probably won't have air-conditioning, but a phone and TV will most likely be in every room. And chances are you'll have a private bathroom—although it might be small. Some in-room amenities might be available, such as a hair dryer and a trouser press.

$$$ ($225–$300) Amenities (hair dryers, trouser presses, tea-making and coffeemaking equipment, special soaps and shampoos) become standard at this level. So do pretty lobbies with elevators. The in-room TV will most likely be hooked up to a satellite dish or cable network. Breakfast or afternoon tea might be included but generally is not. There will probably be an on-site restaurant. Rooms will be larger and have double-glazed windows (unless the hotel is on The Historic Register) to cut down on noise. Bathrooms in this price range are generally roomy and comfortable (although, as usual, this depends on the age of the hotel and how recently it's been refurbished), with combination bathtub-showers.

$$$$ ($300–$400) A full range of amenities and entertainment options will be in every room. There will probably be two or more phones and perhaps a modem jack for personal computers. Rooms will be large and well decorated, with minibars. Bathrooms will be spacious and generally equipped with a bath *and* shower. Breakfast will not be included, but you'll be able to order whatever you want from a high-priced room service or eat in a good on-site restaurant.

Dollars & Sense

You might be able to save as much as 20% or more by traveling in the off-season: mid-October to mid-December or January to March. Always ask whether any special discounts are in effect. In some cases, you might be able to stay for 7 nights for the price of 6, or a child under 12 might be able to stay for free in the parents' room. If you're willing to share a bathroom, you can save money that way, too.

$$$$$ ($400 and up) You're paying for the name, the location, and the prestige. At these Rolls-Royce hotels, there'll be 24-hour room service and probably access to a spa or health club. There'll be one or more bars and gourmet restaurants. The lobbies will be sumptuous and so will all the detailing. The staff will be at your command. Rooms will have everything, from entertainment centers to heated towel racks. Security will be tight.

Tourist Traps

When making your room reservations, always ask what the **cancellation policy** is. If your plans change, you don't want to end up paying for a room you never slept in. At some hotels, you can cancel a room with 24 hours notice and get your money back; at others, you might have to let the hotel know 5 days in advance.

Taxing Matters

There's no escaping that loathsome **17.5%** *value-added tax* (VAT). In general, it will be figured into the quoted price of the hotel room (except at the upper end of the price scale) and not added on as an unpleasant surprise afterward. It is included in all my recommended hotels unless otherwise noted (the listing will say "rates exclusive of VAT").

Tourist Traps

That phone in your hotel room is just waiting to suck money out of your wallet. Think twice before dialing out. A local call that costs 20p at a phone booth might cost you anywhere from £1 to £2 ($1.65 to $3.30) or even more. If you'll be making a lot of phone calls, get a phone card (see the details in appendix A, "London from A to Z—Facts at Your Fingertips") and use a phone outside the hotel.

What Kind of Place Is Right for You?

Accommodations in London come in a variety of shapes, sizes, and flavors, although they can basically be divided into two categories: hotels and bed-and-breakfast inns. What follows is a general discussion of the quirks and perks of each type.

The ABCs of B&Bs

The range of comfort and service you'll find in B&Bs varies widely. Keep in mind that B&Bs are former homes—old homes at that. The plumbing can be cranky and the water temperature variable. B&Bs often do not have elevators, so you might have to carry your luggage up steep, narrow stairs. If you have a physical disability or any type of physical limitation, B&Bs might not be for you. Most B&B rooms will contain a washbasin, but you might have to share a bathroom. The standards of cleanliness in the shared bathrooms are high, but some travelers prefer to keep their hygiene to themselves. Rooms with private bathrooms or showers (but no toilet) are often available, but the bathrooms are generally small and the showers sometimes so minuscule that even Twiggy would find them cramped.

Many of the lower-priced B&Bs are fairly nondescript when it comes to decor. Coming back to a small room with mismatched furniture, orange walls, and a tiny bathroom down the hall with no hot water might be the price you pay for the low price you pay. The more popular B&B choices—that is, the ones with a touch of class—are predictably more expensive.

Hotels, Schmotels

London has a wide choice of hotels. In some of the less expensive ones, you'll get breakfast with your room. At others, like The Fielding in Covent Garden, you can pay a small additional supplement for it. At the four-star hotels, you'll pay through the nose if you eat breakfast on the premises.

In recent years London has seen the opening of a few **boutique hotels.** The Covent Garden Hotel and the Dorset Square Hotel in Marylebone are two of the best. These hotels are midrange in size if not price; sumptuously furnished, they offer state-of-the-art amenities and full service.

You might also want to consider staying in one of London's older deluxe hotels. The Cadogan in Knightsbridge, The Gore in South Kensington, and Hazlitt's 1718 in Soho have all been around for a century or more. In them you will find a distinctly English kind of style, full of charm and character.

There are also large modern high-rise hotels such as the Hyatt Carlton Tower in Knightsbridge. Some of these hotels cater to large groups and might feel rather anonymous. On the other hand, they are generally well equipped for travelers with disabilities and families with children.

At the top of the hotel spectrum, in terms of price and prestige, are those landmarks of elegance—The Dorchester, Claridge's, The Park Lane, and The Savoy. These famous hotels are considered among the best in the world. In them, you can expect glamorous public rooms, generously proportioned and well-decorated rooms with private bathrooms, on-site health clubs or access to ones nearby, and top-of-the-line service.

Gimme the Best Room in the Joint

Somebody has to get the best room in the house. It might as well be you.

Always ask for a **corner room.** They're usually larger, quieter, closer to the elevator, and have more windows and light than standard rooms. And they don't always cost more.

When you make your reservation, ask whether the hotel is renovating; if it is, request a room away from the renovation work. Some London hotels now offer **nonsmoking rooms;** by all means ask for one if smoke bothers you. Inquire, too, about the location of the restaurants and bars in the hotel—these could be a source of irritating noise.

If you aren't happy with your room when you arrive, talk to the front desk. If they have another room, they should be happy to accommodate you, within reason.

Smoke Gets in Your Eyes

The British, and Europeans in general, are less concerned about smoke-free environments than Americans. This is slowly beginning to change, but you'll find that many London hotels and B&Bs don't have exclusively no-smoking rooms. Some do, and some reserve a floor for nonsmokers. There's no general rule about this: All you can do is ask whether no-smoking rooms are available.

Where Else Can I Look for a Place to Stay?

In the next chapter, I give you a rich sampling of Central London hotels in all price ranges. But you might want to check out other options. You can use this all-purpose Web site to investigate your choices and to make hotel reservations:

➤ **www.demon.co.uk/hotel-uk**

The London Hotels On-Line Reservations System

Extra! Extra!

SeniorsSearch—U.K. (www.ageofreason.com/ssuk/shotels.htm) is a Web site for seniors looking for special hotels and other forms of accommodation, including home and apartment exchanges.

Hotel Strategies for Families Traveling with Kids

Although the bulk of their clients are business travelers staying for short hauls, each of the major international hotel chains does its best to create the impression that they're fully geared for family fun. Look for special summer packages at most hotel chains between June and August. Some of the most consistently generous offers come from the **Forte** (**☎ 800/435-4542**) and **Hilton International** (**☎ 800/445-8667**) chains, but it all depends on the specific branch. For best results, call the 800 number and ask about special family packages.

London also has some less expensive options that are happy to accommodate traveling families. Some of these hotels have rooms with three or four beds. The problem here might be that the entire family must share one small bathroom or a bathroom down the hall. In the next chapter, all hotels suitable for families with kids are noted with the special "Kids" icon.

What If I Didn't Plan Ahead?

I'll say it again: It's not a good idea to arrive in London without a hotel reservation. If you do arrive roomless, your first option is to start calling the hotels directly. You can also book rooms through the following two official London tourist agencies, but you'll have to do it in person because neither has phone service. In the high season, expect long lines at both agencies:

- **The Britain Visitor Centre,** 1 Regent St. (tube: Piccadilly Circus), is open Monday through Friday from 9am to 6:30pm and Saturday through Sunday from 10am to 4pm.
- **The Tourist Information Centre,** forecourt of Victoria Station (tube: Victoria), is open from Easter (on a Sunday between March 22 and April 25) through October daily from 8am to 7pm. It's open November through Easter, Monday through Saturday, from 8am to 6pm, and Sunday from 9am to 4pm.

Private agencies also can help you find a room. One of the best options is the **British Hotel Reservation Centre,** 13 Grosvenor Gardens, London SW1W OBD (☎ **0800/716-298** or 0171/824-8232; hotels@bhrc.co.uk; www.bhrc.co.uk), open 7 days a week from 6am to midnight. This agency provides free reservations and discounted rates at all the leading hotel groups and the major independents. It has a reservations desk (open 6am to midnight) at the Underground station of Heathrow Airport.

First Option Hotel Reservations, 5–11 Lavington St., London SE1 0NZ (☎ **0345/110-011;** fax 0171/945-6016), is another hotel booking service. It has kiosks at the following Central London rail stations: **Victoria,** by Platform 9 (☎ 0171/828-4646); **King's Cross,** by Platform 8 (☎ 0171/837-5681); **Euston** (☎ 0171/388-7435); **Paddington** (☎ 0171/723-0184); and **Charing Cross** (☎ 0171/976-1171).

The following agencies can arrange a London B&B room for you: **Bed & Breakfast** (☎ **800/367-4668** or 423/690-8484) and **Worldwide Bed & Breakfast Association** (☎ **800/852-2632** in the U.S. or 0181/742-9123; fax 0181/749-7084). **The London Bed and Breakfast Agency Limited** (☎ **0171/586-2768;** fax 0171/586-6567) is another reputable agency that can provide inexpensive accommodations in selected private homes.

Chapter 6

London Hotels from A to Z

In This Chapter

- Quick indexes of hotels by location and price
- Reviews of London's best hotels
- A worksheet to help you make your choice

Price and **location** are the two biggest factors to keep in mind when choosing a London hotel. After you know where you want to stay and how much you want to pay, you can begin tracking down the hotel that's right for you. I've stayed in my share of dumps and didn't enjoy the experience. Neither would you. So there are no dumps included in my recommended hotels. Basically what I've tried to do is give you good choices in all price ranges. I've included everything from the no-frills to the all-frills. These choices cover all kinds of accommodations, from simple B&Bs to the queen bees of luxury.

In chapter 5 I explained the kinds of hotels you'll find and gave a brief rundown on the Central London neighborhoods that are most convenient for visitors. In this chapter the individual hotels are marked with $ symbols so you'll know the price range. The first index in this chapter lists hotels by **location.** The second index ranks them by **price.** Following the indexes, the hotels are listed **alphabetically.** This is the easiest way for you to flip back and forth among price, location, and description. At the end of the chapter, a worksheet will help you comparison shop for the hotels that appeal to you.

Keep in mind that the quoted prices are the nondiscounted rack rate for a double room. I have used an average conversion rate of £1 = $1.65; exchange

What the Dollar Signs Mean

$	=	$150 and less
$$	=	$150–$225
$$$	=	$225–$300
$$$$	=	$300–$400
$$$$$	=	$400 and up

rates vary from day to day, so these prices are meant only to be a guide. Unless otherwise noted, the prices **include VAT** (value-added tax). For those listings that do not include VAT, you will need to add another 17.5% to the quoted rate (but this generally applies only to the crème de la crème hotels).

Kids Whenever you see the special "Kids" icon in front of a hotel name, it means that the hotel is suitable for families with children. These hotels will have rooms with three or four beds (called *triples* or *quads),* adjoining rooms, or baby-sitting among their services.

Unless otherwise noted, all hotels listed below come with a **private bathroom.** Your private bathroom won't necessarily come with both a shower and a tub, though; you might get one or the other. If having a tub is important to you, ask when making your reservation.

Quick Picks—London's Hotels at a Glance
Hotel Index by Location

Bayswater

The Byron Hotel $$

Belgravia

Diplomat Hotel $$

Bloomsbury

Academy Hotel $$

Blooms Hotel $$$$

Crescent Hotel $

Harlingford Hotel $

Hotel Russell $$$

Jenkins Hotel $

Chelsea

Blair House Hotel $$

The Cadogan $$$$

Wilbraham Hotel $$

Covent Garden

Covent Garden Hotel $$$$$

Fielding Hotel $$

Earl's Court

Aaron House $

Philbeach Hotel $

Kensington

Abbey House $

Avonmore Hotel $

Vicarage Private Hotel $

Knightsbridge

Claverley Hotel $$

Knightsbridge Hotel $$

Marylebone

Boston Court Hotel $

Bryanston Court Hotel $$

Dorset Square Hotel $$$

Durrants Hotel $$

Edward Lear Hotel $

Hart House Hotel $

Hotel La Place $$

Landmark London $$$$$

Mayfair

Ivanhoe Suites Hotel $

Park Lane Hotel $$$$$

Notting Hill

The Abbey Court $$$

The Gate Hotel $

Paddington

Adare House $

Europa House Hotel $

Piccadilly Circus

Regent Palace Hotel $$

Soho

Hazlitt's 1718 $$$

South Kensington

Aster House Hotel $$

Aston's Budget Studios & Aston's Designer Studios and Suites $

The Cranley $$$

Five Sumner Place $$$

The Gallery $$

The Gore $$$$

Harrington Hall $$$

Hotel 167 $

Number Sixteen $$$

The Regency Hotel $$$

Swiss House Hotel $

St. James's

22 Jermyn Street $$$$

The Strand

The Savoy $$$$$

Westminster/Victoria

Caswell Hotel $

James House/Cartref House $

Lime Tree Hotel $$

Tophams Belgravia $$

Hotel Index by Price

$

Aaron House (Earl's Court)

Abbey House (Kensington)

Adare House (Paddington)

Aston's Budget Studios & Aston's Designer Studios and Suites (South Kensington)

Avalon Hotel (Bloomsbury)

Avonmore Hotel (Kensington)

Boston Court Hotel (Marylebone)

Caswell Hotel (Westminster/Victoria)

Crescent Hotel (Bloomsbury)

Edward Lear Hotel (Marylebone)

Europa House Hotel (Paddington)

The Gate Hotel (Notting Hill)

Harlingford Hotel (Bloomsbury)

Hart House Hotel (Marylebone)

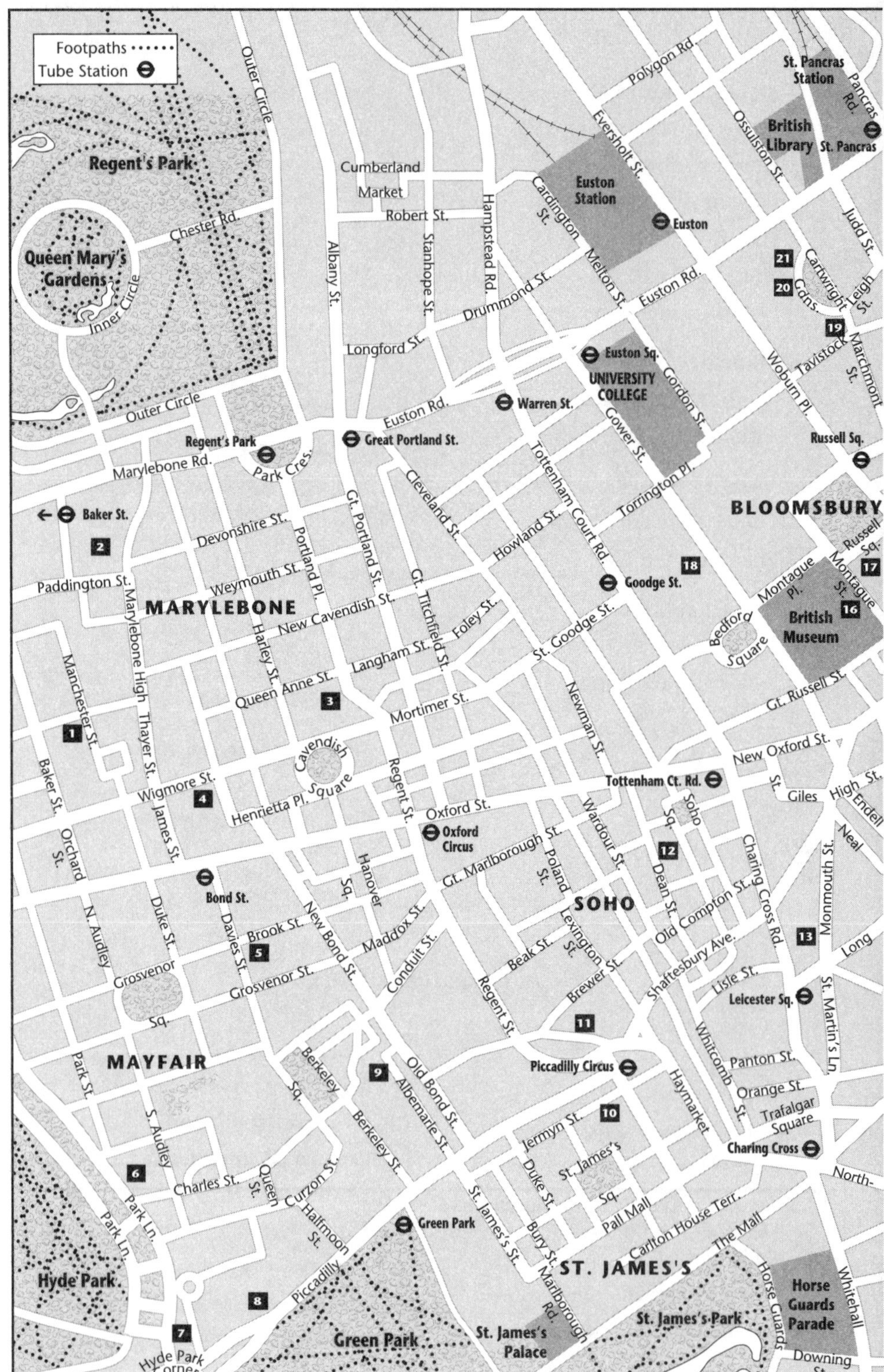

Footpaths
Tube Station
Regent's Park
Queen Mary's Gardens
Inner Circle
Outer Circle
Chester Rd.
Cumberland Market
Robert St.
Albany St.
Stanhope St.
Hampstead Rd.
Polygon Rd.
Eversholt St.
Euston Station
Euston
Cardington St.
Melton St.
St. Pancras Station
Pancras Rd.
British Library
St. Pancras
Ossulston St.
Judd St.
Cartwright Gdns.
Leigh St.
Drummond St.
Euston Rd.
Longford St.
Euston Sq.
UNIVERSITY COLLEGE
Gordon St.
Gower St.
Woburn Pl.
Tavistock
Marchmont St.
Warren St.
Regent's Park
Great Portland St.
Park Cres.
Marylebone Rd.
Russell Sq.
Baker St.
Devonshire St.
Portland Pl.
Gt. Portland St.
Cleveland St.
Tottenham Court Rd.
Torrington Pl.
Howland St.
BLOOMSBURY
Russell Sq.
Montague Pl.
Montague St.
British Museum
Paddington St.
Weymouth St.
MARYLEBONE
Marylebone High St.
New Cavendish St.
Gt. Titchfield St.
Foley St.
Goodge St.
Bedford Square
Harley St.
Langham St.
St. Goodge St.
Manchester St.
Queen Anne St.
Mortimer St.
Newman St.
Gt. Russell St.
Thayer St.
Cavendish Square
New Oxford St.
Baker St.
Wigmore St.
Henrietta Pl.
Regent St.
Tottenham Ct. Rd.
St. Giles High St.
Endell
James St.
Oxford St.
Oxford Circus
Wardour St.
Soho Sq.
Orchard St.
Hanover Sq.
Gt. Marlborough St.
Poland St.
Dean St.
Charing Cross Rd.
Neal
Monmouth St.
Bond St.
SOHO
Old Compton St.
Duke St.
Davies St.
Brook St.
New Bond St.
Maddox St.
Lexington St.
Beak St.
Shaftesbury Ave.
Long
N. Audley
Grosvenor Sq.
Grosvenor St.
Conduit St.
Brewer St.
Lisle St.
Leicester Sq.
St. Martin's Ln.
Regent St.
Whitcomb St.
MAYFAIR
Park St.
Berkeley Sq.
Old Bond St.
Albemarle St.
Piccadilly Circus
Panton St.
Haymarket
Orange St.
Trafalgar Square
S. Audley
Berkeley St.
Jermyn St.
St. James's Sq.
Charing Cross
Charles St.
Queen St.
Curzon St.
Duke St.
North-
Park Ln.
Halfmoon St.
St. James's St.
Pall Mall
Carlton House Terr.
Green Park
Bury St.
The Mall
Whitehall
Hyde Park
Piccadilly
ST. JAMES'S
Horse Guards Parade
Horse Guards
Marlborough Rd.
St. James's Park
Green Park
St. James's Palace
Hyde Park Corner
Downing St.
1
2
3
4
5
6
7
8
9
10
11
12
13
16
17
18
19
20
21

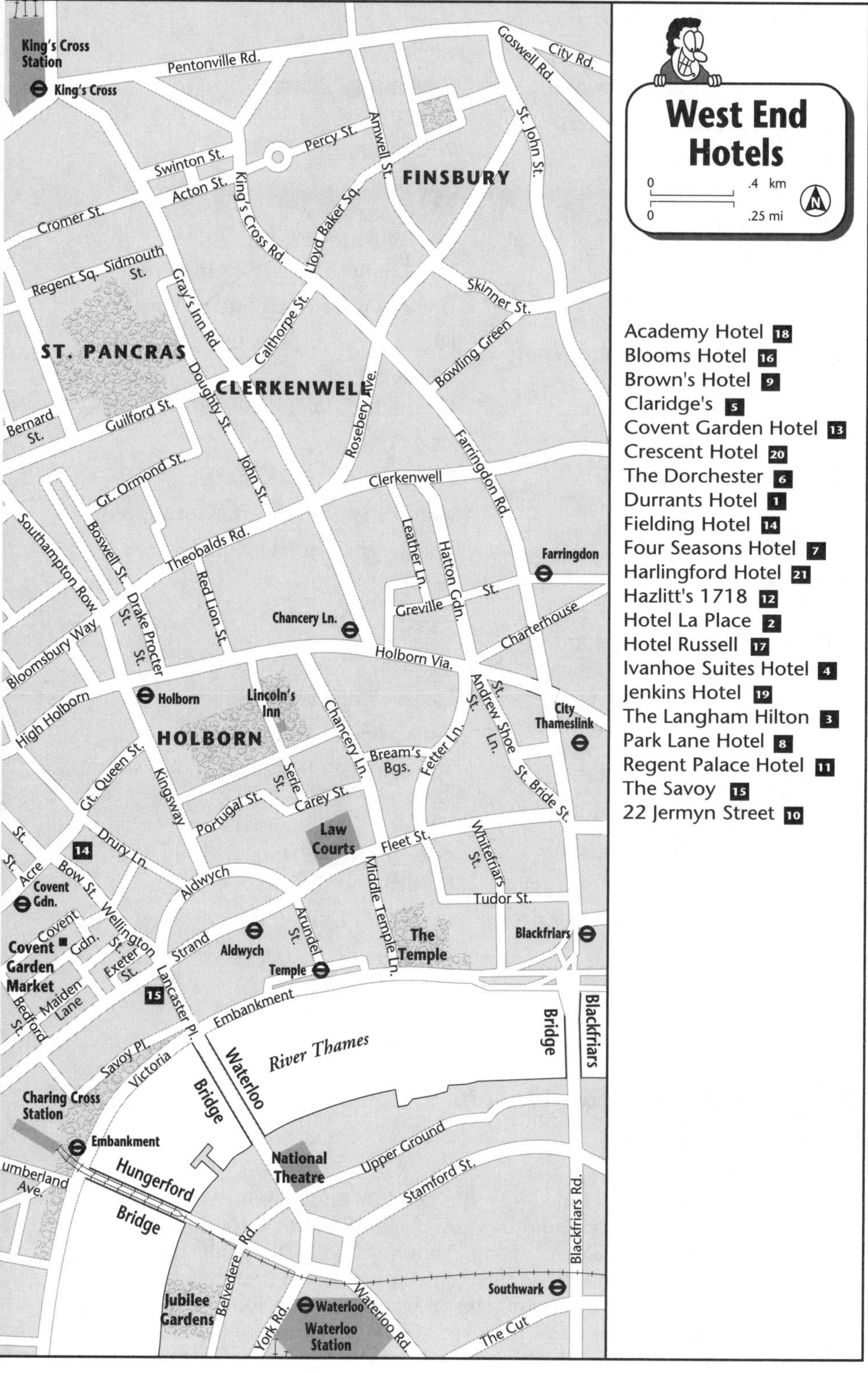
West End Hotels
0 .4 km
0 .25 mi
N
Academy Hotel 18
Blooms Hotel 16
Brown's Hotel 9
Claridge's 5
Covent Garden Hotel 13
Crescent Hotel 20
The Dorchester 6
Durrants Hotel 1
Fielding Hotel 14
Four Seasons Hotel 7
Harlingford Hotel 21
Hazlitt's 1718 12
Hotel La Place 2
Hotel Russell 17
Ivanhoe Suites Hotel 4
Jenkins Hotel 19
The Langham Hilton 3
Park Lane Hotel 8
Regent Palace Hotel 11
The Savoy 15
22 Jermyn Street 10
King's Cross Station
King's Cross
Pentonville Rd.
Goswell Rd.
City Rd.
St. John St.
Percy St.
Amwell St.
FINSBURY
Swinton St.
Acton St.
King's Cross Rd.
Lloyd Baker Sq.
Cromer St.
Regent Sq.
Sidmouth St.
Gray's Inn Rd.
Skinner St.
Calthorpe St.
Bowling Green
ST. PANCRAS
CLERKENWELL
Rosebery Ave.
Doughty St.
Guilford St.
Bernard St.
Farringdon Rd.
Gt. Ormond St.
John St.
Clerkenwell
Southampton Row
Boswell St.
Theobalds Rd.
Leather Ln.
Hatton Gdn.
Farringdon
Red Lion St.
Drake St.
Procter St.
Greville St.
Bloomsbury Way
Chancery Ln.
Charterhouse
Holborn Via.
High Holborn
Holborn
Lincoln's Inn
Chancery Ln.
St. Andrew St.
Shoe Ln.
City Thameslink
HOLBORN
Gt. Queen St.
Kingsway
Serle St.
Bream's Bgs.
Fetter Ln.
St. Bride St.
Portugal St.
Carey St.
Law Courts
Fleet St.
Whitefriars St.
Drury Ln.
St.
Acre
Bow St.
Covent Gdn.
Aldwych
Middle Temple Ln.
Tudor St.
Wellington St.
Covent Gdn.
Covent Garden Market
Exeter St.
Strand
Aldwych
Arundel St.
The Temple
Blackfriars
Temple
Maiden Lane
Bedford St.
Lancaster Pl.
Embankment
Blackfriars Bridge
River Thames
Waterloo Bridge
Savoy Pl.
Victoria
Charing Cross Station
Embankment
Hungerford Bridge
National Theatre
Upper Ground
umberland Ave.
Stamford St.
Blackfriars Rd.
Belvedere Rd.
Jubilee Gardens
Waterloo
Waterloo Station
York Rd.
Waterloo Rd.
Southwark
The Cut

Hotel 167 (South Kensington)

Ivanhoe Suites Hotel (Mayfair)

James House/Cartref House (Westminster/Victoria)

Jenkins Hotel (Bloomsbury)

Philbeach Hotel (Earl's Court)

Swiss House Hotel (South Kensington)

Vicarage Private Hotel (Kensington)

$$

Academy Hotel (Bloomsbury)

Aster House Hotel (South Kensington)

Blair House Hotel (Chelsea)

Bryanston Court Hotel (Marylebone)

The Byron (Paddington & Bayswater)

Claverley Hotel (Knightsbridge)

Diplomat Hotel (Belgravia)

Durrants Hotel (Marylebone)

Fielding Hotel (Covent Garden)

The Gallery (South Kensington)

Hotel La Place (Marylebone)

Knightsbridge Hotel (Knightsbridge)

Lime Tree Hotel (Westminster/Victoria)

Regent Palace Hotel (Piccadilly Circus)

Tophams Belgravia (Westminster/Victoria)

Wilbraham Hotel (Chelsea)

$$$

The Abbey Court (Notting Hill)

The Cranley (South Kensington)

Dorset Square Hotel (Marylebone)

Five Sumner Place (South Kensington)

Harrington Hall (South Kensington)

Hazlitt's 1718 (Soho)

Hotel Russell (Bloomsbury)

Number Sixteen (South Kensington)

The Regency Hotel (South Kensington)

$$$$

22 Jermyn Street (St. James's)

Blooms Hotel (Bloomsbury)

The Cadogan Hotel (Chelsea)

The Gore (South Kensington)

$$$$$

Covent Garden Hotel (Covent Garden)

Landmark London (Marylebone)

Park Lane Hotel (Mayfair)

The Savoy (The Strand)

My Favorite London Hotels

22 Jermyn Street

$$$$. St. James's.

This Victorian town-house hotel, just off Piccadilly on an exclusive street where almost every shop has a Royal Warrant, underwent a radical restoration in 1990 and became a chic, upscale boutique hotel. The public rooms are filled with greenery and the rooms richly appointed in traditional English style, with fresh flowers and chintz everywhere you look. The bathrooms are just as nice. There's 24-hour room service and lots of amenities.

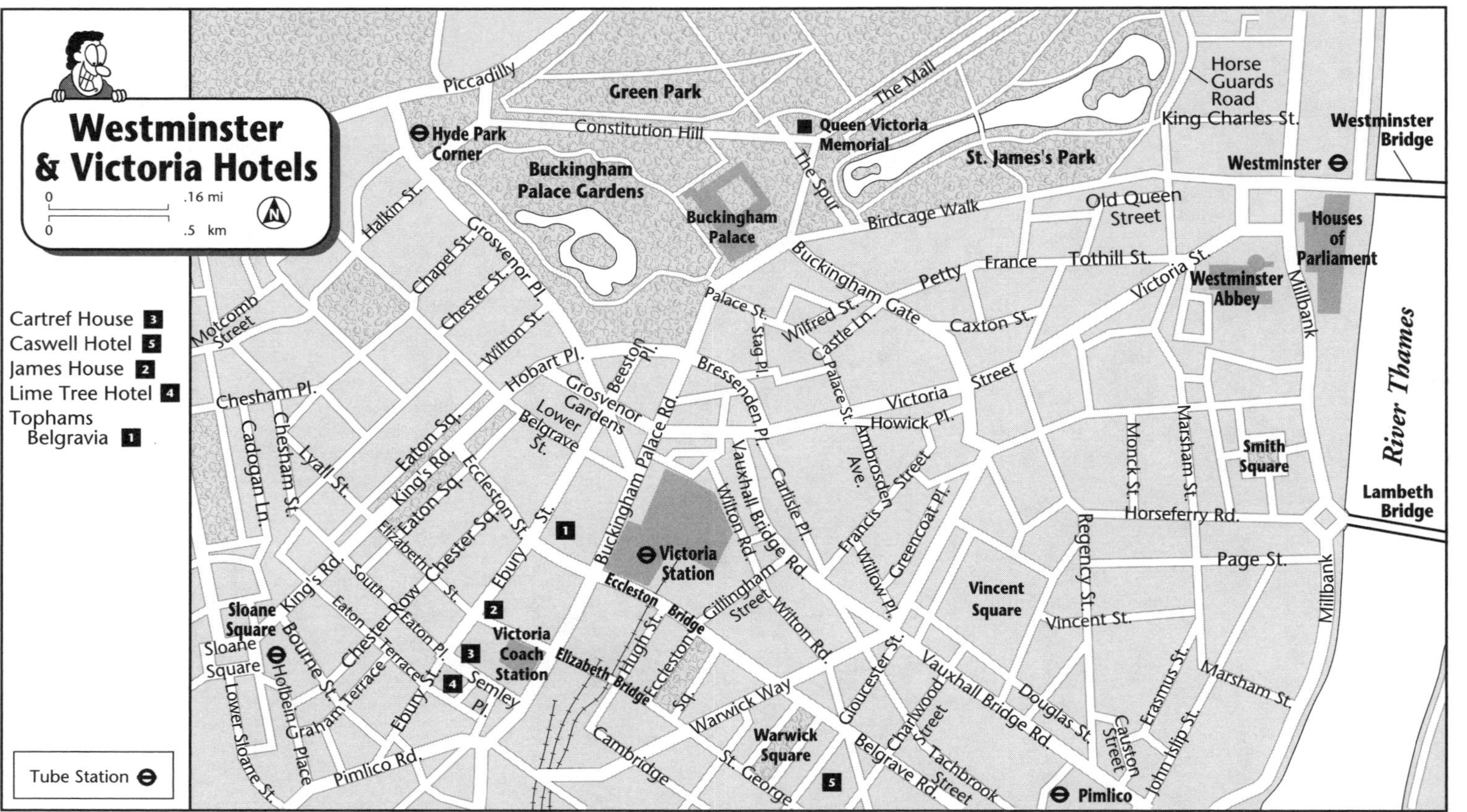

Westminster & Victoria Hotels
0 .16 mi
0 .5 km
Cartref House 3
Caswell Hotel 5
James House 2
Lime Tree Hotel 4
Tophams Belgravia 1
Tube Station
Piccadilly
Green Park
Hyde Park Corner
Constitution Hill
Queen Victoria Memorial
The Mall
St. James's Park
Horse Guards Road
King Charles St.
Westminster Bridge
Westminster
Buckingham Palace Gardens
Buckingham Palace
The Spur
Birdcage Walk
Old Queen Street
Houses of Parliament
Tothill St.
Victoria St.
Westminster Abbey
Millbank
River Thames
Halkin St.
Chapel St.
Grosvenor Pl.
Chester St.
Wilton St.
Motcomb Street
Buckingham Gate
Palace St.
Petty France
Caxton St.
Wilfred St.
Castle Ln.
Stag Pl.
Hobart Pl.
Beeston Pl.
Grosvenor Gardens
Lower Belgrave St.
Bressenden Pl.
Palace St.
Victoria Street
Howick Pl.
Chesham Pl.
Cadogan Ln.
Chesham St.
Lyall St.
Eaton Sq.
King's Rd.
Eaton Sq.
Eccleston St.
Buckingham Palace Rd.
Vauxhall Bridge Rd.
Carlisle Pl.
Ambrosden Ave.
Francis Street
Greencoat Pl.
Monck St.
Marsham St.
Smith Square
Lambeth Bridge
Horseferry Rd.
Regency St.
Page St.
Elizabeth St.
Chester Sq.
Ebury St.
Victoria Station
Wilton Rd.
Willow Pl.
Vincent Square
Vincent St.
Millbank
Sloane Square
King's Rd.
South Eaton Pl.
Chester Row
Eccleston Bridge
Gillingham Street
Wilton Rd.
Victoria Coach Station
Sloane Square
Bourne St.
Eaton Terrace
Eaton Pl.
Elizabeth Bridge
Hugh St.
Eccleston Sq.
Gloucester St.
Vauxhall Bridge Rd.
Douglas St.
Marsham St.
Erasmus St.
Lower Sloane St.
Holbein Place
Graham Terrace
Ebury St.
Semley Pl.
Warwick Way
Charlwood Street
Causton Street
John Islip St.
Pimlico Rd.
Cambridge
Warwick Square
St. George
Belgrave Rd.
Tachbrook Street
Pimlico

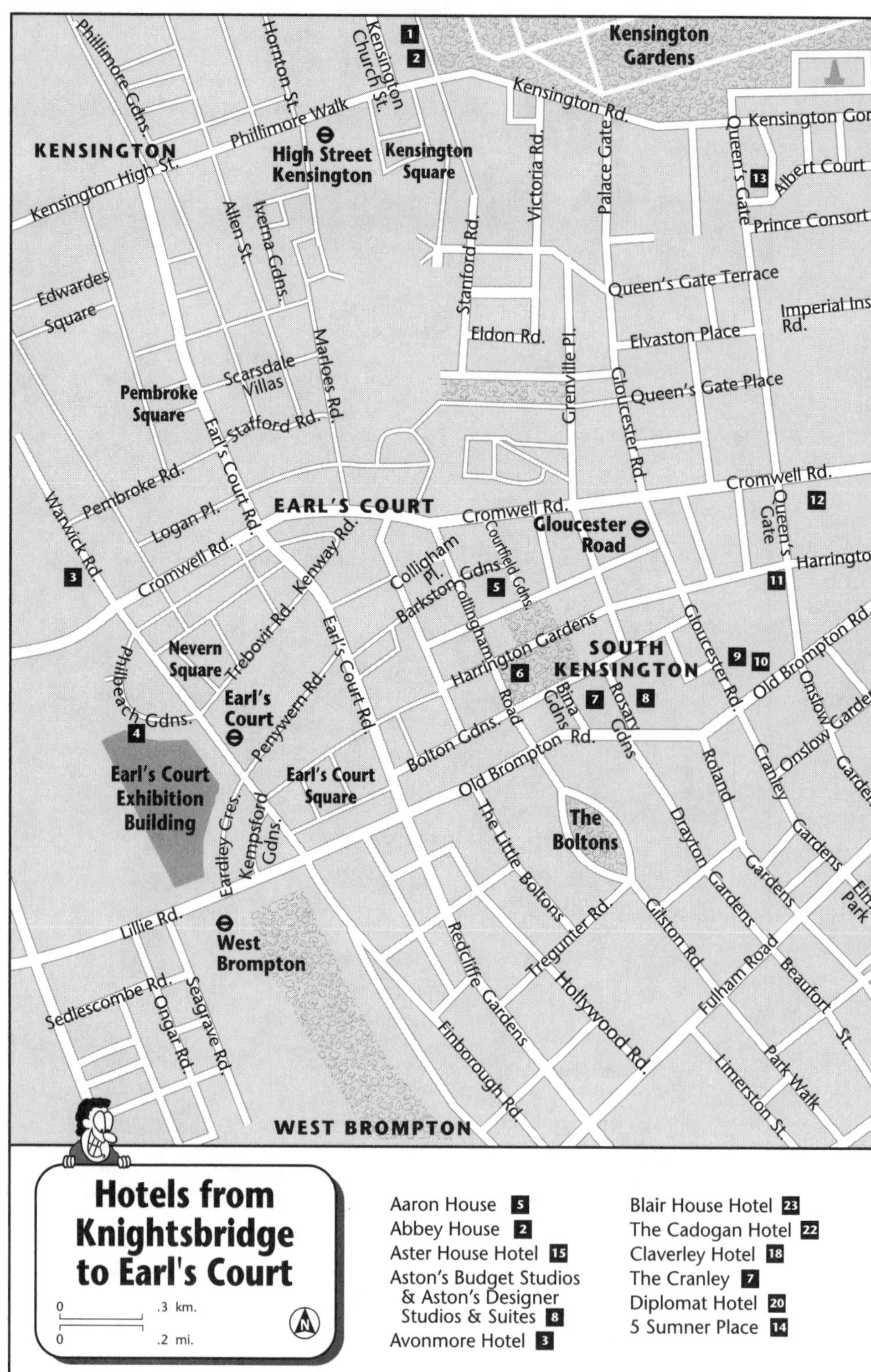
Hotels from Knightsbridge to Earl's Court
0 .3 km.
0 .2 mi.
Aaron House 5
Abbey House 2
Aster House Hotel 15
Aston's Budget Studios & Aston's Designer Studios & Suites 8
Avonmore Hotel 3
Blair House Hotel 23
The Cadogan Hotel 22
Claverley Hotel 18
The Cranley 7
Diplomat Hotel 20
5 Sumner Place 14
Kensington Gardens
KENSINGTON
High Street Kensington
Kensington Square
EARL'S COURT
Gloucester Road
SOUTH KENSINGTON
Earl's Court
West Brompton
WEST BROMPTON
Earl's Court Exhibition Building
The Boltons
Pembroke Square
Nevern Square
Earl's Court Square
Edwardes Square
Kensington High St.
Phillimore Walk
Phillimore Gdns.
Hornton St.
Kensington Church St.
Kensington Rd.
Kensington Gore
Albert Court
Prince Consort
Queen's Gate
Queen's Gate Terrace
Imperial Inst. Rd.
Elvaston Place
Queen's Gate Place
Palace Gate
Victoria Rd.
Stanford Rd.
Eldon Rd.
Grenville Pl.
Gloucester Rd.
Allen St.
Iverna Gdns.
Marloes Rd.
Scarsdale Villas
Stafford Rd.
Earl's Court Rd.
Pembroke Rd.
Logan Pl.
Cromwell Rd.
Warwick Rd.
Kenway Rd.
Trebovir Rd.
Penywern Rd.
Philbeach Gdns.
Collingham Pl.
Barkston Gdns.
Courtfield Gdns.
Collingham Road
Harrington Gardens
Harrington
Old Brompton Rd.
Onslow Gardens
Bina Gdns
Rosary Gdns
Bolton Gdns.
Roland Gardens
Cranley Gardens
Drayton Gardens
The Little Boltons
Eardley Cres.
Kempsford Gdns.
Lillie Rd.
Sedlescombe Rd.
Ongar Rd.
Seagrave Rd.
Redcliffe Gardens
Finborough Rd.
Tregunter Rd.
Hollywood Rd.
Gilston Rd.
Fulham Road
Beaufort St.
Elm Park
Park Walk
Limerston St.

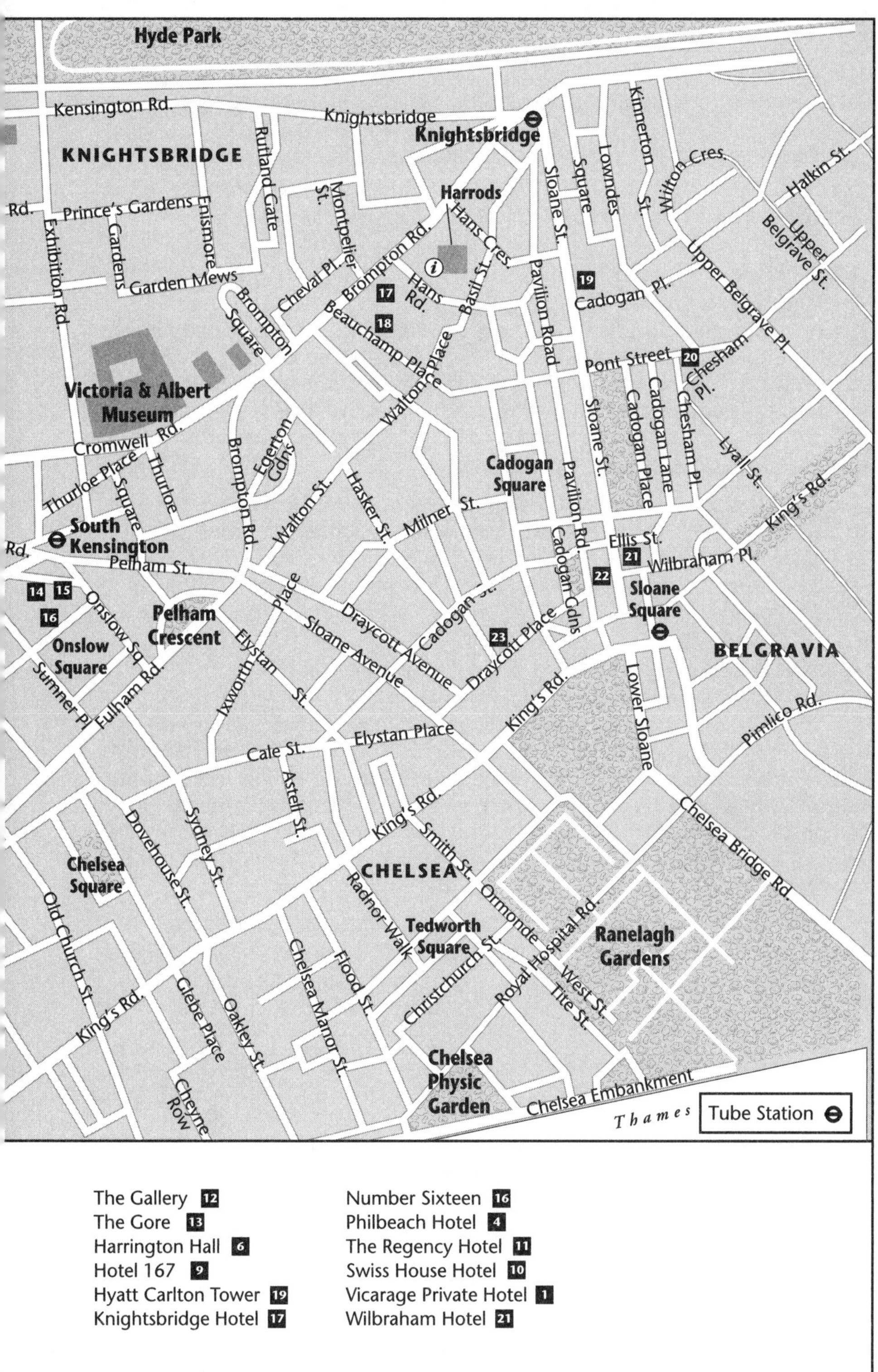

The Gallery 12
The Gore 13
Harrington Hall 6
Hotel 167 9
Hyatt Carlton Tower 19
Knightsbridge Hotel 17
Number Sixteen 16
Philbeach Hotel 4
The Regency Hotel 11
Swiss House Hotel 10
Vicarage Private Hotel 1
Wilbraham Hotel 21

22 Jermyn St. (just south of Piccadilly Circus), London SW1Y 6HL. ☎ ***800/ 682-7808*** *in the U.S., or 0171/734-2353. Fax 0171/734-0750. www.22jermyn. com. E-mail: office@22jermyn.com.* ***Tube:*** *Piccadilly Circus, take Lower Regent Street exit; Jermyn Street is the first right outside the station.* ***Rack rates:*** *£205 ($338) double; rates do not include VAT (17.5%). AE, DC, MC, V.*

Kids **Aaron House**

$. Earl's Court.

The Earl's Court area is filled with budget B&Bs, but this former family home on a Victorian square is a standout. It's been modernized and upgraded but still retains its original tile entry and ornately carved interior staircase leading to the 23 comfortable and well-kept bedrooms. The largest rooms overlook the street, which can be noisy at times. It's not glamorous, but it is clean, friendly, affordable, and convenient.

17 Courtfield Gardens (west of Gloucester Rd. tube station), London SW5 OPD. ☎ ***0171/370-3991.*** *Fax 0171/373-2303.* ***Tube:*** *Gloucester Rd., then a 10-minute walk west on Courtfield Rd. to Courtfield Gardens.* ***Rack rates:*** *£50 ($83) double without bathroom, £61 ($101) double with bathroom. Continental breakfast included. MC, V.*

Kids **The Abbey Court**

$$$. Notting Hill.

This small, graceful hotel in a renovated mid-Victorian town house near Kensington Gardens has a flower-filled patio in front and a conservatory in back where breakfast is served. Furnished with taste and charm, its 25 rooms feature 18th- and 19th-century country antiques and marble bathrooms equipped with a Jacuzzi bath, shower, and heated towel racks. There's no elevator in the five-story hotel, but there is a concierge, and baby-sitting can be arranged.

20 Pembridge Gardens, London W2 4DU. ☎ ***0171/221-7518.*** *Fax 0171/792-0858.* ***Tube:*** *Notting Hill Gate, then a 5-minute walk north on Pembridge Gardens Rd.* ***Rack rates:*** *£130–£145 ($215–$239) double. Breakfast included. AE, MC, V.*

Kids **Abbey House**

$. Kensington.

For peace, tranquillity, and affordability in a very good location (next to Kensington Gardens and Palace), this small, family-run B&B can't be beat. The 1860s-era building has been completely modernized but retains many original features. The 16 spacious guest rooms (some triples and quads) have central heating and washbasins; every two units share a bathroom. Decor tends toward the frilly, but there's an overall cheerful charm.

11 Vicarage Gate (off Kensington Church St.), London W8 4AG. ☎ ***0171/ 727-2594.*** ***Tube:*** *High Street Kensington, then a 10-minute walk east on Kensington High St. and north on Kensington Church St.* ***Rack rates:*** *£65 ($107) double with shared bathroom. English breakfast included. No credit cards.*

Academy Hotel

$$. Bloomsbury.

Price and location (the British Museum, the theatre district, and Covent Garden are within walking distance) offset the neutrally bland guest rooms and sometimes tacky detailing in this 55-unit hotel housed in three Georgian row houses. Every room has a bathroom, although these tend to be minuscule. There are some nice features, though: original glass panels, colonnades, intricate exterior plasterwork, an elegant bar, a library room, a secluded patio garden, and a restaurant serving modern European food.

*17–25 Gower St. (near the British Museum), London WC1E 6HG. ☎ **800/678-3096** in the U.S., or 0171/631-4115. Fax 0171/636-3442. **Tube:** Goodge St., then a 10-minute walk east on Chenies St. and south on Gower St. **Rack rates:** £115 ($190) double with shared bathroom, £125 ($206) double with private bathroom. AE, DC, MC, V.*

Adare House

$. Paddington.

Sussex Gardens tends to be crammed with featureless B&Bs, but this well-maintained property, recently refurbished by the new owners, still retains a modest, homey ambiance. Most of the 20 rooms are quite small, but they're immaculately clean, comfortably furnished, and all have private bathrooms. Hyde Park is within easy walking distance.

*153 Sussex Gardens (near Paddington Station), London W2 2RY. ☎ **0171/262-0633.** Fax 0171/706-1859. E-mail: adare.hotel@virgin.net. **Tube:** Paddington, then a 5-minute walk south on London St. and west on Sussex Gardens Rd. **Rack rates:** £58–£69 ($96–$114) double with shower. English breakfast included. MC, V.*

Aster House Hotel

$$. South Kensington.

Located at the end of an early Victorian terrace built in 1848, Aster House is so discreet that there's not even a sign outside. This 12-unit, nonsmoking B&B is a charmer, especially for the price (hotels offering similar amenities may charge £250 a night). Each bedroom is individually decorated in English country house style, many with four-poster, half-canopied beds and silk wallpaper. The showers are a bit too cozy for real comfort. Breakfasts, served in the glassed-in garden conservatory, are more health conscious than what you would expect from an English B&B.

*3 Sumner Place (near Onslow Square), London SW7 3EE. ☎ **0171/581-5888.** Fax 0171/584-4925. E-mail: asterhouse@btinternet.com. **Tube:** South Kensington, then a 5-minute walk west on Old Brompton Rd. and south on Sumner Place. **Rack rates:** £115–£145 ($190–$240) double. Buffet continental breakfast included. MC, V.*

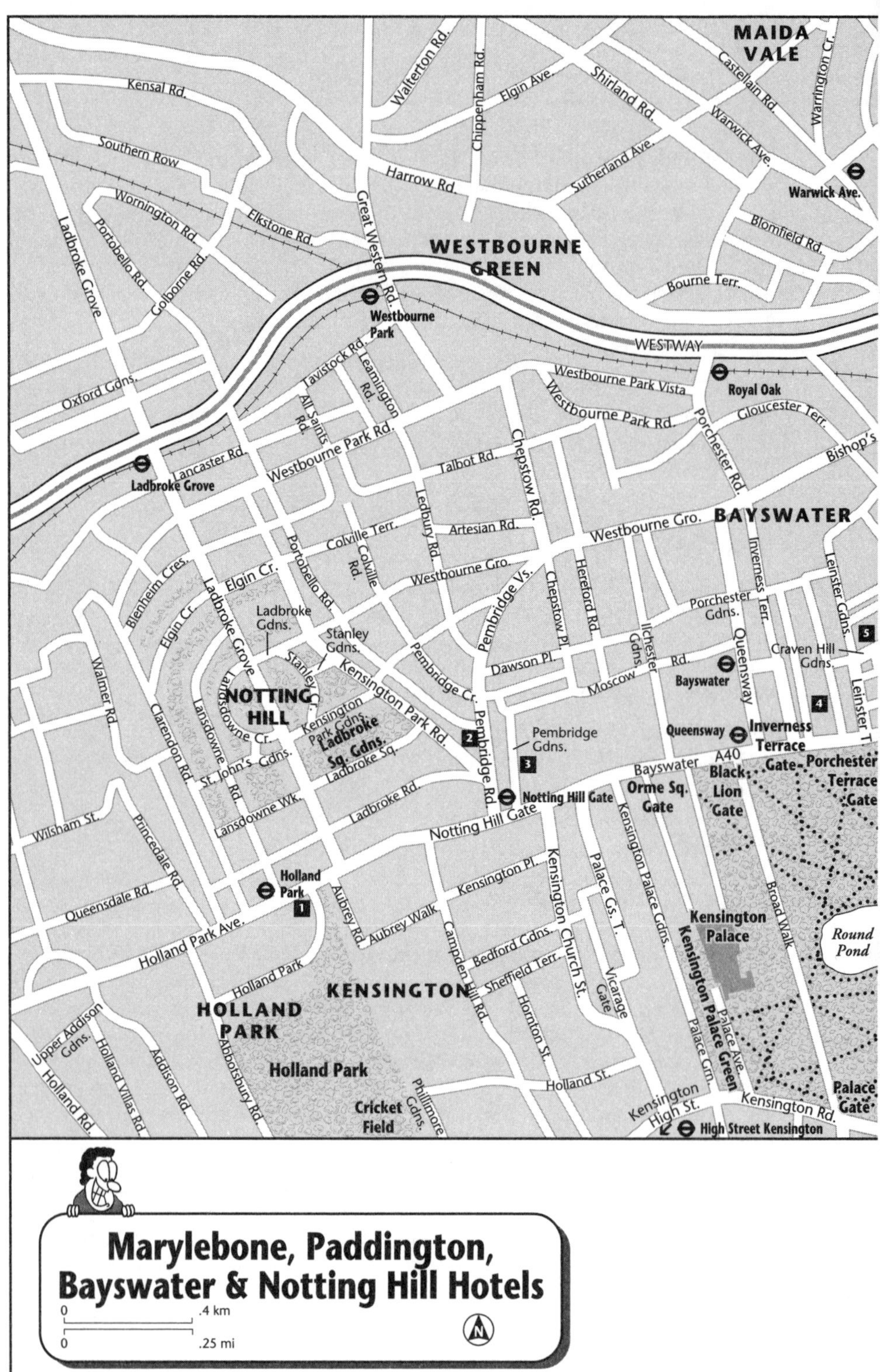
MAIDA VALE
WESTBOURNE GREEN
BAYSWATER
NOTTING HILL
KENSINGTON
HOLLAND PARK
Kensal Rd.
Southern Row
Wornington Rd.
Elkstone Rd.
Ladbroke Grove
Portobello Rd.
Golborne Rd.
Walterton Rd.
Chippenham Rd.
Elgin Ave.
Shirland Rd.
Castellain Rd.
Warrington Cr.
Warwick Ave.
Sutherland Ave.
Harrow Rd.
Great Western Rd.
Warwick Ave.
Blomfield Rd.
Bourne Terr.
Westbourne Park
WESTWAY
Royal Oak
Tavistock Rd.
Leamington Rd.
All Saints Rd.
Oxford Gdns.
Westbourne Park Vista
Westbourne Park Rd.
Gloucester Terr.
Porchester Rd.
Bishop's
Lancaster Rd.
Ladbroke Grove
Talbot Rd.
Chepstow Rd.
Ledbury Rd.
Artesian Rd.
Westbourne Gro.
Colville Terr.
Colville Rd.
Inverness Terr.
Leinster Gdns.
Blenheim Cres.
Elgin Cr.
Hereford Rd.
Chepstow Pl.
Pembridge Vs.
Ladbroke Gdns.
Stanley Gdns.
Stanley Cr.
Porchester Gdns.
Queensway
Craven Hill Gdns.
Ilchester Gdns.
Dawson Pl.
Moscow Rd.
Bayswater
Kensington Park Rd.
Pembridge Cr.
Walmer Rd.
Clarendon Rd.
Lansdowne Rd.
Lansdowne Cr.
Kensington Park Gdns.
Ladbroke Sq. Gdns.
Ladbroke Sq.
St. John's Gdns.
Pembridge Gdns.
Pembridge Rd.
Queensway
Inverness Terrace Gate
Leinster T.
Bayswater A40
Black Lion Gate
Porchester Terrace Gate
Orme Sq. Gate
Notting Hill Gate
Lansdowne Wk.
Ladbroke Rd.
Wilsham St.
Princedale Rd.
Holland Park
Queensdale Rd.
Aubrey Rd.
Aubrey Walk
Kensington Pl.
Kensington Church St.
Palace Gs. T.
Kensington Palace Gdns.
Broad Walk
Kensington Palace
Round Pond
Holland Park Ave.
Campden Hill Rd.
Bedford Gdns.
Sheffield Terr.
Vicarage Gate
Kensington Palace Green
Palace Ave.
Palace Grn.
Upper Addison Gdns.
Holland Villas Rd.
Addison Rd.
Abbotsbury Rd.
Holland Park
Hornton St.
Holland St.
Cricket Field
Phillimore Gdns.
Holland Rd.
Kensington High St.
Kensington Rd.
Palace Gate
High Street Kensington
1
2
3
4
5
Marylebone, Paddington, Bayswater & Notting Hill Hotels
0 .4 km
0 .25 mi
N

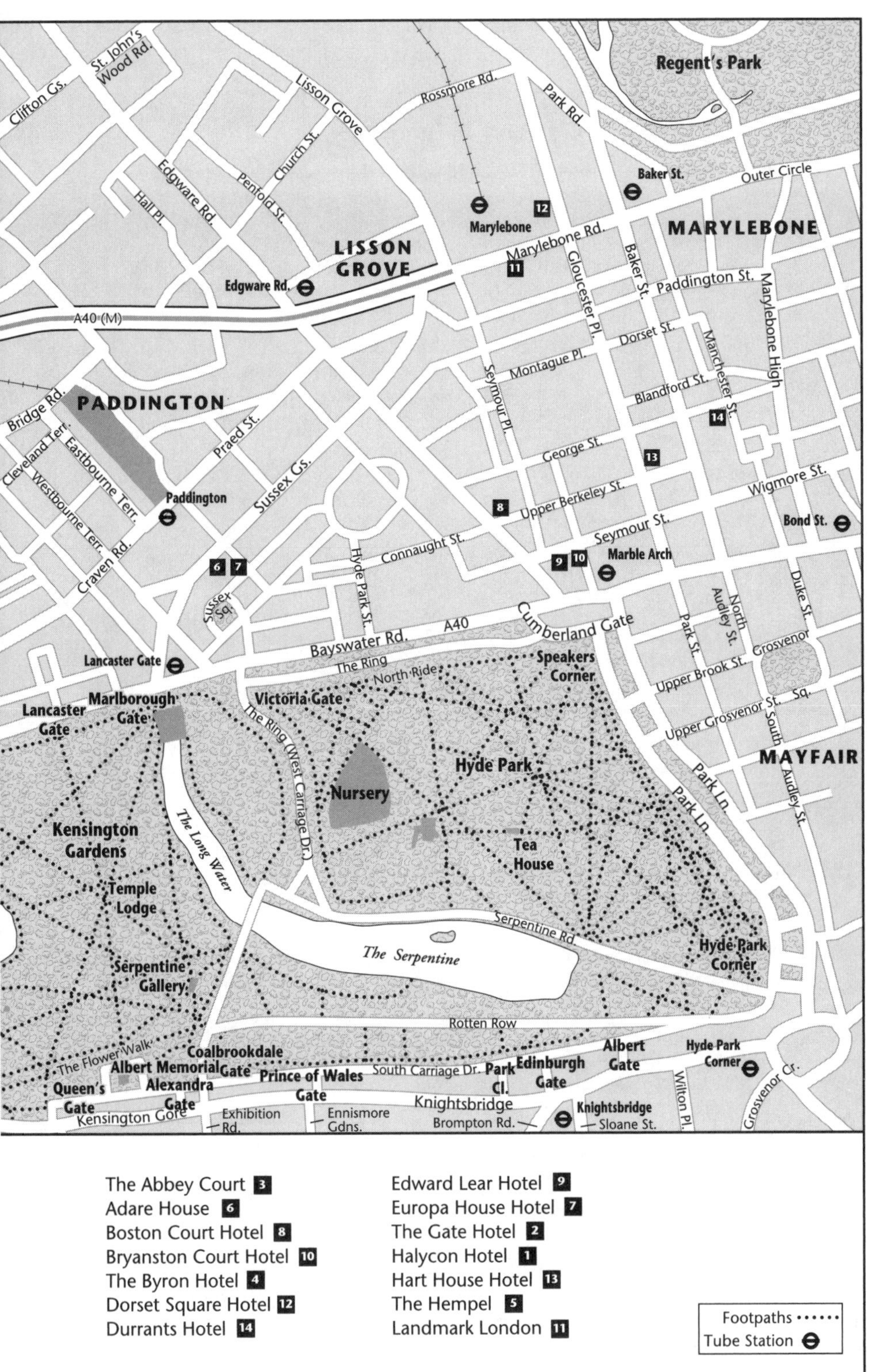

The Abbey Court 3
Adare House 6
Boston Court Hotel 8
Bryanston Court Hotel 10
The Byron Hotel 4
Dorset Square Hotel 12
Durrants Hotel 14
Edward Lear Hotel 9
Europa House Hotel 7
The Gate Hotel 2
Halycon Hotel 1
Hart House Hotel 13
The Hempel 5
Landmark London 11

Big-Buck Splurges

For the most part, I've kept my list of London hotels in the affordable range, with a few high-end glamour-puss places thrown in. What about all those famous London hotels you've always heard about—Claridge's, The Dorchester, and so on? It's true they're fabulous, filled with every comfort and ultra-civilized amenity you can think of. It's also true that most of us don't want to sink $400 plus a night into a hotel room. But, hey, maybe you do have some pounds to burn. If so, here's a list of some of London's truly great $$$$$ hotels:

- **Brown's Hotel.** 29–34 Albemarle St. (near Berkeley Square), London W1X 4BP. ☎ **0171/493-6020.** Fax 0171/493-9381. E-mail: brownshotel@ukbusiness.com.
- **Claridge's.** Brook St. (near Grosvenor Square), London W1A 2JQ. ☎ **800/223-6800** in the U.S., or 0171/629-8860. Fax 0171/499-2210. Web site: www.savoy-group.co.uk. E-mail: info@claridges.co.uk.
- **The Dorchester.** 53 Park Lane (on the east side of Hyde Park), London W1A 2HJ. ☎ **800/727-9820** in the U.S., or 0171/629-8888. Fax 0171/409-0114.
- **Four Seasons Hotel.** Hamilton Place, Park Lane (opposite Hyde Park Corner), London W1A 1AZ. ☎ **800/332-3442** in the U.S., or 0171/499-0888. Fax 0171/493-1895. Web site: www.fshr.com. E-mail: World.Reservations@fourseasons.com.
- **Halcyon Hotel.** 81 Holland Park (on the northeastern corner of Holland Park and Holland Park Ave.), London W11 3RZ. ☎ **800/595-5416** and 800/457-4000 in the U.S., or 0171/727-7288. E-mail: halcyonhotel@compuserve.com.
- **The Hempel.** 31–35 Craven Hill Gardens (just north of Kensington Gardens), London W2 3EA. ☎ **800/747-1337** in the U.S., or 0171/298-9000. Fax 0171/402-4666. Web site: www.hempelhotel.com. E-mail: the-hempel@easynet.co.uk.
- **Hyatt Carlton Tower.** 2 Cadogan Place (just north of Sloane Square), London SW1 X9PY. ☎ **800/233-1234** in the U.S., or 0171/245-6570. Fax 0171/235-9129. Web site www.hyatt.com.
- **The Langham Hilton.** 1 Portland Place (north of Oxford Circus), London W1N 3JA. ☎ **800/445-8667** in the U.S., or 0171/636-1000. Fax 0171/323-2340. Web site www.hilton.com.

Kids Aston's Budget Studios & Aston's Designer Studios and Suites

$. South Kensington.

Located on a quiet street in the heart of South Kensington, this carefully restored row of Victorian town houses offers value-packed self-catering accommodations, including three and four bedrooms ideal for families. Budget units have a compact kitchenette; a small bathroom; and bright, functional furnishings. The more expensive designer studios, also with kitchens, feature marble bathrooms with showers, better-quality contemporary furnishings, and daily maid service. Electricity is metered, so in the colder months you need to allow a few extra pounds a week to stay warm. Weekly rentals are preferred, but daily rentals are accepted.

39 Rosary Gardens (off Hereford Square), London SW7 4NQ. ☎ ***800/525-2810*** *in the U.S., or 0171/370-0737. Fax 0171/835-1419.* ***Tube:*** *Gloucester Rd., then a 5-minute walk south on Gloucester Rd. and west on Hereford Square; Rosary Gardens is 1 block farther west.* ***Rack rates:*** *Budget studios £65 ($107) double with shared bathroom, £74 ($122) double with private bathroom; designer studios £110 ($182) double with private bathroom. Rates do not include VAT (17.5%). MC, V.*

Kids Avonmore Hotel

$. Kensington.

This small, award-winning hotel, once voted the best private hotel in London, is located in a quiet neighborhood that's easily accessible to West End theatres and shops. You'd be hard pressed to find more for your money: Each of the nine tastefully decorated rooms (all with wall-to-wall carpeting) has an array of amenities not usually found in this price range. An English breakfast is served in a cheerful breakfast room, and there's a bar and limited room service.

66 Avonmore Rd. (northwest of Earl's Court), London W14 8RS. ☎ ***0171/603-4296.*** *Fax 0171/603-4035. www.cityscan.co.uk./avonmore.* ***Tube:*** *West Kensington, then a 5-minute walk north on North End Rd. and east on Gorleston St. to Avonmore Rd.* ***Rack rates:*** *£78 ($129) double with shared bathroom, £88 ($145) double with private bathroom. English breakfast included. AE, MC, V.*

Blair House Hotel

$$. Chelsea.

This small, comfortable hotel in the heart of Chelsea is housed in an older building that's been completely refurbished. The rooms are individually decorated with an emphasis on flowery prints. There's a shower and toilet in every room, and all have amenities usually found in higher-priced hotels. If traffic noise bothers you, ask for a quieter room in the back. You can have breakfast served in your room.

34 Draycott Place (west of Sloane Square), London SW3 2SA. ☎ ***0171/581-2323.*** *Fax 0171/823-7752.* ***Tube:*** *Sloane Square, then a 5-minute walk west on Symons St. (at the northwest corner of the square) to Draycott Place.* ***Rack rates:*** *£105– £115 ($173–$190) double. Continental breakfast included. AE, DC, MC, V.*

Kids Blooms Hotel

$$$$. Bloomsbury.

Guests in this beautifully restored town house can take morning coffee or light summer meals in a walled garden overlooking the British Museum. With its cozy fireplace, period art, and copies of *Country Life* in the magazine rack, the 27-room hotel evokes a country-home atmosphere. Bedrooms are individually designed with traditional elegance and muted colors. There are ground-floor rooms for travelers with disabilities.

7 Montague St. (next to the British Museum), London WC1B 5BP. ☎ ***0171/323-1717.*** *Fax 0171/636-6498. E-mail: blooms@mermaid.co.uk.* ***Tube:*** *Russell Square, then a 10-minute walk west on Bernard St. and around Russell Square to Montague St., at the northwest corner of the square.* ***Rack rates:*** *£185–£195 ($305–$322) double. English breakfast included. AE, DC, MC, V.*

Boston Court Hotel

$. Marylebone.

This unfrilly 13-unit hotel on a street brimming with B&Bs offers affordable accommodations in a centrally located Victorian-era building within walking distance of Oxford Street shopping and Hyde Park. Rooms are small and what you might call utilitarian, with a no-nonsense approach to decorating, but all have private showers and small refrigerators.

26 Upper Berkeley St. (near Marble Arch), London W1H 7PF. ☎ ***0171/723-1445.*** *Fax 0171/262-8823.* ***Tube:*** *Marble Arch, then a 10-minute walk west on Bayswater Rd., north on Edgware Rd., and east on Upper Berkeley St.* ***Rack rates:*** *£55 ($91) double with shower only, £75 ($124) double with shower and toilet. Continental breakfast included. MC, V.*

Best Hotels for Travelers with Disabilities

- Blooms Hotel (Bloomsbury, $$$$)
- Claridge's (Mayfair, $$$$$)
- The Dorchester (Mayfair, $$$$$)
- Dorset Square Hotel (Marylebone, $$$)
- Four Seasons Hotel (Mayfair, $$$$$)
- Landmark London (Marylebone, $$$$$)
- The Langham Hilton (Marylebone, $$$$$)

Bryanston Court Hotel

$$. Marylebone.

Three houses were joined to form this 200-year-old hotel, one of the finest moderately priced hotels in Central London, in a neighborhood with many attractive squares. Family owned and operated, the Bryanston Court has small rooms (and equally small bathrooms) that are comfortably furnished and well maintained. Just *don't* let them send you down to the basement room, or you'll feel like Cinderella before she met Prince Charming. There's a comfy bar with a fireplace in the back of the lounge.

56–60 Great Cumberland Place (near Marble Arch), London W1H 7FD. ☎ ***0171/262-3141.*** *Fax 0171/262-7248.* ***Tube:*** *Marble Arch, then a 5-minute walk north on Great Cumberland Place to Bryanston Place.* ***Rack rates:*** *£110 ($182) double. Continental breakfast included. AE, DC, MC, V.*

The Byron Hotel

$$. Bayswater.

The staff at this pleasant, family-run hotel just north of Kensington Gardens is unusually helpful, and this place is a standout in terms of the amenities you get for the price you pay. The 45-room Byron occupies a Victorian house that's been thoroughly modernized but hasn't lost its traditional appeal. Rooms have ample closets, tile bathrooms, and good lighting. An elevator services all floors, and breakfast is served in a bright and cheery room.

36–38 Queensborough Terrace (off Bayswater Rd.), London W2 3SH. ☎ ***0171/243-0987.*** *Fax 0171/792-1957. E-mail: byronhotel@capricorn.com.* ***Tube:*** *Queensway, then a 5-minute walk east on Bayswater Rd. and north on Queensborough Terrace.* ***Rack rates:*** *£105 ($173). English or continental breakfast included. AE, DC, MC, V.*

The Cadogan Hotel

$$$$. Chelsea.

Memories of the Victorian era haunt this beautiful hotel located close to all the exclusive Knightsbridge shops. The Cadogan (pronounced Ca-*dug*-en) is the hotel where Oscar Wilde was staying when he was arrested. (Room 118 is now called the Oscar Wilde Suite.) With its small, wood-paneled lobby and sumptuously furnished drawing room (good for afternoon tea), it is truly like stepping into another era. The large rooms, many of them overlooking the gardens in Cadogan Place, are quietly tasteful and splendidly comfortable, with large bathrooms. The sedate Edwardian restaurant is known for its excellent cuisine.

75 Sloane St. (near Sloane Square), London SW1X 9SG. ☎ ***800/260-8338*** *in the U.S., or 0171/235-7141. Fax 0171/245-0994. E-mail: info@thecadogan.u-net.com.* ***Tube:*** *Sloane Square, then a 5-minute walk north on Sloane St.* ***Rack rates:*** *£195–£230 ($322–$380) double. AE, MC, V.*

Caswell Hotel

$. Westminster/Victoria.

The Caswell lies on a cul-de-sac that's a calm oasis in an otherwise busy area. Beyond the chintz-filled lobby, the decor is understated: There are four floors of nicely furnished bedrooms, many without a private bathroom, but each with amenities usually found in higher-priced hotels. The staff is extremely thoughtful and considerate, which accounts for a lot of repeat business.

25 Gloucester St. (near Warwick Square), London SW1V 2DB. ☎ ***0171/834-6345.*** ***Tube:*** *Victoria, then a 15-minute walk southeast on Belgrave Rd. and southwest on Gloucester St.* ***Rack rates:*** *£54 ($89) double without bathroom, £75 ($124) double with bathroom. English breakfast included. MC, V.*

Claverley Hotel

$$. Knightsbridge.

Set on a quiet cul-de-sac in Knightsbridge a few blocks from Harrods, this small, cozy place is generally considered to be one of the best B&Bs in

London. Public rooms are accented with Georgian-era accessories, 19th-century oil portraits, and a collection of elegant antiques and leather-covered sofas. Most of the 29 guest rooms have wall-to-wall carpeting, upholstered armchairs, and marble bathrooms with power showers. The English breakfast is outstanding.

13–14 Beaufort Gardens (off Brompton Rd.), London SW3 1PS. ☎ ***800/747-0398*** *in the U.S., or 0171/589-8541. Fax 0171/584-3410.* ***Tube:*** *Knightsbridge, then a 10-minute walk south on Brompton Rd. and southeast on Beaufort Gardens.* ***Rack rates:*** *£120–£180 ($192–$256) double. English breakfast included. AE, DC, MC, V.*

Covent Garden Hotel

$$$$$. Covent Garden.

This stylishly luxurious boutique hotel near Covent Garden Market was created from an 1850s French hospital and dispensary. No two rooms are alike, and many have large windows looking out over the rooftops of London. The decor is a lush mixture of antiques and fine contemporary furniture, and the granite-tiled bathrooms with spacious glass-walled showers and heated towel racks are among the best in London. The wood-paneled public rooms are equally luxe. Brasserie Max serves up eclectic bistro food and is a chic place to lunch. There's a small gym on the premises.

10 Monmouth St. (near Covent Garden Market), London WC2H 9HB. ☎ ***800/553-6674*** *in the U.S. or 0171/806-1000. www.firmdale.com. E-mail: covent@firmdale.com.* ***Tube:*** *Leicester Square, then a 5-minute walk north on St. Martin's Lane, which becomes Monmouth St.* ***Rack rates:*** *£200–£295 ($330–$487) double. AE, MC, V.*

Kids The Cranley

$$$. South Kensington.

Situated on a quiet street near South Kensington's famous museums, the Cranley is housed in a trio of restored 1875 town houses. It's a real find for this price category, with luxuriously appointed public rooms and 37 bright, high-ceilinged rooms featuring original plasterwork and concealed kitchens. The white-tiled bathrooms are large and nicely finished with a tub and shower. Suites on the ground (first) floor open onto a charming private garden and have Jacuzzis. Breakfast is served in a pleasantly tony dining room.

10–12 Bina Gardens (off Brompton Rd.), London SW5 OLA. ☎ ***800/448-8355*** *in the U.S., or 0171/373-0123. Fax 0171/373-9497. www.thecranley.co.uk. E-mail: thecranley@compuserve.com.* ***Tube:*** *Gloucester Rd., then a 5-minute walk south on Gloucester Rd., west on Brompton Rd., and north on Bina Gardens.* ***Rack rates:*** *£140–£170 ($231–$281) double. Continental breakfast included. AE, DC, MC, V.*

Crescent Hotel

$. Bloomsbury.

For 4 decades, travelers have been returning to the well-run, comfortably elegant Crescent, located north of Russell Square in the heart of academic London. The 24 rooms range from small singles with shared bathrooms to more spacious twin, double, and family rooms with private plumbing (although the bathrooms are very small). There are a lot of thoughtful extras in each room, and guests have access to the adjacent gardens with private tennis courts.

49–50 Cartwright Gardens (near Tavistock Square), London WC1H 9EL. ☎ ***0171/ 387-1515.*** *Fax 0171/383-2054.* ***Tube:*** *Russell Square, then a 10-minute walk north on Marchmont St., which becomes Cartwright Gardens.* ***Rack rates:*** *£60 ($99) double with shared bathroom, £75 ($124) double with bathroom. English breakfast included. MC, V.*

Diplomat Hotel

$$. Belgravia.

Part of the Diplomat's charm is that it is a small, reasonably priced hotel in an otherwise prohibitively expensive area. The lobby area features a partially gilded circular staircase and a cherub-studded chandelier from the Regency era. The 27 high-ceilinged guest rooms are tastefully done in a Victorian style. The hotel is not exactly state-of-the-art, but it's very well maintained and a cut above the average for this price range.

2 Chesham St. (just south of Belgrave Square), London SW1X 3DT. ☎ ***0171/ 235-1544.*** *Fax 0171/259-6153.* ***Tube:*** *Sloane Square, then a 10-minute walk northeast on Cliveden and north on Eaton Place, which becomes Chesham St.* ***Rack rates:*** *£125–£155 ($192–$240) double. English buffet breakfast included. AE, DC, MC, V.*

Dorset Square Hotel

$$$. Marylebone.

This small, sophisticated luxury hotel is housed in a beautifully restored Regency town house overlooking Dorset Square—a leafy private garden surrounded by tall, graceful buildings. Aggressively gorgeous inside and out, the hotel is the epitome of traditional English style. All the rooms are different; all are filled with a superlative mixture of antiques, original oils, fine furniture, fresh flowers, and lots of richly textured fabrics. The bathrooms are marble and mahogany. It's a place that makes you feel like purring; it's so comfortable you can't wait to get back in the evening.

39–40 Dorset Square (just west of Regent's Park), London NW1 6QN. ☎ ***800/ 553-6674*** *in the U.S. or 0171/723-7874. Fax 0171/724-3328. www.firmdale.com. E-mail: Dorset@firmdale.com.* ***Tube:*** *Marylebone, then a 5-minute walk east on Melcombe to Dorset Square.* ***Rack rates:*** *£130–£190 ($215–$314) double; rates do not include 17.5% VAT. AE, MC, V.*

Kids Durrants Hotel

$$. Marylebone.

Established in 1789 off Manchester Square, directly across from the Wallace Collection (see page xx), this historic hotel makes for an atmospheric Central London retreat. It's quintessentially English, with pine-and-mahogany-paneled public areas, a wonderful Georgian room that serves as a restaurant, and even an 18th-century letter-writing room. The wood-paneled guest quarters are generously proportioned (for the most part), nicely furnished, and have decent-sized bathrooms.

George St. (across from the Wallace Collection), London W1H 6BJ. ☎ ***0171/935-8131.*** *Fax 0171/487-3510.* ***Tube:*** *Bond St., then a 5-minute walk west on Oxford St. and north on Duke St. and Manchester St.* ***Rack rates:*** *£130–£135 ($215–$223) double. AE, MC, V.*

Edward Lear Hotel

$. Marylebone.

This popular budget hotel close to Marble Arch occupies a pair of brick town houses dating from 1780. One of them was the London home of the 19th-century artist and nonsense poet Edward Lear, whose illustrated limericks decorate the walls of the sitting room. Steep stairs lead up to the rooms, which are fairly small but comfortable. One drawback is that fewer than half the rooms have private bathrooms; another is that the area has a lot of traffic noise. Rooms in the rear are quieter.

28–30 Seymour St. (near Marble Arch), London W1H 5WD. ☎ ***0171/402-5401.*** *Fax 0171/706-3766. www.edlear.com. E-mail: edwardlear@aol.com.* ***Tube:*** *Marble Arch, then 1 block north to Seymour St.* ***Rack rates:*** *£60 ($99) double without bathroom, £89.50 ($148) double with bathroom. English breakfast included. MC, V.*

Kids Europa House Hotel

$. Paddington.

This family-run budget hotel attracts those who want a private shower with their room but don't want to pay too much extra for the luxury. As in most B&Bs along Sussex Gardens, the bedrooms here are a bit cramped, but they're well-kept, sometimes color-coordinated, and each has a bathroom. Some rooms are custom built for groups, with three, four, or five beds, which makes them good for families. A hearty English breakfast is served in the bright dining room every morning.

151 Sussex Gardens (near Paddington Station), London W2 2RY. ☎ ***0171/402-1923*** *or 0171/723-7343. Fax 0171/224-9331. www.smoothhound.co.uk/hotels/europa.html. E-mail: europahouse@enterprise.net.* ***Tube:*** *Paddington, then a 5-minute walk south on London St. to Sussex Gardens.* ***Rack rates:*** *£50–£68 ($83–$112) double. English breakfast included. AE, MC, V.*

Fielding Hotel

$$. Covent Garden.

The Fielding Hotel is located on a beautiful old London street (now pedestrians only) lit by 19th-century gaslights and just steps away from the Royal Opera House. There's no elevator; stairways are steep and narrow; and the rather cramped rooms, filled with white wicker furniture, show little sign of decor perception. Those quibbles aside, this quirky hotel is an excellent value. Every room has a small shower and a toilet. Breakfast is available for a modest £2.50 to £4 ($4 to $7). And Smokey, an ancient parrot, presides over the tiny bar for residents.

4 Broad Court, Bow St., London WC2B 5QZ. ☎ ***0171/836-8305.*** *Fax 0171/497-0064.* ***Tube:*** *Covent Garden.* ***Rack rates:*** *£88–£98 ($145–$162) double. AE, DC, MC, V.*

Five Sumner Place

$$$. South Kensington.

One of the best B&Bs in Kensington, this little charmer occupies a landmark Victorian terrace house that's been completely restored in an elegant English style. Rooms are comfortably and traditionally furnished, and all have private bathrooms (a few have refrigerators as well). There's a full range of services; breakfast is served in a Victorian-style conservatory.

Best Rooms with a View

Park Lane Hotel (Mayfair, $$$$$)

The Savoy (The Strand, $$$$$)

5 Sumner Place (just east of Onslow Square), London SW7 3EE. ☎ ***0171/584-7586.*** *Fax 0171/823-9962. E-mail: no.5@dial.pipex.com.* ***Tube:*** *South Kensington, then a 5-minute walk west on Brompton Rd. and south on Sumner Place.* ***Rack rates:*** *£141 ($233) double. English breakfast included. AE, MC, V.*

The Gallery

$$. South Kensington.

Two splendid Georgian residences were completely restored and converted into this remarkable and relatively unknown hotel near all the cultural and retail attractions in South Kensington and Knightsbridge. Bedrooms are individually designed and elegantly decorated with half-canopied beds and luxurious marble-tiled bathrooms with brass fittings. A team of butlers takes care of everything. The lounge, with its rich mahogany paneling and moldings and deep colors, has the ambiance of a private club.

8–10 Queensberry Place (opposite the Museum of Natural History), London SW7 2EA. ☎ ***0171/915-0000.*** *Fax 0171/915-4400. www.eeh.co.uk. E-mail: gallery@eeh.co.uk.* ***Tube:*** *South Kensington, then a 5-minute walk west on Thurloe St. and Harrington Rd. and north on Queensberry Place.* ***Rack rates:*** *£115 ($190) double; rates do not include VAT (17.5%). Buffet English breakfast included. AE, DC, MC, V.*

The Gate Hotel

$. Notting Hill.

This is the only hotel along the entire length of Portobello Road, with its antiques and bric-a-brac stalls. The tiny three-story building dates from the 1820s (when people were much smaller), so the bedrooms are cramped but atmospheric, and the stairs are very steep. Rooms are color coordinated and have en-suite bathrooms. Kensington Gardens is a 5-minute walk away.

6 Portobello Rd., London W11 3DG. ☎ ***0171/221-2403.*** *Fax 0171/221-9128. www.smoothhound.co.uk/hotels/gate.html. E-mail: gatehotel@aol.com.* ***Tube:*** *Notting Hill Gate, then a 5-minute walk north on Pembridge Rd. and northwest on Portobello Rd.* ***Rack rates:*** *£75–£78 ($124–$129) double. Continental breakfast included. MC, V.*

The Gore

$$$$. South Kensington.

Lovers of true Victoriana will love The Gore, located on a busy road near Kensington Gardens and Royal Albert Hall. The hotel has been in more or less continuous operation since 1892 and is loaded with historic charm: lots of walnut and mahogany paneling, potted palms, oriental rugs, and walls covered with 19th-century prints. Every room is different, but all are remarkable for their high-quality antiques and furnishings. Even the toilets, concealed within old commodes, are noteworthy. Bistro 190, just off the lobby, is hip and popular.

189 Queen's Gate (south of Kensington Gardens), London SW7 5EX. ☎ ***800/ 637-7200*** *in the U.S., or 0171/584-6601. Fax 0171/589-8127. E-mail: reservations@gorehotels.co.uk.* ***Tube:*** *Gloucester Rd., then a 10-minute walk east on Cromwell Rd. and north on Queen's Gate.* ***Rack rates:*** *£163–£245 ($269–$404) double; rates do not include VAT (17.5%). AE, DC, MC, V.*

Kids Harlingford Hotel

$. Bloomsbury.

Set in the heart of Bloomsbury, this personable hotel is composed of three 1820s-era town houses joined together with a bewildering array of staircases (no elevators) and hallways. The 44 bedrooms are comfortable and inviting and are graced with floral prints and double-glazed windows to cut down on noise. Bathrooms are very small, however. The best rooms are on the second and third levels; say no to the darker rooms on the ground level. Guests have use of the tennis courts in Cartwright Gardens.

61–63 Cartwright Gardens (north of Russell Square), London WC1H 9EL. ☎ ***0171/ 387-1551.*** *Fax 0171/387-4616.* ***Tube:*** *Russell Square, then a 10-minute walk northwest on Woburn Place, east on Tavistock Square and north on Marchmont St.* ***Rack rates:*** *£81 ($134) double. English breakfast included. AE, DC. MC, V.*

Harrington Hall

$$$. South Kensington.

This six-story 1870s terrace house is one of the most inviting addresses in the South Kensington area. The beautifully designed classical lobby sets the tone for 200 tasteful and stylish bedrooms (some much larger than others); flowery fabrics and patterned carpets create a High English ambiance. There's 24-hour room service and a fitness center with a gym, a sauna, and showers.

5–25 Harrington Gardens (south of Kensington Gardens), London SW7 4JW. ☎ ***800/44-UTELL*** *in the U.S., or 0171/396-9696. Fax 0171/396-9090. www.harringtonhall.co.uk. E-mail: harringtonsales@compuserve.com.* ***Tube:*** *Gloucester Rd., then a 5-minute walk south on Gloucester Rd. and west on Harrington Gardens.* ***Rack rates:*** *£160 ($256) double. AE, DC, MC, V.*

Kids

Hart House Hotel

$. Marylebone.

Cozy and convenient, this well-preserved Georgian mansion-cum-hotel lies within easy walking distance of West End theatres, shopping areas, and parks. The 16 rooms—done in a combination of styles and furnishings ranging from Portobello antique to modern—are spick-and-span; not all have private bathrooms. No. 7 is a triple with a big bathroom and shower; no. 11, on the top floor, is a brightly lit aerie.

51 Gloucester Place, Portman Square (just north of Marble Arch), London W1H 3PE. ☎ ***0171/935-2288.*** *Fax 0171/935-8516.* ***Tube:*** *Marble Arch, then a 5-minute walk north on Gloucester Place.* ***Rack rates:*** *£75 ($124) double without bathroom, £93 ($153) double with bathroom. English breakfast included. AE, MC, V.*

Hazlitt's 1718

$$$. Soho.

Staying in this intimate, historic gem, built in 1718, is a delight, in part because of its old-fashioned atmosphere. The hotel has installed lovely bathrooms, many with claw-foot tubs, but there is no elevator. The Georgian-era rooms are charming and elegant, filled with mahogany and pine furnishings and antiques. It's quieter in the back; the front rooms are lighter, but restrictions on historic properties don't allow for double glazing of the windows. The location couldn't be better: Step out the door and you're smack dab in the heart of hip Soho. There's a small sitting room downstairs, and you can order a continental breakfast for £7.25 ($12).

6 Frith St., Soho Square (just west of Charing Cross Rd.), London W1V 5TZ. ☎ ***0171/434-1771.*** *Fax 0171/439-1524.* ***Tube:*** *Tottenham Court Rd., then a 10-minute walk west on Oxford St. and south on Soho St. to Frith St. at the south end of Soho Square.* ***Rack rates:*** *£163 ($269) double; rates do not include VAT (17.5%). AE, DC, MC, V.*

Hotel 167

$. South Kensington.

Hotel 167 is one of the more fashionable guest houses in the South Ken area, attracting a hip young crowd that likes the price and business travelers who like its central location. Every room has a decent-sized bathroom, some with a shower, others with a tub, and the overall ambiance is clean, bright, and attractive. The rooms are furnished with a mixture of fabrics and styles, all tending to the beige-brown end of the palette. Nearby tube stations make access to the rest of London a snap, and the neighborhood itself is charming, busy, and fun to explore.

167 Old Brompton Rd., London SW5 OAN. ☎ ***0171/373-0672.*** *Fax 0171/373-3360.* ***Tube:*** *South Kensington, then a 10-minute walk west on Old Brompton Rd.* ***Rack rates:*** *£78–£90 ($129–$149) double. Continental breakfast included. AE, DC, MC, V.*

Kids

Hotel La Place

$$. Marylebone.

One of the most desirable hotels north of Oxford Street, this Victorian-era building, in the vicinity of Madame Tussaud's, isn't particularly distinguished outside, but the interior was recently refurbished to boutique-hotel standards. The moderately sized bedrooms are done in a classic English style, with mahogany furnishings, brocades, and opulently swagged windows. The bathrooms are as nice as the rooms. The hotel's **Jardin** is a chic, intimate wine bar and restaurant.

17 Nottingham Place (near the southwest corner of Regent's Park), London W1M 3FF. ☎ ***0171/486-2323.*** *Fax 0171/486-4335. www.hotellaplace.com. E-mail: reservations@hotellaplace.com.* ***Tube:*** *Baker Street, then a 5-minute walk east on Marylebone Rd. and south on Nottingham Place.* ***Rack rates:*** *£105–£165 ($173–$272) double. English breakfast included. AE, DC, MC, V.*

Hotel Russell

$$$. Bloomsbury.

For about 100 years, the massive red-brick Hotel Russell has been looking down on Russell Square, the heart of Bloomsbury. This is a castle-size establishment in the grand Victorian style, with an imposing marble staircase, gleaming wood paneling, and crystal chandeliers. The rooms are furnished in an uninspired traditional style, but they all have decent bathrooms. Virginia Woolf would turn over in her grave if she knew that the hotel has a restaurant named after her and that it serves burgers and grills.

Russell Square, London WC1B 5BE. ☎ ***0171/837-6470.*** *Fax 0171/837-2857. www.forte-hotels.com. E-mail: hotelrussell@ukbusiness.com.* ***Tube:*** *Russell Square; the hotel sits right on the square, and you can't miss it.* ***Rack rates:*** *£179 ($275) double. AE, MC, V.*

Ivanhoe Suites Hotel

$. Mayfair.

Situated above a restaurant on a pedestrian street full of boutiques and restaurants, and close to even more shopping on New and Old Bond streets, this town-house hotel has eight stylishly furnished rooms with private bathrooms, sitting areas, and fridge/bars. It offers an unusual number of services for a hotel this small and this inexpensive, including room service and babysitting. Hyde Park is 5 minutes away.

1 St. Christopher's Place, Barrett St. Piazza (just north of Oxford St.), London W1M 5HB. ☎ ***0171/935-1047.*** *Fax 0171/224-0563.* ***Tube:*** *Bond St., then a 2-minute walk north on Gees Court to St. Christopher's Place.* ***Rack rates:*** *£79 ($130) double. Continental breakfast included. AE, DC, MC, V.*

Kids James House/Cartref House

$. Westminster/Victoria.

Generally considered one of the top 10 B&Bs in London, James House and Cartref House (across the street), deserve the accolades. Each room is individually designed; some of the large ones have bunk beds that make them suitable for families. Fewer than half have private bathrooms. The English breakfast is extremely generous, and everything is kept in tip-top order. There's no elevator, but guests don't seem to mind. It doesn't matter which house you're assigned to; both are winners.

108 and 129 Ebury St. (near Victoria Station), London SW1W 9QD. James House ☎ ***0171/730-7338;*** *Cartref House* ☎ ***0171/730-6176.*** *Fax 0171/730-7338. E-mail: jamescartref@compuserve.com.* ***Tube:*** *Victoria, then a 10-minute walk north on Grosvenor Gardens and south on Ebury St.* ***Rack rates:*** *£60 ($99) double without bathroom, £70 ($116) double with bathroom. English breakfast included. AE, MC, V.*

Kids Jenkins Hotel

$. Bloomsbury.

This completely nonsmoking hotel has its drawbacks: The rooms are small, there's no elevator, fewer than half the units have private bathrooms, and there's no reception room or sitting room. But let's hear it for the pluses: a bit of Georgian charm, a great location near the British Museum and West End theatres, a nice comfortable feel, a full breakfast, and a wonderfully low price. It's a place where you can settle in and feel at home.

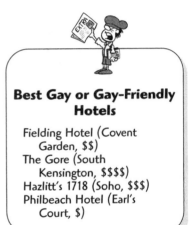

Best Gay or Gay-Friendly Hotels

- Fielding Hotel (Covent Garden, $$)
- The Gore (South Kensington, $$$$)
- Hazlitt's 1718 (Soho, $$$)
- Philbeach Hotel (Earl's Court, $)

45 Cartwright Gardens (just south of Euston Station), London WC1H 9EH. ☎ ***0171/387-2067.*** *Fax 0171/383-3139. E-mail: reservations@jenkinshotel.demon.co.uk.* ***Tube:*** *Euston, then a 5-minute walk east on Euston Rd. and south on Mabledon Place to the south end of Cartwright Gardens.* ***Rack rates:*** *£62 ($102) double without bathroom, £72 ($119) double with shower and toilet. English breakfast included. MC, V.*

Knightsbridge Hotel

$$. Knightsbridge.

This family-run hotel sits on a tree-lined, traffic-free square between fashionable Beauchamp Place and Harrods, with many of the city's top theatres and museums close at hand. Small and unpretentious, with a subdued Victorian ambiance, it's been recently renovated to a high standard. All the well-furnished rooms have a private bathroom and more amenities than you'd expect for the price. There's even a small health club with a steam room and a spa for guests' use.

12 Beaufort Gardens (just south of Harrods), London SW3 1PT. ☎ ***0171/589-9271.*** *Fax 0171/823-9692. www.knightsbridge.co.uk.* ***Tube:*** *Knightsbridge, then a 5-minute walk west on Brompton Rd. and south on Beaufort Gardens.* ***Rack rates:*** *£135 ($223) double. English breakfast included. AE, MC, V.*

Kids

Landmark London

$$$$$. Marylebone.

This was the finest Victorian railway hotel in England when it opened in 1899, and millions of dollars' worth of renovations have recently restored it to its former glory—and then some. Almost nobody pays the rack rates here, so ask and see what they're offering: You might land a real deal. The hotel is in a great location, particularly if you're traveling with children: Madame Tussaud's is a half-block away, and Regent's Park is a 5-minute walk. The rooms are unusually large, and they come with marble bathrooms, blonde-wood furnishings, and modern paintings. Every amenity is available, including baby-sitting, a large health club, and an indoor pool. It has special rooms for guests with disabilities.

222 Marylebone Rd. (half a block from Madame Tussaud's), London NW1 6JQ. ☎ ***800/457-4000*** *in the U.S. or 0171/631-8000. Fax 0171/631-8080. www.landmarklondon.co.uk.* ***Tube:*** *Baker St., then a 5-minute walk west on Marylebone Rd.* ***Rack rates:*** *£245–£267 ($404–$441) double; rates do not include VAT (17.5%). AE, DC, MC, V.*

Lime Tree Hotel

$$. Westminster/Victoria.

A good choice for budget travelers, this cozy hotel is within easy reach of Buckingham Palace, Westminster Abbey, and the Houses of Parliament. The 26 bedrooms, scattered over four floors of a brick-fronted town house, are furnished simply but are generally larger and offer more amenities than you find in this price range. The en-suite bathrooms are small but serviceable. The front rooms have small balconies overlooking Ebury Street; rooms in the back are quieter and look out over the hotel's small rear garden. Breakfasts are generous.

135–137 Ebury St. (near Victoria Station), London SW1W 9RA. ☎ ***0171/730-8191.*** *Fax 0171/730-7865.* ***Tube:*** *Victoria, then a 5-minute walk north on Grosvenor Gardens and south on Ebury St.* ***Rack rates:*** *£90–£100 ($149–$165) double. English breakfast included. AE, MC, V.*

Number Sixteen

$$$. South Kensington.

City gardeners will appreciate the award-winning gardens in the front and rear of this luxurious and idyllic pension housed in four early-Victorian town houses. The rooms are decorated with an eclectic mix of English antiques and modern paintings, and the bathrooms have enough room to move around. On chilly days, a fire roars in the drawing room's fireplace. Breakfast is served in the privacy of your bedroom, but if the weather's fine, you can have breakfast in the garden, with its bubbling fountain and fish pond.

*16 Sumner Place (north of Onslow Square), London SW7 3EG. ☎ **800/592-5387** in the U.S., or 0171/589-5232. Fax 0171/584-8615. **Tube:** South Kensington, then a 5-minute walk west on Brompton Rd. and south on Sumner Place. **Rack rates:** £110 ($182) double without bathroom, £160–£190 ($264–$314) double with bathroom. Continental breakfast included. AE, DC, MC, V.*

Most Romantic Hotels

22 Jermyn Street (St. James's, $$$$)
Blooms Hotel (Bloomsbury, $$$$)
The Cadogan (Chelsea, $$$$)
Covent Garden Hotel (Covent Garden, $$$$$)
Dorset Square Hotel (Marylebone, $$$)
The Gallery (South Kensington, $$)
The Gore (South Kensington, $$$$)
Hazlitt's 1718 (Soho, $$$)
Hotel La Place (Marylebone, $$)
Park Lane Hotel (Mayfair, $$$$$)
The Savoy (The Strand, $$$$$)

Park Lane Hotel

$$$$$. Mayfair.

This prestigious landmark hotel opened in 1927 and is sometimes called the Iron Lady of Piccadilly—not because it's torture to stay here, but because she's so well built. The cheapest rooms—those not yet remodeled—are quiet and fairly spacious but lack air-conditioning. Far more enticing are the renovated executive rooms and suites, all of which have beautiful marble bathrooms and are decorated with a warm mixture of classic English furnishings. No two rooms are alike, and the price goes up according to location (particularly if it's a suite overlooking Green Park), size, and decor. The **Palm Court Lounge** is a swank place for afternoon tea (see chapter 11).

*Piccadilly (across from Green Park), London W1Y 8BX. ☎ **800/325-3535** in the U.S., or 0171/499-6321. Fax 0171/499-1965. www.ittsheraton.com. **Tube:** Green Park, then a 5-minute walk southwest along Piccadilly. **Rack rates:** £280–£330 ($462–$545) double. AE, DC, MC, V.*

Philbeach Hotel

$. Earl's Court.

Opened in 1978, the Philbeach is the largest and most established of the exclusively gay hotels in Earl's Court. Occupying a large Victorian house on a Victorian crescent, it's relaxed and less pompous than the gay New York Hotel next door. There's a baroque quality to the decor, which favors an eclectic mix of paintings and furniture. About half the 40 rooms have bathrooms (with minuscule showers). There's a TV lounge, an intimate basement bar popular with drag queens, and a glass-walled dining room off the garden for breakfast. In the evening, this becomes a good French restaurant called **Wilde About Oscar.**

30–31 Philbeach Gardens (near Earl's Court Exhibition Centre), London SW5 9EB. ☎ ***0171/373-1244.*** *Fax 0171/244-0149.* ***Tube:*** *Earl's Court, take the Warwick Rd. exit; the hotel is a 5-minute walk north on Warwick St. and west on Philbeach Gardens.* ***Rack rates:*** *£55 ($91) double without bathroom, £70 ($116) double with bathroom. English breakfast included. AE, DC, MC, V.*

The Regency Hotel

$$$. South Kensington.

Close to the great South Kensington museums and Knightsbridge shopping, this recently refitted hotel occupies six Victorian terrace houses. It's quite a picture of English elegance, with a Chippendale fireplace and five Empire chandeliers suspended vertically, one on top of the other, in one of the stairwells. The modern guest rooms are subdued and attractive, with good-sized bathrooms. There's a health club with steam rooms, saunas, and a sensory-deprivation tank if you need it.

100 Queen's Gate (near Museum of Natural History), London SW7 5AG. ☎ ***800/ 328-9898*** *in the U.S., or 0171/370-4595. Fax 0171/370-5555. E-mail: regency.london@dial.pipex.com.* ***Tube:*** *Gloucester Rd., then a 10-minute walk east on Cromwell Rd. and north on Queen's Gate.* ***Rack rates:*** *£139 ($229) double. AE, DC, MC, V.*

Regent Palace Hotel

$$. Piccadilly Circus.

One of the largest hotels in Europe, the Regent Palace sits at the edge of Piccadilly Circus near the bright lights of London's Theatreland. It's far from glamorous and staunchly adheres to its rather utilitarian 1915 design. None of the 950 simply furnished rooms contains a private bathroom, but they do have a sink and the shared facilities in the hallways are adequate. It's easy to feel anonymous amid the endless flow of tourists—but step out the door and you're right in the heart of the West End. There's a currency exchange and a theatre-booking agency on the premises, and the hotel's **The Carvery** is a good (and inexpensive) place to dine (see chapter 10).

12 Sherwood St. (just north of Piccadilly Circus), London W1A 4BZ. ☎ ***0171/ 734-7000.*** *Fax 0171/734-6435.* ***Tube:*** *Piccadilly Circus, then a 2-minute walk north on Sherwood St.* ***Rack rates:*** *£103 ($170) double with shared bathroom. English breakfast included. AE, DC, MC, V.*

The Savoy

$$$$$. The Strand.

The Savoy, established in 1889, is synonymous with luxury, and it's not only close to Theatreland—it also has the Savoy Theatre on the premises. The opulent eight-story landmark hotel has 15 types of rooms, including some famous art deco ones with their original features. They are all spacious, and the decor throughout is splendid. The bathrooms, as large as some hotel rooms, are clad in red-and-white marble and have enormous glass-walled showers and heated towel racks. The most expensive rooms have river views; others look out over the hotel courtyard. **The Savoy Grill** is one of London's most famous restaurants (see chapter 10), and in the **Thames Foyer** you can get a superlative English tea.

The Strand (just north of Waterloo Bridge), London WC2R 0EU. ☎ ***800/ 63-SAVOY*** *in the U.S. or 0171/836-4343. Fax 0171/240-6040. www.savoy-group.co.uk. E-mail: info@savoy.co.uk.* ***Tube:*** *Charing Cross, then a 5-minute walk east along The Strand.* ***Rack rates:*** *£295–£305 ($487–$503) double; rates do not include VAT (17.5%). AE, DC, MC, V.*

Kids Swiss House Hotel

$. South Kensington.

Swiss House, in the heart of South Ken (and right next door to Hotel 167), is a comfortable bargain B&B. It's not what you'd call stylish, and it lacks an elevator, but the rooms are clean and perfectly adequate, with pale walls, floral-print bedspreads, serviceable furniture, and small bathrooms. The doubles in back are quieter and have views out into a garden. The hotel is known as a good place for budget travelers, so it's wise to book early. Babysitting services can be arranged.

171 Old Brompton Rd. (south of Gloucester Rd. tube station), London SW5 0AN. ☎ ***0171/373-2769.*** *Fax 0171/373-4983. www.webscape.co.uk/swiss-house/index.html. E-mail: recep@swiss-hh.demon.co.uk.* ***Tube:*** *Gloucester Rd., then a 5-minute walk south on Gloucester Rd. and east on Old Brompton Rd.* ***Rack rates:*** *£77–£85 ($127–$140) double with bathroom. Continental breakfast included. AE, DC, MC, V.*

Tophams Belgravia

$$. Westminster/Victoria.

Housed in five small, interconnected row houses with flower-filled window boxes out front, Tophams was completely renovated in 1997. The best of the guest rooms are comfortably appointed with private baths and four-poster beds. The restaurant offers both traditional and modern English cooking for lunch and dinner. And the location is great, especially if you're planning to cover a lot of ground by tube or train: Victoria Station is just around the corner.

28 Ebury St. (near Victoria Station), London SW1W 0LU. ☎ ***0171/730-8147.*** *Fax 0171/823-5966. www.tophams.com. E-mail: tophams-belgravia@compuserve.com.* ***Tube:*** *Victoria, then a 5-minute walk north on Grosvenor Gardens and south on Ebury St.* ***Rack rates:*** *£100 ($165) double without bathroom, £120–£140 ($198–$221) double with bathroom. AE, DC, MC, V.*

Vicarage Private Hotel

$. Kensington.

Tops for old-fashioned English charm, affordable prices, and hospitality, the Vicarage is located on a residential garden square close to High Street Kensington, and Kensington Palace. Individually furnished in a country-house style, the bedrooms can accommodate up to four. No. 19 on the top floor is a particularly charming aerie. The biggest drawback is that there are no private bathrooms, but the guests don't seem to mind because many come back year after year.

10 Vicarage Gate (west of Kensington Gardens), London W8 4AG. ☎ ***0171/229-4030.*** *Fax 0171/792-5989. www.londonvicaragehotel.com. E-mail: reservations@londonvicaragehotel.com.* ***Tube:*** *Kensington High St., then a 10-minute walk east on Kensington High St. and north on Kensington Church St.* ***Rack rate:*** *£63 ($104) double with shared bathroom. English breakfast included. No credit cards.*

Wilbraham Hotel

$$. Chelsea.

Set on a quiet residential street, just a few hundred yards from Sloane Square, this old-fashioned hotel is a bit faded but very well maintained and not without a certain dated charm. The traditionally furnished, wood-paneled bedrooms have fireplaces, leaded-glass windows, and heated towel racks in the bathroom. There's an attractive lounge where you can order drinks and simple meals.

1–5 Wilbraham Place (off Sloane St.), London SW1X 9AE. ☎ ***0171/730-8296.*** *Fax 0171/730-6815.* ***Tube:*** *Sloane Square, then a 5-minute walk north on Sloane St. and east on Wilbraham Place.* ***Rack rates:*** *£105 ($155) double. No credit cards.*

Help! I'm So Confused!

For some people, the decision about where to stay is an easy one. Maybe you've always dreamed of splurging on a room at The Savoy or the Park Lane Hotel. Maybe you want to stay right in the middle of all the action on Piccadilly Circus. Or you might not have a clear preference, and that's where organization comes into the picture. Some people charge lots of money for getting other people organized, but we'll throw it in for free.

You probably read through the reviews in this chapter and said, at least a few times, "Hey, that one sounds good." If you put a little check mark next to those, you're ahead of the game (if not, we hope you have a good memory), but it would still be a royal pain in the butt to flip among a few dozen pages comparing and contrasting hotels. So what you want to do is jot down the names and vital statistics of those places on the following chart, get everything lined up and orderly, and then scan the lines to see how they stack up against each other. As you rank the choices in your mind, rank them in the column on the right, too; that way, you can have your preferences all ready when making reservations, and if there's no room at your number-1 choice, just move right on to number 2.

Hotel Preferences Worksheet

Hotel	Location	Price per night

Advantages	Disadvantages	Your Ranking (1–10)

Part 3

Learning Your Way Around London

Daydreaming about a place is convenient and lots of fun: You don't have to concern yourself with the nitty-gritty of getting from point A to point B. But when you actually reach your destination, reality sets in. You're not familiar with the subways (maybe you've never ridden in one), with how the bus system works, when the trains run, or how to get a taxi. You have to rely on maps, timetables, tickets, and all the rest. In London, at least, you won't have to worry about driving—at least I hope you won't, because having a car in London is a sure-fire way to not enjoy yourself.

London is a big place, no doubt about it. Unless you can afford to take a taxi everywhere you go, you'll need to familiarize yourself with public transportation—the Underground (subway) in particular—and London's neighborhoods. It's not that difficult, and once you get the hang of it, you'll be whizzing around like a native. In this chapter, we'll cover all the basics. You might be surprised at how quickly you can learn your way around London.

Chapter 7

Getting Your Bearings

In This Chapter

- Smooth landings: How to get from the airport to your hotel
- North, south, east, west: How to get yourself oriented
- Helping hands

London is one of the world's largest cities, in both size and population. And I won't pretend that it's always the easiest city to find your way around in. As you might expect from a place that's been growing since Roman times, the streets are not laid out in an orderly grid. But traveling higgledy-piggledy through London's streets is part of its enduring charm. Many of the London neighborhoods were once small villages, and a village-like character is still evident. Later on in this chapter, you'll learn more about the neighborhood boundaries. But first you have to get from the airport (or train station) into Central London.

You've Just Arrived—Now What?

Chances are you'll be coming into Heathrow or Gatwick Airport; both handle the bulk of London's international flights. You don't have to expect any weird surprises. The airports handle hundreds of thousands of visitors a day and are geared toward moving people efficiently from point A to point B. If you get lost or confused, don't be afraid to ask for help. The English are invariably polite and helpful.

NORTH SEA
Glasgow
Edinburgh
SCOTLAND
Northumberland Nat'l Park
Newcastle upon Tyne
Carlisle
Belfast
NORTHUMBRIA
Solway Firth
THE LAKE DISTRICT
Lake District Nat'l Park
North York Moors Nat'l Park
NORTHERN IRELAND
Isle of Man
Yorkshire Dales Nat'l Park
YORKSHIRE
York
IRISH SEA
Blackpool
Leeds
Liverpool Bay
Manchester
Liverpool
Peak District Nat'l Park
Chester
Lincoln
LINCOLNSHIRE
THE NORTHWEST
EAST MIDLANDS
The Wash
Nottingham
ENGLAND
Norwich
Leicester
EAST ANGLIA
Birmingham
Ely
WARWICKSHIRE
THE COTSWOLDS
Cambridge
Stratford-upon-Avon
Bedford
Aldeburgh
WALES
Woodstock
St. George's Channel
Buckingham
Dedham
Swansea
Oxford
AVON
LONDON
Cardiff
OXFORDSHIRE
Windsor
Bath
THAMES VALLEY
Bristol Channel
Bristol
Canterbury
WILTSHIRE
SURREY
Exmoor Nat'l Park
SOMERSET
KENT
Dover
HAMPSHIRE
Strait of Dover
Salisbury
WEST SUSSEX
EAST SUSSEX
Southampton
Brighton
DEVON
DORSET
Hastings
Calais
Portsmouth
Dartmoor Nat'l Park
Lyme Bay
Isle of Wight
CORNWALL
Plymouth
English Channel
Land's End
Lizard Point
Cherbourg
Le Havre
Channel Islands
England
0
50 mi
0
80 km
N
FRANCE

What Time Is It?

One thing to keep in mind is that the U.K., like the rest of Europe, uses the 24-hour clock for timetables. That means 0530 is 5:30am, 1200 is noon, and 1830 is 6:30pm. It's not really confusing: Just continue counting up from noon—1300 = 1pm, 1400 = 2pm, 1500 = 3pm, and so on up to 2400 (midnight). In this guide, we'll stick to the system you know best—am and pm.

If You Arrive at Heathrow

Located about 15 miles west of Central London, Heathrow is the largest of London's airports. In fact, it's the busiest airport in the world, with four passenger terminals serving flights from around the globe. The corridors are surrealistically long, but there are moving walkways to make the trek easier. And signposts are everywhere so that you won't get lost. **Terminal 1** is mainly for short-haul British Airways flights, **Terminal 2** is for the European services of non-British airlines, **Terminal 3** handles non-British long-haul flights, and **Terminal 4** is used for British Airways intercontinental flights and the super-fast Concorde. You'll probably arrive at Terminal 3 or 4.

After you clear Customs (see the box, below), you'll enter the main concourse of your terminal. All sorts of services are available, including hotel-booking agencies (see "What If I Didn't Plan Ahead?" in chapter 5), theatre-booking services, and several banks and Bureaux de Change where you can swap your dollars (or traveler's checks) for pounds and pence. If you want to pick up a free map and general tourist information, there's a **Tourist Information Centre** (open daily 8:30am–6pm) in the underground concourse of Terminals 1, 2, and 3.

You have several options for getting into the city from Heathrow. If you want to travel as cheaply as possible, take the Underground. To reach your hotel on the Underground, you might have to change trains or take a cab from the Underground station to your hotel.

London Underground—Piccadilly Line (**☎ 0171/222-1234**), hereafter called **the Underground** or **the tube,** is the cheapest mode of public transportation for most Central London destinations. All terminals link up with the tube system. Follow the large Underground signs to the ticket booth. The **Piccadilly Line** gets you into Central London in about 40 minutes. The fare is £3.30 ($5.50). The one potential hassle with the Underground is that the trains do not have luggage racks. And if it's rush hour, they'll be packed.

From Heathrow Terminal 1, 2, or 3, Underground trains run every 5 to 9 minutes Monday through Saturday from 5:13am to 11:54pm, Sunday from 6:03am to 11:02pm. From Terminal 4, trains run Monday through Saturday from 5:08am to 11:49pm, Sunday from 5:58am to 11:57pm.

No Sweat—Navigating Your Way Through Passport Control & Customs

Have your passport ready, because your first stop at Heathrow or any of the airports will be Passport Control. It's a fairly routine procedure. On the plane, you receive a **landing card** to be filled out. Present this completed form and your passport to the passport official. He or she may ask you how long you will be staying (less than 3 months if you don't have a visa), where you'll be staying (on the landing card, you will have written this information already), whether the trip is for business or pleasure (don't be afraid to say pleasure), what your next destination will be, and how much money you have with you. The last question is not snoopy impertinence: They want to verify that you won't burden the country by applying for some kind of welfare or national health insurance benefits.

After your passport is stamped, you'll proceed on to pick up your luggage. From there you'll wend your way out through Customs Hall. Chances are you'll be able to walk right through. You might be stopped for a random luggage search, however. Don't take it personally if this happens. Unless you're smuggling in contraband, you have nothing to worry about.

If the Underground has closed, the **N97** night bus connects Heathrow with Central London. Buses (located in front of the terminals) run every 30 minutes Monday through Saturday from midnight to 5am, Sunday from 11pm to 5:30am. The trip takes about an hour; a one-way fare is £1.50 ($2.50) before 4:30am, £1.20 ($2) after 4:30am.

For more information on the Underground, including discount passes (called Travelcards), see chapter 8.

The **Airbus** (☎ **0181/400-6655**) might be a better alternative to the Underground if you have lots of heavy luggage. There are two routes—the A1 and the A2. Travel time for both is about 1 hour. The fare is £6.00 ($10).

Dollars & Sense

Unless you're on an escorted tour or have purchased a package that includes hotel transfers, you'll need to have some pounds and pence to pay for your trip from the airport to Central London. You'll find places in the airport to exchange currency, but a better idea is to **buy some British pounds before you leave the States.** Just get as much as you'll need to get you from the airport to downtown, where you will typically find better exchange rates. You can buy foreign currency in the United States at any bank; shop around for the best rate.

Buses depart about every 30 minutes from the front of each terminal, not far from Customs Hall; look for signposts.

The **A1** goes from Heathrow to **Victoria Station** via Cromwell Road, Knightsbridge, and Hyde Park Corner. Buses run from Terminal 1 6:54am to 10:54pm, Terminal 2 6:50am to 10:50pm, Terminal 3 5:35am to 10:58pm, and Terminal 4 5:20am to 10:35pm. The **A2** goes to **King's Cross Station** via Bayswater, Marble Arch, Euston, and Russell Square. Buses run from Terminal 1 6:44am to 11:24pm, Terminal 2 6:40am to 10:20pm, Terminal 3 5:20am to 10:28pm, and Terminal 4 5:05am to 10:05pm.

FastTrain (☎ **0845/600-1515**) is a new (as of June 1998) dedicated train line that runs from all four Heathrow terminals to **Paddington Station** in just 35 minutes. The trains, which have air-conditioning, ergonomically designed seating, and lots of luggage space, are considerably more luxurious than the Underground. Using this service does require a simple bus-to-train transfer, however. You can catch a FastTrain bus outside your arrival terminal. The bus will take you directly to the FastTrain. The fare is £5 ($8.25). You can purchase tickets at Heathrow (at the Speedlink sales desk and selected Bureaux de Change) or on board the train.

If you're so jet-lagged that you're seeing double, and you have two cranky kids and a load of luggage to deal with, you might want the luxury of taking a **taxi** (☎ **0181/745-5325**) directly to your hotel. Taxis are especially cost-effective if four or five people are traveling together. You can order a taxi at the **Taxi Information booths** found in all four terminals. Expect to pay about £28 to £35 ($46 to $58) plus tip. The trip should take about 45 minutes. Cabs are available 24 hours a day. Wheelchair facilities are available at all times for travelers with disabilities.

Extra! Extra!

If you're a jittery first-time traveler and want hand-held service from Heathrow or Gatwick Airport directly to your hotel, try **Hotelink** (☎ **888/722-5269** in the U.S.; 01293/552-251 in the U.K.). You need to reserve a seat on one of its air-conditioned minivans before you leave. (You can't book this service once you arrive.) The per-person cost is $21 from Gatwick and $30 from Heathrow. A company representative will meet you outside of Customs Hall at either airport and direct you to the minivan. Travel time from Heathrow to your hotel is usually about an hour; from Gatwick, which doesn't have a direct highway link to Central London, the trip could take up to 2 hours if traffic is bad. Because this is a reserved-seat service, you might have to wait some additional time at the airport until all the passengers have arrived.

If You Arrive at Gatwick

Gatwick, considerably smaller than Heathrow, lies about 28 miles south of Central London. It was once used only for charters but now handles international flights from several U.S. airlines. Many travelers prefer Gatwick to Heathrow. It has two terminals: North and South. International flights come in at the **South Terminal.** Gatwick provides the same array of services that Heathrow does, except that there's no office of the British Tourist Authority. It has fewer transportation options for getting into Central London than Heathrow does. The hands-down winner here is the Gatwick Express train. The highway system into London is far less efficient than from Heathrow, so buses, minivans, or cabs can end up taking 2 to 3 hours if there's a snarl.

Your best bet for getting into Central London from Gatwick is the handy Gatwick Express train (**☎ 0345/484-950**), which is right in the terminal. It will whiz you from the airport to Victoria Station in about half an hour for £8.90 ($15). Trains run every 15 minutes from 5am to 11pm and every hour from 11pm to 4:30am.

You can save a couple of bucks by taking the local **Connex South-Central** train (**☎ 0345/484-950**), which also runs to Victoria and usually takes only about 5 minutes longer. The fare is £7.50 ($12). There are four trains an hour during the day; trains run hourly at night. Another train service is **Thameslink** (**☎ 0345/484-950**), which runs between Gatwick and King's Cross Station. The fare is £8.90 ($15). Service is every 15 minutes from 3:45am to 12:15am; trip time is about 45 minutes.

Two companies provide 24-hour **taxi service** between Gatwick and Central London: **Gatwick Airport Cars** (**☎ 01293/562-2291**) and **Gatwick Goldlines Cars** (**☎ 01293/568-368**). You can order a taxi at the **Taxi Information booth** when you arrive. Fares for both companies are the same: £55 ($91) plus tip. The journey takes about 90 minutes.

If You Arrive at Another Airport

Stansted Located about 33 miles northeast of Central London, Stansted is a new (the Queen opened it in 1991), single-terminal airport used for national and European flights. The **Stansted Express Train** (**☎ 0345/484-950**) to Liverpool Street Station takes 45 minutes and costs £10 ($17). Trains run every half-hour from 6am to 11:59pm. A taxi fare into the city averages about £50 ($83) plus tip.

London City Airport One of London's best-kept secrets, London City Airport is a mere 6 miles east of the center of the city. But it only services European destinations. A **Red Route shuttle bus** (**☎ 0171/474-5555**) takes passengers from the airport to Liverpool Street Station in 25 minutes for £3 ($5). The buses run every 10 minutes from 6:40am to 10:30pm. A **taxi** costs about £18 ($30) plus tip.

Luton Luton, a small independent airport 33 miles northwest of the city, services European charter flights. **Greenline** coaches (**☎ 0181/668-7261**) run from the airport to Central London every hour from 5:30am to midnight; the trip takes about 70 minutes and costs £6 ($10). There is also a 24-hour **Railair Coach Link** to Luton Station (3 miles away) that connects with the Luton Flyer train to London Bridge, Blackfriars, Farringdon, and King's Cross stations in Central London. The fare is £10.10 ($17); trip time is 1 hour. **Taxis** into the city cost £38 to £45 ($63 to $74).

Which Way to the Tower? Orienting Yourself in London

From its beginnings as a Roman garrison town nearly 2,000 years ago, London has grown steadily and in a somewhat pell-mell fashion, swallowing up what were once small villages. Today, Greater London encompasses a whopping 622 square miles. The main tourist portion of London is only a fraction of that (25 square miles at the most), so don't be alarmed. The distances you'll travel are sometimes considerable, but they're generally a whiz on London's Underground system (called "the tube"). To reach your final destination, you might have to walk some distance—but rarely more than 10 minutes—from the tube stop. Luckily, London is flat. For walkers, it's a dream.

Many visitors—and even some Londoners—are often confounded by London's size, its confusing (and sometimes oddly named) streets, and its seemingly endless plethora of neighborhoods. To help you find your way around, I strongly suggest that you buy a copy of ***London A to Z.*** You can pick up this book at a bookstore or newsagent in the airport or train station.

Extra! Extra!

When you go to the bookstore or news agent to purchase your copy of *London A to Z,* remember: The Brits say "zed" instead of "z."

Londoners orient themselves by **neighborhood.** Sounds logical enough, but the problem is that it's often difficult to tell where one neighborhood begins and another leaves off. For orientation purposes, I'm going to give you major streets as boundary markers; however, the neighborhoods frequently creep beyond these principal arteries.

All London street addresses include a designation such as **SW1** or **EC1.** These are the **postal areas.** The system dates back to the time when the original post office was at St. Martin-le-Grand in the city. Postal districts are thus related to where they lie geographically from there. Addresses in the city of London, the easternmost portion of Central London, for example, have designations such as EC2, EC3, or EC4. As you move west, the code changes to W (West), WC (West Central), SW, NW, and so on. You don't really need to bother yourself with postal areas except when you're looking up streets in ***London A to Z*** (many streets in different parts of London have the same name) or sending something by mail. When you actually hit the streets, the postal-area designations are not as important as the nearest tube stop.

How to Tell Your Bloomsbury from Your Marylebone: London's Neighborhoods in Brief

Let's start by breaking this enormous megalopolis down into manageable sections. The first thing you need to know is that London grew up along the north and south banks of the **River Thames.** It's impossible to overestimate the importance of this great tidal river to London's growth and importance. It snakes through the city in a long, loose S curve. London's major tourist sites, hotels, and restaurants are on the river's **north bank,** whereas many of the city's famous performing arts venues are located on the **South Bank.**

Extra! Extra!

A **London Underground** map is as indispensable as *London A to Z* (which includes an Underground map). You can pick up a tube map at any Underground ticket office.

Central London, on the north bank of the Thames, is considered the **city center.** Londoners think of it as the area encompassed by the Circle Line Underground route, with Paddington Station tube stop at the northwest corner, Earl's Court tube stop at the southwest corner, Tower Hill tube stop at the southeast corner, and Liverpool Street Station tube stop at the northeast corner. Central London is divided into three areas: **the City, the West End,** and **West London.** Let's start at the City and move west from there.

Where It All Began: The City of London

The City of London is a self-governing entity that extends south from Chiswell Street to the Thames. To the west it's bounded by Chancery Lane; to the east it's bounded by the **Tower of London,** its most important historical monument. Fleet Street, once the heart of newspaper publishing, cuts through the center of the district to Ludgate Circus, where it becomes Ludgate and leads to **St. Paul's Cathedral.** Perched on the top of this ancient area is **the City,** which covers the original 1 square mile the Romans called Londinium. Today this is the Wall Street of England—home to the Bank of England, the Royal Exchange, and the stock exchange. It's also where you'll find the **Museum of London** and the **Barbican,** a mega-arts complex of theatres and concert halls. Liverpool Street Station is the main railroad terminus in this eastern portion of Central London. Major tube stops: Blackfriars, Tower Hill, St. Paul's, Liverpool Street Station, Bank, Barbican, and Moorgate.

Everywhere You Want to Be: The West End 'Hoods

The West End (that is, west of the city of London) is what you might loosely call "downtown" London. For most people it's synonymous with the theatres, entertainment, and shopping areas found around Piccadilly Circus and Leicester Square. But the West End actually includes a host of neighborhoods.

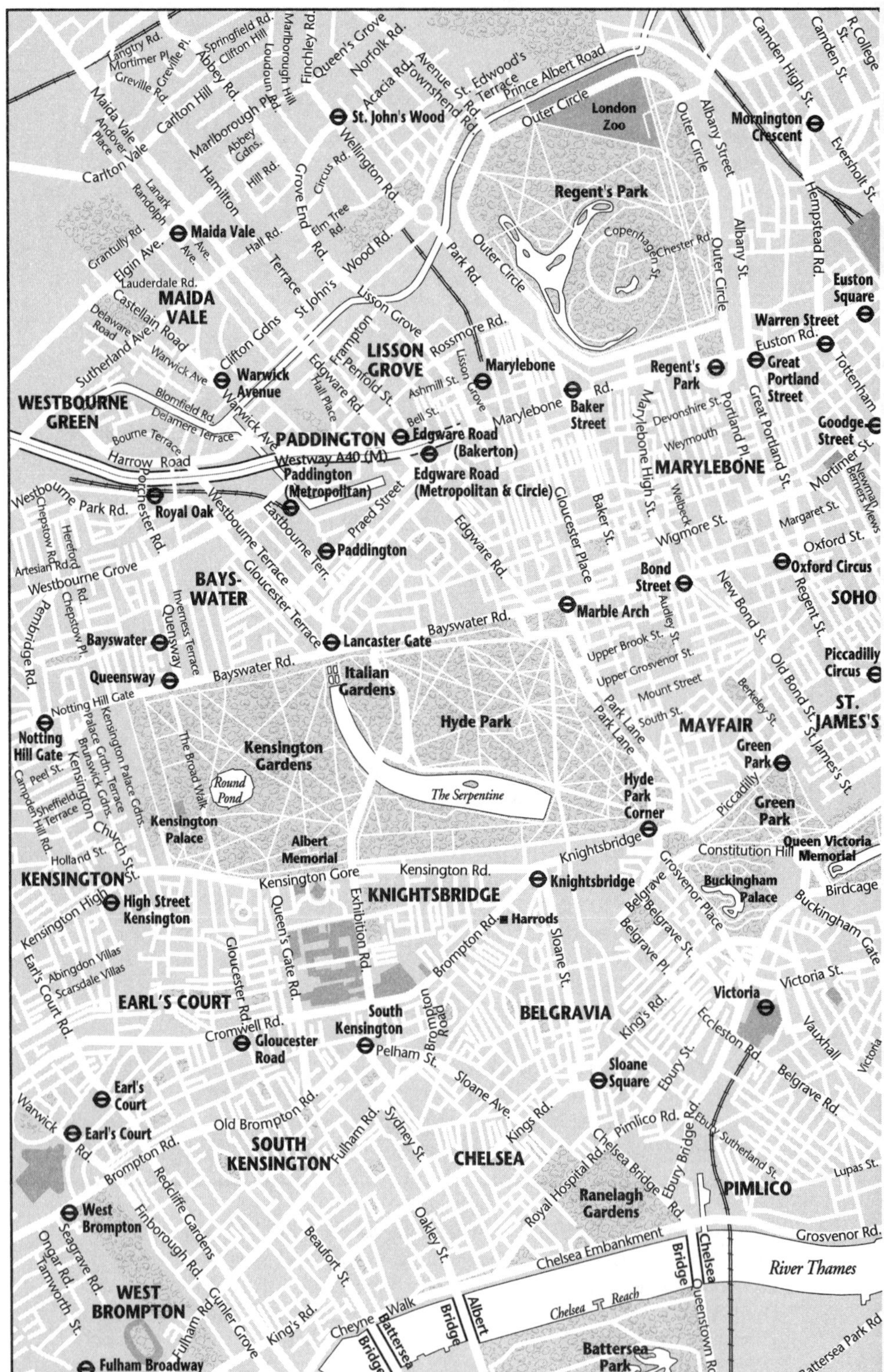

MAIDA VALE
WESTBOURNE GREEN
LISSON GROVE
PADDINGTON
MARYLEBONE
BAYSWATER
SOHO
MAYFAIR
ST. JAMES'S
KENSINGTON
KNIGHTSBRIDGE
EARL'S COURT
BELGRAVIA
SOUTH KENSINGTON
CHELSEA
PIMLICO
WEST BROMPTON
St. John's Wood
Maida Vale
Warwick Avenue
Marylebone
Baker Street
Regent's Park
Great Portland Street
Warren Street
Euston Square
Mornington Crescent
Goodge Street
Edgware Road (Bakerton)
Edgware Road (Metropolitan & Circle)
Paddington (Metropolitan)
Paddington
Royal Oak
Bayswater
Queensway
Notting Hill Gate
Lancaster Gate
Marble Arch
Bond Street
Oxford Circus
Piccadilly Circus
Green Park
Hyde Park Corner
Knightsbridge
High Street Kensington
Gloucester Road
South Kensington
Sloane Square
Victoria
Earl's Court
West Brompton
Fulham Broadway
London Zoo
Regent's Park
Hyde Park
Kensington Gardens
Italian Gardens
The Serpentine
Round Pond
Kensington Palace
Albert Memorial
Buckingham Palace
Queen Victoria Memorial
Harrods
Ranelagh Gardens
Battersea Park
River Thames
Chelsea Reach
Chelsea Bridge
Albert Bridge
Battersea Bridge
Prince Albert Road
Outer Circle
Westway A40 (M)
Harrow Road
Bayswater Rd.
Notting Hill Gate
Kensington Rd.
Kensington Gore
Knightsbridge
Constitution Hill
Piccadilly
Park Lane
Oxford St.
Wigmore St.
Marylebone Rd.
Euston Rd.
Cromwell Rd.
Brompton Rd.
Old Brompton Rd.
Fulham Rd.
King's Rd.
Chelsea Embankment
Grosvenor Rd.
Victoria St.
Buckingham Gate
Birdcage
Sloane St.
Edgware Rd.
Baker St.
Gloucester Place
Regent St.
New Bond St.
Old Bond St.
Praed Street
Lisson Grove
Park Rd.
Wellington Rd.
Abbey Rd.
Maida Vale
Camden High St.
Hampstead Rd.
Tottenham

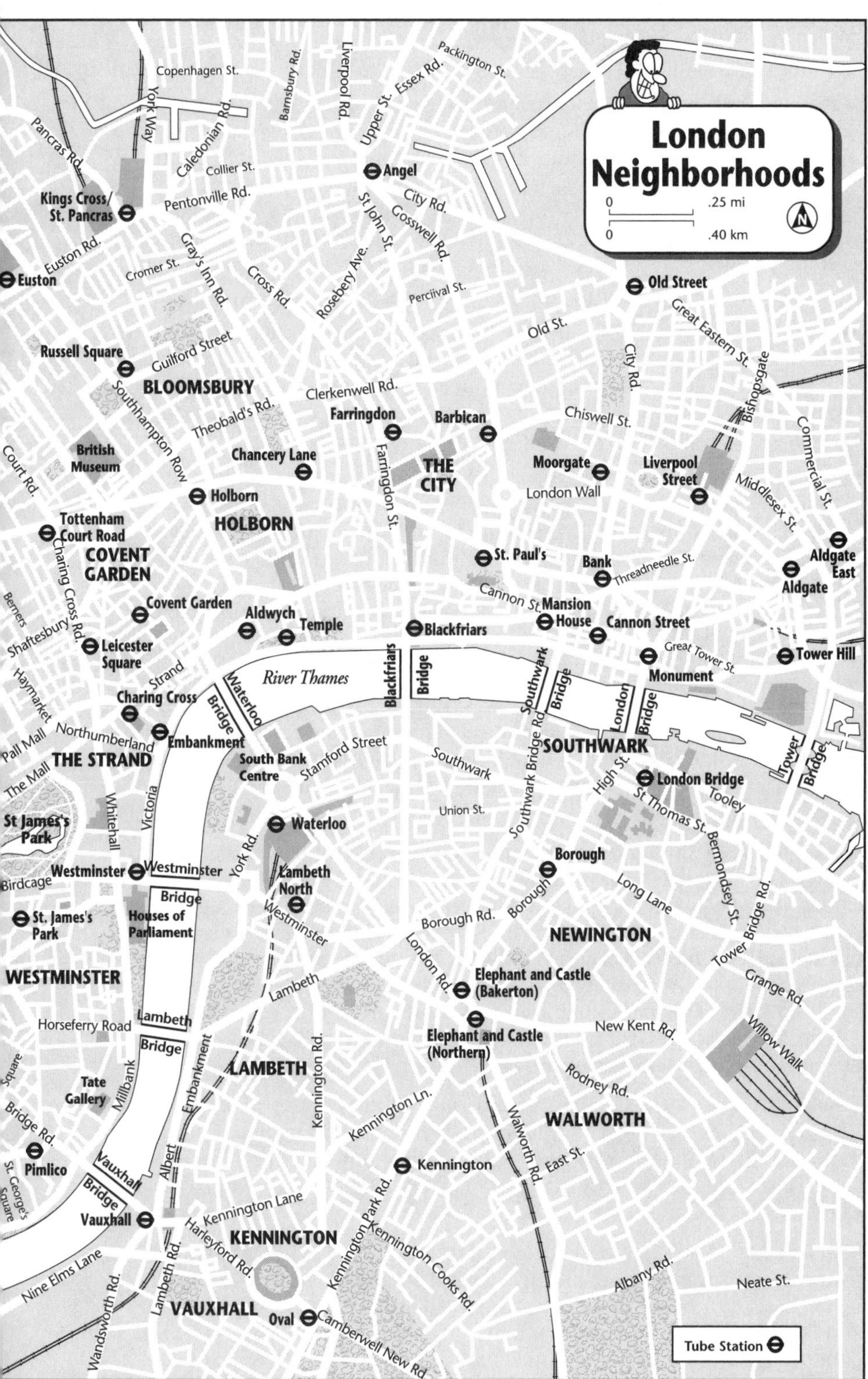
London Neighborhoods
0 .25 mi
0 .40 km
Tube Station
BLOOMSBURY
HOLBORN
COVENT GARDEN
THE STRAND
THE CITY
SOUTHWARK
WESTMINSTER
LAMBETH
NEWINGTON
WALWORTH
KENNINGTON
VAUXHALL
Kings Cross/ St. Pancras
Euston
Russell Square
Angel
Old Street
Farringdon
Barbican
Chancery Lane
Holborn
Moorgate
Liverpool Street
Tottenham Court Road
St. Paul's
Bank
Aldgate East
Aldgate
Covent Garden
Aldwych
Temple
Blackfriars
Mansion House
Cannon Street
Leicester Square
Monument
Tower Hill
Charing Cross
Embankment
London Bridge
Waterloo
Westminster
Lambeth North
Borough
St. James's Park
Elephant and Castle (Bakerton)
Elephant and Castle (Northern)
Kennington
Pimlico
Vauxhall
Oval
British Museum
South Bank Centre
Houses of Parliament
Tate Gallery
St James's Park
River Thames
Waterloo Bridge
Blackfriars Bridge
Southwark Bridge
London Bridge
Tower Bridge
Westminster Bridge
Lambeth Bridge
Vauxhall Bridge
Copenhagen St.
York Way
Caledonian Rd.
Barnsbury Rd.
Liverpool Rd.
Upper St.
Essex Rd.
Packington St.
Pancras Rd.
Collier St.
Pentonville Rd.
City Rd.
St John St.
Goswell Rd.
Euston Rd.
Cromer St.
Gray's Inn Rd.
Cross Rd.
Rosebery Ave.
Perciival St.
Old St.
Great Eastern St.
City Rd.
Bishopsgate
Guilford Street
Southampton Row
Theobald's Rd.
Clerkenwell Rd.
Chiswell St.
Commercial St.
Court Rd.
Farringdon St.
London Wall
Middlesex St.
Charing Cross Rd.
Threadneedle St.
Berners
Shaftesbury
Cannon St.
Great Tower St.
Strand
Haymarket
Pall Mall
Northumberland
The Mall
Southwark Bridge Rd.
Stamford Street
Southwark
High St.
Tooley
St Thomas St.
Whitehall
Victoria
Union St.
Southwark Bridge Rd.
York Rd.
Birdcage
Long Lane
Bermondsey St.
Westminster
Borough Rd.
Borough
Tower Bridge Rd.
London Rd.
Lambeth
Grange Rd.
Horseferry Road
New Kent Rd.
Willow Walk
Square
Embankment
Kennington Rd.
Millbank
Rodney Rd.
Bridge Rd.
Kennington Ln.
Walworth Rd.
East St.
St. George's Square
Albert
Kennington Lane
Kennington Park Rd.
Harleyford Rd.
Kennington Cooks Rd.
Nine Elms Lane
Lambeth Rd.
Albany Rd.
Neate St.
Wandsworth Rd.
Camberwell New Rd

Holborn Abutting the City of London to the west is the old borough of Holborn, the legal heart of London. Barristers, solicitors, and law clerks scurry to and fro among the Inns of Court, Lincoln's Inn Fields, and the Royal Courts of Justice and Old Bailey. This "in-between" district is bounded roughly by Theobald's Road to the north; Farringdon Road to the east; the Thames to the south; and Kingsway, Aldwych, and Lancaster Place to the west. Major tube stops: Holborn, Temple, Blackfriars, and Aldwych.

Covent Garden & The Strand The northern section of The Strand, the area west of Holborn, is Covent Garden, with Shaftesbury Avenue as its northern boundary. The Strand, a major street that runs from Trafalgar Square to Fleet Street, is the principal thoroughfare along the southern edge, with Charing Cross Road to the west, and Kingsway, Aldwych, and Lancaster Place to the east. Major tube stops: Covent Garden, Leicester Square, and Charing Cross.

Bloomsbury Just north of Covent Garden, New Oxford Street and Bloomsbury Way mark the beginnings of the Bloomsbury district. Home of the **British Museum** and several colleges and universities, this intellectual pocket of Central London is bounded on the east by Woburn Place and Southampton Row, to the north by Euston Road, and to the west by Tottenham Court Road. Major tube stops: Euston Square, Russell Square, Goodge Street, and Tottenham Court Road.

Soho The Soho neighborhood consists of the warren of densely packed streets north of Shaftesbury Avenue, west of Charing Cross Road, east of Regent Street, and south of Oxford Street. This lively area is full of restaurants and nightclubs. London's Gay Village is centered around Old Compton Street. Major tube stops: Leicester Square, Covent Garden, and Tottenham Court Road.

Piccadilly Circus, Leicester Square & Charing Cross Think of this area just west of The Strand as "downtown" London, or Theatreland. Piccadilly Circus, the area's major traffic hub and best-known tourist destination, feeds into Regent Street and Piccadilly. The **Royal Academy of Arts** is just west of **Piccadilly Circus. Leicester Square** and Shaftesbury Avenue, a few minutes' walk to the east, are where most of the West End theatres are located. From Leicester Square, Charing Cross Road runs south to Trafalgar Square, the National Gallery, and Charing Cross Station. Major tube stops: Piccadilly Circus, Leicester Square, and Charing Cross.

Mayfair Elegant and exclusive Mayfair is comfortably nestled between Regent Street on the east, Oxford Street on the north, Piccadilly on the south, and Hyde Park on the west. This is luxury-hotel and luxury-shopping land. Tube stops: Piccadilly Circus, Bond Street, Marble Arch, and Hyde Park Corner.

Marylebone Marylebone, the neighborhood north of Mayfair and west of Bloomsbury, is capped to the north by giant **Regent's Park** (Marylebone Road runs south of the park). Great Portland Street is the eastern boundary, and Edgware Road is the western. In a sense, you might call this "Medical London," because it has several hospitals and the famous Harley Street

Clinic. But perhaps the most famous street in Marylebone is Baker Street, home of the fictional Sherlock Holmes. Madame Tussaud's is on Marylebone Road. Tube stops: Baker Street, Marylebone, and Regent's Park.

Cool Britannia

Madame Tussaud, born Marie Grosholtz in Strasbourg, France, in 1761, was taken on as a child trainee by Dr. Philippe Curtius, a doctor and wax modeler. During the French Revolution, Marie had the grisly job of making death masks from the heads of guillotined prisoners. When Curtius died, he left his wax-model exhibition to Marie. In 1835 she took her wax collection to London. The models were bequeathed to her two sons, and in 1884 Madame Tussaud's wax exhibition moved to Marylebone Road, where it's been ever since. See chapter 13 for details.

St. James's St. James's, considered "Royal London," is a posh green haven that begins at Piccadilly and includes **Green Park** and **St. James's Park,** with **Buckingham Palace** between them. Pall Mall runs roughly east-west into the area and meets the north-south St. James's Street. Regent Street is the eastern boundary. Tube stops: St. James's Park and Green Park.

Westminster Westminster, situated to the east and south of St. James's, draws visitors to **Westminster Abbey** and the **Houses of Parliament,** the seat of British government. Westminster extends from Northumberland Avenue, just south of Charing Cross, to Vauxhall Bridge Road, with the Thames to the east and St. James's Park to the west. Victoria Station, on the northwestern perimeter, is a kind of center axis among Westminster, Belgravia, and Pimlico. Tube stops: Westminster, St. James's Park, and Victoria.

Pimlico Pimlico, the pie-shaped wedge of residential London that extends west roughly from Vauxhall Bridge Road to Buckingham Palace Road, with Victoria Station crowning it to the north, is the home of the **Tate Gallery.** Tube stops: Pimlico and Victoria.

Wait, There's More: Central London Beyond the West End

Belgravia Belgravia, the posh quarter long favored by aristocrats, begins west of Victoria Station and Green Park and extends south to the river and west to Sloane Street. It's bounded to the north by Hyde Park. Belgravia is where many foreign embassies are located. Tube stops: Victoria, Hyde Park Corner, and Sloane Square.

Knightsbridge West of Belgravia is the fashionable residential and shopping district of Knightsbridge, bounded to the north by Hyde Park. Running along its western perimeter is Brompton Road, and running through it is Beauchamp Place. Harrods on Brompton Road is the neighborhood's chief attraction. Tube stops: Knightsbridge and Sloane Square.

Cool Britannia

Harrods, founded in 1901, has been called "the Notre Dame of department stores"—they'll even arrange your burial. The store truly lives up to its motto, "everything for everyone, everywhere." In 1975 one customer who had his doubts called Harrods at midnight requesting that a baby elephant be delivered to the home of the governor of California and his First Lady, Mr. and Mrs. Ronald Reagan in Sacramento. The animal arrived safely. (Nancy even sent a thank-you note.)

Chelsea Chelsea, situated below Knightsbridge and west of Belgravia, begins at Sloane Square and runs south to Thameside Cheyne Walk and Chelsea Embankment. The area is bounded by King's Road to the north and Chelsea Bridge Road to the east. To the west it extends as far as Earl's Court Road, Redcliffe Gardens, and Edith Grove. It's a charming, expensive neighborhood filled with 18th- and 19th-century town houses where many of London's writers and artists once lived. Tube stop: Sloane Square.

South Kensington **Kensington Gardens** and **Hyde Park** form the green northern boundary of South Kensington. Frequently referred to as Museumland, South Ken is hopping with hotels, restaurants, and tourists. It's bounded to the west by Palace Gate and Gloucester Road, to the south by Fulham Road, and to the east by busy Brompton Road. Tube stops: Gloucester Road and South Kensington.

Kensington The residential neighborhood of Kensington fills in the gap between **Kensington Gardens** and **Holland Park,** with Notting Hill Gate and Bayswater Road marking it off to the north. Kensington Church Street runs north-south between Notting Hill Gate and Kensington High Street. With its preponderance of well-kept 19th-century homes, Kensington is tony, sedate, and attractive without being pretentious. The shops along Kensington High Street and Kensington Church Street draw shoppers from around the city. Tube stop: High Street Kensington.

Earl's Court Beginning south of West Cromwell Road and extending down to Lillie Road and Brompton Road is the down-to-earth Earl's Court neighborhood. Its western boundary is North End Road; to the east is Earl's Court Road. You won't find any major tourist attractions in Earl's Court, which has long been a haven for budget travelers (particularly Australians) and a neighborhood favored by gays and lesbians. It's gradually being spruced up, but there are many streets that still look a bit frayed. Tube stop: Earl's Court.

Notting Hill Notting Hill and the rising subneighborhood of Notting Hill Gate begin north of Holland Park, Kensington Gardens, and Hyde Park (Holland Park Avenue and Bayswater Road run along the northern perimeter of the parks). The area is bounded by Clarendon Road to the west, Queensway to the east, and Wesbourne Grove to the north. Portobello Road runs north-south through the center. Notting Hill is another London neighborhood in transition: Neglect is now giving way to a fresh new hipness as restaurants and clubs move in. The most famous street, **Portobello Road,** has long been the site of a popular antiques and bric-a-brac market. Tube stops: Notting Hill Gate, Bayswater, and Queensway.

Bayswater & Paddington Bayswater picks up where Notting Hill ends, running east to meet Marylebone at Edgware Road. The roaring A40 (Westway) highway acts as its northern boundary. Paddington Station is in the northwestern corner of Bayswater. This area is fairly commercial and not particularly attractive. There are no major tourist attractions, but there are lots of budget B&Bs. Tube stops: Paddington, Lancaster Gate, Marble Arch, and Edgware Road.

Culturesville: The South Bank

It's unlikely that you'll be staying on the South Bank, but you might be going there for a play, an exhibition, or a concert at one of its internationally known arts and performance venues or museums. The **Royal National Theatre** (actually three theatres), the **South Bank Centre** (which contains **Royal Festival Hall** and two smaller concert halls), the **Hayward Gallery,** the **National Film Theatre,** and the **Museum of the Moving Image** are all clustered beside the river within easy walking distance of Waterloo Station. For a more scenic route to the South Bank, take the tube to Embankment, on the north bank, and walk across the Thames on the Hungerford Pedestrian Bridge. The **Jubilee Walkway,** a breezy riverside path, extends south from the arts complexes to the **London Aquarium** and north to the new **Globe Theatre** (based on an Elizabethan outdoor theatre), **Southwark Cathedral,** and **Tower Bridge.** Tube stops: Waterloo and London Bridge.

Street Smarts: Where to Get Information & Guidance After You Reach London

The **British Travel Centre,** 1 Regent St., Piccadilly Circus, SW1 (tube: Piccadilly Circus), provides tourist information to walk-in visitors (there's no phone assistance). The office is open Monday to Friday from 9am to 6:30pm, and Saturday and Sunday from 10am to 4pm. There are hotel and theatre-booking agencies; a Bureaux de Change; and lots of free brochures on river trips, walking tours, and day trips from London.

The main **Tourist Information Centre,** run by the London Tourist Board, is in the forecourt of Victoria Station (tube: Victoria). It, too, has booking services and free literature on London attractions and entertainment, as well as an excellent bookshop. There are other Tourist Information Centres at

Liverpool Street Station; Waterloo International Station; and in the basement of **Selfridges** department store, 400 Oxford St. (tube: Bond Street).

Extra! Extra!

Kids If you're traveling with kids, you can call **Kidsline** at ☎ **0171/222-8070** (Monday to Friday 4 to 6pm and summer holidays 9am to 4pm) for tips on kid-friendly places to go and things to see. The London Tourist Board also has a special **children's information line** (☎ **01839/123-404**) and publishes a leaflet called ***Where to Take Children,*** which you can pick up at a Tourist Information Centre.

Visitorcall (☎ **0839/123-456**) provides 24-hour information, updated daily, on everything that's going on. At 49p (80¢) a minute, this service is not cheap, but it's reliable.

For current listings and reviews of everything that's going on, buy a copy of ***Time Out.*** It hits newsstands on Wednesday and costs £1.80 ($3).

Mind Your Teas & Queues

When you're in London, you'll be speaking English. American English is perfectly fine, of course, and will be understood everywhere. But English English does have a few quirks. (See chapter 9 for food terms.)

English	American English
Bonnet	Hood of a car
Cheers	Goodbye (or when raising a glass)
Cinema	Movie ("Theatre" is only live theatre.)
Coach	A long-distance bus
Concessions	Special discounts for students, senior citizens, and those with disabilities
Cooker	Stove
Jumper	Sweater
'Kew	Thank you
Knickers	Underwear
Loo	Rest room ("I need to use the loo.")
Lorry	Truck
Mate	Male friend
Queue	To line up (The Brits are excellent queuers.)
Ta	Thank you
Tea time	Between 3:30 and 6pm

Chapter 8

Getting Around London

In This Chapter

- Go with the flow: Using London's mass transit
- Getting around by taxi
- Getting around on foot

Whether you're grinding through rush-hour traffic on top of a double-decker bus, whizzing through the labyrinth of tunnels on a packed Underground train, or nervously eyeing the meter in a London cab, making your way around London is part of the overall London experience. I always use the Underground because it's fast and relatively inexpensive with a Travelcard (see below). The Underground (often referred to as "the tube") and the buses put you in close contact with Londoners going about their daily routines. That means they're great places to people watch. Plus, they're safe.

For general London travel information, call ☎ **0171/222-1234.** You can get free bus and Underground maps and timetables, and buy Travelcards and bus passes (see below) at the **London Travel Information Centres.** They are located at the following Underground stations: King's Cross, Liverpool Street, Oxford Circus, Piccadilly Circus, St. James's Park, and Heathrow terminals 1, 2, and 3. You can buy Travelcards and bus passes at other major Underground stations as well. *Note: To purchase anything other than a 1-day pass for the Underground or the bus, you need a photo ID.*

Traveling by Tube: The London Underground

London has one of the oldest and most comprehensive subway systems in the world. "The tube" is fast, convenient, and everyone but the royals uses it. Everything in London is cued to the nearest **tube stops,** which are clearly marked with a red circle and blue crossbar. Most of the city's main attractions are close to a tube stop, and there's always a tube map and a neighborhood map near the entrances to help you orient yourself.

There are **13 lines** that crisscross the city and intersect at various stations where you can change from one train to the next. Every line is **color coded** on Underground maps (Bakerloo is brown, Central is red, and so on), making it easy to plan your route. All you need to know is the direction in which you're heading. After you figure out which line you need to take, look on the map for the name of the last stop in the direction you need to go. The name of the last stop on the line is marked on the front of the train and sometimes on electronic signboards that tell you which train is arriving. Every line is clearly marked by signposts in the Underground stations. It's likely that at some point on your Underground trip, you'll have to transfer from one line to another; stations where you can do this are clearly marked on the Underground map.

Extra! Extra!

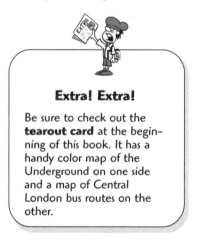

Be sure to check out the **tearout card** at the beginning of this book. It has a handy color map of the Underground on one side and a map of Central London bus routes on the other.

Every tube station is different. Some, such as Covent Garden, have elevators to the trains (and an optional stairway if you want a workout). Others, like Leicester Square and Piccadilly Circus, have very long escalators. Still others have stairways. In major stations that handle more than one line, there are long (but clearly marked) tunnels from one line to another.

Many of the trains have been modernized; others are older. Most of them have cushioned seats that haven't been ripped to shreds by vandals. The trains are not air-conditioned, and during weekday **rush hours** (8 to 10am, 5 to 7pm), they can be packed and stuffy. Smoking is not permitted on any of the trains. The trains are safe, and the passengers are generally considerate. The only times to think twice about taking the tube are on Friday and Saturday nights after 10:30pm, when drinkers are leaving the pubs. It won't be dangerous, but inebriated louts can be obnoxious. The only drawback to the Underground is that service generally stops at about midnight (sometimes a little earlier). Keep this in mind when you're out painting the town red. You'll have to take a taxi or one of the night buses.

How Do I Get Outta Here?

Most of the Underground system operates with **automated entry and exit gates.** You feed your ticket into the slot it disappears and pops up again like a piece of toast, the turnstile bangs open, and you remove your ticket and pass through. At the other end you do the same thing to get out—but the machine keeps the ticket (unless it's a Travelcard, which is returned to you). Ticket collectors are located at some stations.

You've Got a Ticket to Ride

You can purchase Underground **tickets** at the ticket window or from one of the automated machines found in most stations. At the ticket window, simply tell the ticket seller what station you're going to. Fares are posted.

For fare purposes, the city is divided into zones. **Zone 1** covers all of Central London. **Zone 6** extends as far as Heathrow to the west and Upminster to the east. Make sure that your ticket covers all the zones you will be traveling through. If it doesn't, you might have to pay a £10 ($16.50) penalty fare.

A **single-fare one-way ticket** within one zone costs £1.30 ($2.25) for an adult and 60p ($1) for a child 5 to 15 years of age. This is the most you will pay to reach any sight within Central London. Tickets are valid for use on the day of issue only.

The Ins & Outs of Travelcards

To make the most of London's public transportation, consider purchasing a 1-day, weekend, 1-week, or 1-month **Travelcard,** which allows unlimited travel by Underground *and* bus. A **1-day** Travelcard for zones 1 and 2 (everything in Central London) costs £3.50 ($6) for an adult and £1.80 ($3) for a child; it's valid after 9:30am on weekdays (in other words, after the morning rush hour) and all day Saturday and Sunday. The **weekend** version is good for one zone only and costs £5.20 ($8.50) for adults and £2.70 ($4.50) for children. A **1-week** Travelcard costs £13 ($21.50) for adults and £5.20 ($8.50) for children; a **1-month** Travelcard is £50 ($82.50) for adults and £20 ($32) for children. You (and your children) must show a photo ID to buy a weekend, 1-week, or 1-month Travelcard.

The **Family Travelcard** is good for families of one or two adults traveling with one to four children. These Travelcards are valid after 9:30am Monday to Friday and all day on Saturday and Sunday. Rates for 1 day of travel in zones 1 and 2 are £2.80 ($4.50) per adult and 60p ($1) per child.

Time-Savers

If you're going to be traveling by Underground, you can save time and money by purchasing a book of 10 tickets, called a **carnet.** Carnet tickets are valid in one zone only. The price is £10 ($16.50) for an adult and £5 ($8.25) for a child. With a carnet, you save £3.50 ($5.75) over single fares and don't have to wait in line to buy your ticket.

Double the Fun, Double the Headache: Getting Around by Bus

Time-Savers

Remember, if you want to purchase anything other than a 1-day **Travelcard or bus pass,** you (and your children) must show a photo ID.

You probably already know what London buses look like, right? Yes, those distinctive red **double-decker buses** are very much a part of London's snarled traffic scene. But not all London buses are double-deckers, and some are not red. And unless you have plenty of time or a claustrophobic aversion to the Underground, you're better off (timewise, at least) taking the tube or walking (during rush hour, buses creep along at about the same pace as a pedestrian). The one other drawback to bus travel, especially for first-time visitors, is that you need to know the streets of London so that you can get off at the correct stop. Get a **free bus map** at one of the **Travel Information Centres** (see above), or you might become hopelessly lost. On the plus side, riding the bus is cheaper than taking the tube, there are no escalators/elevators/tunnels to contend with, and you get to see the sights as you travel.

Bus stops are clearly marked by concrete posts with a red or white sign on top that says **London Transport Bus Service.** Another sign shows the routes of the buses that stop there. If the sign on top is red, it's a **request stop,** and you must hail the approaching bus as you would a taxi (don't whistle, just put up your hand). If the sign is not red, the bus will stop automatically. Be sure to check the destination sign in front of the bus to make certain it's going the entire route.

Unlike the Underground, buses run around the clock. But around midnight, buses change their destination prefix to "N" (for "night," obviously) and change their routes as well. Fares on night buses are generally double the daytime rates (see below).

Fare Game

The bus network is divided into four fare zones. **Zone 1** covers all of the main Central London tourist sites. (Zone 4 is the equivalent of zones 4, 5, and 6 on the Underground.)

It used to be that there was always a conductor on board the bus who went around and collected fares with a polite "'kew" (thank you). Nowadays the driver often doubles as the conductor. When you board, tell the driver (or conductor, if there is one) where you are going. They will tell you the fare. If you have a Travelcard or bus pass, show it to them. Have some coins with you if you're paying because they will not change banknotes.

A **one-zone bus fare** is 90p ($1.50) for adults and 40p (65¢) for children 5 to 15. Please note that child fares are not available after 10pm, and children 14 and 15 years old must have a Photocard to obtain the child rate. (When you have your child's passport photo taken, be sure to get a few extras made. The photo is attached to the travel pass.)

If you're going no more than three stops, you can get a **short hop ticket** for 60p ($1) for adults, or 40p (65¢) for children. Ask the driver (or conductor) if you're unsure.

Dollars & Sense

A 1-day bus pass is a good thing to have if you plan to travel a lot by bus. You can use the pass all day (before 9:30am even on weekdays, unlike the Travelcard), but it is not valid on N-prefixed night buses (see below). You can purchase this and longer-period bus passes at most Underground stations, at selected newsagents, and at the Travel Information Centres. A 1-day four-zone pass costs £2.70 ($4.50) for adults and £1.40 ($2.30) for children 5 to 15. A weekly bus pass is £12 ($20) for adults and £5.20 ($9) for children 5 to 15 with a child-rate photocard. (When you have your child's passport photo taken, be sure to get a few extras made. The photo is attached to the travel pass.) A monthly bus pass is £46.10 ($76) for adults and £20 ($33) for children.

In the Wee Hours: Night Buses

The pubs close at 11pm, the tube stops running about 11:30pm, and at the witching hour of midnight, buses become **night (N) buses,** which means they change their routes and double their fares. Your 1-day bus pass and family or weekend Travelcard will not be good on a night bus. Nearly all night buses pass through Trafalgar Square, Central London's late-night mecca for insomniacs.

Cool Britannia

When it comes to finding a street address, London cabbies are among the most knowledgeable in the world. Their rigorous training, which includes an exhaustive street test called "The Knowledge," gives them an encyclopedic grasp of the terrain.

Home, James, and Don't Spare the Horsepower: London by Taxi

It's hard not to love the roomy, old-fashioned, black London taxis. These blasts from the past still exist, but these days you'll also find many newer and smaller taxis. London cabs of any size or color are not cheap. The fare starts at £1.40 ($2.30), with 40p (70¢) for each additional passenger. On Saturday there's an additional 40p (70¢) charge, and on Sunday it's 60p ($1). If you have luggage, there's a surcharge for that, too. Then, after 8pm, another 40p (70¢) is tacked on—except for Saturdays, when it's 60p ($1). After all this, the meter leaps 20p (35¢) every 111 yards.

You can hail a cab on the street. If a cab is available, its yellow "For Hire" sign on the roof is lit. You can get radio cabs by calling ☎ **0171/272-0272** or 0171/253-5000. If you call for a cab, the meter starts ticking when the taxi receives notification from the dispatcher.

Tip your cabbie 15% of the total fare.

Pounding the Pavement

Sure, you can hop around town via tube, bus, or cab. But if you really want to get acquainted with the charming hodgepodge and monumental grandeur of London, bring along a good pair of walking shoes and let your feet do some of the work. Everywhere you turn, you'll see enticing side streets, country like lanes, little mews (former stables converted into homes), and leafy garden squares.

London is a walker's paradise, but even Central London is much too large to cover entirely on foot. Do try, however, to give yourself at least some time just to wander about. All of Chelsea is best explored on foot; start at Sloane Square or busy King's Road and meander southwest toward Cheyne Walk along the river. The same is true of bustling, cafe-laden Soho, just north of Shaftesbury Avenue, and the pedestrian-only precincts of the Covent Garden area just south of it. South Kensington, with its great museums, is full of charming side streets and squares. Even more atmospheric is the area in and around Lincoln's Inn Fields in Holborn, where a quiet whiff of old London pervades the beautiful 17th-century courts of law. At night, the Houses of Parliament, Big Ben, and Westminster Abbey are all floodlit and form an impressive sight; to get there, walk down Whitehall from Charing Cross.

Extra! Extra!

One of the **best scenic walks** in London is the **Jubilee Walkway,** which runs along the South Bank from Lambeth Bridge to Tower Bridge, offering great Thameside views of the North Bank along the way, and continues on the North Bank from the Tower of London all the way down to the Houses of Parliament. This walk is marked on the London map distributed free by the British Tourist Authority. The walk will take you most of a day, but you'll see so much of London that you won't regret it.

London has some of the most beautiful **parks** in the world, and the only way to experience them is on foot. The Green Park tube stop provides convenient access to Green Park from the north; from the tube stop, you can walk down to Constitution Hill, a major thoroughfare closed to traffic on Sundays, and on to Buckingham Palace. From there you can continue east into St. James's Park via Pall Mall (also traffic-free on Sundays), passing Clarence House and St. James's Palace, or stroll along the shores of St. James's Park Lake. You can enter Hyde Park from the Hyde Park Corner tube stop; head west into this massive green lung via the paths that parallel the north and south banks of the Serpentine, Hyde Park's lake. After you cross Serpentine Bridge, you're in Kensington Gardens; the famous statue of Peter Pan is to the north, and Kensington Palace is on the western perimeter, beyond Round Pond. Marylebone, to the north, is where you'll find Regent's Park, with the London Zoo in the northern section and Queen Mary's Gardens roughly in the center.

Part 4

London's Best Restaurants

Sometimes I wonder if I love to travel because I like to eat but hate to cook. Traveling is the perfect excuse to eat out all the time! I don't have to plan meals—just figure out where to find them. Someone else will do the cooking and wash the dishes. All I have to do is pay.

Dining out is one of the great pleasures of a trip. It can also be a big fat hassle if you don't know where to go or what to order. ("Kippers" might sound cute and delicious, but do you really like smoked fish?) In London, picking a place can be particularly difficult, because you have literally thousands of restaurants to choose from. You don't want to end up in a place where you need a buzz saw to cut the steak. Then, too, except for the ubiquitous fast-food chains and sandwich bars, London is not really a place where it's all that easy to eat on the run. The British set great store in sitting down to enjoy a "proper" meal or tea.

The following chapters should help set you straight about the London dining scene. This chapter gives you the general lowdown—the kinds of restaurants you'll find (from pubs and fish-and-chip joints to the hottest haute havens) and the variety of cuisine. You'll get tips on how to eat well for less (we're all trying to lose a few pounds, but there are ways to save a few pounds as well) and other tidbits of useful information.

My A-to-Z list of recommended London restaurants is in chapter 10. I've tried to include as many low- to moderately priced restaurants as possible, but if you're a real "foodie," you'll find some truly great places where you can sink your teeth into a true gourmet meal. Chapter 11 provides further options: places for tea, spots for quick(er) bites, and venues that will provide solace to your sweet tooth.

Chapter 9

The Lowdown on the London Dining Scene

In This Chapter

- The trendiest of the trendy: London's premier tables
- British cuisine: It's not so bad anymore—really
- The scoop on London's ethnic eats
- How to cut costs without cutting corners
- Tips on when to dine and what to wear

It'll probably come as no surprise to you that the dining options in London are almost inexhaustible. At last count, the city had some 5,700 restaurants serving the cuisine of more than 60 countries. New places are opening every day, but in the volatile restaurant business you never know how long they'll be around. Places that are hot today might be passé tomorrow. In this chapter, I'll give you the rundown on London's dining scene: new trends, ethnic tastes, and tips on finding decent chow that won't bankrupt your pocketbook.

The Leaders of the Pack

To become or remain a culinary hot spot in London, a restaurant must have one or more of the following: a celebrity owner, a celebrity chef, memorable food, a long-standing reputation, a fabulous view, a chic location, or some kind of special ambiance. One of the newer trends is the mega-eatery—a place that can hold up to several hundred diners at one time.

When it comes to designing can't-miss London restaurants, Sir Terence Conran leads the pack with his Oxo Tower Restaurant and the adjacent

Oxo Tower Brasserie perched above the Thames on the South Bank; **Le Pont de la Tour,** overlooking Tower Bridge; and **Bluebird,** his bright Chelsea restaurant. Other hot/haute spots include Chelsea's **Aubergine,** where the classic French cooking earns two *Michelin Guide* stars; **The Savoy Grill,** a power-player hangout in the Savoy Hotel; **Zafferano,** a superlative Italian restaurant in tony Knightsbridge; and the stylish **L'Odeon,** where window tables provide a bird's-eye view of Piccadilly Circus.

Time-Savers

Only a handful of top London restaurants—including all those listed under "The Leaders of the Pack"—require booking more than a week in advance. At most places it's usually possible to get a table on fairly short notice, especially if you're willing to dine before 7pm or after 9pm. If that fails, try for lunch instead.

Cuisine, Cuisine

"Plain English cooking" was often just that—dull and unimaginative. It was summed up in that old saying: "The French live to eat but the English eat to live." English cooking was often called "hearty" for lack of a better (or worse) word. The best dishes were—and remain—game, lamb, meat and fish pies, and the ever-popular roast beef with Yorkshire pudding (a crispy concoction made with drippings and served with gravy). At the lower end were—and are—greasy fish-and-chips, gluey steak and kidney pie, and bangers and mash (sausage and mashed potatoes) with a side of cold peas and carrots. In the past few years, however, there has been a renewed interest in and respect for traditional English fare. When it's done well, it's both hearty *and* delicious.

In the last decade or so, London has been in the grip of a gastronomic revolution. **"Modern British"** cuisine takes old standards and jazzes them up with foreign influences and ingredients, mostly from France (sauces), the Mediterranean (olive oil, oregano, garlic), and northern Italy (pasta, polenta, risotto). Besides Modern British, London foodies continue to favor classic French and Italian cuisine. Other new influences making their way into Modern British cooking come from Thailand and Morocco (couscous).

Indian cooking, one of the more pleasant reminders of "The Empire," has been a favorite ethnic food for some time. London is filled with Indian restaurants (about 1,500 of them) serving curries and dishes cooked in clay tandoor pots. ***Balti,*** a thick curry from Pakistan, is the new ethnic "must-try" dish.

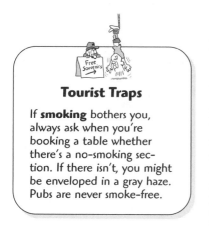

Tourist Traps

If **smoking** bothers you, always ask when you're booking a table whether there's a no-smoking section. If there isn't, you might be enveloped in a gray haze. Pubs are never smoke-free.

Location, Location, Location

You'll find all sorts of restaurants all over London (see chapter 10 for an index of restaurants by neighborhood). Unlike in some other large cities, **ethnic restaurants** are not really confined to one particular area of London, either. There are a few exceptions to this, however: You'll find a cluster of Chinese restaurants along Lisle, Wardour, and Gerrard streets in Soho's **Chinatown.** And **Notting Hill** has long been a standby for low-price Indian and Caribbean restaurants. But otherwise, ethnic joints are scattered all over. In terms of sheer variety, **Soho** and neighboring **Covent Garden** offer the most choices in the West End, with British, African, Caribbean, Mongolian, American (North and South), French, Italian, Spanish, Thai, Korean, Japanese, Middle Eastern, Eastern European, Modern European, Turkish, and vegetarian restaurants all represented. **Soho** is also particularly rich in cafes. **South Kensington** is another eclectic grab bag of culinary choices.

The Price Is Right

The restaurant listings in chapter 10 give you two price elements for each restaurant: the price range of the main courses on the menu and a dollar symbol that gives you an idea of the average cost of dinner for one person, including an appetizer (called a "starter" in the U.K.), a main course, dessert (sometimes called "afters"), one drink (not wine or beer), tax, and tip.

At places marked with **$,** the average dinner price is $25 or less. Plan to shell out between $25 and $35 at places marked with **$$.** Restaurants with **$$$** will set you back $35 to $50. Going for broke? Expect to pay $50 and more at **$$$$** restaurants.

Please bear in mind that the $ symbols denote the *average* price for a meal; if you order the most expensive entree and a bottle of wine, a $$ restaurant might become a $$$$ restaurant. On the other hand, if you order from a set-price menu, a $$$$ restaurant tab might go down to $$.

Eating More for Less

Not all of us can afford to cough up $50 a night for dinner, even on a holiday. So where do you go for lower cost meals? Pubs, cafes, sandwich bars, pizza places, and fast-food restaurants. In short, places where you're not paying for custom cooking and personal service. I've listed some of these places in chapter 11, "Light Bites and Munchies." But here's another tip: Always look to see whether the restaurant of your choice has a **set-price menu.**

More and more of London's top restaurants offer two- and three-course (or more) fixed-priced meals that can slash your tab in half. Sometimes these are called pre- or post-theatre menus, which means they're served only from about 5:30 to 7pm and after 9:30pm. Wine is generally fairly expensive, so forgo that if price is an issue. Lunch prices are often half of dinner prices, and the food is the same.

Pub Grub

Eating in pubs is often the best way to get a good meal for a low price. At most pubs the food is traditional and nothing fancy: meat pies and mash (mashed potatoes), **fish-and-chips,** mixed grills (sausages and a chop or cutlet), salads, sandwiches, and the famous **ploughman's lunch** of bread and cheese or pâté. In many pubs the food is prepackaged and frozen, and then microwaved. Lately, however, many pubs have become virtually indistinguishable from casual restaurants—except that there are more people drinking. The food is fresh, more adventurous, and better prepared at these places.

Extra! Extra!

The **legal drinking age** in the U.K. is 18, although kids over 16 can be served beer or cider with a meal in restaurants.

Reservations are not accepted at a pub: They're drop-in places, and finding a table at lunchtime is not always easy. Pub grub is generally washed down by beer, the British national drink. Pubs tend to be smoky, so avoid them if you are allergic to smoke. Unless a pub has a special "children's certificate," kids under 14 are only allowed into the gardens and separate family rooms.

Wine Bars

Wine bars are more sophisticated versions of pubs. You can eat well (sometimes very well), but a meal in a wine bar will cost you more than at a pub. And you'll drink wine instead of beer. Wine bars are more upscale than pubs and usually less smoky. As in pubs, children under 14 are not permitted in wine bars except in gardens or family rooms.

Extra! Extra!

Gays and lesbians on the lookout for low-priced meals in groovy, gay-friendly environments flock to Soho's newest phenomenon: the gay cafe-bar. These trendy-chic hangouts serve good, low-priced meals and pay serious attention to decor.

Cafes

Yes, London has plenty of these, too. Cafes serve a limited menu, usually on the light side and usually for not too much money. You can stop in for just a coffee or pot of tea and a sandwich. But when you see the cakes and other sweets, you might decide to indulge.

Check, Please

The annoying 17.5% VAT (value-added tax) is automatically added to your bill, and a moderate "cover charge" for bread (even if you don't eat it) might be tacked on as well. But look at the menu to see whether a **service charge** has been added to your tab. If it has, you're not expected to leave any further gratuities. If the menu says "service not included," you should leave an additional tip of at least 15%.

Tourist Traps

Be aware that the words **"service charge"** on a bill mean that a gratuity has already been added. Some places hoping to cash in on tourist gullibility might be tacky enough to include a service charge in your final bill and *also* have a space for "gratuity" on your credit-card receipt. Don't be conned into double tipping.

At What Time Do We Dine, Dear?

As a general rule, breakfast is served from 7:30 to 9:30am, lunch from 12:30 to 2:30pm, and dinner from 7 to 9:30pm. Afternoon tea time is 3:30 to 5:30pm. To add a bit of confusion, lunch is often called dinner, and dinner may be called supper. Brunch remains brunch and is generally served from 1 to 4pm on weekends.

Top Hat & Tails? Dressing to Dine

London, like the rest of the world, is becoming more and more casual. You can wear whatever you like (within reason) at all but the most upscale restaurants. At the same time, fashion-conscious Londoners are quick to spot the gauche and the gaudy. They tend to play down garish Hollywood-style glamour in favor of sedate stylishness. At a trendy place or any $$$ and $$$$ restaurant, you'll want to dress up rather than down. Leave the running shoes and blue jeans back at the hotel. Don a dressy jacket and wear a shirt and tie (or a nice sweater). Ladies: A basic black dress will come in handy if you're going to "swan about" in tony eateries.

What's an Aubergine, Anyway?

Even though you speak the same language (well, sort of), you might encounter a few unfamiliar terms on restaurant menus. To help you save face before you stuff your face, here are a few that might trip you up:

English	American English
Aubergine	Eggplant
Bangers	Sausages
Biscuit	Cracker or cookie
Bubble and squeak	Mashed potatoes mixed with cabbage or meat and then fried
Chips	French fries
Cornish pasties	Pastries filled with meat, onion, and vegetables
Cottage pie	Ground meat and mashed potatoes in a pie
Crisps	Potato chips
Crumpet	Similar to an English muffin, with more holes
Fry-up	Big English breakfast of eggs, sausage/bacon, baked beans, and so on
Jacket potato	Baked potato served with various toppings
Jelly	Jell-O
Joint	Meat roasted on the bone
Liquor	A green, salty, parsley-based gravy
Marrow	Squash
Mash	Mashed potatoes
Mince	Ground meat, usually beef
Ploughman's lunch	Pub grub consisting of crusty bread with cheese or pâté
Pudding	Dessert
Rasher	Slice of bacon
Shepherd's pie	A baked pie of meat and vegetables covered with gravy and mashed potatoes
Steak-and-kidney pie	A pastry-topped pie of steak, kidneys, and mushrooms in gravy
Sultana	Raisin
Trifle	Sponge cake soaked in sherry, layered with raspberry preserves, covered with custard sauce, and capped with whipped cream
Welsh rarebit	Welsh rabbit—melted Cheddar cheese and mustard or Worcestershire sauce served on toast

Chapter 10

London Restaurants A to Z

In This Chapter

- Restaurant indexes by location, price, and cuisine
- Full reviews of my favorite restaurants in town
- The best places for kids, breakfast, spotting celebs, and more

Ready, set, eat! This chapter gets to the meat of the matter (excuse the pun) with succinct and snappy reviews of London's best (in my humble opinion) places to chow. As you can imagine, with more than 5,700 restaurants to choose from, it hasn't been easy honing this list down to a manageable size. What I've tried to do is cover as much of Central London as possible. None of the places here is hard to get to—you can reach them all by taking the tube and then walking.

I've included several of the oldest and most well-respected restaurants that serve traditional English food. But since "Rule Britannia" is now "Cool Britannia," I've included just as many that serve "Modern British" cuisine or hybrids of British/French and British/Continental. I've also put in some of London's better pubs, where you can eat English food at easy-on-the-pocket prices.

I know there are travelers who always yearn for American-style chow wherever they go, so I've included places where you can get a hamburger, a bowl of chili, or a plate of ribs. And because some of you are traveling with kids, I've listed family-friendly places where the kids won't groan about the food (but you never know), and you won't groan about traveling with kids. Family-friendly restaurants are always marked with a "Kids" icon. There are several $ places that will let all of you eat without having to break the kids' piggy bank. You'll find many more kid-friendly choices in chapter 11, "Light Bites & Munchies."

But hey—you're on holiday in one of the world's great gastronomic capitals. Why not try Indian, Chinese, French, Italian, or some other ethnic cuisine? There are many to choose from on this list. And although most of my recommendations are in the moderate price range ($$ and $$$), there are some expensive ($$$$) joints for those who want to dress up and rub elbows with the smart set.

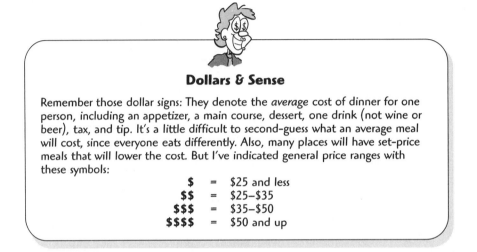

Dollars & Sense

Remember those dollar signs: They denote the *average* cost of dinner for one person, including an appetizer, a main course, dessert, one drink (not wine or beer), tax, and tip. It's a little difficult to second-guess what an average meal will cost, since everyone eats differently. Also, many places will have set-price meals that will lower the cost. But I've indicated general price ranges with these symbols:

$	=	$25 and less
$$	=	$25–$35
$$$	=	$35–$50
$$$$	=	$50 and up

Quick Picks: London's Restaurants at a Glance

Restaurant Index by Location

Bayswater

Veronica's $$

Bloomsbury

Museum Street Café $$

North Sea Fish Restaurant $$

Chelsea

Aubergine $$$$

Bluebird $$$

Chelsea Kitchen $

English House $$

The City

Café Spice Namaste $$

Dickens Inn by the Tower $

Fox & Anchor $

The George & Vulture $$

Poons in the City $$$

Ye Olde Cheshire Cheese $$

Covent Garden

Food for Thought $

Joe Allen $$

Porter's English Restaurant $$

Rules $$$

Kensington

Devonshire Arms $

Maggie Jones $$

Knightsbridge

Chicago Rib Shack $$

The Oratory $$

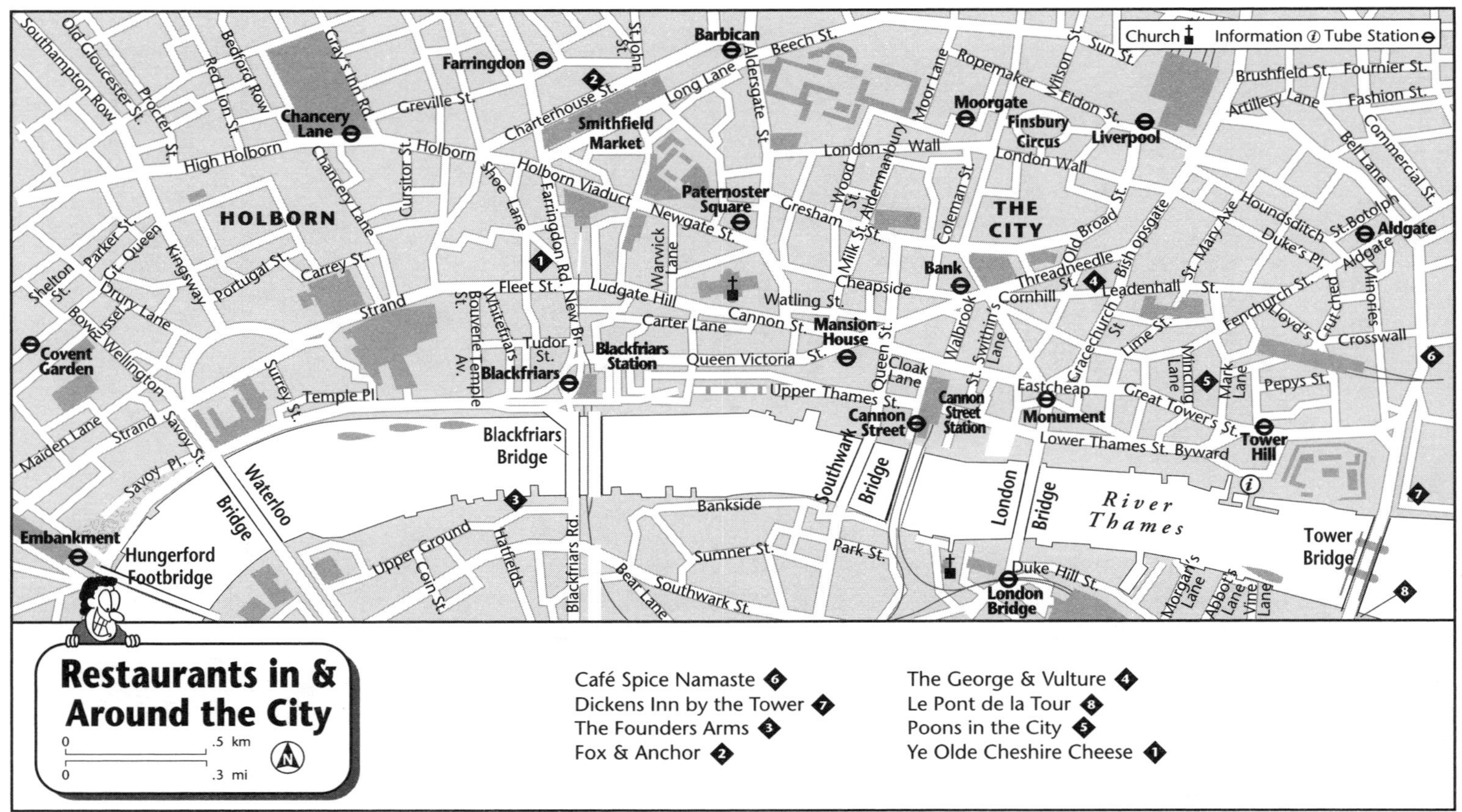

Restaurants in & Around the City
Church
Information
Tube Station
0 .5 km
0 .3 mi
N
Café Spice Namaste 6
Dickens Inn by the Tower 7
The Founders Arms 3
Fox & Anchor 2
The George & Vulture 4
Le Pont de la Tour 8
Poons in the City 5
Ye Olde Cheshire Cheese 1
HOLBORN
THE CITY
River Thames
Farringdon
Barbican
Moorgate
Liverpool
Aldgate
Chancery Lane
Paternoster Square
Bank
Mansion House
Blackfriars
Blackfriars Station
Cannon Street
Cannon Street Station
Monument
Tower Hill
London Bridge
Covent Garden
Embankment
Smithfield Market
Finsbury Circus
Blackfriars Bridge
Waterloo Bridge
Southwark Bridge
London Bridge
Tower Bridge
Hungerford Footbridge

San Lorenzo $$$

Vong $$$

Zafferano $$$

Marylebone

Langan's Bistro $$

Odin's $$$

Mayfair

Chez Nico at Ninety Park Lane $$$$

Hard Rock Cafe $$

Pizzeria Condotti $

Notting Hill

Clarke's $$$

Piccadilly Circus/ Leicester Square

The Carvery $$

The Granary $

L'Odeon $$$$

The Stockpot $

Soho

Au Jardin des Gourmets $$$

Chiang Mai $$

Crank's In London $

Ed's Easy Diner $

The Gay Hussar $$$$

The Ivy $$

Wagamama Noodle Bar $

South Bank

The Founders Arms $

Le Pont de la Tour $$$$

Oxo Tower Brasserie $$$

South Kensington

The Bombay Brasserie $$$$

Brasserie St. Quentin $$

Noor Jahan $$

St. James's

Fortnum & Mason $$

Gourmet Pizza Company $

Quaglino's $$$$

The Strand

The George $

RS Hispaniola $$$

The Savoy Grill $$$$

Simpson's-in-the-Strand $$$

Westminster/Victoria

Ebury Wine Bar $$

Ken Lo's Memories of China $$$$

Shepherd's $$$

Restaurant Index by Price

$$$$

Aubergine (Chelsea)

The Bombay Brasserie (South Kensington)

Chez Nico at Ninety Park Lane (Mayfair)

The Gay Hussar (Soho)

Ken Lo's Memories of China (Wesminster/Victoria)

L'Odeon (Picadilly Circus/ Leicester Square)

Le Pont de la Tour (South Bank)

Quaglino's (St. James's)

The Savoy Grill (The Strand)

$$$

Au Jardin des Gourmets (Soho)

Bluebird (Chelsea)

Clarke's (Notting Hill)

Odin's (Marylebone)

Oxo Tower Brasserie (South Bank)

Poons in the City (The City)

RS Hispaniola (The Strand)

Rules (Covent Garden)

San Lorenzo (Knightsbridge)

Shepherd's (Westminster/Victoria)

Simpson's-in-the-Strand (The Strand)

Vong (Knightsbridge)

Zafferano (Knightsbridge)

$$

Brasserie St. Quentin (South Kensington)

Café Spice Namaste (The City)

The Carvery (Picadilly Circus/Leicester Square)

Chiang Mai (Soho)

Chicago Rib Shack (Knightsbridge)

Ebury Wine Bar (Westminster/Victoria)

English House (Chelsea)

Fortnum & Mason (St. James's)

The George & Vulture (The City)

Hard Rock Cafe (Mayfair)

The Ivy (Soho)

Joe Allen (Covent Garden)

Langan's Bistro (Marylebone)

Maggie Jones (Kensington)

Museum Street Café (Bloomsbury)

Noor Jahan (South Kensington)

North Sea Fish Restaurant (Bloomsbury)

The Oratory (Knightsbridge)

Porter's English Restaurant (Covent Garden)

Veronica's (Bayswater)

Ye Olde Cheshire Cheese (The City)

$

Chelsea Kitchen (Chelsea)

Crank's In London (Soho)

Devonshire Arms (Kensington)

Dickens Inn by the Tower (The City)

Ed's Easy Diner (Soho)

Food for Thought (Covent Garden)

The Founders Arms (South Bank)

Fox & Anchor (The City)

The George (The Strand)

Gourmet Pizza Company (St. James's)

The Granary (Piccadilly Circus/Leicester Square)

Pizzeria Condotti (Mayfair)

The Stockpot (Picadilly Circus/Leicester Square)

Wagamama Noodle Bar (Soho)

Restaurant Index by Cuisine

British

The Carvery (Picadilly Circus/Leicester Square, $$)

Devonshire Arms (Kensington, $)

Dickens Inn by the Tower (The City, $)

Ebury Wine Bar (Westminster/Victoria, $$)

English House (Chelsea, $$)

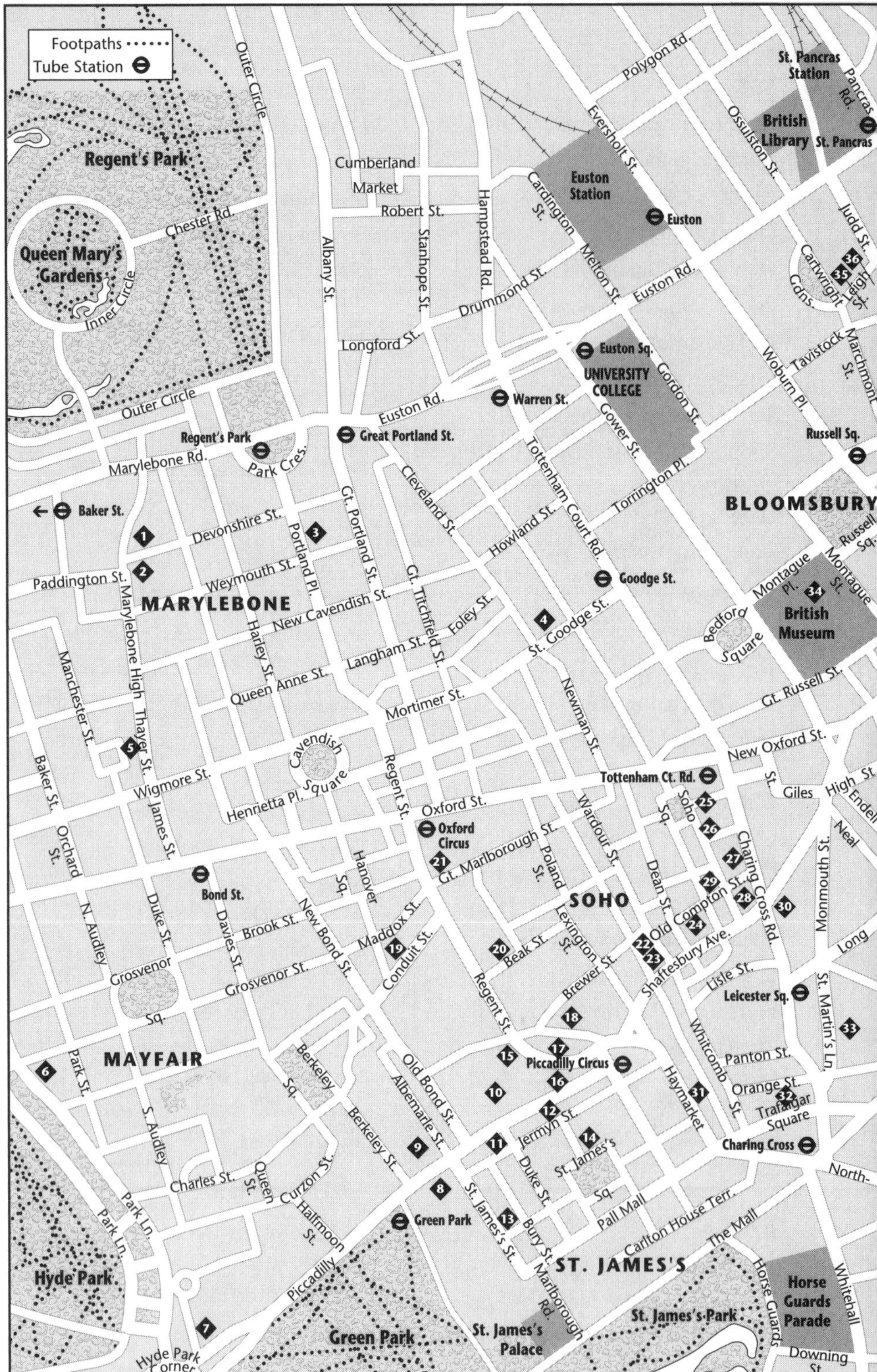

Footpaths
Tube Station
Regent's Park
Queen Mary's Gardens
Outer Circle
Inner Circle
Chester Rd.
Cumberland Market
Robert St.
Albany St.
Stanhope St.
Hampstead Rd.
Polygon Rd.
Eversholt St.
St. Pancras Station
Pancras Rd.
British Library
St. Pancras
Ossulston St.
Euston Station
Cardington St.
Euston
Melton St.
Euston Rd.
Drummond St.
Longford St.
Judd St.
Cartwright Gdns.
Leigh St.
36
35
Euston Sq.
UNIVERSITY COLLEGE
Gordon St.
Woburn Pl.
Tavistock
Marchmont St.
Warren St.
Euston Rd.
Regent's Park
Great Portland St.
Park Cres.
Marylebone Rd.
Gower St.
Tottenham Court Rd.
Torrington Pl.
Russell Sq.
Cleveland St.
BLOOMSBURY
Baker St.
1
Devonshire St.
3
Portland Pl.
Gt. Portland St.
Howland St.
Russell Sq.
Montague Pl.
Montague St.
2
Paddington St.
Weymouth St.
Gt. Titchfield St.
Goodge St.
34
British Museum
MARYLEBONE
New Cavendish St.
Foley St.
4
St. Goodge St.
Bedford Square
Marylebone High
Manchester St.
Harley St.
Langham St.
Queen Anne St.
Mortimer St.
Newman St.
Gt. Russell St.
Thayer St.
5
Cavendish Square
Wigmore St.
James St.
Baker St.
Henrietta Pl.
Regent St.
New Oxford St.
Tottenham Ct. Rd.
St. Giles High St.
Endell
Oxford St.
Soho Sq.
25
26
Oxford Circus
Orchard St.
21
Gt. Marlborough St.
Poland St.
Wardour St.
Neal
27
Charing Cross Rd.
Bond St.
Hanover Sq.
Dean St.
29
Old Compton St.
28
Monmouth St.
SOHO
30
N. Audley
Duke St.
Davies St.
Brook St.
New Bond St.
Maddox St.
19
Conduit St.
20
Beak St.
Lexington St.
24
22
23
Shaftesbury Ave.
Long
Grosvenor Sq.
Grosvenor St.
Regent St.
Brewer St.
Lisle St.
Leicester Sq.
St. Martin's Ln.
18
Whitcomb St.
33
6
Park St.
MAYFAIR
Berkeley Sq.
Old Bond St.
Albemarle St.
15
17
Piccadilly Circus
Panton St.
16
Haymarket
10
31
Orange St.
32
Trafalgar Square
S. Audley
Berkeley St.
12
Jermyn St.
9
11
14
St. James's Sq.
Charing Cross
Duke St.
North-
Charles St.
Queen St.
Curzon St.
8
Park Ln.
Halfmoon St.
Green Park
St. James's St.
13
Bury St.
Pall Mall
Carlton House Terr.
The Mall
Hyde Park
Piccadilly
ST. JAMES'S
Marlborough Rd.
Horse Guards
Horse Guards Parade
Whitehall
7
St. James's Park
Green Park
St. James's Palace
Hyde Park Corner
Downing St.

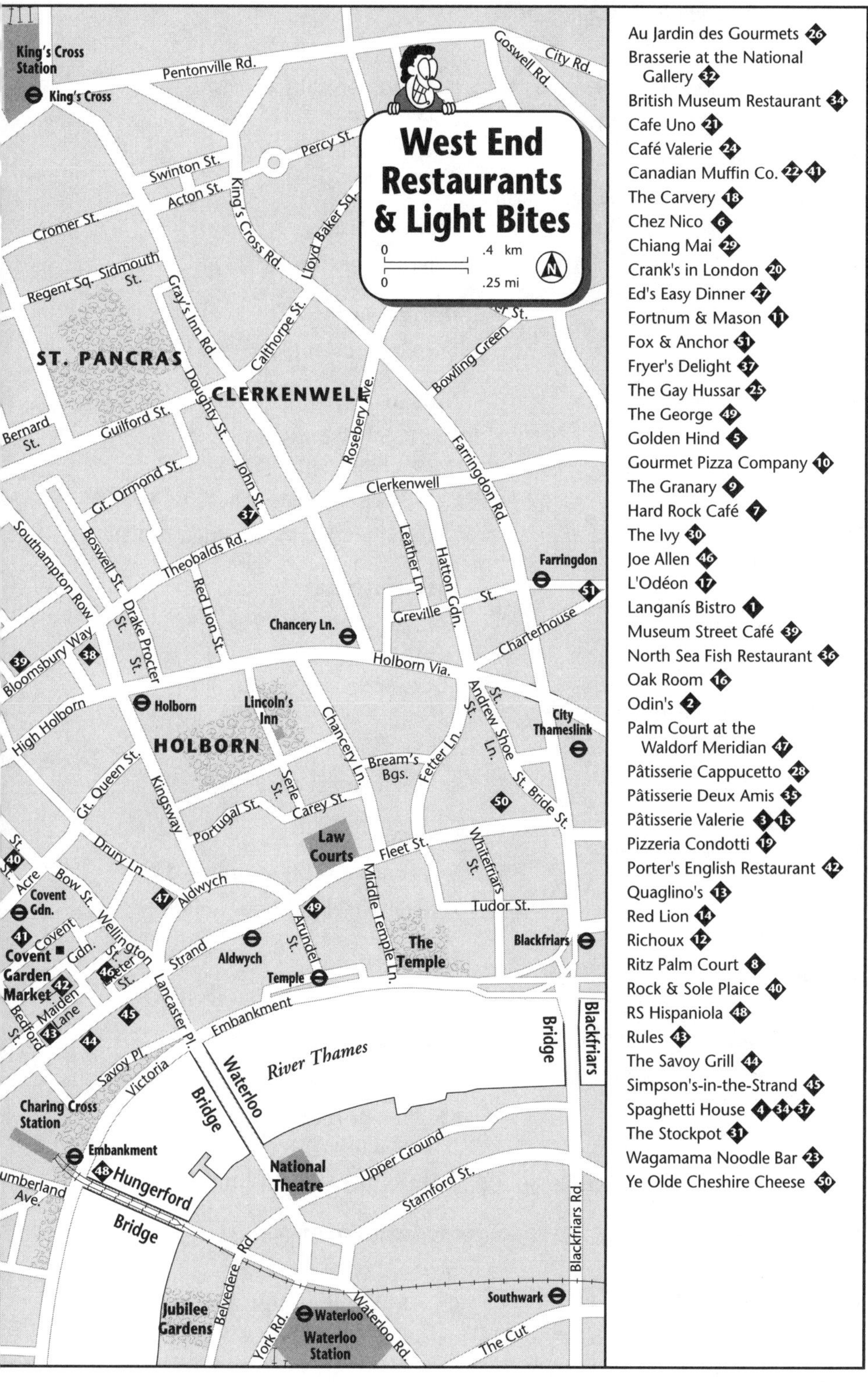
West End Restaurants & Light Bites
0 .4 km
0 .25 mi
Au Jardin des Gourmets 26
Brasserie at the National Gallery 32
British Museum Restaurant 34
Cafe Uno 21
Café Valerie 24
Canadian Muffin Co. 22 41
The Carvery 18
Chez Nico 6
Chiang Mai 29
Crank's in London 20
Ed's Easy Dinner 27
Fortnum & Mason 11
Fox & Anchor 51
Fryer's Delight 37
The Gay Hussar 25
The George 49
Golden Hind 5
Gourmet Pizza Company 10
The Granary 9
Hard Rock Café 7
The Ivy 30
Joe Allen 46
L'Odéon 17
Langanís Bistro 1
Museum Street Café 39
North Sea Fish Restaurant 36
Oak Room 16
Odin's 2
Palm Court at the Waldorf Meridian 47
Pâtisserie Cappucetto 28
Pâtisserie Deux Amis 35
Pâtisserie Valerie 3 15
Pizzeria Condotti 19
Porter's English Restaurant 42
Quaglino's 13
Red Lion 14
Richoux 12
Ritz Palm Court 8
Rock & Sole Plaice 40
RS Hispaniola 48
Rules 43
The Savoy Grill 44
Simpson's-in-the-Strand 45
Spaghetti House 4 34 37
The Stockpot 31
Wagamama Noodle Bar 23
Ye Olde Cheshire Cheese 50

Fortnum & Mason (St. James's, $$)

Fox & Anchor (The City, $)

The George (The Strand, $)

The George & Vulture (The City, $$)

The Granary (Piccadilly Circus/Leicester Square, $)

Maggie Jones (Kensington, $$)

Porter's English Restaurant (Covent Garden, $$)

Rules (Covent Garden, $$$)

The Savoy Grill (The Strand, $$$$)

Shepherd's (Westminster/ Victoria, $$$)

Simpson's-in-the-Strand (The Strand, $$$)

Veronica's (Bayswater, $$)

Ye Olde Cheshire Cheese (The City, $$)

British/Continental

The Stockpot (Picadilly Circus/Leicester Square, $)

British/French

The Ivy (Soho, $$)

Langan's Bistro (Marylebone, $$)

RS Hispaniola (The Strand, $$$)

Chinese

Ken Lo's Memories of China (Westminster/Victoria, $$$$)

Poons in the City (The City, $$$)

French

Au Jardin des Gourmets (Soho, $$$)

Aubergine (Chelsea, $$$$)

Brasserie St. Quentin (South Kensington, $$)

Chez Nico at Ninety Park Lane (Mayfair, $$$$)

L'Odeon (Picadilly Circus/ Leicester Square, $$$$)

Oxo Tower Brasserie (South Bank, $$$)

French/Thai

Vong (Knightsbridge, $$$)

Hungarian

The Gay Hussar (Soho, $$$$)

Indian

The Bombay Brasserie (South Kensington, $$$$)

Café Spice Namaste (The City, $$)

Noor Jahan (South Kensington, $$)

International

Chelsea Kitchen (Chelsea, $)

L'Odeon (Picadilly Circus/ Leicester Square, $$$$)

Le Pont de la Tour (South Bank, $$$$)

Odin's (Marylebone, $$$)

Italian

San Lorenzo (Knightsbridge, $$$)

Zafferano (Knightsbridge, $$$)

Japanese

Wagamama Noodle Bar (Soho, $)

Modern British

The Founders Arms (South Bank, $)

Museum Street Café (Bloomsbury, $$)

The Oratory (Knightsbridge, $$)

Modern European

Bluebird (Chelsea, $$$)

Clarke's (Notting Hill, $$$)

Quaglino's (St. James's, $$$$)

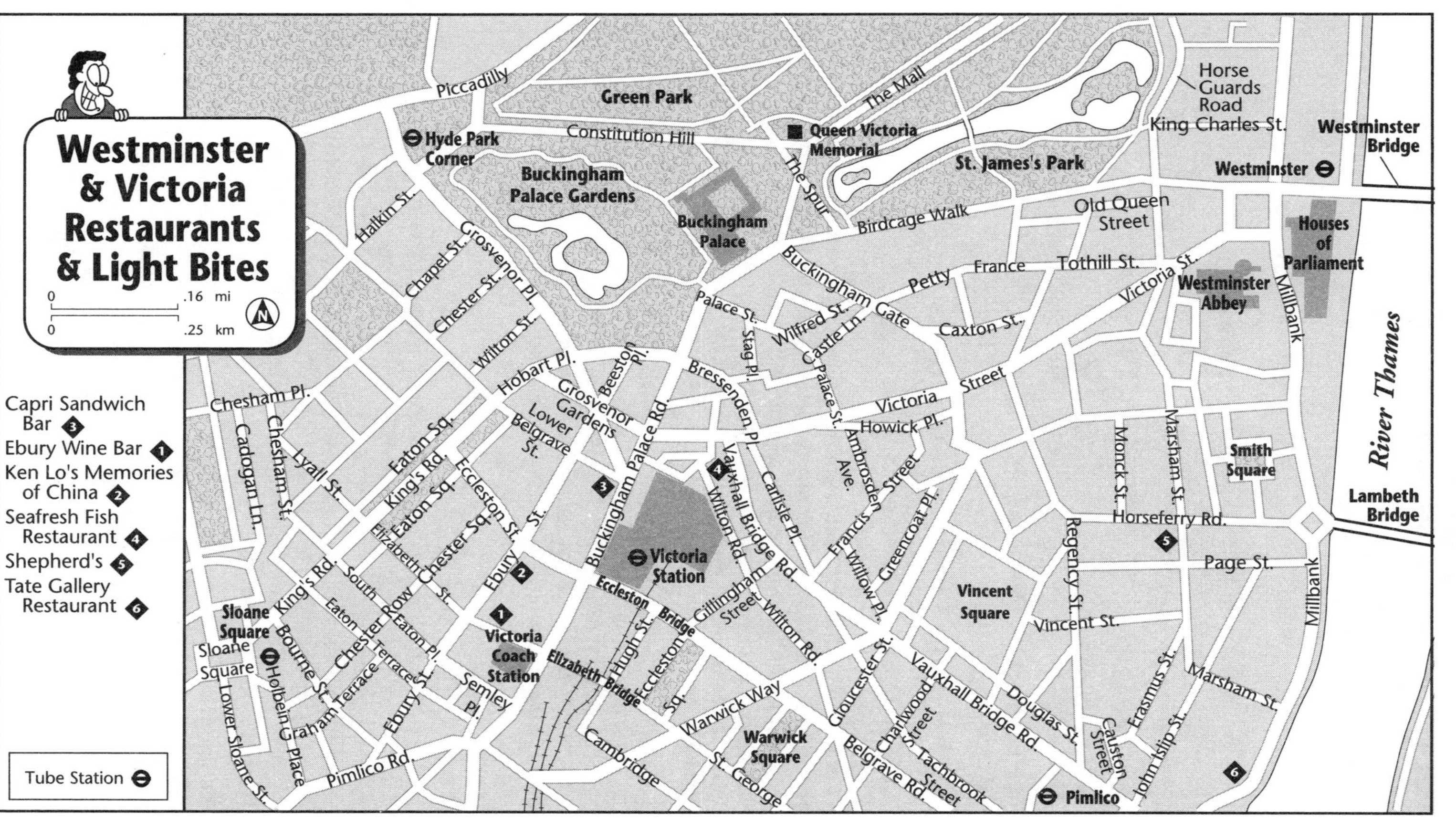

Westminster & Victoria Restaurants & Light Bites
0 .16 mi
0 .25 km
Capri Sandwich Bar 3
Ebury Wine Bar 1
Ken Lo's Memories of China 2
Seafresh Fish Restaurant 4
Shepherd's 5
Tate Gallery Restaurant 6
Tube Station
Piccadilly
Green Park
The Mall
Constitution Hill
Hyde Park Corner
Queen Victoria Memorial
St. James's Park
Horse Guards Road
King Charles St.
Westminster Bridge
Westminster
Buckingham Palace Gardens
Buckingham Palace
The Spur
Birdcage Walk
Old Queen Street
Houses of Parliament
Halkin St.
Grosvenor Pl.
Chapel St.
Chester St.
Buckingham Gate
Petty France
Tothill St.
Victoria St.
Westminster Abbey
Millbank
Palace St.
Wilfred St.
Castle Ln.
Caxton St.
Stag Pl.
Wilton St.
Hobart Pl.
Beeston Pl.
Bressenden Pl.
Palace St.
Victoria Street
Howick Pl.
River Thames
Chesham Pl.
Grosvenor Gardens
Lower Belgrave St.
Buckingham Palace Rd.
Ambrosden Ave.
Cadogan Ln.
Chesham St.
Lyall St.
Eaton Sq.
King's Rd.
Eccleston St.
Vauxhall Bridge Rd.
Wilton Rd.
Carlisle Pl.
Francis Street
Greencoat Pl.
Monck St.
Marsham St.
Smith Square
Lambeth Bridge
Horseferry Rd.
Regency St.
Elizabeth St.
Chester Sq.
Ebury St.
Victoria Station
Willow Pl.
Page St.
King's Rd.
South Eaton Pl.
Eccleston Bridge
Gillingham Street
Vincent Square
Millbank
Sloane Square
Eaton Terrace
Chester Row
Victoria Coach Station
Hugh St.
Vincent St.
Bourne St.
Ebury St.
Semley Pl.
Elizabeth Bridge
Eccleston Sq.
Gloucester St.
Vauxhall Bridge Rd.
Douglas St.
Erasmus St.
Marsham St.
Holbein Place
Graham Terrace
Warwick Way
Charlwood Street
Causton Street
John Islip St.
Lower Sloane St.
Pimlico Rd.
Cambridge
Warwick Square
St. George
Belgrave Rd.
Tachbrook Street
Pimlico

North American

Chicago Rib Shack (Knightsbridge, $$)

Ed's Easy Diner (Soho, $)

Hard Rock Cafe (Mayfair, $$)

Joe Allen (Covent Garden, $$)

Pizza/Pasta

Gourmet Pizza Company (St. James's, $)

Pizzeria Condotti (Mayfair, $)

Seafood

North Sea Fish Restaurant (Bloomsbury, $$)

Thai

Chiang Mai (Soho, $$)

Vegetarian

Crank's In London (Soho, $)

Food for Thought (Covent Garden, $)

My Favorite London Restaurants

Au Jardin des Gourmets

$$$. Soho. FRENCH.

Devotees of traditional French cuisine have gathered in this second-floor restaurant since 1931. The comprehensive à la carte menu changes with the seasons. It may feature poached salmon with mussels flavored with orange and basil, roast rump of lamb with young herbs on a bed of couscous and Provençale vegetables, or roast saddle of rabbit. Vegetarian options are also available.

5 Greek St. (off Soho Square), W1. ☎ ***0171/437-1816. Tube:*** *Tottenham Court Rd., then a 5-minute walk south on Charing Cross Rd. and west on Manette St. to Greek St.* ***Reservations:*** *Required.* ***Main courses:*** *2 courses £25 ($41); 3 courses £30 ($50); fixed-price 2-course lunch or pre-theatre dinner £16.50 ($27). AE, DC, MC, V.* ***Open:*** *Mon–Fri 12:15–2:30pm and 6:30–11:15pm; Sat 6:30–11:15pm.*

Aubergine

$$$$. Chelsea. FRENCH.

This is one of the top "name" restaurants in London, with celebs, royals, and commoners all vying for one of the 14 tables, so if you do get in, you'll want to look reasonably chic when you arrive. Every dish (you choose from a set menu), from the fish and lighter Mediterranean-style choices to pigeon with wild-mushroom ravioli and fillet of venison with braised baby turnips, is a culinary achievement of the highest order. Cap off your meal with the celebrated cappuccino of white beans with grated truffle.

11 Park Walk, SW10. ☎ ***0171/352-3449. Tube:*** *Sloane Square, then a 10-minute walk southwest on King's Rd. to Park Walk; or take bus 11, 19, 22, or 211 southwest on King's Rd. from the tube station.* ***Reservations:*** *Required 2 months in advance.* ***Main courses:*** *Fixed-price lunch £24 ($40) 2 courses, £45 ($74) 3 courses; fixed-price dinner £45 ($74) 3 courses £55 ($90) 7 courses. AE, DC, MC, V.* ***Open:*** *Mon–Fri noon–2:15pm and 7–10:30pm; Sat 7–10:30pm.*

Bluebird

$$$. Chelsea. MODERN EUROPEAN.

Sir Terence Conran transformed a former car-repair garage into this sleek and appealing place with a gleaming chrome bar, skylights, and an open kitchen with a wood-burning stove. It's definitely upscale, but comfortable and refreshingly unpretentious. The menu emphasizes hearty, cooked-to-order cuisine. Fish and fresh shellfish (oysters, clams) and crustaceans (lobster, crab) are standouts, as are the grilled meats (veal, lamb, pigeon, organic chicken). There's a cafe and food store on the first floor.

350 King's Rd., SW3. ☎ ***0171/559-1000. Tube:*** *Sloane Square, then a 10-minute walk south on King's Rd.; or take bus 19, 22, or 49 from the tube station.* ***Reservations:*** *Recommended.* ***Main courses:*** *£9.75–£30 ($16–$50); set lunch (12:30–3pm)/pre-theatre menu (6–7pm) £12.75–£15.75 ($21–$26). AE, DC, MC, V.* ***Open:*** *Mon–Fri noon–3:30pm and 6–11:30pm, Sat 11am–4pm and 6–11:30pm, Sun 11am–4pm and 6–10:30pm.*

The Bombay Brasserie

$$$$. South Kensington. INDIAN.

The trappings of British colonialism set the stage in the restaurant's huge dining room, but ask for a table in the more pleasant conservatory. The menu ranges throughout the Indian subcontinent. All main courses are served with potatoes, vegetable of the day, and a lentil dish. I recommend the mixed grill, the lamb dhansak (cooked with spicy lentils and puréed vegetables), the chicken biryani (meat, fish, or vegetables and rice flavored with saffron or turmeric), and the chicken korma rizala with cashew-nut paste and purée of fresh coriander. The lunch buffet approaches a bargain at this otherwise expensive eatery, which is popular with late-night diners.

Courtfield Close, Courtfield Rd., SW7. ☎ ***0171/370-4040. Tube:*** *Gloucester Rd.; the restaurant is across the street adjoining Bailey's Hotel.* ***Reservations:*** *Recommended for dinner.* ***Main courses:*** *£13.75–£16.95 ($23–$28); buffet lunch £15.95 ($26); set dinner £34.10 ($56). AE, DC, MC, V.* ***Open:*** *Daily 12:30–3pm and 7:30–11:30pm.*

Brasserie St. Quentin

$$. South Kensington. FRENCH.

The most authentic-looking French brasserie in London, St. Quentin's attracts a fair share of London's French community (always a good sign for a French restaurant outside of France). Amid mirrors and crystal chandeliers, you can dine on roast cod in pepper cream sauce, grilled tuna with tomato and pepper salsa, or stuffed leg of rabbit. Hors d'oeuvres worth trying are the Cornish crab with crème fraîche and the terrine of duck liver with walnut dressing.

243 Brompton Rd., SW3. ☎ ***0171/581-5131. Tube:*** *South Kensington, then a 5-minute walk east on Brompton Rd.* ***Reservations:*** *Required.* ***Main courses:*** *£11.25–£24 ($19–$40); fixed-price lunch £13.50 ($22) for 2 courses, £16.50 ($27) for 3 courses; set-price 2-course dinner (6:30–7:30pm) £10 ($17). AE, DC, MC, V.* ***Open:*** *Mon–Sat noon–3pm and 6:30–11:30pm, Sun noon–3:30pm and 6:30–11pm.*

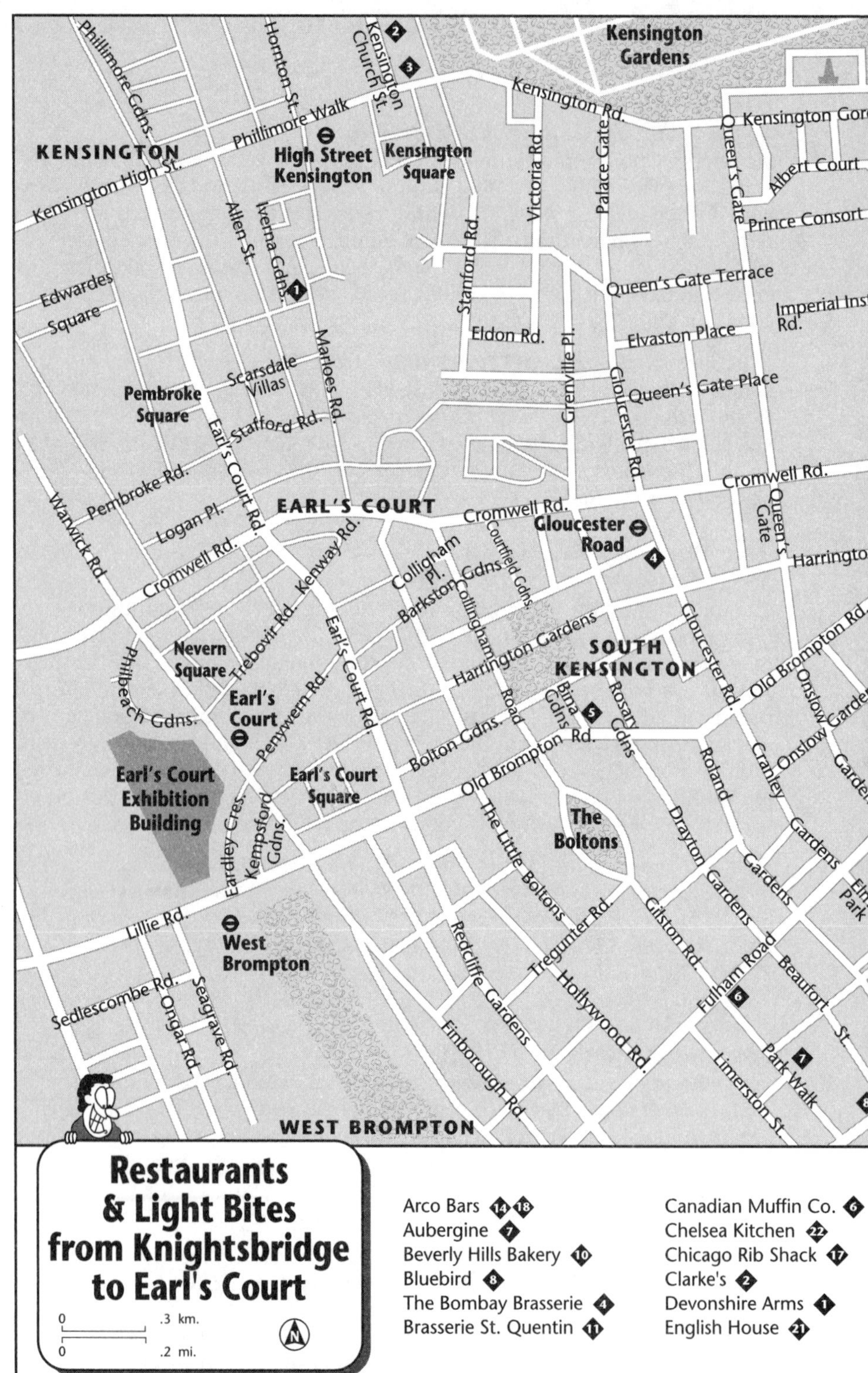
Restaurants
& Light Bites
from Knightsbridge
to Earl's Court
0 .3 km.
0 .2 mi.
N
Arco Bars 14 18
Aubergine 7
Beverly Hills Bakery 10
Bluebird 8
The Bombay Brasserie 4
Brasserie St. Quentin 11
Canadian Muffin Co. 6
Chelsea Kitchen 22
Chicago Rib Shack 17
Clarke's 2
Devonshire Arms 1
English House 21
KENSINGTON
EARL'S COURT
SOUTH KENSINGTON
WEST BROMPTON
Kensington Gardens
High Street Kensington
Kensington Square
Gloucester Road
Earl's Court
West Brompton
Edwardes Square
Pembroke Square
Nevern Square
Earl's Court Square
Earl's Court Exhibition Building
The Boltons
Phillimore Gdns.
Hornton St.
Kensington Church St.
Phillimore Walk
Kensington High St.
Kensington Rd.
Kensington Gore
Albert Court
Prince Consort
Queen's Gate
Victoria Rd.
Palace Gate
Allen St.
Iverna Gdns.
Stanford Rd.
Queen's Gate Terrace
Imperial Inst. Rd.
Eldon Rd.
Elvaston Place
Grenville Pl.
Gloucester Rd.
Queen's Gate Place
Scarsdale Villas
Marloes Rd.
Stafford Rd.
Earl's Court Rd.
Pembroke Rd.
Logan Pl.
Warwick Rd.
Cromwell Rd.
Kenway Rd.
Collingham Pl.
Courtfield Gdns.
Barkston Gdns.
Collingham Road
Harrington
Harrington Gardens
Trebovir Rd.
Philbeach Gdns.
Penywern Rd.
Bolton Gdns.
Bina Gdns.
Rosary Gdns.
Old Brompton Rd.
Onslow Gardens
Roland
Cranley Gardens
Eardley Cres.
Kempsford Gdns.
The Little Boltons
Drayton Gardens
Elm Park
Lillie Rd.
Tregunter Rd.
Gilston Rd.
Fulham Road
Beaufort St.
Redcliffe Gardens
Hollywood Rd.
Sedlescombe Rd.
Ongar Rd.
Seagrave Rd.
Finborough Rd.
Limerston St.
Park Walk

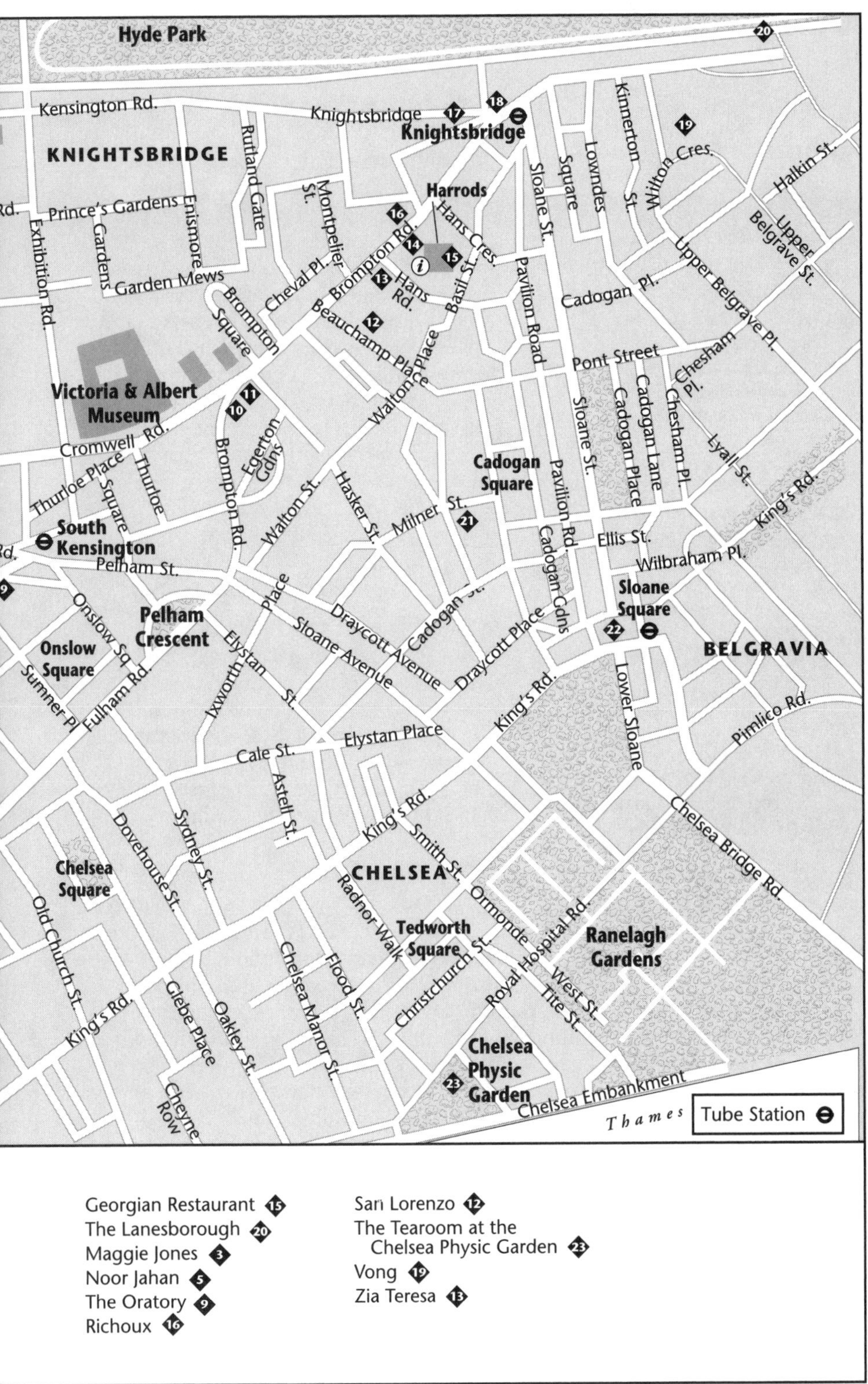

Hyde Park
Kensington Rd.
Knightsbridge
Knightsbridge
KNIGHTSBRIDGE
Rutland Gate
Montpelier St.
Harrods
Hans Cres.
Sloane St.
Lowndes Square
Kinnerton St.
Wilton Cres.
Halkin St.
Upper Belgrave St.
Prince's Gardens
Ennismore Gardens
Gardens
Exhibition Rd.
Garden Mews
Brompton Square
Cheval Pl.
Brompton Rd.
Hans Rd.
Basil St.
Pavilion Road
Cadogan Pl.
Upper Belgrave Pl.
Beauchamp Place
Walton Place
Pont Street
Chesham Pl.
Victoria & Albert Museum
Cromwell Rd.
Egerton Gdns
Brompton Rd.
Sloane St.
Cadogan Place
Cadogan Lane
Chesham Pl.
Lyall St.
Thurloe Place
Thurloe Square
Thurloe
Walton St.
Hasker St.
Cadogan Square
Pavilion Rd.
King's Rd.
Milner St.
Ellis St.
South Kensington
Pelham St.
Wilbraham Pl.
Cadogan Gdns
Sloane Square
Onslow Sq.
Pelham Crescent
Place
Draycott Avenue
Cadogan St.
Draycott Place
Onslow Square
Elystan St.
Sloane Avenue
BELGRAVIA
Sumner Pl.
Fulham Rd.
Ixworth
Lower Sloane
Pimlico Rd.
King's Rd.
Elystan Place
Cale St.
Astell St.
Chelsea Bridge Rd.
Dovehouse St.
Sydney St.
King's Rd.
Smith St.
Chelsea Square
CHELSEA
Radnor Walk
Ormonde
Old Church St.
Tedworth Square
Royal Hospital Rd.
Ranelagh Gardens
Chelsea Manor St.
Flood St.
Christchurch St.
West St.
Tite St.
King's Rd.
Glebe Place
Oakley St.
Chelsea Physic Garden
Cheyne Row
Chelsea Embankment
Thames
Tube Station
Georgian Restaurant 15
The Lanesborough 20
Maggie Jones 3
Noor Jahan 5
The Oratory 9
Richoux 16
San Lorenzo 12
The Tearoom at the Chelsea Physic Garden 23
Vong 19
Zia Teresa 13

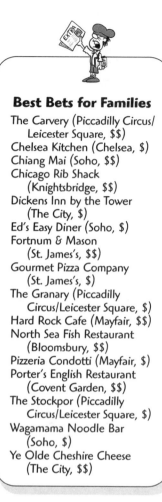

Best Bets for Families

The Carvery (Piccadilly Circus/ Leicester Square, $$)
Chelsea Kitchen (Chelsea, $)
Chiang Mai (Soho, $$)
Chicago Rib Shack (Knightsbridge, $$)
Dickens Inn by the Tower (The City, $)
Ed's Easy Diner (Soho, $)
Fortnum & Mason (St. James's, $$)
Gourmet Pizza Company (St. James's, $)
The Granary (Piccadilly Circus/Leicester Square, $)
Hard Rock Cafe (Mayfair, $$)
North Sea Fish Restaurant (Bloomsbury, $$)
Pizzeria Condotti (Mayfair, $)
Porter's English Restaurant (Covent Garden, $$)
The Stockpor (Piccadilly Circus/Leicester Square, $)
Wagamama Noodle Bar (Soho, $)
Ye Olde Cheshire Cheese (The City, $$)

Café Spice Namaste

$$. The City. INDIAN.

The competition among Indian restaurants in London is stiff, but this one remains a perennial favorite for the consistently high quality of its food (the homemade chutneys alone are worth the trip). Housed in a landmark Victorian hall near Tower Bridge, it has a kitchen that concentrates on spicy southern and northern Indian dishes with a strong Portuguese influence, such as Goa's signature dish, *sorpotel* (diced kidney, liver, and pork slow-cooked and served in an oniony stew). There are excellent chicken, duck, lamb, and fish dishes, served mild to spicy hot, as well as unusual offerings such as emu and venison. All dishes come with fresh vegetables and Indian bread.

16 Prescot St., E1. ☎ ***0171/488-9242. Tube:*** *Tower Hill, then a 5-minute walk north on Minories St. and east on Goodman's Yard, which becomes Prescot St. after you cross Mansell St.* ***Reservations:*** *Required.* ***Main courses:*** *£8–£10 ($13–$17). AE, DC, MC, V.* ***Open:*** *Mon–Sat noon–3pm and 6–10:30pm.*

The Carvery

$$. Piccadilly Circus/Leicester Square. BRITISH.

This renowned establishment in the heart of Theatreland has a one-price-all-you-can-eat policy. You can choose from a wide range of appetizers. Then, at the buffet carving table, a chef will slice you a roast leg of Southdown lamb with mint sauce or a roast leg of English pork with applesauce. After that, you can help yourself to buttered peas, roast potatoes, new carrots, and gravy. Cold food, assorted fresh salads, and desserts are available as well.

Regent Palace Hotel, 12 Sherwood St. (entrance on Glasshouse St.), W1. ☎ ***0171/488-4600. Tube:*** *Piccadilly Circus, then a 2-minute walk west on Glasshouse St.* ***Reservations:*** *Recommended.* ***Main courses:*** *All-you-can-eat meals £17.50 ($29) or £12.50 ($21) from 5:15–7pm; £7.75 ($13) for children 5–16, free for those under 5. AE, DC, MC, V.* ***Open:*** *Mon–Thurs 12:15–2:30pm and 5:30–10:30pm; Fri 12:15–2:30pm and 5:30pm–midnight; Sat 12:15–2:30pm and 5:30pm–midnight; Sun 6–10:30pm.*

Kids Chelsea Kitchen

$. Chelsea. INTERNATIONAL.

Chelsea Kitchen has been feeding local residents and drop-ins (or dropouts) since 1961, so it's considered something of an institution. It's a simple place, dinerlike in atmosphere, where the food and clientele move fast. Staple menu items usually include leek-and-potato soup, chicken Kiev, chicken parmigiana, steaks, sandwiches, and burgers.

98 King's Rd. (off Sloane Square), SW3. ☎ ***0171/589-1330. Tube:*** *Sloane Square; the restaurant is at the beginning of King's Rd. just west of the square.* ***Reservations:*** *Recommended.* ***Main courses:*** *£3–£5.50 ($5–$9), fixed-price menu £6 ($10). No credit cards.* ***Open:*** *Daily 8am–11:15pm.*

Chez Nico at Ninety Park Lane

$$$$. Mayfair. FRENCH.

A proper Mayfair drawing-room atmosphere sets the tone for the opulent cuisine at this stylish, post-nouvelle restaurant. The dishes are constantly being reinvented, but not to worry: Everything is sublime and memorable. You might start with quail salad with sweetbreads flavored with an almond vinaigrette. The main courses, creatively and flexibly adapted to local fresh ingredients (sometimes with a hint of Asia and the Middle East), might include chargrilled sea bass with basil purée or roasted scallops accented with sesame seeds.

In Grosvenor House, 90 Park Lane, W1. ☎ ***0171/409-1290.*** *Fax 0171/355-4877.* ***Tube:*** *Marble Arch, then a 5-minute walk south on Park Lane.* ***Reservations:*** *Required at least 7 days in advance for dinner, 2 days for lunch.* ***Main courses:*** *Fixed-price 3-course lunch £32 ($53); à la carte dinner £50 ($83) for 2 courses, £62 ($102) for 3 courses. AE, DC, MC, V.* ***Open:*** *Mon–Fri noon–2pm and 7–11pm; Sat 7–11pm.*

Kids Chiang Mai

$$. Soho. THAI.

Named after the ancient northern capital of Thailand (a region known for its rich, spicy foods), this pleasant, unpretentious place is good for hot-and-sour beef and chicken dishes, pad Thai noodles with various toppings, and vegetarian meals. Order a couple of different courses and share. It's located next door to Ronnie Scott's, the most famous jazz club in England, so it's a good stop for an early dinner before a night on the town. Children's specials are available.

48 Frith St. (off Soho Square), W1. ☎ ***0171/437-7444. Reservations:*** *Not necessary.* ***Tube:*** *Tottenham Court Rd., then a 5-minute walk west on Oxford St. and south on Soho St.; Frith St. is at the southwest corner of Soho Square.* ***Main courses:*** *£6–£9 ($10–$15). AE, MC, V.* ***Open:*** *Mon–Sat noon–3pm and 6–11pm; Sun 6–10:30pm.*

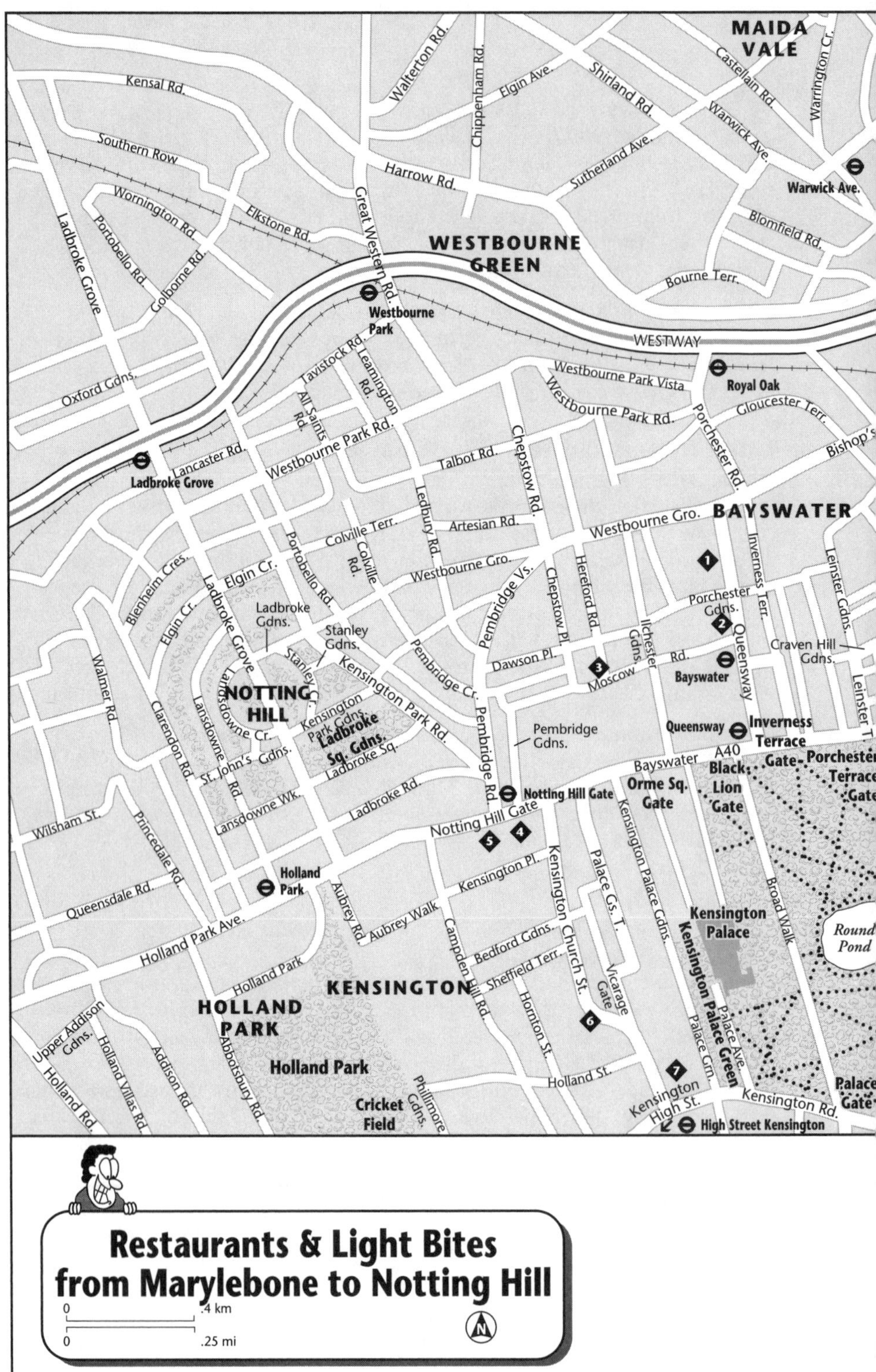

Restaurants & Light Bites from Marylebone to Notting Hill

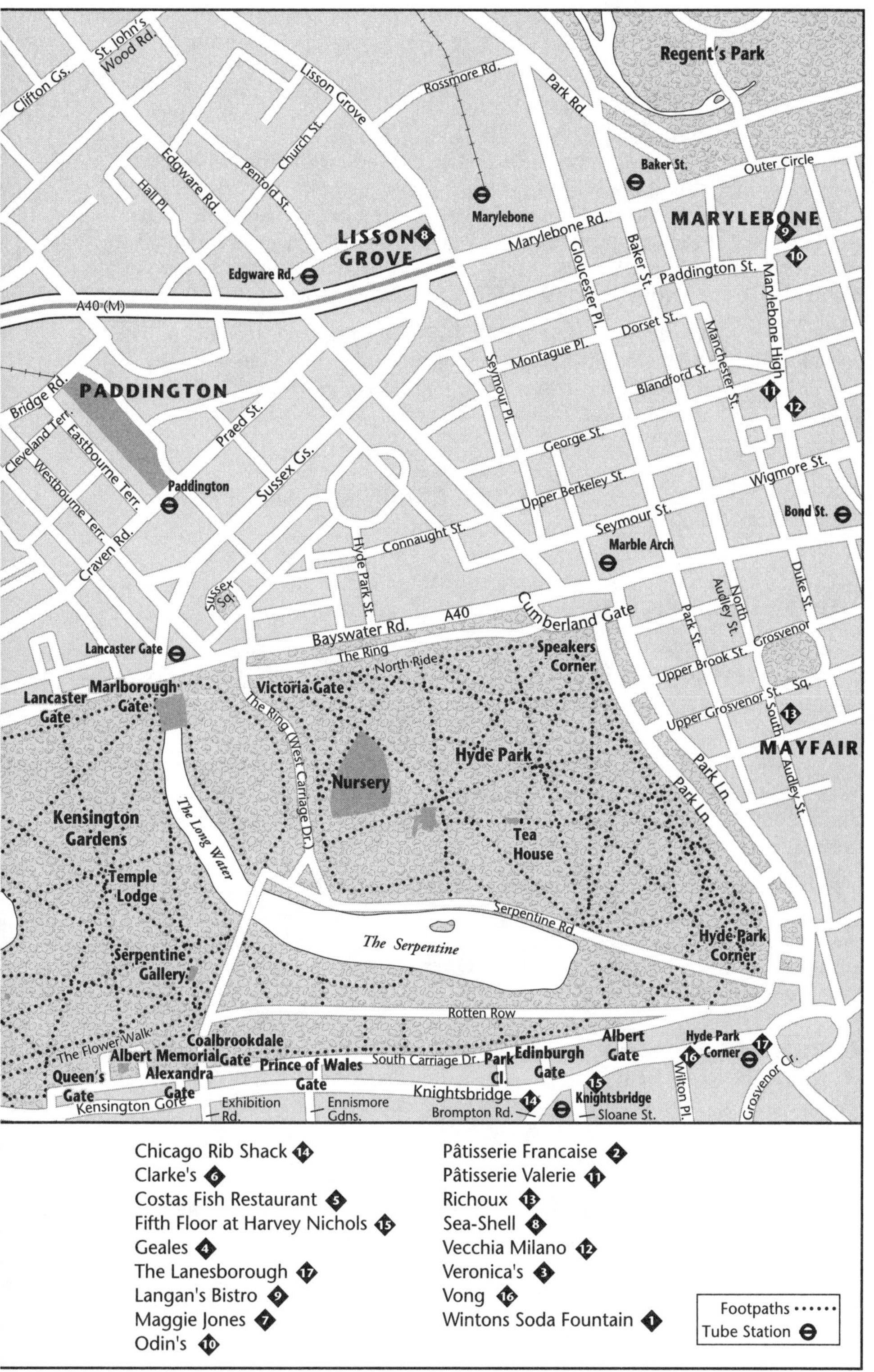
Regent's Park
St. John's Wood Rd.
Clifton Gs.
Lisson Grove
Rossmore Rd.
Park Rd.
Church St.
Penfold St.
Edgware Rd.
Hall Pl.
Baker St.
Outer Circle
Marylebone
MARYLEBONE
LISSON GROVE
Marylebone Rd.
Edgware Rd.
A40 (M)
Gloucester Pl.
Baker St.
Paddington St.
Marylebone High
Dorset St.
Manchester St.
Montague Pl.
Seymour Pl.
Blandford St.
PADDINGTON
Bridge Rd.
Cleveland Terr.
Eastbourne Terr.
Westbourne Terr.
Praed St.
Paddington
Sussex Gs.
George St.
Upper Berkeley St.
Wigmore St.
Bond St.
Seymour St.
Marble Arch
Connaught St.
Hyde Park St.
Craven Rd.
Sussex Sq.
Cumberland Gate
Duke St.
North Audley St.
Park St.
Bayswater Rd.
A40
Lancaster Gate
The Ring
North Ride
Speakers Corner
Grosvenor Sq.
Upper Brook St.
Upper Grosvenor St.
South Audley St.
MAYFAIR
Lancaster Gate
Marlborough Gate
Victoria Gate
The Ring (West Carriage Dr.)
Nursery
Hyde Park
Park Ln.
Kensington Gardens
The Long Water
Tea House
Temple Lodge
Serpentine Rd.
The Serpentine
Hyde Park Corner
Serpentine Gallery
Rotten Row
The Flower Walk
Coalbrookdale Gate
Albert Memorial
Albert Gate
Hyde Park Corner
Queen's Gate
Alexandra Gate
Prince of Wales Gate
South Carriage Dr.
Park Cl.
Edinburgh Gate
Wilton Pl.
Grosvenor Cr.
Kensington Gore
Exhibition Rd.
Ennismore Gdns.
Knightsbridge
Brompton Rd.
Knightsbridge
Sloane St.
Chicago Rib Shack 14
Clarke's 6
Costas Fish Restaurant 5
Fifth Floor at Harvey Nichols 15
Geales 4
The Lanesborough 17
Langan's Bistro 9
Maggie Jones 7
Odin's 10
Pâtisserie Francaise 2
Pâtisserie Valerie 11
Richoux 13
Sea-Shell 8
Vecchia Milano 12
Veronica's 3
Vong 16
Wintons Soda Fountain 1
Footpaths
Tube Station

Chicago Rib Shack

$$. Knightsbridge. NORTH AMERICAN.

Got a hankering for real American barbecue cooked in imported smoking ovens and marinated in a sauce made with 15 ingredients? At this restaurant, just 100 yards from Harrods, diners are encouraged to eat with their fingers (bibs and hot towels are provided). A TV screen tuned to a sports channel is suspended in the bar; otherwise, you're surrounded by Victorian architectural elements salvaged from demolished buildings all over the country.

1 Raphael St., SW7. ☎ ***0171/581-5595. Tube:*** *Knightsbridge, then a 5-minute walk southwest on Brompton Rd., north on Knightsbridge Green, and west on Raphael St.* ***Reservations:*** *Accepted, except Sat.* ***Main courses:*** *£6.45–£15 ($11–$25). AE, MC, V.* ***Open:*** *Daily 11:45am–11:45pm.*

Best Bets for Breakfast

Ed's Easy Diner (Soho, $)
Fox & Anchor (The City, $)

Clarke's

$$$. Notting Hill. MODERN EUROPEAN.

Chef Sally Clarke's bright, modern restaurant is one of the hottest eateries in town. Some people are put off by the fixed-price menu, which offers no choices, but you probably won't mind after you taste the food. The menu changes daily but emphasizes chargrilled foods with herbs and seasonal vegetables. A typical meal might include an appetizer of poached cod with anchovy-and-basil mayonnaise; grilled breast of chicken with black truffle, crisp polenta, and arugula; and a warm pear-and-raisin puff pastry with maple-syrup ice cream.

124 Kensington Church St., W8. ☎ ***0171/221-9225. Tube:*** *Notting Hill Gate, then a 5-minute walk south on Kensington Church St.* ***Reservations:*** *Recommended.* ***Main courses:*** *Fixed-price lunches £8–£14 ($13–$23); fixed-price 4-course dinner £40 ($66). AE, DC, MC, V.* ***Open:*** *Mon–Fri 12:30–2pm and 7–10pm. Closed Sat and Sun.*

Crank's In London

$. Soho. VEGETARIAN.

Located just off Carnaby Street, this is the headquarters of a chain of self-service vegetarian restaurants with seven other branches in London. The wood-and-wicker decor is appropriate for this all-natural cuisine. Organic white and stone-ground flour are used for breads and rolls. The uncooked vegetable salad is especially good, and there's always a hot stew of savory vegetables served with a salad. Homemade honey cake, cheesecake, and tarts are featured.

8 Marshall St., W1 ☎ ***0171/437-9431. Tube:*** *Oxford Circus, then a 5-minute walk south on Regent St. and east on Foubert's Place to Marshall St.* ***Reservations:*** *Not accepted.* ***Main courses:*** *£5–£6.45 ($8–$11); 2-course set meal (Sat only) £6.95 ($11). AE, DC, MC, V.* ***Open:*** *Mon–Tues and Fri–Sat 8am–8pm; Wed–Thurs 8am–9pm.*

Devonshire Arms

$. Kensington. BRITISH.

This mid-19th-century pub is a good place for lunch if you're shopping on Kensington High Street. It's large enough that you can always get a seat, and the food is way above average. There's a self-service section to one side for quick daily specials; otherwise, your meal is prepared and brought to your table. The big mixed grill, with rump steak, pork sausage, gammon (cured or smoked ham), lamb cutlet, fried egg, chips, and sautéed mushrooms will set you up for the rest of the day. The club sandwich is great, and so is the vegetarian lasagna.

37 Marloes Rd., W8. ☎ ***0171/937-0710.*** *Reservations not accepted.* ***Tube:*** *High Street Kensington, then a 5-minute walk west on Kensington High St. and south on Wright's Lane to Marloes Rd.* ***Main courses:*** *£5.95–£6.50 ($10–$11). AE, MC, V.* ***Open:*** *Mon–Sat 11am–11pm; Sun noon–10:30pm (food served noon–3pm).*

Kids Dickens Inn by the Tower

$. The City. BRITISH.

Even fussy kids will find something they like at this former spice warehouse, now a three-story restaurant with sweeping Thames and Tower Bridge views. The ground-floor **Tavern Room** serves lasagna, soup, sandwiches, and chili. **Pizza on the Dock,** one floor above, offers four sizes of pizzas. **Wheeler's,** on the top floor, is a relatively formal (geared more toward adults) dining room that serves Modern British cuisine; specials include steaks, chargrilled brochette of wild mushrooms, and baked fillet of cod.

St. Katherine's Way (near the Tower of London), E1. ☎ ***0171/488-2208. Tube:*** *Tower Hill, then a 10-minute walk east on Tower Hill East and south on St. Katherine's Street to St. Katherine's Way.* ***Reservations:*** *Recommended.* ***Main courses:*** *Wheeler's £10–£22 ($17–$36); Tavern Room snacks and platters £3.75–£6 ($6–$10); Pizza on the Dock pizzas £5.75–£23 ($9–$38). AE, DC, MC, V.* ***Open:*** *Wheeler's, daily noon–3pm and 6:30–10:30pm; Tavern Room, daily 11am–11pm; Pizza on the Dock, daily noon–10pm.*

Ebury Wine Bar

$$. Westminster/Victoria. BRITISH/INTERNATIONAL.

This is a popular and attractive wine bar with a surprisingly good and varied menu and excellent wines. The narrow, woodsy interior is reminiscent of a Paris bistro. In addition to steaks, the oft-changing menu features traditional dishes, such as Cumberland sausages, meat loaf, and roast pork, but you might find something with a Pacific Rim influence as well (like Thai fish balls).

139 Ebury St., SW1. ☎ ***0171/730-5447. Tube:*** *Victoria, then a 10-minute walk west on Belgrave St. and south on Ebury St.* ***Reservations:*** *Recommended.* ***Main courses:*** *£17–£22 ($28–$36); set-price Sun lunch £14 ($23) for 2 courses, £17 ($28) for 3 courses. AE, DC, MC, V.* ***Open:*** *Daily 11am–11pm.*

Kids Ed's Easy Diner

$. Soho. NORTH AMERICAN.

At London's version of an old American diner, you perch on stools around a wraparound counter and listen to old songs blaring from the jukebox. This Ed's is a bit more authentic than the version at the Pepsi Trocadero in Piccadilly Circus but still attracts a fair share of teens on the town. If you're lonely for all the comforting, cholesterol-laden chow no one's supposed to eat anymore, you'll find big hamburgers served with fries or onion rings, giant kosher weenies slathered with cheddar cheese, chili, tuna melts, and grilled cheese sandwiches. Loosen your belt if you're ordering the lumberjack's breakfast.

12 Moor St. (off Cambridge Circus), W1. ☎ ***0171/439-1955. Tube:*** *Leicester Square, then a 5-minute walk north on Charing Cross Rd. and west on Moor St.* ***Reservations:*** *Not accepted.* ***Main courses:*** *£4.50–£5.50 ($7–$9). MC, V.* ***Open:*** *Mon–Thurs 11:30am–midnight; Fri 11:30am–1am; Sat 9am–1am; Sun 9am–11pm.*

English House

$$. Chelsea. BRITISH.

With a name like English House, the food has to be English. Dining at this tiny, elegant restaurant is like being a guest in a Victorian house. The menu is seasonal, so you might start with a pumpkin-and-rosemary soup or grilled pigeon breast with bean compote. Main courses generally include roast lamb with bubble and squeak (cabbage and potatoes) and braised ham hock with corn and mashed apples. Game is available in season, as is fresh fish of the day. Summer berries in season predominate on the pudding (dessert) menu.

3 Milner St., SW3. ☎ ***0171/584-3002. Tube:*** *Sloane Square, then a 10-minute walk north on Cadogan Gardens to Milner St., west off of Cadogan Square.* ***Reservations:*** *Required.* ***Main courses:*** *£8–£17 ($13–$28); fixed-price lunch £15.25 ($25); fixed-price dinner (Sun only) £20.75 ($34). AE, DC, MC, V.* ***Open:*** *Mon–Sat 12:30–2:30pm and 7:30–11:15pm; Sun 12:30–2pm and 7:30–9:45pm.*

Cool Britannia

Sirloin, so the story goes, got its name from James I when he was a guest at Houghton Tower in Lancashire. He knighted the leg of beef put before him with his dagger, crying "Arise, Sir Loin."

Food For Thought

$. Covent Garden. VEGETARIAN.

This simple basement hole-in-the-wall is a pleasant respite from the hubbub of Covent Garden with all its expensive restaurants geared toward carnivores. The menu changes constantly, but there's always a daily soup (such as carrot and fresh coriander) and a couple of good main courses. You might find sweet and tangy Jamaican curry or pasta with a not-very-spicy sauce made of roasted red peppers and tomatoes. There are daily quiche and salad specials. The desserts generally include apple and rhubarb crumble and fruit with yogurt. Service is cafeteria-style.

31 Neal St., WC2. ☎ ***0171/836-0239. Tube:*** *Covent Garden, then a 2-minute walk north on Neal St.* ***Reservations:*** *Not accepted.* ***Main courses:*** *£3–£5.50 ($5–$9). No credit cards.* ***Open:*** *Mon–Sat noon–3:30pm and 5:30–8:15pm; Sun noon–4pm.*

Kids

Fortnum & Mason

$$. St. James's. BRITISH.

Fortnum & Mason is a posh, legendary London store famous for its food section (see chapter 15), but it also has three restaurants: the mezzanine-level **Patio** (lunch and tea), the lower-level **Fountain** (breakfast, lunch, tea, and dinner), and the fourth-floor **St. James's** (lunch and afternoon tea). Although these places are crowded with tourists, they remain pleasant spots where you can get a good meal and a glimpse of the fading empire. The Patio's luncheon menu offers an assortment of pricey sandwiches and main courses. The Fountain specializes in hot and cold pies (steak and kidney, curried fish and banana, chicken, and game) and Welsh rarebit prepared with Guinness stout. The more well-heeled dine at the St. James's, where the menu is even more traditionally British. For starters, try the kipper mousse (chilled smoked fish mousse) or potato and Stilton (a rich, waxy cheese) brûlée; main courses include pies and roast rib of Scottish beef.

181 Piccadilly, W1. ☎ ***0171/734-8040. Tube:*** *Piccadilly Circus, then a 5-minute walk west on Piccadilly.* ***Reservations:*** *Accepted for St. James's only.* ***Main courses:*** *£7.50–£15.95 ($12–$26). AE, DC, MC, V.* ***Open:*** *St. James's and the Patio, Mon–Sat 9:30am–5:30pm; Fountain, Mon–Sat 9am–8pm.*

The Founders Arms

$. South Bank. MODERN BRITISH.

This modern pub-restaurant sits right on the Thames on the South Bank, a few minutes' walk from the South Bank Centre. You can sit inside or out beside the river. Although there are some pub favorites, such as smoked sausage and mash, pork/stuffing/apricot pie, and lamb's liver and bacon on bubble and squeak (cabbage and potatoes), other dishes are more ambitious. You can get mussels in white-wine-and-cream sauce, chargrilled chicken, a good hot seafood salad, homemade salmon and crab fishcakes, and a Lebanese lamb casserole. Pasta, fresh fish, and other daily specials are listed on a blackboard.

52 Hopton St., SE1. ☎ ***0171/928-1899. Tube:*** *Waterloo, then a 10-minute walk north along the Thames path in front of the National Theatre; the pub is right on the path.* ***Reservations:*** *Recommended for dinner.* ***Main courses:*** *£4.95–£9.95 ($8–$16). AE, MC, V.* ***Open:*** *Mon–Sat noon–9pm; Sun noon–8:30pm.*

Fox & Anchor

$. The City. BRITISH.

For an authentic taste of early-morning London, this unique pub is tops. It's been serving gargantuan breakfasts to butchers from the nearby Smithfield meat market since 1898, and you'll also rub elbows with nurses coming off their night shifts, city clerks, and tycoons. The "full house" breakfast plate comes with at least eight items, including sausage, bacon, kidneys, eggs, beans, black pudding, and a fried slice of bread, along with unlimited tea or coffee, toast, and jam. If you're in a festive mood, order a Black Velvet (champagne with Guinness) or a Bucks Fizz (orange juice and champagne—what Americans call a mimosa).

115 Charterhouse St., EC1. ☎ ***0171/253-4838. Tube:*** *Barbican, then a 5-minute walk north on Aldersgate and west on Charterhouse St.* ***Reservations:*** *Recommended.* ***Main courses:*** *"Full house" breakfast £7 ($11); steak breakfast £4.50–£9.80 ($7–$16). AE, DC, MC, V.* ***Open:*** *Mon–Fri 7–10:30am and noon–2:15pm.*

The Gay Hussar

$$$$. Soho. HUNGARIAN.

The Gay Hussar, generally considered the best Hungarian restaurant outside of Hungary, is gay in the old ha-ha sense of the word. The cuisine is undeniably authentic: chilled wild-cherry soup, smoked Hungarian sausage, cabbage stuffed with minced veal and rice, perfectly done chicken served in mild paprika sauce with cucumber salad and noodles, mouth-watering roast duck with red cabbage and caraway potatoes, and, of course, veal goulash with egg dumplings. Portions are immoderately large, but if you have room for dessert, try the poppyseed strudel or walnut pancakes.

2 Greek St. (off Soho Square), W1. ☎ ***0171/437-0973. Tube:*** *Tottenham Court, then a 5-minute walk west on Oxford St. and south on Soho St.; Greek St. is at the southeast corner of Soho Square.* ***Reservations:*** *Recommended.* ***Main courses:*** *£20–£25 ($33–$41); fixed-price lunch £16 ($26). AE, DC, MC, V.* ***Open:*** *Mon–Sat 12:15–2:30pm and 5:30–10:45pm.*

The George

$. The Strand. BRITISH.

Located opposite the Royal Courts of Justice, The George dates from 1723 and is a favorite pub of barristers. Much of the original structure is still intact. Hot and cold platters, including bangers and mash (sausages and mashed potatoes), fish-and-chips, steak-and-kidney pie, and lasagna, are served from a food counter at the back. Additional seating is available in the basement, where a headless cavalier is said to haunt the premises, evidently looking for his head *and* a drink.

213 The Strand, WC2. ☎ ***0171/427-0941. Tube:*** *Temple, then a 5-minute walk north on Arundel St. and east on The Strand.* ***Reservations:*** *Not accepted.* ***Main courses:*** *Bar platters £3–£6.30 ($5–$10). DC, V.* ***Open:*** *Mon–Fri 11am–11pm; Sat 11am–3pm (food served Mon–Sat 11:30am–2:30pm).*

The George & Vulture

$$. The City. BRITISH.

This historic city pub, dating from 1660, serves English lunches on its three floors. Daily specials are offered, as well as a regular menu that includes a mixed grill, a loin chop, and fried Dover sole fillets. Potatoes and buttered cabbage are the standard vegetables, and the apple tart is always reliable. The system is to arrive and give your name, and then retire to the Jamaican pub opposite for a drink; you're fetched when your table is ready. Afterward you can explore the maze of pubs, shops, wine houses, and other old buildings near the tavern.

3 Castle Court, Cornhill, EC3. ☎ ***0171/626-9710. Tube:*** *Bank, then a 5-minute walk east on Cornhill.* ***Reservations:*** *Accepted only if you agree to arrive by 12:45pm.* ***Main courses:*** *£6.45–£12.45 ($11–$21). AE, DC, MC, V.* ***Open:*** *Mon–Fri noon–2:30pm.*

Kids Gourmet Pizza Company

$. St. James's. PIZZA/PASTA.

If you're in the West End and want an economical lunch or dinner, stop in here for a pizza. It's a large, bright, pleasant place frequented by the area's shop and office workers. You can choose from 15 pizzas (this is pizza as in pie, not slice). Everything from a BLT version to one with Cajun chicken and prawns is available. The crusts are light and crispy, the toppings fresh and flavorful. Instead of pizza, you might want to try the wild-mushroom tortellini with chopped basil, tomato, and olive oil.

Best Bets for Celebrity Spotting

Aubergine (Chelsea, $$$$)
Joe Allen (Covent Garden, $$)

7–9 Swallow Walk (off Piccadilly), W1. ☎ ***0171/734-5182. Tube:*** *Piccadilly Circus, then a 5-minute walk west on Piccadilly and north on Swallow St.* ***Reservations:*** *Not accepted.* ***Main courses:*** *Pizzas £4.80–£8.45 ($8–$14), pastas £6.60–£8.45 ($11–$14). AE, DC, MC, V.* ***Open:*** *Mon–Sat noon–11pm; Sun noon–10:30pm.*

Kids The Granary

$. Piccadilly Circus/Leicester Square. BRITISH.

This country-style restaurant serves a simple but flavorful array of home-cooked dishes, listed daily on a blackboard. The daily specials might include lamb casserole with mint and lemon; pan-fried cod; and avocados stuffed with prawns, spinach, and cheese. Vegetarian meals include mushrooms stuffed with mixed vegetables, stuffed eggplant with curry sauce, and vegetarian lasagna. Tempting desserts are bread-and-butter pudding and brown Betty (both served hot). Large portions guarantee that you won't go hungry.

39 Albemarle St., W1. ☎ ***0171/493-2978. Tube:*** *Green Park, then a 5-minute walk east on Piccadilly to Albermarle St.; or Piccadilly Circus, then a 5-minute walk west on Piccadilly.* ***Reservations:*** *Not necessary.* ***Main courses:*** *£7–£8.60 ($11–$14). MC, V.* ***Open:*** *Mon–Fri 11:30am–8pm; Sat–Sun noon–2:30pm.*

Kids

Hard Rock Cafe

$$. Mayfair. NORTH AMERICAN.

This is the original Hard Rock, now a worldwide chain of rock-and-roll/American-roadside-diner-themed restaurants serving up good food and service with a smile. Teenagers like the rock 'n' roll memorabilia and loud music, as well as the juicy burgers and shakes. There are tasty vegetarian dishes, too. Portions are generous, and the price of a main dish includes a salad and fries or a baked potato. The fajitas are always a good choice, and homemade apple pie is one of the better desserts. If you come in the evening, be prepared to stand in line.

150 Old Park Lane, W1. ☎ ***0171/629-0382. Tube:*** *Hyde Park Corner, take the Park Lane exit; Old Park Lane is just to the east of Park Lane.* ***Reservations:*** *Not accepted; expect to wait in line to be seated.* ***Main courses:*** *£8.50–£15 ($14–$25). AE, MC, V.* ***Open:*** *Sun–Thurs 11:30am–12:30am; Fri–Sat 11:30am–1am.*

The Ivy

$$. Soho. BRITISH/FRENCH.

The Ivy, with its 1930s look, tiny bar, glamour-scene crowd, and later-than-usual hours, is one of the hippest places to dine after the theatre. The menu is simple, and the cooking is notable for the skillful preparation of fresh ingredients. Popular dishes include white asparagus with sea kale and truffle butter; seared scallops with spinach, sorrel, and bacon; and salmon fish cakes. You'll also find Mediterranean fish soup, a great mixed grill, and wonderful English desserts, such as sticky toffee and caramelized bread-and-butter pudding.

1–5 West St., WC2. ☎ ***0171/836-4751. Tube:*** *Leicester Square, then a 5-minute walk north on Charing Cross Rd.; West St. is at the southeastern end of Cambridge Circus.* ***Reservations:*** *Required.* ***Main courses:*** *£8.50–£16 ($14–$26); Sat–Sun set lunch £15.50 ($26). AE, DC, MC, V.* ***Open:*** *Daily noon–3pm and 5:30pm–midnight.*

Joe Allen

$$. Covent Garden. NORTH AMERICAN.

Joe Allen's, with its checkered tablecloths and crowded dining room, is the sort of gabby place where actors often come after a performance to wolf down a bowl of chili con carne or gnaw on a plate of barbecued ribs. It keeps a low profile on a back street in Covent Garden. The food, American classics with some international twists thrown in, is sturdy and dependable, and the set menu is a real value: After a starter (maybe smoked haddock vichyssoise), you can choose main courses like pan-fried Parmesan-crusted lemon sole, Cajun chicken breast, or grilled spicy Italian sausages. If you're feeling homesick, console yourself with a burger, a brownie, and a Coke. Come before the show for the best prices, and come after for potential star gazing.

13 Exeter St., WC2. ☎ ***0171/836-0651. Tube:*** *Covent Garden, then a 5-minute walk south past the Market to Burleigh St. on the southeast corner of the Piazza and west on Exeter St.* ***Reservations:*** *Recommended.* ***Main courses:*** *£6.50–£13.50 ($11–$22); pre-theatre dinner £12–£14 ($20–$22); set lunch menu Mon–Fri £11–£13 ($18–$21); Sun brunch £13.50–£15.50 ($22–$26). AE, MC, V.* ***Open:*** *Mon–Fri noon–12:45am; Sat 11:30am–12:45am; Sun 11:30am–11:30pm.*

Ken Lo's Memories of China

$$$$. Westminster/Victoria. CHINESE.

Founded by the late Ken Lo, author of more than 30 cookbooks and once the host of a TV cooking show, this remains one of the better (and certainly one of the more expensive) Pan-Chinese restaurants in London. The interior decor is appealingly minimalist, the service impeccable. Spanning broadly divergent regions of China, the ambitious menu features Cantonese quick-fried beef in oyster sauce, lobster with handmade noodles, pomegranate prawn balls, and "bang-bang chicken" (a Szechuan dish), among many others.

Best Bets for a Pre-theatre Meal

The Ivy (Soho, $$)
Jardin des Gourmets (Soho, $$$)
Joe Allen (Covent Garden, $$)
L'Odeon (Piccadilly Circus/Leicester Square, $$$$)
Quaglino's (St. James's, $$$$)
Rules (Covent Garden, $$$)
Simpons's-in-the-Strand (The Strand, $$$)

67–69 Ebury St. (near Victoria Station), SW1. ☎ ***0171/730-7734. Tube:*** *Victoria Station, then a 10-minute walk west on Belgrave St. and south on Ebury St.* ***Reservations:*** *Recommended.* ***Main courses:*** *£10–£30 ($17–$50); fixed-price lunch £19.50–£22 ($32–$36); fixed-price 3-course dinner £27.50 ($45), fixed-price 5-course dinner £30 ($50), after-theatre 3-course dinner £24.50 ($40). AE, DC, MC, V.* ***Open:*** *Mon–Sat noon–2:30pm; daily 7–11:15pm.*

Langan's Bistro

$$. Marylebone. BRITISH/FRENCH.

Set behind a brightly colored storefront, the dining room of this busy bistro is covered with clusters of Japanese parasols, rococo mirrors, paintings, and old photographs. The menu is English with an underplayed French influence. Depending on the season, the fixed-price menu might start with chicken livers or a pepper-and-brie tartlet and move on to brochette of lamb or poached salmon. There are also old standbys, such as bangers and mash and calf's liver and bacon. The dessert extravaganza known as "Mrs. Langan's chocolate pudding" is a must for chocoholics.

26 Devonshire St., W1. ☎ ***0171/935-4531. Tube:*** *Regent's Park, then a 5-minute walk south on Portland Place and west on Devonshire St.* ***Reservations:*** *Recommended.* ***Main courses:*** *fixed-price 2-course lunch or dinner £18.50 ($31), fixed-price 3-course lunch or dinner £20.50 ($34). AE, DC, MC, V.* ***Open:*** *Mon–Fri 12:30–2:30pm and 6:30–11:30pm; Sat 6:30–11:30pm.*

L'Odeon

$$$$. Piccadilly Circus/Leicester Square. FRENCH/INTERNATIONAL.
Dressy L'Odeon created quite a stir when it opened, as much for its size and super-sophisticated interior as for its food. Located in Nash Terrace, the huge second-floor dining room has semicircular windows overlooking the bustle of Regent Street and Piccadilly Circus. The cuisine is Gallic with international overtones, always fresh, and always beautifully presented. Main courses might include poached salmon with orange zest, roast chicken with Parmesan, calf's liver with braised cabbage, or braised lamb. The service is efficient but rather impersonal.

65 Regent St. (entrance at Air St.), W1. ☎ ***0171/287-1400. Tube:*** *Piccadilly Circus; Air St. is the first turn on the south side of Regent St.* ***Reservations:*** *Essential.* ***Main courses:*** *£14–£25 ($23–$41); lunch and pre-theatre menus £15.50–£19.50 ($26–$32). AE, DC, MC, V.* ***Open:*** *Mon–Sat noon–2:45pm and 5:30–11:30pm; Sun noon–3:30pm and 7–10:30pm.*

Le Pont de la Tour

$$$$. South Bank. INTERNATIONAL.
The ubiquitous Sir Terence Conran is the force behind this upscale wine-and-dine emporium built in a mid-19th-century warehouse with magnificent views of the Thames and Tower Bridge. Amid the brash hubbub of the **Bar and Grill,** you can dine on ham-and–foie gras terrine; a half-lobster with roast peppers, olives, and fennel; or a heaping platter of fresh shellfish. The menu in the larger and more formal **Restaurant** offers dishes such as roast squab pigeon with morel (mushroom)-and-truffle sauce, braised lamb shank with rosemary jus and carrot-and-parsnip purée, and an excellent Dover sole.

36D Shad Thames, Butler's Wharf, SE1. ☎ ***0171/403-8403. Tube:*** *London Bridge, then a 10–15 minute walk east on Tooley St. and north on Lafon St. to Shad Thames.* ***Reservations:*** *Not accepted in the Bar and Grill, recommended in the Restaurant.* ***Main courses:*** *Bar and Grill £9–£18 ($15–$30); Restaurant £16–£24 ($26–$40); fixed-price 3-course lunch £27.50 ($45). AE, DC, MC, V.* ***Open:*** *Restaurant Mon–Fri noon–3pm and 6–11:30pm, Sat 6–11:30pm, Sun 12:30–3pm and 6–11pm; Bar and Grill daily 11:30am–midnight.*

Maggie Jones

$$. Kensington. BRITISH.

English cuisine is all that's served at this three-story restaurant with pine tables. Menu items include grilled leg of lamb chop with rosemary, grilled trout with almonds, and Maggie's famous fish pie. Desserts include treacle (molasses) tarts. Everything is reliably cooked and good, but never thrilling. By the way, the place is named after Princess Margaret, who used to eat here.

6 Old Court Place (off Kensington Church St.), W8. ☎ ***0171/937-6462. Tube:*** *High Street Kensington, then a 5-minute walk east on Kensington High St., north on Kensington Church St., and east on Old Court Place.* ***Reservations:*** *Required.* ***Main courses:*** *£5–£17 ($8–$28). AE, MC, V.* ***Open:*** *Daily 12:30–2:30pm and 6:30–11pm.*

Museum Street Café

$$. Bloomsbury. MODERN BRITISH.

For a good lunch after visiting the British Museum, or a good early supper in Bloomsbury, you might want to stop in at this pleasant, informal restaurant that's low on frills and high on quality. The kitchen comes up with creative dishes such as salmon-and-coconut soup with lime, chili, and coriander; dill-and-leek tart with smoked salmon; chargrilled corn-fed chicken with pesto; and rabbit chili with chipotle sauce. Lunch choices change daily, dinner choices change every week, and everything is ordered from a fixed-price menu.

47 Museum St., WC1. ☎ ***0171/405-3211. Tube:*** *Tottenham Court Rd., then a 5-minute walk east on New Oxford St. and north on Museum St.; from the museum itself, it's a 2-minute walk from Great Russell St. down Museum St.* ***Reservations:*** *Required.* ***Main courses:*** *Lunch £14.50 ($24) for 2 courses, £17.50 ($29) for 3 courses; dinner £19.50 ($32) for 2 courses, £23.50 ($39) for 3 courses. AE, MC, V.* ***Open:*** *Mon 12:30–2:15pm (last order); Tues–Fri 12:30–2:15pm (last order) and 6:30–9:15pm.*

Noor Jahan

$$. South Kensington. INDIAN.

Small, unpretentious, and always reliable for good Indian food, Noor Jahan is a neighborhood favorite in South Ken. Marinated chicken and lamb dishes cooked Tandoor style in a clay oven are moist and flavorful. Chicken tikka (boneless chicken marinated in yogurt, ginger, garlic, and peppercorns and broiled in a clay oven), a staple of northern India, is one specialty worth trying. So are the biryani dishes; chicken, lamb, or prawns are mixed with basmati rice, fried in ghee (clarified butter), and served with a mixed vegetable curry. If you're unfamiliar with Indian food, the waiters will gladly explain the various dishes.

2A Bina Gardens (off Old Brompton Rd.), SW5. ☎ ***0171/373-6522. Tube:*** *Gloucester Rd., then a 5-minute walk south on Gloucester Rd., west on Brompton Rd., north on Bina Gardens.* ***Reservations:*** *Recommended.* ***Main courses:*** *£7.50–£15 ($12–$25); set menu £18.50 ($31). AE, DC, MC, V.* ***Open:*** *Daily noon–2:45pm and 6–11:45pm.*

Kids North Sea Fish Restaurant

$$. Bloomsbury. SEAFOOD.

If you get a craving for "real" fish-and-chips (not the generic frozen stuff that often passes for it), definitely try this unassuming and inexpensive "chippie" in Bloomsbury where the fish is *always* fresh that day. The place itself is bright and comfortable (and generally crowded). You might want to start with grilled fresh sardines or a fish cake before digging into a main course of cod or haddock. The fish is most often served battered and deep-fried, but you can also order it grilled. The chips are almost as good as the fish.

7–8 Leigh St. (off Cartwright Gardens), WC1. ☎ ***0171/387-5892. Tube:*** *Russell Square, then a 10-minute walk north on Marchmont Place and east on Leigh St.* ***Reservations:*** *Recommended.* ***Main courses:*** *Fish platters £6–£13.75 ($10–$23). AE, DC, MC, V.* ***Open:*** *Mon–Sat noon–2pm and 5:30–10pm.*

Odin's

$$$. Marylebone. INTERNATIONAL.

Set next door to its slightly less-expensive twin, Langan's Bistro (see above; the actor Michael Caine owns both), this elegant restaurant has sufficient elbow room and an eclectic decor. The set menu changes with the seasons: Typical fare might include forest mushrooms in brioche, braised leeks glazed with mustard and tomato sauce, roast duck with applesauce and sage-and-onion stuffing, or roast fillet of sea bass with a juniper cream sauce. Oddly enough, Odin's is not open on weekends.

27 Devonshire St., W1. ☎ ***0171/935-7296. Tube:*** *Regent's Park, then a 5-minute walk south on Portland Place and west on Devonshire St.* ***Reservations:*** *Required.* ***Main courses:*** *fixed-price 2-course lunch or dinner £24 ($40), fixed-price 3-course lunch or dinner £26 ($43). AE, DC, MC, V.* ***Open:*** *Mon–Fri 12:30–2:30pm and 6:30–11pm.*

The Oratory

$$. Knightsbridge. MODERN BRITISH.

Close to the Victoria and Albert Museum and Knightsbridge shopping, this funky bistro serves up some of the best and least-expensive food in swanky South Ken. The high-ceilinged room has enormous glass chandeliers, patterned walls and ceilings, and wooden tables with wrought-iron chairs. Take note of the daily specials on the blackboard, especially any pasta dishes. The homemade fish cakes, stir-fried prawns with noodles, and breast of chicken stuffed with Parma ham and fontina cheese are all noteworthy. For dessert, the sticky toffee pudding with ice cream is a melt-in-the-mouth delight.

232 Brompton Rd., SW3. ☎ ***0171/584-3493. Tube:*** *Knightsbridge or South Kensington.* ***Main courses:*** *£4.50–£9 ($7–$15); set-menu lunch £7.95 ($13). MC, V.* ***Open:*** *Mon–Sat 11:30am–11pm; Sun 11:30am–5pm.*

Oxo Tower Brasserie

$$$. South Bank. FRENCH.

Book well in advance and plead for a window table at this smooth, sleek, and stylish brasserie perched atop the landmark Oxo Tower on the South Bank. The Brasserie is less chichi than the adjacent Oxo Tower Restaurant, but the food is marvelous, costs about half of what you'd pay to dine on tablecloths, and the superlative river-and-city views are just as sublime.

Oxo Tower Wharf, Barge House St., SE1. ☎ ***0171/803-3888. Tube:*** *Waterloo; the easiest foot route is to head west to the South Bank Centre and then follow the Thames pathway north to the Oxo Tower (about a 10–15 minute walk).* ***Reservations:*** *Essential at least 1 or 2 weeks in advance.* ***Main courses:*** *£12.50–£14.50 ($21–$24). AE, DC, MC, V.* ***Open:*** *Daily noon–3pm and 5:30–11pm.*

Kids Pizzeria Condotti

$. Mayfair. PIZZA/PASTA.

With its fresh flowers and art-covered walls, this place just off Regent Street is a nice family-friendly haven where the light, crisp pizzas arrive bubbling hot from the oven. Choices range from a simple margarita with mozzarella and tomato to the "American hot," with mozzarella, pepperoni, sausages, and hot peppers. There are plenty of fresh salads and pastas to choose from, as well as a good, reasonably priced wine list. You might want to finish off with a scoop of creamy tartufo ice cream made with chocolate liqueur.

4 Mill St., W1. ☎ ***0171/499-1308. Tube:*** *Oxford Circus, then a 5-minute walk south on Regent St., west on Conduit St., and north on Mill St.* ***Reservations:*** *Not required.* ***Main courses:*** *Pizzas £5–£7 ($8–$12), pastas £6.30 ($10), salads £6–£8 ($10–$13). AE, DC, MC, V.* ***Open:*** *Mon–Sat 11:30am–midnight; Sun noon–11pm.*

Best Tables with a View

Dickens Inn by the Tower (The City, $)
L'Odeon (Piccadilly Circus/Leicester Square, $$$$)
La Pont de la Tour (South Bank, $$$$)
Oxo Tower Brasserie (South Bank, $$$)
RS Hispaniola (The Strand, $$$)

Poons in the City

$$$. The City. CHINESE.

Located on the ground floor of an office block less than a 5-minute walk from the Tower of London, Poons is famous for Cantonese specialties such as *lap yuk soom* (similar to tacos, with finely chopped wind-dried bacon) and braised honeycomb (a Chinese version of Yorkshire pudding and gravy). Pan-fried dumplings and deep-fried scallops make excellent starters. Dishes also feature crispy, aromatic duck; prawns with cashew nuts; and barbecued pork. At the end of the L-shaped restaurant, there's a simpler and less-expensive 80-seat express cafe with stir-fries and snacks.

2 Minster Pavement, Minster Court, Mincing Lane, EC3. ☎ ***0171/626-0126. Tube:*** *Tower Hill.* ***Reservations:*** *Recommended for lunch.* ***Main courses:*** *£5.15–£7.80 ($8–$13); fixed-price lunch and dinner £22.50–£32 ($37–$53); express cafe fixed-price lunch £5.15–£22.50 ($8–$37) per person (minimum of 2). AE, DC, MC, V.* ***Open:*** *Mon–Fri noon–10:30pm.*

Kids

Porter's English Restaurant

$$. Covent Garden. BRITISH.

This comfortable, informal restaurant is a great place to introduce your kids to the venerable staples of traditional British cuisine. It specializes in classic English pies, including Old English fish pie; lamb-and-apricot pie; and ham, leek, and cheese pie. The main courses, accompanied by vegetables and side dishes, are so generous that you can bypass the appetizers. If you don't want a pie, try the bangers and mash, grilled sirloin, lamb steaks, or pork chops. The puddings, including bread-and-butter pudding and steamed syrup sponge, are the real puddings (in the American sense); they're served hot or cold, with whipped cream or custard. Kids love them (and so do adults).

17 Henrietta St., WC2. ☎ ***0171/836-6466. Tube:*** *Covent Garden, then a 5-minute walk south on James St.; Henrietta St. is at the southwest corner behind Covent Garden Market.* ***Reservations:*** *Recommended.* ***Main courses:*** *£8 ($13); fixed-price menu £16.50 ($27). AE, DC, MC, V.* ***Open:*** *Mon–Sat noon–11:30pm, Sun noon–10:30pm.*

Quaglino's

$$$$. St. James's. MODERN EUROPEAN.

If you want to mix food with some glamorous fun, head for this mega-eatery with a huge sunken dining room that's reminiscent of an ocean liner. The shellfish are always excellent, but other menu items can be hit or miss, and there can be delays in service. But people come to Quaglino's for the showy buzz, not the culinary finesse. The menu changes often, but your choices might include goat cheese and caramelized onion tart, seared salmon with potato pancakes, or roasted cod and ox cheek with chargrilled vegetables. The desserts are delectable. This is one of the rare London restaurants with a rest room for patrons with disabilities.

16 Bury St., SW1. ☎ ***0171/930-6767.*** *Fax 0171/839 2866.* ***Tube:*** *Green Park, then a 10-minute walk northeast on Piccadilly, southeast on St. James's St., and east on King St. to Bury St.* ***Reservations:*** *Essential (book 2 weeks in advance).* ***Main courses:*** *£10.50–£19.50 ($17–$32); fixed-price 3-course menu (available only at lunch and for pre-theatre dinner between 5:30 and 6:30pm) £14.50–£19.50 ($24–$32). AE, DC, MC, V.* ***Open:*** *Daily noon–3pm and 5:30–11:30pm.*

R.S. Hispaniola

$$$. The Strand. BRITISH/FRENCH.

Permanently moored beside the Thames, this large, comfortably outfitted former passenger boat provides good food and spectacular views of the passing river traffic. The frequently changing menu offers a variety of sturdy and generally well-prepared dishes. On any given night, you might find flambéed Mediterranean prawns with garlic, fried fish cakes with tartar sauce, poached halibut on a bed of creamed spinach, Dover sole meunière, rack of lamb flavored with rosemary and shallots, and several vegetarian dishes. There's live music on most nights, and the place can be fun and romantic, if a bit touristy.

River Thames, Victoria Embankment, Charing Cross, WC2. ☎ ***0171/839-3011. Tube:*** *Embankment; the restaurant is moored in the Thames a few steps from the station.* ***Reservations:*** *Recommended.* ***Main courses:*** *£9.50–£19.50 ($16–$32); £15 ($25) minimum per person. AE, DC, MC, V.* ***Open:*** *Mon–Fri noon–2pm and 6–10:30pm; Sat 6–10:30pm. Closed Dec 24–Jan 4.*

Rules

$$$. Covent Garden. BRITISH.

London's oldest restaurant, Rules was founded in 1798 and is decorated with 2 centuries' worth of prints, cartoons, and paintings. If you want to eat classic British cuisine in a memorable (nay, venerable) setting, put on something reasonably dressy and head for Maiden Lane. If you're game for game, go for it—that's what Rules is famous for. Game birds shot at the restaurant's hunting seat are roasted to order from September to February. In recent years, they've added a few vegetarian dishes, and fish is also available.

35 Maiden Lane, WC2. ☎ ***0171/836-5314. Tube:*** *Covent Garden, then a 5-minute walk south on James St. to Southampton St. behind Covent Garden Market and west on Maiden Lane.* ***Reservations:*** *Essential.* ***Main courses:*** *£14–£17 ($23–$28); pre- and post-theatre meals Mon–Fri 3–6pm and 10:30–11:30pm £15.95 ($26); Sat–Sun lunch £17.95 ($29). AE, DC, MC, V.* ***Open:*** *Daily noon–midnight.*

San Lorenzo

$$$. Knightsbridge. ITALIAN.

Once a favorite of Princess Di, this fashionable restaurant specializes in the cuisine of Tuscany and Piedmont. Seasonal fish, game, and vegetables appear in dishes such as homemade fettuccine with salmon, risotto with fresh asparagus, and partridge in white-wine sauce. The food is reliably good, but some diners complain that there's too much attitude that goes along with it.

22 Beauchamp Place, SW3. ☎ ***0171/584-1074. Tube:*** *Knightsbridge, then a 5-minute walk southwest on Brompton Rd. and south on Beauchamp Place.* ***Reservations:*** *Required.* ***Main courses:*** *£14.50–£20 ($24–$33). No credit cards.* ***Open:*** *Mon–Sat 12:30–3pm and 7:30–11:30pm.*

The Savoy Grill

$$$$. The Strand. BRITISH.

Like the hotel that houses it, The Savoy Grill caters to the rich, the powerful, the prestigious, and anyone else who can dress up and pay for a meal. You can expect impeccable service in the spacious but low-key dining room.

If you like old-fashioned meat dishes, choose the daily special "from the trolley": saddle of lamb, roast sirloin, beef Wellington, and pot-roasted guinea hen with a horseradish crust. The chef tarts up other traditional British dishes with some interesting mixes, such as roast duck with caramelized oranges, asparagus, and pancetta; pan-fried salmon with mushroom risotto; and fish cakes with roasted tomato-and-fennel compote.

The Savoy Hotel, The Strand, WC2. ☎ ***0171/240-6040. Tube:*** *Charing Cross, then a 5-minute walk east along The Strand.* ***Reservations:*** *Essential.* ***Main courses:*** *£15–£37 ($25–$61). AE, DC, MC, V.* ***Open:*** *Mon–Fri 12:30–2:30pm and 6–11:15pm; Sat 6–11:15pm.*

Shepherd's

$$$. Westminster/Victoria. BRITISH.

About equidistant between the Tate Gallery and Big Ben, this popular restaurant has a loyal clientele of barristers and members of Parliament (a bell rings in the dining room summoning them back to the House of Commons when it's time to vote). Amid a nook-and-cranny setting of leather banquettes, sober 19th-century accessories, and English portraits and landscapes, you can dine on rib of Scottish beef served with Yorkshire pudding and other traditional dishes. You choose everything from a fixed-price menu, but the number of options is impressive.

Marsham Court, Marsham St. (at the corner of Page St.), SW1. ☎ ***0171/834-9552. Tube:*** *Westminster, then a 10-minute walk south on St. Margaret Place and Millbank, and west on Westminster St. to Page and Marsham streets; or Pimlico, then north on Bessboro St., John Islip St., and Marsham St.* ***Reservations:*** *Recommended.* ***Main courses:*** *Fixed-price meals £22 ($36) for 2 courses, £24 ($40) for 3 courses. AE, DC, MC, V.* ***Open:*** *Mon–Fri 12:30–2:45pm and 6:30–11:30pm.*

Simpson's-in-the-Strand

$$$. The Strand. BRITISH.

Simpson's, in business since 1828, boasts an army of formal waiters serving the best of staunchly traditional English food. You'll find an array of the best roasts in London: sirloin of beef, saddle of mutton with red-currant jelly, and Aylesbury duckling. (Remember to tip the tail-coated carver.) For a pudding (dessert), you might order the treacle roll and custard or Stilton with vintage port.

100 The Strand (next to the Savoy Hotel), WC2. ☎ ***0171/836-9112. Tube:*** *Charing Cross, then a 5-minute walk east along The Strand.* ***Reservations:*** *Required. Jacket and tie required for men.* ***Main courses:*** *£17.50–£25 ($29–$41); fixed-price 2-course lunch and pre-theatre dinner £12.50 ($21); fixed-price breakfast £11.50 ($19). AE, DC, MC, V.* ***Open:*** *Mon–Fri 7am–2:30pm and 6–11pm; Sat and Sun noon–2:30pm and 6–11pm.*

The Stockpot

$. Piccadilly Circus/Leicester Square. BRITISH/ CONTINENTAL.

This simple, two-level restaurant in the heart of the West End offers some of the best dining bargains in Central London. It's not refined cooking by any stretch, but it's filling and satisfying, and kids are welcome. The dishes are kept simple. The fixed-price daily menu will offer something like minestrone soup, spaghetti Bolognese (the eternal favorite), braised lamb, and apple crumble. There's a share-the-table policy during peak dining hours.

40 Panton St. (off Haymarket, opposite the Comedy Theatre), SW1. ☎ ***0171/ 839-5142. Tube:*** *Piccadilly Circus, then a 5-minute walk south on Haymarket and east on Panton St.* ***Reservations:*** *Accepted for dinner.* ***Main courses:*** *£2.30–£5.55 ($4–$9); fixed-price 2-course lunch £3.20 ($5); fixed-price 3-course dinner £6 ($10). No credit cards.* ***Open:*** *Mon–Sat 7am–11:30pm; Sun 7am–10pm.*

Veronica's

$$. Bayswater. BRITISH.

Veronica's is a celebration of historical and regional cuisine in the British Isles, with an imaginative modern twist. One month the chef might focus on Scotland, the next on Victorian foods. Your appetizer might be an Elizabethan salad called salmagundi, made with crunchy pickled vegetables, or Tweed Kettle, a 19th-century recipe to improve the taste of salmon. Many dishes are vegetarian, and everything tastes better when followed with a British farmhouse cheese or a pudding. The restaurant is bright and attractive, and the service is warm and efficient.

Best Bests for Soaking Up "the Scene"

The Ivy (Soho, $$)
Quaglino's (St. James's, $$$$)
Vong (Knightsbridge, $$$)

3 Hereford Rd., W2. ☎ ***0171/229-5079. Tube:*** *Bayswater, then a 5-minute walk west on Moscow Rd. and north on Hereford Rd.* ***Reservations:*** *Required.* ***Main courses:*** *£10.50–£17.50 ($17–$29); fixed-price meals £12.50–£16.50 ($21–$27). AE, DC, MC, V.* ***Open:*** *Mon–Fri noon–3pm and 6:30pm–midnight; Sat 6:30pm–midnight.*

Vong

$$$. Knightsbridge. FRENCH/THAI.

This minimalist restaurant on three levels is a chic hangout for food groupies who can't get enough of owner/chef Jean-Georges Vongerichten's French/ Thai food. The cooking is subtle, innovative, and inspired, as you'll see (or taste) if you order the black-plate sampler of six starters. You can dine on perfectly roasted halibut or a sublime lobster-and-daikon (a white radish from Japan) roll with rosemary-and-ginger sauce. The exotic desserts include a salad of banana and passion fruit with white-pepper ice cream.

In the Berkeley Hotel, Wilton Place, SW1. ☎ ***0171/235-1010. Tube:*** *Knightsbridge, then a 5-minute walk east on Knightsbridge and south on Wilton Place.* ***Reservations:*** *Required 7 days in advance.* ***Main courses:*** *£9–£26.75 ($15–$44); tasting menu £45 ($74); fixed-price dinner £27 ($45) for 2 courses, £36.50 ($60) for 3 courses; pre- and post-theatre dinner £17.50 ($29). AE, DC, MC, V.* ***Open:*** *Mon–Sat noon–2:30pm and 6–11:30pm.*

Kids Wagamama Noodle Bar

$. Soho. JAPANESE.

If you're exploring Soho and want a good, nutritious meal in a smoke-free environment, try this sleek, trend-setting noodle bar modeled after the ramen shops of Japan. You pass along a stark, glowing corridor with a busy open kitchen and descend to a large open room with communal tables on the lower level. The specialties here are ramen (Chinese-style thread noodles served in soups with various toppings) and the fat white noodles called *udon.* Rice dishes, vegetarian dishes, dumplings, vegetable and chicken skewers, and tempura are also on the menu.

10A Lexington St., W1. ☎ ***0171/292-0990. Tube:*** *Piccadilly Circus, then a 5-minute walk north on Shaftesbury Ave. and Windmill St., which becomes Lexington St.* ***Reservations:*** *Not accepted.* ***Main courses:*** *£3.50–£7.60 ($6–$13). MC, V.* ***Open:*** *Mon–Sat noon–11pm; Sun 12:30–10:00pm.*

Kids Ye Olde Cheshire Cheese

$$. The City. BRITISH.

Established in 1667 and a one-time haunt of Charles Dickens, Ye Olde Cheshire Cheese is London's most famous chophouse. You'll find six bars and two dining rooms in this place, which is perennially popular with families and tourists looking for some Olde London atmosphere. The house specialties include "ye famous pudding" (steak, kidney, mushrooms, and game), Scottish roast beef with Yorkshire pudding and horseradish sauce, and Dover sole. If those choices put the kids off, they can choose sandwiches and salads.

Wine Office Court, 145 Fleet St., EC4. ☎ ***0171/353-6170. Tube:*** *Blackfriars, then a 10-minute walk north on New Bridge St. and west on Fleet St.* ***Main courses:*** *£7–£15 ($12–$25). AE, DC, MC, V.* ***Open:*** *Mon–Sat noon–9:30pm, Sun noon–2:30pm and 6–9:30pm; drinks and bar snacks daily 11:30am–11pm.*

Zafferano

$$$. Knightsbridge. ITALIAN.

If you want what is perhaps the best Italian food in London, served in a quietly elegant, attitude-free restaurant, you'll find it at Zafferano (you might not find a table, though, unless you reserve in advance). The pastas are perfectly cooked. Main courses such as roast rabbit with Parma ham and polenta, chargrilled chicken, and tuna with rocket (arugula)-and-tomato salad are deliciously simple and tender. For dessert, try the sublime lemon-and-marscapone tart. Everything is ordered from a set menu.

15 Lowndes St., SW1. ☎ ***0171/235-5800. Tube:*** *Knightsbridge, then a 5-minute walk south on Sloane St., east on Cadogan Place, and north on Lowndes St.* ***Reservations:*** *Essential.* ***Main courses:*** *Set lunch £16.50–£19.50 ($27–$32), set dinner £24.50–£28.50 ($40–$47). AE, MC, V.* ***Open:*** *Mon–Sat noon–2:30pm and 7–11pm.*

Chapter 11

Light Bites & Munchies

In This Chapter

- Where to find a fast snack: fish-and-chips, meat pies, and more
- The best places for a spot of tea
- Where to take the kiddies
- Where to satisfy your sweet tooth

You'll rarely see an adult Londoner eating on the street or in the subway, the way New Yorkers do. It's just not done. Nor will you find street vendors selling food from carts (the exception being ice-cream vans in the parks and in front of some of the major sites). When it comes to eating, even the most frantic Londoner likes a proper "sit down." This is the price you pay for civilization. So what's a tourist in a rush to do?

There are fast-food restaurants all over Central London, including **Burger King, KFC,** and **McDonalds.** The kids will spot these places immediately and begin clamoring. But here are some alternatives.

Museum Cafes & Restaurants

Many London museums have cafes where you can pop in for a sandwich or snack and a cup of coffee or tea before, after, or in-between perusing the galleries. The following "Big Three" also have good restaurants where you can dine in comfort.

If you're exploring the British Museum, the **British Museum Restaurant** (☎ **0171/323-8256**) is a good and reasonably priced place for lunch or a late-afternoon snack. It's on the lobby level of the East Wing. The cafeteria-style format offers a few hot specials (including a vegetarian selection), fresh salads, fish and cold meat dishes, and desserts.

Located on the second floor in the Sainsbury Wing, **the Brasserie at the National Gallery** (☎ **0171/737-2885**) is a large and rather elegant restaurant that has a complete lunch menu (including wine). In the afternoon it serves tea with cakes and sandwiches. Main courses range from £7.75 to £12.50 ($13 to $21); fixed-price lunches are £7.95 to £11.75 ($13 to $19), and set-price afternoon teas are £5.95 to £7.50 ($10 to $12). It's open for lunch daily from noon to 3pm and for afternoon tea from 3 to 5:30pm.

The **Tate Gallery Restaurant,** on the lower level of the museum, offers what might be the best bargains for superior wines anywhere in Britain. The food menu changes every month but usually includes items such as pheasant casserole, Oxford sausage with mashed potatoes, and a selection of vegetarian dishes. It's a bit pricey for lunch, with main courses going for £10 to £16 ($16 to $26), although there's a fixed-price two-course lunch for £15.75 ($25) and a fixed-price three-course lunch for £18.50 ($30). It's open Monday to Saturday from noon to 3pm.

Between the Bread: London Sandwich Bars

Sandwich bars are a faster and cheaper alternative to sit-down restaurants and pubs. They usually open early for breakfast and close in the afternoon. There's often a counter or booths where you can eat; or you can take your sandwich and go to the nearest park for an alfresco lunch. Coffee, tea, and nonalcoholic beverages are sold. One tip: At a sandwich bar, make sure that the sandwiches are "freshly cut"—that means they haven't been sitting around in the display case for hours.

If you've blown a wad at Harrods and suddenly want to economize, just across the street is **Arco Bars of Knightsbridge,** 46 Hans Crescent (☎ **0171/585-6454;** tube: Knightsbridge); they have a smaller location just around the corner from the Knightsbridge tube station at 16 Brompton Arcade (☎ **0171/584-3136**). Both are open from 8am to 6pm. Near Victoria Station, there's an imaginative variety of sandwiches to be had at **Capri Sandwich Bar,** 16 Belgrave Rd. (☎ **0171/834-1989;** tube: Victoria), open from 7:30am to 3:30pm. If you're in the vicinity of Euston Station, try the unpretentious and cheerful **Giovanni's Sandwich Bar,** 152 North Gower St. at Euston Road (☎ **0171/383-0531;** tube: Euston), open from 6:30am to 4pm.

Kids Fish & Chips

In England, a fish-and-chips place is called a **"chippie."** At some chippies the food is wonderful, at others it's hideous. At the good places (the only ones I'll recommend), the fish (usually cod, haddock, or plaice) is fresh, the batter crisp, and the fries (chips) hand-cut. The following restaurants all have sit-down and takeaway (take-out) service; families with kids are welcome at all of them.

North Sea Fish Restaurant, 7–8 Leigh St. (☎ **0171/387-5892;** tube: Russell Square), has takeaway service from noon to 2:30pm and 5:30 to 11:30pm Monday through Saturday. If the weather is good, take your meal over to Russell Square in the heart of Bloomsbury.

In Covent Garden, try **Rock & Sole Plaice,** 47 Endell St. (☎ **0171/836-3785;** tube: Covent Garden). Use the all-day takeaway service and find a place to eat in the crowded Covent Garden Piazza. This is the most expensive of the chippies (because of its location); expect to pay at least £10 ($17) for a meal.

If you're in Holborn exploring legal London, try **Fryer's Delight,** 19 Theobald Rd. (☎ **0171/405-4114;** tube: Chancery Lane or Holborn), across from the Holborn Police Station. A plate of cod-and-chips is less than £4 ($7); takeaway is available from noon to 11pm.

A few blocks south of Madame Tussaud's is the **Golden Hind,** 73 Marylebone Lane (☎ **0171/486-3644;** tube: Baker St. or Bond St.), another bargain chippie where an average meal costs £5 ($8). Within easy walking distance to the west of Madame Tussaud's is **Sea-Shell,** 49–51 Lisson Grove (☎ **0171/723-8703;** tube: Marylebone), considered one of the best chippies in London; they have another location in the city near St. Paul's Cathedral at Gutter Lane, Gresham Street (☎ **0171/606-696;** tube: St. Paul's).

Near Victoria Station, you can get a good cod fillet and great chips for around £7 ($12) at **Seafresh Fish Restaurant,** 80–81 Wilton Rd. (☎ **0171/828-0747;** tube: Victoria).

Notting Hill has two inexpensive and worthwhile fish-and-chips joints: **Costas Fish Restaurant,** 18 Hillgate St. (☎ **0171/727-4310;** tube: Notting Hill Gate), and **Geales,** 2 Farmer St. (☎ **0171/727-7969;** tube: Notting Hill Gate). Both are good if you've been poking around the antiques and whatnot stands along Portobello Road.

Consuming Consumers: Department Store Restaurants

Sometimes the best way to catch a bite while you're shopping is to head for the department store's restaurant. Be aware that these might be convenient, but they are not cheap.

Fortnum & Mason, 181 Piccadilly (☎ **0171/734-8040;** tube: Piccadilly; see chapter 15) has three restaurants to choose from, **The Fountain** being the least expensive.

Harrods, in addition to its ice-cream parlor (see below) and awe-inspiring Food Hall, has **Harrods Famous Deli Counter** (☎ **0171/730-1234**), where you perch on stools (no reservations) and pay too much for what's called "traditional Jewish food" but often isn't.

Harvey Nichols (Harvey Nicks) is another Knightsbridge emporium with a restaurant: **Fifth Floor at Harvey Nichols,** 109–125 Knightsbridge

(☎ **0171/235-5250;** tube: Knightsbridge). It's open for lunch and dinner, but eating here is pretty expensive. A better bet is the cafe near the ground (first) floor entrance, where you can get a cup of tea and a salad or light meal. Like Harrods, it has a fabulous food emporium where you can buy now, eat later.

Tea for Two, Please: Tearooms & Patisseries

Yes, they drink coffee, but mostly the Brits drink tea. In fact, they swill down some 171 million cups a day. It might be served fast-food style in paper cups, home-style in mugs, or more elegantly in bone china (see "Traditional Afternoon Teas," below). Here are some down-to-earth neighborhood tearooms and patisseries where you can get a good cup of tea and a pastry, muffin, scone, or plate of tea sandwiches for about £3 to £10 ($5 to $17).

In Knightsbridge: Beverly Hills Bakery, 3 Edgerton Terrace (☎ **0171/584-4401;** tube: Knightsbridge), is noted for its muffins and serves light lunches from noon on.

In Soho and Covent Garden: Canadian Muffin Company, with three locations in Central London, specializes in low-fat, low-sugar, and fat-free muffins that you can wolf down with coffee or tea. You'll find outlets in Covent Garden at 5 King St. (☎ **0171/379-1525;** tube: Covent Garden) and in Soho at 9 Brewer St. (☎ **0171/287-3555;** tube: Leicester Square). There's also **Café Valerie,** 8 Russell St. (☎ **0171/240-0064;** tube: Covent Garden). You might have to stand in line at Soho's **Patisserie Valerie,** 44 Old Compton St. (☎ **0171/437-3466;** tube: Leicester Square or Tottenham Court Rd.), which has been around since 1926 and serves a mouthwatering array of pastries. Another great place to try in Soho is **Patisserie Cappucetto,** 809 Moor St. (☎ **0171/437-9472;** tube Leicester Square), which serves breakfast, sandwiches, soups, and superb desserts.

In Marylebone: There are also two **Patisserie Valerie** branches in Marylebone: one at 105 Marylebone High St. (☎ **0171/935-6240;** tube: Bond St. or Baker St.) and the other near Regent's Park at 66 Portland Place (☎ **0171/580-5533;** tube: Great Portland St.).

Extra! Extra!

The three old-fashioned **Richoux** tearooms, all in choice locations, serve food all day long and won't strain your budget: **Richoux-Knightsbridge,** 215 Brompton Rd. (☎ **0171/823-9971;** tube: Knightsbridge, across from Harrods); **Richoux-Mayfair,** 41a South Audley St. (☎ **0171/629-5228;** tube: Bond St. or Green Park); and **Richoux-Piccadilly,** 172 Piccadilly (☎ **0171/493-2204;** tube: Piccadilly Circus).

In St James's: There's another **Patisserie Valerie** in St. James's at 79–81 Regent St. (☎ **0171/439-0090;** tube: Piccadilly Circus).

In South Kensington: There's a branch of Canadian Muffin Company at 353 Fulham Rd. (☎ **0171/351-0015;** tube: South Kensington).

In Bloomsbury: A good choice for a quick bite is **Patisserie Deux Amis,** 63 Judd St. (☎ **0171/383-7029;** tube: Russell Square).

In Bayswater: A tempting array of French pastries is available at **Patisserie Française,** 127 Queensway (☎ **0171/229-0746;** tube: Bayswater or Queensway).

Cool Britannia

So what exactly is the difference between afternoon tea and high tea, you ask? **Afternoon tea** is tea with cakes and/or sandwiches. **High tea** is a more elaborate affair: It's a light supper with a hot dish, followed by dessert and tea.

Traditional Afternoon Teas

There's tea (drunk all day long), and then there's **tea,** a more elaborate and dressy afternoon affair. A traditional afternoon English tea—with cakes, sandwiches, and scones with clotted cream (also called Devonshire cream) and jam "taken" in a high-toned hotel or restaurant—can be a nice alternative to lunch or dinner. Keep in mind that these rather lavish affairs are expensive. You're paying for the location, the food, and the service. But at any one of the following, you'll get a very memorable traditional tea:

- **Palm Court Lounge.** In the Park Lane Hotel, Piccadilly, W1. ☎ **0171/499-6321. Tube:** Hyde Park Corner or Green Park. **Reservations:** Required. **Afternoon tea:** £14 ($22). AE, DC, MC, V. **Teatime:** Daily 3:30–6:30pm.
- **Oak Room Lounge.** In Le Meridien, 21 Piccadilly, W1. ☎ **0171/734-8000. Tube:** Piccadilly Circus or Green Park. **Reservations:** Not accepted. **Afternoon tea:** £13.50–£19.50 ($22–$31). AE, DC, MC, V. **Teatime:** Daily 3:30–6pm.
- **Ritz Palm Court.** In the Ritz Hotel, Piccadilly, W1. ☎ **0171/493-8181. Tube:** Green Park. **Reservations:** Required at least 8 weeks in advance. Jeans and sneakers not acceptable. Jacket and tie required for men. **Afternoon tea:** £23.50 ($38). AE, DC, MC, V. **Teatime:** Daily 2–6pm.
- **St. James Restaurant & The Fountain Restaurant.** In Fortnum & Mason, 181 Piccadilly, W1. ☎ **0171/734-8040. Tube:** Piccadilly Circus. **Full tea:** St. James £10.50–£12.25 ($17–$20), The Fountain £7–£10 ($11–$16). AE, DC, MC, V. **Teatime:** St. James Mon–Sat 3–5:30pm, The Fountain Mon–Sat 3–6pm.

- **Palm Court at the Waldorf Meridien.** In the Waldorf Hotel, Aldwych, WC2. ☎ **0171/836-2400. Tube:** Covent Garden. **Reservations:** Required. Jacket and tie for men at tea dance. **Afternoon tea:** £17–£20 ($27–$32). **Tea dance:** £24–£27 ($38–$43). AE, DC, MC, V. **Teatime:** Afternoon tea Mon–Fri 3–5:30pm, tea dance (with live music) Sat 2:30–5:30pm and Sun 4–6:30pm.
- **The Georgian Restaurant.** On the 4th floor of Harrods, 87–135 Brompton Rd., SW1. ☎ **0171/225-6800. Tube:** Knightsbridge. **High tea:** £15.50 ($25) per person. AE, DC, MC, V. **Teatime:** Mon–Sat 3:45–5:30pm (last order).
- **The Lanesborough.** Hyde Park Corner, SW1. ☎ **0171/259-5599. Tube**: Hyde Park Corner. **Reservations:** Required. **High tea:** £18.50 ($30), with strawberries and champagne £22.50 ($36), pot of tea £3.50 ($5.60). AE, DC, MC, V. **Teatime:** Daily 3:30–5:30pm (last order).

Meat Pies & Jellied Eels: Yum, Yum!

Londoners have been eating meat (and fish) pies and jellied eels for centuries; they were a kind of cheap fast food long before Big Macs hit the scene. Meat pies and jellied eels (which are just what they sound like—eels in gelatin) are served with mashed potatoes (mash) and a green, salty, parsley-based gravy called "liquor." Unfortunately, many of the old pie shops in Central London have hit the dust. But near the Tower of London, not far from London Bridge, you'll find **Manze's,** 84 Tower Bridge Rd. (☎ **0171/407-2985;** tube: London Bridge). It's open Monday 11am to 2pm, Tuesday through Thursday 10:30am to 2pm, Friday 10am to 2:15pm, and Saturday 10am to 2:45pm.

Kids Pasta on the Run

Want a quick, filling meal for not too much dough? Pop into one of London's pasta parlors for a plate of spaghetti or cannelloni. These places are open for lunch and dinner, and you can get a set-price meal for about £10 ($16.50). The most ubiquitous chain is **Spaghetti House,** which has several locations in Central London: in Bloomsbury at 20 Sicilian Ave. (☎ **0171/405-5215;** tube Holborn), near Leicester Square at 30 St. Martin's Lane (☎ **0171/836-1626;** tube: Leicester Square), in Marylebone (**Vecchia Milano**) at 74 Welbeck St. (☎ **0171/935-2371;** tube: Bond St.), in Knightsbridge (**Zia Teresa**) at 6 Hans Rd. (☎ **0171/589-7634;** tube: Knightsbridge), and in Bloomsbury at 15 Goodge St. (☎ **0171/636-66582;** tube: Goodge St.). Children are welcome at all these locations; high chairs and reduced-price kids' portions are available. Another big pasta chain, **Cafe Uno,** which has more than 20 branches, also provides these items for kids. The most popular is in Soho at 5 Argyll St. (☎ **0171/437-2503;** tube: Oxford Circus).

Kids Ice-Cream Parlors

If you or the kids have a hankering for an ice cream, **Häagen-Dazs** has several well-placed branches in tourist-heavy sections of London: 14 Leicester

Square (☎ **0171/287-9577;** tube: Leicester Square); Unit 6, Covent Garden Piazza (☎ **0171/240-0436;** tube: Covent Garden); and 83 Gloucester Rd. (☎ **0171/373-9988;** tube: Gloucester Rd.). They're open from 10am to midnight.

More upscale (and overpriced) is **Harrods Ice Cream Parlour & Crêperie,** 87 Brompton Rd. (☎ **0171/225-6628;** tube: Knightsbridge), on the fourth floor of Harrods department store. It's open Monday, Tuesday, and Saturday 10am to 5:30pm, and Wednesday through Friday 10am to 6:30pm.

Farther west in Bayswater, you'll find **Wintons Soda Fountain** on the second floor of Whiteley's Shopping Centre, 151 Queensway (☎ **0171/229-8489;** tube: Bayswater or Queensway). It's open Monday through Thursday and Sunday 11am to 10pm, and Friday and Saturday 11am to 11pm. **Regent Milk Bar,** 362 Edgware Rd. (☎ **0171/723-8669;** tube: Edgware Rd.), is a classic 1950s milk bar offering 20 flavors of ice cream. Popular with families, it's open daily from 9:30am to 5:30pm.

Where to Have a Picnic

Everyone loves a picnic, but eating alfresco in London is often a dicey affair. Rain can quickly put a damper on a picnic hamper. But on balmy spring days and warm summer afternoons, it's fun to pack up some sandwiches and head to a green, leafy spot for an outdoor nosh. In the area around the West End, you'll find all the necessary provisions in delis and sandwich shops (or expensive Fortnum & Mason). In neighborhoods outside the West End (South Kensington or Marylebone, for example), you can stop in at a supermarket and generally find packaged sandwiches, crisps (potato chips), and drinks.

In the West End, the Embankment Gardens is a good picnic spot. You'll find this green, flower-filled strip of park (you'll have to sit on benches instead of the grass) right next to the Embankment tube station, below the Savoy Hotel. It looks out on the Thames, and traffic along the Embankment can be distracting, but it's pretty nonetheless.

A favorite picnicking spot in the city—especially with children—is **Kensington Gardens.** Here you'll find vast green lawns, play areas, splashing fountains, Kensington Palace, and the famous statue of Peter Pan. The park is close to all the great museums in South Kensington. Adjacent **Hyde Park** is another relaxing spot, particularly along the shores of Serpentine Lake. You can buy sandwiches and snacks at the Dell Restaurant (see "Hyde Park" in chapter 13) at the east end of the lake. In the summer, bandstand concerts are given in the park.

The "royal parks"—**Green Park** and **St. James's Park**—are more sedate. Here you can spread out on the grass under a leafy London plane tree within eyeshot of Buckingham Palace.

Across the Thames, on the **South Bank,** you'll find benches along the riverside promenade close to Royal Festival Hall and the National Theatre. There are trees and flowers but no lawns for lazing; on the other hand, you're right next to the mighty Thames.

Part 5

Ready, Set, Go! Exploring London

After you arrive at your hotel, unpack, freshen up, and look at a map or two, the real fun begins. You're ready to step out into London. This is always a magical moment. Even if you're so jet-lagged you can't see straight, it's a good idea to go out for an exploratory stroll. Walking is a good way to recharge your batteries.

Where to begin when there's so much to see and do? If you're traveling with children, have very limited time, or are simply a bit nervous about exploring on your own, you'll find the list of guided-tour possibilities in chapter 12 quite helpful. Given London's size, a guided tour can be fun and relaxing even if you're the kind of traveler who normally craves complete independence. On the other hand, if you're raring to see the city's top attractions on your own, you'll find them—along with directions, opening hours, and admission prices—in chapter 13. One of the great things about London sightseeing, though, is that it can be as general or as specialized as you want. Browsing through chapter 14, which gives you a rundown of other intriguing museums and sights (not the most popular, but definitely worth considering), you'll see just how much this great city has to offer. Check out chapter 15 for some great tips on how to make the most of your shopping in London, as well as specific places to visit. In chapter 16, you'll find eight great walking-tour itineraries. These guide you to many of London's most-visited historic sights but have the added advantage of introducing you to special London neighborhoods. Then, chapter 17 will help you design your own day-by-day itineraries: These commonsense tips and strategies will help you maximize your sightseeing time without having a nervous breakdown in the process.

Chapter 12

Should I Just Take a Guided Tour?

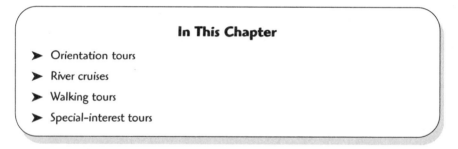

In This Chapter

- Orientation tours
- River cruises
- Walking tours
- Special-interest tours

Confronted by the immenseness and complexity of London, many first-time visitors just don't know where or how to begin their explorations. With a limited amount of time and so much ground to cover, I'll admit it can be daunting. But, hey, that's why you bought this book in the first place, right? I'll help you figure it all out. The first step is to carefully read through the list of top sights in the next chapter (and the additional sights in chapter 14) and decide what it is that's really important for you to see. Are you a culture vulture, a history buff, or a garden fan? Using public transportation, you can get to every sight that's listed and spend as much or as little time at each as you want.

But what if you want to get a general overview of the city first? Or you're just not able to navigate the Underground or walk for any distance? Or you have only a couple of days and still want to cover the principal sights, such as Westminster Abbey, Buckingham Palace, and the Tower of London? That's where a guided tour comes in handy.

Who, Me? Take a Guided Tour?

Guided tours are often pooh-poohed as the most boring way to see the sights. Nowadays, and especially in London, that's baloney. There are many tours that can open up this fascinating city to you in ways that are fun and exciting. They reduce the complications of finding your way around and allow you to concentrate on aspects of London that are of particular interest.

By Bus, Boat, or Pavement: Which London Tour Is Right for Me?

When it comes to sightseeing tours of London, you're limited only by your imagination, stamina, and pocketbook. You can tour London in a luxury motor coach equipped with rest rooms or from the top of a double-decker. These ways are listed under "Where Am I? Orientation Tours" below. You can sail down the Thames on one of the boats described in "River Dance: Thames Cruises." Or you can hoof it with a walking tour. There's something to be said for all of these choices.

Of course the best way to fully experience any city is to get out and explore it on your own. You can learn so much by getting lost! But sometimes exploring on your own is easier after you've oriented yourself with a tour. You might want to bring along a copy of ***Frommer's Memorable Walks in London,*** which has 11 self-guided perambulations of London's most historic and colorful neighborhoods. And check out chapter 16 of this book, which contains eight special walking tours.

Where Am I? Orientation Tours

You'll notice in the following list that all but one of the general sightseeing companies offer variations of **two basic half-day orientation tours.** One tour is an excursion that covers sights in the West End and includes a stop-off visit at Westminster Abbey and a chance to see the Changing of the Guard at Buckingham Palace. The second basic tour heads east into the city, with stops at St. Paul's Cathedral and the Tower of London.

Time-Savers

You can reserve tickets for all the orientation tours discussed in this chapter at the London Tourist Board and London Transport Information Centres, at most Central London hotels, or through your travel agent.

London Pride Sightseeing (☎ **01708/631-122**) provides a variety of tours on a fleet of double-decker buses, many of them open on top. All their tours offer hop-on/hop-off service at 90 boarding points throughout the city (look for London Pride bus-stop signs; they are everywhere). You're free to pick and choose where you want to stop and spend more time. **The Grand Tour** lasts 90 minutes and passes every major site in Central London and the South Bank; tours start from Piccadilly Circus (tube: Piccadilly Circus) outside the Trocadero on Coventry Street and depart every 15 minutes daily, year-round, from 9am to 6pm (9am to 9pm in the summer). **Cityrama,** a 2-hour sightseeing tour of the principal sights, offers prerecorded commentary in eight languages; tours leave from Cockspur Street on Trafalgar Square (tube: Charing Cross) every half hour daily from 9am to 5pm. London Pride's **Green Route** circuit links all the major museums (and Harrods); buses leave from Russell Square in Bloomsbury. You don't have to book in advance for any of these tours, and you can pay on the bus. Full-day tours are also available, some of which include a cruise on the Thames. A ticket good for 24 hours on all London Pride Sightseeing routes costs £12 ($20) for adults and £6 ($10) for children under 16.

Tourist Traps

Keep in mind that the **Changing of the Guard** at Buckingham Palace is no longer a daily occurrence; it happens every other day from August 1 to March 31 (although this is subject to change; see chapter 13 for details). If it's not going on the day you take your tour, you'll be taken to see the Household Calvary in Whitehall instead.

Original London Sightseeing Tours, Jews Row, London SW18 (☎ **0181/877-1722**), is another all-purpose sightseeing company that uses open-topped double-decker buses (ideal for photo ops). Pickups are at Victoria Coach Station, Marble Arch, Haymarket, and Baker Street. Tours cost £12 ($20) for adults and £6 ($10) for children under the age of 16.

More expensive, and more individualized, are the tours offered by **Visitors Sightseeing Tours,** Departure Lounge, Royal National Hotel, Bedford Way (☎ **0171/636-7175;** tube: Russell Square). Tours, available Monday through Saturday, are conducted on luxury buses with certified guides; tour prices vary according to itinerary.

Extra! Extra!

On Wednesday, Friday, and Sunday, **Visitors Sightseeing Tours** offers a macabre evening (6:50pm) tour called **"Ghosts, Ghouls & Ancient Taverns"** that explores sights associated with Jack the Ripper and the medieval plague and stops in at a couple of pubs along the way. The cost is £15 ($25); the tour is not recommended for children under 14. You can reserve seats by calling direct (☎ **0171/636-7175**).

Another tour company with many different guided excursions to choose from is **Golden Tours,** 4 Fountain Square, 123–151 Buckingham Palace Rd. (☎ **800/456-6303** in the U.S., or 0171/233-7030; e-mail Goldtour@aol.com). Their buses are comfy and have rest rooms, and the certified guides have a certifiable sense of humor. **Tour 1 (Historic & Modern London),** offered daily, is a full-day outing that includes the West End, Westminster Abbey, the Changing of the Guard, the City of London, St. Paul's Cathedral, the Tower of London, and a cruise from the Tower down to Charing Cross Pier; a pub lunch is included along the way, as well as tea aboard ship. The cost is £49.50 ($82) for adults and £42.50 ($70) for kids under 16; all admission prices are included, so this one turns out to be a real winner in terms of what you see and how much you pay. Tours depart from the office at Buckingham Palace Road and other points in Central London; courtesy pickup service is also offered from several hotels. You can book your tickets directly or at Selfridges department store.

River Dance: Thames Cruises

Sightseeing tours in London are not confined to the land. A cruise down the majestic Thames is a marvelous way to take in the sights of the city. Sightseeing boats regularly ply the river between Westminster and the Tower of London. Some continue downstream to Greenwich (see chapter 14)—site of the Prime Meridian Line, the *Cutty Sark,* and the Old Royal Observatory—and upstream to Kew Gardens and Hampton Court. Along the way, many of London's greatest monuments—the Houses of Parliament, Westminster Abbey, St. Paul's Cathedral, the Tower and Tower Bridge—can be seen. Boat tours are surefire kid-pleasers, but adults will find them just as enjoyable. The main departure points along the Thames are at Westminster Pier (tube: Westminster), Charing Cross Pier (tube: Charing Cross), Temple Pier (tube: Temple), Tower Pier (tube: Tower Hill), and Greenwich Pier (a few minutes from Greenwich Station). For recorded information on what's available, call ☎ **0839/123432.**

Evan Evans (☎ **0181/332-2222;** fax 0181/784-2835; e-mail reservations@evanevans.co.uk; www.evanevans.co.uk), in addition to daily coach tours of London, offers three river cruises. A daily luncheon cruise on board the *Silver Bonito* costs £14.50 ($24) per person. Another daily offering starts with a guided bus tour of the city and continues down the Thames on board a chartered vessel; the price is £17 ($28) for adults and £15 ($25) for children ages 3 to 17. A full-day tour, offered daily, takes in Westminster Abbey, continues through Westminster to Buckingham Palace for the Changing of the Guard, includes a lunch cruise on the Thames, and returns by bus to St. Paul's and the Tower of London. The price is £49.50 ($82) for adults and £45.50 ($75) for children.

Catamaran Cruisers (☎ **0171/839-1034**) runs a year-round fleet of boats on the Thames from Charing Cross Pier to the Tower of London and Greenwich. A round-trip ticket from Charing Cross to the Tower is £5.80 ($10) for adults and £3.30 ($5) for children under 16. From Charing Cross to Greenwich, the round-trip fare is £7 ($12) for adults and £3.80 ($6) for children. From May to September, they have a nightly 45-minute circular cruise from Charing Cross Pier (6:30, 7:30, and 10:30pm) that passes most of London's major floodlit monuments; the cost is £5.60 ($9) for adults and £3.60 ($6) for children. All the boats provide live commentary and have a fully licensed bar on board.

One of London's best and most affordable sightseeing cruises is the hour-long **Royal River Thames Cruise** (☎ **0171/930-4097**) from Westminster to Greenwich. From November to March, hourly departures take place from 10:40am to 3:20pm from Westminster Pier. From April to October, boats leave about every half hour from 10:00am to 5pm. In the summer, the boats have both open and closed decks. Light refreshments and bar service are available on all boats. The round-trip cost is £6.70 ($11) for adults, £5.50 ($9) for senior citizens, and £3.50 ($6) for children. A family rate of £18 ($30) for two adults and three children is also available.

Dining on the River

Bateaux London, Charing Cross Pier, Victoria Embankment (☎ **0171/925-2215**), offers a nightly dinner cruise that leaves Temple Pier at 8pm and returns at 10:30pm. The cruise, which includes a four-course dinner with live music and after-dinner dancing, costs £53 ($87) per person. A 1-hour lunch cruise with a three-course set-menu meal and live commentary is offered Monday through Saturday and costs £19.50 ($32) per person. It departs from Temple Pier at 12:30pm. A 2-hour (three-course) Sunday lunch cruise departs from Charing Cross Pier at 12:45pm; it costs £26 ($43) per person. Reservations are required for all of these, and there's a "smart casual" dress code.

Walkie-Talkies: Walking Tours of London

A walking tour is a fabulous, affordable way to see London from street level in the company of a truly knowledgeable guide. For history, literature, and architecture buffs, these tours are great, and older kids generally have a good time as well.

London Walks, P.O. Box 1708, London NW6 4LW (☎ **0171/624-3978;** http://london.walks.com; e-mail londonwalks@mail.bogo.co.uk), is the oldest established walking-tour company in London. It has a terrific array of tours, including Jack the Ripper's London and The Beatles' Magical Mystery Tour. There are different walks every day of the week, rain or shine; they last about 2 hours and end near an Underground station. There is no need to reserve in advance. A London Walk costs £4.50 ($7) for adults and £3.50 ($6) for students with ID; kids are free if accompanied by a parent. Write, e-mail, or call for more information, or pick up a brochure at the Tourist Informa-tion Centre in the forecourt of Victoria Station.

Another company offering walking tours is **Citisights of London,** 213 Brooke Rd., London E5 8AB (☎ **0181/806-4325;** e-mail KPFlude@aol.com; www.aoll.mrmbrtd.com\LinHamlon\chr.html).

Stepping Out, 32 Elvendon Rd. (☎ **0180/881-2933**), offers guided walking tours of Southwark on the South Bank. One offbeat theme walk called "Brothels, Bishops and the Bard," explores the Clink (the oldest prison in London), Shakespeare's memorial window in Southwark Cathedral, and the site of the original Globe Theatre.

Visitors with a special interest in London history can call **Historical Walks of London,** 3 Florence Rd., South Croydon (☎ **0181/668-4019**), for information on current offerings.

London Pub Walks (☎ **0181/883-2656**) combines a walking tour with a pub crawl; as you visit old pubs, you learn the history of English beer. Walks depart from the Temple tube stop every Friday at 7:30pm. There's no need to book in advance, and the cost is £4 ($7).

For gays and lesbians, there's a weekly, independently operated **Gay Walk** that costs £5 ($8). Check the Gay listings in *Time Out* magazine for times and departure points.

London Garden Tours

Expo Garden Tours, 70 Great Oak, Dept. 8, Redding, CT 06896 (☎ **800/448-2685;** e-mail gardentrav@aol.com; http://gardennet.com/ExpoGardenTours/), specializes in English garden tours. Two of their offerings include tours of public and private gardens in the countryside plus a visit to the Chelsea Flower Show in London in May. **Select Travel Service,** 99 Bauer Dr., Oakland, NJ 07436 (☎ **800/752-6787;** www.SelectTravel.com; e-mail info@selectTravel.com), also provides tours of the Spring-time Extravaganza in Chelsea. Both must be booked before you leave the States.

Chapter 13

London's Top Sights from A to Z

In This Chapter

- The top attractions indexed by location and type
- Full write-ups of the "A" list sights, including what to see, when to see it, and how much it will cost
- Worksheet to help you budget your sightseeing time

At last we come to the meat and potatoes (or roast beef and Yorkshire pudding) of your trip: the sights of London. This dazzling metropolis has 2,000 years of history behind it, and it's loaded with famous monuments, fabulous museums, fascinating historical buildings, and flower-filled parks. Seeing everything would take a lifetime, but with some sound planning, you'll be able to dip and delve into London as deeply as your time and energy allow. You might be covering a lot of ground, but if you augment my directions with a ***London A to Z*** map, you're unlikely to get lost. And even if you do—so what? That's part of the adventure of travel. If you get lost or turned around, just ask any passerby. Londoners are unfailingly polite and uncommonly helpful.

Since this is a city with 150 museums, 600 art galleries, and countless places of interest, considerable planning is needed for sightseeing. You can use the **worksheet** at the end of this chapter for just that. As you read through the list of sights, put a check mark next to the "must-sees" (or whatever sounds interesting). Then, when you've finished reading up on all the sights, list all the check-marked attractions on the worksheet at the end of the chapter, making note of the best time to visit and how long you expect to spend there. Next, go back over your list and rank each attraction on a scale of 1 to 5 (with 1s being your must-not-leave-London-before-I-see-this attractions). The sights in this chapter are the most important, but they represent only the tip of the iceberg. There's plenty more to choose from in chapter 14. Chapter 17 gives you additional useful information about planning workable itineraries.

The sights of London are arranged in alphabetical order and are cross-referenced when necessary. Whenever there's something that children will enjoy, it's marked with a "Kids" icon.

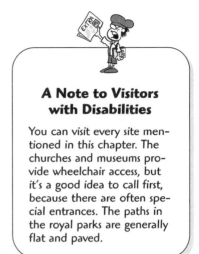

A Note to Visitors with Disabilities

You can visit every site mentioned in this chapter. The churches and museums provide wheelchair access, but it's a good idea to call first, because there are often special entrances. The paths in the royal parks are generally flat and paved.

Quick Picks—London's Top Attractions at a Glance
Index by Location

Bloomsbury

British Museum

City of London

Museum of London

St. Paul's Cathedral

Tower of London

Covent Garden

Covent Garden Market & Piazza

Kensington & South Kensington

Kensington Gardens

Kensington Palace

Natural History Museum

Science Museum

Victoria and Albert Museum

Marylebone

London Zoo

Madame Tussaud's

Regent's Park

Piccadilly Circus, Leicester Square & Charing Cross

Leicester Square

Piccadilly Circus

Pimlico

Tate Gallery

St. James's

Buckingham Palace

National Gallery

National Portrait Gallery

St. James's Park/Green Park

Trafalgar Square

Westminster

Houses of Parliament/Big Ben

Hyde Park

Westminster Abbey

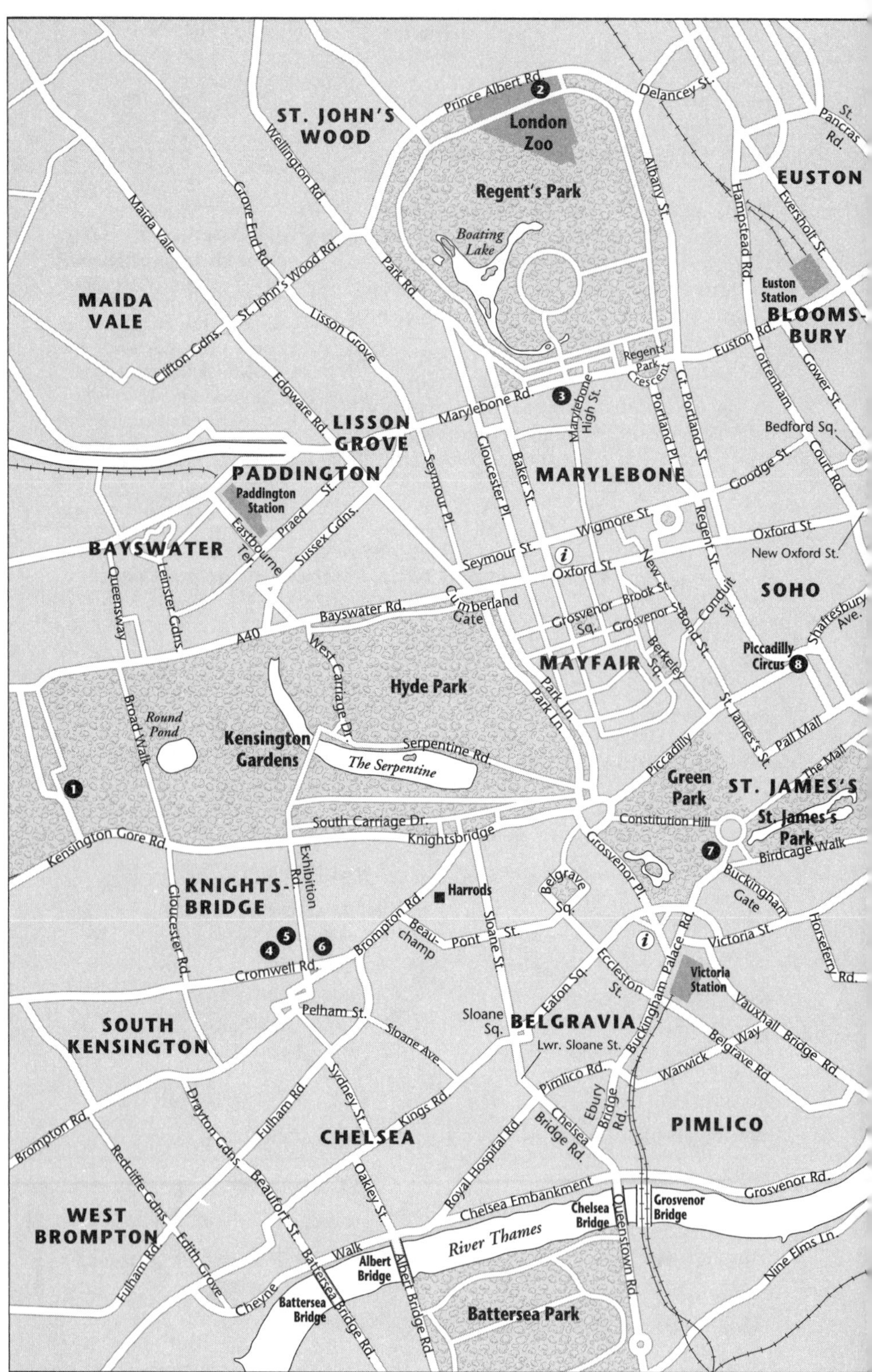

Prince Albert Rd.
Delancey St.
St. Pancras Rd.
ST. JOHN'S WOOD
London Zoo
Regent's Park
EUSTON
Wellington Rd.
Albany St.
Hampstead Rd.
Eversholt St.
Maida Vale
Grove End Rd.
Boating Lake
St. John's Wood Rd.
Park Rd.
Euston Station
MAIDA VALE
BLOOMSBURY
Lisson Grove
Clifton Gdns.
Regents' Park Crescent
Euston Rd.
Tottenham
Gower St.
Edgware Rd.
Marylebone Rd.
Marylebone High St.
Portland Pl.
Gt. Portland St.
LISSON GROVE
Bedford Sq.
Court Rd.
Seymour Pl.
Gloucester Pl.
Baker St.
PADDINGTON
MARYLEBONE
Goodge St.
Paddington Station
Praed St.
Eastbourne Ter.
Sussex Gdns.
Wigmore St.
Regent St.
Oxford St.
BAYSWATER
New Oxford St.
Leinster Gdns.
Queensway
Seymour St.
Oxford St.
New Bond St.
Cumberland Gate
Brook St.
Conduit St.
SOHO
Bayswater Rd.
Grosvenor Sq.
Grosvenor St.
Shaftesbury Ave.
A40
West Carriage Dr.
Berkeley Sq.
MAYFAIR
Piccadilly Circus
Hyde Park
Park Ln.
Broad Walk
Round Pond
St. James's St.
Pall Mall
Kensington Gardens
Serpentine Rd.
The Serpentine
Piccadilly
The Mall
Green Park
ST. JAMES'S
St. James's Park
Constitution Hill
South Carriage Dr.
Kensington Gore Rd.
Knightsbridge
Birdcage Walk
Grosvenor Pl.
Exhibition Rd.
Belgrave Sq.
Buckingham Gate
KNIGHTSBRIDGE
Harrods
Gloucester Rd.
Brompton Rd.
Beauchamp
Sloane St.
Pont St.
Buckingham Palace Rd.
Victoria St.
Horseferry Rd.
Cromwell Rd.
Eccleston St.
Eaton Sq.
Victoria Station
Pelham St.
Vauxhall Bridge Rd.
SOUTH KENSINGTON
Sloane Sq.
BELGRAVIA
Sloane Ave.
Lwr. Sloane St.
Belgrave Rd.
Warwick Way
Drayton Gdns.
Fulham Rd.
Sydney St.
Pimlico Rd.
Brompton Rd.
Kings Rd.
Chelsea Bridge Rd.
Ebury Bridge Rd.
Royal Hospital Rd.
CHELSEA
PIMLICO
Redcliffe Gdns.
Beaufort St.
Oakley St.
Chelsea Embankment
Grosvenor Rd.
WEST BROMPTON
Chelsea Bridge
Grosvenor Bridge
Queenstown Rd.
Edith Grove
River Thames
Nine Elms Ln.
Fulham Rd.
Cheyne Walk
Albert Bridge
Battersea Bridge
Battersea Bridge Rd.
Albert Bridge Rd.
Battersea Park
1
2
3
4
5
6
7
8

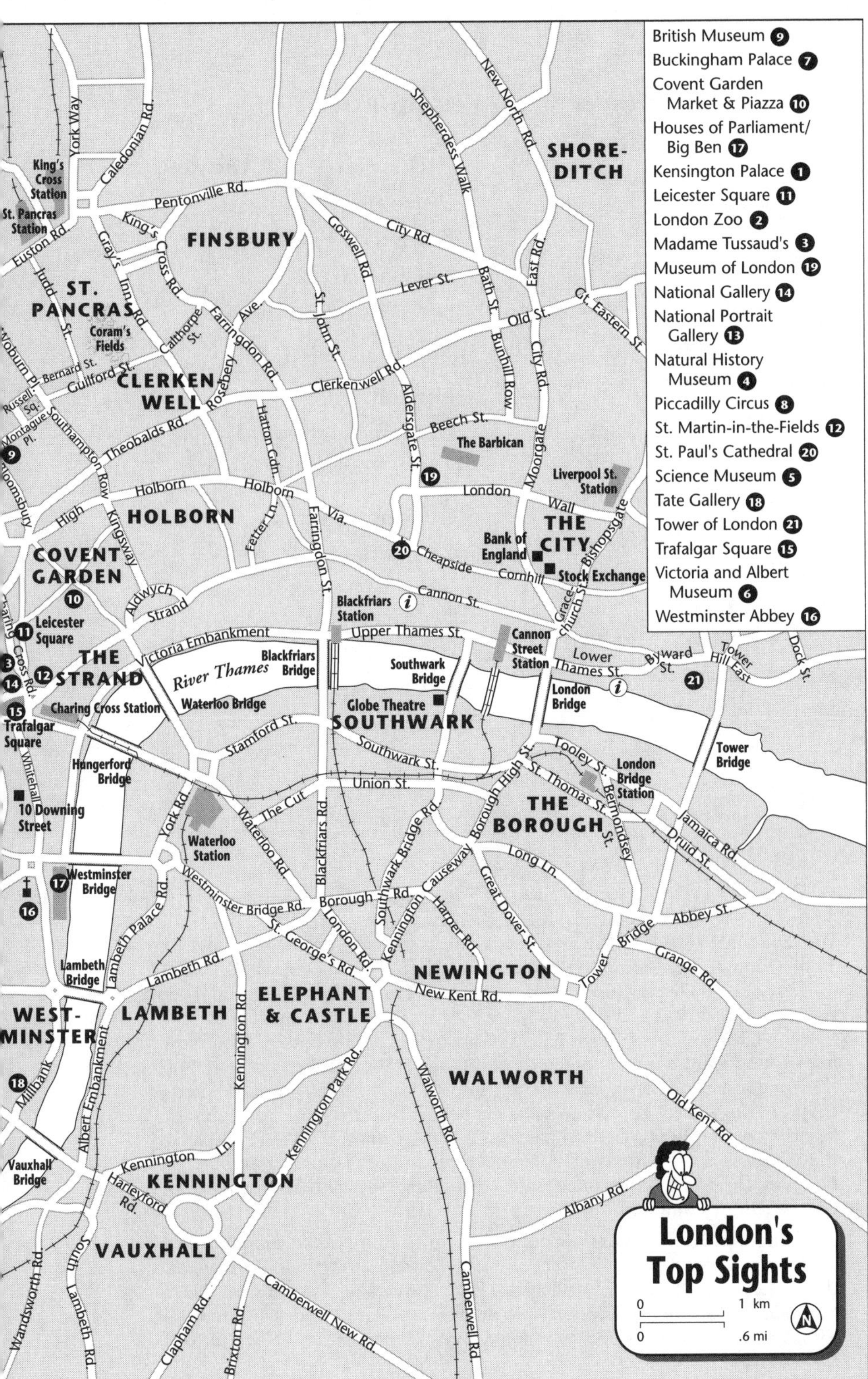
London's Top Sights
British Museum 9
Buckingham Palace 7
Covent Garden Market & Piazza 10
Houses of Parliament/ Big Ben 17
Kensington Palace 1
Leicester Square 11
London Zoo 2
Madame Tussaud's 3
Museum of London 19
National Gallery 14
National Portrait Gallery 13
Natural History Museum 4
Piccadilly Circus 8
St. Martin-in-the-Fields 12
St. Paul's Cathedral 20
Science Museum 5
Tate Gallery 18
Tower of London 21
Trafalgar Square 15
Victoria and Albert Museum 6
Westminster Abbey 16
0 1 km
0 .6 mi
N
SHORE-DITCH
FINSBURY
ST. PANCRAS
CLERKEN-WELL
HOLBORN
COVENT GARDEN
THE STRAND
THE CITY
SOUTHWARK
THE BOROUGH
NEWINGTON
ELEPHANT & CASTLE
LAMBETH
WEST-MINSTER
WALWORTH
KENNINGTON
VAUXHALL
King's Cross Station
St. Pancras Station
Coram's Fields
The Barbican
Liverpool St. Station
Bank of England
Stock Exchange
Blackfriars Station
Cannon Street Station
River Thames
Blackfriars Bridge
Southwark Bridge
London Bridge
Tower Bridge
Waterloo Bridge
Globe Theatre
Charing Cross Station
Trafalgar Square
Leicester Square
Hungerford Bridge
10 Downing Street
Waterloo Station
London Bridge Station
Westminster Bridge
Lambeth Bridge
Vauxhall Bridge
Pentonville Rd.
Caledonian Rd.
York Way
Euston Rd.
King's Cross Rd.
Gray's Inn Rd.
Judd St.
City Rd.
Goswell Rd.
Shepherdess Walk
New North Rd.
East Rd.
Lever St.
Bath St.
Old St.
Gt. Eastern St.
Bunhill Row
City Rd.
St. John St.
Farringdon Rd.
Rosebery Ave.
Calthorpe St.
Guilford St.
Bernard St.
Woburn Pl.
Russell Sq.
Montague Pl.
Bloomsbury
Southampton Row
Theobalds Rd.
Clerkenwell Rd.
Aldersgate St.
Beech St.
Moorgate
Hatton Gdn.
Holborn
Holborn Via.
London Wall
Bishopsgate
High Holborn
Kingsway
Fetter Ln.
Farringdon St.
Cheapside
Cornhill
Cannon St.
Aldwych
Strand
Victoria Embankment
Upper Thames St.
Lower Thames St.
Gracechurch St.
Byward St.
Tower Hill East
Dock St.
Charing Cross Rd.
Whitehall
Stamford St.
Southwark St.
Union St.
Tooley St.
St. Thomas St.
Bermondsey St.
Jamaica Rd.
Druid St.
The Cut
Waterloo Rd.
York Rd.
Blackfriars Rd.
Southwark Bridge Rd.
Borough High St.
Long Ln.
Westminster Bridge Rd.
Borough Rd.
Lambeth Palace Rd.
London Rd.
St. George's Rd.
Harper Rd.
Great Dover St.
Kennington Causeway
Abbey St.
Tower Bridge Rd.
Grange Rd.
Lambeth Rd.
New Kent Rd.
Kennington Rd.
Millbank
Albert Embankment
Kennington Park Rd.
Walworth Rd.
Old Kent Rd.
Kennington Ln.
Harleyford Rd.
Albany Rd.
Wandsworth Rd.
South Lambeth Rd.
Clapham Rd.
Brixton Rd.
Camberwell New Rd.
Camberwell Rd.

Index by Type of Attraction

Museums
British Museum
Madame Tussaud's
Museum of London
National Gallery
National Portrait Gallery
Natural History Museum
Science Museum
Tate Gallery
Victoria and Albert Museum

Palaces & Other Historic Buildings
Buckingham Palace
Houses of Parliament/Big Ben
Kensington Palace
Tower of London

Parks, Gardens & the Zoo
Hyde Park
Kensington Gardens
London Zoo
Regent's Park
St. James's Park/Green Park

Churches
St. Paul's Cathedral
Westminster Abbey

Famous Squares
Covent Garden Market and Piazza
Leicester Square
Piccadilly Circus
Trafalgar Square

Dollars & Sense

The London **White Card** is a money-saving pass that provides admittance to 15 museums and galleries. Adult cards cost £16 ($26) for 3 days or £26 ($43) for 7 days; a family pass (up to two adults and four children 16 or under) costs £32 ($53) for 3 days and £50 ($82) for 7 days. White Cards are sold at the Britain Visitor Centre, 1 Regent St., SW1 (tube: Piccadilly Circus); the Tourist Information Centre in the forecourt of Victoria Station (tube: Victoria); and the London Visitor Centre at Waterloo International (tube: Waterloo). See chapter 7 for more information on these tourist-board offices. You can also buy the London White Card in participating museums and galleries, including the Victoria and Albert Museum, Museum of London, London Transport Museum, Design Museum, Imperial War Museum, Hayward Gallery, and Natural History Museum.

With one **London for Less** discount card, up to four people can get a week's worth of reduced-price admissions to many London attractions not covered by the White Card, including Buckingham Palace, Madame Tussaud's, St. Paul's Cathedral, the Tower of London, and many more. London for Less cards cost $19.95 + $4.95 shipping and handling; you can order one by calling ☎ **888/463-6753.**

The Top Sights

British Museum

Bloomsbury.

One of the world's greatest repositories of art and antiquities, the British Museum is so huge that you'd need a month just to scratch the surface. Wandering through its 94 galleries, you can't help but be struck by humankind's enduring creative spirit. There are permanent displays of antiquities from Egypt, Western Asia, Greece, and Rome, as well as prehistoric and Romano-British, Medieval, Renaissance, Modern, and Oriental collections. The most famous of the museum's countless treasures are the **Elgin Marbles,** the sculptures that once adorned the Parthenon (and which Greece wants returned); the **Rosetta Stone** (which allowed archaeologists to decipher Egyptian hieroglyphics); the **Egyptian mummies;** and the **Sutton Hoo Treasure,** an Anglo-Saxon burial ship believed to be the tomb of a 7th-century East Anglian king. There's a museum cafe (see chapter 11) and a very good bookshop and card store.

Extra! Extra!

The incredible literary cache that was once housed in the British Museum (including its rare copy of the Magna Carta) has been moved to a remarkable new gallery space in North London. For details see "British Library Exhibition Centre" in chapter 14.

Great Russell St. (between Bloomsbury St. and Montgomery St.), WC1. ☎ ***0171/ 636-1555. Tube:*** *Russell Square, then a 5-minute walk south on Montgomery St., along the west side of Russell Square, to the museum entrance on Great Russell St.* ***Admission:*** *Free.* ***Open:*** *Mon–Sat 10am–5pm, Sun 2:30–6pm. Closed Jan 1, Good Friday, Dec 24–26. Most of the museum has wheelchair access via elevators; call first for entrance information.*

Time-Savers

If you have only limited time to cover the highlights of the British Museum (and not get lost in the $2^1/_2$ miles of galleries), consider taking one of the £6 ($10) hour-long guided tours. They are offered Monday to Saturday at 10:45am, 11:15am, 1:45pm, and 2:15pm; and on Sundays at 3pm, 3:20pm, and 3:45pm. Tickets are available at the information desk.

Cool Britannia

In 1993 the Queen allowed Buckingham Palace to be opened to the public for the first time; it will remain open at least to the year 2000. What you see on a palace tour: 18 rooms, most of them Baroque, filled with some of the world's finest works of art. You can see where the Queen and members of the Royal Family receive guests on official occasions. At the end of the visit, you leave via the Bow Room and the gardens where the Queen's garden parties are held each summer.

Buckingham Palace

St. James's.

All the scandal, intrigue, tragedy, power, wealth, and tradition associated with the British monarchy is hidden behind the monumental facade of Buckingham Palace, the London residence of the British sovereign since Victoria ascended the throne in 1837. An impressive early-18th-century pile, the palace was rebuilt in 1825 and further modified in 1913. The pageantry of the **Changing of the Guard** is no longer a daily occurrence (see below), but in August and September, when the royal family is not in residence, you can buy a ticket and get a glimpse of the impressive state-rooms used by Queen Elizabeth II. You can also visit (throughout the year) **the Queen's Gallery,** which features changing exhibitions of works from the Royal Collection, and **the Royal Mews,** one of the finest working stables in existence, where the magnificent Gold State Coach and other royal conveyances are housed.

Buckingham Palace Rd., SW1. Palace Visitor Office, Queen's Gallery, and Royal Mews ☎ ***0171/839 1377*** *(9:30am–5:30pm) or 0171/799-2331 (24-hour recorded information).* ***Tube:*** *St. James's Park, then a 10-minute walk north on Queen Anne's Gate and west on Birdcage Walk to Buckingham Gate; or Green Park (from the tube stop you walk directly south through the park to the palace).* ***Admission:*** *Palace tours £9 ($15) adults, £6.50 ($12) seniors over age 60, £5 ($8) children under age 17. Queen's Gallery £4 ($7) adults, £3 ($5) seniors, £2 ($4) children. Royal Mews £4 ($7) adults, £2 ($4) children. Family ticket for Queen's Gallery and*

Time-Savers

You can charge tickets for Buckingham Palace tours by calling ☎ **0171/321-2233;** all phone-charged tickets are £9.50 ($16), but you save yourself the time and bother of queuing up for tickets outside the palace. Tickets purchased in advance guarantee entry at a specific time. All other ticket holders should be prepared to spend upwards of an hour in line before getting inside the palace and sometimes that long at the ticket office beforehand.

Royal Mews £10 ($17). Visitors with disabilities must prebook for palace tours; Royal Mews is wheelchair accessible, but Queen's Gallery is not. The ticket office, across from the palace, opens at 9am and closes after the last ticket is sold. ***Open:*** *Palace Aug 6–Oct 4 daily 9:30am–4:30pm. Queen's Gallery (entrance on Buckingham Palace Rd.) daily 9:30am–4:30pm, closed Mar 28, Dec 25–26. Royal Mews Jan 1–March 24 and Oct 3–Dec 31 Wed noon–4pm; March 25–Aug 3 Tues–Thurs noon–4pm; Aug 4–Oct 2 Mon–Thurs 10:30am–4:30pm; closed Dec 24. The Changing of the Guard generally takes place daily at 11:15am April–July and then every other day Aug–March, although this is subject to change. For more information on Royal Mews opening hours and the Changing of the Guard, both of which change with bewildering frequency, you can phone* ***Visitorcall*** *at* ☎ ***01839/123-456.***

Extra! Extra!

Just what's going on during the **Changing of the Guard?** It's carried out by the Foot Guards of the Household Division of the Army, the Queen's personal guard. The Old Guard forms in the Palace forecourt before going off duty and handing everything over to the New Guard, which leaves Wellington Barracks at 11:27am precisely and marches to the Palace via Birdcage Walk, usually accompanied by a band. The Guard consists of three officers and 40 men but is reduced when the Queen is away. The entire ceremony takes around 40 minutes. If you can't find a spot at the front of the railings of Buckingham Palace, you can see pretty well from the Victoria Memorial in front of the palace.

If you miss the Changing of the Guard, or it's not on the day you're there, you can get an eyeful of London pageantry by attending the **Mounted Guard Changing Ceremony** at the **Horse Guards Building** in Whitehall. It takes place Monday through Saturday at 11am, and Sunday at 10am. No ticket is required, but arrive early for a good view. To get there, take the tube to Charing Cross and walk south from Trafalgar Square along Whitehall (about a 5-minute walk); the Horse Guards Building will be on your right.

Kids Covent Garden Market and Piazza

Covent Garden used to be a teeming, raucous public market where loud-mouthed vendors hawked everything from fish to flowers (remember Eliza Doolittle in *My Fair Lady?)*. In 1970, the market moved out and the area became the site of one of London's earliest and most successful "urban recycling" schemes. The market buildings now house dozens of upscale shops and eating and drinking establishments, but the wrought-iron stalls in the former flower market are loaded with more downmarket vendors selling the good, the bad, and the ugly. The Piazza in front is probably the most popular public gathering point outside of Trafalgar Square. Covent Garden is also the home of the **Royal Opera House** (see chapter 19) and the **Theatre Museum** (see chapter 14).

Tube: *Covent Garden. When you come out of the tube stop you're in Covent Garden. The Market and Piazza are a 2-minute walk south in a pedestrian-only zone.*

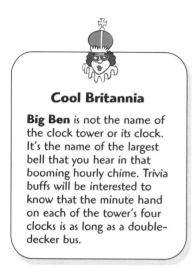

Cool Britannia

Big Ben is not the name of the clock tower or its clock. It's the name of the largest bell that you hear in that booming hourly chime. Trivia buffs will be interested to know that the minute hand on each of the tower's four clocks is as long as a double-decker bus.

Houses of Parliament/ Big Ben

Westminster.

The Thames-side Houses of Parliament, with the landmark clock tower known as Big Ben, are an undeniably impressive example of Victorian architecture doing its "Neo-Gothic" thing. Designed by Sir Charles Barry and A. W. N. Pugin, the buildings were completed in 1857. Covering some 8 acres, they occupy the site of an 11th-century palace of Edward the Confessor. At one end (Old Palace Yard) is the **Jewel House,** built in 1366 and once the treasury house of Edward III, who reigned from 1327 to 1377. For most visitors, a glimpse of the exterior is sufficient, but if you want to sit in the **Stranger's Gallery** to hear the squabbling that passes for debate, you can line up (pardon me, *queue*) for tickets at the St. Stephen's entrance.

Bridge Street and Parliament Square, SW1. House of Commons ☎ ***0171/219-4272;*** *House of Lords* ☎ ***0171/219-3107. Tube:*** *Westminster; you'll see Big Ben directly across Bridge St.* ***Admission:*** *Free. Join the queue at the St. Stephen's entrance.* ***Open:*** *House of Lords Mon–Wed from 2:30pm, Thurs from 3pm. House of Commons Mon–Tues and Thurs from 3:30pm, Wed and Fri from 10am. Visitors interested in obtaining a pass to the Stranger's Gallery should line up at least an hour before. Parliament is not in session late July to mid-October or weekends.*

Hyde Park

Westminster.

At one time the private boar- and deer-hunting domain of Henry VIII and other royals, Hyde Park is now the largest and most popular of the Central London parks—and one of the biggest urban "green lungs" in the world. With adjoining Kensington Gardens (see below), it encompasses 630 acres of landscaped lawns, flower beds, avenues of trees, and the 41-acre lake known as the **Serpentine,** where you can row and sail model boats. **Rotten Row,** the park's famous 300-year-old riding track, was the country's first public road to be lit at night. At the northeastern tip, near Marble Arch, is

Speakers' Corner, a famous Sunday-morning venting spot for all forms of orating humanity. Free band concerts are held in the park's band shell on Sundays and bank holidays from May to August. The **Dell Restaurant** (☎ **0171/706-0464**), at the east end of the Serpentine, offers cafeteria-style food and drinks Monday through Friday from 10am to 4pm in the winter (until 5pm on weekends) and 10am to 6pm in the summer (until 7pm on weekends).

Bounded by Knightsbridge to the south, Bayswater Road to the north, and Park Lane to the east. ***☎ 0171/298-2100. Tube:*** *Marble Arch or Lancaster Gate on the north side (the park is directly across Bayswater Rd.); or Hyde Park Corner, which is in the southeast corner of the park.* ***Open:*** *Daily year-round from dawn to midnight.*

Kids Kensington Gardens

Kensington.

Adjoining Hyde Park to the west (there's no clear boundary, but think of it as west of the Serpentine), Kensington Gardens was formed from land taken from Hyde Park after William and Mary moved into what is now **Kensington Palace** (see below) in 1689. It's a well-manicured oasis, especially popular with children, who love the famous statue of **Peter Pan,** located north of the Serpentine Bridge. The park is also home to the **Albert Memorial,** the lovely **Italian Gardens,** and the **Serpentine Gallery** (☎ **0171/402-6075l;** open daily 10am to 6pm; closed December 24 to 27 and January 1; admission free), which is gaining a reputation for showing cutting-edge art.

Bounded by Kensington Palace Gardens and Palace Green on the west, Bayswater Rd. on the north, Kensington Rd. and Kensington Gore on the south. ***☎ 0171/298-2100. Tube:*** *High Street Kensington, then a 10-minute walk east on Kensington High St.; or Queensway, which is directly across from the northwest corner of the park.* ***Open:*** *Daily year-round from dawn to midnight.*

Kensington Palace

Kensington.

One wing of Kensington Palace was Princess Diana's London home after her divorce from Prince Charles. After her death, tens of thousands of mourners gathered in front of the palace and left a sea of floral tributes. Acquired by William III in 1689 and remodeled by Sir Christopher Wren, the palace was used as a royal residence until 1760. Victoria was born here, and it was here, in 1837, that she was informed that she was the new Queen of England (and could move to the grander Buckingham Palace). Since the palace is still the home of Princess Margaret and other lesser royals, much of it is closed off to visitors. But you can see the **State Apartments** and visit the **Royal Ceremonial Dress Collection,** which takes visitors through the process of being presented at court, from the first visit to the tailor to the final curtsy or bow.

Extra! Extra!

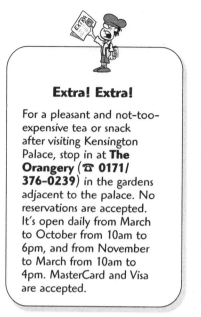

For a pleasant and not-too-expensive tea or snack after visiting Kensington Palace, stop in at **The Orangery** (☎ **0171/376-0239**) in the gardens adjacent to the palace. No reservations are accepted. It's open daily from March to October from 10am to 6pm, and from November to March from 10am to 4pm. MasterCard and Visa are accepted.

The Broad Walk, Kensington Gardens, W8. **☎ *0171/937-9561.* *Tube:*** *Queensway on the north side, then a 10-minute walk south through the park to the palace entrance; or High Street Kensington on the southwest side, then a 10-minute walk through the park.* ***Admission:*** *£7.50 ($12) adults, £5.90 ($9) seniors and children 5 and older.* ***Open:*** *Daily 10am–5pm (Mon–Fri by guided tour; weekends you can wander through on your own). The palace has some stairs but is accessible for persons with disabilities; call first.*

Leicester Square

Laid out in 1665 as a dueling ground, Leicester (pronounced *Lester)* Square is now a pedestrian zone for West End entertainment. In the center, surrounded by movie theatres, restaurants, and a lot of neon, is **Leicester Square Gardens,** with four corner gates named for William Hogarth, Sir Joshua Reynolds, John Hunter, and Sir Isaac Newton, all of whom once lived or worked in the area. There are also statues of William Shakespeare and Charlie Chaplin (a bow to theatre and cinema). A **half-price ticket booth** (no phone) for theatre, opera, and dance is located at the south end of the square (see chapter 16). You probably won't want to linger very long in Leicester Square; it has a city buzz but not a lot of character. If you're traveling with kids, this is one place with a rest room (coin-operated).

Tube: *Leicester Square, then a 5-minute walk west across Charing Cross Rd.*

London Zoo

Marylebone.

The London Zoo is Britain's largest, with an aquarium, a reptile house, and a children's zoo. Unfortunately, the famous panda is gone, and some parts of the 36-acre compound could use refurbishment, but there are still about 8,000 animals in various specie-specific houses. The best are the **Insect House** (bird-eating spiders), the **Reptile House** (huge monitor lizards and a 15-foot python), the **Sobell Pavilion for Apes and Monkeys,** and the **Lion Terraces.** In **Moonlight World,** special lighting effects simulate night for the nocturnal creatures so that you can see them in action. Many families budget almost an entire day here, watching the penguins being fed, enjoying an animal ride in the summer, and meeting elephants on their walks around the zoo.

North end of Regent's Park, NW1. **☎ *0171/722-3333.* *Tube:*** *Regent's Park, then bus C2 north on Albany St. to Delaney St. (10 minutes), or a half-hour walk north through the park; or Camden Town, then bus 274 south on Parkway and west on*

Delaney St. (about 10 minutes). ***Admission:*** *£8.50 ($14) adults; £7.50 ($12) seniors, students, and persons with disabilities; £6.50 ($11) children ages 4–14; family ticket (2 adults/2 children) £26 ($43); free for children under 4.* ***Open:*** *Mar–Sept daily 10am–5:30pm; Oct–Feb daily 10am–4pm.*

Extra! Extra!

Kids Want to arrive at the London Zoo by water? **London Waterbus Co.** (☎ **0171/482-2550**) operates single and return trips in snug, converted canal boats along Regent's Canal from Warwick Crescent in Little Venice to Camden Lock Market. To catch the boat, take the tube to Warwick Avenue, walk south across Regent's Canal, and you'll see the landing stage. Trips from both locks depart daily from 10am to 5pm.

Kids Madame Tussaud's

Marylebone.

Eerily lifelike figures have made the century-old Madame Tussaud's world famous. But do you really want to shell out a hefty sum to look at a bunch of boring wax dummies? The original moldings of members of the French court, to whom Madame Tussaud had direct access (quite literally, since she made molds of their heads after they were guillotined during the French Revolution), are undeniably fascinating. And animatronic gadgetry makes the "Spirit of London" theme ride fun. But the modern superstars (Cybill Shepherd was the latest addition) and the Chamber of Horrors are the stuff tourist traps are made of. Do you really want to see one of Jack the Ripper's victims lying in a pool of blood, or pay money to see the likenesses of mass-murderers like Gary Gilmore and Charles Manson? There are better stars to be seen next door, at the new planetarium (see chapter 14).

Marylebone Rd., NW1. ☎ ***0171/935-6861.*** ***Tube:*** *Baker St., then a 2-minute walk east on Marylebone Rd.* ***Admission:*** *£9.25 ($15) adults, £6.75 ($11) seniors, £6.10 ($10) children 5–16; free for children under 5. Combination tickets including the new planetarium £11.50 ($19) adults, £7.55 ($12) children under 16.* ***Open:*** *Daily 9am–5:30pm.*

Tourist Traps

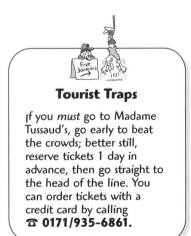

If you *must* go to Madame Tussaud's, go early to beat the crowds; better still, reserve tickets 1 day in advance, then go straight to the head of the line. You can order tickets with a credit card by calling ☎ **0171/935-6861.**

Cool Britannia

When it was announced that the Prince and Princess of Wales were separating, their mannequins at Madame Tussaud's were moved slightly apart. When they were divorced, Diana was moved to the end of the royal line, but since her death, she has been brought down from the royal enclosure so that people can get closer to her.

Wheelchair accessible via elevators, but call first because only 3 chairs can be accommodated at a time.

Museum of London

The City of London.

If you're captivated with London and want to know more about it, this is the place to go. It's probably the most comprehensive city museum in the world. It's located in the original 1-square-mile Londinium of the Romans overlooking the city's Roman and medieval walls. Incorporating archeological finds; paintings and prints; social, industrial, and historical artifacts; and costumes, maps, and models, the museum traces the city's history from prehistoric times to the 20th century. Of special interest is the gilt-and-scarlet **Lord Mayor's Coach,** built in 1757 and weighing in at 3 tons.

150 London Wall (in the Barbican district near St. Paul's Cathedral), EC2. ☎ ***0171/600-3699. Tube:*** *St. Paul's, then a 10-minute walk north on St. Martin Le Grand and Aldersgate.* ***Admission:*** *£5 ($8) adults; £3 ($5) children, students, and seniors; family ticket (2 adults/3 children) £12 ($20). Admission free after 4:30pm.* ***Open:*** *Mon–Sat 10am–5:50pm, Sun noon–5:50pm. The entire museum has flat, ramped, or elevator access for wheelchair users.*

National Gallery

St. James's.

The National Gallery possesses one of the world's most dazzlingly comprehensive collections of British and European paintings. All the major schools from the 13th to the 20th centuries are represented, but the Italians get the lion's share of wall space, with artists like Leonardo da Vinci, Botticelli, and Raphael on the roster. The French impressionist, post-impressionist, and neo-impressionist works by Monet, Manet, Seurat, Cézanne, and Degas, as well as those by van Gogh (Dutch), are shimmering and sublime. And since you're on English soil, you'd be well advised to check out at least a few of the stunning seascapes by J. M. W. Turner, landscapes by Constable, and society portraits by Sir Joshua Reynolds. And don't forget the Rembrandts. There's a good restaurant for lunch, tea, or snacks on the second floor.

Trafalgar Square, WC2. ☎ ***0171/839-3321. Tube:*** *Charing Cross, then a 2-minute walk north across Trafalgar Square.* ***Admission:*** *Free, but there's a charge for special exhibitions, usually around £5 ($8).* ***Open:*** *Mon–Tues and Thurs–Sat 10am–6pm, Wed 10am–8pm, Sun noon–6pm. Closed Jan 1, Good Friday, Dec 24–26. The entire museum is wheelchair accessible.*

Time-Savers

Like the British Museum, the **National Gallery** has too much for a mere mortal to comprehend in a single visit, so again the best advice is to be selective. A computer information center allows you to design a tour based on your personal preferences (a maximum of 10 paintings from the 2,200 entries) and prints out a customized tour map. You can also rent a portable audio tour guide for £3 ($5). Every painting has a reference number. When you see something you like, punch in the appropriate number and a mellifluous voice will give you the lowdown on it.

National Portrait Gallery

St. James's.

There's more life in many of these portraits than you'll ever find at Madame Tussaud's. On five fascinating floors, every famous English face you've ever wanted to see is represented in a pictorial Who's Who that ranges from Sir Walter Raleigh, Shakespeare (wearing a gold earring), and Queen Elizabeth I to the Brontë sisters, Winston Churchill, Oscar Wilde, Sir Noel Coward, Mick Jagger, and Princess Diana. It's all arranged in chronological order and it's a real feast.

St. Martin's Place (off Trafalgar Square behind the National Gallery), WC2. ☎ ***0171/306-0055. Tube:*** *Leicester Square, then a 2-minute walk south on Charing Cross Rd.* ***Admission:*** *Free. Audio tour £3 ($5) donation.* ***Open:*** *Mon–Sat 10am–6pm, Sun noon–6pm. All but the landing galleries are wheelchair accessible; call first for entry instructions.*

Kids Natural History Museum

South Kensington.

The most popular attraction in this enormous Victorian-era museum is the huge dinosaur exhibit, with 14 complete skeletons and a trio of full-size robotic Deinonychus lunching on a freshly killed Tenontosaurus. But this is the home of the national collections of living and fossil plants, animals, and minerals, so there are magnificent specimens and exciting displays relating to natural history everywhere you look. "Creepy Crawlies" is another popular kid-pleaser. The sparkling gems and crystals in the Mineral Gallery are literally dazzling, and in the Meteorite Pavilion you can see fragments of rock that have crashed into the earth from the farthest reaches of the galaxy.

Cromwell Rd., SW7. ☎ ***0171/938-9123. Tube:*** *South Kensington; the tube station is on the corner of Cromwell Rd. and Exhibition Rd., at the corner of the museum.* ***Admission:*** *£6 ($10) adults, £3.20 ($5) seniors and students, £3 ($5) children 5–17; free for children 4 and under; £16 ($26) family ticket (2 adults/*

4 children). Free admission Mon–Fri after 4:30pm and Sat–Sun after 5pm. ***Open:*** *Mon–Sat 10am–5:50pm, Sun 11am–5:50pm. Nearly all the galleries are flat or ramped for wheelchair users; call for instructions on entering the building.*

Piccadilly Circus

Glowing with neon and bursting with all manner of tourist glitz, Piccadilly Circus, along with neighboring Leicester Square (see above), is London's equivalent to New York's Times Square. It's the beginning of the West End, and not what you'd call fashionable, but everyone who comes to London wants to see it. As traffic wheels around the famous **statue of Eros,** jostling crowds pack the pavement and an international contingent of teens heads for the **Pepsi Trocadero,** the area's mega-entertainment center (see chapter 14). Regent Street, at the west side of the circus, and Piccadilly, at the south end, are major shopping streets (see chapter 15).

Tube: *Piccadilly Circus and you're there.*

Cool Britannia

Piccadilly, traditionally the western road out of town, was named for the "picadil," a ruffled collar created by a 17th-century tailor named Robert Baker.

Regent's Park

Marylebone.

Regent's Park, 400 acres of green, mostly open parkland fringed by imposing Regency terraces, is the home of the London Zoo (see above), among other things. People come here to play soccer, cricket, tennis, and softball; boat in the lake; visit **Queen Mary's Rose Garden** (with an outdoor theater; see chapter 18); and let their kids have fun in the many playgrounds. During the summer, concerts are performed in the bandstand at lunchtime and in the evening, and puppet shows and other children's activities are on tap weekdays throughout August. The northernmost section of the park rises to the summit of Primrose Hill, which provides fine views of Westminster and the City.

Just north of Marylebone Rd. and surrounded by Outer Circle Rd. ***☎ 0171/486-7905.*** *Advance booking for Open Air Theatre (operating late May–early Sept)* ***☎ 0171/486-2431. Tube:*** *Regent's Park or Baker St., then a 5-minute walk north to the south end of the park; for the London Zoo, see above.* ***Open:*** *Daily 5am to dusk. There are rest rooms that include facilities for persons with disabilities and a diaper-changing room by Chester Gate on the east side of the park.*

Science Museum

South Kensington.

This innovative museum, named 1997 Visitor Attraction of the Year by the English Tourist Board, covers the history and development of science and technology. The state-of-the-art interactive displays are challenging, brain-tickling, and fun for 7- to 12-year-old kids, and the Garden galleries provide construction areas, sound and light shows, and games for younger kids. On display are rarities such as an 1813 steam locomotive, Arkwright's spinning machine, Talbot's first camera, and Edison's original phonograph.

Exhibition Rd., London SW7. ☎ ***0171/938-8080. Tube:*** *South Kensington; an exit marked by a signpost in the Underground station goes directly to the museum.* ***Admission:*** *£6.50 ($11) adults, £3.50 ($6) children. Free admission after 4:30pm.* ***Open:*** *Daily 10am–6pm. All galleries are wheelchair accessible.*

St. James's Park/Green Park

St. James's.

Buckingham Palace (see above) forms the centerpiece of these two adjoining royal parks acquired by Henry VIII in the early 16th century. St James's Park, the prettier of the two, was landscaped in 1827 by John Nash in a picturesque English style with an ornamental lake and promenades. **The Mall,** the processional route between the Palace and Whitehall and Horse Guards Parade, is the route used for major ceremonial occasions. **St. James's Palace,** the abode of Prince Charles and the boys, and adjacent **Clarence House,** residence of the Queen Mum, are located between The Mall and **Pall Mall,** a broad avenue that runs from Trafalgar Square to St. James's Palace. Neither residence is open to visitors.

Bounded by Piccadilly to the north, Regent St. to the east, Birdcage Walk and Buckingham Palace Rd. to the south, and Grosvenor Place to the west. ☎ ***0171/930-1793. Tube:*** *Green Park tube station is right at the northeast corner of Green Park; from St. James's Park tube station, it's a 5-minute walk north on Queen Anne's Gate to Birdcage Walk, the southern perimeter of St. James's Park.* ***Open:*** *Daily from dawn to dusk.*

Cool Britannia

Green Park is called Green Park because it's the only royal park without any flower beds. Why? One popular story has it that one day, as Charles II was perambulating through the park with his entourage, he announced that he was going to pick a flower and give it to the most beautiful lady present. This happened to be a milkmaid and not Queen Catherine, his wife. The Queen, bitten by the green-eyed monster of jealousy, was so incensed that she commanded that all the flowers be removed from the park.

St. Paul's Cathedral

The City of London.

The great architect Sir Christopher Wren was called upon to design this huge and harmonious Renaissance-leaning-toward-Baroque edifice after the Great

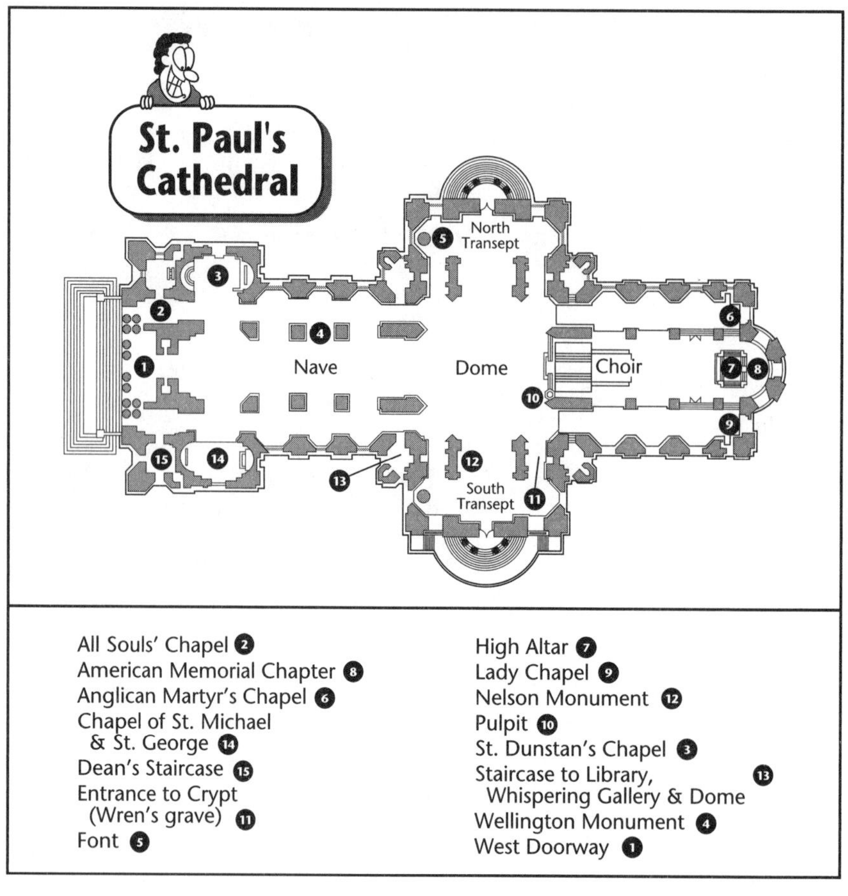

Fire of 1666 destroyed the City's old cathedral. The surrounding area was wiped out in Nazi bombing raids, so Wren's masterpiece, capped by the most famous dome in London, rises majestically above a crowded sea of disconcertingly banal office buildings. Inside, there's not much in the way of art except for the exceptionally beautiful choir stalls carved by Grinling Gibbons. Sir Christopher Wren lies in the crypt, as do those famous national heroes the Duke of Wellington and Lord Nelson. You can climb up to the **Whispering Gallery** for a bit of acoustical fun or gasp your way up to the very top for a breathtaking (literally) view of London. Many will want to see St. Paul's simply because it was here that Lady Diana Spencer wed Prince Charles in what was prematurely billed as "the fairytale wedding of the century."

St. Paul's Churchyard, Ludgate Hill, EC4. ☎ ***0171/246-8348. Tube:*** *St. Paul's, then a 5-minute walk west on Ludgate to the cathedral entrance on St. Paul's Churchyard.* ***Admission:*** *£4 ($7) adults, £3.50 ($6) seniors and students, £2 ($3) children to enter the church; an additional £3.50 ($6) adults, £3 ($5) seniors and students, £1.50 ($2) children to enter the galleries; family ticket (2 adults/ 2 children) £9 ($15) to enter the church, an additional £7.50 ($12) to enter the galleries. Tours lasting 90 minutes to 2 hours take place at 11:30am, 1:30pm,* *and 2pm; the cost is £2 ($3) adults, £1 ($1.65) children under 10. Audio tours available from 8:30am–3:30pm; the cost is £3 ($5) adults, £2.50 ($4) children, £7 ($12) family.* ***Open:*** *Mon–Sat 8:30am–4pm; galleries 9:30am–4pm; no sightseeing on Sun (services only). The cathedral is wheelchair accessible by the service entrance near the South Transept; ring the bell for assistance.*

Tate Gallery

Pimlico.

If you like the dreamy works of the British Pre-Raphaelite school, the celestial visions of William Blake, the satirical works of William Hogarth, the genteel portraits by Sir Joshua Reynolds, the bucolic landscapes of John Constable, the shimmering seascapes of J. M. W. Turner, the sculptures of Henry Moore, or the disturbing canvases of Francis Bacon, make a point to visit the Tate Gallery, a major repository for British art. Equally grand is the collection of international modern art, with important works by Matisse, Dali, Modigliani, Munch, Bonnard, Picasso, and Mark Rothko. *(Note:* The Tate's prestigious collection of 20th-century art will be moved to the new Tate Gallery of Modern Art in the renovated Bankside Power Station sometime in the year 2000.) There's a restaurant and a cafe on the lower level.

Millbank, Pimlico, SW1. ☎ ***0171/887-8000. Tube:*** *Pimlico, then a 10-minute walk south on Vauxhall Bridge Rd. to the river and north on Millbank to the museum entrance.* ***Bus:*** *For a more scenic route, take bus 77A, which runs south along The Strand and Whitehall to the museum entrance on Millbank.* ***Admission:*** *Free. There are varying admission fees for special exhibitions; for advance ticket sales, call* ☎ ***0171/420-0055.*** *Audio tours £3 ($5).* ***Open:*** *Daily 10am–5:40pm. Most of the galleries are wheelchair accessible, but call first for details on entry.*

Extra! Extra!

If work proceeds on time, by the spring of 2000, the Tate's 20th-century collections will have a new home in the converted Bankside Power Station on the South Bank, between Blackfriars and Vauxhall bridges. The South Bank complex will be called the Tate Gallery of Modern Art; the old Tate will change its name to the Tate Gallery of British Art.

Time-Savers

The secret to avoiding the Tower's notoriously long lines, especially to see the crown jewels, is to arrive the moment the gates open, before the hordes descend in the afternoon. Choose a day other than Sunday if you can—crowds are at their worst then.

Cool Britannia

As you wander around visiting the various sites at the Tower of London, you'll notice huge **black ravens** hopping around and squawking. There's an old legend that says the world will end when the ravens leave the Tower. Their wings have been clipped as a precaution.

Tower of London

The City of London.

The City's best-known and oldest historic site, the Tower was built by William the Conqueror in 1066 and served as his fortress and later as a prison, holding famous captives such as Sir Walter Raleigh and Princess Elizabeth. Ann Boleyn and Catherine Howard (two of the six wives of Henry VIII), the 9-day queen Lady Jane Grey, and Sir Thomas More were among those who got their heads chopped off on **Tower Green.** According to Shakespeare, the two little princes (the sons of Edward IV) were murdered in the **Bloody Tower** by henchmen of Richard III—but many modern historians refute this story. There's enough here to keep you occupied for several hours, but make sure that you save time for the **crown jewels,** which include the largest diamond in the world (the 530-carat Star of Africa) and other breathtaking gems set into royal robes, swords, sceptres, and crowns.

You can attend the nightly **Ceremony of the Keys,** the ceremonial locking up of the Tower by the Yeoman Warders. For free tickets, write to the Ceremony of the Keys, Waterloo Block, Tower of London, London EC3N 4AB, and request a specific date, but also list alternate dates. At least 6 weeks' notice is required. All requests must be accompanied by a

Extra! Extra!

In the bad old days, important prisoners often arrived at the Tower by boat. You can, too. There's daily ferry service between Westminster Pier, Charing Cross Pier, and Tower Pier. **Catamaran Cruisers (☎ 0171/839-1034)** is one outfit that runs ferries between Charing Cross Pier to the Tower. A round-trip ticket is £5.80 ($10) for adults and £3.30 ($5) for children under 16.

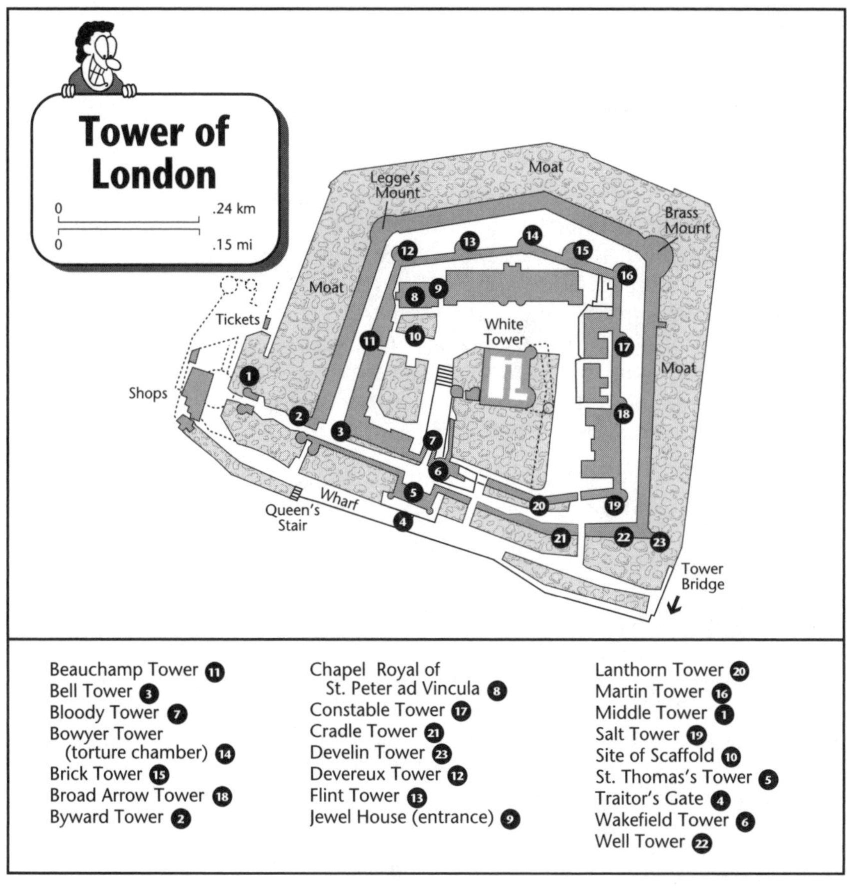

stamped, self-addressed envelope (British stamps only) or two International Reply coupons. With ticket in hand, you'll be admitted by a Yeoman Warder at 9:35pm.

Tower Hill, EC3. ☎ ***0171/709-0765. Tube:*** *Tower Hill, then a 10-minute walk west and south on Tower Hill.* ***Bus:*** *You can take the eastbound bus 25 from Marble Arch, Oxford Circus, or St. Paul's; it stops at Tower Hill, north of the entrance.* ***Admission:*** *£9.50 ($16) adults, £7.15 ($12) seniors and students, £6.25 ($10) children 5–15; free for children under 5; £28.40 ($47) family ticket for 5 (but no more than 2 adults). Free 1-hour guided* ***tours*** *of the entire compound are given by the Yeoman Warders (also known as "Beefeaters") every half-hour, starting at 9:25am from the Middle Tower near the main entrance. The last guided walk starts at about 3:30pm in the summer, 2:30pm in the winter, weather permitting.* ***Open:*** *Mar–Oct Mon–Sat 9am–6pm, Sun 10am–6pm; Nov–Feb Tues–Sat 9am–5pm, Sun 10am–5pm. Closed Jan 1, Dec 24–26. There is wheelchair access onto the grounds, but many of the historic buildings cannot accommodate wheelchairs.*

Trafalgar Square

St. James's.

A popular gathering spot for tourists, pigeons, political demonstrations, Christmas revels, and raucous New Year's Eve festivities, Trafalgar Square is a roaringly busy traffic interchange surrounded by imposing historic buildings, such as St. Martin-in-the-Fields church (see below) and the National Gallery (see above). The square honors the military hero Horatio, Viscount Nelson (1758–1805), who lost his life at the Battle of Trafalgar. **Nelson's Column,** with fountains and four bronze lions at its base, rises some 145 feet above the square. At the top, a 14-foot-high statue of Nelson (5 ft. 4 in. tall in real life) looks commandingly toward **Admiralty Arch,** passed through by state and royal processions between Buckingham Place and St. Paul's Cathedral.

If the Neoclassical church on the northeast corner of Trafalgar Square looks vaguely familiar, perhaps it's because it was the precursor for dozens of similar-looking churches throughout colonial New England. Designed by James Gibbs, a disciple of Sir Christopher Wren, **St. Martin-in-the-Fields** (☎ 0171/437-6023) was completed in 1726, and a 185-foot tower was added about 100 years later. The Academy of St. Martin-in-the-Fields, a famous ensemble, frequently performs here. Lunchtime concerts are held on Monday, Tuesday, and Friday at 1pm; and evening concerts are held on Thursday through Saturday at 7:30pm. Tickets range from £6 to £15 ($10 to $24); for reservations by credit card, call % 0171/839-8362. The church is open Monday through Saturday from 10am to 6pm, and Sunday from noon to 6pm; admission is free.

Extra! Extra!

One of the West End's most pleasant restaurants is located in the crypt of St. Martin-in-the-Fields on Trafalgar Square. The floor may be paved with gravestones, but there's nothing eerie or macabre about **Cafe-in-the-Crypt** (**☎ 0171/839-4342**), which serves up helpings of traditional English home cooking Monday through Saturday from 10am to 8pm, and Sunday from noon to 6pm.

Kids In addition to the cafe, the busy crypt of St. Martin-in-the-Fields contains the **London Brass Rubbing Centre** (**☎ 0171/437-6023**), which provides paper, metallic waxes, and instructions on how to rub your own replica of historic brasses. There are 88 exact copies to choose from. Prices range from £2 to £15 ($3 to $24). This is a great rainy-day pastime and a wonderful diversion for kids 10 and up.

Bounded on the north by Trafalgar, on the west by Cockspur St., and on the east by Whitehall. ***Tube:*** *Charing Cross; there is an exit from the Underground station to the square.*

Victoria and Albert Museum

South Kensington.

The Victoria and Albert (known as "the V&A") is the national museum of art and design. It's not as dauntingly huge as the British Museum, but it does have 145 galleries filled with fine and decorative arts from around the world. Highlights include superbly decorated period rooms, a collection spanning 400 years of European fashion, cartoons by Raphael (designs for tapestries in the Sistine Chapel), the Silver Galleries, and the largest assemblage of Renaissance sculpture outside of Italy and Indian art outside of India. The museum's newest addition is the Canon Photography Gallery, showing work by celebrated photographers.

Cromwell Rd., SW7. ***☎ 0171/938-8500. Tube:*** *South Kensington; the museum is across the street from the Underground station.* ***Admission:*** *£5 ($8) adults, £3 ($5) senior citizens; free for students with ID and children under 18.* ***Open:*** *Mon noon–5:45pm, Tues–Sun 10am–5:45pm. Wheelchair accessible (about 95% of the exhibits are step free).*

Westminster Abbey

Westminster.

It's just a short stroll from the Neo-Gothic Houses of Parliament to the truly magnificent Gothic splendor of Westminster Abbey. Though the present abbey dates mostly from the 13th and 14th centuries, there's been a church on this spot for more than 1,000 years. Since 1066, when William the Conquerer became the first English monarch to be crowned here, every successive British sovereign, except two (Edward V and Edward VIII), has sat in the **Coronation Chair** and received the crown and sceptre. In September 1997, the abbey was the site of Princess Diana's funeral. In the **Royal Chapels** you can see the **Henry VII chapel** with its delicate fan vaulting, and the tomb of Queen Elizabeth I, buried in the same vault as her Catholic half-sister, Mary I, and not far from her rival, Mary Queen of Scots. In **Poets' Corner,** some of England's greatest writers (including Chaucer, Dickens, and Hardy) are interred or memorialized.

Broad Sanctuary, SW1. ***☎ 0171/222-5152. Tube:*** *Westminster, then a 5-minute walk; cross traffic-laden Bridge St., head west, following Parliament Square to Broad Sanctuary.* ***Bus:*** *The 77A going south along The Strand, Whitehall, and Millbank stops near the Houses of Parliament, near the Abbey.* ***Admission:*** *Abbey £5 ($8) adults, £3 ($5) seniors and students, £2.50 ($4) children; Chapter House, Pyx Chamber, and Museum £2.50 ($4) adults, £1.30 ($2) children (price is reduced for those who have already paid to enter the Abbey). College Garden free, but "donations invited." Guided tours led by an abbey verger £8 ($13) (tickets available at Enquiry Desk in the Abbey); other guided tours £3 ($5); call for times.* ***Open:***

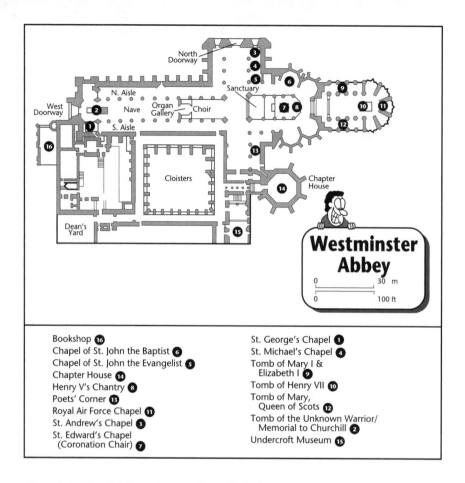

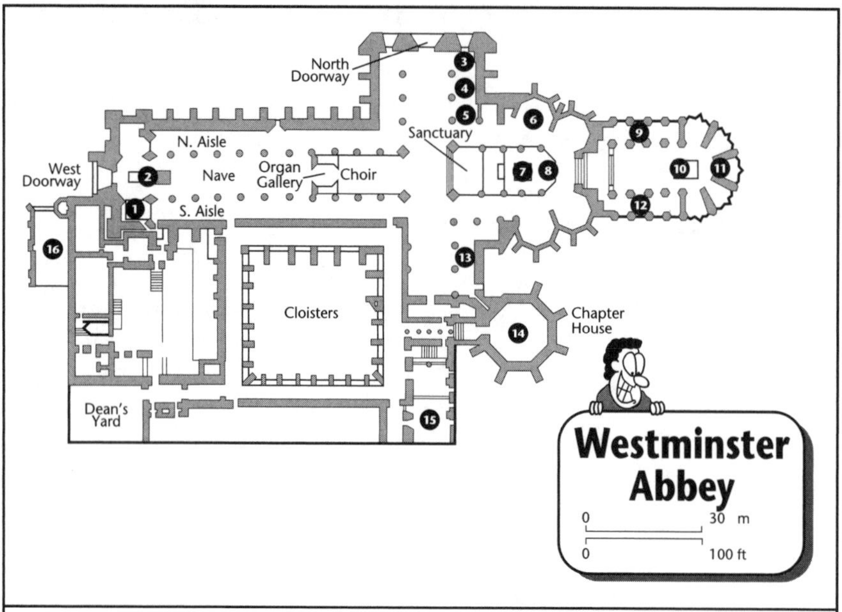

Westminster Abbey

North Doorway
West Doorway
N. Aisle
Nave
Organ Gallery
Choir
Sanctuary
S. Aisle
Cloisters
Chapter House
Dean's Yard

0 — 30 m
0 — 100 ft

- Bookshop 16
- Chapel of St. John the Baptist 6
- Chapel of St. John the Evangelist 5
- Chapter House 14
- Henry V's Chantry 8
- Poets' Corner 13
- Royal Air Force Chapel 11
- St. Andrew's Chapel 3
- St. Edward's Chapel (Coronation Chair) 7
- St. George's Chapel 1
- St. Michael's Chapel 4
- Tomb of Mary I & Elizabeth I 9
- Tomb of Henry VII 10
- Tomb of Mary, Queen of Scots 12
- Tomb of the Unknown Warrior/ Memorial to Churchill 2
- Undercroft Museum 15

Cathedral Mon–Fri 9am–4:45pm (last admission 3:45pm), Sat 9:15am–1:45pm; no sightseeing on Sun (services only). Cloisters daily 10am–6pm. Chapter House, Pyx Chamber, and Museum daily 10:30am–4pm. College Garden Tues and Thurs 10am–6pm. Ramped wheelchair access via the Cloisters; ring bell for assistance.

Cool Britannia

In 1995, 100 years after his release from Reading Gaol, the immortal genius of Oscar Wilde was finally recognized by the Church of England with a blue abstract-design memorial window in Westminster Abbey. But since his name is nowhere to be seen, it's the kind of dubious honor that would no doubt provoke a witty quip from the great man. Maybe something like, "Clear glass wasn't good enough for me; it had to be stained."

Worksheet: Your Must-See Attractions

Enter the attractions you would like most to visit to see how they'll fit into your schedule. You'll refer to this worksheet later on in chapter 17 when you begin planning your trip itinerary.

Attraction and location	Amount of time you expect to spend there	Best day and time to go

Chapter 14

More Fun Stuff to Do

In This Chapter

- More sights and activities for history buffs, art lovers, bookworms, kids, and others
- More royal castles and palaces
- Sights to see just outside London

Right-o, you've marveled at Westminster Abbey, seen where the Queen lives, wandered through St. Paul's Cathedral, toured the Tower of London, and feasted your eyes on the masterpieces in the British Museum and the National Gallery. And you think you've seen London. Well, you've seen a *bit* of London.

In this chapter you'll discover how much you *haven't* seen: magical gardens, palatial mansions, special museums, ancient corners, modern developments, landmark churches, and lots of themed attractions that will fill you and the kids in on the history of majestic London Town. You can pick and choose from the categories below to find things that will tickle your fancy and round out your visit.

I've also included four major attractions—Hampstead Heath, Kew Gardens, Windsor Castle, and Hampton Palace—that are not in Central London but close to it and easily accessible by tube or train. Visiting them will take up the better part of a day, but you can easily get back in time for a play or concert in the evening.

Accessible London

The following sights are fully or partially wheelchair accessible; visitors with disabilities should call the attraction to find out about special entrances, ramps, and elevator locations:

Bank of England Museum
Barbican Centre
Bethnal Green Museum of Childhood
Bramah Tea & Coffee Museum
British Library Exhibition Galleries
Chelsea Physic Garden
Design Museum
Hampton Court (East Molesey, Surrey)
Hayward Gallery
Imperial War Museum
Inns of Court
Kew Gardens (Richmond, Surrey)
London Aquarium
London Dungeon
London Planetarium
London Transport Museum
Museum of Mankind (British Museum)
Museum of the Moving Image
Rock Circus
Royal Academy of Art
St. Martin-in-the-Fields
Theatre Museum
Tower Bridge Experience
The Wallace Collection

London for the History Buff

You won't want to miss the **Cabinet War Rooms,** in Westminster at Clive Steps, King Charles Street, SW1 (☎ **0171/930-6961**). Give yourself at least an hour to explore the famous World War II bunker used by Winston Churchill and his chiefs of staff during "England's darkest hour." In this history-laden labyrinth of 21 underground rooms, the Prime Minister and his War Cabinet planned out the military campaigns of World War II. It's all been meticulously preserved, right down to the cigar waiting by Churchill's bed. Admission is £4.40 ($7) for adults and £2.20 ($4) for children; a free audio tour comes with your ticket. It's open daily from 10am to 6pm (last admission 5:15pm). Tube: Westminster, then a 10-minute walk west (stay on the north side of the street) to Parliament Street, turn right to reach King Charles Street.

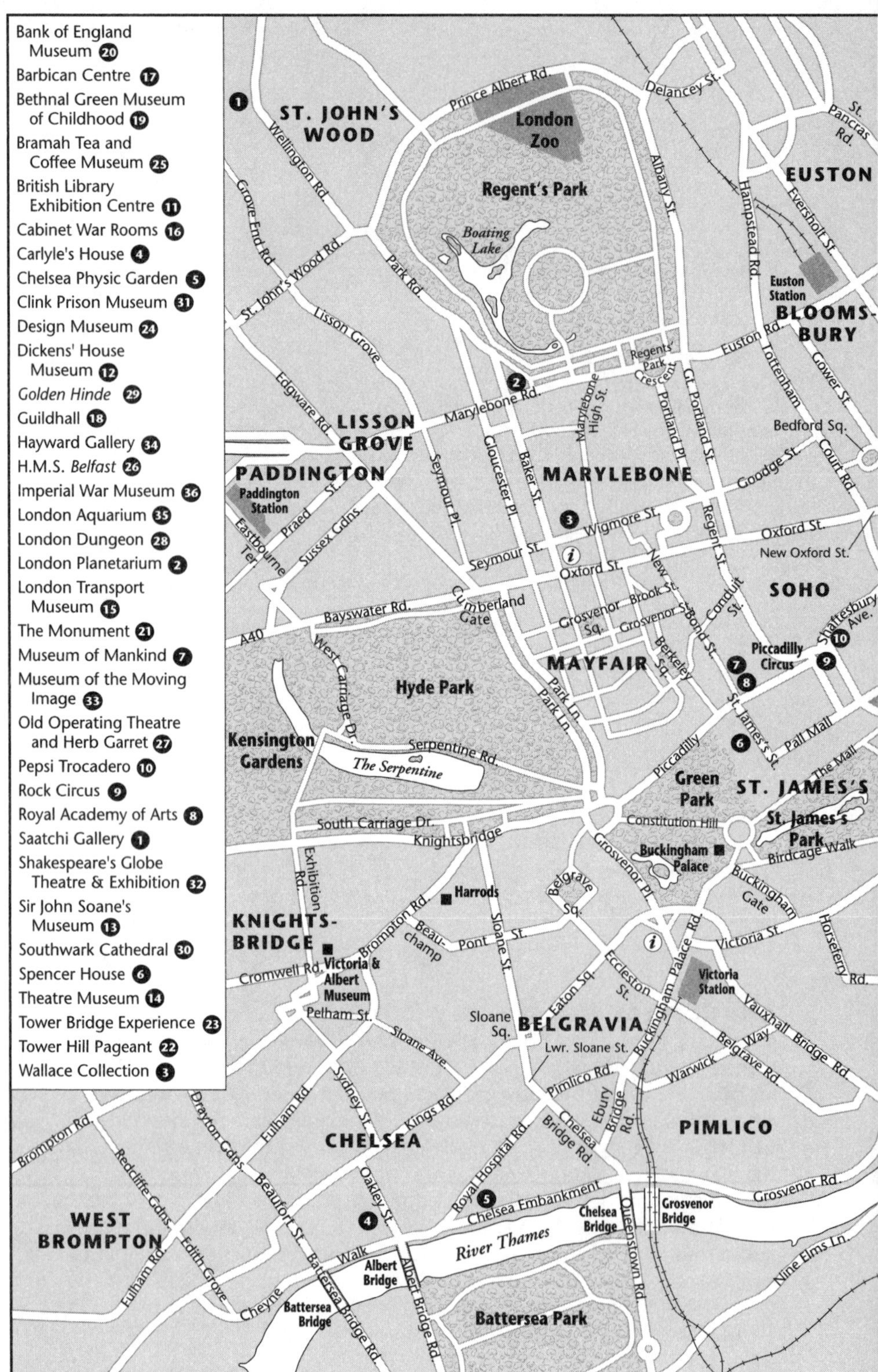
Bank of England Museum 20
Barbican Centre 17
Bethnal Green Museum of Childhood 19
Bramah Tea and Coffee Museum 25
British Library Exhibition Centre 11
Cabinet War Rooms 16
Carlyle's House 4
Chelsea Physic Garden 5
Clink Prison Museum 31
Design Museum 24
Dickens' House Museum 12
Golden Hinde 29
Guildhall 18
Hayward Gallery 34
H.M.S. *Belfast* 26
Imperial War Museum 36
London Aquarium 35
London Dungeon 28
London Planetarium 2
London Transport Museum 15
The Monument 21
Museum of Mankind 7
Museum of the Moving Image 33
Old Operating Theatre and Herb Garret 27
Pepsi Trocadero 10
Rock Circus 9
Royal Academy of Arts 8
Saatchi Gallery 1
Shakespeare's Globe Theatre & Exhibition 32
Sir John Soane's Museum 13
Southwark Cathedral 30
Spencer House 6
Theatre Museum 14
Tower Bridge Experience 23
Tower Hill Pageant 22
Wallace Collection 3
ST. JOHN'S WOOD
Prince Albert Rd.
London Zoo
Delancey St.
St. Pancras Rd.
EUSTON
Regent's Park
Boating Lake
Albany St.
Hampstead Rd.
Eversholt St.
Euston Station
BLOOMSBURY
Wellington Rd.
Grove End Rd.
St. John's Wood Rd.
Park Rd.
Lisson Grove
Edgware Rd.
Regents' Park Crescent
Euston Rd.
Tottenham
Gower St.
Marylebone Rd.
Marylebone High St.
Portland Pl.
Gt. Portland St.
Bedford Sq.
LISSON GROVE
PADDINGTON
Paddington Station
Praed St.
Eastbourne Ter.
Sussex Gdns.
Seymour Pl.
Gloucester Pl.
Baker St.
MARYLEBONE
Goodge St.
Court Rd.
Wigmore St.
Regent St.
Oxford St.
New Oxford St.
Seymour St.
Oxford St.
New Bond St.
SOHO
Bayswater Rd.
A40
Cumberland Gate
Grosvenor Sq.
Brook St.
Grosvenor St.
Conduit St.
Shaftesbury Ave.
West Carriage Dr.
MAYFAIR
Berkeley Sq.
Piccadilly Circus
Hyde Park
Park Ln.
St. James's St.
Pall Mall
Kensington Gardens
Serpentine Rd.
The Serpentine
Piccadilly
Green Park
ST. JAMES'S
The Mall
St. James's Park
South Carriage Dr.
Constitution Hill
Knightsbridge
Birdcage Walk
Buckingham Palace
Grosvenor Pl.
Exhibition Rd.
Belgrave Sq.
Buckingham Gate
Harrods
KNIGHTSBRIDGE
Brompton Rd.
Beauchamp
Pont St.
Sloane St.
Buckingham Palace Rd.
Victoria St.
Horseferry Rd.
Victoria & Albert Museum
Cromwell Rd.
Eaton Sq.
Eccleston St.
Victoria Station
Pelham St.
Sloane Sq.
BELGRAVIA
Vauxhall Bridge Rd.
Sloane Ave.
Lwr. Sloane St.
Belgrave Rd.
Warwick Way
Brompton Rd.
Drayton Gdns.
Fulham Rd.
Sydney St.
Kings Rd.
Pimlico Rd.
Ebury Bridge Rd.
Chelsea Bridge Rd.
Royal Hospital Rd.
PIMLICO
CHELSEA
Redcliffe Gdns.
Beaufort St.
Oakley St.
Chelsea Embankment
Grosvenor Rd.
WEST BROMPTON
Chelsea Bridge
Queenstown Rd.
Grosvenor Bridge
River Thames
Fulham Rd.
Edith Grove
Cheyne Walk
Albert Bridge
Albert Bridge Rd.
Nine Elms Ln.
Battersea Bridge
Battersea Bridge Rd.
Battersea Park

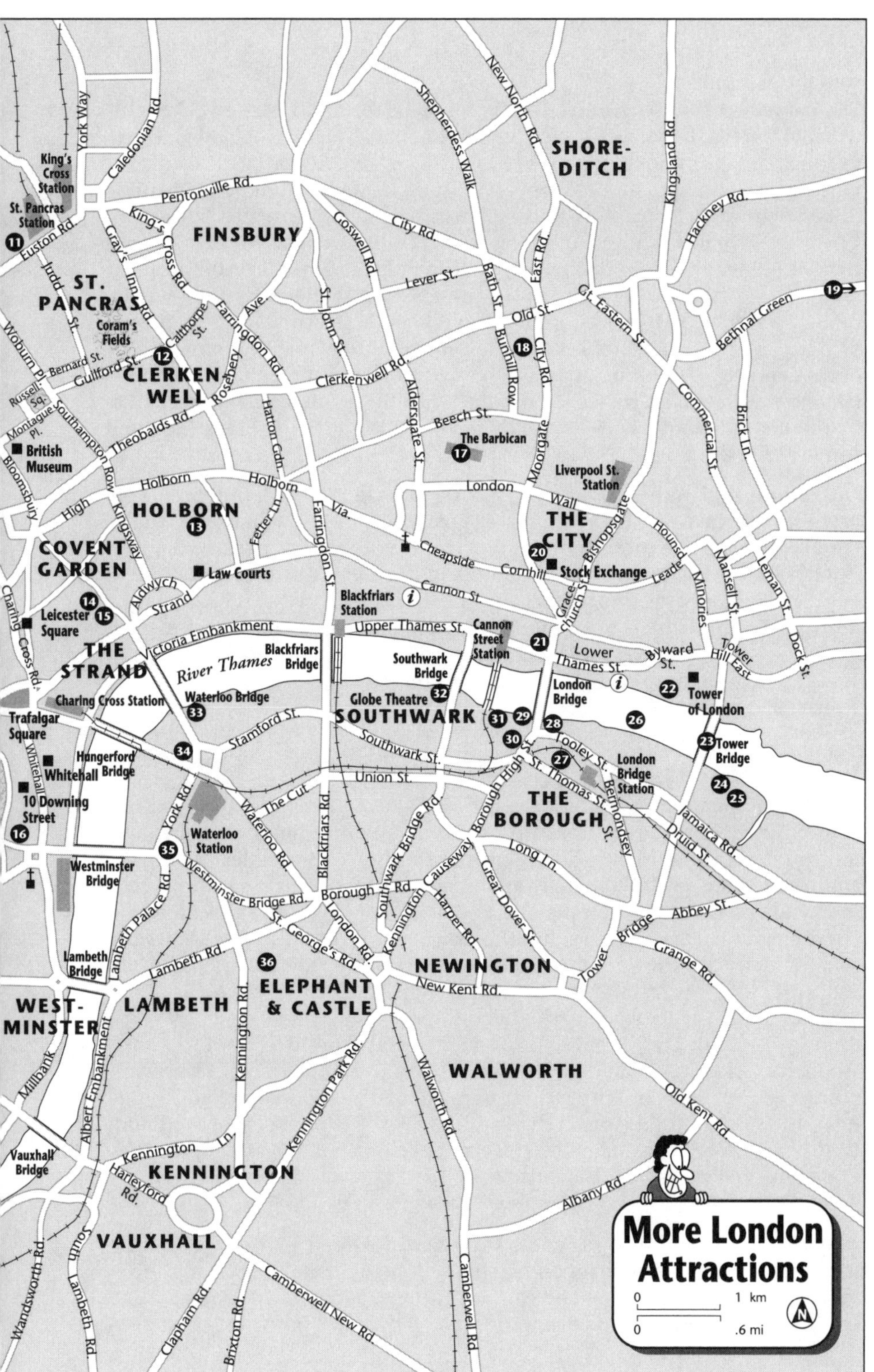
More London Attractions
SHORE-DITCH
FINSBURY
ST. PANCRAS
CLERKEN-WELL
HOLBORN
COVENT GARDEN
THE STRAND
THE CITY
SOUTHWARK
THE BOROUGH
NEWINGTON
ELEPHANT & CASTLE
WEST-MINSTER
LAMBETH
WALWORTH
KENNINGTON
VAUXHALL
King's Cross Station
St. Pancras Station
Coram's Fields
British Museum
The Barbican
Liverpool St. Station
Law Courts
Stock Exchange
Blackfriars Station
Cannon Street Station
Leicester Square
Charing Cross Station
Trafalgar Square
Whitehall
10 Downing Street
Waterloo Station
Westminster Bridge
Lambeth Bridge
Vauxhall Bridge
Hungerford Bridge
Waterloo Bridge
Blackfriars Bridge
Southwark Bridge
London Bridge
London Bridge Station
Tower Bridge
Tower of London
Globe Theatre
River Thames
0 1 km
0 .6 mi

The **Imperial War Museum,** Lambeth Road, SE1 (☎ **0171/416-5320**), which occupies the former insane asylum known as Bedlam, is now devoted to the insanity of war (though it's billed as "fun" and "exciting"). A wide range of weapons and equipment is on display: a Mark V tank, a Battle of Britain Spitfire, a German one-man submarine, and a rifle carried by Lawrence of Arabia. Multimedia shows explain the Blitz and trench warfare. Other exhibits include coded messages, forged documents, and equipment used by spies from World War I to the present day. At the turn of the millennium a permanent Holocaust gallery will open. There's enough to keep you preoccupied for a couple of hours. It's open daily from 10am to 6pm, and admission is £5 ($8) for adults, £4 ($6) for seniors and students, and £2.50 ($4) for children; admittance is free after 4:30. Tube: Lambeth North, then a 10-minute walk south on Kennington (south of Westminster Bridge Rd.) and east on Lambeth Road.

Guildhall, off Gresham Street, EC2 (☎ **0171/606-3030**), dating from 1411, is the seat of the City of London's local government (presided over by the Lord Mayor). It's the most important secular Gothic structure in London. The exterior suffers from some jarring 1960s additions, but the interior, with its Great Hall used for ceremonial occasions and medieval crypt, is beautifully restored. The building is open Monday through Saturday from 10am to 5pm; it may be closed for ceremonial occasions, so call ahead. Admission is free. Tube: Bank, then west on Poultry and right on Ironmongers Row; it's about a 10-minute walk.

London for the Art Lover

The **Barbican Centre,** Barbican Centre, EC2 (☎ **0171/382-7105**), which dates from the 1970s, is a "total arts-and-living" complex of apartments, restaurants, cinemas, theatres, concert halls, and two art galleries. It's huge and some would say brutally ugly and unnecessarily confusing—but if you follow the yellow pedestrian markers you won't get lost. The Barbican Art Gallery mounts major exhibitions, the Concourse Gallery has free shows of contemporary art, the Barbican Theatre is the home of the illustrious Royal Shakespeare Company, and the London Symphony Orchestra plays at Barbican Hall. The Barbican Art Gallery is open Monday and Thursday through Saturday from 10am to 6:45pm, Tuesday 10am to 5:45pm, Wednesday 10am to 7:45pm, and Sunday noon to 6:45pm. The Concourse Gallery is open Monday through Saturday from 10am to 7:30pm, and Sunday noon to 7:30pm. Admission to the Barbican Centre is £5 ($8) for adults and £3 ($5) for children; Monday to Friday all tickets are £3 ($5) after 5pm. The Concourse Gallery is free. Tube: Barbican, then a 10-minute walk across Beech Street to the Barbican complex; follow the signs.

Opened by Elizabeth II in 1968, the **Hayward Gallery,** part of the South Bank Centre, presents a changing program of major contemporary and historical exhibits from Europe and the U.S. It closes between exhibitions, so it's best to call or check the arts listings in *Time Out* to find out whether there's an exhibition you want to see. The gallery is on Belvedere Road, SE1 (☎ **0171/928-3144,** or ☎ 0171/261-0127 for recorded information; advance ticket sales for exhibitions ☎ 0171/960-4242). Take the tube to Waterloo, then it's a 10-minute walk northwest; follow the signs to the South Bank Centre. During exhibitions, the gallery is open Thursday through Monday from 10am to 6pm, and Tuesday and Wednesday from 10am to 8pm. The admission fee varies according to the exhibition, but it's usually £6 ($10) for adults, £3.50 ($6) for students, seniors, and children; free for children under 12; and £12 ($19) for a family ticket.

The **Royal Academy of Arts,** located in the 18th-century Burlington House, Piccadilly W1 (☎ **0171/439-7438,** or ☎ 0171/300-8000 for advance ticket reservations), has major art exhibitions throughout the year and mounts a famous (and usually packed) Summer Exhibition of works from around the U.K. selected by jury. Expect long lines; plus, there are *no* interactive exhibitions in this institution, so think twice before bringing the kiddies. It's open Monday through Saturday from 10am to 6pm (last admission 5:30 pm), and Sunday from 10am to 8:30pm (last admission 8pm). Admission varies according to the exhibition, but expect to pay around £7 ($12) for adults, £2.50 ($4) for children 11 to 18, and £1 ($2) for children under 11. Tube: Piccadilly Circus, then a 10-minute walk down Piccadilly; the Academy is on the north side of the street just before the Burlington Arcade.

Advertising and media mogul Charles Saatchi has assembled a brilliant collection of contemporary art, and it's all beautifully displayed in a white-on-white space in northwest London. You enter the **Saatchi Gallery,** 98A Boundary Rd., NW8 (☎ **0171/624-8299**), through the unmarked metal gateway of a former paint warehouse. Consisting of more than 1,000 paintings and sculptures, the collection's main focus is works by young British artists, although Americans are represented as well. Some of the work, such as Damien Hirst's 14-foot tiger shark preserved in a formaldehyde-filled tank, are controversial. If you've ever wondered what many Brits think American tourists look like, catch Duane Hanson's *Tourists II.* The gallery is open Thursday through Sunday from noon to 6pm. Admission is £4 ($6) for adults and free for children under 12; admission is free on Thursdays. Tube: Swiss Cottage, then a 10-minute walk south on Finchley Road and west on Boundary Road.

London for the Bookish

The **British Library Exhibition Centre,** Euston Rd., NW1 (☎ **0171/412-7332**), opened in 1998 and houses some of the world's most famous books, maps, manuscripts, and documents. Treasures include a copy of the Magna Carta, the illustrated *Lindisfarne Gospel* from Ireland, *The Diamond Sutra* (the world's earliest-dated printed book), Shakespeare's first folio, and handwritten manuscripts by authors such as Jane Austen and Thomas Hardy. Multimedia exhibitions and a "Workshop of Words, Sounds, and Images" trace the story of book production. Give it at least an hour—more if you're the literary type. It's open Monday and Wednesday through Friday 9:30am to

6pm, Tuesday 9:30am to 8pm, Saturday 9:30am to 5pm, and Sunday 11am to 5pm. Admission is free. Tube: King's Cross/St. Pancras, then a 10-minute walk west on Euston Road; the museum entrance is just beyond Midland Road.

You don't need to be a literary aficionado to appreciate the pretty 1708 Queen Anne terrace house where Thomas Carlyle (author of *The French Revolution*) and his wife Jane (a wit and noted letter writer) lived from 1834 to 1881. Located in Chelsea, **Carlyle's House,** 24 Cheyne Row, SW3 (☎ **0171/352-7087**), is furnished as it was during their residence and gives you a vivid picture of Victorian domestic life. Carlyle's not-so-soundproof "soundproof" study in the skylit attic is filled with memorabilia. You can browse through in about a half-hour. It's open from Easter through October, Wednesday through Sunday, 2 to 5pm; and on bank holidays from 11am to 5pm. Admission is £3.30 ($5) for adults and £1.60 ($3) for children. Tube: Sloane Square, then a 25-minute walk south on Lower Sloane Street and Hospital Road to Cheyne Walk, and north on Cheyne Row; or from Sloane Square, take bus 11, 19, or 22.

No one wrote more passionately about Victorian England than Charles Dickens. Throughout his lifetime, Dickens lived in many places, but he and his family called the house at 48 Doughty St., WC1, in Bloomsbury, now the **Dickens' House Museum** (☎ **0171/405-2127**), home from 1837 to 1839. This is where he penned such famous works as *The Pickwick Papers, Oliver Twist,* and *Nicholas Nickleby.* The museum contains the most comprehensive Dickens library in the world and portraits, illustrations, and rooms furnished exactly as they were in Dickens's time. The museum is open Monday through Friday from 9:45am to 5:30pm and Saturday from 10am to 5pm. Admission is £3.50 ($6) for adults and £1.50 ($2) for children. Tube: Russell Square, then a 10-minute walk up Guilford Street; turn right on Doughty Street; the museum is on the east side of the street.

More Museums of All Shapes, Sorts & Sizes

How nice to have a museum about money that doesn't cost a cent to enter. The Bank of England's beginnings date back to 1694, when funds were needed to finance the war against Louis XIV. The **Bank of England Museum,** Threadneedle Street, EC2 (☎ **0171/601-5545**), housed in the enormous Bank of England building, chronicles changes in the banking industry since then. On display are documents from famous customers (George Washington among them), gold bullion, bank notes (forged and real), and coins. Interactive video displays demonstrate today's high-tech world of finance and a reconstructed 18th-century banking hall. You can see it all in less than an hour. The museum is open Monday through Friday from 10am to 5pm. Tube: Bank, then a 5-minute walk east on Threadneedle Street; turn left on Bartholomew's Lane for the museum entrance.

If you think your HMO at home is bad, get a load of this place . . . The roof garret of the church of St. Thomas, once attached to St. Thomas's Hospital, contains Britain's oldest operating theatre, dating from 1821. The theatre, where students could witness surgical procedures, was in use long before the advent of anesthesia in 1846 (before that, if you had a limb amputated all you got was a blindfold). The array of mid-19th-century "state-of-the-art" medical instruments, including amputation saws, on display at the **Old Operating Theatre and Herb Garret,** 9A St. Thomas St., Southwark, SE1 (☎ **0171/955-4791**), will make you shudder. The garret was also used for storing and curing medicinal herbs. You'll walk away grateful for the medical advances of the last 150 years. Admission is £2.50 ($4) for adults and £1.70 ($3) for children. The theatre is open Tuesday through Sunday from 10am to 4pm. Tube: London Bridge, then a 5-minute walk east on St. Thomas Street.

Calling all caffeine junkies. Set among the old tea warehouses of Butlers Wharf on the South Bank, the **Bramah Tea and Coffee Museum** (The Clove Building, Maguire St., Butlers Wharf, SE1; ☎ **0171/378-0222**) explores the history and traditions of two important beverages—tea and coffee. It illustrates how tea was brought into Europe by the Dutch in the 17th century, studies the 18th-century London phenomena of "Tea and Leisure Gardens," examines the reasons why tea became so popular in England, and discusses the reasons behind the Boston Tea Party. And that's only the beginning. Plus, it smells delicious. There's a good cafe on the premises where—surprise, surprise—you can get an excellent cup of perfectly infused tea or ground roast coffee. The museum is open daily from 10am to 6pm, and admission is £3.50 ($6) for adults, £2 ($3.30) for children. Tube: London Bridge, then a 10-minute walk east along the riverside path to Shad Thames and left of Maguire Street.

It's a bit difficult to get to the **Design Museum** (Butlers Wharf, SE1; ☎ **0171/378-6055**) on the South Bank, but it's worth it if you're a design enthusiast—or if you just want to see the role that commercial design plays in our everyday lives. Classical, kitsch, modern, surreal, and innovative, from Le Corbusier chairs to the Coke bottle, it's all chronicled here. It's the sort of place that makes visitors say, "We had one of those when I was growing up." Plus there are great river views. It's open daily from 11:30am to 6pm; admission is £5.25 ($9) for adults and £4 ($6) for children. Tube: Tower Hill, then a half-hour walk across Tower Bridge to Butler's Wharf east of the bridge on the South Bank.

The house of Sir John Soane (1753–1837), architect of the Bank of England, is an eccentric treasure-trove of ancient sculpture, artifacts, and art mixed in with strange architectural perspectives, fool-the-eye mirrors, flying arches, and domes. Located in Holborn, **Sir John Soane's Museum,** 13 Lincoln's Inn Fields, WC2 (☎ **0171/430-0175**), is rarely crowded, which makes spending an hour here even more of a treat. The oldest piece in the house is the 3,300-year-old sarcophagus of Pharaoh Seti I. Top prize in the picture gallery goes to William Hogarth's satirical and sometimes bawdy series from *The Rake's Progress*. The house is open Tuesday through Saturday from 10am to 5pm and the first Tuesday of each month from 6 to 9pm. Admission is free, but donations are invited. Tours are given Saturday at 2:30pm; tickets are £3 ($5) and are distributed at 2pm on a first-come, first-served basis; call

☎ **0171/405-2107** for details. Tube: Holborn, then a 5-minute walk south on Kingsway to Lincoln's Inn Fields; the museum entrance is on the north side of the street.

All the world's a stage at the **Theatre Museum,** Russell Street, WC2 (☎ **0171/836-7891**). At this branch museum of the Victoria and Albert Museum, you can enjoy an hour or so perusing the grandly named National Collections of the Performing Arts. British theatre, ballet, opera, music-hall pantomime, puppets, circus, and rock and pop music—both past and present—are represented. Activities include daily stage makeup demonstrations and costume workshops that use costumes from the Royal Shakespeare Company and the Royal National Theatre. The museum is open Tuesday through Sunday from 11am to 7pm. Admission is £3.50 ($6) for adults and £2 ($3) for seniors and children 5 to 17. Tube: Covent Garden, then a 5-minute walk south to Russell Street on the east side of Covent Garden Piazza.

London for the Young (& the Young at Heart)

You and your little ones will enjoy the **Bethnal Green Museum of Childhood,** Cambridge Heath Road, E2 (☎ **0181/980-2415**), a branch of the Victoria and Albert Museum specializing in toys from past and present, including fully furnished dollhouses ranging from simple cottages to miniature mansions. It's an enchanting place to wile away a couple of hours. It's open Monday through Thursday and Saturday from 10am to 5:50pm, and on Sunday from 2:30 to 5:50pm. It's closed May 1, December 25, and January 1. Admission is free. Tube: Bethnal Green, then a 5-minute walk north on Cambridge Heath Road to the museum entrance on the east side of the street.

Kids The capital's first world-class aquarium, the **London Aquarium,** Bridge Road, SE1 (☎ **0171/967-8000**), on the South Bank, is home to some 350 species of fish and aquatic invertebrates, including sharks, graceful stingrays, man-eating piranha, and sea scorpions. Elaborate exhibits, with enormous floor-to-ceiling tanks, re-create all sorts of marine habitats. Plan on spending at least 2 hours—longer if you can't pull the kids away. It's open daily from 10am to 6pm (last admission 5pm); admission is £7 ($12) for adults and £5 ($8) for children. Tube: Waterloo, then a 10-minute walk south along York Road to Westminster Bridge Road.

Kids Now partnered with Madame Tussaud's, which is right next door, the **London Planetarium,** Marylebone Road, NW1 (☎ **0171/486-1121**), takes you on a journey to the stars. In a show that's both instructive and entertaining, the audience accompanies a spaceship of travelers forced to desert their planet and travel through the solar system, visiting its major landmarks and witnessing spectacular cosmic activity. There are lots of kid-friendly hands-on exhibits (including one that lets you see what shape or weight you'd be on other planets). You can also hear Stephen Hawking talk about mysterious black holes. Give this at least a couple of hours. It's open daily from 10am to 5:30pm, with shows beginning daily at 10:20am and taking place every 40 minutes until 5pm. Admission is £5.85 ($10) for adults,

£4.65 ($8) for seniors, and £3.85 ($7) for children 5 to 17. Children under 5 are not admitted. Combined tickets for Madame Tussaud's and the Planetarium cost £11.50 ($19) for adults and £7.55 ($12) for children. Tube: Baker Street, then a 2-minute walk east on Marylebone Road.

Kids Let's hear it for public transportation! Housed in a splendid Victorian building (once the Flower Market at Covent Garden), the **London Transport Museum** (The Piazza, Covent Garden, WC2; ☎ **0171/379-6344**) recounts the development of the city's famous Underground and red-bus system. Several new KidZones with interactive exhibits allow younger visitors to operate the controls of a tube train, get their tickets punched, and play with touch-screen technology. After 2 hours, you might have to drag them away. It's open Saturday through Thursday from 10am to 6pm and Friday from 11am to 6pm (last admission at 5:15pm). Admission is £4.95 ($8) for adults, £2.95 ($5) for children, and £13 ($21) for a family ticket; children under 5 get in free. Tube: Covent Garden, then a 5-minute walk west to the Piazza; the museum is in the southeast corner.

Tourist Traps

Know before you go: Kids under 5 are not admitted to the **London Planetarium.**

Kids The **Museum of Mankind,** the incredible ethnographic collections of the British Museum, was housed in Mayfair until 1998, when it moved back to its parent museum in Bloomsbury. The galleries are filled with curiosities—everything from a pair of polar-bear slacks worn by Eskimos to Sioux war bonnets and a curious Hawaiian god with a Mohawk haircut, found by Captain Cook and shipped back to London. The collection is located in the British Museum, Great Russell St., WC1 (☎ **0171/730-0717**). It's open Monday through Saturday from 10am to 5pm and Sunday from 2:30 to 6pm; it's closed January 1, Good Friday, in early May, and December 24 to 26. Admission is free. Tube: Russell Square, then a 10-minute walk south on Montgomery Street, along the west side of Russell Square, to the museum entrance on Great Russell Street.

Kids Lights! Cameras! Action! The **Museum of the Moving Image,** South Bank (underneath Waterloo Bridge), SE1 (☎ **0171/401-2636**), provides an exhaustive and wonderfully entertaining history of the moving image. You can even audition for your own starring role. Ready for your close-up? Give yourself a couple of hours to see it all. It's open daily from 10am to 6pm (last admission 5pm). Admission is £6 ($10) for adults, £5.25 ($9) for students, £4.50 ($7) for children and seniors, and £17 ($28) for a family ticket (up to two adults and two children). Tube: Waterloo, then a 5-minute walk north on Waterloo Road; the museum is on the east side of Waterloo Bridge.

Kids Tower Hill is loaded with history—and here's a way to get the kids interested in it. A thousand years before construction began on the

Tower of London in 1065, Romans roamed the muddy lanes of nearby Londinium. At **Tower Hill Pageant,** Tower Hill Terrace, EC3 (☎ **0171/709-0081**), you can board a car and whiz through 2,000 years of city history in under an hour. You might call this "Senssurround," since the realistic scenes of London's waterfront come complete with sounds and smells. It's open daily April through October from 9:30am to 5:30pm, and November through March from 9:30am to 4:30pm. Admission is £6.45 ($11) for adults, £4.45 ($7) for children 4 to 16, and £15.95 ($26) for a family ticket. Tube: Tower Hill, then a 15-minute walk to the southwest corner of Tower Hill.

Tourist Traps

The international Pepsi Generation (your kids, and don't even try to keep them away) gravitates toward the **Pepsi Trocadero** (☎ **0171/439-1791**), a "total entertainment complex" located right on Piccadilly Circus. The lead attraction is **Segaworld,** with six rides, including a virtual reality "Space Mission" trip; "Max Drop," the world's first indoor free-fall ride (don't eat for at least an hour before); and 400 ear-splitting, eye-popping video games and simulators. The U.K.'s first IMAX 3-D Cinema (☎ **0171/494-4153**) screens an underwater adventure called *Aqua Planet.* Rock Circus, the other big attraction, is described below. **Planet Hollywood,** the ersatz **Rainforest Cafe** (which doesn't pretend its proceeds go to support the rain forests), and the 1950s-style **Ed's Easy Diner** are among the theme restaurants on the glitzed-up premises. The Trocadero Centre, with its shops and restaurants, is open daily and admission is free. All the individual attractions are priced separately: IMAX theatre tickets are £6.95 ($11) for adults and £5.50 ($9) for children; admission to Segaworld is free, but each game and ride will set you back 20p (50¢) to £3 ($5).

Rock Circus (☎ **0171/734-7203**), a popular outpost of Madame Tussaud's, presents the history of rock and pop music from Bill Haley and the Beatles to Sting and Madonna. The audio-animatronic performers move and sing golden oldies and more recent chart-toppers in an eerily lifelike way. There's lots of memorabilia and a sensory overload of videos and personal stereo sound. Of course it's always disconcerting for adults to hear the songs they grew up with as "oldies." It's open Wednesday through Monday from 11am (10am in the summer) to 9 or 10pm; it opens at noon on Tuesdays. Admission is £8 ($13) for adults, £7 ($12) for seniors and students, £6.50 ($11) for children under 16, and £20 ($32) for a family ticket.

Dungeons Without Dragons

Ever wonder where the phrase "throw him in the clink" came from? Well, now you know: The Clink was the jail attached to the Bishops of Winchester's palace. The former prison is gone, but the **Clink Prison Museum,** 1 Clink St. (☎ **0171/403-6515**), near the original site, will interest history buffs. You'll probably need only about an hour in "the clink" to see it all. It's open daily 10am to 6pm; admission is £4 ($7) for adults, £3 ($5) for seniors and students, and £2 ($3) for children. Tube: London Bridge, then a 10-minute walk across Duke Street and west along the river; the prison is just beyond Southwark Cathedral.

Kids Don't bring younger kids, because they'll be reduced to traumatized mush, but teens will probably love the grisly re-creations of medieval torture and executions at the **London Dungeon,** 28–34 Tooley St., SE1 (☎ **0171/403-0606**). There's a scream (literally) around every corner. If you're looking for a Jack-the-Ripper experience or are in the mood to witness a simulated burning at the stake, this is the place. Tolling bells, dripping water, and caged rats make it even more oppressive. If you're hungry after all the murder and mayhem, you're in luck: There's a Pizza Hut on the premises. The dungeon is open daily from 10am to 6:30pm (last admission 5:30pm). Admission is £8.95 ($15) for adults and £6.50 ($11) for students, seniors, and children under 15. Tube: London Bridge; the exhibition is just south as you exit the tube station. Not recommended for young children.

If you're looking for another sight guaranteed to give you the willies, check out the **Old Operating Theatre and Herb Garret.** (See "More Museums of All Shapes, Sorts & Sizes," above, for details.)

Tourist Traps

The **London Dungeon** is pretty intense, with plenty of blood and guts to go around. It's *not* recommended for young children.

Shakespeare Sights

After years of fundraising and construction delays, the South Bank finally has a full-size replica of Shakespeare's Globe Theatre. **Shakespeare's Globe Theatre & Exhibition,** New Globe Walk, Bankside, SE1 (☎ **0171/902-1500**), is located just east of its original site. Watching a Shakespeare play from one of the benches in this roofless "wooden O" is a wonderful experience, though it can be hard on the backside. On guided tours through the theatre and its workshops, you'll learn more about Shakespeare and Elizabethan theatre: what audiences were like, the rivalry between theatres, the cruel bear-baiting shows, and the notorious Southwark Stews—a nearby area where prostitutes plied their trade from at least the 14th century. It's open daily May through September 9am to 12:30pm and 2 to 4pm; October through April, it's open from 10am to 5pm. Tours are £5 ($8) for adults and £3 ($5) for children. Tube: Mansion House, then a 20-minute walk across Southwark Bridge; the theatre is visible on the west side along the river.

Southwark (pronounced *Suth*-ick) **Cathedral** (Montague Close, London Bridge, SE1; ☎ **0171/407-3708**), London's second-oldest church (after Westminster Abbey), is located in what was London's first theatre district (as well as a Church-sanctioned center of prostitution). Although partially rebuilt in 1890, there's still a lot of history associated with this 15th-century church. Shakespeare and Chaucer worshipped here. You can see it all, including the memorial to the Bard and a 13th-century wooden effigy of a knight, in less than 30 minutes. Lunchtime concerts are regularly given on Monday and Tuesday; call for exact times and schedules. The cathedral is open daily 8:30am to 6pm; admission is free, but a £2 ($3) donation is suggested. Tube: London Bridge, then a 10-minute walk across London Bridge Road to Cathedral Street.

Extra! Extra!

If you're exploring Southwark or planning to see a Shakespeare play at The Globe, you can have a snack, tea, or a full meal in the theatre itself. No reservations are required at **The Globe Cafe,** open daily 10am to 11pm. If you want lunch or dinner, it's a good idea to reserve ahead at **The Globe Restaurant** (☎ **0171/928-9444**), open for lunch from noon to 2:30pm and for dinner from 5:30 to 11pm.

Shipshape London

Kids A massive Royal Navy cruiser built in 1938 and used in World War II, the **H.M.S. *Belfast*** (Morgan's Lane, Tooley Street, SE1; ☎ **0171/407-6434**) is now moored on the south bank of the Thames near London Bridge and opposite the Tower of London. Tours of this floating, 10,500-ton museum take in all seven decks. There are exhibits devoted to the history of the ship and the Royal Navy, and you can even witness a re-created surface battle. Plan to spend at least 90 minutes here. It's open daily from 10am to 6pm (last admission 5:15pm). Admission is £4.70 ($8) for adults and £2.40 ($4) for children. Tube: London Bridge, then a 10-minute walk north across Tooley Street and north on Hays Lane toward the entrance on the river.

Kids Also on the South Bank is a full-scale reconstruction of Sir Francis Drake's 16th-century flagship, the ***Golden Hinde*** (St. Mary Overie Dock, Cathedral Street, London, SE1; ☎ **0171/403-0123**). This *Golden Hinde* was built in Devon but launched in San Francisco in 1973 to commemorate Drake's claiming of California. Like the original, it circumnavigated the globe, sailing over 140,000 miles, before becoming a permanent floating museum in 1996. A crew in period costumes gives tours of the fully rigged ship, once the home to 20 officers and gentlemen and between 40 and 60 crew members. The ship is open April through October from 10am to 6pm, and November through March from 10am to 5pm; admission is £2.30 ($4) for adults and £1.50 ($2.50) for children. Tube: London Bridge, then a 5-minute walk west on Bedale and Cathedral streets.

A Fabulous View

Kids In the new world of interpretive sightseeing, everything seems to offer an "experience," so why not Tower Bridge? At the aptly named **Tower Bridge Experience** (☎ **0171/378-1928**), you'll find "Harry," a Victorian bridge worker brought to life by animatronics. He'll tell you the story of this famous drawbridge with its pinnacled towers and how the mechanism for raising the bridge for ship traffic actually works. Along the way you'll meet the architect's ghost and visit a miniature music-hall show. Once there, the "experience" takes about an hour, and the fabulous views of the Thames from the bridge's walkways are alone worth the trip. It's open daily from 9:30am to 6pm (last admission 4:45pm); it's closed December 24 through 26 and January 1. Admission is £5.95 ($10) for adults and £3.95 ($7) for seniors, students, and children 5 to 15. Tube: Tower Hill, then a 10-minute walk south to the north pier of Tower Bridge.

It's not just any monument, it's **The Monument.** Designed by Sir Christopher Wren, this 202-foot-high Doric column commemorates the Great Fire of London, which swept through London in 1662. The Great Fire allegedly began in nearby Pudding Lane. The Monument—located, of all places, on Monument Street—is the tallest isolated stone column in the world. You'll appreciate just how tall it is if you climb the 311 steps to the wonderful viewing platform at the top. It's open Monday through Friday 10am to 5:40pm, and Saturday through Sunday 2 to 5:40pm. Admission is £1 ($1.65) for adults and 50p (80¢) for children. The phone is ☎ **0171/626-2717.** Tube: The Monument stop lets you out right across from the Monument.

Where to See How the Other Half Lived

The late Princess Diana was probably the most famous Spencer who never lived in **Spencer House,** 27 St. James's Place, SW1 (☎ **0171/499-8620**), the family's ancestral London home. One of London's most beautiful buildings, the house was built in 1766 for the first Earl Spencer, but it hasn't been a private residence since 1927. Restored and opened as a museum in 1990, its rooms are filled with period furniture and art loans from Queen Elizabeth, the Tate Gallery, and the Victoria and Albert. Guided tours take less than an hour. The house is open Sunday from 10:30am to 4:45pm; it's closed January and August. Admission is £6 ($10) for adults and £5 ($8) for children under 16; children under 10 are not admitted. Tube: Green Park, then a 10-minute walk south down Queen's Walk to St. James's Place on your left.

The palatial "town house" of the late Lady Wallace in Marylebone is the setting for the **Wallace Collection** (Hertford House, Manchester Square, W1; ☎ **0171/935-0687**), a breathtaking collection of art and armaments. The collection of French works is outstanding, but you'll also find masterworks from the Dutch, English, Spanish, and Italian schools. Vying for your attention are collections of decorative art and ornaments from 18th-century France and European and Asian armaments. You'll need at least an hour just to give everything a cursory glance. The house is open year-round Monday through Saturday 10am to 5pm, Sunday 2 to 5pm (April through September Sunday 11am to 5pm). Admission is free. Tube: Baker Street, then a 10-minute walk south on Baker Street to the museum entrance on the north side of Manchester Square.

Where to Stop & Smell the Roses

Hidden behind high brick walls is the **Chelsea Physic Garden** (Swan Walk, 66 Royal Hospital Rd., SW3), the second-oldest surviving botanical garden in England and one of the prettiest spots in London. The Chelsea Physic Garden was founded in 1673 by the Worshipful Society of Apothecaries to develop medicinal and commercial plant species. Cottonseeds from this garden launched an industry in the new colony of Georgia. You'll see some 7,000 exotic herbs, shrubs, trees, and flowers, as well as England's earliest rock garden. It's small enough (3½ acres) to wander through in an hour, but plant lovers will want to linger. The garden is open from April through October on Wednesdays from noon to 5pm and on Sundays from 2 to 6pm; it's open daily from 2 to 5pm during the Chelsea Flower Show in May. Admission is £3.50 ($5) for adults and £1.80 ($3) for students and children 5 to 15. Tube: Sloane Square, then a 20-minute walk south on Lower Sloane Street and west to the end of Royal Hospital Road; or from Sloane Square, you can catch southbound bus 11, 19, or 22.

The **Royal Botanic Gardens** (also known as the **Kew Gardens**) in Kew, 9 miles southwest of Central London (☎ **0181/940-1171**), are a feast for the eyes (and nose). This trip, including travel time and garden browsing, will take the better part of a day but is well worth it. On display in the 300-acre gardens is a marvelous array of specimens first planted in the 17th and 18th centuries. Orchids and palms are nurtured in the Victorian "glass pavilion" hothouse. There's also a lake, aquatic gardens, a Chinese pagoda, and even a royal palace. Kew Palace, the smallest and most picturesque of the former royal compounds, is where King George III went off his rocker. Queen Charlotte's Cottage was the mad king's summer retreat.

The gardens are open daily from 9:30am to dusk; they're closed December 25 and January 1. The Glasshouse closes at 4:45pm. Kew Palace and Queen Charlotte's Cottage are open daily in April through October from 11am to 5:30pm. Admission to the gardens is £5 ($8) for adults, £3.50 ($6) for seniors, £2.50 ($4) for children 5 to 16, and free for children under 5; a family ticket is £13 ($21). Admission is reduced to £3.50 ($6) within 45 minutes of the conservatory's closing. Admission is free to wheelchair users, the blind, and vision-impaired visitors. One-hour tours are available in March through November daily at 11am and 2pm; tickets, available at the Information Desk, cost £1 ($2) per person per hour. Call ☎ **0181/332-5623** for information. Tube: Kew Gardens, then a 10-minute walk west on Broomfield Street to the Victoria Gate entrance on Kew Road.

Extra! Extra!

Tired of the tube? You can take a boat upstream to Kew Gardens (and farther to Hampton Court) instead. Boats operated by **Westminster Passenger Service Association** (☎ **0171/930-2062**) leave from Westminster Pier daily between April and October from 10:15am to 2pm; the fare for the one-way, 90-minute journey is £6 ($10) for adults and £3 ($5) for children. The last boat from Kew usually departs around 5:30pm (depending on the tide).

A Quaint Village Just a Tube Ride Away

Although it's only 20 minutes by tube from Central London, **Hampstead** remains a village of charm and character, filled with Regency and Georgian houses favored by artists and writers from John Keats to John le Carré. Along **Flask Walk,** the village's pedestrian mall, you'll find a quirky mix of historic pubs, shops, and chic boutiques; the village itself has lots of old alleys, steps, courts, and groves just begging to be explored. Adjacent **Hampstead Heath** is 800 acres of high parkland where Londoners come to sun worship, fly kites, fish the ponds, swim, picnic, and jog. On a clear day you can see St. Paul's Cathedral and even the hills of Kent. An excursion here will take up at least half a day or more. Tube: Hampstead (the tube stop is a minute from Flask Walk) or Hampstead Heath. (Parliament Hill, right behind the tube stop, leads up into the park itself.)

Cool Britannia

Kenwood, Hampstead Lane, NW3 (☎ **0181/348-1286**), is a lovely neoclassical villa designed by Robert Adam on the shore of Kenwood Lake in the northern section of Hampstead Heath. Inside you'll find a small but impressive collection of paintings and jewelry. A cafeteria is located in the former coach house. The Kenwood Lakeside concert bowl beside the house is the sublime setting for outdoor symphony concerts in the summer; call ☎ **0171/413-1443** for concert information. Kenwood is open daily in April through October from 10am to 6pm, and in November through March from 10am to 4pm; it's closed December 24 and 25. Admission is free. Tube: Archway, then bus 210 west along Highgate and Hampstead Lane. For Kenwood Lakeside, take the tube to East Finchley; a free shuttle bus is provided from the tube stop for concert-goers.

More Royal Castles & Palaces

Located in Windsor, Berkshire, 20 miles from the center of London, **Windsor Castle (☎ 01753/868-286)** is one of the queen's official residences. The castle, its imposing skyline of towers and battlements rising from the center of the 4,800-acre Great Park, was constructed by William the Conquerer some 900 years ago and has been used as a royal residence ever since. The State Apartments open to visitors range from the intimate chambers of Charles II to the enormous Waterloo Chamber, built to commemorate the victory over Napoleon in 1815. All are superbly furnished with important works of art from the Royal Collection. From the ramparts of Windsor, you can look down on the playing fields of Eton College, where countless aristocratic boys have been educated. You can explore the famous school (all the Royals go there) by strolling across the Thames Bridge. Give yourself a full day for this excursion. The castle is open daily (except March 28, June 16, December 25 to 26, and January 1) November through February from 10am to 4pm (last admission 3pm) and March through October from 10am to 5:30pm (last admission 4pm). Admission is £9.80 ($17) for adults, £7 ($12) for seniors and students, and £5 ($8) for children 16 and under; a family ticket (for four) costs £21.50 ($35).

How to get there: The trip by train from Waterloo or Paddington Station takes 50 minutes and involves a transfer at Slough to the Slough–Windsor shuttle train. There are more than a dozen trains per day, with fares starting at £6.20 ($10) round-trip.

In 1514, Cardinal Wolsey began building the superb Tudor Hampton Court in East Moseley, Surrey, 13 miles west of London on the north side of the Thames. But that greedy monarch Henry VIII (of six wives fame) wanted a pretty home in the country. In 1525, he grabbed Hampton Court for himself and made **Hampton Court Palace (☎ 0181/781-9500)** a royal residence, which it remained until 1760. One of his wives, Anne Boleyn (mother of Elizabeth I), supposedly haunts the place to this day, though you'd think the hordes of tourists would've scared her away by now. Later Hampton Court was much altered by Sir Christopher Wren for William and Mary; Wren also designed the famous Maze, where you can wander in dizzy confusion. Inside the enormous palace (something of a maze itself), you'll see various state apartments and private rooms. The manicured Thames-side gardens alone are worth the trip. You'll need a full day for this excursion. There's a cafe and restaurant on the grounds.

The palace is open from mid-March to mid-October daily from 9:30am to 6pm; the rest of the year, it's open Monday 10:15am to 6pm and Tuesday through Sunday 9:30am to 6pm; it's closed December 24 to 26. Admission is £9.25 ($15) for adults, £7 ($12) for seniors and students, and £6.10 ($10) for children.

How to get there: The simplest way is to take the **train** from London's Waterloo Station to Hampton Court Station; the trip takes half an hour and costs £4.30 ($7) round-trip. The **boat** trip from Westminster Pier (daily at

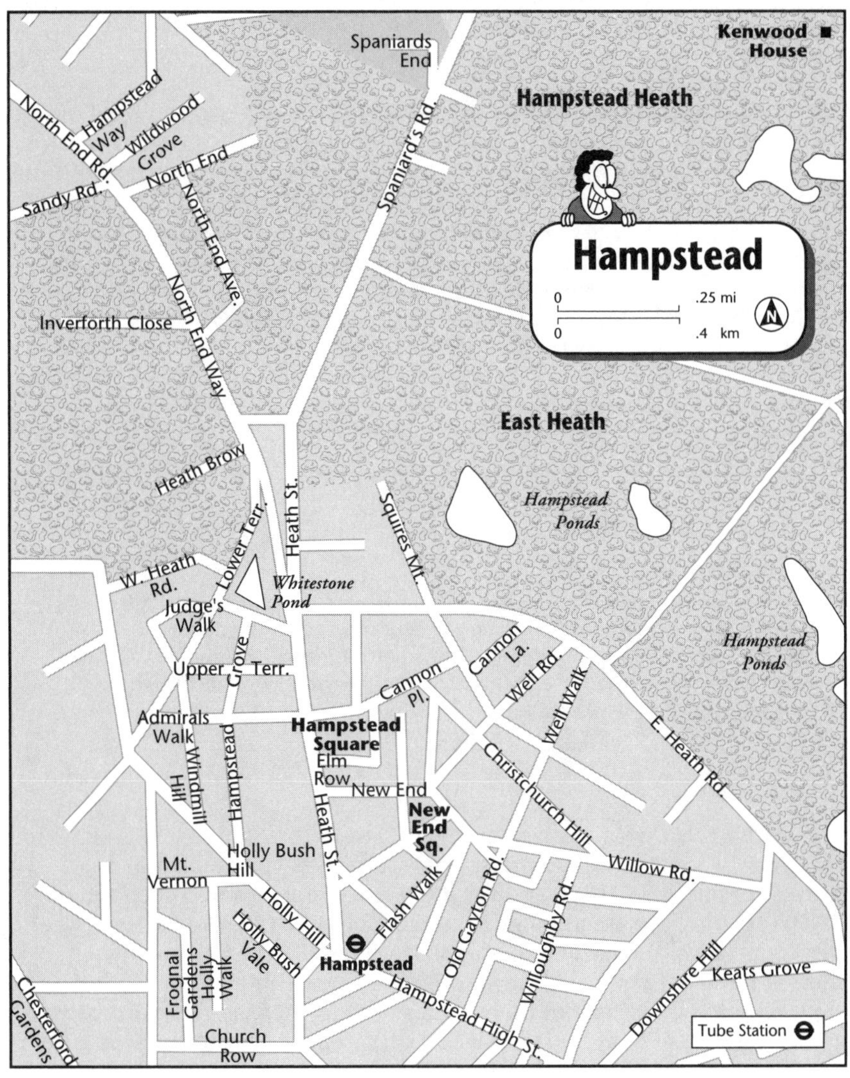

11am and noon April to October) is more scenic but takes about 3½ hours and costs £8 ($13) for adults and £4 ($7) for children round-trip; boats stop at Kew Gardens (see above) on the way. Call **Westminster Passenger Service Association** (☎ **0171/930-4097**) for more information.

Greenwich: The Center of Time

Kids Time is money in Greenwich, a town and borough of Greater London, about 4 miles east of the City. The world's clocks are set according to Greenwich Mean Time, and tourists flock here to stand on the prime meridian, the line from which the world's longitude is measured.

Greenwich is also famous for its maritime history. Berthed on the Thames is the last of the tea-clipper ships, the majestic 19th-century ***Cutty Sark***

(☎ **0181/858-3445**), open Monday through Saturday 10am to 5pm and Sunday noon to 5pm. Admission is £3.50 ($6) for adults and £2.50 ($4) for seniors and children 5 to 16; family tickets are £8.50 ($14). Not far from the *Cutty Sark* on the Thames is the **Royal Naval College,** King William Walk (off Romney Road; ☎ **0181/858-2154**); its imposing Great Hall (where the body of Lord Nelson lay in state in 1805) and chapel are open to visitors daily from 2:30 to 4:45pm (admission is free). The buildings were designed by Sir Christopher Wren in 1696 on the site of Greenwich Palace, which stood here from 1422 to 1620.

Tourist Traps

Greenwich's newest attraction, the **Millennium Dome** (www.mx2000.co.uk), is being readied (with endless financial setbacks) for its opening in the year 2000. Though nobody seems quite sure what the dome will contain, it's the subject of endless hype, and local promoters are grandly predicting that 12 million visitors will come to see it.

In **Greenwich Park,** marked clearly by signposts from the town, you'll find three very worthwhile attractions. One ticket gives you admission to all three. The cost is £5 ($8) for adults, £4 ($7) for seniors and students, and £2.50 ($4) for children. The phone number (☎ **0181/858-4422**) and opening hours (daily 10am to 5pm) are the same for all. The **National Maritime Museum** is dedicated to Britain's seafaring past. The paintings of ships tend to be boring, but there are also sailing crafts and models, as well as an extensive exhibit on Lord Nelson, which includes some 600 of his personal artifacts (including the coat he was wearing when he was shot at the Battle of Trafalgar). Adjacent to the museum is the splendidly restored **Queen's House.** You can visit the royal apartments on a self-guided tour that takes about 30 minutes. Next, huff your way up the hill in the park to explore the **Old Royal Observatory,** "the center of time and space." This is where you'll find the **prime meridian line** (longitude 0°) and the millennium countdown clock. Of particular interest here is the collection of original 18th-century chronometers (marked H1, H2, H3, and H4), beautiful instruments that were developed to help mariners chart longitude by time instead of by the stars. There's enough in Greenwich to keep you fully occupied for a full day, and it's a great outing for kids.

Time-Savers

The **Greenwich Tourist Information Centre,** 46 Greenwich Church St. (☎ **0181/858-6376**), is open in April through October daily from 10am to 5pm. In November through March, it's open Monday through Thursday from 11:15am to 4:30pm, and Friday through Sunday from 10am to 5pm. The center offers daily (at 12:15pm and 2:15pm) 1½- to 2-hour **walking tours** of the town's principal sights for £4 ($6). Reservations are not necessary, but it's a good idea to call first to make certain that there haven't been any schedule changes. If you take the walking tour, you get 50% off the admission to the National Maritime Museum, Queen's House, and Old Royal Observatory.

How to get there: The easiest and most interesting route is by Docklands Light Rail from Tower Hill Gateway, which takes you past Canary Wharf and all the new Docklands development; the one-way fare is £1.60 ($3), and 80p ($1.50) if you have a Travelcard. Take the train to Island Gardens, the last stop, and then walk through the foot tunnel beneath the Thames to Greenwich. You'll come out next to the *Cutty Sark*. All the attractions in Greenwich are clearly marked with signposts.

Grabbing a Meal in Greenwich

The town is full of restaurants. One of the best places for lunch is **Green Village Restaurant,** 11–13 Greenwich Church St. (☎ **0181/858-2348**). The restaurant serves several kinds of fresh fish (try the fish pie if it's available), American-style burgers, salads, and omelets. It's open daily from 11am to 11pm.

Chapter 15

Charge It! A Shopper's Guide to London

In This Chapter

- The big department stores
- Shopping areas & specialty shops
- How to get your VAT back
- How to save a bundle on sales
- Duty-free airport shopping: Is it worth it?

Shoppers beware: You're about to enter one of the greatest shopping cities in the world. Years ago, every time I was in London, I would go on a book-buying rampage. Books, at least "back then," cost half of what they did in the States. Then I'd rush over to Fortnum & Mason to stock up on tea. That's no longer necessary, since my neighborhood food store began to stock Earl Grey and other imported teas. I'd also make a point of visiting Floris on Jermyn Street, because it has some of the best soaps in the world. That's something I still do. I also like to give myself an hour or so to wander through Harrods, where people watching is as fun as shopping.

When you think of shopping in London, what comes to mind? Silky cashmere sweaters? Burberry raincoats? Hand-tailored suits and shirts? Tartan plaids? Irish linens? Silver spoons? Old engravings? Bone china? Whatever you think of, you'll be able to find it somewhere in London. What you won't find are a lot of bargains, except during the department stores' big blowout sales in January and July (see below). Your best bet is to ignore anything American and concentrate on British goods. You can also do well with French products; values are almost as good as what you'd find in Paris.

Just as the British market has made inroads into America (think of Laura Ashley), so too have American stores made inroads into London (The GAP is everywhere). But for every homogenized chain and megastore, there are still hundreds of small, enticing specialty shops and boutiques to delight the eye and empty the pocketbook.

Dollars & Sense

Bargain hunters should zero in on goods that are manufactured in England. Anything from **The Body Shop, Filofax,** or **Dr. Marten's** (all covered below) will cost about half of what it does in the States. Other things to look for include woolens and cashmeres, English brands of bone china, antiques, used silver, old maps and engravings, and rare books.

Shopping Hours

Normal shopping hours are Monday through Saturday 10am to 5:30pm, with a late closing (7 or 8pm) on Wednesday or Thursday night. Stores may legally be open for 6 hours on Sunday, usually from 11am to 5pm.

Taxing Matters

VAT (value-added tax) in London and throughout the U.K. is **17.5%.** It's already included in the price you see on the price tag. (Maybe that's why everything seems so expensive.) As a non-EU (Economic Union) resident, you can get a VAT refund (see below), but every store requires you to purchase a minimum amount to qualify; the exact amount varies from store to store, but the minimum you have to spend is £50 ($82). VAT is not charged on goods shipped out of the country, no matter what you spend. Many London shops will help you beat the VAT rap by shipping for you.

Dollars & Sense

Shipping goods from London stores might seem like a great way to beat the VAT tax and avoid the hassle of lugging large packages home with you. But beware: Shipping can *double* the cost of your purchase. You might also have to pay U.S. duties when the goods arrive. To save money, if you're really loaded down, consider paying for excess baggage (rates vary with the airline).

Extra! Extra!

One of the best-kept secrets of London shopping is that the minimum expenditure needed to qualify for a refund on VAT is only £50 ($82). Not every store honors this minimum: It's £100 ($165) at Harrods, £75 ($124) at Selfridges, and £62 ($102) at Hermès. But it's far easier to qualify for a tax refund in Britain than almost any other country in the European Union.

How to Claim Your VAT Refund

If you know what to do, you can get back about 15% of the 17.5% VAT tax. The process is a bit complicated but worth it if you've dropped a wad shopping in London. Here's what you do:

1. First, ask the store whether they do VAT refunds and what their minimum purchase is.
2. If you've spent the minimum amount, ask for the VAT refund paperwork. The retailer will have to fill out a portion.
3. Fill out your portion of the form.
4. Present the form—along with the goods—at the Customs office in the airport. Allow a half hour to stand in line. ***Remember:*** You're required to show the goods at your time of departure, so don't pack them in your checked luggage; put them in your carry-on instead.
5. After you have the paperwork stamped by the Customs officials, you have two choices. You can mail in the papers and receive your refund in a British check (no!) or a credit-card refund (yes!), or you can go directly to the **Cash VAT Refund** desk at the airport and get your refund in cash. The bad news: If you accept cash other than sterling, you will lose money on the conversion rate. Many stores charge a flat fee for processing your refund, so £3 to £5 ($5 to $8) may be automatically deducted from the total refund. But if you get back 15%, you might be saving a bundle.

Note: If you're traveling to **other countries** within the European Union, you do not apply for your VAT refund at the London airport. At your final destination, prior to departure from the EU, you file for all your VAT refunds at one time.

Tourist Traps

Be alert to any merchant who tells you that you can get VAT refund forms at the airport. It's not true. You must get a refund form from the retailer, and it must be completed by the retailer at the time of purchase. Don't leave the store without a completed refund form.

I Need a Drugstore!

In England, a drugstore is called a chemists' shop. All over London you'll find **Boots The Chemist,** the drugstore with a million branches. In terms of size and convenience, the best one is just across the street from Harrods at 72 Brompton Rd., SW3 (☎ **0171/589-6557;** tube: Knightsbridge). The house brands of beauty products are worth checking out as inexpensive gift items. Global and Naturalistic are two lines that are Boots' versions of The Body Shop, and the Boots knockoff of Chanel makeup is called No. 7. They also sell film, pantyhose (called tights), sandwiches, and all of life's little necessities.

How to Save a Bundle: The London Sales

Stores in London have traditionally held two sale periods—one in January and the other in July. Modern life has changed this somewhat, since July sales may now begin in June or even earlier. The January sale remains the big event of the year, usually starting after the first week in January (when round-trip airfares are in the low range). If you find enough bargains, savings on January sale items might earn back your travel money.

Discounts can range from 25% to 50% at leading department stores, such as Harrods and Selfridges. At Harrods the best buys are on Harrods logo souvenirs, English china (seconds are trucked in from factories in Stoke-on-Trent), and English designer brands like Jaeger. Harrods has the most famous January sale in London, but it's not the only show in town. Just about every other store—save Boots—also has a big sale at this time.

On the Way Home: Duty-Free Airport Shopping

Duty-free shopping at airports is big business. Heathrow's Terminal 4 is now a virtual shopping mall, but each terminal has a good bit of shopping, with not a lot of crossover between brands. You might be sorely tempted, if you didn't get in any London shopping, to spend your preboarding time by looking for something to take home.

Just remember this: Not everything in a duty-free area is a bargain. Prices at the airport for items like souvenirs and candy bars are actually higher than on the streets of London. Duty-free prices on luxury goods are usually fair but not rock bottom by any means. Liquor and cigarettes usually are much cheaper than you'd ever find back home. Airport stores often have special promotions and coupons that allow for pounds off at the time of the purchase. A word to the wise: Don't save all your shopping until you get to the airport, and have some idea of prices beforehand so you know when to pounce.

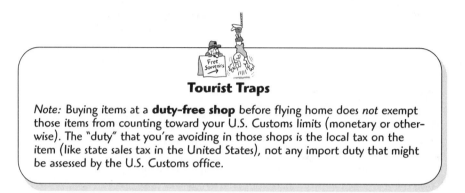

Tourist Traps

Note: Buying items at a **duty-free shop** before flying home does *not* exempt those items from counting toward your U.S. Customs limits (monetary or otherwise). The "duty" that you're avoiding in those shops is the local tax on the item (like state sales tax in the United States), not any import duty that might be assessed by the U.S. Customs office.

Getting Your Stuff Through Customs

Technically, there are no limits on how much loot you can bring back into the **United States** from a trip abroad, but the customs authority does put limits on how much you can bring back for free. You may bring home $400 worth of goods duty-free, provided you've been out of the country at least 48 hours and haven't used the exemption in the past 30 days. This limit includes not more than 1 liter of an alcoholic beverage (you must, of course, be over 21), 200 cigarettes, and 100 cigars. Antiques over 100 years old and works of art are exempt from the $400 limit, as is anything you mail home from abroad. You may mail up to $200 worth of goods to yourself (marked "for personal use") and up to $100 worth to others (marked "unsolicited gift") once each day, as long as the package does not include alcohol or tobacco products. You'll have to pay an import duty on anything over these limits. You'll be charged a flat rate of 10% duty on the next $1,000 worth of purchases. Be sure to have your receipts with you. For more specific guidance, write to the **U.S. Customs Service,** P.O. Box 7407, Washington, DC 20044 (☎ **202/927-6724**), and request the free pamphlet *Know Before You Go.* Or check out the details on the Customs Department Web site (**www.customs.ustreas.gov**).

Returning **Canadian** citizens are allowed a $300 exemption and can bring back duty-free 200 cigarettes, 2.2 pounds of tobacco, 40 imperial ounces (1.2 qt.) of liquor, and 50 cigars. All valuables that you're taking with you to the U.K., such as expensive cameras, should be declared on the Y-38 form before departure from Canada. For a clear summary of Canadian rules, write for the booklet *I Declare,* issued by Revenue Canada, 2265 St. Laurent Blvd., Ottawa K1G 4KE (☎ **800/461-9999** or 613/993-0534).

The Biggies: London Department Stores

When it comes to department stores, London is tops. Yes, all those little shops on every London street are enticing, but these behemoths can save you time because they carry under their roofs just about everything you could ever dream of. The following are the biggest and most well known of London's shopping emporiums.

Harrods, 87–135 Brompton Rd., Knightsbridge, SW1 (☎ **0171/730-1234**), which might be the most famous department store in the world, is a 10-minute walk south of the Knightsbridge tube station along Brompton Road. As firmly entrenched in London life as Buckingham Palace, this enormous emporium is not only Shopping personified, it offers some of the best people-watching opportunities in the city. There are 300 departments, and the sheer range, variety, and quality of merchandise is dazzling. Best of all are the food halls, stocked with a huge variety of foods and several cafes. Carrying around the famous green plastic Harrods bag they give you with every purchase conveys a certain sense of accomplishment.

Just north of the Knightsbridge tube stop is **Harvey Nichols,** 109–125 Knightsbridge, SW1 (☎ **0171/235-5000**), which was the late Princess Diana's department store of choice. Harvey Nicks, as it's called, doesn't compete with Harrods because it has a much more upmarket, fashionable image. It has its own gourmet food hall and fancy restaurant, The Fifth Floor, and it's crammed with designer home furnishings, gifts, and fashions. Women's clothing is the largest segment of its business, as you might know if you're a fan of the TV series *Absolutely Fabulous.*

Fortnum & Mason, 181 Piccadilly, W1 (☎ **0171/734-8040;** Tube: Piccadilly Circus), just a hop and a skip from Daks Simpson and down the street from the Ritz, is the world's most elegant grocery store. The grocery department carries the finest foods from around the world, and on the other floors you'll find bone china; crystal-cut glass; and leather, antiques, and stationery departments. Dining choices here include the Patio & Buttery, St. James's, and The Fountain Restaurant (see chapter 10, "London Restaurants from A to Z").

Cool Britannia

Fortnum & Mason holds two royal warrants and is the Queen's London grocer. Of course you'll never see Her Majesty wandering through the aisles with a shopping basket on her arm. Someone else in the Royal Household takes care of the shopping.

Liberty PLC, 214–220 Regent St., W1 (☎ **0171/734-1234**), an easy 10-minute stroll south from the Oxford Circus tube stop, is celebrated for its Liberty Prints—top-echelon fabrics, typically in floral patterns, that are prized by decorators for the way they add a sense of Englishness to a room. The front part of the store isn't particularly distinctive, but other parts of the place have been restored to Tudor-style splendor with half-timbering and lots of wood paneling. There are six floors of fashion, china, and home furnishings, as well as the famous Liberty Print fashion fabrics, upholstery fabrics, scarves, ties, luggage, and gifts.

Fenwick of Bond Street, 63 New Bond St., W1 (☎ **0171/629-9161**), located south of the Bond Street tube station and a short walk west from Liberty, is a high-style women's fashion store that has been around since 1891. Fenwick (pronounced *Fen*-ick) offers an excellent collection of designer womenswear, ranging from moderately priced ready-to-wear items to more expensive designer fashions. A wide range of lingerie in all price ranges is also sold.

From Liberty or Fenwick, you can walk north to **Selfridges** at 400 Oxford St., W1 (☎ **0171/629-1234;** tube: Bond Street or Marble Arch). This is one of the largest department stores in Europe, with more than 500 divisions selling everything from artificial flowers to groceries. The store has recently been redone to attract a more upscale clientele, but the size of the store allows it to feature less-expensive, mass-marketed lines as well. The Miss Selfridge boutique, located on one side of the store near the cosmetics department, features teen fashions, hotshot clothes, accessories, makeup, and moderately priced cutting-edge fashions. There's a cafe tucked into this side of the store.

Finally, I have to mention good old **Marks & Spencer,** 458 Oxford St., W1 (☎ **0171/935-7954;** tube: Marble Arch), a private-label department store good for basics of all kinds. The goods are good quality, if rather conservative, and the stores tend to be unfussy. There's another branch at 173 Oxford St., W1 (☎ **0171/437-7722;** tube: Oxford Circus).

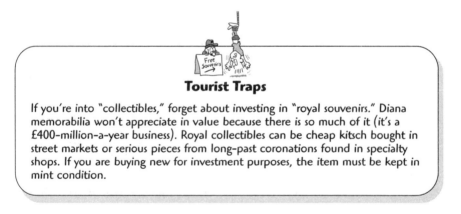

Tourist Traps

If you're into "collectibles," forget about investing in "royal souvenirs." Diana memorabilia won't appreciate in value because there is so much of it (it's a £400-million-a-year business). Royal collectibles can be cheap kitsch bought in street markets or serious pieces from long-past coronations found in specialty shops. If you are buying new for investment purposes, the item must be kept in mint condition.

London's Prime Shopping Grounds

If you've hit any of the department stores listed above, you've already been in London's two prime shopping areas: **Knightsbridge** and the **West End.** Several key streets in both areas house some of London's finest retail stores. All are compactly located in a niche or neighborhood so you can easily stroll and shop.

Most of the department stores, designer shops, and multiples (chain stores) have their flagships in the West End. The key streets are **Oxford Street** for affordable shopping, **Regent Street** for fancier shops and more upscale department stores and specialty dealers, **Piccadilly** for older established department stores, **Jermyn Street** for traditional English luxury goods, and **Bond Street** for chic, upscale fashion boutiques. The **Covent Garden** area is great for all-purpose shopping, and there's a special shopping nook around **Leicester Square.**

Dollars & Sense

British retailers now have the option to charge more for goods and services bought by credit card, although they are obliged to display a clear indication that differentiated pricing applies.

Piccadilly

Piccadilly Circus is considered the heart of London, but for shopping purposes you're better off striking out south from the Piccadilly tube stop along Piccadilly (the street) or northwest along Regent Street. Piccadilly Circus is dominated by entertainment complexes like Pepsi Trocadero, but there's one megastore, Tower Records, that you might want to check out, and the big Burberry store is on Haymarket, just east of the tube stop.

Tower Records, 1 Piccadilly Circus, W1 (☎ **0171/439-2500;** tube: Piccadilly Circus), is one of the largest record and CD stores in Europe. It's practically a tourist attraction in its own right. All I can say is that it's enormous and glowing with orange and red neon. You can avoid it, but you can't overlook it.

Burberry, 18–22 Haymarket, SW1 (☎ **0171/930-3343**), sells those famous raincoats, plus excellent men's shirts, sportswear, knitwear, and accessories.

If you're a walker, the Piccadilly Circus tube will get you to all the stores on Piccadilly (including **Fortnum & Mason;** see "The Biggies: London Department Stores" above), Regent, and Jermyn streets, and many on Bond Street. Piccadilly (the street) runs southwest from Piccadilly Circus.

Hatchards, 187 Piccadilly, W1 (☎ **0171/439-9921**), established in 1797, is London's most historic and atmospheric bookstore.

Jermyn Street

Two-block-long Jermyn Street, one of St. James's most exclusive little nooks, lies 1 block south of Piccadilly between St. James's Street and Duke Street. Here you'll find posh, high-end men's haberdasher's and toiletries shops, many of which have been doing business for centuries and hold royal warrants.

If you walk south on St. James's Street from Jermyn Street, you'll come to **Farlows** at 5 Pall Mall, SW1 (☎ **0171/839-2423**), famous for fishing and shooting equipment and classic country clothing.

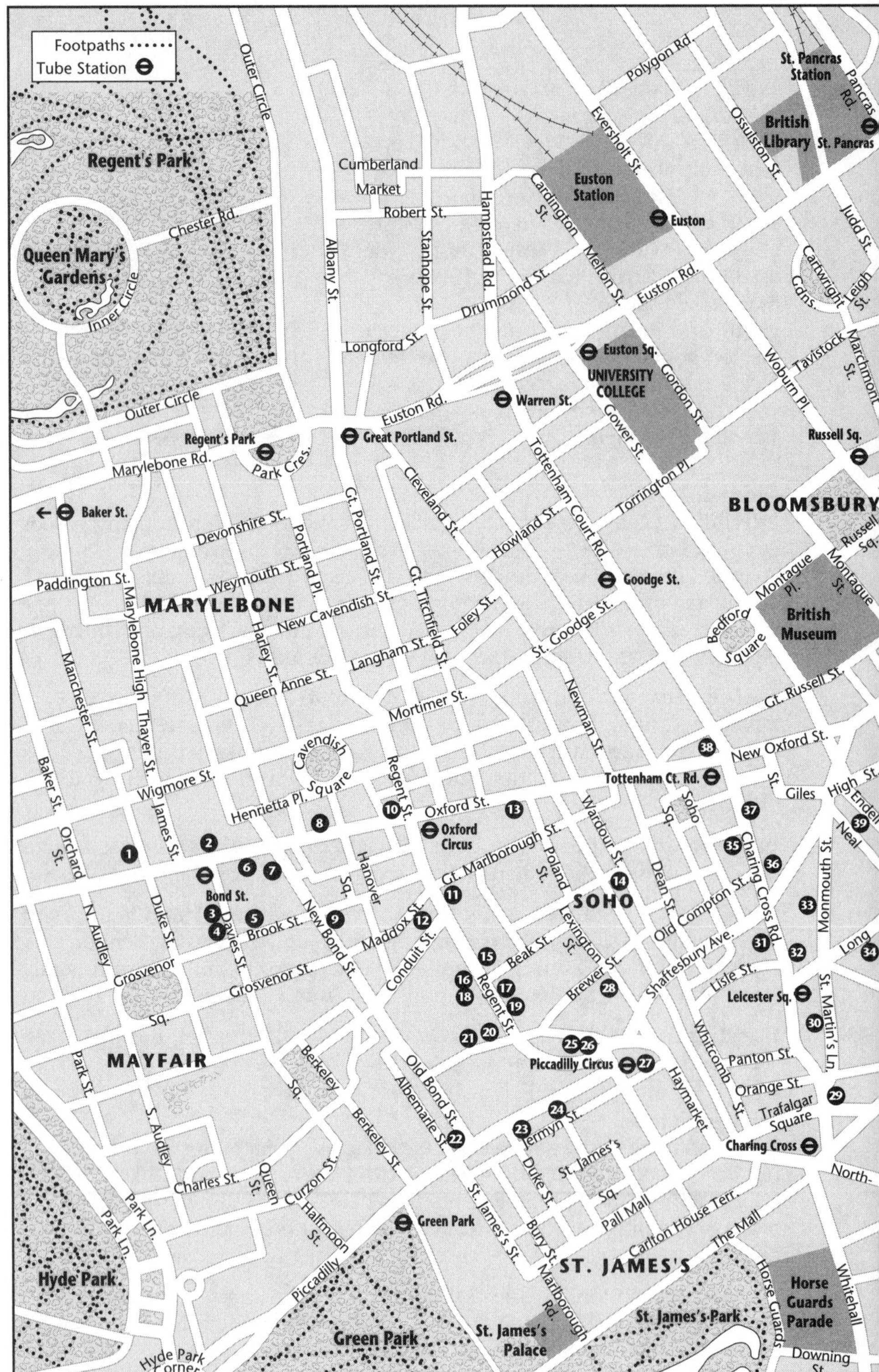

Footpaths
Tube Station
Regent's Park
Queen Mary's Gardens
Inner Circle
Outer Circle
Chester Rd.
Cumberland Market
Robert St.
Albany St.
Stanhope St.
Hampstead Rd.
Polygon Rd.
Eversholt St.
Euston Station
Euston
Cardington St.
Melton St.
Drummond St.
Euston Rd.
Longford St.
Euston Sq.
UNIVERSITY COLLEGE
Gordon St.
Gower St.
Warren St.
Great Portland St.
Regent's Park
Park Cres.
Marylebone Rd.
Baker St.
St. Pancras Station
British Library
St. Pancras
Pancras Rd.
Ossulston St.
Judd St.
Cartwright Gdns.
Leigh St.
Woburn Pl.
Tavistock
Marchmont St.
Russell Sq.
BLOOMSBURY
Russell Sq.
Montague Pl.
Montague St.
British Museum
Bedford Square
Gt. Russell St.
Torrington Pl.
Tottenham Court Rd.
Goodge St.
Howland St.
Cleveland St.
Devonshire St.
Weymouth St.
Paddington St.
MARYLEBONE
Portland Pl.
Gt. Portland St.
Gt. Titchfield St.
New Cavendish St.
Foley St.
St. Goodge St.
Langham St.
Harley St.
Queen Anne St.
Mortimer St.
Marylebone High St.
Manchester St.
Thayer St.
Cavendish Square
Wigmore St.
Regent St.
Henrietta Pl.
Newman St.
New Oxford St.
Tottenham Ct. Rd.
St. Giles High St.
Endell
Neal
Soho Sq.
Baker St.
Orchard St.
James St.
Oxford St.
Oxford Circus
Gt. Marlborough St.
Poland St.
Wardour St.
Dean St.
Charing Cross Rd.
Monmouth St.
Bond St.
Hanover Sq.
New Bond St.
Davies St.
Brook St.
Maddox St.
SOHO
Old Compton St.
N. Audley
Duke St.
Grosvenor Sq.
Grosvenor St.
Conduit St.
Beak St.
Lexington St.
Brewer St.
Shaftesbury Ave.
Lisle St.
Leicester Sq.
Long
St. Martin's Ln.
Regent St.
MAYFAIR
Park St.
Berkeley Sq.
Old Bond St.
Albemarle St.
Piccadilly Circus
Haymarket
Whitcomb St.
Panton St.
Orange St.
Trafalgar Square
Charing Cross
North-
S. Audley
Berkeley St.
Jermyn St.
St. James's Sq.
Duke St.
Charles St.
Queen St.
Curzon St.
Halfmoon St.
Park Ln.
Park Ln.
Green Park
St. James's St.
Bury St.
Pall Mall
Carlton House Terr.
The Mall
ST. JAMES'S
Marlborough Rd.
Horse Guards
Horse Guards Parade
Whitehall
Hyde Park
Piccadilly
Green Park
St. James's Palace
St. James's Park
Hyde Park Corner
Downing St.

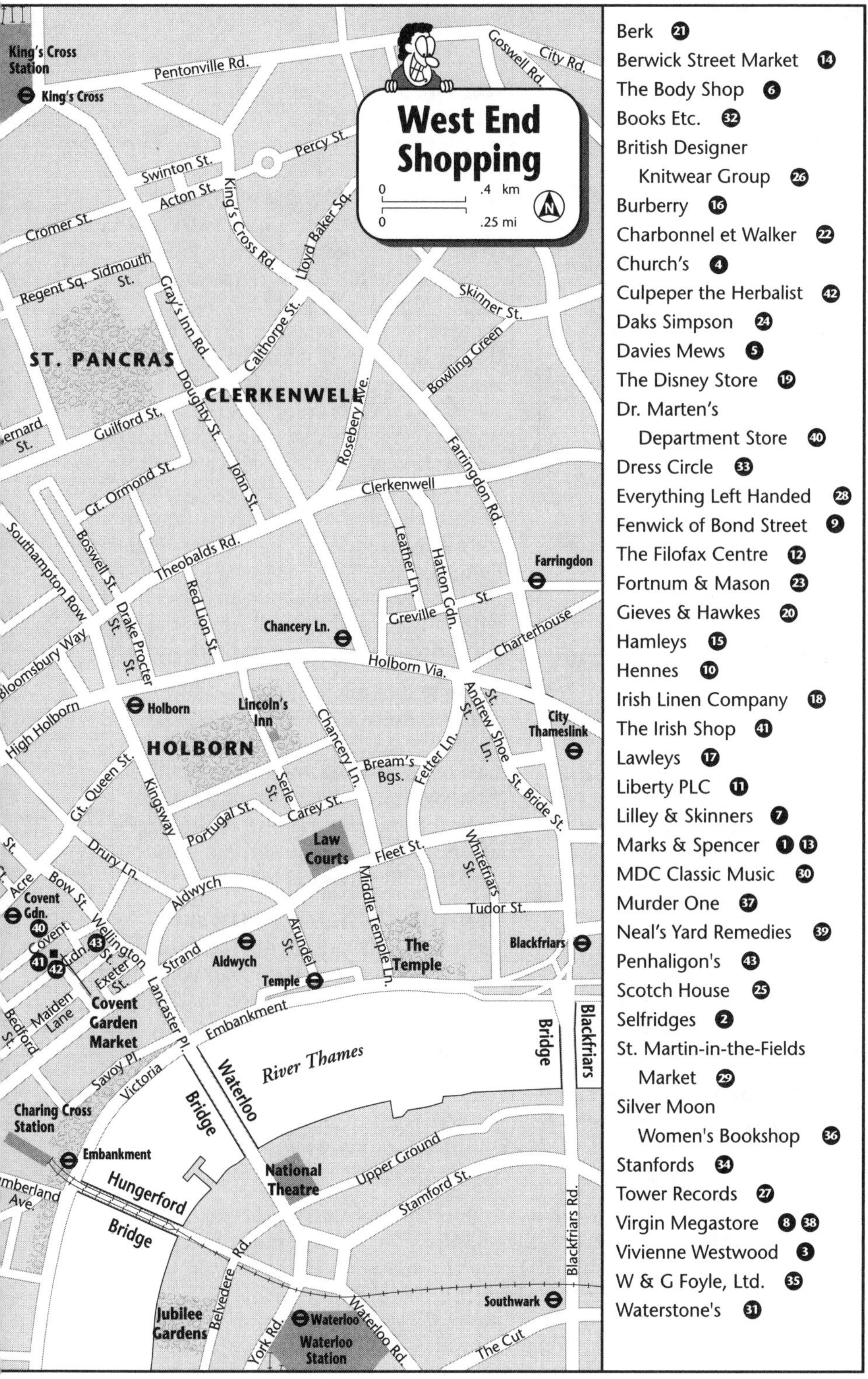
West End Shopping
0 .4 km
0 .25 mi
N
King's Cross Station
King's Cross
Pentonville Rd.
Goswell Rd.
City Rd.
Percy St.
Swinton St.
Acton St.
King's Cross Rd.
Lloyd Baker Sq.
Cromer St.
Regent Sq.
Sidmouth St.
Gray's Inn Rd.
Calthorpe St.
Skinner St.
Bowling Green
ST. PANCRAS
Doughty St.
CLERKENWELL
Rosebery Ave.
Guilford St.
John St.
Farringdon Rd.
Gt. Ormond St.
Clerkenwell
Southampton Row
Boswell St.
Theobalds Rd.
Leather Ln.
Hatton Gdn.
Farringdon
Red Lion St.
Drake St.
Procter St.
Chancery Ln.
Greville St.
Charterhouse
Bloomsbury Way
Holborn Via.
High Holborn
Holborn
Lincoln's Inn
Chancery Ln.
St. Andrew St.
Shoe Ln.
City Thameslink
HOLBORN
Gt. Queen St.
Kingsway
Serle St.
Bream's Bgs.
Fetter Ln.
St. Bride St.
Portugal St.
Carey St.
Law Courts
Fleet St.
Whitefriars St.
Drury Ln.
Aldwych
Middle Temple Ln.
Tudor St.
Bow St.
Covent Gdn.
Wellington St.
Arundel St.
The Temple
Blackfriars
Strand
Aldwych
Temple
Exeter St.
Lancaster Pl.
Maiden Lane
Covent Garden Market
Bedford St.
Embankment
Bridge
Blackfriars
River Thames
Waterloo
Savoy Pl.
Victoria
Bridge
Charing Cross Station
Embankment
Hungerford
National Theatre
Upper Ground
Stamford St.
Bridge
Blackfriars Rd.
Belvedere Rd.
Southwark
Jubilee Gardens
Waterloo
Waterloo Station
York Rd.
Waterloo Rd.
The Cut
Berk 21
Berwick Street Market 14
The Body Shop 6
Books Etc. 32
British Designer Knitwear Group 26
Burberry 16
Charbonnel et Walker 22
Church's 4
Culpeper the Herbalist 42
Daks Simpson 24
Davies Mews 5
The Disney Store 19
Dr. Marten's Department Store 40
Dress Circle 33
Everything Left Handed 28
Fenwick of Bond Street 9
The Filofax Centre 12
Fortnum & Mason 23
Gieves & Hawkes 20
Hamleys 15
Hennes 10
Irish Linen Company 18
The Irish Shop 41
Lawleys 17
Liberty PLC 11
Lilley & Skinners 7
Marks & Spencer 1 13
MDC Classic Music 30
Murder One 37
Neal's Yard Remedies 39
Penhaligon's 43
Scotch House 25
Selfridges 2
St. Martin-in-the-Fields Market 29
Silver Moon Women's Bookshop 36
Stanfords 34
Tower Records 27
Virgin Megastore 8 38
Vivienne Westwood 3
W & G Foyle, Ltd. 35
Waterstone's 31

Regent Street

There's a majestic look to Regent Street, which begins in a grand sweeping curve on the west side of Piccadilly Circus and heads north to intersect with Oxford Street. Regent Street is lined with upscale department stores and specialty boutiques. Savile Row, synonymous with hand-tailored men's suits, lies 1 block to the west of Regent Street. Its wild counterpart—or at least it was in the early Beatles' years—is Carnaby Street, now a rather sad tourist attraction trying to trade in on a vanished past; it's a block east of Regent Street. Finally, if you're shopping in this area, make a point to visit the Burlington Arcade, which runs from Regent Street to Savile Row. This famous glass-roofed, Regency-era passage, lit by wrought-iron lamps and decorated with clusters of ferns and flowers, is lined with intriguing shops and boutiques.

Extra! Extra!

Left-handed folks are usually in the minority—except at **Everything Left Handed,** 57 Brewer St., W1 (off Regent Street; ☎ **0171/ 437-3910**). This unique store sells practical items—everything from scissors to corkscrews—for all the lefties in the world.

Extra! Extra!

For hot-off-the-catwalk women's knockoffs that won't last more than a season, go to **Hennes,** 261 Regent St., W1 (☎ **0171/ 493-4004**).

If you're looking for Royal Doulton, Minton, Royal Crown Derby, Wedgwood, Spode, or Aynsley china, stop in at **Lawleys,** 154 Regent St., W1 (☎ **0171/ 734-3184;** tube: Piccadilly Circus or Oxford Circus); it has one of the largest inventories of china in Britain. (The January and July sales are excellent.)

At **British Designer Knitwear Group,** 2–6 Quadrant Arcade, 80 Regent St., W1 (☎ **0171/734-5786**), you'll find woolens from all over the British Islands, including the Scottish Shetlands. Some of the woolens are handmade; many of the designers are well known. Some have a tweedy English look, while others are more high fashion.

Scotch House, 84–86 Regent St., W1 (☎ **0171/734-5966**), has a worldwide reputation for its comprehensive selection of cashmere and wool knitwear for men, women, and children. It also sells tartan garments and accessories, as well as Scottish tweed classics.

Kids Do I need to tell you what you'll find at the **Disney Store,** 140 Regent St., W1 (☎ **0171/287-6558**), which you'll see as you walk farther north toward Oxford Street? If you're looking for non-Disney toys, you couldn't do any better than **Hamleys,** 1 block from the Disney Store at 188–196 Regent St., W1 ☎**0171/734-3161**). The finest toy shop in the world, it stocks more than 35,000 toys and games on seven floors of fun and magic. You can get everything from cuddly stuffed animals and dolls to radio-controlled cars, train sets, model kits, board games, outdoor toys, and computer games.

Gieves & Hawkes, 1 Savile Row, W1 (☎ **0171/434-2001;** tube: Piccadilly Circus), offers good-quality cotton shirts, silk ties, Shetland sweaters, and ready-to-wear and tailor-made suits. The list of clients includes the Prince of Wales.

Irish Linen Company, 35–36 Burlington Arcade, W1 (☎ **0171/493-8949**), carries items crafted of Irish linen, including hand-embroidered handkerchiefs and bed and table linens.

Berk, 46 Burlington Arcade, Piccadilly, W1 (☎ **0171/493-0028**), boasts one of the largest collections of cashmere sweaters in London, as well as capes, stoles, scarves, and camel's-hair sweaters.

Dollars & Sense

Chronic organizers who can't live without their Filofax should head immediately for **The Filofax Centre,** 21 Conduit St., W1 (☎ **0171/499-0457**). At this store on Conduit Street, which leads west from Regent Street, you'll find the entire range of inserts and books at prices that are at least half off the U.S. rate.

Oxford Street

Winded and broke from all that shopping on Regent Street, maybe you've finally made it as far north as Oxford Street. An alternative would be to come here first, getting out at the Oxford Circus, Bond Street, or Tottenham Court Road tube stop. Oxford Street is more affordable than Regent Street—not as tony, but there's plenty of pickings.

Lilley & Skinners, 360 Oxford St., W1 (☎ **0171/560-2000;** tube: Bond Street), is the largest shoe store in Europe, displaying many different brands over three floors.

Dollars & Sense

The U.K.-based **Body Shop** stores are now found all over the U.S., but prices at their London branches are drastically lower. You can stock up on their politically and environmentally correct beauty, bath, and aromatherapy products at **The Body Shop,** 375 Oxford St., W1 (☎ **0171/409-7868;** tube: Bond Street). You'll find other branches in every shopping zone in London.

Virgin Megastore, a giant musical grocery megastore, has two Oxford Street locations. The larger is at 14–16 Oxford St., W1 (☎ **0171/631-1234;** tube: Tottenham Court Road); the other is at 527 Oxford St., W1 (☎ **0171/491-8582;** tube: Oxford Circus). Hundreds of thousands of current CDs in every genre are sold, and you can hear releases on headphones at listening stations before making purchases.

Extra! Extra!

If you love all things chocolate, make a point to stop in at **Charbonnel et Walker,** 1 The Royal Arcade, 28 Old Bond St., W1 (☎ **0171/491-0939;** tube: Green Park), famous for its hot chocolate (buy it by the tin) and its strawberries-and-cream chocolates.

Bond Street

Bond Street, which runs parallel to Regent Street on the west and connects Piccadilly with Oxford Street, is London's equivalent to New York's Fifth Avenue. Divided into New (northern section) and Old (southern section), Bond Street is the hot address for all the hotshot international designers. Here and on adjacent streets, you'll find a large conglomeration of very expensive fashion boutiques. Davies Street, which runs south from outside the Bond Street tube station, is just one of the choicer streets in the area; Davies Mews is an upscale shopping zone noted for its antiques dealers. You can access the area from the north by the Bond Street tube stop and from the south by Green Park.

Vivienne Westwood, 6 Davies St., W1 (☎ **0171/629-3757;** tube: Bond Street), is one of the hottest British designers for women; this flagship store carries a full range of jackets, skirts, trousers, blouses, dresses, and evening dresses.

Church's, 13 New Bond St., W1 (☎ **0171/493-1474;** tube: Bond Street), sells classy shoes said to be recognizable to all the snobby maitres d'hôtel in London.

Leicester Square

You don't want to shop in Leicester Square itself because there's nothing there but giant movie palaces and touristy restaurants (and the reduced-price ticket booth). St. Martin's Lane, to one side of the Leicester Square tube station, is a pleasant promenade lined with shops selling rare books, prints, and posters, some of them relating to the performing arts. Monmouth Street, which runs north from the tube station, and theater-lined Haymarket are other areas to explore.

Dress Circle, 57–59 Monmouth St., WC2 (☎ **0171/240-2227;** tube: Leicester Square), specializes in show-business memorabilia from all West End and Broadway shows.

MDC Classic Music, 31–32 St. Martin's Lane, WC2 (☎ **0171/240-0270;** tube: Leicester Square), is the largest independent retailer of classical music in the U.K., with 20,000 CDs in stock and 50,000 on database. You'll receive expert knowledge and personal service.

Charing Cross Road

Charing Cross Road is the haunt of book lovers like myself. It's known for its extraordinary number of bookstores, selling both new and old volumes. Many of these places sell maps and guides, so if you haven't yet picked up a copy of *London A to Z,* look for it here. To easily reach all of the bookstores, get out at the Charing Cross, Leicester Square, or Tottenham Court Road tube stop.

W & G Foyle, Ltd., 113–119 Charing Cross Rd., WC2 (☎ **0171/439-8501;** tube: Tottenham Court Road), claims to be the world's largest bookstore, with an impressive array of hardcovers and paperbacks, as well as travel maps, records, videotapes, and sheet music.

Silver Moon Women's Bookshop, 64–68 Charing Cross Rd. (☎ **0171/836-7906;** tube: Charing Cross Road), stocks thousands of titles by and about women, plus videos, jewelry, and a large selection of lesbian-related books.

Books Etc., 120 Charing Cross Rd. (☎ **0171/379-6836;** tube: Charing Cross Road), stocks a lot of remainders—publishers' overstock that they unload at a discount.

Waterstone's, 121 Charing Cross Rd. (☎ **0171/434-4291;** tube: Tottenham Court Road), is a U.K. chain with branches all over London; you'll find all the latest releases and well-stocked sections of books currently in print.

Murder One, 71–73 Charing Cross Rd., WC2 (☎ **0171/734-3485;** tube: Leicester Square), specializes in crime, romance, science fiction, and horror books. Crime and science fiction magazines, some of them obscure, are also available.

Extra! Extra!

Thoroughly lost? Go to the Leicester Square tube station and head northeast along Long Acre. There you'll find **Stanfords,** 12–14 Long Acre, WC2 (☎ **0171/836-1321**), established in 1852 and today the world's largest map shop. Many of its maps, which include worldwide touring and survey maps, are unavailable elsewhere. It's also London's best travel bookstore (with a complete selection of Frommer's guides!).

Soho

The tired old sex shops in Soho—that fascinating warren of streets just west of Charing Cross Road—are being converted into cutting-edge designer shops. But they're not all gone. **Berwick Street Market** (tube: Oxford Circus or Tottenham Court Road) might be the only street market in the world that's flanked by strip clubs, porno stores, and adult-movie dens. Don't let that put you off, though, because the market is humming from 8am to 5pm 6 days a week (closed Sunday), with an array of stalls and booths selling the best and cheapest fruit and vegetables in town. It also hawks items that are potentially collectors' items: ancient records, tapes, books, and old magazines.

Covent Garden

I'll bet you're ready to drop, but try to save some of that shopping energy for Covent Garden, home of what might be the most famous "market" in all of England. **Covent Garden Market (☎ 0171/ 836-9136;** tube: Covent Garden) is really several different markets, open daily from 9am to 5pm. It can be a little confusing until you dive in and explore it all. **Apple Market** is the fun, bustling market in the courtyard, where traders sell . . . well, everything. Much of it is what the English call "collectible nostalgia": glassware and ceramics, leather goods, toys, clothes, hats, and jewelry. On Mondays antiques dealers take over. On the back side is **Jubilee Market** (**☎ 0171/836-2139**), a sort of fancy hippie-ish market with cheap clothes and books. **Covent Garden Market** itself (in the superbly restored hall on

Dollars & Sense

Covent Garden Market and its surrounding streets (all accessed by the Covent Garden tube stop) are loaded with herbalists and shops selling excellent English soaps and toiletries. The more famous of them have outlets in large American cities, but the prices here are much better. Here are the ones to look out for:

- **Culpeper the Herbalist,** 8 The Market, Covent Garden, WC2 (**☎ 0171/379-6698**), with food, bath, and aromatherapy products as well as dream pillows, candles, sachets, and many a shopper's fave: the aromatherapy fan.
- **Penhaligon's,** 41 Wellington St., WC2 (**☎ 0171/836-2150**), an exclusive-line Victorian perfumery dedicated to good grooming, with a large selection of perfumes, after-shaves, soaps, and bath oils for women and men.
- **Neal's Yard Remedies,** 15 Neal's Yard, WC2 (**☎ 0171/379-7222**), noted the world over for its chichi bath, beauty, and aromatherapy products in cobalt-blue bottles.

The Piazza) is one of the best shopping opportunities in London. Specialty shops sell fashions and herbs, gifts and toys, books and personalized dollhouses, hand-rolled cigars, automata, you name it. You'll find bookshops and branches of famous stores (**Hamleys, The Body Shop**), and prices are moderate.

Walking along the pedestrian-only zone from the Covent Garden tube stop down to the various markets on The Piazza, you'll pass **Dr. Marten's Department Store,** 1–4 King St., WC2 (☎ **0171/497-1460**), the flagship store for the internationally famous (just ask your kids) "Doc Marts" shoes. Prices are far better than they are in the States.

Farther along, at 14 King St., is **The Irish Shop** (☎ **0171/379-3625**), which sells a wide variety of articles shipped directly from Ireland, including colorful knitwear, traditional Irish linens, hand-knitted Aran fisherman's sweaters, and Celtic jewelry.

Knightsbridge

The home of **Harrods** and **Harvey Nichols** (see "The Biggies: London Department Stores" above), Knightsbridge is London's second-most-famous retail district. It runs east-west along the southern side of Hyde Park. **Brompton Road** (think "Harrods") runs southwest from the **Knightsbridge** tube stop. **Beauchamp Place** (pronounced *Beecham),* one of the streets running south from Brompton Road, is only 1 block long, but it's very "Sloane Ranger," featuring the kinds of shops where young British aristos buy their clothing for "the season." **Cheval Place,** running parallel to Brompton Road to the north, is lined with designer resale shops. **Sloane Street,** where you'll find plenty more fashion boutiques, runs south from the Knightsbridge tube stop to Sloane Square and the beginning of Chelsea.

Katharine Hamnett, 20 Sloane St., SW1 (☎ **0171/823-1002;** tube: Knightsbridge), earned the title of "bad girl of Brit fashion" for her "slut dresses." She has a complete line of men's and women's daywear and eveningwear using "nature-friendly" fabrics.

Map House, 54 Beauchamp Place, SW3 (☎ **0171/589-4325;** tube: Knightsbridge), is an ideal place to find an offbeat souvenir, or maybe an antique map, an engraving, or an old print of London. A century-old original engraving can cost as little as £5 ($8).

Reject China Shop, 183 Brompton Rd., SW3 (☎ **0171/581-0739;** tube: Knightsbridge), near Harrods, sells seconds (not as many as you might think, though) along with first-quality pieces of Royal Doulton, Spode, and Wedgwood china.

Chelsea

Sloane Street, around Sloane Square tube stop, is chock-a-block with more designer shops, but what Chelsea is really famous for is King's Road (tube: Sloane Square). It's the area's main street and, along with Carnaby Street, is branded in Londoners' minds as the street of the Swinging Sixties. It's still

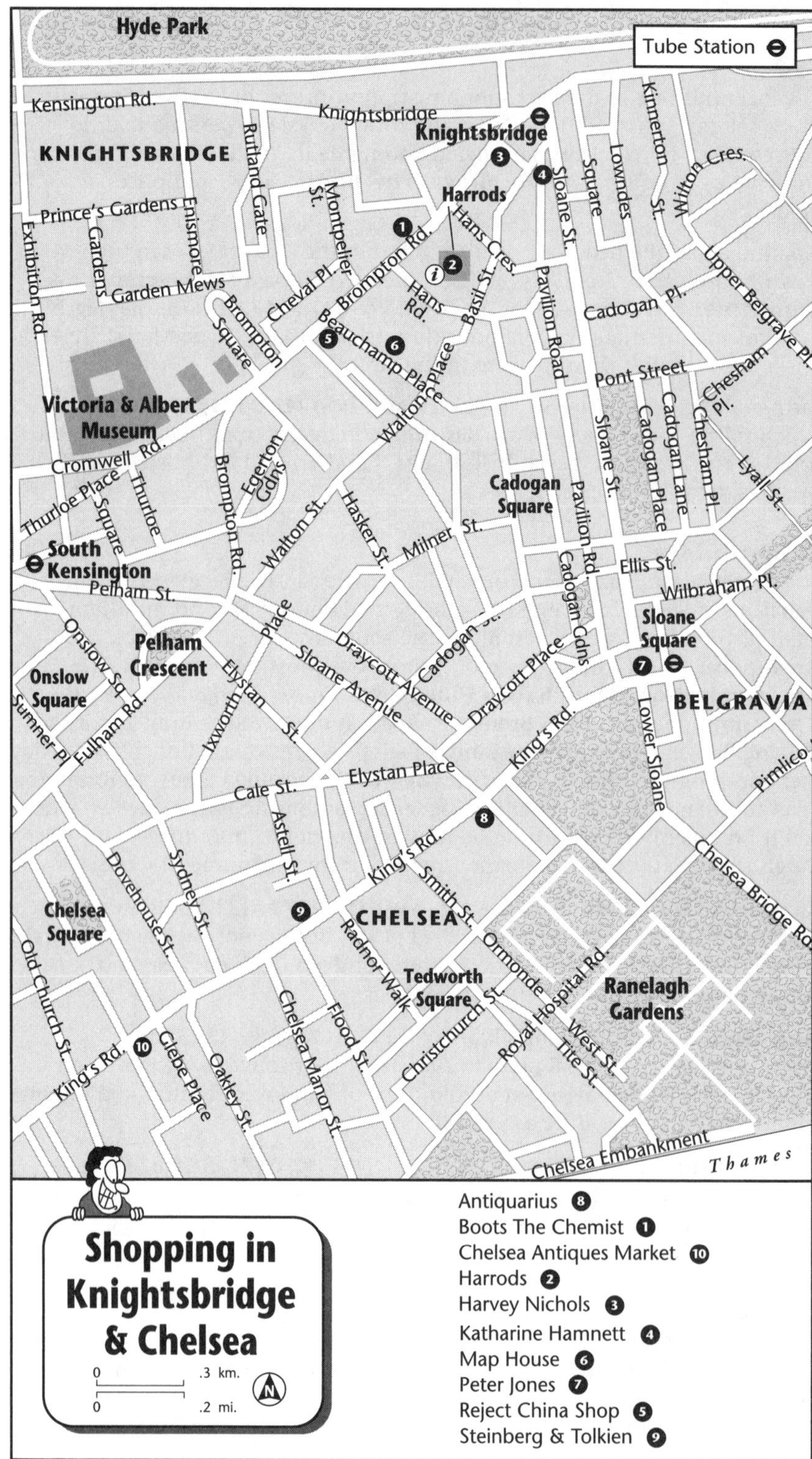

Hyde Park
Tube Station
Kensington Rd.
Knightsbridge
Knightsbridge
KNIGHTSBRIDGE
Rutland Gate
Montpelier St.
Harrods
Prince's Gardens
Ennismore Gardens
Ennismore Garden Mews
Exhibition Rd.
Hans Cres.
Sloane St.
Lowndes Square
Kinnerton St.
Wilton Cres.
Brompton Rd.
Cheval Pl.
Hans Rd.
Basil St.
Pavilion Road
Cadogan Pl.
Upper Belgrave Pl.
Brompton Square
Beauchamp Place
Walton Place
Pont Street
Chesham Pl.
Victoria & Albert Museum
Cromwell Rd.
Thurloe Place
Thurloe Square
Thurloe
Brompton Rd.
Egerton Gdns
Hasker St.
Walton St.
Cadogan Square
Pavilion Rd
Sloane St.
Cadogan Place
Cadogan Lane
Chesham Pl.
Lyall St.
Milner St.
South Kensington
Pelham St.
Ellis St.
Wilbraham Pl.
Cadogan Gdns
Sloane Square
Onslow Sq
Pelham Crescent
Onslow Square
Elystan Place
Sloane Avenue
Draycott Avenue
Cadogan St.
Draycott Place
BELGRAVIA
Sumner Pl.
Fulham Rd.
Ixworth Place
Elystan St.
King's Rd.
Lower Sloane St.
Pimlico Rd.
Elystan Place
Cale St.
Astell St.
King's Rd.
Chelsea Bridge Rd.
Dovehouse St.
Sydney St.
Smith St.
Chelsea Square
CHELSEA
Radnor Walk
Ormonde
Tedworth Square
Royal Hospital Rd.
Ranelagh Gardens
Old Church St.
Chelsea Manor St.
Flood St.
Christchurch St.
West St.
Tite St.
King's Rd.
Glebe Place
Oakley St.
Chelsea Embankment
Thames
Shopping in Knightsbridge & Chelsea
0 .3 km.
0 .2 mi.
N
Antiquarius 8
Boots The Chemist 1
Chelsea Antiques Market 10
Harrods 2
Harvey Nichols 3
Katharine Hamnett 4
Map House 6
Peter Jones 7
Reject China Shop 5
Steinberg & Tolkien 9

popular with the young crowd, but it's becoming more and more a lineup of markets and "multistores"—large or small conglomerations of indoor stands, stalls, and booths within one building or enclosure. About one-third of King's Road is devoted to these kinds of antiques markets, another third houses design trade showrooms and household wares stores, and the remaining third is faithful to the area's teenybopper roots. King's Road begins on the west side of Sloane Square tube stop.

Peter Jones, Sloane Square, SW1 (☎ **0171/730-3434**), was founded in 1877 and rebuilt in 1936. This Chelsea emporium is known for household goods, household fabrics and trims, china, glass, soft furnishings, and linens. The linen department is one of the best in London.

Sheltered in a rambling old building, **Chelsea Antiques Market,** 245A–253 King's Rd., SW3 (☎ **0171/352-5686**), offers endless bric-a-brac browsing possibilities for the curio addict. It's definitely a good place to search out old or rare books. You're likely to run across Staffordshire dogs, shaving mugs, Edwardian buckles and clasps, ivory-handled razors, old velours, lace gowns, wooden tea caddies—and that's just the beginning. It's closed on Sundays.

Another good market to try is **Antiquarius,** 131–141 King's Rd., SW3 (☎ **0171/351-5353**), where more than 120 dealers offer specialized merchandise—usually of the small, domestic variety, such as antique and period jewelry, porcelain, silver, first-edition books, boxes, clocks, prints, and paintings.

Steinberg & Tolkien, 193 King's Rd., SW3 (☎ **0171/376-3660**), is London's leading dealer in vintage costume jewelry and clothing.

Kensington

Now we come to Kensington, west of Knightsbridge, which you can reach by taking the tube to **Kensington High Street,** which just happens to be the area's preeminent shopping street. A lot of the retail around here caters to the "street-chic" teens. Although you'll find a few staples of basic British fashion on this strip, most of the stores feature stretchy items that are very, very short; very, very tight; and very, very black. **Kensington Church Street,** which runs north to Notting Hill, is one of the city's main shopping avenues for antiques, selling everything from antique furniture to impressionist paintings.

Kids **Children's Book Centre,** 237 Kensington High St., W8 (☎ **0171/937-7497**), is the best place in London to go for children's books. Fiction is arranged according to age, up to 16. You'll also find videos and toys for kids.

Notting Hill

Kensington Church Street dead-ends at the Notting Hill Gate tube station, which is the jumping-off point for **Portobello Market,** the famous London street market along Portobello Road, about 2 blocks north of the tube stop. Portobello (market and road) is a magnet for collectors of virtually anything—from precious junk to precious antiques. It's mainly a fun happening, open

Tourist Traps

Portobello Market has become synonymous with antiques. But don't take the stallholder's word for it that the beat-up violin he's trying to push on you is a genuine Stradivarius. It might just as well have been "nicked" from an East End pawnshop.

Saturdays from 6am to 5pm. I'm not telling you not to explore Portobello Road and Market. You might find that perfect Regency commode you've been looking for. But mixed in with the good stuff is a lot of overpriced junk. And the bargain days of the 1970s are pretty much over. Now that everything's been "discovered" and designated a "collectible," the prices are often higher than they should be. My best advice is simply to treat this as a browsing event. *Warning: This is prime pickpocketing territory, so keep an eye or a hand on your wallet or purse.*

Time-Savers

Some 90 **antiques and art shops** along Portobello Road are open during the week when the street market is closed. This is actually a better time for the serious collector to shop because you'll get more attention from dealers and you won't be distracted by the throngs of shoppers.

Chapter 16

Battle Plans for Seeing the Sights—Eight Great Itineraries

In This Chapter

- Eight easy-to-follow, self-guided city tours to help you see it all without knocking yourself out

With limited time and so many things to see and do, it's easy to boomerang around London from sight to sight via the Underground. There's nothing wrong with this approach, except that it doesn't give you much of a feel for the city and its constituent parts. That's why I've compiled the following eight itineraries, which concentrate on selected areas and include many of London's most-visited attractions. These are, for the most part, walking itineraries.

Luckily, London is a walker's dream. Yes, the streets (not to mention the mews, the closes, the courts, and the yards) can be confusing. What would you expect in a city that's 2,000 years old? But many of London's major sights are concentrated in specific areas, and walking is the best way to take in a number of them at one time. When you're strolling in London it's always a good idea to have a copy of *London A to Z* with you.

Each of the eight itineraries in this chapter is easy to do, easy to walk, and takes up the better part of a day. Each includes a lunch stop in the area. For exact street addresses, opening hours, admission prices, and additional information on the sights mentioned below, see chapters 13 and 14. You can find fuller descriptions of the restaurants in chapters 10 and 11.

Itinerary 1—Trafalgar Square, the National Gallery, St. James's Park & Buckingham Palace

After breakfast, start your day at Trafalgar Square before heading to the National Gallery, which is directly across the street. You can have lunch at the museum's restaurant or in the restaurant beneath St. Martin-in-the-Fields church on the east side of the square. After lunch, cross over to Admiralty Arch, which spans the entrance to The Mall, a processional boulevard at the southwest corner of Trafalgar Square. Stroll down the Mall, through St. James's Park, to Buckingham Palace. You'll pass St. James's Palace and Clarence House along the way.

1. **Trafalgar Square.** The Charing Cross tube stop is right across the street from Trafalgar Square, London's grandest and certainly most famous plaza. You can see the square and its monuments in less than half an hour. If you're tempted to feed the pigeons, be aware that the minute you hold out food, they'll descend like something out of Hitchcock's *The Birds* and you might regret your generosity. For a description of the square, see chapter 13.

2. **The National Gallery.** A visit to this great art museum, located on the north side of Trafalgar Square, can easily take up the better part of a day. Arrive early (opening time is 10am except Sundays, when it opens at noon) and allow a minimum of 2 hours to see the art. Renting one of the self-guided audio tours will help you to hone in on the most important paintings in the collection. See chapter 13 for a description of what's on view.

3. **Lunchtime.** You can have a convenient (and rather elegant) lunch at **the Brasserie at the National Gallery** (**☎ 0171/737-2885**), located on the second floor in the Sainsbury Wing (see chapter 11). Alternatively, head across the street to **St. Martin-in-the-Fields** church on the east side of Trafalgar Square. Here you'll find **Cafe-in-the-Crypt** (**☎ 0171/839-4342**), which serves up helpings of traditional English home cooking (see chapter 13). Afterward spend a few minutes looking around the church itself.

4. **St. James's Park.** Passing beneath **Admiralty Arch,** at the southwest corner of Trafalgar Square, you will enter **The Mall,** which forms the northern boundary of St. James's Park. Strolling down The Mall is most pleasurable on Sundays, when it's closed to traffic. The Mall will take you past **St. James's Palace** (on your right), the primary royal residence from 1698 to 1837, and today the London home of Prince Charles and his two sons. **Clarence House,** the official London home of the Queen Mother, lies to the south of St. James's Palace. (Note: St. James's Palace and Clarence House are not open to visitors.)

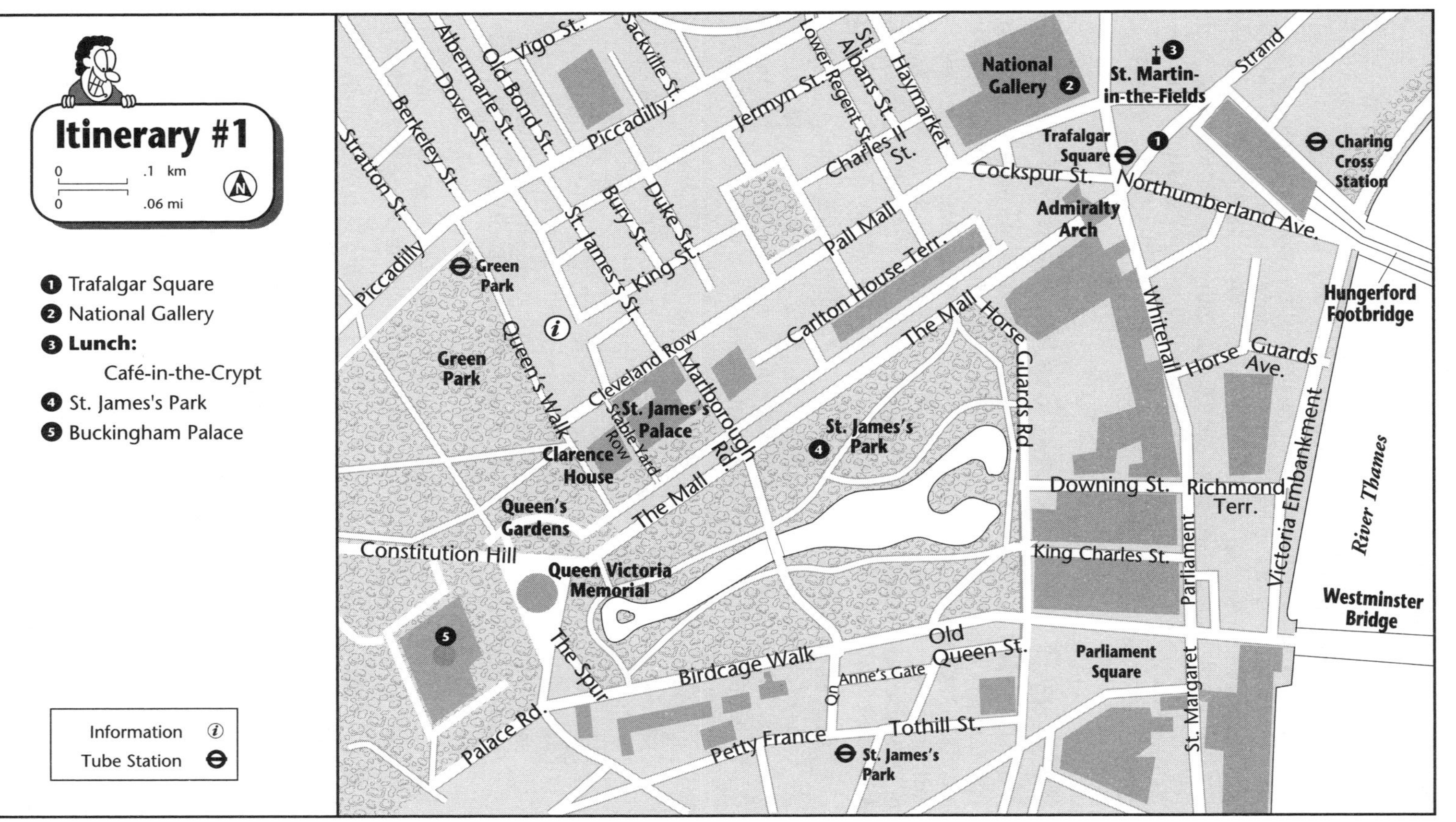

Itinerary #1
0 .1 km
0 .06 mi
N
1 Trafalgar Square
2 National Gallery
3 Lunch:
Café-in-the-Crypt
4 St. James's Park
5 Buckingham Palace
Information
Tube Station
Vigo St.
Sackville St.
Albermarle St.
Old Bond St.
Dover St.
Berkeley St.
Stratton St.
Piccadilly
Jermyn St.
Lower Regent St.
St. Albans St.
Haymarket
Charles II St.
National Gallery
St. Martin-in-the-Fields
Strand
Trafalgar Square
Charing Cross Station
Cockspur St.
Northumberland Ave.
Admiralty Arch
Pall Mall
Duke St.
Bury St.
King St.
St. James's St.
Green Park
Carlton House Terr.
The Mall
Horse Guards Rd.
Whitehall
Horse Guards Ave.
Hungerford Footbridge
Victoria Embankment
River Thames
Cleveland Row
Marlborough Rd.
St. James's Palace
Stable Yard Row
St. James's Park
Queen's Walk
Clarence House
Queen's Gardens
Constitution Hill
Queen Victoria Memorial
Downing St.
Richmond Terr.
King Charles St.
Parliament
Westminster Bridge
The Spur
Birdcage Walk
Old Queen St.
Qu Anne's Gate
Parliament Square
St. Margaret
Palace Rd.
Petty France
Tothill St.
St. James's Park

5. **Buckingham Palace.** It should take you about 45 minutes to reach Buckingham Palace from Trafalgar Square. For details on touring the **State Rooms** of Buckingham Palace during August and September, see chapter 13. It's best to reserve tickets in advance for a specific entry time; otherwise, you will have to wait in line for up to an hour to get in. If you're not touring the palace itself, allow yourself about an hour to visit the **Queen's Gallery** and another hour to see the **Royal Mews,** but check opening days and hours for the latter before you arrive.

Itinerary 2—Green Park, Buckingham Palace, Pall Mall, Trafalgar Square, the National Gallery & Soho

This itinerary takes in some of the same sights as Itinerary 1 but reverses the order and uses a different route. Start your day by strolling through Green Park (tube: Green Park) to Buckingham Palace. Lunch at the National Gallery or St. Martin-in-the-Fields church before visiting the National Gallery itself. Afterward, head north along Charing Cross Road to nearby Soho.

1. **Buckingham Palace.** Before you start out, check to see whether the Changing of the Guard ceremony is taking place that day (at 11:30am; see chapter 13 for details). If it is, time your arrival at Buckingham Palace for no later than 11am. After watching the ceremony, you can visit the Queen's Gallery and/or the Royal Mews. (See chapter 13 and step 5 in Itinerary 1.) From the palace, head northeast along The Mall, past Clarence House and St. James's Palace (see step 4 in Itinerary 1), to Marlborough Road.

2. **Pall Mall.** Turn left on Marlborough to Pall Mall, (pronounced *pell mell*). This tony street is lined with exclusive "gentlemen's clubs." On the north side are the sedate 18th-century precincts of **St. James's Square.** Stroll northeast on Pall Mall to Trafalgar Square, which you should reach in about half an hour.

3. **Lunchtime.** See step 3 in Itinerary 1 for my recommended lunch spots, either in the National Gallery or St. Martin-in-the-Fields church.

4. **The National Gallery.** See step 2 in Itinerary 1. Spend your afternoon taking in the art.

5. **Soho.** From the National Gallery, head north on Charing Cross Road, where you might want to do some book shopping. You might also want to stop at the reduced-price tickets booth in **Leicester Square** (left off Charing Cross Road) to pick up a ticket for a West End show that night. At Shaftesbury Avenue, cross north and head into Soho, a great place for dinner (see chapter 10 for recommended Soho restaurants).

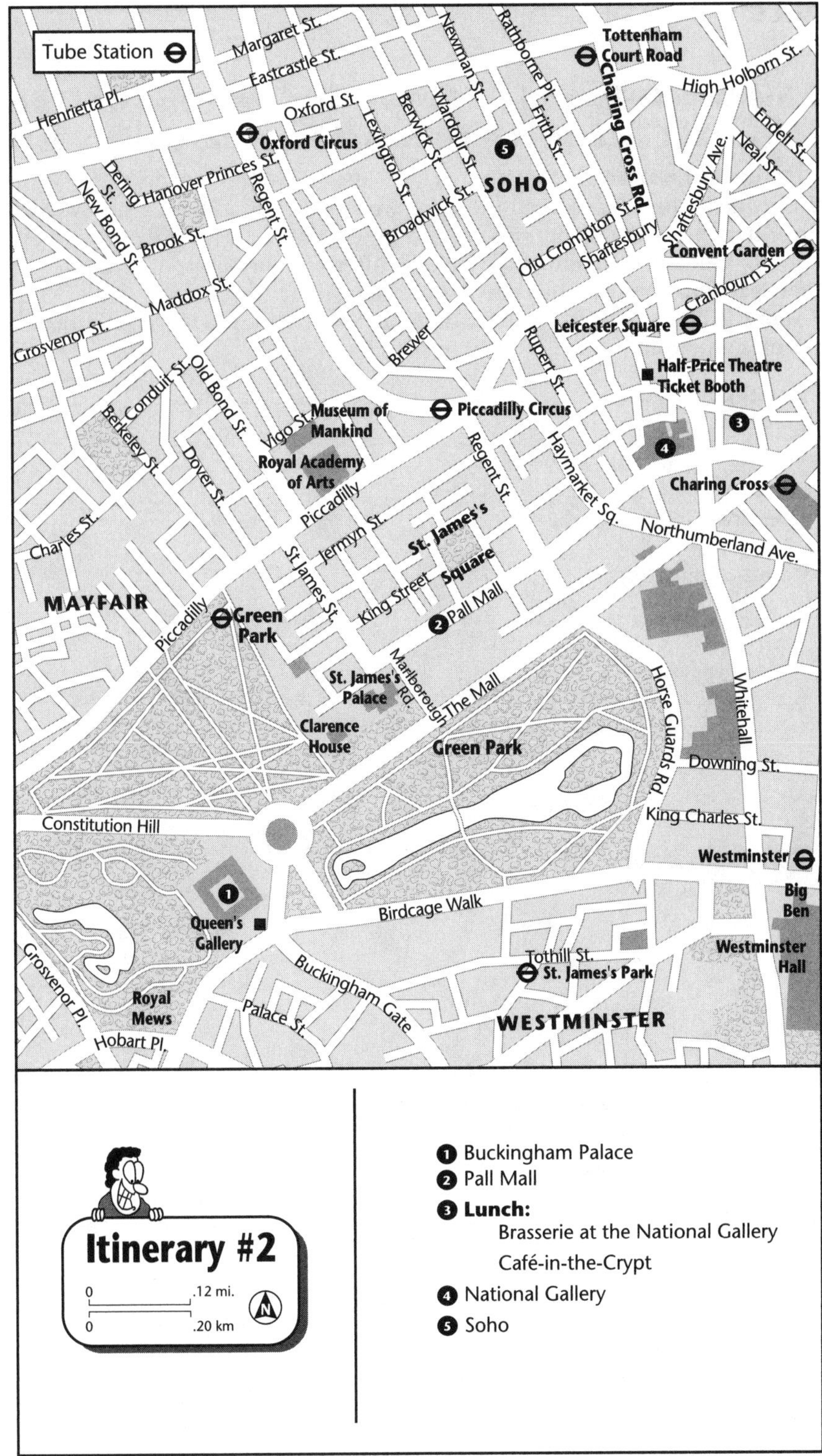

Tube Station
Margaret St.
Eastcastle St.
Henrietta Pl.
Oxford St.
Oxford Circus
Newman St.
Rathbone Pl.
Tottenham Court Road
Charing Cross Rd.
High Holborn St.
Endell St.
Neal St.
Shaftesbury Ave.
Berwick St.
Wardour St.
Lexington St.
Frith St.
SOHO
Dering St.
Hanover Princes St.
Regent St.
New Bond St.
Brook St.
Broadwick St.
Old Crompton St.
Shaftesbury
Convent Garden
Cranbourn St.
Maddox St.
Grosvenor St.
Brewer
Rupert St.
Leicester Square
Half-Price Theatre Ticket Booth
Conduit St.
Old Bond St.
Berkeley St.
Vigo St.
Museum of Mankind
Piccadilly Circus
Royal Academy of Arts
Dover St.
Haymarket Sq.
Charing Cross
Piccadilly
Jermyn St.
St. James's Square
Northumberland Ave.
Charles St.
St James St.
King Street
Pall Mall
MAYFAIR
Green Park
Marlborough Rd.
St. James's Palace
The Mall
Clarence House
Horse Guards Rd.
Whitehall
Downing St.
King Charles St.
Constitution Hill
Westminster
Big Ben
Birdcage Walk
Queen's Gallery
Westminster Hall
Tothill St.
St. James's Park
Grosvenor Pl.
Royal Mews
Buckingham Gate
Palace St.
Hobart Pl.
WESTMINSTER
Itinerary #2
0 .12 mi.
0 .20 km
N
1 Buckingham Palace
2 Pall Mall
3 Lunch:
Brasserie at the National Gallery
Café-in-the-Crypt
4 National Gallery
5 Soho

Itinerary 3—Piccadilly Circus, Trafalgar Square, the National Gallery, the National Portrait Gallery & Covent Garden

This itinerary combines plenty of shopping opportunities with visits to two great museums. The day begins at bustling Piccadilly Circus (tube: Piccadilly Circus), the heart of London's West End. After a shopping stroll, head to Trafalgar Square to visit the National Gallery and the National Portrait Gallery. When you've finished with the museums, head to Covent Garden for more shopping and/or dinner.

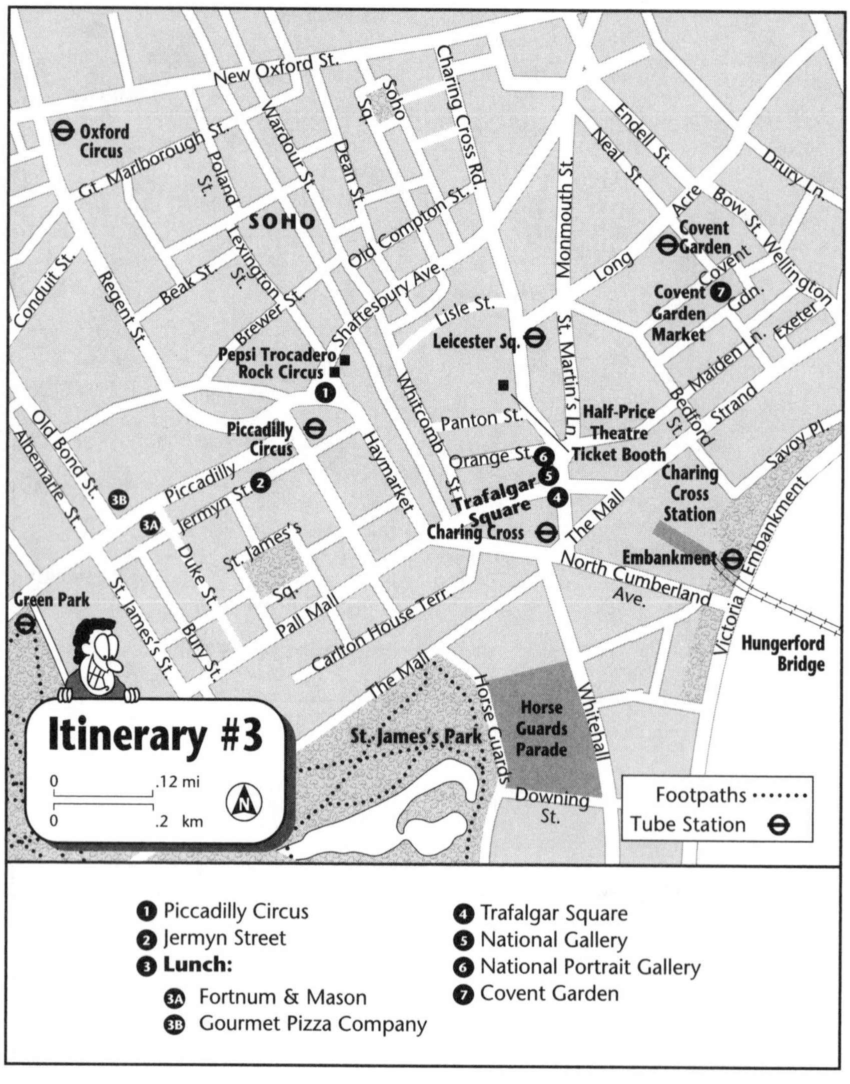

1. **Piccadilly Circus.** It may be famous, but you don't need to spend much time wandering around Piccadilly Circus. The adjacent streets—Piccadilly, Jermyn Street, and Regent Street—are more interesting if you're a shopper. If you're with kids, you might want to stop in at the Pepsi Trocadero (allot at least half an hour for them to play the video games) or Rock Circus, a branch of Madame Tussaud's (give this about an hour); see chapter 14 for details on both.
2. **Shopping stroll.** If you're in a shopping mood, head west along Piccadilly, turn south at St. James's Street, and backtrack east along Jermyn Street. Then continue south on Regent Street and east on Pall Mall to Trafalgar Square. (Alternatively, if you're not interested in shopping, from Piccadilly Circus head south along Regent Street and turn east on Pall Mall to reach Trafalgar Square.)
3. **Lunchtime.** If you've taken the shopping route along Piccadilly (the street—not the Circus) or Jermyn Street, have lunch at either **The Fountain** or **The Patio** (☎ **0171/734-8040** for both) in **Fortnum & Mason,** 181 Piccadilly, one of London's most famous department stores. Or head over to nearby **Gourmet Pizza Company,** 7–9 Swallow Walk (☎ **0171/734-5182**), north of Piccadilly (see chapter 10 for details on all three). Otherwise, you can have lunch at the **National Gallery** or **St. Martin-in-the-Fields** at Trafalgar Square (see step 3 in Itinerary 1).
4. **Trafalgar Square.** See step 1 in Itinerary 1.
5. **The National Gallery.** See step 2 in Itinerary 1.
6. **The National Portrait Gallery.** It's right behind the National Gallery, and it's well worth your time. Allow 1 hour minimum (it's easy to become so engrossed that you end up spending more time than you anticipated). Renting one of the self-guided audio tours is a good idea. From the museum, walk north on Charing Cross, east on Long Acre, and south on James Street to Covent Garden.
7. **Covent Garden.** As you head north on Charing Cross Road, you might want to stop at the reduced-price tickets booth in **Leicester Square** (just west of Charing Cross Road) to see whether you can get a ticket for a show that evening. There are plenty of interesting shops in and around Covent Garden Market; Covent Garden Piazza is a lively tourist hub. The Covent Garden area is also filled with restaurants, so it's a perfect spot for dinner.

Itinerary 4—The British Museum, Oxford Street, Hyde Park & Harrods

Following breakfast, start your day at the British Museum. Have lunch at the museum or the nearby Museum Street Café. After lunch, continue south on Museum Street to New Oxford Street. You can spend some of your afternoon shopping on Oxford Street to Marble Arch. From Marble Arch, you can stroll

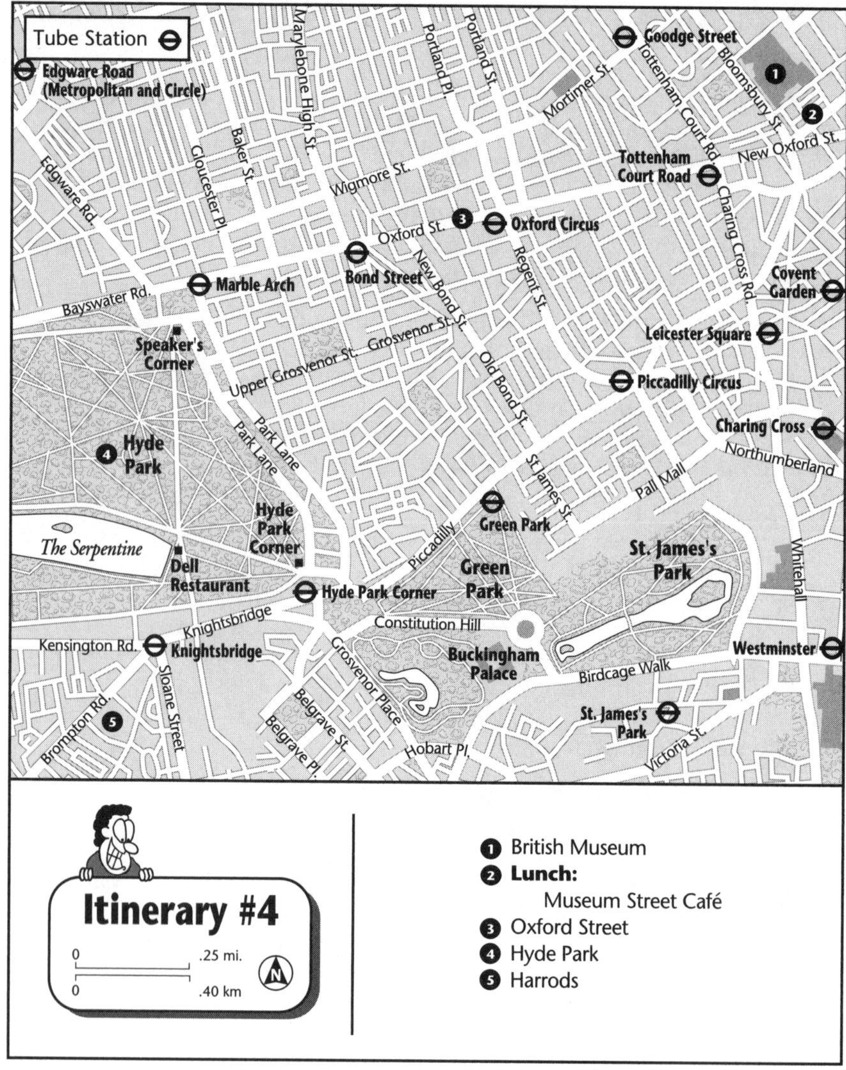

south through Hyde Park to Hyde Park Corner. Here you'll be at the eastern end of Knightsbridge, an area famed for its exclusive shops and Harrods department store.

1. **British Museum.** This great museum has enough to keep you occupied for several days; if you want to see only the highlights, allow yourself a minimum of 2 hours. The museum opens at 10am except on Sundays, when it opens at 2:30pm.

2. **Lunchtime.** For a simple, convenient, and inexpensive lunch, eat at the **British Museum Restaurant** (☎ **0171/323-8256;** see chapter 11). You'll find much better food at the **Museum Street Café** (☎ **0171/405-3211**) at 47 Museum St., less than a 5-minute walk away. It's open for lunch Monday to Friday 12:30 to 2:15pm only,

though; see chapter 10. After lunch, continue south on Museum Street to New Oxford Street. As you head west, it becomes Oxford Street.

3. **Oxford Street.** This retail artery is generally less chic and more affordable than Regent Street or Jermyn Street, though by the time you hit Bond Street the prices start rising. For a general rundown on Oxford Street shopping, see chapter 15. Continue on Oxford Street until you reach Hyde Park.

   If shopping doesn't interest you or you want to save your shopping time for Harrods, hop on the Central Line tube at Tottenham Court Road and take it to Marble Arch. For a more scenic ride, take the no. 10 or no. 73 bus west on Oxford Street to Marble Arch (if you don't feel like walking through Hyde Park, the no. 10 will take you all the way to Knightsbridge).

4. **Hyde Park.** One of London's best-loved green spaces, Hyde Park is a wonderful place for a refreshing afternoon stroll. Marble Arch and the famous **Speaker's Corner** are located at the park's northeastern corner. Allow yourself a leisurely hour to get from there to Hyde Park Corner at the southeastern corner, perhaps stopping for tea and a snack at the **Dell Restaurant** (**☎ 0171/706-0464**) at the east end of the Serpentine; see chapter 13. Once you reach Hyde Park Corner, you'll be at the eastern end of Knightsbridge. You can reach Harrods by following Knightsbridge west to Brompton Road and then continuing southwest on Brompton Road.

5. **Harrods.** The most famous department store in London—and perhaps the world—is a must for most visitors. On your way there, you'll pass dozens of upscale shops in the Knightsbridge area. Knightsbridge is a fine, if rather expensive, place to dine; adjacent South Kensington, to the west, is another option. For a list of Knightsbridge and South Kensington restaurants, see chapter 10.

Itinerary 5—The Tower of London, Tower Bridge, Southwark & St. Paul's Cathedral

The morning's first stop is the Tower of London. Afterward, treat yourself to a lunch of Indian food at Café Spice Namaste on Prescot Street or sample the Chinese menu at Poons in the City on Mincing Lane. After lunch, head south and cross Tower Bridge to Southwark on the south side of the Thames. Take Queens' Walk, the riverside path, west to London Bridge (if you have time, you might want to visit the H.M.S. *Belfast,* which you'll pass on the way). Take the Northern Line tube from London Bridge to Monument and change there for the Central Line, which takes you to St. Paul's (tube: St. Paul's).

Both of these City restaurants are about a 5-minute walk from the Tower Hill tube station.

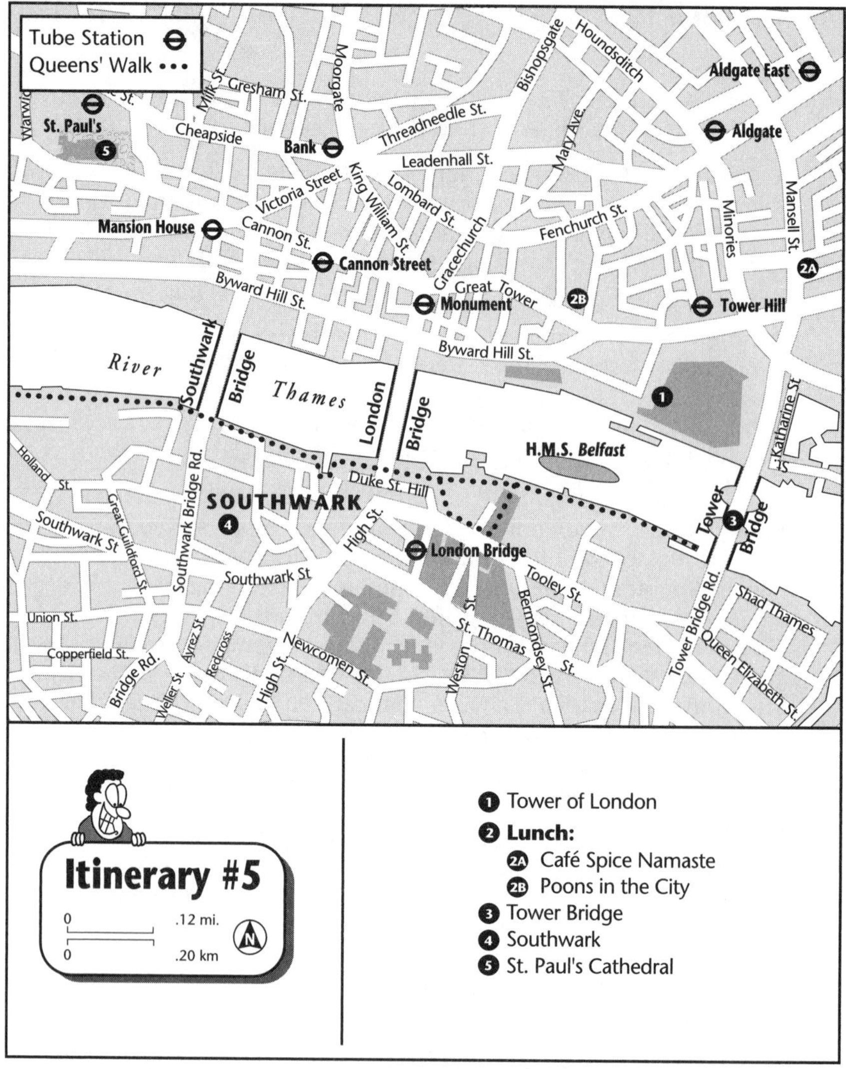

1. **Tower of London.** Try to be at the Tower when the gates open (either 9am or 10am, depending on the day and season; see chapter 13) and immediately join one of the 1-hour guided tours led by the Beefeaters. Afterward you can explore further on your own, visiting the crown jewels and other historic sites. Allow a minimum of 2 hours.

2. **Lunchtime.** If you want to sample some of the best Indian food in London, reserve in advance for lunch at **Café Spice Namaste,** 16 Prescot St. (**☎ 0171/488-9242**). Or, for excellent Chinese food, try **Poons in the City,** 2 Minster Pavement, Minster Court, Mincing Lane (**☎ 0171/626-0126**). Both of these City restaurants are a 5-minute walk from the Tower Hill tube stop; for directions and more information on them, see the listings in chapter 10.

3. **Tower Bridge.** As you cross Tower Bridge, the view of the Thames, the City, and all of London is breathtaking. You might want to spend an hour visiting the **Tower Bridge Experience,** located at the north pier (see chapter 14).

4. **Southwark.** Though most tourists never cross the river to Southwark, the area is filled with many historic sights and contains some interesting new commercial developments (for Southwark Cathedral and other Southwark sights, see chapter 14). **Queens' Walk,** along the south bank of the Thames, provides views of the Tower of London and the City and takes you past the **H.M.S. *Belfast*** (see chapter 14). If you visit this ship, you'll need to allot a minimum of 90 minutes. Otherwise, continue west to Hays Lane, turn south to Tooley Street, and take Tooley Street west to the London Bridge station, where you can catch the tube to St. Paul's (changing at Monument).

5. **St. Paul's Cathedral.** You'll want to spend at least an hour in St. Paul's, but be aware that the cathedral closes at 4pm and is not open for sightseeing on Sundays.

Itinerary 6—Tate Gallery, Houses of Parliament, Westminster Abbey & the South Bank

After breakfast, take the tube to the Pimlico Station, the closest stop to the Tate Gallery. The route to the Tate (south on Vauxhall Bridge Road and north along Millbank) is marked by signposts. Have lunch at the Tate and then head to the Houses of Parliament and Big Ben. You'll see Westminster Abbey to the west; it's less than a 5-minute walk from the Houses of Parliament. After you visit the Abbey, cross over Westminster Bridge and stroll north along the Thames to the South Bank Centre. (You might want to schedule this itinerary for a day when you have tickets for a concert or a play at the National Theatre.) Alternatively, you can catch a boat at Westminster Pier and take it north to Charing Cross Pier.

1. **Tate Gallery.** The Tate is open daily at 10am. Allow yourself at least 90 minutes to see the collections. Renting a self-guided audio tour will add to your enjoyment (see chapter 13 for more details).

2. **Lunchtime.** The **Tate Gallery Restaurant** (**☎ 0171/887-8000**) is a fine place to have lunch; it's open Monday to Saturday from noon until 3pm (see chapter 11). After lunch, continue north on Millbank (you can also take the no. 77a bus) to the Houses of Parliament and Big Ben.

3. **Houses of Parliament.** Unless you're hearing a debate (see chapter 13 for details), you won't be able to get inside the Houses of Parliament. Viewing the exterior, Big Ben, and Parliament Square will probably take you no more than 15 minutes to a half hour. Give yourself a few extra minutes to visit **Victoria Tower Gardens,** on the south side of the Houses of Parliament; here you'll find a copy of Auguste Rodin's masterpiece, *The Burghers of Calais.*

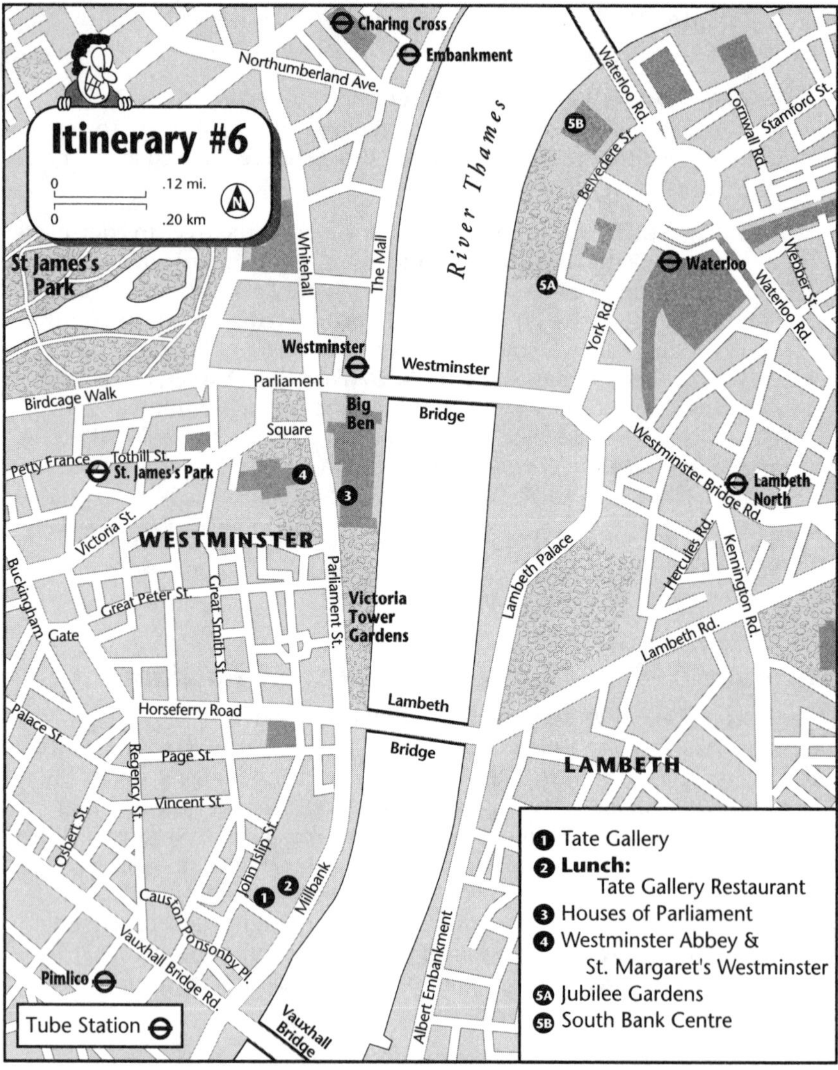

4. **Westminster Abbey.** The crowds can be daunting, no matter what time you arrive. Give yourself a minimum of 1 hour and don't be surprised if the sheer volume of visitors slows your tour down to a crawl. Afterward, take another 15 minutes to visit the Abbey gardens and the adjacent church of **St. Margaret's Westminster,** the parish church of the House of Commons since 1614.

5. **The South Bank.** Cross via Westminster Bridge to the south bank of the Thames (you're actually walking east). The bridge offers a wonderful view of the Houses of Parliament and Big Ben. At the opposite side of the bridge, walk north on York Road and turn left at Chichly Street to the riverside **Jubilee Gardens** (an enormous Ferris wheel, called the Millennium Wheel, is scheduled to be erected here by mid-1999). From here you can walk north to the **South Bank Centre** (see

chapter 19). Alternatively, from the Houses of Parliament you can catch a boat from Westminster Pier beside Westminster Bridge and enjoy a short Thames cruise north to Charing Cross Pier (see chapter 12).

Itinerary 7—Westminster Abbey, Houses of Parliament, Cabinet War Rooms, Whitehall, Downing Street, Horse Guards & Trafalgar Square

This itinerary includes some of the same sights as Itinerary 6 but takes you up Whitehall, the area's most important street. Begin at Westminster Abbey and then have a look at the Houses of Parliament and Big Ben. Afterward, have a pub lunch at the Red Lion Public House, on Parliament Street on the north side of Parliament Square. Following lunch, stroll to the Cabinet War Rooms. After your visit, return to Parliament Street and head north; the street almost immediately becomes Whitehall. You'll pass Downing Street and the Horse Guards on your way to Trafalgar Square.

1. **Westminster Abbey.** The Abbey opens its doors at 9am Monday through Friday and on Saturdays at 9:15am; it is not open for sightseeing on Sundays. See chapter 13 and step 4 in Itinerary 6.
2. **Houses of Parliament.** See chapter 13 and step 3 in Itinerary 6.
3. **Lunchtime. Red Lion Public House,** 48 Parliament St. (☎ **0171/930-5826**), has a good selection of hot daily specials as well as sandwiches and, of course, beers and soft drinks. After lunch, walk north on Parliament Street 1 block and turn left on King Charles Street to reach the Cabinet War Rooms.
4. **Cabinet War Rooms.** This historically evocative site is usually not very crowded (lucky for you). Using the self-guided audio tour, your visit should take you about an hour; see chapter 14.
5. **Whitehall.** This broad avenue between the Houses of Parliament and Trafalgar Square is where major governmental departments have their offices. When you return to Parliament Street after visiting the Cabinet War Rooms, turn left (north). After 1 block, you will come to **Downing Street,** where the British Prime Minister lives at No. 10. The street has heavy security, so you won't get more than a peek through barred gates. Continuing north you'll come to two stern-faced guards on horseback (on duty until 4pm). Soldiers of the Queen's Household Division, they are known as the **Horse Guards.** You can pass by them to have a look at the **Horse Guards Parade,** where the yearly Trooping the Colour ceremony is held in honor of the Queen's birthday. Almost directly opposite the Horse Guards is the **Banqueting House.** Completed in 1622, it was the first true Renaissance building in London (it is not open to the public).
6. **Trafalgar Square.** At the end of Whitehall, you will come to Trafalgar Square; see chapter 13 and step 1 of Itinerary 1 for details.

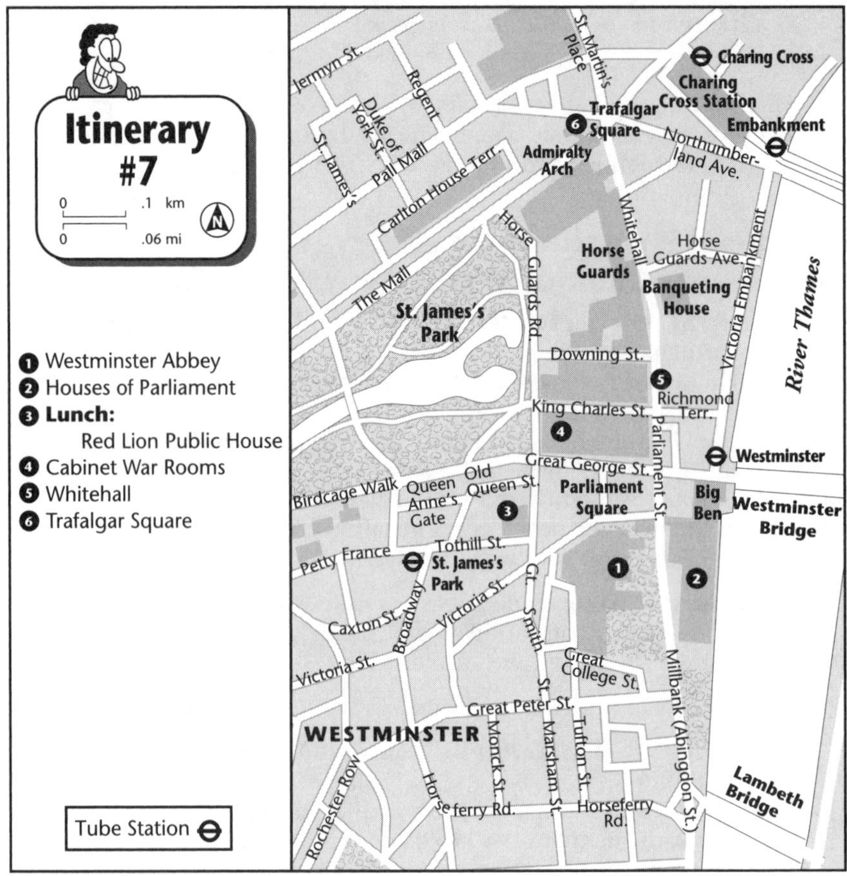

Itinerary 8—South Kensington Museums, Kensington Gardens & Kensington Palace

Begin your day in one of the great South Kensington museums. Take your pick: the Victoria and Albert, the Museum of Natural History, or the Science Museum. Have lunch at The Oratory on Brompton Road. Then backtrack to the museums and head north on Exhibition Road to Kensington Gardens. Stroll west through the gardens to round off your day with a visit to Kensington Palace and tea at the Orangery.

1. **South Kensington Museums.** Choosing among the three major South Kensington museums—the **Natural History Museum,** the **Science Museum,** and the **Victoria and Albert Museum**—is entirely a matter of taste; see chapter 13 for a description of each. If you're traveling with kids, the Natural History Museum or the Science Museum is probably a better choice than the Victoria and Albert. On most days the museums open at 10am; on Sundays the Natural History Museum opens at 11am, and on Mondays the Victoria and Albert opens at noon. Give yourself a minimum of 2 hours at whatever museum you choose.

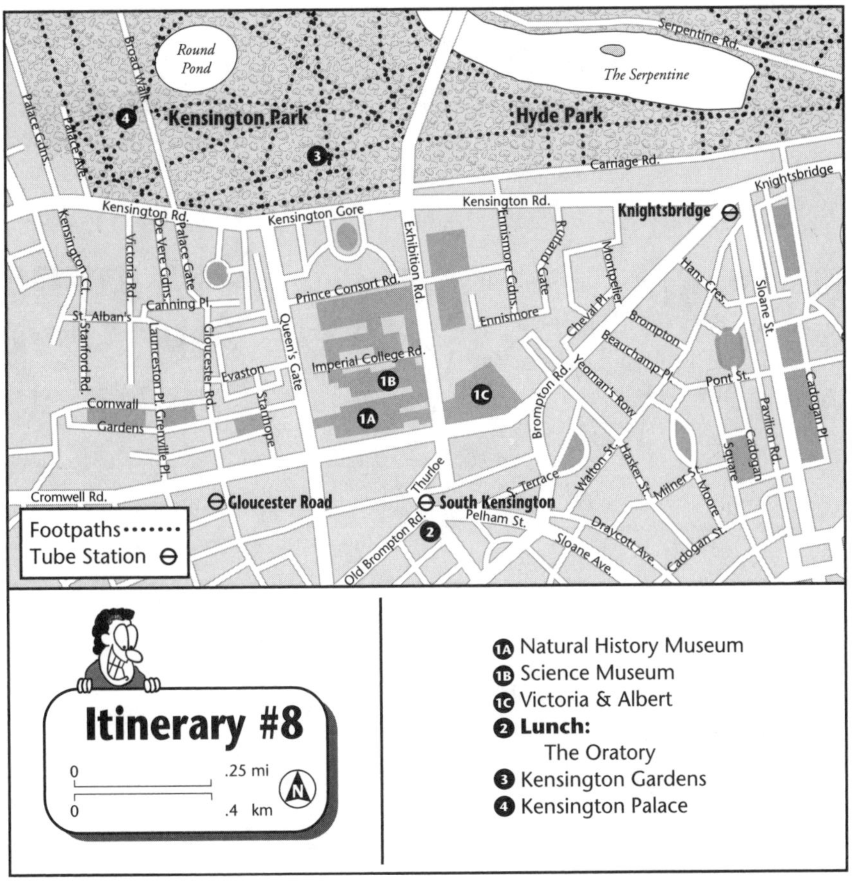

2. **Lunchtime.** Enjoy a relaxed, bistro-style lunch in Knightsbridge at **The Oratory** (☎ **0171/584-3493**) at 232 Brompton Rd., about a 10-minute walk from the museums (see chapter 10).

3. **Kensington Gardens.** If you backtrack from the restaurant to Exhibition Road, where the museums are located, it will take you about 15 minutes to walk to Kensington Gardens. After you enter the park, head west toward Kensington Palace. You can enjoy more of the gardens after you've toured the palace.

4. **Kensington Palace.** The palace is open daily until 5pm, but you'll have to arrive by 4pm. Give yourself at least 1 hour; Monday through Friday, you might have to wait a bit, since you will be part of a guided tour. After your visit, you might want to stop in for tea at **The Orangery** (☎ **0171/376-0239**) in the gardens adjacent to the palace; it closes at 6pm from March through October and at 4pm the rest of the year (see chapter 13).

Chapter 17

Designing Your Own Itinerary

In This Chapter

- Budgeting Your Time
- Pacing Yourself
- Tough Choices

If you've been reading this guide through from beginning to end, you should by now have a sense of the size and scope of London. You should also have a physical list of your "must-sees" (remember that worksheet you did back in chapter 13?) and a mental tally of other museums you'd like to visit, gardens you'd like to stroll, and shopping streets you'd like to browse. Well, now comes the fun part: trying to fit it all in.

Even a lifelong resident of London can't hope to see everything this city has to offer. But you, with limited time, can see more if you organize your days efficiently and with common sense. Disorganized travelers waste a lot of time, show up at a museum on the day it's closed, and end up in the nether regions of Tooting Bec because they hopped the wrong Underground line. The worksheets in this chapter are designed to help you decide what to see and to organize yourself so that you can do it all without knocking yourself out.

Back to the Drawing Board—Your Top Attractions

The first step is to go back to chapter 13, where you rated the top attractions from 1 to 5. Using this list, break down the sights by number: Write in all the #1s, all the #2s, and so on.

#1 Picks

➤ ______________________________
➤ ______________________________
➤ ______________________________
➤ ______________________________
➤ ______________________________
➤ ______________________________
➤ ______________________________
➤ ______________________________
➤ ______________________________
➤ ______________________________

#2 Picks

➤ ______________________________
➤ ______________________________
➤ ______________________________
➤ ______________________________
➤ ______________________________
➤ ______________________________
➤ ______________________________
➤ ______________________________
➤ ______________________________
➤ ______________________________

#3 Picks

➤ ______________________________
➤ ______________________________
➤ ______________________________
➤ ______________________________
➤ ______________________________
➤ ______________________________
➤ ______________________________

- ➤ ______
- ➤ ______
- ➤ ______

#4 Picks

- ➤ ______
- ➤ ______
- ➤ ______
- ➤ ______
- ➤ ______
- ➤ ______
- ➤ ______
- ➤ ______
- ➤ ______
- ➤ ______

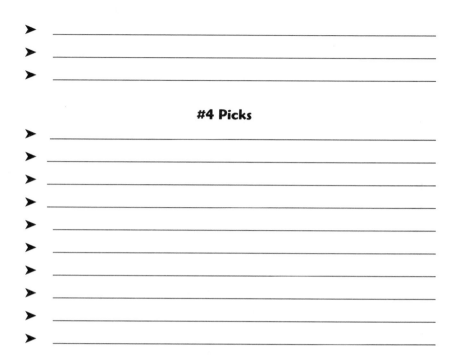

After you've done this, go back to chapter 14 and pick up the "other fun stuff" that fits your particular interests. Assign these attractions a number, and put them into the preceding lists, too.

You're probably now asking why there are no spaces for the #5s. That's because, if you're a typical visitor, there are so many 1s, 2s, and 3s that you won't need the 5s and might not even be able to visit the 4s. What if your #1 list above says "British Museum, Buckingham Palace, Tower of London (reached by boat), Westminster Abbey, Kensington Gardens and Palace, and Museum of Natural History?" That would easily fill 2 *full* days. Day 1 would be your "Palace, Abbey, Tower day," getting up early to take the palace tour (in August and September), visiting the Queen's Gallery and the Royal Mews, watching the Changing of the Guard (if it's happening), having lunch, and then, after spending an hour in Westminster Abbey, taking the 30-minute boat ride to the Tower of London, where you'd spend at least 2 hours in the late afternoon. Day 2 you would start by visiting the British Museum, then wander through Kensington Gardens and the palace, have lunch in South Kensington, and then visit the nearby Natural History Museum. On both days you'd still be able to see a show and have a great dinner at night. You'd also be exhausted.

One word of advice: Try to hit the very top sights on your list early in the day, preferably right when they open, or late in the afternoon. You want to see what's really important to you when you're feeling fresh and when there are fewer people. Using the Underground, you rarely have to wait more than 10 minutes for a train, but boats run on their schedule, not yours, so you might have to wait on the pier for a while. Taking the tube sometimes necessitates a 10- to 15-minute walk to your destination from the tube stop in unfamiliar territory. Keep your ***London A to Z*** with you all day. Trust me: It will come in handy.

Budgeting Your Time

An average top sight takes about 2 hours to visit, once you're actually there and inside. Some (Buckingham Palace and the nearby Queen's Gallery and Royal Mews) take more, others (Westminster Abbey, Kensington Palace) take less. But other variables enter in: whether or not you're taking a guided tour (usually about an hour to 90 minutes, no matter where) or if there are so many people that lines move slowly. It's difficult to allot a certain amount of time to a great institution like the British Museum or the National Gallery, loaded with so many treasures you could easily spend a full day or more. But as a general rule of thumb, you can "do" about three or four sights in a day if you're pushing yourself, fewer if you're not.

Add up the number of 1s and 2s in the above list, and then divide by the number of full days in your trip. If the result is a number larger than 4, you might have a problem, because you can't see six or eight major sights in a day—even superficially. How to get that sights-per-day number down?

- **Lengthen your visit.** This option may or may not be easy for you to do.
- **Split up.** If you are a couple or group, make individual lists as above, and then see if splitting up for a half day or two will provide enough time for everyone to see all his or her favorites.

Time-Savers

If you're on a *really* tight schedule, you might have time to view only the outside of a particular sight or area. It can be enough simply to stroll through Piccadilly Circus and Leicester Square without stopping. Few tourists actually go into the Houses of Parliament; it's the structure itself (and Big Ben) they want to see. The same is true for Buckingham Palace: You might want a glimpse, but it's not that important to traipse through the Queen's Gallery and Royal Mews. If time is of the essence, consider taking one of the guided tours mentioned in chapter 14.

- **Axe the 3s.** In my opinion, it's better to see less and see it well than to spend 30 minutes at the National Gallery, race through Westminster Abbey, hightail it over to St. Paul's, and then arrive exhausted at the Tower of London for a peek at the royal jewels.

Am I Staying in the Right Place?

Take your lists of attractions and put them into the following geographical categories:

The City of London & South Bank (East London)

- ______________________________
- ______________________________
- ______________________________
- ______________________________
- ______________________________
- ______________________________
- ______________________________
- ______________________________
- ______________________________
- ______________________________

The West End (Holborn, Covent Garden & The Strand, Bloomsbury, Soho, Piccadilly Circus & Leicester Square, Mayfair, Marylebone, St. James's, Westminster & Pimlico)

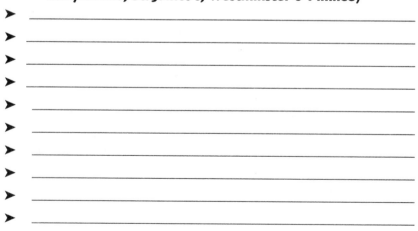

- ______________________________
- ______________________________
- ______________________________
- ______________________________
- ______________________________
- ______________________________
- ______________________________
- ______________________________
- ______________________________
- ______________________________

Central London Beyond the West End (Belgravia, Knightsbridge, Chelsea, South Kensington, Kensington, Earl's Court, Notting Hill, Bayswater & Paddington)

➤ ____________________

➤ ____________________

➤ ____________________

➤ ____________________

➤ ____________________

➤ ____________________

➤ ____________________

➤ ____________________

➤ ____________________

➤ ____________________

If your hotel is in the area with the most entries, you're doing well; you'll be able to get to the first item on your daily agenda in a timely manner, even if you aren't up at the crack of dawn. If you can walk to it, so much the better. If, on the other hand, you've reserved at a hotel that's close to very few of the things you want to see, you'll spend more time commuting. Maybe you should change your hotel.

Time-Savers

Don't forget the season. It's always good in the winter to have a plan B in case it rains. The weather will also partly determine how much walking you can do (or want to do). At a certain point it might become too cold or raw to ride the ferry from Westminster to the Tower, or to stroll in Kensington Gardens comfortably. Also take into account what the sun does to your planning: For instance, the lights in Piccadilly Circus are best at night, but night comes down around 5pm in the winter and 9pm in the summer.

Getting All Your Ducks in a Row

Making your plan concrete may also help make your ideal trip doable. Take a map and mark the locations of all the sights you've listed so far; then mark your hotel. Now try to find clusters of activities that naturally group together. Avoid the Ricochet Rabbit approach to sightseeing (Tower of London—Madame Tussaud's—Kensington Palace—Westminster Abbey). Don't let the city's size and complicated layout throw you for a loop. You can see Kensington Palace in the morning and then stroll through Kensington Gardens on the way to the Victoria and Albert or the Natural History Museum in South Kensington in the afternoon. And remember: In London you're rarely far from a tube station, although you might have to change trains.

Fill-Ins

Fill-ins are things you do on the way to someplace else. Shopping is a natural; go back to chapter 15 and pick out the specific stores and neighborhoods you want to spend time in. List them here.

Shopping

- ______________________________
- ______________________________
- ______________________________
- ______________________________
- ______________________________
- ______________________________
- ______________________________
- ______________________________
- ______________________________
- ______________________________

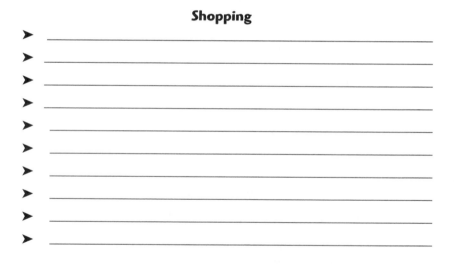

Locate these on the map and figure out what sights they lie between. Allow different amounts of time, depending on whether you're just window-shopping or really planning to graze these places. If you intend to buy a suit at Harvey Nichols in Knightsbridge or get all your Christmas shopping done at Harrods, it might become an attraction-length process.

Dining is another fill-in. Leave the question of dinner aside for now. If there are specific places where you want to lunch, locate them on the map in terms of your clusters of sights. If you have no "musts," use the listings in chapters 10 and 11 to pick out some lunchtime options for each of the clusters so you won't go hungry. List the lunch restaurants below.

Lunch

- ______________________________
- ______________________________
- ______________________________
- ______________________________
- ______________________________
- ______________________________
- ______________________________
- ______________________________
- ______________________________
- ______________________________

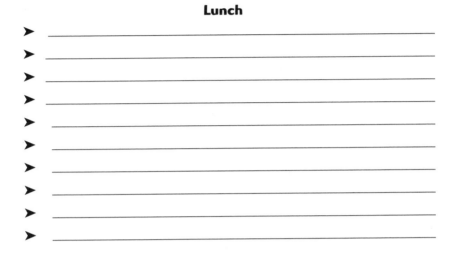

Sketching Out Your Itineraries

Now you're ready to plot some itineraries. At its most basic, an itinerary should be something like this:

> Breakfast at [hotel/place/neighborhood]. See [attraction] in the morning. Lunch at [place/neighborhood] or [alternative]. Walk or take the tube/bus to [attraction]; visit in the afternoon.

Of course, you can fit another attraction into the morning and/or afternoon ("walk across Tower Bridge after visiting the Tower") and leave room for shopping ("exit tube at Bond Street, shop like crazy, and then walk to The Wallace Collection").

DAY 1

Morning:

Lunch:

Afternoon:

Dinner:

Evening:

DAY 2

Morning:

Lunch:

Afternoon:

Dinner:

Evening:

DAY 3

Morning:

Lunch:

Afternoon:

Dinner:

Evening:

DAY 4

Morning:

Lunch:

Afternoon:

Dinner:

Evening:

DAY 5

Morning:

Lunch:

Afternoon:

Dinner:

Evening:

Planning Your Nighttime Right

There's a certain magic that descends upon London—especially in the West End—when night falls, the lights begin to glow, and people head for restaurants, theatres, and pubs. Unless you've got adrenaline to spare, it might be best to unwind a little before you begin your round of after-dark itineraries. You could schedule yourself so that when the museum closes at 5:30pm you come out the door and stand facing that great restaurant you wanted to try, but that would be just a little bit *too* organized—and also exhausting. Give yourself a minibreak before you head out again. You'll probably need some down time between the end of your sightseeing day and the beginning of your evening's activities, so I suggest that you head back to your hotel to take a shower or bath and then curl up with a novel or the evening paper for an hour, or maybe catch a quick snooze to recharge your batteries. This plan also allows you to think about your nightlife plans as a separate mini-itinerary; rather than plan your nightlife by where you end your sightseeing, you can plan a separate sortie from your hotel and hit the town refreshed, dolled up in your evening best (or funkiest), and ready for action.

Spontaneity rules the night, so check out the nightlife recommendations in the following chapters and do what comes naturally—but don't forget to keep track of any dinner reservations or theatre/concert tickets you've booked in advance. Write them here.

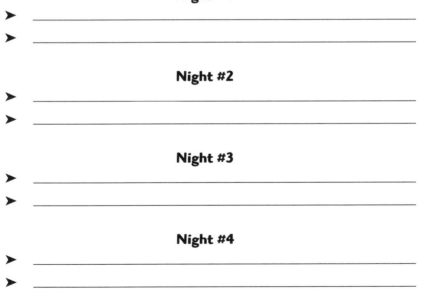

Night #1

➤ ______________________________

➤ ______________________________

Night #2

➤ ______________________________

➤ ______________________________

Night #3

➤ ______________________________

➤ ______________________________

Night #4

➤ ______________________________

➤ ______________________________

For the nights that are blank, you might want to write in tentative options, such as "dinner in [neighborhood]; go to [club/pub/bar] afterward?"

Lastly, keep geography and transportation time enough in mind so that you don't find yourself finishing up your day at a pub in South Kensington with only half an hour before you have to get to a West End theatre. Remember to leave time not only for resting, showering, changing, and dressing, but for that other pleasure of London: the fortuitous and unexpected things that happen when you finally *slow down.*

Part 6

On the Town: Nightlife & Entertainment

London, for some of us, is synonymous with the performing arts. Year-round, on every evening of the week, someone's performing something somewhere. Planning a night out isn't the problem; choosing from all the possibilities is where the difficulty lies.

For most visitors, a trip to London wouldn't be complete without seeing a play or a musical. And rightly so: Theatre is the most popular of the city's diverse cultural activities. You can be thrilled down to your toenails by the spectacle of a megamusical hit, laugh until your stomach aches at a comedy, gasp at the twists and turns of a drama, or just sit back and let the sound of those wonderful Shakespearean voices wash over you.

But if theatre is not your thing, you won't be lacking for other diversions. There's also grand opera, performed by two different opera companies; symphonic concerts by London's and the world's leading orchestras; modern and classical ballet; and countless musical recitals by chamber groups and internationally known artists.

Nightlife in London is certainly not restricted to highbrows, however. Pubs are British institutions, and going out for an evening of pub crawling (or restricting yourself to a "pint" at one place) is a good way to see and meet Londoners. You'll find bars where you can enjoy a relaxing drink after a day of intensive sightseeing. You'll also see jazz clubs and cabarets.

I'll be covering all of the above in the following three chapters, but in the end, the choice is up to you.

Chapter 18

The Play's the Thing: The London Theatre Scene

In This Chapter

- How to find out what's on
- How to get tickets
- What to wear
- What about dinner?

When it comes to theatre, London is the greatest. For sheer diversity of offerings and overall excellence (and intelligence) of performance standards, it's right up there at the top. The city's theatrical reputation boomed during the Elizabethan era, when Shakespeare and other playwrights were staging their plays in a theatre district on the South Bank. Except for a brief hiatus during Cromwell's Puritan era, it hasn't stopped since. Maybe, in part, this is because the British still value the glory of the spoken word and the sound of a trained voice.

London's theatre scene may have started on the South Bank, but today plays and musicals are staged all over London. The "big" shows (musicals and commercial hits) are concentrated mostly in the **West End,** but you'll find major theatre venues at the Barbican and on the South Bank as well. Just as important to the theatrical vitality of London are the city's many **"fringe"** venues. "Fringe" is the equivalent of off- or off-off-Broadway.

Keep in mind that theatre in London is big business. With 100 theatres—about 50 in the West End alone—it's even bigger than New York. What this means is that you should think about booking a seat before you go, especially if you want to see one of the hot musicals. Some of these shows are sold out months in advance.

In addition to the information that's given here, refer to chapter 4.

The Play May Be the Thing . . . but What's Playing?

You can find details for all London shows, concerts, and other performances in the daily London newspapers: the *Daily Telegraph,* the *Evening Standard,* the *Guardian,* the *Independent,* and the *Times.* You can also check in the weekly magazines ***Time Out*** and ***What's On in London,*** available at all newsagents. Another good source is the free booklet ***London Planner,*** available at the British Travel Centre, 1 Regent Street, or by mail from a BTA travel office (see chapter 1 for addresses).

Extra! Extra!

For the most comprehensive listings of everything that's going on in London, plus thumbnail synopses of the plots and (usually scathing) critical opinion, buy a copy of the weekly magazine ***Time Out.*** It's available at London newsstands on Wednesdays and costs £1.80 ($3).

The **Web** is one of the best places to search in advance for information on plays and performances currently running in London. The following Web sites are useful; see chapter 4 for more information on these sites: www.OfficialLondonTheatre.co.uk, www.keithprowse.com, www.albemarlelondon.com, www.timeout.co.uk, www.telegraph.co.uk, www.thetimes.co.uk, and www.thisislondon.co.uk.

How Do I Book a Theatre Seat?

If you're in London and have found a show you want to see but don't yet have tickets, the best thing you can do is go directly to the theatre's box office. I don't know how many times I've been told that a West End show was officially sold out and then gone to the box office and purchased a seat without any problem. There are always cancellations and house seats that only go on sale the day of the performance or an hour before. Plus, if you buy directly from the box office, you don't have to pay the commission fee (up to 30%) charged by ticket agencies.

Ticket Agencies

All over the West End you'll see ticket agencies blaring the news that they have tickets to such-and-so (always a big "sold-out" hit). Most of these places are legitimate, though their commission fees vary. I recommend that you go to one of the following trustworthy agencies.

Edwards & Edwards–Globaltickets has two drop-in London branches: Palace Theatre, Shaftesbury Ave., W1 (☎ **0171/734-4555;** tube: Leicester Square); and at the British Visitor Center, 1 Regent St., SW1

(☎ 0171/839-3952; tube: Piccadilly Circus). They're open Monday through Friday 10:15am to 6:15pm, Saturday 10am to 4pm, and Sunday 10am to 4pm. You'll pay a 20% commission on top of the ticket price.

Time-Savers

If you don't have time to go to the box office and have a major credit card handy, call the office directly. Phone numbers are listed in all the major papers and in ***Time Out.*** Many London theatres accept bookings via telephone at regular prices (plus a minimal telephone-booking fee) with a credit card. They'll hold your tickets for you at the box office, where you can pick them up any time up to a half-hour before the curtain.

Albemarle Booking Agency, 74 Mortimer St., London, W1 (☎ **017/ 637 9041;** tube: Oxford Circus or Goodge Street), is another long-established agency. Its commission fee is 22%.

If you want to book by phone, there are two trustworthy agencies you can try; both accept credit-card booking 24-hours a day and charge a 25% commission: **First Call** (☎ **0171/240-7941**) and **Ticketmaster** (☎ **0171/ 413-3321**). You can pick up your tickets at the box office. If you are making a telephone booking, the agent must tell you the face value of the ticket, the location, and whether you will have a restricted view. If there's any doubt in your mind, buy your tickets elsewhere.

How Do I Reserve a Seat Before I Arrive?

If you've got your heart set on seeing a specific show, you can reserve in advance through **Edwards & Edwards–Globaltickets,** which has telephone box offices around the world. In the **U.S.,** call ☎ **800/223-6108.** In **Australia,** call ☎ **1300/363-163.** In **Canada,** call ☎ **800/223-6108.** In Ireland, call ☎ **1/667-5323.** In South Africa, call ☎ **11/788-0810.** They'll mail tickets to your home, fax you a confirmation, or leave your tickets at the box office; a booking and handling fee of up to 20% is added to the ticket price.

Dollars & Sense

Many London theatres offer **standby seats,** sold an hour before the performance, to students and seniors with proper identification. Matinees are also somewhat cheaper than evening performances.

Keith Prowse/Firstcall also has an office in the United States that allows you to reserve seats before you leave home: Suite 1000, 234 W. 44th St., New York, NY 10036 (☎ **800/669-8687** or

212/398-1430). The fee for booking a ticket from the U.S. is 35% of the ticket price.

Dollars & Sense

The **Society of London Theatres** (☎ **0171/836-0971**) operates a **half-price tickets booth** in Leicester Square (tube: Leicester Square). Tickets are sold only on the day of the performance, Monday through Saturday from noon to 6:30pm and from noon to 2pm for matinees (which may be on Wednesday, Thursday, or Saturday). This is a cash-only affair; no credit cards or traveler's checks are accepted. A nominal fee (less than $5) is added to the price. The most popular shows won't be available, but you might luck out. Tickets for the English National Opera and other events are sometimes available as well. You might want to stop by in any case to pick up a free copy of ***The Official London Theatre Guide,*** which lists every show with its address and phone number and includes a map of the West End theatre district.

Another option in the U.S. is **Theatre Direct International (TDI)** (☎ **800/334-8457**), which specializes in fringe-production tickets but has tickets to most London shows.

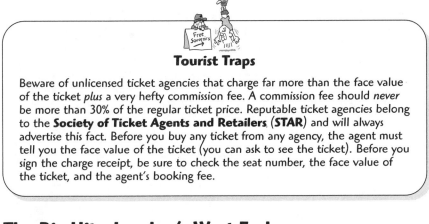

Tourist Traps

Beware of unlicensed ticket agencies that charge far more than the face value of the ticket *plus* a very hefty commission fee. A commission fee should *never* be more than 30% of the regular ticket price. Reputable ticket agencies belong to the **Society of Ticket Agents and Retailers** (**STAR**) and will always advertise this fact. Before you buy any ticket from any agency, the agent must tell you the face value of the ticket (you can ask to see the ticket). Before you sign the charge receipt, be sure to check the seat number, the face value of the ticket, and the agent's booking fee.

The Big Hits: London's West End

The West End theatre district—or **Theatreland,** as it's now called—is concentrated mostly in the area around Piccadilly Circus, Leicester Square, and Covent Garden. But the theatres at the Barbican Centre and South Bank Centre (see below) are theatrically considered West End venues as well.

Tourist Traps

Wave away those pesky **scalpers** who hang out in front of megahit shows. They may indeed be selling (for an astronomical price) a valid ticket. But some of these touts, as they're called, also forge tickets, which means you'll be out of cash and out of a show. By law, any tout must tell you the face value of the ticket so you'll know exactly what its markup is. The best advice: Don't deal with them.

Dollars & Sense

Some of London's larger and ritzier hotels—The Savoy and The Dorchester, for instance—have dedicated theatre desks. And they'd be happy to book a seat for you . . . with about a 30% commission tacked on to the actual ticket price. This holds true for just about any theatre booking through a hotel concierge or theatre desk.

Major British stars with international screen reputations regularly perform in the West End. You might see Dame Judi Dench, Ralph Fiennes, Vanessa Redgrave, Helen Mirren, or Alan Bates. You're just as likely to see a show starring someone you've never heard of but who's well known in England. You can expect the production values to be topnotch and the performers outstanding. (Whether you like the play itself is another matter.) You can also expect to find a few American plays, since the crossover between London and New York grows greater every year.

Extra! Extra!

Many of the airlines that fly to London offer special **theatre packages** or will book **theatre** seats as an add-on service. The thing to remember is that the airlines' package offerings are strictly confined to a list of about 10 of the long-established hits (most of them musicals) that everyone wants to see. See chapter 3 for more information on airline **theatre** packages.

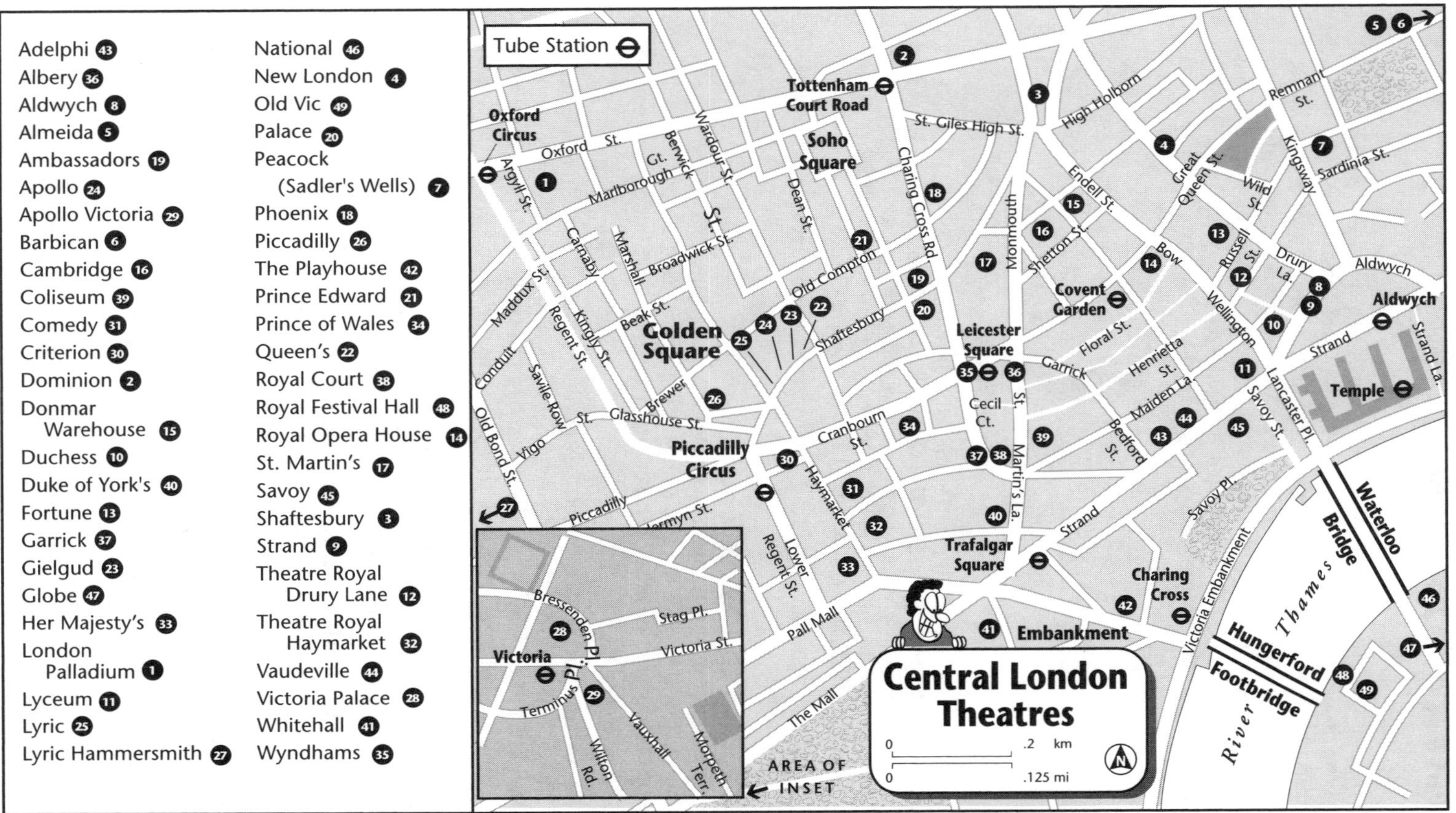

Central London Theatres
Tube Station
Adelphi 43
Albery 36
Aldwych 8
Almeida 5
Ambassadors 19
Apollo 24
Apollo Victoria 29
Barbican 6
Cambridge 16
Coliseum 39
Comedy 31
Criterion 30
Dominion 2
Donmar Warehouse 15
Duchess 10
Duke of York's 40
Fortune 13
Garrick 37
Gielgud 23
Globe 47
Her Majesty's 33
London Palladium 1
Lyceum 11
Lyric 25
Lyric Hammersmith 27
National 46
New London 4
Old Vic 49
Palace 20
Peacock (Sadler's Wells) 7
Phoenix 18
Piccadilly 26
The Playhouse 42
Prince Edward 21
Prince of Wales 34
Queen's 22
Royal Court 38
Royal Festival Hall 48
Royal Opera House 14
St. Martin's 17
Savoy 45
Shaftesbury 3
Strand 9
Theatre Royal Drury Lane 12
Theatre Royal Haymarket 32
Vaudeville 44
Victoria Palace 28
Whitehall 41
Wyndhams 35
Oxford Circus
Tottenham Court Road
Soho Square
Golden Square
Piccadilly Circus
Leicester Square
Covent Garden
Trafalgar Square
Charing Cross
Embankment
Aldwych
Temple
Victoria
Waterloo Bridge
Hungerford Footbridge
River Thames
AREA OF INSET
0 .2 km
0 .125 mi

Some of the shows in the West End have been running for years and still show no signs of vacating their premises. There are also new plays, old chestnuts, and revivals of the classics. Plus Shakespeare, of course. You can expect to pay approximately $50 to $75 for a ticket (this is the price at the box office). In general, there are evening performances Monday through Saturday and, depending on the show, matinees on Wednesday or Thursday and Saturday. Recently some shows have added Sunday performances as well.

Extra! Extra!

The same Society of London Theatres that operates the half-price tickets booth in Leicester Square publishes ***The Complete Guide to London's West End Theatres,*** which has seating plans for every theatre. It costs £9.95 ($17), and you can purchase it from its office at Bedford Chambers, The Piazza, Covent Garden, WC2 (☎ **0171/836-3193;** tube: Covent Garden).

Beyond the West End

The number of theatres in Theatreland makes listing each and every one impossible, but there are two outstanding venues that should be mentioned. Both are located outside of the central theatre district but are still considered part of it.

Barbican Centre, Silk Street, EC2 (tube: Barbican), a multiarts center in the City of London (see chapter 14) is the London home of the prestigious **Royal Shakespeare Company** (☎ **0171/638-8891**). They perform in the 1,156-seat Barbican Theatre. Other plays are performed in The Pit, a 200-seat studio theatre. Ticket prices vary from show to show, but in general cost less than commercial hits in the West End. There are bars, cafes, and restaurants in the complex. The box office is open daily from 9am to 8pm. For 24-hour recorded information on all Barbican Centre events, call ☎ **0171/638-7297.**

The **South Bank Centre,** South Bank, SE1 (tube: Waterloo), is home to the **Royal National Theatre** (☎ **0171/452-3000**), which performs in three theatres: the 1,160-seat Olivier, the 890-seat Lyttelton, and the smaller theatre-in-the-round Cottesloe. Ticket prices are lower than at the commercial theatres on the other side of the river—generally £10 to £25 ($17 to $41) for evening performances and £8 to £20 ($13 to $34) for matinees. Unsold seats are offered at even lower prices 2 hours before the performance. The Royal National performs Shakespeare, but it's just as likely to have in its repertory a new work by David Hare, a revival of a Tennessee Williams play, or a production of a Restoration comedy. Cafes, bars, and a good bookstore are on the premises. The box office is open Monday through Saturday from

10am to 8pm. For information on performances, call ☎ **0171/452-3400** (Monday through Saturday 10am to 11pm).

Extra! Extra!

The newest addition to the South Bank scene is **Shakespeare's Globe Theatre,** New Globe Walk, Bankside, SE1 (☎ **0171/401-9919;** tube: Cannon Street or London Bridge), which presents a May-to-September season of Shakespeare plays in a reconstructed Elizabethan theatre. After a couple of hours the benches can be a bit numbing, but you're seeing Shakespeare performed not far from the original theatre—and you're right beside the Thames.

On the Fringe

I love the glitz and glamour of West End shows as much as the next person, but when my own play, ***Beardsley,*** was produced in London it was "on the fringe." What's "the fringe"? It's London's equivalent to New York's off- or off-off-Broadway. You might, in fact, now hear it referred to as "Off–West End." The plays performed on the fringe are sometimes controversial or experimental, but for true theatre-lovers they can provide a stimulating alternative to the West End.

The performance spaces for fringe productions are usually smaller (sometimes tiny, sometimes above a pub), the ticket prices are much lower (rarely more than £10/$17), and usually there's no sacrifice in artistic excellence. In many ways, fringe theatre is the real theatrical heartbeat of the City. Groups performing on the fringe don't have the big bucks to mount lavish West End–style productions. But they're often hoping that their show will be a critical hit and move to the West End. With the overabundance of acting talent in London, the fringe is where you might see tomorrow's stars acting today and next season's hit in its original bare-bones form.

Fringe theatres and spaces adapted to fringe productions are scattered far and wide, and you'll need to consult ***London A to Z*** or call the theatre for directions on how to find them. The shows have limited runs but are always listed in ***Time Out.***

Seeing the Stars Under the Stars

Want to sit under the stars and watch a good play, usually Shakespeare? **Regent's Park Open Air Theatre,** Regent's Park, NW1 (☎ **0171/486-2431;** tube: Baker Street), has an April through August season. This is a large venue, with real seats but no roof—so rain might cancel the show. It's located on the north side of Queen Mary's Rose Garden.

My God, They've Put Me in the Stalls!

Relax. Buying a ticket in "the stalls" doesn't mean you'll be seated in the powder room. It means you might have one of the best seats in the house. **Stalls** is the British term for first-floor orchestra. Most of the West End theatres are fairly old, which means they might have "boxes" for sale as well. These will be on the sides of the second or third tier.

Theatre Etiquette

Plays in the West End have different curtain times. They might begin at 7:30pm, 8pm, or 8:30pm; matinees can begin at 1:30pm, 2pm, or 2:30pm. Check your ticket to be certain, because if you're late you will not be admitted until the second act or a suitable pause in the action. (If it's a one-act play, good luck.) Londoners take their theatre very seriously (even the comedies), so don't be one of those boorish latecomers who whines that the tube was late. If you come laden with packages, you can check them in the coatroom. Do not tip the usher who shows you to your seat. Talking and noisily unwrapping pieces of candy during the performance will be frowned upon.

So, What Should I Wear?

You certainly don't want to wear a tuxedo or an evening gown, but if you arrive in a sweat suit and running shoes you'll be pretty conspicuous. (No one would be rude enough to say anything, of course.) London theatre audiences are, on the whole, pretty well dressed. This is an evening out, after all. There are no hard-and-fast rules here. Use common sense and "try to look nice," as my mother used to say.

Should I Have Dinner Before or After the Show?

You've got to eat—but do you do it before or after a show? It depends on your eating habits. If you eat beforehand, you might feel too rushed—and hungry again after the show lets out. Eating late is more fun and relaxed, but not every restaurant is open late. You might want to try one of the pretheatre menus offered by many West End restaurants (see chapter 10).

When to Eat

If you decide to dine **before the show,** plan to be seated and ordering no later than **6pm.** Keep in mind that West End restaurants are often crowded with people who are, like you, going to the theatre. On the plus side, timewise, you'll often be within walking distance of the theatre. If you're dining outside of the West End, you'll have to allot extra time to order, eat, pay the bill, get your coats, and then hop on a tube or hail a taxi to make the curtain. You might encounter a delay on the tube, or the taxi might run into heavy traffic.

I'm not a big one for late dining, and in the West End the final curtain rarely goes down before 10:30pm (at the opera it's usually not until 11pm). If you're dining **after the show,** you'll have to ascertain whether the restaurant of your choice is open. (London isn't New York when it comes to late-night dining.) And if you're using the tube as your primary means of transportation, remember that service on most lines ends at 11:30pm. What you might want to do is have dinner before the show and dessert afterward.

Where to Eat

The West End is loaded with restaurants of varying quality. Check out my recommendations in chapter 10 for good places to dine. Piccadilly Circus, Covent Garden, and Soho are all close to major West End theatres. Reserve a table in advance, and when you arrive tell the waiter that you're going to the theatre and need to be out by X time.

If you're not fussy about what you eat and just want to keep your stomach from growling during the performance, you'll find lots of fast-food joints around Leicester Square and Piccadilly Circus. And if you're going farther afield—to the Barbican or South Bank Centre—there are cafes and restaurants on the premises where you can ward off impending hunger pangs with a light meal or a sandwich.

What to Eat

One of the best things you can do is find a West End restaurant (see chapter 10) that serves **pretheatre meals.** These restaurants are geared for the theatre crowd, so they know your time is limited. Pretheatre menus are usually served between 6pm and 7pm, your choices are limited to a set menu, and you're out by 7:30pm or earlier. The prices are usually good values. Just be certain to book a table beforehand.

Chapter 19

The Performing Arts

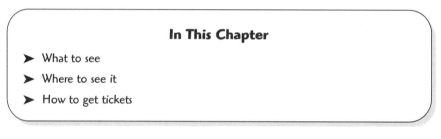

In This Chapter

- What to see
- Where to see it
- How to get tickets

Symphony concerts, chamber music, recitals, modern and classical ballet, rock concerts, cabarets—it's all here, and it's all over London. The Royal Opera, the Royal Ballet, the English National Opera, and the London Symphony Orchestra are just a few of the internationally renowned groups that have their home bases in the nation's capital. But London, as a cultural mecca par excellence, is also a stopover on the international tour circuit. It draws major performing arts companies and solo performers from all over.

Finding Out What's On

The same newspapers, magazines, and brochures that have theatre listings will have information on all other performing arts events (see chapter 18).

For a weeklong list of what's happening, check ***Time Out,*** available at newsstands on Wednesdays and on the Web at **www.timeout.co.uk** (2-week listings). Many London newspapers have Arts or Culture sections in their Sunday editions and can be accessed on the Web. The most comprehensive are the ***Times*** (www.the-times.co.uk) and the ***Telegraph*** (www.telegraph.co.uk).

Before you go, you can call the **British Tourist Authority** (see chapter 1) and request a copy of its monthly ***London Planner,*** which lists all major events; BTA is on the Web at www.visitbritain.com. For more information, consult the list of various sources in chapters 1 and 4.

Two other useful Web sites for current performing arts events are **Leisure London** at **www.thisislondon.co.uk** and **www.culturefinder.com**.

Extra! Extra!

British Music Information Centre, 10 Stratford Place, W1 (☎ **0171/499-8567;** tube: Bond Street), is the city's clearinghouse and resource center for serious music. Open Monday through Friday from noon to 5pm, it provides free telephone and walk-in information on current and upcoming events. Recitals featuring 20th-century British classical compositions are presented here weekly, usually on Tuesday and Thursday at 7:30pm; call ahead for day and time. Tickets are generally about £5 ($8).

Getting Your Tickets

The best thing to do is to go to the box office or call and order tickets by phone. Addresses and box-office numbers for major venues are listed below. With a credit card, you can usually order tickets directly from the box office before you leave home and pick them up once you arrive. **First Call** (☎ **800/669-8687** in the U.S., or 0171/240-7941) and **Ticketmaster** (☎ **0171/413-3321**) accept credit-card bookings 24 hours a day. Also try **Edwards & Edwards–Globaltickets** (☎ **0171/734-4555** or 0171/839-3952; for their London addresses, see chapter 18).

Grand Opera

London has two major opera companies. In terms of international prestige, the Royal Opera wins hands down. It gets the famous international singers and performs operas in their original languages. But in terms of popularity and inventiveness, the English National comes out ahead.

The Royal Opera House, Covent Garden, London, WC2E 9DD (☎ **0171/212-9123** info line), is being refurbished and won't reopen until at least December 1999 (don't hold your breath). Until then, the Royal Opera will be performing its usual September-to-August

Extra! Extra!

Artsline (☎ **0171/388-2227**) provides advice regarding accessibility to London arts and entertainment events for persons with disabilities.

season at temporary homes (the Barbican Centre, the London Coliseum, Royal Albert Hall, Royal Festival Hall, and Sadler's Wells). Ticket prices are £10 to £65 ($17 to $107). For a summary of the opera (and ballet) season, check the Web site at www.royalopera.org.

English National Opera, London Coliseum, St. Martin's Lane, London, WC2N 4ES (☎ **0171/632-8300** for box office—open 24 hours Monday to Saturday; tube: Leicester Square), performs in a big old barn of an auditorium (2,358 seats). The ENO ventures into territory where the traditional Royal Opera would never go. The operas here are all sung in English. Seats range from £5 to £47.50 ($9 to $78), and 100 balcony seats for £2.50 ($4) each go on sale at 10am on the day of the performance. The opera season runs from September to July.

Opera in the Park

Holland Park Theatre, Holland Park, W8 (☎ **0171/602-7856;** tube: Holland Park), has London's most charming outdoor stage. It's set in the ruins of a Jacobean mansion and is used for an August season of opera. Performances are held in a covered auditorium.

Mozart, Mahler & Mussourgsky

Where do you go to hear great music in London? You have several choices.

The **London Symphony Orchestra's** home base is **Barbican Hall** at Barbican Centre, Silk Street, EC2Y 8DS (☎ **0171-638-8891;** tube: Barbican), the concert-hall portion of this giant performing-arts complex in the City of London. You might also catch a performance by the **Royal Philharmonic Orchestra,** which plays concerts both here and at Royal Albert Hall (see below). For 24-hour recorded information on all events at the Barbican, call ☎ **0171/638-8891.** The Royal Opera will be performing here periodically throughout 1999.

About 1,200 classical music and dance concerts are held year-round in the three auditoriums of the **South Bank Centre,** South Bank, SE1 8XX (☎ **0171/960-4242;** tube: Waterloo). Symphonic works performed by all manner of orchestras—some British, some international—take place in **Royal Festival Hall.** Chamber music concerts and dance programs are given in the smaller **Queen Elizabeth Hall,** and recitals are held in the more intimate **Purcell Room.** You can get tickets and information on all three venues at the box office; prices vary for each event. For credit-card bookings, call ☎ **0171/960-4242.**

Another all-purpose venue for classical music is **Royal Albert Hall,** Kensington Gore, SW7 2AP (☎ **0171/589-8212;** tube: Gloucester Road or Knightsbridge). This enormous circular domed concert hall has been a landmark in South Kensington since 1871. The box office is open daily from 9am to 9pm; ticket prices are different for every event. For general information, you can call ☎ **0891/500-252.** This is one of the places where the Royal Opera will be performing until the Royal Opera House refurbishment is completed.

Going to the Proms

One of London's most eagerly awaited summer musical events is the 2-month (mid-July to mid-September) series of classical and pop concerts known as the **Proms.** All Proms concerts are held at **Royal Albert Hall** (see above), where they began in 1895. For Proms concerts, all the seats are removed from the stalls (orchestra level). Reserved seats are available, but true aficionados stand for a close-up look at the orchestras, which come from all over Europe to play here. You can reserve a seat through Ticketmaster or one of the other agencies listed above; for standing room, you have to queue up (be prepared for long lines) on the day of the performance.

Wigmore Hall, 36 Wigmore St., W1 (☎ **0171/935-2141;** tube: Bond Street), is a fine old concert hall, recently restored, where chamber-music concerts and recitals are held.

The Major Minors: Churches with Concert Programs

Many of Central London's churches have concert programs. The best-known are **St. Giles in the Barbican,** Fore Street, EC2 (no tel.; tube: Barbican); **St. James Garlickhythe,** Garlick Hill, EC4 (☎ **0171/236-1719;** tube: Mansion House); **St. Margaret's Westminster,** St. Margaret Street., SW1 (☎ **0171/722-5152;** tube: Westminster); **St. Peter's Eaton Square,** Eaton Square, SW1 (☎ **0171/823-1205;** tube: Victoria); and on the South Bank, **Southwark Cathedral,** Montague Close, London Bridge, SE1 (☎ **0171/928-8800;** tube: London Bridge). Check the listings in ***Time Out*** to see if a concert is scheduled, or call the church directly. There's usually a nominal admission fee.

Music Under the Stars

At 7:30pm on Saturday evenings during August, **Kenwood Lakeside Concerts,** Hampstead Lane, NW3 (☎ **0171/413-1443;** tube: East Finchley), presents outdoor summer concerts at a marvelous lakeside estate in Hampstead Heath. A free shuttle bus runs between the East Finchley tube station and the concert bowl. Allow yourself at least 20 minutes to get to the tube stop from Central London and another 15 minutes for the ride on the shuttle bus.

Concerts by Candlelight

Evening candlelit concerts of Baroque music are performed every Thursday, Friday, and Saturday at 7:30pm in the lovely church of **St. Martin-in-the-Fields,** Trafalgar Square, W1 (☎ **0171/839-8362** for credit-card bookings; tube: Charing Cross). Lunchtime concerts are held on Monday, Tuesday, and Friday at 1pm. (See chapter 13 for more details on the church.)

A Bit of Everything

That's what you'll find at **Sadler's Wells,** Rosebery Avenue, Islington, EC1R 4TN (☎ **0171/713-6000;** tube: Angel). Newly refurbished in 1998, this hall is well known for its dance programs. The **Royal Ballet** and the Royal Opera will be performing here until they move back to the Royal Opera House in Covent Garden. And so will a host of other contemporary dance companies, European theatre and music productions, and solo performers. Sadler's Wells is also the home of the D'Oyly Carte Gilbert & Sullivan company.

On Your Toes: Other Dance Venues

Major contemporary and classical dance companies perform at some of the venues already listed: **Queen Elizabeth Hall** at the South Bank Centre, the London **Coliseum** in the West End, and **Barbican Hall** in the City of London's Barbican Centre (see above for addresses and box-office numbers). **The Place,** 17 Duke's Rd., WC1 (☎ **0171/387-0031;** tube: Euston), is the epicenter for contemporary dance in the U.K. **Riverside Studios,** Crisp Road, W6 (☎ **0181/741-2255;** tube: Hammersmith), is an arts center that showcases both theatre and dance. **Lillian Baylis Theatre,** Arlington Way, EC1 (☎ **0171/713-6000;** tube: Angel), is another performance space for dance.

Humongous Rock Concerts

When Madonna, The Rolling Stones, and Aerosmith tour in the U.K., they need a HUGE arena to hold their shrieking fans. The big groups play at **Wembley Stadium** and **Wembley Arena,** Empire Way, Wembley, Middlesex (☎ **0181/902-0902;** tube: Wembley Park). A much smaller (by that, I mean 70,000 seats smaller) rock 'n' pop venue is **Brixton Academy,** 211 Stockwell Rd., SW9 (☎ **0171/924-9999;** tube: Brixton). Another big-event hall is **Apollo Hammersmith,** Queen Caroline Street, W6 (☎ **0181/741-4868;** tube: Hammersmith). And sometimes old **Royal Albert Hall** (see above) rocks, too.

Forget the Live Stuff—I Want to Go to the Movies

You don't go to "the movies" in England, you go to "the cinema." The city's largest multiplex, where you can catch one of those blockbusters you conveniently missed at home, is **Warner West End,** Leicester Square, WC2 (☎ **0171/437-4347;** tube: Leicester Square). Classics from here, there, and everywhere show up at the **National Film Theatre,** South Bank Centre, SE1 (☎ **0171/249-6876;** tube: Waterloo). At **Odeon Marble Arch,** Edgware Road, W1 (☎ **0171/723-2011;** tube: Marble Arch), Hollywood hits hog the biggest non-IMAX screen (and theatre) in London. French films are often featured at Mayfair's posh **Curzon,** Curzon Street, W1 (☎ **0171/368-1710;** tube: Green Park). The **Lumiere,** St. Martin's Lane, WC2 (☎ **0171/379-3014;** tube: Charing Cross), right in the heart of the West End, is a good first-run art cinema. **Screen on Baker Street,** 96 Baker St., NW1 (☎ **0171/935-2772;** tube: Baker Street), is a smaller, comfortable, independent art-house theatre not far from Madame Tussaud's.

Chapter 20

Hitting the Clubs, Pubs & Bars

In This Chapter

- Where to hear your kind of music live
- Where to dance to your kind of music
- Where to have a drink in your kind of place

London's late-night club scene is hopping with every kind of music imaginable, so if you want to go out and tangle your tail feathers you won't be lacking in places to hear the newest and the loudest. Maybe you'd rather hear some mellow jazz, or listen to the blues, or shake your cha-chas to Latin-American sounds. Or go to a tony hotel bar for a good martini. Or sit back in a historic pub and quaff a pint of ale. I've tried to include something for everyone in this chapter.

Pub Crawling

Central London is awash with wonderful historic pubs where you can sit all evening with a pint of real ale or bitter or stout or cider (or a glass of malt whiskey) and soak up the local color. Or you can do a pub crawl, walking from place to place and sampling the incredibly diverse brews on tap. There's a pub on practically every corner in London, so it's impossible to mention all of them. The ones below offer something out of the ordinary and will provide a memorable—albeit smoky—evening out.

In The City **Cittie of Yorke,** 22 High Holborn, WC1 (☎ **0171/242-7670;** tube: Holborn or Chancery Lane), has the longest bar in Britain and looks like a great medieval hall—appropriate since a pub has existed at this location since 1430. **Seven Stars,** 53 Carey St., WC2 (**☎ 0171/242-8521;** tube: Holborn), at the back of the law courts, is tiny and modest except for its collection of Toby mugs and law-related art. Lots of barristers drink here, so it's a great place to pick up some British legal jargon. **Olde Mitre,** Ely Place, EC1 (**☎ 0171/405-4751;** tube: Chancery Lane), the namesake of an inn built here in 1547, is a small pub with an eccentric assortment of customers. The wedge-shaped **Black Friar,** 174 Queen Victoria St., EC4 (**☎ 0171/236-5650;** tube: Blackfriars), an Edwardian wonder of marble and bronze art nouveau, features bas-reliefs of mad monks, a low-vaulted mosaic ceiling, and seating carved out of gold marble recesses.

West London Loaded with Churchill memorabilia, the Churchill Arms, 119 Kensington Church St., W8 (% 0171/727-4242; tube: Notting Hill Gate or High Street Kensington), hosts an entire week of celebration leading up to his birthday on November 30. Visitors are often welcomed like regulars here, and the overall ambiance is down-to-earth and homey. **Ladbroke Arms,** 54 Ladbroke Rd., W11 (% 0171/727-6648; tube: Holland Park), is that rare pub known for its food. A changing menu includes chicken breast stuffed with avocado and garlic steak in pink peppercorn sauce. With background jazz and rotating art prints, the place strays a bit from the traditional pub environment, but it makes for a pleasant stop and a good meal.

Extra! Extra!

Most pubs adhere to **strict hours** governed by Parliament: Monday through Saturday from 11am to 11pm and Sunday from noon to 10:30pm. Americans take note: No service charge is asked for or expected in a pub, and you never tip the bartender. The best you can do is offer to buy him or her a drink. Ten minutes before closing, a bell rings signaling that it's time to order your last round.

Hot Spots for Cool Jazz

You'll find lots of small, smoky jazz clubs in London where you can groove 'til the wee hours. **Ronnie Scott's,** 47 Frith St., W1 (**☎ 0171/439-0747;** tube: Tottenham Court Road), in Soho, has been London's preeminent jazz club for years. Go here for dependably high-caliber performances. It will cost you, though: You have to order food (meals or snacks), and the admission is £15 ($25). For something trendier with fewer tourists, try the **Blue Note,** 1 Hoxton Square, N1 (**☎ 0171/729-8440;** tube: Old Street), in Islington. It has an innovative and wide-ranging musical program. Cover ranges from £3 to £10 ($5 to $17).

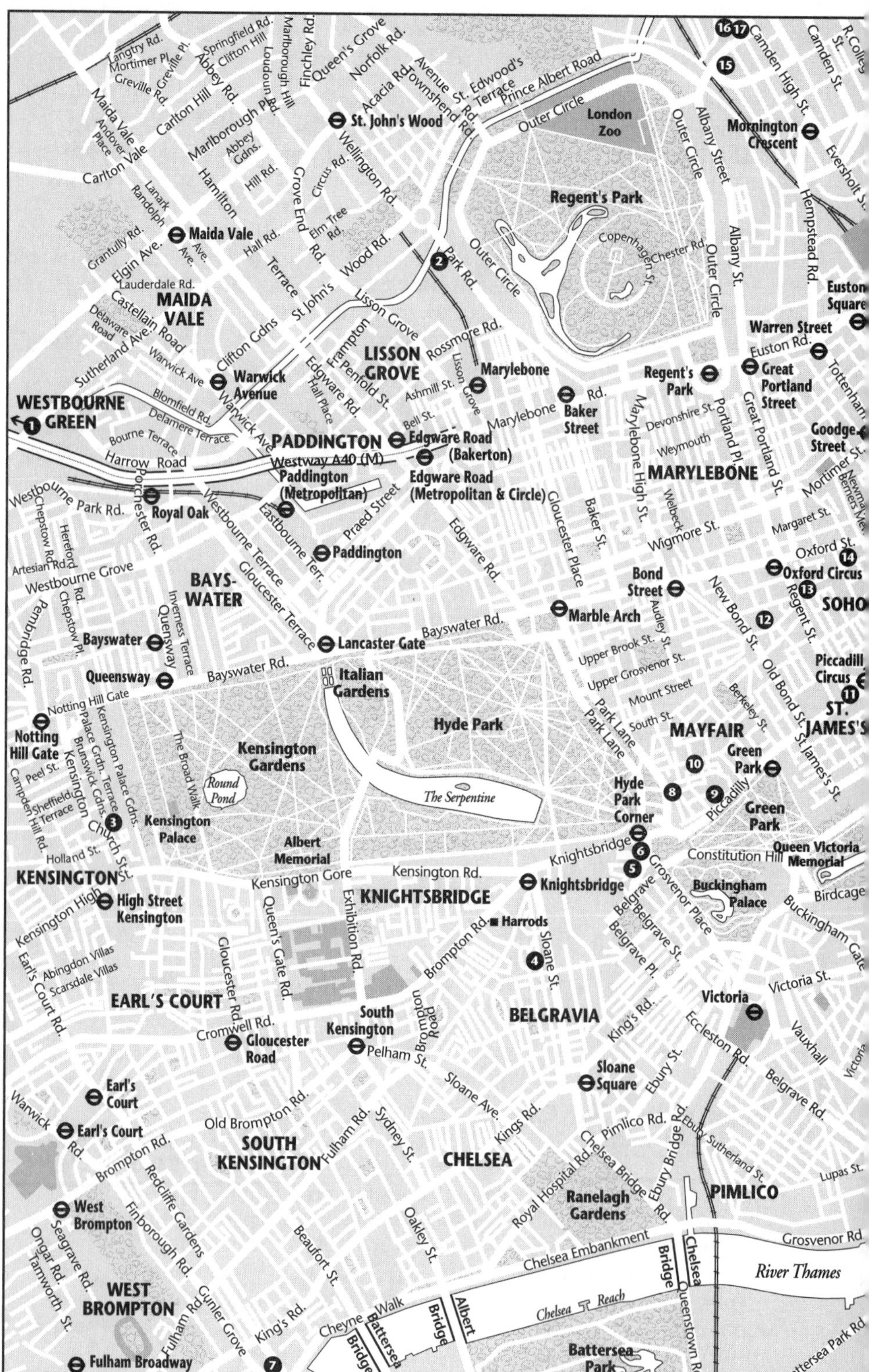

Langtry Rd.
Mortimer Pl.
Greville Pl.
Greville Rd.
Springfield Rd.
Clifton Hill
Abbey Rd.
Marlborough Hill
Loudoun Rd.
Finchley Rd.
Queen's Grove
Norfolk Rd.
Avenue Rd.
St. Edwood's Terrace
Townshend Rd.
Prince Albert Road
Acacia Rd.
St. John's Wood
Maida Vale
Andover Place
Carlton Hill
Carlton Vale
Marlborough Pl.
Abbey Gdns.
Hill Rd.
Circus Rd.
Wellington Rd.
Outer Circle
London Zoo
Regent's Park
Copenhagen St.
Chester Rd.
Lanark
Randolph
Hamilton
Grove End Rd.
Elm Tree Rd.
Maida Vale
Ave.
Ave.
Hall Rd.
Grantully Rd.
Elgin Ave.
Terrace
Wood Rd.
Park Rd.
Lauderdale Rd.
MAIDA VALE
Castellain Road
Delaware Road
St. John's
Lisson Grove
Rossmore Rd.
Sutherland Ave.
Warwick Ave
Clifton Gdns
Frampton
Penfold St.
Edgware Rd.
Hall Place
LISSON GROVE
Lisson Grove
Marylebone
Ashmill St.
Warwick Avenue
WESTBOURNE GREEN
Blomfield Rd.
Delamere Terrace
Bourne Terrace
Warwick Ave
Bell St.
PADDINGTON
Edgware Road
Edgware Road (Bakerton)
Marylebone Rd.
Baker Street
Harrow Road
Westway A40 (M)
Paddington (Metropolitan)
Edgware Road (Metropolitan & Circle)
Westbourne Park Rd.
Chepstow Rd.
Porchester Rd.
Royal Oak
Westbourne Terrace
Eastbourne Terr.
Praed Street
Hereford Rd.
Artesian Rd.
Westbourne Grove
Paddington
Edgware Rd.
Gloucester Place
Baker St.
BAYS-WATER
Gloucester Terrace
Pembridge Rd.
Chepstow Pl.
Inverness Terrace
Queensway
Bayswater
Queensway
Lancaster Gate
Bayswater Rd.
Bayswater Rd.
Marble Arch
Italian Gardens
Notting Hill Gate
Notting Hill Gate
Kensington Palace Gdns.
Palace Grdn. Terrace
Brunswick Gdns.
Kensington Church St.
Peel St.
Sheffield Terrace
Campden Hill Rd.
Holland St.
The Broad Walk
Round Pond
Kensington Gardens
Kensington Palace
Hyde Park
The Serpentine
Albert Memorial
KENSINGTON
High Street Kensington
Kensington High
Kensington Gore
Kensington Rd.
KNIGHTSBRIDGE
Knightsbridge
Knightsbridge
Queen's Gate Rd.
Exhibition Rd.
Gloucester Rd.
Brompton Rd.
Harrods
Sloane St.
Earl's Court Rd.
Abingdon Villas
Scarsdale Villas
EARL'S COURT
Cromwell Rd.
Gloucester Road
South Kensington
Brompton Road
Pelham St.
BELGRAVIA
Sloane Ave.
Sloane Square
Earl's Court
Earl's Court
Warwick Rd.
Brompton Rd.
Old Brompton Rd.
SOUTH KENSINGTON
Fulham Rd.
Sydney St.
CHELSEA
Kings Rd.
Redcliffe Gardens
Finborough Rd.
West Brompton
Seagrave Rd.
Ongar Rd.
Tamworth St.
WEST BROMPTON
Fulham Rd.
Gunter Grove
Beaufort St.
Oakley St.
King's Rd.
Fulham Broadway
Cheyne Walk
Battersea Bridge
Albert Bridge
Chelsea Reach
Chelsea Embankment
Royal Hospital Rd.
Ranelagh Gardens
Chelsea Bridge Rd.
Ebury Bridge Rd.
Chelsea Bridge
Queenstown Rd.
Battersea Park
River Thames
Grosvenor Rd.
Battersea Park Rd.
PIMLICO
Pimlico Rd.
Ebury St.
Ebury Bridge Rd.
Sutherland St.
Lupus St.
Belgrave Rd.
Eccleston Rd.
Victoria
Victoria St.
Vauxhall
King's Rd.
Belgrave Pl.
Belgrave St.
Belgrave
Grosvenor Place
Buckingham Palace
Buckingham Gate
Birdcage
Queen Victoria Memorial
Constitution Hill
Green Park
Hyde Park Corner
Piccadilly
Green Park
MAYFAIR
Park Lane
Park Lane
South St.
Mount Street
Berkeley St.
Upper Grosvenor St.
Upper Brook St.
Audley St.
St. James's St.
ST. JAMES'S
Old Bond St.
Piccadilly Circus
SOHO
Regent St.
New Bond St.
Bond Street
Oxford Circus
Oxford St.
Margaret St.
Wigmore St.
Welbeck
MARYLEBONE
Marylebone High St.
Weymouth
Devonshire St.
Portland Pl.
Great Portland St.
Mortimer St.
Berners
Newman
Goodge Street
Regent's Park
Great Portland Street
Euston Rd.
Warren Street
Tottenham
Euston Square
Albany St.
Albany Street
Outer Circle
Hempstead Rd.
Mornington Crescent
Eversholt St.
Camden High St.
Camden St.
R. College St.

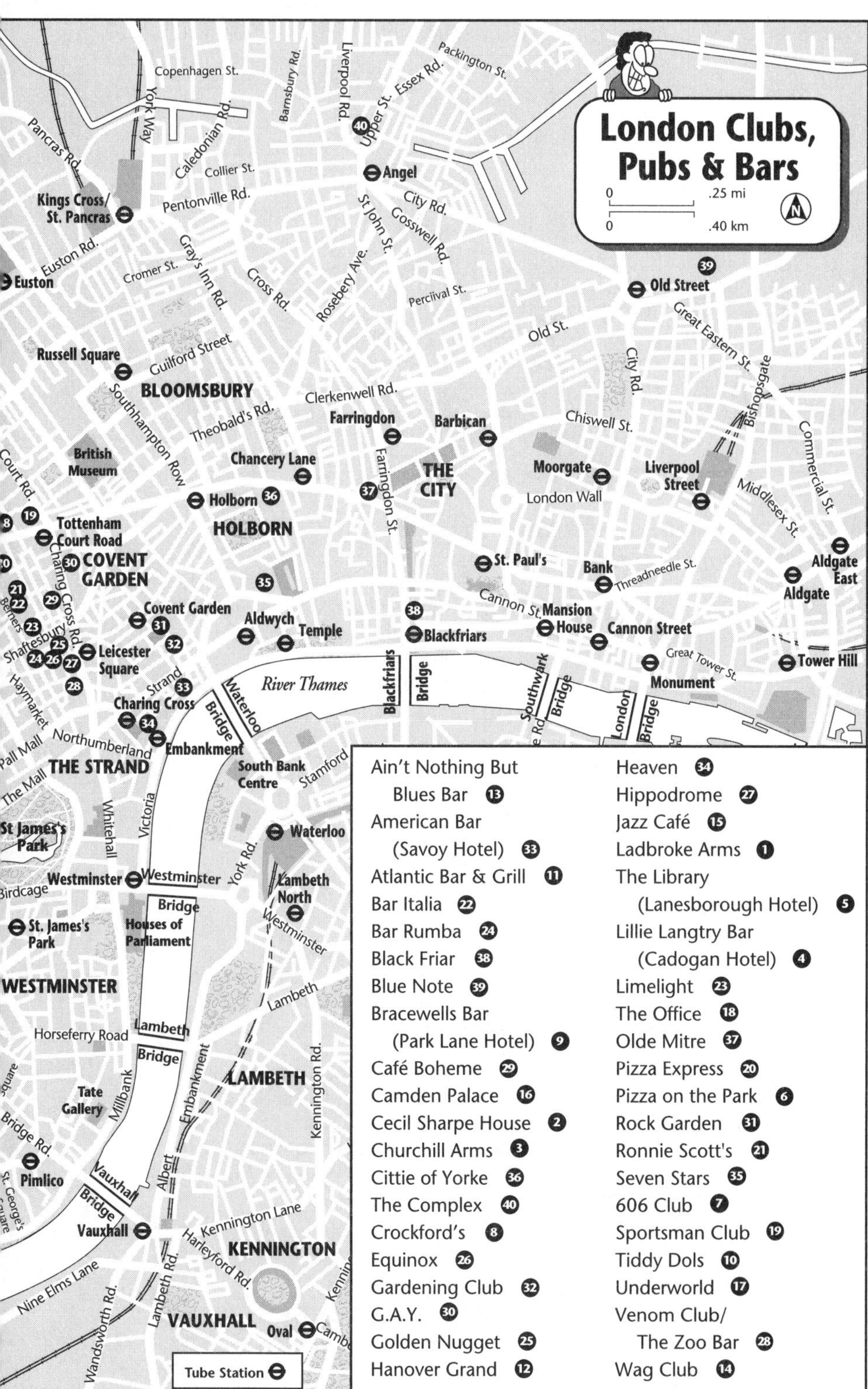
London Clubs, Pubs & Bars
0 .25 mi
0 .40 km
N
Copenhagen St.
York Way
Pancras Rd.
Caledonian Rd.
Barnsbury Rd.
Liverpool Rd.
Upper St.
Essex Rd.
Packington St.
Collier St.
Angel
Kings Cross/ St. Pancras
Pentonville Rd.
City Rd.
Goswell Rd.
St John St.
Euston Rd.
Euston
Cromer St.
Gray's Inn Rd.
Cross Rd.
Rosebery Ave.
Percival St.
Old Street
Great Eastern St.
Old St.
City Rd.
Bishopsgate
Russell Square
Guilford Street
BLOOMSBURY
Southampton Row
Theobald's Rd.
Clerkenwell Rd.
Farringdon
Barbican
Chiswell St.
Commercial St.
British Museum
Chancery Lane
Farringdon St.
THE CITY
Moorgate
London Wall
Liverpool Street
Middlesex St.
Court Rd.
Holborn
HOLBORN
Tottenham Court Road
Charing Cross Rd.
COVENT GARDEN
St. Paul's
Bank
Threadneedle St.
Aldgate East
Aldgate
Berners
Shaftesbury
Covent Garden
Aldwych
Temple
Cannon St.
Mansion House
Cannon Street
Blackfriars
Leicester Square
Great Tower St.
Tower Hill
Monument
Haymarket
Strand
River Thames
Waterloo Bridge
Blackfriars Bridge
Southwark Bridge
London Bridge
Charing Cross
Embankment
Pall Mall
Northumberland
THE STRAND
The Mall
South Bank Centre
Stamford
St James's Park
Whitehall
Victoria
Waterloo
Birdcage
Westminster
Westminster Bridge
York Rd.
Lambeth North
St. James's Park
Houses of Parliament
Westminster
WESTMINSTER
Lambeth
Horseferry Road
Lambeth Bridge
Embankment
LAMBETH
Kennington Rd.
Tate Gallery
Millbank
Bridge Rd.
Pimlico
Vauxhall Bridge
Albert
St. George's Square
Vauxhall
Kennington Lane
Harleyford Rd.
KENNINGTON
Nine Elms Lane
Wandsworth Rd.
Lambeth Rd.
VAUXHALL
Oval
Tube Station
Ain't Nothing But Blues Bar 13
American Bar (Savoy Hotel) 33
Atlantic Bar & Grill 11
Bar Italia 22
Bar Rumba 24
Black Friar 38
Blue Note 39
Bracewells Bar (Park Lane Hotel) 9
Café Boheme 29
Camden Palace 16
Cecil Sharpe House 2
Churchill Arms 3
Cittie of Yorke 36
The Complex 40
Crockford's 8
Equinox 26
Gardening Club 32
G.A.Y. 30
Golden Nugget 25
Hanover Grand 12
Heaven 34
Hippodrome 27
Jazz Café 15
Ladbroke Arms 1
The Library (Lanesborough Hotel) 5
Lillie Langtry Bar (Cadogan Hotel) 4
Limelight 23
The Office 18
Olde Mitre 37
Pizza Express 20
Pizza on the Park 6
Rock Garden 31
Ronnie Scott's 21
Seven Stars 35
606 Club 7
Sportsman Club 19
Tiddy Dols 10
Underworld 17
Venom Club/ The Zoo Bar 28
Wag Club 14

Cool Britannia

If you're accustomed to ordering a Bud Light, the names of British beers on tap in a pub might make your head swim. You'll find Courage Best, Directors, Old Speckled Hen, John Smiths, Wadworths 6X, Adams, Tetleys, Brakspears, Friary Meux, and Ind Coope Burton, to name just a few. Although you can get a "hard" drink at both bars and pubs, when you're in a pub you're better off confining yourself to beer. Pubs are affiliated with one particular brewery and sell only that company's ales (you order either a pint or a half-pint). But they'll also have bitter, stout, lager, and bottled beers.

In Earl's Court there's the **606 Club,** 90 Lots Rd., SW10 (☎ **0171/352-5953;** tube: Earl's Court or Fulham Broadway), a basement club where young British jazz musicians play. There's no cover to get in, but you have to order something to eat, and a charge of £4.25 ($7) Monday through Thursday and Sunday—and about $1 more on Fridays and Saturdays—is added to your bill to pay the musicians (they have to eat, too). You can find good food and diverse music (Afro-Latin jazz to rap) at **Jazz Café,** 5 Parkway, NW1 (☎ **0171/916-6060;** tube: Camden Town). Admission is £6 to £16 ($10 to $26).

Extra! Extra!

How about a pizza with your jazz? There are two places where you can enjoy both at the same time. In Soho, try **Pizza Express,** 10 Dean St., W1 (☎ **0171/439-8722;** tube: Tottenham Court Road). Big names from the American jazz scene regularly perform in this intimate venue. It's open daily from noon to midnight. Music is served up Monday through Saturday from 9pm and Sunday from 11am to 3pm; admission is £8 to £20 ($13 to $33). In Knightsbridge there's **Pizza on the Park,** 11 Knightsbridge, SW1 (☎ **0171/235-5273;** tube: Hyde Park Corner), where mainstream jazz is performed in the basement Jazz Room. It's open Monday through Saturday from 8pm to midnight and Sunday from 9pm to midnight; admission is £12 to £18 ($20 to $30). The cover charges at both do not include food.

Nothing but the Blues

Ain't Nothing But Blues Bar, 20 Kingly St., W1 (☎ **0171/287-0514;** tube: Oxford Circus), the only true-blue blues venue in town, features local acts and touring American bands; expect long lines on weekends. The cover charge is £3 to £5 ($5 to $8) Fridays and Saturdays; you get in free before 9:30pm.

Where to Shake 'n' Sweat to Live Music

London is swinging with so many specialized sounds that it's impossible to keep track of them all. The cosmopolitan stew of different cultures has led to categories like drum 'n' bass, indie, Asian underground (or tabla 'n' bass, as it's called), chemical beats (don't ask), break beats, techno, trance, psychedelic (you might remember an earlier version of that from the 1960s), and many others.

The club scene has boomed big time—but I have to warn you: This is very much a youth scene. If you're a woman under 30 and can squeeze into a leather miniskirt and a sleeveless zip-up top, or a man under 30 who wears Doc Martens and an earring, you'll probably fit in. The following dance clubs frequently have live bands; the action doesn't really get hot until around midnight.

Rock Garden, The Piazza, Covent Garden, WC2 (☎ **0171/836-4052;** tube: Covent Garden), is a big basement dance club with young bands performing funk, blues, and rock and pop; the cover is £5 to £8 ($8 to $13). **The Complex,** 1–5 Parkfield St., N1 (☎ **0171/288-1986;** tube: Angel), in Islington, has four floors with different dance vibes on each.

Wag Club, 35 Wardour St., W1 (☎ **071/437-5534;** tube: Leicester Square or Piccadilly Circus), is a split-level affair that's one of the more stylish live-music places in town. The downstairs stage usually attracts cutting-edge rock bands, while a DJ spins dance records upstairs. The door policy can be selective. The cover is £3 to £10 ($5 to $17); it's closed on Mondays.

Underworld, 174 Camden High St., NW1 (☎ **0171/482-1932;** tube: Camden Town), has lots of well-known (at least in London) bands and is generally standing room only. It's open different hours for club and band nights, so call to find out what's going on; admission is £3.50 to £15 ($6 to $25).

Where to Go-Go to Disco

Equinox, Leicester Square, WC2 (☎ **0171/437-1446;** tube: Leicester Square), with the largest dance floor in London, is a lavishly illuminated club boasting one of the largest lighting rigs in Europe. A crowd as varied as London itself dances to virtually every kind of music, including dance hall, pop, rock, and Latin. The cover charge is £5 to £12 ($8 to $19). It's closed on Sundays.

Hippodrome, corner of Cranbourn Street and Charing Cross Road, WC2 (☎ **0171/437-4311;** tube: Leicester Square), is a cavernous place with a great sound system and lights to match. It was Lady Di's favorite scene in her bar-hopping days. It's tacky, touristy, and packed on weekends. The cover charge is £4 to £12 ($6.40 to $20). It's closed on Sundays.

Limelight, 136 Shaftesbury Ave., WC2 (☎ **0171/434-0572;** tube: Leicester Square), housed inside an 18th-century Welsh chapel, is a large dance club with plenty of Gothic nooks and crannies. DJs spin the latest house music. The cover charge is £4 to £8 ($6 to $13) before 10pm and £8 to £12 ($13 to $19) after 10pm.

Venom Club/The Zoo Bar, 13–18 Bear St., WC2 (☎ **0171/839-4188;** tube: Leicester Square), has the slickest, flashiest, most psychedelic decor in London, and even 35-year-olds come here. Expect a trendy Euro-androgynous crowd and music so loud you have to use sign language. The cover is £3 to £5 ($5 to $8) after 10pm.

Bar Rumba, 26 Shaftesbury Ave., W1 (☎ **0171/287-2715;** tube: Piccadilly Circus), has a different musical theme every night: jazz fusion, phat funk, hip-hop, drum 'n' bass, soul, R&B, and swing. The minimum age for admittance is 21 on Saturday and Sunday; Monday through Friday, it's 18. The cover charge is £3 to £12 ($5 to $20). **Hanover Grand,** 6 Hanover St., W1 (☎ **0171/499-7977;** tube: Oxford Circus), is funky and down and dirty on Thursday, otherwise cutting-edge, and always crowded. Age and gender are not always easy to distinguish. The cover is £5 to £15 ($8 to $24). It's closed Sundays.

The Office, 3–5 Rathbone Place, W1 (☎ **0171/636-1598;** tube: Tottenham Court Road), is an eclectic club popular on Wednesday nights when there's easy listening and board games from 6pm to 2am. Other nights are more traditional recorded pop, rock, soul, and disco. The cover is £5 ($8). **Camden Palace,** 1A Camden High St., NW1 (☎ **0171/387-0428;** tube: Camden Town), housed in a former theatre, draws a young all-night crowd addicted to trendy downtown costumes. The music varies from night to night, so it's a good idea to call in advance. A live band performs on Tuesdays. The cover charge is £5 ($8) on Tuesdays and Wednesdays, and £7 to £20 ($11 to $32) on Fridays and Saturdays.

A Meal & a Song

Performers at **Tiddy Dols,** 55 Shepherd Market, Mayfair, W1 (☎ **0171/499-2357;** tube: Green Park), housed in nine small Georgian town houses, entertain diners with madrigals, Noel Coward ditties, Gilbert and Sullivan tunes, vaudeville, and music-hall songs. Main courses range from £11.50 to £15.25 ($19 to $25); set dinners are £22 ($37). It's open Monday through Saturday from 6 to 11:30pm and Sunday from 6 to 11pm. There is no cover charge.

Where to Go If You're Feeling Folksy

The focal point of the folk revival in the 1960s, **Cecil Sharpe House,** 2 Regent's Park Rd., NW1 (☎ **0171/485-2206;** tube: Camden Town), continues to treasure and nurture the folk-music style. Here you'll find a whole range of traditional English music and dance. It's open different nights; call to see what's happening. There is no cover charge.

Where to Go for a Classy Cocktail

The choices below are elegant and dressy, the surroundings far removed from the hurly-burly of the London streets. They're perfect places for a pre- or post-theatre drink, or if you're looking for a quietly romantic spot to unwind. And since they're all in grand hotels, it's a perfect opportunity to check out the surroundings (for your next trip).

American Bar, Savoy Hotel, The Strand, WC2 (☎ **0171/836-4343;** tube: Charing Cross Road or Embankment), is one of the most sophisticated gathering places in London. The bartender is known for his special concoctions—"Savoy Affair" and "Prince of Wales"—as well as what is reputedly the best martini in town. Men must wear a jacket and tie. **Bracewells Bar,** Park Lane Hotel, Piccadilly, W1 (☎ **0171/499-6321;** tube: Green Park or Hyde Park), is chic, nostalgic, and elegant, with a plush decor of Chinese lacquer, comfortable sofas, and soft lighting.

The Library, Lanesborough Hotel, 1 Lanesborough Place, SW1 (☎ **0171/259-5599;** tube: Hyde Park Corner), is one of London's most posh drinking retreats, with its high ceilings, leather chesterfields, oil paintings, and grand windows. Its collection of ancient cognacs is unparalleled in London.

Lillie Langtry Bar, The Cadogan Hotel, Sloane Street, SW1 (☎ **0171/235-7141;** tube: Sloane Square or Knightsbridge), epitomizes the charm and elegance of the Edwardian era. Lillie Langtry, the turn-of-the-century actress and society beauty (and the mistress of Edward VII), once lived here. Oscar Wilde—arrested in this very hotel—is honored on the drinks menu by his favorite libation, the Hock and Seltzer. (See chapter 6 for a description of the hotel.)

Into the Wee Hours

Except for the all-night discos, London tends to keep pretty early hours. Restaurants and bars routinely close before midnight. But if you're a real night owl, a few places in restless, nightclubby Soho stay open late.

Bar Italia, 22 Frith St., W1 (☎ **0171/437-4520;** tube: Tottenham Court Road), is open round-the-clock for coffee and has a limited snack menu. **Atlantic Bar & Grill,** 20 Glasshouse St., W1 (☎ **0171/734-4888;** tube: Piccadilly Circus), is open for drinks Monday through Saturday until 3am; you might have to wait in line until there's room. You can get a drink until 3am Monday through Wednesday, until midnight on Sunday, and 24 hours a day Thursday through Saturday at **Café Boheme,** 13–17 Old Compton St., W1 (☎ **0171/734-0623;** tube: Tottenham Court Road or Leicester Square).

Where to Go for a Laugh

Comedy Spot, The Spot, Maiden Lane, WC2 (☎ **0171/379-5900;** tube: Covent Garden), is a bar-restaurant with DJs and singers every night except Monday, when "spotlight comedy" takes the stage. If you're into stand-up comedy, English-style, this is one of the best places in town. The cover charge is £4 ($6) after 8pm on Friday and Saturday.

The Comedy Store, 1A Oxendon St., off Piccadilly Circus, SW1 (☎ **0142/691-4433;** tube: Piccadilly Circus), inspired by American comedy clubs, is London's best showcase for established and rising comic talent. Visitors must be 18 and older. Reserve tickets through Ticketmaster (☎ **0171/344-4444**). The cover charge is £10 ($17) Tuesday through Thursday and £11 to £12 ($19 to $20) Friday through Sunday.

Where Life Is a Cabaret

Madame Jo-Jo's, 8–10 Brewer St., Soho, W1 (☎ **0171/734-2473;** tube: Leicester Square), has been a fixture of the drag/cabaret scene for years; the shows produced in its plush theatre-bar are campy and fun, enjoyed by both gays and straights. It's open nightly from 10pm to 4am. Tickets are £8 to £10 ($14 to $17) and £5 ($9) on Wednesday.

Gaming Clubs

London was quite a gambling town until Queen Victoria's reign squelched all games of chance. It was only in 1960 that gambling was again permitted in bona fide gaming clubs. This is definitely not Las Vegas–style gambling, though. At a gambling club you're required to become a member and wait 24 hours before you can play at the tables. Games are cash only and commonly include roulette, blackjack, Punto Banco, and baccarat. Men must wear a jacket and tie in all of the establishments below; hours for each club are 2pm to 4am daily.

Crockford's, 30 Curzon St., W1 (☎ **0171/493-7777;** tube: Green Park), is a 150-year-old club with a large international clientele. It has American roulette, Punto Banco, and blackjack. **Golden Nugget,** 22 Shaftesbury Ave., W1 (☎ **0171/439-0099;** tube: Piccadilly Circus), is where gamblers go to play blackjack, Punto Banco, and roulette. **Sportsman Club,** 3 Tottenham Court Rd., W1 (☎ **0171/637-5464;** tube: Tottenham Court Road), offers a dice table along with American roulette, blackjack, and Punto Banco.

Gay Clubs & Discos

Check the Gay listings in ***Time Out*** to find out what's going on, since many clubs have special gay nights. In terms of size, central location, and continued popularity, the best gay (and everyone else) disco in London is **Heaven,** Under the Arches, Villiers Street, WC2 (☎ **0171/839-5210;** tube: Charing Cross or Embankment); it's open different hours nightly, it's packed, and it's attitude-free fun. **G.A.Y.,** London Astoria, 157 Charing Cross Rd., Soho, WC2 (☎ **0171/434-9592;** tube: Tottenham Court Road), is the biggest gay dance venue in Europe. It's open Saturdays from 10:30pm to 5am. **Gardening Club,** 4 The Piazza, Covent Garden, WC2 (☎ **0171/836-4052;** tube: Covent Garden), in the hiply renovated cellars beneath Covent Garden, hosts a Queer Nation night Thursdays from 9pm to 3am that attracts lots of foreign visitors.

Part 7

Day Trips from London

The Brits love to complain about how "far" everything is, but to Americans and others accustomed to vast distances, practically every place in England could be considered a side trip from London. Given its relatively small size and comprehensive train network, England is a snap to explore. In chapter 14 I included the easiest side trips from London: Kew Gardens, Hampton Court Palace, Windsor Palace, and Greenwich. In this section I'll take you a bit farther afield to some of England's most beautiful towns and venerable sites. From London you can reach Bath and Oxford in 90 minutes or less by train. The train trip to Salisbury takes about 2 hours (and then involves a further bus trip if you're going to Stonehenge); Stratford is about 3 hours away by train. If you get an early start, you can explore all of these places, have lunch, and still be back in London in time for dinner (and maybe even a show).

Chapter 21

Can I *Really* Get There & Back in a Day? Yes You Can!

In This Chapter

- The best day trips from London
- How to get there
- What to see and do once you arrive

This chapter includes four fascinating day trips from London: Bath, Oxford, Salisbury and Stonehenge, and Stratford-upon-Avon—with everything you need to know to get there, get around, and get back to London.

If you're going to travel around England by train, consider getting a **Brit-Rail pass.** These passes, which must be purchased before you arrive, offer considerable savings over individual fares. There's a slew of options: a choice of either first or second class, senior passes for those over 60, travel time periods from 8 consecutive days to 1 month, and Flexipasses allowing you to travel a certain number of days within a set time period. The **BritRail Southeast pass** will get you to four of the towns in this chapter (but not to Bath or Stratford-upon-Avon). The cost for first-class travel for any 3 days in an 8-day period is $94 for adults and $27 for children (5 to 15 years of age); second-class tickets are $69 for adults and $18 for children. There are also 4-day and 7-day Southeast passes. You can order BritRail passes from your travel agent or by calling ☎ **888-BRITRAIL** (in the U.S.) or **800-555-BRIT** (in Canada).

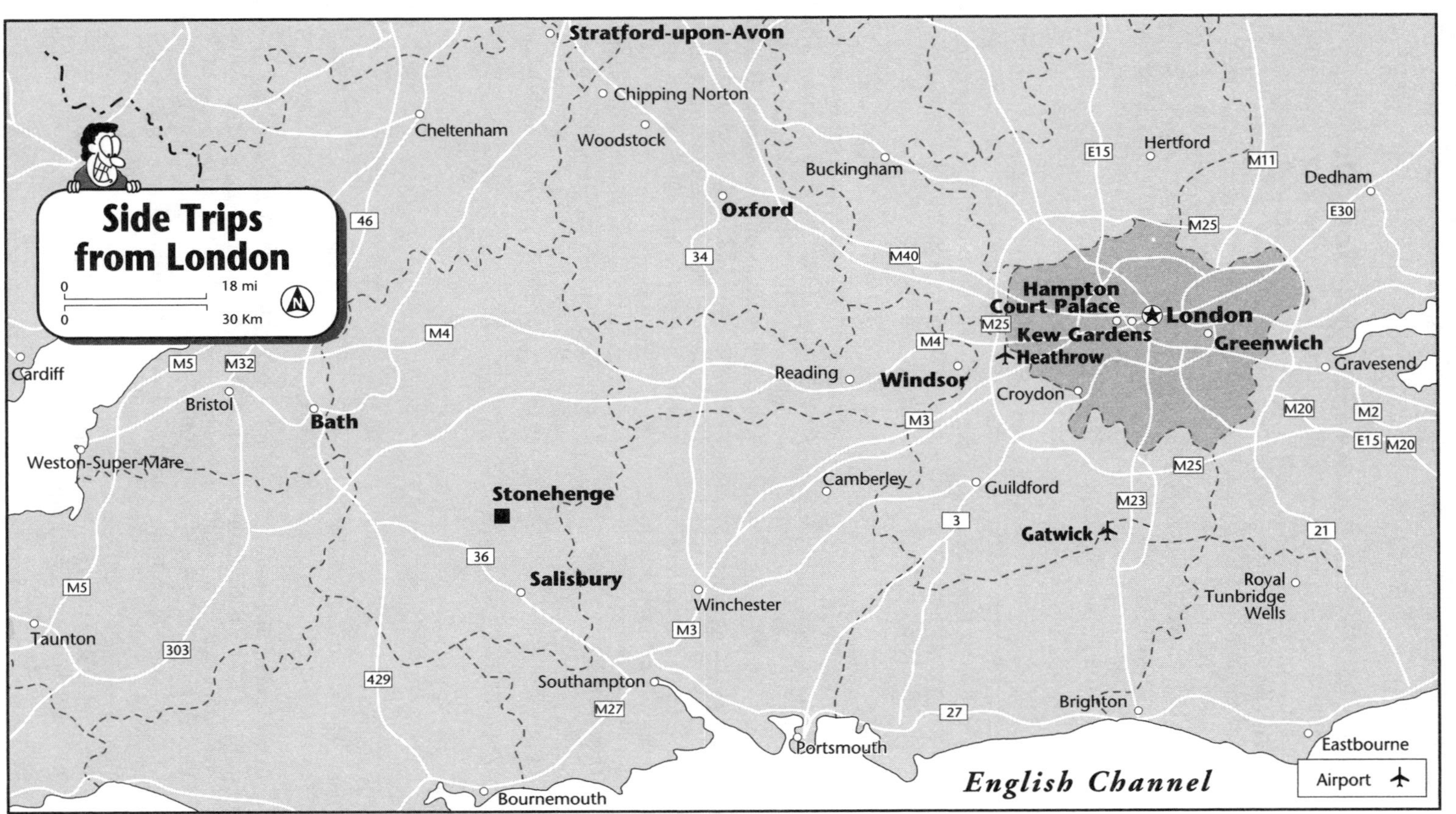
Side Trips
from London
0
18 mi
0
30 Km
N
Stratford-upon-Avon
Chipping Norton
Cheltenham
Woodstock
Hertford
Buckingham
Dedham
Oxford
Hampton
Court Palace
London
Kew Gardens
Greenwich
Heathrow
Gravesend
Cardiff
Reading
Windsor
Bristol
Croydon
Bath
Weston-Super-Mare
Camberley
Guildford
Stonehenge
Gatwick
Salisbury
Royal
Tunbridge
Wells
Winchester
Taunton
Southampton
Brighton
Portsmouth
Eastbourne
English Channel
Airport
Bournemouth
E15
M11
46
M25
E30
34
M40
M25
M4
M4
M5
M32
M20
M2
M3
E15
M20
M25
M23
3
21
36
M5
M3
303
429
M27
27

Bath: Hot Water & Cool Georgian Splendor

A beautiful spa town on the Avon River, Bath is 115 miles west of London. In ancient times the area was known far and wide for its hot mineral springs, which drew the Celts and later the Romans, who settled here in A.D. 75 and built a huge bath complex to soak their weary bones. Centuries later, in 1702, Queen Anne dipped her royal bod into the soothing, sulfurous waters and sparked a trend that transformed Bath into an ultra-fashionable spa. Aristocrats, socialites, social climbers, and flamboyant dandies like Beau Nash held sway. A demure visitor named Jane Austen used Bath as an upwardly genteel setting for her class-conscious plots.

The town you see today is a fabulous legacy from the Georgian era, filled with remarkable curving crescents and classically inspired buildings built of honey-colored stone. Highlights include the **Roman Baths Museum** and adjoining **Pump Room** (where water was, and continues to be, sipped to musical accompaniment), the adjacent **Abbey,** the Assembly Rooms (once used for balls and gaming), and the various crescents.

Getting to Bath

Trains for Bath leave from London's Paddington Station at least every hour; the trip takes about 90 minutes.

The hot, healing waters of Bath's mineral springs were considered sacred by ancient British tribes, but it was the Romans who built the enormous bath complex that forms the nucleus of the **Roman Baths Museum** (☎ **01225/477-785**) located beside Bath Abbey. Upon entering you're given a portable self-guided audio tour that's keyed to everything on display, including the original Roman baths and heating system; it's fun, informative, and very well done. It's open daily from 9:30am to 5:30pm, and admission is £6.30 ($11).

Time-Savers

Bath's **Tourist Information Centre** (☎ **01225/477-761**), located in the center of town on the square in front of Bath Abbey, offers **free guided walks** that leave from outside the Pump Room on Monday through Friday at 10:30am and 2pm, Saturday at 10:30am, and Sunday at 10:30am and 2:30pm. From May through September, additional walks are offered at 7pm on Tuesday, Friday, and Saturday. The information center is open June through September, Monday through Saturday, from 9:30am to 7pm, and Sunday from 10am to 6pm. In October through May, it's open Monday through Saturday from 9:30am to 5pm and Sunday from 10am to 4pm.

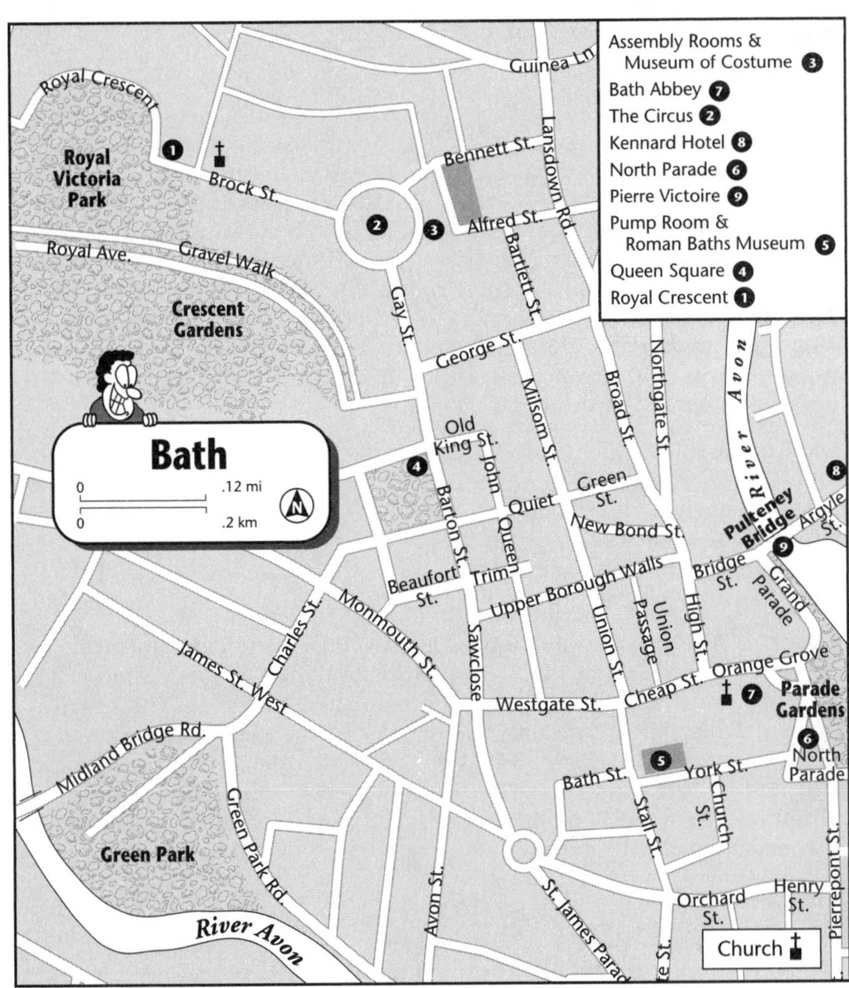

Overlooking the Roman baths is the late-18th-century **Pump Room** (**☎ 01225/444-477**), where the fashionable congregated to sip the vile-tasting but supposedly salubrious water; you can enter as part of your ticket and taste it for yourself (it's *not* Perrier). The Pump Room is an amusingly old-fashioned place for "elevenses" (morning tea), lunch, or afternoon tea, usually with live musical accompaniment. Main courses are £8.50 to £9.95 ($14 to $16); a fixed-price lunch menu is £11.50 to £12.95 ($19 to $21); afternoon teas are £5.75 to £8 ($9 to $13). American Express, MasterCard, and Visa are accepted. It's open Monday through Saturday from 9:30am to 4:40pm and Sunday from 10:30am to 4:30pm.

Bath Abbey dominates the adjacent square. Step inside for a look at the graceful fan vaulting, the great East Window, and the unexpectedly simple memorial to Beau Nash, the most flamboyant of the dandies who frequented Bath in its heyday. It's open from April through October, Monday through Saturday, from 9am to 6pm (and until 4:30pm from November to March); it's open Sundays year-round from 1 to 2:30pm and 4:30 to 5:30pm. Admission is by donation.

Bath is a wonderful walking town, filled with beautiful squares and long, sweeping residential **crescents.** Stroll along the **North Parade** and the **South Parade, Queen Square** (where Jane Austen once lived), and **The Circus,** and be sure to have a look at the **Royal Crescent,** a magnificent curving row of 30 town houses designed in 1767 by John Wood the Younger. Regarded as the epitome of Palladian style in England, the Royal Crescent is now designated a World Heritage site. **No. 1 Royal Crescent** (☎ **01225/ 428-126**) is a beautifully restored 18th-century house with period furnishings. It's open in March through October, Tuesday through Sunday, from 10:30am to 5pm; in November it's open Tuesday through Sunday from 10:30am to 4pm. Admission is £3.50 ($6).

Another classic building worth visiting is the **Assembly Rooms,** Bennett Street (☎ **01225/477-789**), the site of all the grand balls and social climbing in 18th-century Bath. Admission is free unless you want to visit the excellent **Museum of Costume,** which is part of the complex (£3.50/$6). Both are open Monday through Saturday from 10am to 4:30pm and Sunday from 11am to 4:30pm.

Built in 1770 and obviously inspired by the Ponte Vecchio in Florence, **Pulteney Bridge** spans the Avon a few blocks south of the Assembly Rooms. It's one of the few bridges in Europe lined with shops and restaurants, including the picturesque and popular eatery **Pierre Victoire,** 16 Argyle Street (☎ **01225/334-334**). The Modern British menu changes daily and features three-course fixed-price lunches; you need to book in advance on weekends. The fixed-price lunch is £5.90 ($10). MasterCard and Visa are accepted. It's open daily from noon to 3pm and 6 to 11pm.

A Place to Sleep in Bath

If you'd like to spend the night, try the **Kennard Hotel,** 11 Henrietta St., Bath, BA2 6LL (☎ **01225/310-472;** fax 01225/460-054; e-mail kennard@dirconco.uk; www.kennard.co.uk). On the east side of Pulteney Bridge, within walking distance of everything in Bath, this elegant hotel occupies a beautifully restored Georgian town house built in 1794. Room rates are £78 to £88 ($129 to $145) for a double; breakfast is included. American Express, MasterCard, and Visa are accepted.

Oxford: You Don't Need a Degree to Enjoy It

Oxford University, one of the oldest, greatest, and most revered universities in the world, dominates the town of Oxford, about 54 miles northwest of London. Its skyline pierced by ancient, tawny towers and spires, Oxford has been a center of learning for 7 centuries (the city itself was founded by the Saxons in the 10th century). Roger Bacon, Sir Walter Raleigh, John Donne,

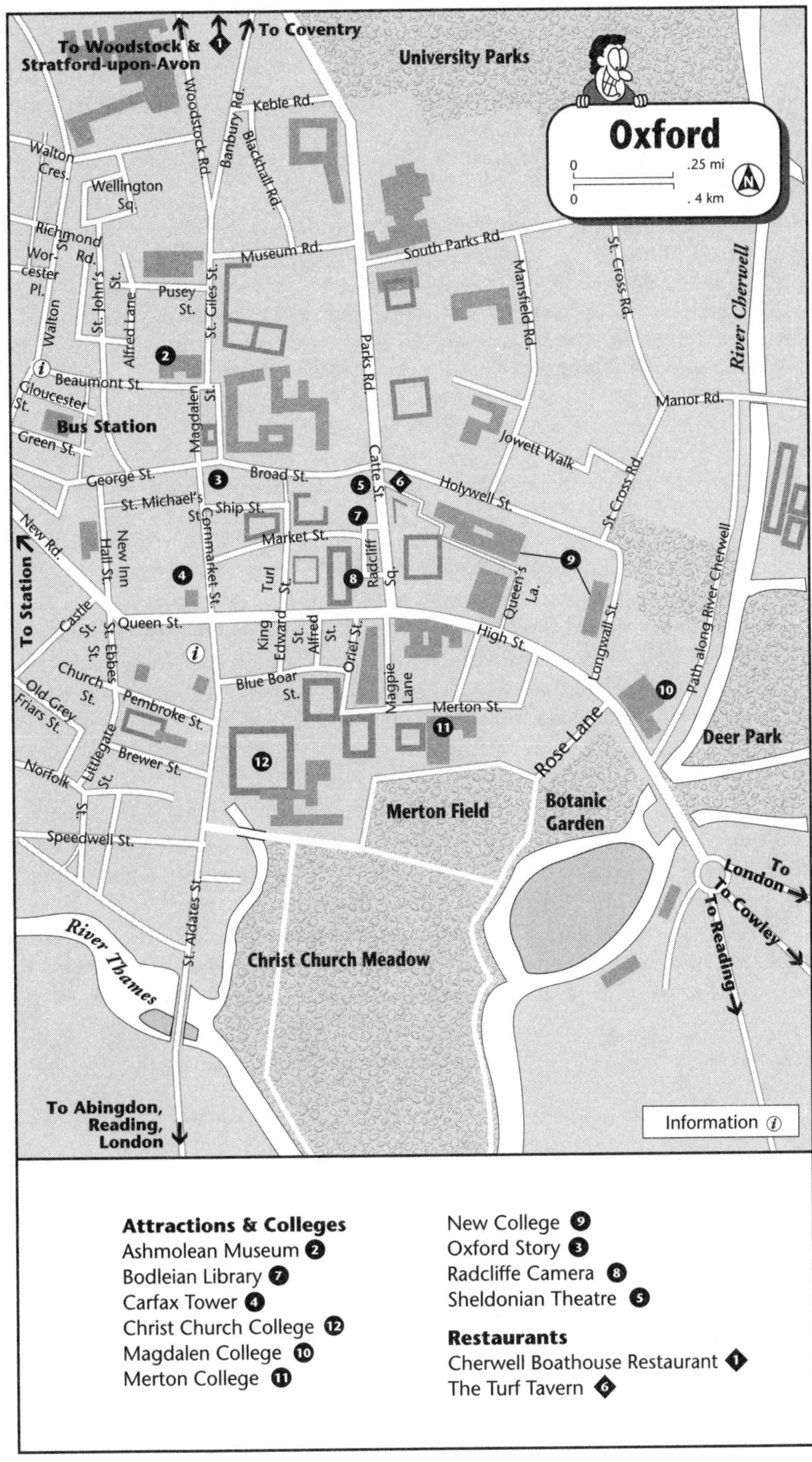

Oxford
0 .25 mi
0 . 4 km
To Woodstock & Stratford-upon-Avon
To Coventry
University Parks
Keble Rd.
Woodstock Rd.
Banbury Rd.
Blackhall Rd.
Walton Cres.
Wellington Sq.
Richmond Rd.
Worcester Pl.
Walton St.
St. John's St.
Alfred Lane
Pusey St.
St. Giles St.
Museum Rd.
South Parks Rd.
Mansfield Rd.
St. Cross Rd.
River Cherwell
Parks Rd.
Beaumont St.
Gloucester St.
Bus Station
Green St.
Magdalen St.
George St.
Broad St.
Catte St.
Holywell St.
Jowett Walk
Manor Rd.
St. Michael's St.
Ship St.
Market St.
New Rd.
New Inn Hall St.
Cornmarket St.
Turl St.
Radcliff Sq.
Queen's La.
Longwall St.
Path along River Cherwell
To Station
Castle St.
St. Ebbes St.
Queen St.
King Edward St.
Alfred St.
Oriel St.
High St.
Church St.
Blue Boar St.
Magpie Lane
Merton St.
Old Grey Friars St.
Pembroke St.
Brewer St.
Littlegate St.
Norfolk St.
Rose Lane
Deer Park
Speedwell St.
Merton Field
Botanic Garden
To London
To Cowley
To Reading
River Thames
St. Aldates St.
Christ Church Meadow
To Abingdon, Reading, London
Information
Attractions & Colleges
Ashmolean Museum 2
Bodleian Library 7
Carfax Tower 4
Christ Church College 12
Magdalen College 10
Merton College 11
New College 9
Oxford Story 3
Radcliffe Camera 8
Sheldonian Theatre 5
Restaurants
Cherwell Boathouse Restaurant 1
The Turf Tavern 6

Sir Christopher Wren, Samuel Johnson, Edward Gibbon, William Penn, John Wesley, Lewis Carroll, T. E. Lawrence, W. H. Auden, and Margaret Thatcher are just a few of the distinguished alumni who have taken degrees here. Even President Bill Clinton studied at Oxford.

Although academically oriented, Oxford is far from dull. Its long sweep of a main street (**The High**) buzzes with a cosmopolitan mix of locals, students, black-gowned dons, and foreign visitors. What you'll want to do here is tour some of the beautiful **historic colleges,** each sequestered away within its own quadrangle (or quad) built around an interior courtyard; stroll along the lovely **Cherwell River** and visit the **Ashmoleon Museum.**

Getting to Oxford

Trains to Oxford leave from London's Paddington Station (☎ **0345/484-950**) every hour; the trip takes about 75 minutes. A same-day round-trip ticket (day return) costs £12.40 ($20).

By car, take **M40** west from London and follow the signs. Note, however, that parking is a nightmare in Oxford.

Many Americans arriving at Oxford ask, "Where's the campus?" There isn't just one—35 widely dispersed colleges serve some 11,000 students. Instead of trying to see all of them (impossible in a day), focus on seeing a handful of the better-known ones. Faced with an overabundance of tourists, the colleges have restricted visiting to certain hours and to groups of six or fewer, and there are areas where visitors aren't allowed at all. Before heading off, check with the tourist office to find out when and what colleges you can visit.

Time-Savers

The **Oxford Tourist Information Centre** (☎ **01865/726-871**), open Monday through Saturday from 9:30am to 5pm and in the summer also on Sundays from 10am to 3pm, is at the Old School Gloucester Green, opposite the bus station. It sells a comprehensive range of maps and brochures and conducts daily 2-hour **walking tours** of the town and its major colleges (but not New College or Christ Church). Tours leave daily at 11am and 2pm; the cost is £4 ($6) for adults and £2.50 ($4) for children.

A good way to start your tour is with a bird's-eye view of the colleges from the top of **Carfax Tower ☎ 01865/792-653**), located in the center of the city just north of the information center. The tower is all that remains from St. Martin's Church, where William Shakespeare once stood as godfather for a fellow playwright. It's open daily in November through March from 10:30am to 3:30pm and in April through October from 10am to 5:30pm. Admission is £1.20 ($2) for adults and 60p ($1) for children.

East of Carfax, at the north end of Radcliffe Square, is the **Bodleian Library,** Broad Street (**☎ 01865/277-000**), the oldest library in the world (originally established in 1450); it's open Monday through Friday from 9am to 7pm and Saturday from 9am to 1pm. The **Radcliffe Camera,** the domed building just south of the Bodleian, is the library's reading room; it dates from 1737 (no tourist access). To one side of the Bodleian is the **Sheldonian Theatre,** Broad Street (**☎ 01865/277-299**), which dates from 1669 and was the first major work by Sir Christopher Wren, designed when he was a professor of astronomy at Oxford. It's used for lectures and concerts, and you'll see great city views from the cupola. It's open daily from 10am to 12:30pm and 2 to 4:30pm; admission is £1.50 ($2.50) for adults and £1 ($1.65) for children.

Christ Church College Christ Church College (**☎ 01865/276-499**), facing St. Aldate's Street, was begun in 1525. It has the largest quadrangle of any college in Oxford and a chapel with 15th-century pillars and impressive fan vaulting. Tom Tower houses Great Tom, the 18,000-pound bell that rings nightly at 9:05pm, signaling the closing of the college gates. Several notable portraits, including works by Thomas Gainsborough and Sir Joshua Reynolds, hang in the 16th-century Great Hall. The college and chapel are open daily from 9am to 5:30pm. Admission is £3 ($5) for adults and £2 ($3.20) for children; a family ticket costs £6 ($10).

Magdalen College Founded in 1458, Magdalen College (pronounced *Maud*-lin) on High Street (**☎ 01865/276-000**) boasts the oldest **botanic garden** in England and the most extensive grounds of any Oxford college; there's even a deer park. The 15th-century **bell tower,** one of the town's most famous landmarks, is reflected in the waters of the Cherwell River. You can cross a small footbridge and stroll through the water meadows along the path known as Addison's Walk. The college is open daily from noon to 6pm from Easter to September; off-season, it's open daily from 2 to 6pm. Admission is £2 ($3.20) for adults and £1 ($1.65) for children.

Merton College Merton College (**☎ 01865/276-310**), dating from 1264, stands near Merton Street, the only medieval cobbled street left in Oxford. The college is noted for its 14th-century library, said to be the oldest college library in England (admission is £1/$1.65). On display is an astrolabe (an astronomical instrument used for measuring the altitude of the sun and stars) thought to have belonged to Chaucer. The library and college are open Monday through Friday from 2 to 4pm, and Saturday and Sunday from 10am to 4pm; both are closed for 1 week at Easter and Christmas.

New College New College (☎ **01865/279-555**), on New College Lane, contains the first quadrangle to be built in Oxford (14th century); it was the architectural boilerplate for the quadrangles in many other colleges. In the antechapel is Sir Jacob Epstein's remarkable modern sculpture of Lazarus and a fine El Greco study of St. James. In the gardens, you can see remnants of the old city wall. You can visit the college daily from Easter through September from 11am to 5pm; during the off-season, the hours are daily from 2 to 4pm.

Ashmoleon Museum If you have time, round out your visit to Oxford with a stroll through the Ashmoleon Museum, Beaumont Street (☎ **01865/278-000**), the oldest museum in Britain. The collections of the University of Oxford—European and Asian art, silver, ceramics, and antiquities from ancient Egypt, Greece, and Rome—are housed in a beautiful classical building dating from the 1840s. It's open Tuesday through Saturday from 10am to 4pm and Sunday from 2 to 4pm. Admission is free.

Extra! Extra!

The Oxford Story, 6 Broad St. (☎ **01865/790-055**), has packaged Oxford's complexities into a concise and entertaining audiovisual tour. The exhibition, spanning 800 years of the city's history, reviews some of the architectural and historical features that you might otherwise miss. You're also filled in on the backgrounds of the colleges and those who have passed through their portals. It's open daily from 9:30am to 5:30pm; admission is £5 ($8) for adults, £4 ($6.30) for children, and £15 ($24) for a family ticket (two adults and two children).

Where to Get a Bite to Eat One of the best places to eat in Oxford is the **Cherwell Boathouse Restaurant,** on Bardwell Road (☎ **01865/552-746**). It's right on the Cherwell River and serves Modern British and French cuisine. Before dinner you can try punting; there's a rental agency on the other side of the boathouse. Main courses range from £9 to £14 ($14 to $22); the fixed-price dinner is £18.50 ($30), the fixed-price lunch is £17.50 ($28), and half-price kids' meals are available. It's open Tuesday from 6 to 11:30pm, Wednesday through Saturday from noon to 2pm and 6 to 11:30pm, and Sunday from noon to 2pm; it's closed December 24 through 30.

For less-expensive pub grub (salads, soups, sandwiches, beef pie, chili con carne) or a pint of beer, try **The Turf Tavern,** 4 Bath Place (☎ **01865/243-235**). Dating back to the 13th century, it has served the likes of Thomas Hardy, Richard Burton and Elizabeth Taylor, and President Bill Clinton, who was a frequent visitor during his student days at Oxford. You can reach the pub via St. Helen's Passage, which stretches between Holywell Street and New College Lane. Food is served Monday through Saturday only from noon to 2:30pm. Main courses are £3 to £5 ($5 to $8).

Stratford-upon-Avon: In the Footsteps of the Bard

Do I need to tell you whose commercialized spirit pervades this market town on the Avon River, 91 miles northwest of London? Stratford-upon-Avon is a shrine to the world's greatest playwright, William Shakespeare, who was born, lived much of his life, and is buried here. In the summer months, crowds of international tourists overrun the town, which aggressively hustles its Shakespeare connection in every conceivable way. Stratford has many Elizabethan and Jacobean buildings, and the charms of its once-bucolic setting have not been completely lost—it's just difficult to find a quiet spot to enjoy them. Besides the literary pilgrimage sights, the top draw in Stratford is the Royal Shakespeare Theatre, where Britain's foremost actors perform. After visiting the shrines and seeing a play, there's really not much reason to stick around.

Getting to Stratford-upon-Avon

Oddly enough, there are no direct **trains** from London. From Paddington Station, you take a train to Leamington Spa and pick up a local connection for Stratford-upon-Avon. The journey takes about 3 hours at a cost of £20 ($33) for a round-trip ticket. Call ☎ **0345/484-950** for information and schedules. Stratford's train station, on Alcester Road (☎ **01203/555-211**), is closed on Sundays from October to May, so you'll have to rely on the bus or drive. Eight **National Express buses** (☎ **0990/808-080**) leave daily from Victoria Coach Station, with a trip time of 3¼ hours. A single-day round-trip ticket costs £13.50 ($22), except on Friday when the price is £16 ($26). To drive from London, take the **M40** toward Oxford and continue to Stratford-upon-Avon on **A34.**

Stratford's **Tourist Information Centre,** Bridgefoot (☎ **01789/293-127**), provides information and maps of the town and its principal sites. It's open March through October, Monday through Saturday, from 9am to 6pm and Sunday from 11am to 5pm; in November through February, it's open Monday through Saturday from 9am to 5pm.

A logical place to begin your tour is at **Shakespeare's Birthplace,** Henley Street (☎ **01789/204-016**), where the Bard, son of a glover and a leather-worker, first saw the light of day on April 23, 1564. Filled with Shakespeare memorabilia, it's actually two 16th-century half-timbered houses joined together: His father's shop was on one side and the family residence on the other. After visiting the bedroom where wee Willie was (probably) born, the Elizabethan kitchen, and the Shakespeare Museum (which illustrates his life and times), you can walk through the garden. The modern **Shakespeare Centre** next door is a library, exhibition space, and study center. It's open March 20 through October 19 daily from 9am to 5pm (it opens at 9:30am on Sunday); off-season, it's open daily from 9:30am to 4pm (it opens at 10am on Sunday). It's closed December 24 to 26. Admission is £4.50 ($7) for adults and £2 ($3.30) for children.

Time-Savers

Guided tours of Stratford-upon-Avon leave from near the **Guide Friday Tourism Center,** Civic Hall, Rother Street (☎ **01789/294-466**). Open-top double-decker buses depart every 15 minutes daily from 9:30am to 5:30pm in the summer. You can take a 1-hour ride without stops, or you can get off and on at any or all of the town's five Shakespeare properties. Tour tickets are valid all day. The tours are £8 ($13) for adults, £6 ($10) for senior citizens and students, and £2.50 ($4) for children under 12.

To visit **Anne Hathaway's Cottage,** Cottage Lane, Shottery (☎ **01789/292-100**), about 1 mile south of Stratford, take a bus from Bridge Street, or better still, walk there along the well-marked country path from Evesham Place. Anne Hathaway, whose family was yeomen farmers, lived in this lovely thatched cottage before she married 18-year-old Shakespeare (a May-September marriage in reverse: Anne was much older than Will). Many original 16th-century furnishings, including the courting settle, are preserved inside the house, which was occupied by Anne's descendants until 1892. Before leaving, be sure to stroll through the beautiful garden and orchard. It's open March 20 through October 19 daily from 9:30am to 5pm; off-season, it's open daily from 9:30am to 4pm (it opens at 10am on Sunday). It's closed January 1, Good Friday, and December 24 to 26. Admission is £3.50 ($6) for adults and £1.50 ($2.50) for children.

In 1610, when Shakespeare was a relatively prosperous man whose plays had been seen by Queen Elizabeth, he retired to **New Place,** Chapel Street (☎ **01789/204-016**), a Stratford house that he purchased a few years earlier and where he was to die in 1616. The house was later torn down. To reach the site from his birthplace, walk east on Henley Street and south on High Street, which becomes Chapel Street. Of New Place itself, only the garden remains. You enter through **Nash's House,** which belonged to Thomas Nash, husband of Shakespeare's granddaughter. The house contains

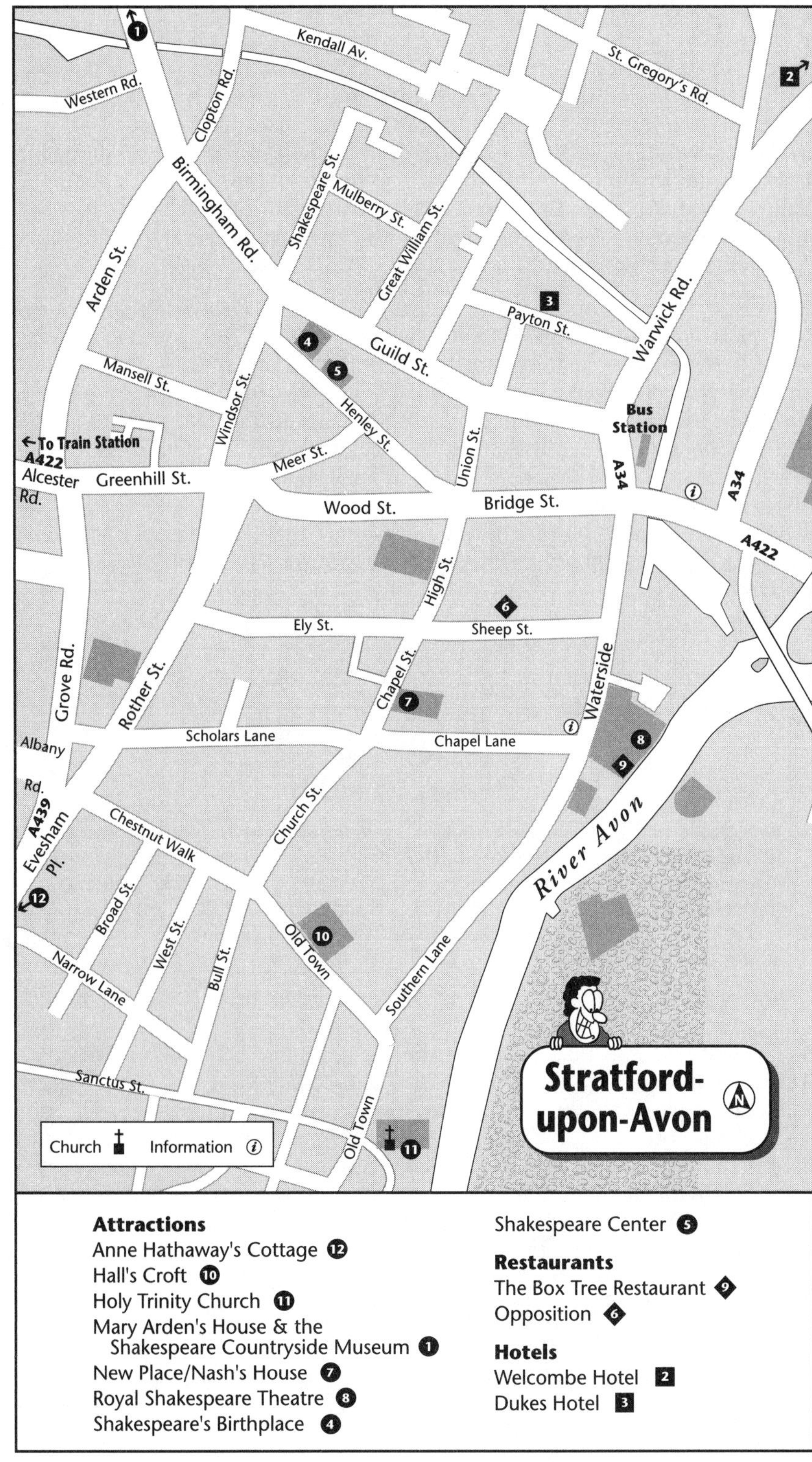

Stratford-upon-Avon
Kendall Av.
St. Gregory's Rd.
Western Rd.
Clopton Rd.
Birmingham Rd.
Shakespeare St.
Mulberry St.
Great William St.
Arden St.
Payton St.
Guild St.
Warwick Rd.
Mansell St.
Windsor St.
Henley St.
Union St.
Bus Station
To Train Station
A422
Alcester Rd.
Greenhill St.
Meer St.
Wood St.
Bridge St.
A34
A34
A422
High St.
Ely St.
Sheep St.
Grove Rd.
Rother St.
Chapel St.
Waterside
Scholars Lane
Chapel Lane
Albany Rd.
A439
Evesham Pl.
Chestnut Walk
Church St.
River Avon
Broad St.
West St.
Bull St.
Old Town
Southern Lane
Narrow Lane
Sanctus St.
Old Town
Church
Information
Attractions
Anne Hathaway's Cottage 12
Hall's Croft 10
Holy Trinity Church 11
Mary Arden's House & the Shakespeare Countryside Museum 1
New Place/Nash's House 7
Royal Shakespeare Theatre 8
Shakespeare's Birthplace 4
Shakespeare Center 5
Restaurants
The Box Tree Restaurant 9
Opposition 6
Hotels
Welcombe Hotel 2
Dukes Hotel 3

16th-century period rooms and an exhibition illustrating the history of Stratford. Adjoining the house is Knott Garden, landscaped in an Elizabethan style. The house is open from March 20 to October 19 daily from 9:30am to 5pm (it opens at 10am on Sunday); off-season, it's open daily from 10am to 4pm (it opens at 10:30am on Sunday). It opens at 1:30pm on January 1 and Good Friday; it's closed December 24 to 26. Admission is £3 ($5) for adults and £1.50 ($2.50) for children.

From New Place, continue south on Chapel and Church streets and turn east on Old Town to reach **Hall's Croft,** Old Town (☎ **01789/292-107**), a magnificent Tudor house with a walled garden. Here, Shakespeare's daughter Susanna probably lived with her husband, Dr. John Hall. The house is furnished in the style of a middle-class 17th-century home. On view are exhibits illustrating the theory and practice of medicine in Dr. Hall's time. It's open March 20 to October 19 daily from 9:30am to 5pm (it opens at 10am on Sunday); off-season, it's open daily from 10am to 4pm (it opens at 10:30am on Sunday). On January 1 and Good Friday, it opens at 1:30pm; it's closed December 24 to 26. Admission is £3 ($5) for adults and £1.50 ($2.50) for children.

Dollars & Sense

One ticket will get you into the five sites administered by the **Shakespeare Birthplace Trust:** Shakespeare's Birthplace, Anne Hathaway's Cottage, New Place/Nash's House, Mary Arden's House, and Hall's Croft. You can pick up the ticket at your first stop. It costs £10 ($17) for adults, £9 ($14) for seniors and students, £5 ($8) for children, and £26 ($42) for a family ticket (two adults, three children).

Shakespeare died on his birthday at the age of 52 and is buried in **Holy Trinity Church,** Old Town (☎ **01789/266-316**), a beautiful parish church in an attractive setting near the Avon River. It's a bit odd that the inscription on the tomb of the man who wrote some of the world's most enduring lines is little more than doggerel, ending with "and curst be he who moves my bones." Obviously he didn't want to leave Stratford—ever. You can visit the church March through October, Monday through Saturday, from 8:30am to 6pm, and Sunday from 2 to 5pm. You can visit in November through February, Monday through Saturday, from 8:30am to 4pm, and on Sunday from 2 to 5pm. Admission to the church is free, but a small donation is requested to see the tomb.

About 3½ miles north of Stratford on the A34 (Birmingham) road is the last of the five Shakespeare shrines: **Mary Arden's House & the Shakespeare**

Countryside Museum, Wilmcote (☎ **01789/204-016**). This Tudor farmstead, with its old stone dovecote and outbuildings, was reputedly the girlhood home of Shakespeare's mother. The house contains country furniture and domestic utensils; in the barns, stable, cowshed, and farmyard, there's an extensive collection of farming implements illustrating life and work in the local countryside from Shakespeare's time to the present. It's open March 20 through October 19 daily from 9:30am to 5pm (it opens at 10am on Sunday); off-season, you can visit daily from 10am to 4pm (it opens at 10:30am on Sunday). On January 1 and Good Friday, it opens at 1:30pm; it's closed December 24 to 26. Admission is £4 ($7) for adults and £2 ($3.30) for children.

All the World's a Stage—Especially at Stratford

The **Royal Shakespeare Theatre,** Waterside, Stratford-upon-Avon, CV37 6BB (☎ **01789/295-623**), is a major showcase for the Royal Shakespeare Company, which typically stages five Shakespeare plays during a season that runs from November until September. You can reserve seats through a North American or English travel or ticket agent (see chapters 4 and 18). A few tickets are always held for sale on the day of a performance, but it might be too late for a good seat if you wait until you arrive in Stratford. The box office is open Monday through Saturday from 9am to 8pm, but it closes at 6pm on days when there are no performances. Ticket prices range from £6 to £46 ($10 to $74).

During the long theatre season, it's best to reserve in advance if you're planning to sleep, perchance to dream, in Stratford. However, the **Tourist Information Center** (see above) will help you find accommodations.

Where to Rest Thy Weary Head If you're feeling to the manor born, stay in the **Welcombe Hotel,** Warwick Rd., Stratford-upon-Avon, Warwickshire, CV37 ONR (☎ **01789/295-252;** fax 01789/414-666; www.welcombe.co.uk). Located 1½ miles northeast of the town center, this luxurious, full-service hotel is housed in one of the country's great Jacobean houses. It has an 18-hole golf course and is surrounded by 157 acres of grounds. The largest bedrooms are big enough for tennis matches; in the smaller rooms you'd have to content yourself with Ping-Pong. Room rates range from £150 to £160 ($248 to $264) for a double. Rates include an English breakfast. American Express, Diners Club, MasterCard, and Visa are accepted.

Smaller and less glamorous, but charming for the price, is **Dukes,** Payton St., Stratford-upon-Avon, Warwickshire, CV37 6UA (☎ **01789/269-300;** fax 01789/414-700; www.astanet.com/get/dukeshtl). Located in the center of

Stratford, close to Shakespeare's birthplace, the hotel was formed from two Georgian town houses. The nicely restored public areas and bedrooms are attractive, there are many amenities usually found in more-expensive hotels, and the hotel's restaurant serves good English and continental cuisine. No children under 12 are accepted here. Rooms go for £70 to £115 ($116 to $190) for a double. Rates include an English breakfast. American Express, Diners Club, MasterCard, and Visa are accepted.

Where to Eat The River Avon and its gliding white swans provide a quietly dramatic backdrop for diners at The **Box Tree Restaurant,** Waterside (☎ **01789/293-226**), located in the Royal Shakespeare Theatre. The menu offers a bit of everything—French, Italian, and English—and you can dine by candlelight after a performance. Reservations are required (there's a special phone for reservations in the theatre lobby). The matinee lunch is £16.50 ($27); main courses at dinner are around £25.50 ($42). American Express, MasterCard, and Visa are accepted. It's open Thursday through Saturday from noon to 2:30pm and Monday through Saturday from 5:45pm to midnight.

Moderately priced bistro fare is served up in historic but refreshingly unpretentious surroundings at **Opposition,** 13 Sheep Street (☎ **01789/269-980**), housed in a 16th-century building in the heart of Stratford. Morning coffee, teacakes, and croissants are available Monday to Saturday from 11am to noon. Lunch and dinner choices are a mixture of traditional and Modern British cuisine. Reservations are recommended. Main courses range from £6 to £15 ($10 to $24). MasterCard and Visa are accepted. It's open from 11am to 2pm and 5:30 to 11pm.

Salisbury & Stonehenge: Gothic Splendor & Prehistoric Mysteries

The tall, slender spire of Salisbury Cathedral rises up from the plains of Wiltshire like a finger pointing toward heaven. Salisbury, or New Sarum as it was once called, lies in the valley of the Avon River, 90 miles southwest of London. Filled with Tudor inns and tearooms and dominated by its beautiful cathedral, this lovely old market town is often overlooked by visitors eager to see Stonehenge, about 9 miles away.

Getting to Salisbury

From London's Waterloo Station there are hourly **Network Express trains** to Salisbury; the journey takes 2 hours. For information and schedules, call ☎ **0345/484-950.** If you're driving from London, head west on **M3** to the end of the run, continuing the rest of the way on **A30.**

Salisbury's **Tourist Information Centre,** Fish Row (☎ **01722/334-956**), is open October through April, Monday through Saturday, from 9:30am to 5pm; and in May, Monday through Saturday, from 9:30am to 5pm and Sunday from 10:30am to 4:30pm. In June and September, it's open Monday through

Saturday from 9:30am to 6pm and Sunday from 10:30am to 4:30pm. In July and August, it's open Monday through Saturday from 9:30am to 7pm and Sunday from 10:30am to 5pm.

Even if Stonehenge is your real goal in this neck of the woods, try to spend a bit of time wandering through **Salisbury Cathedral,** The Close (☎ **01722/323-279**). Despite an ill-conceived renovation in the 18th century, this 13th-century structure remains the best example of the Early English, or Perpendicular, style in all of England.

At 404 feet, its spire is the tallest in the country. The beautiful 13th-century octagonal chapter house possesses one of the four surviving original texts of the Magna Carta. Adding to the serene beauty of the cathedral are the cloisters and an exceptionally large close, consisting of about 75 buildings. The cathedral is open May through August daily from 8:30am to 8:30pm, and in September through April daily from 8am to 6:30pm. The suggested donation for admission is £2.50 ($4) for the cathedral and 30p (50¢) for the chapter house.

Extra! Extra!

The **Brass Rubbing Centre** (☎ **01722/323-279**), located in the cathedral cloisters, has a number of exact replicas molded from the original cathedral brasses: medieval and Tudor knights and ladies, famous historical faces, and even Celtic designs. The £3 ($5) average charge for each rubbing includes materials and instructions. The center is open in mid-June through September, Monday through Saturday, from 10am to 6pm and on Sunday from 11:15am to 4pm.

In the town of Wilton, 3 miles west of Salisbury on A30, is one of England's great country estates: **Wilton House** (☎ **01722/746-729**). It's believed that Shakespeare's troupe entertained here. Several centuries later, it was at Wilton House that General Eisenhower and his advisers made preparations for the D-Day landings at Normandy. The house is filled with beautifully maintained furnishings and world-class art, including paintings by Van Dyck, Rubens, Brueghel, and Reynolds. You can visit a reconstructed Tudor kitchen and Victorian laundry plus The Wareham Bears, a collection of some 200 miniature dressed teddy bears.

The 21-acre grounds include rose and water gardens, riverside and woodland walks, and a huge adventure playground for children. The house is open from Easter through October daily from 11am to 6pm (last admission 5pm); admission is £6.75 ($11) for adults, £4 ($7) for children 5 to 15, and free for children under 5. If you're without wheels, you can take the bus that stops on New Canal, just north of the Salisbury train station; check with the tourist office for schedules.

About 9 miles north of Salisbury, at the junction of A303 and A344/A360, is one of the world's most-renowned prehistoric sites: the prehistoric stone circle known as **Stonehenge** (☎ **01980/624-715**). If you're not driving, hop on one of the Wilts & Dorset **buses** that depart at frequent intervals from Salisbury's coach station near the Market Place, north of the train station and just west of the tourist information center; the trip takes about 30 minutes.

Tourist Traps

Stonehenge is one of England's most popular attractions, and the **crowds** can reach epidemic proportions as the day wears on, so it's best to arrive as early as possible. (The site opens at either 9 or 9:30am, depending on the season.)

Believed to be from 3,500 to 5,000 years old, Stonehenge is a stone circle of megalithic pillars and lintels built on the flat Salisbury Plain. Many folks are disappointed when they actually see the site, which is not as huge as modern-day megasensibilities expect and is now surrounded by a fence that keeps visitors 50 feet from the stones. Keep in mind, however, what a remarkable achievement, both in terms of design and engineering skills, Stonehenge represents. Many of the stones, which weigh several tons, were mined and moved from sites as far away as southern Wales in a time before forklifts, trucks, and dynamite.

Who were the people who built it and what does it all mean? The old belief that Stonehenge was built by the Druids has been discredited. (It's probably older than the Celtic Druids.) One popular theory maintains that the site was an astronomical observatory, because it's aligned to the summer equinox and capable of predicting eclipses. Obviously, it was a shrine and/or ceremonial gathering place of some kind. But in an age that thinks it knows everything, Stonehenge still keeps its awe-inspiring mysteries to itself. You can visit the site daily from March 16 to May and from September to October 15 from 9:30am to 6pm, June to August from 9am to 7pm, and October 16 to March 15 from 9:30am to 4pm. Admission is £3.90 ($6) for adults, £2.90 ($5) for students and seniors, and £2 ($3.30) for children.

Where to Stay & Dine A good hotel choice for a Salisbury sojourn is the **White Hart,** 1 St. John St., Salisbury, Wiltshire, SP1 2SD (☎ **01722/327-476;** fax 01722/412-761). A Salisbury landmark since Georgian times, it has accommodations in the older section of the building or in a new motel-like section in the rear. The hotel was completely refurbished in 1995 and has a good restaurant. Room rates are £110 to £140 ($176 to $224) for a double. American Express, Diners Club, MasterCard, and Visa are accepted.

If you're looking for an inexpensive but atmospheric (and smoke-free) B&B, try **The New Inn & Old House,** 39–47 New St., Salisbury, Wiltshire, SP1 2PH (☎ **01722/327-679**). This 15th-century building, with a walled garden backing up to the Cathedral Close Wall, has well-appointed oak-beamed bedrooms. The Inn restaurant serves reasonably priced meals. A double goes for £50 to £70 ($83 to $116). Rates include a continental breakfast. American Express, MasterCard, and Visa are accepted.

For homemade, uncomplicated, and wholesome food in the center of Salisbury, go to **Harper's Restaurant,** 7–9 Ox Row, Market Square (☎ **01722/333-118**). You can order from two different menus—one featuring cost-conscious bistro-style platters, and the other a longer menu that includes all-vegetarian pasta dishes. Reservations are recommended. Main courses range from £8.50 to £12.50 ($14 to $21), and fixed-price three-course meals go for £8 ($13) at lunch and £13 ($21) at dinner. American Express, Diners Club, MasterCard, and Visa are accepted. It's open Monday through Saturday from noon to 2pm and 6:30 to 9:30pm and Sunday from 6 to 9:30pm; it's closed on Sunday in October through May.

Another good choice is the **Salisbury Haunch of Venison,** 1 Minster Street (☎ **01722/322-024**). This creaky-timbered, 1320 chophouse and pub serves English roasts and grills. The house specialty is roast haunch of venison with garlic and juniper berries. Main courses range from £9 to £12 ($15 to $20); pub platters go for £4 to £6 ($7 to $10). American Express, Diners Club, MasterCard, and Visa are accepted. The restaurant is open daily from noon to 3pm and Monday through Saturday from 7 to 9:30pm. The pub is open Monday through Saturday from 11am to 11pm and on Sunday from noon to 3pm and 7 to 11pm. It's closed Christmas through Easter.

Appendix A

London from A to Z—Facts at Your Fingertips

American Express The main Amex office is at 6 Haymarket, SW1 (☎ **0171/930-4411;** tube: Piccadilly Circus). Full services are available Monday to Friday 9am to 5:30pm and Saturday 9am to 4pm. At other times (Saturday 4 to 6pm and Sunday 10am to 6pm), only the foreign-exchange bureau is open.

Area Codes London has two telephone area codes: 0171 and 0181. The **0171** area code is for Central London within a 4-mile radius of Charing Cross (including the City, Knightsbridge, Oxford Street, and as far south as Brixton). The **0181** area code is for outer London (including Heathrow Airport, Wimbledon, and Greenwich). Within London, you'll need to dial the area code when calling from one section of the city to the other, but not within a section. The country code for England is 44; see "Telephone" below for instructions on how to dial.

Baby-Sitters Baby-sitting organizations are discussed in chapter 1.

Business Hours Banks are usually open Monday to Friday 9:30am to 3:30pm. Business offices are open Monday to Friday 9am to 5pm; the lunch break lasts an hour, but most places stay open during that time. Pubs and bars are allowed to stay open from 11am to 11pm on Monday to Saturday and from noon to 10:30pm on Sunday. London stores generally open at 9am and close at 5:30pm, staying open until 7pm on Wednesday or Thursday. Most central shops close on Saturday around 1pm.

Climate Climate is discussed in chapter 1.

Currency Exchange Currency exchange is discussed in chapter 2.

Dentists For dental emergencies, call **Eastman Dental Hospital** (☎ **0171/915-1000;** tube: King's Cross).

Doctors In an emergency, contact **Doctor's Call** (☎ **07000/372-255**). Some hotels also have physicians on call. **Medical Express,** 117A Harley

St., W1 (☎ **0171/499-1991;** tube: Regent's Park), is a private British clinic; it's not part of the free British medical establishment. For filling the British equivalent of a U.S. prescription, there's sometimes a surcharge of £20 ($32) on top of the cost of the medications. The clinic is open Monday to Friday 9am to 6pm and Saturday 9:30am to 2:30pm.

Documents Required See chapter 4, "Tying Up the Loose Ends."

Drugstores In Britain they're called chemist shops. Every police station in the country has a list of emergency chemists (dial 0 and ask the operator for the local police). One of the most centrally located chemists, keeping long hours, is **Bliss the Chemist,** 5 Marble Arch, W1 (☎ **0171/723-6116;** tube: Marble Arch), open daily 9am to midnight. Every London neighborhood has a branch of **Boots,** Britain's leading pharmacy.

Electricity British current is 240 volts, AC cycle, roughly twice the voltage of North American current, which is 115 to 120 volts, AC cycle. You probably won't be able to plug the flat pins of your appliance's plugs into the holes of British wall outlets without suitable converters or adapters. Some (but not all) hotels supply these for guests. Experienced travelers bring their own transformers. An electrical supply shop will also have what you need. Be forewarned that you'll destroy the inner workings of your appliance (and possibly start a fire as well) if you plug an American appliance directly into a European electrical outlet without a transformer.

Embassies & High Commissions We hope you won't need such services, but in case you lose your passport or have some other emergency, here's a list of addresses and phone numbers:

- **Australia** The high commission is at **Australia House,** The Strand, WC2 (☎ **0171/379-4334;** tube: Charing Cross or Aldwych); it's open Monday to Friday from 10am to 4pm.
- **Canada** The high commission is located at **MacDonald House,** 38 Grosvenor Square, W1 (☎ **0171/258-6600;** tube: Bond Street); it's open Monday to Friday from 8 to 11am.
- **Ireland** The embassy is at 17 Grosvenor Place, SW1 (☎ **0171/235-2171;** tube: Hyde Park Corner); it's open Monday to Friday from 9:30am to 1pm and 2:15 to 5pm.
- **New Zealand** The high commission is at **New Zealand House,** 80 Haymarket at Pall Mall, SW1 (☎ **0171/930-8422;** tube: Charing Cross or Piccadilly Circus); it's open Monday to Friday from 9am to 5pm.
- **The United States** The embassy is located at 24 Grosvenor Square, W1 (☎ **0171/499-9000;** tube: Bond Street). For passport and visa information, go to the **U.S. Passport & Citizenship Unit,** 55–56 Upper Brook St., W1 (☎ **0171/499-9000,** ext. 2563 or 2564; tube: Marble Arch or Bond Street). Hours are Monday to Friday from 8:30am to noon and from 2 to 4pm (there are no afternoon hours on Tuesday).

Emergencies For police, fire, or an ambulance, dial ☎ **999.**

Holidays U.K. holidays are discussed in chapter 1.

Hospitals The following offer emergency care in London 24 hours a day, with the first treatment free under the National Health Service: **Royal Free Hospital,** Pond St., NW3 (☎ **0171/794-0500;** tube: Belsize Park); and **University College Hospital,** Grafton Way, WC1 (☎ **0171/387-9300;** tube: Warren Street or Euston Square). Many other London hospitals also have accident and emergency departments.

Hot lines For **police or medical emergencies,** dial ☎ **999** (no coins required). If you're in some sort of **legal emergency,** call Release at ☎ **0171/729-9904,** 24 hours a day. The **Rape Crisis Line** is ☎ **0171/837-1600,** accepting calls after 6pm. **Samaritans,** 46 Marshall St., W1 (☎ **0171/734-2800;** tube: Oxford Circus or Piccadilly Circus), maintains a crisis hotline that helps with all kinds of trouble, even threatened suicides, from 9am to 9pm. **Alcoholics Anonymous** (☎ **0171/352-3001**) answers its hotline daily from 10am to 10pm. The **AIDS 24-hour hotline** is ☎ **0800/567-123.**

Information See chapters 1 and 7 for where to get visitor information before you leave home and after you arrive in London.

Liquor Laws No alcohol is served to anyone under 18. Children under 16 aren't allowed in pubs, except in certain rooms, and then only when accompanied by a parent or guardian. Don't drink and drive; penalties for drunk driving are stiff, even if you're an overseas visitor. Restaurants are allowed to serve liquor during the same hours as pubs; however, only people who are eating a meal on the premises can be served a drink. A meal, incidentally, is defined as "substantial refreshment." And you have to eat and drink sitting down. In hotels, liquor may be served from 11am to 11pm to both residents and nonresidents; after 11pm, only residents may be served.

Mail An airmail letter to North America costs 43p (70¢) for 10 grams, and postcards require a 35p (55¢) stamp; letters generally take 7 to 10 days to arrive from the United States. See "Post Offices" below for locations.

Money See chapter 2, "Money Matters."

Newspapers/Magazines The *Times, Telegraph, Daily Mail,* and *Manchester Guardian* are all dailies carrying the latest news. The *International Herald Tribune,* published in Paris, and an international edition of *USA Today,* beamed via satellite, are available daily. Copies of *Time* and *Newsweek* are also sold at most newsstands. Magazines such as *Time Out, City Limits,* and *Where* contain lots of useful information about the latest happenings in London.

Police In an emergency, dial ☎ **999** (no coins required). You can also go to one of the local police branches in Central London, including **New Scotland Yard,** Broadway, SW1 (☎ **0171/230-1212;** tube: St. James's Park).

Post Offices The **Main Post Office** is at 24 William IV St. (☎ **0171/930-9580;** tube: Charing Cross). It operates as three separate businesses: inland and international postal service and banking (open Monday to Saturday 8:30am to 8pm); philatelic postage stamp sales (open Monday to Saturday 8am to 8pm); and the post shop, selling greeting cards and stationery (open Monday to Saturday from 8am to 8pm). Other post offices and sub–post offices are open Monday to Friday 9am to 5:30pm and on Saturday 9am to 12:30pm. Many sub–post offices and some main post offices close for an hour at lunchtime.

Radio There are 24-hour radio channels operating throughout the United Kingdom, including London. They offer mostly pop music and chat shows at night. Some "pirate" radio stations add more spice. So-called legal FM stations are BBC1 (104.8); BBC2 (89.1); BBC3 (between 90 and 92); and the classical station, BBC4 (95). There is also the BBC Greater London Radio (94.9) station, with lots of rock, plus LBC Crown (97.3), with news and reports of "what's on" in London. Pop/rock U.S. style is heard on Capital FM (95.8); and if you like jazz, reggae, or salsa, tune in to Choice FM (96.9). Jazz FM (102.2) also offers blues and big-band music.

Rest Rooms They're marked by "public toilets" signs on streets, parks, and tube stations; many are automatic, and are sterilized after each use. The English often call toilets "loos." You'll also find well-maintained lavatories that can be used by anybody in all larger public buildings, such as museums and art galleries, large department stores, and railway stations. It's not really acceptable to use the lavatories in hotels, restaurants, and pubs if you're not a customer, but we can't say that we always stick to this rule. Public lavatories are usually free, but you might need a small coin to get in or to use a proper washroom.

Smoking Most U.S. cigarette brands are available in London. Antismoking laws are tougher than ever: Smoking is strictly forbidden in the Underground (on the cars and the platforms) and on buses, and it's increasingly frowned upon in many other places. But London still isn't a particularly friendly place for the nonsmoker. Most restaurants have nonsmoking tables, but they're usually separated from the smoking section by only a little bit of space. Nonsmoking rooms are available in the bigger hotels. Although some of the smaller hotels claim that they have no-smoking rooms, we've often found that this means that the room is smoke-free only during our visit; if you're bothered by the odor, ask to be shown another room.

Taxes To encourage energy conservation, the British government levies a 25% tax on gasoline ("petrol"). There is also a 17.5% national value-added tax (VAT) that is added to all hotel and restaurant bills and will be included in the price of many items you purchase. This can be refunded if you shop at stores that participate in the Retail Export Scheme (signs are posted in the window). See "How to Claim Your VAT Refund" in chapter 15.

In October 1994, Britain imposed a **departure tax:** £5 ($8) for flights within Britain and the European Union or £10 ($16) for passengers flying elsewhere, including to the United States. Your airline ticket may or may not include this tax. Ask in advance to avoid a surprise at the gate.

Taxis See chapter 8, "Getting Around London."

Telephone For **directory assistance** in London, dial ☎ **142;** for the rest of Britain, call ☎ **192.** The country code for the United Kingdom is **44.** London has two city codes, **0171** in central London and **0181** in outer London. (City codes are necessary when dialing from outside the code.) If you're calling London from outside the U.K., drop the initial zero from the city code. To call London from the United States, dial **011-44-171** or 011-44-181, and then the seven-digit local number. ***Note:*** As of June 1999, a new city code **020**, will replace 0171 and 0181. The new city code will be followed by an eight-digit number beginning with either a 7 or an 8 (7 for a number that had a 0171 code, 8 for a number that had a 0181 code. From the United States, you will need to dial 011-44-20 and then the new eight-digit number. If you're within the United Kingdom but not in London, use 020 followed by the new eight-digit number. If you're calling within London, simply leave off the code and dial only the eight-digit number.

There are three types of public pay phones: those taking only coins, those accepting only phonecards (called Cardphones), and those taking both phonecards and credit cards. At coin-operated phones, insert your coins before dialing. The minimum charge is 10p (15¢).

Phonecards are available in four values—£2 ($3.20), £4 ($6.40), £10 ($16), and £20 ($32)—and are reusable until the total value has expired. Cards can be purchased from newsstands and post offices. Finally, the credit-call pay phone operates on credit cards—Access (MasterCard), Visa, American Express, and Diners Club—and is most common at airports and large railway stations.

Phone numbers in Britain outside of the major cities consist of an exchange name plus a telephone number. To dial the number, you'll need the code of the exchange being called. Information sheets on call-box walls give the codes in most instances. If your code isn't there, call the operator by dialing ☎ **100.**

In London, phone numbers consist of the exchange code and number (seven digits or more). These digits are all you need to dial if you are calling from within the same city. If you're calling from elsewhere, you will need to prefix them with the dialing code for the city. Again, you'll find these codes on the call-box information sheets or by dialing the operator (☎ **100**).

To make an international call from London, dial the international access code (00), then the country code, then the area code, and finally the local number. Or call through one of the following long-distance access codes: **AT&T USA Direct** (☎ 0800/890-011), **Canada Direct** (☎ 0800/890-016), **Australia** (☎ 0800/890-061), and **New Zealand** (☎ 0800/890-064). Common country codes are **USA** and **Canada,** 1; **Australia,** 61; **New Zealand,** 64; and **South Africa,** 27.

Time England follows Greenwich Mean Time (5 hours ahead of Eastern Standard Time). Most of the year, including the summer, Britain is 5 hours ahead of the time observed on the East Coast of the United States. Because the U.S. and Britain observe daylight saving time at slightly different times of year, there's a brief period (about a week) in autumn when Britain is only 4 hours ahead of New York, and a brief period in spring when it's 6 hours ahead of New York.

Tipping In restaurants, service charges ranging from 15% to 20% are usually added to the bill. Sometimes this is clearly marked; at other times, it isn't. When in doubt, ask. If service isn't included, it's customary to add 15% to the bill. Sommeliers get about £1 ($1.60) per bottle of wine served. Tipping in pubs isn't common, although in cocktail bars the server usually gets about 75p ($1.20) per round of drinks.

Hotels, like restaurants, often add a service charge of 10% to 15% to most bills. In smaller B&Bs, the tip isn't likely to be included. Therefore, tip for special service, such as for the person who served you breakfast. If several persons have served you in a B&B, many guests ask that 10% or 15% be added to the bill and divided among the staff.

It's standard to tip taxi drivers 10% to 15% of the fare, although a tip for a taxi driver should never be less than 30p (50¢), even for a short run. Barbers and hairdressers expect 10% to 15%. Tour guides expect £2 ($3.20), although it's not mandatory. Gas station attendants are rarely tipped, and theater ushers don't expect tips.

Transit Information Call ☎ **0171/222-1234** 24 hours a day.

Weather Call ☎ **0171/922-8844** for current weather information, but chances are the line will be busy.

Appendix B

Toll-Free Phone Numbers & Web Sites for Airlines & Hotels

Airlines

Air New Zealand
☎ 800/262-2468
www.airnz.co.nz/

American Airlines
☎ 800/433-7300
www.americanair.com

American Trans Air
☎ 800/435-9282
www.ata.com/

British Airways
☎ 800/AIRWAYS
www.british-airways.com

Continental Airlines
☎ 800/231-0856
www.flycontinental.com

Delta Air Lines
☎ 800/241-4141
www.delta-air.com

Icelandair
☎ 800/223-5500
www.icelandair.is

Northwest Airlines
☎ 800/447-4747
www.nwa.com

Trans World Airlines
☎ 800/892-4141
www.twa.com

United Airlines
☎ 800/538-2929
www.ual.com

Virgin Atlantic Airways
☎ 800/862-8621
www.virgin.com

Major London Hotel Chains

Forte and Le Meridien Hotels & Resorts
☎ 800/225-5843
www.forte-hotels.com/

Hilton International
☎ 800/HILTONS
www.hilton.com

Hyatt Hotels and Resorts
☎ 800/228-3336
www.hyatt.com

Inter-Continental Hotels and Resorts
☎ 800/327-0200
www.interconti.com

Sheraton Hotels & Resorts
☎ 800/325-3535
www.sheraton.com

Thistle Hotels
☎ 800/847-4358
www.thistlehotels.com/

Index

Page numbers in *italics* refer to maps.

A

A.A. Guide for the Disabled Traveller, 15
Aaron House, 86
AARP (American Association of Retired Persons), 13, 30
Abbey Court, The, 86
Abbey House, 86
About Family Travel, 11
Academy Hotel, 87
Academy of St. Martin-in-the-Fields, 210
Access America, 53
Accessible Journeys, 17
Access in London, 15
Access to the Underground, 17
Access to Travel Magazine, 16
Access Tours, 17
Accommodations, 61–107
- Bayswater, 70
- Belgravia, 68
- Bloomsbury, 66
- Central London, 63
- Charing Cross Road, 66
- Chelsea, 68–69
- children staying in same room with you, 30
- choosing a neighborhood for, 63, 66–70
- cost of, 77–78
  - cost-cutting strategies, 29, 30
  - discounts, 71, 72
  - off-season rates, 29, 72
  - phone calls, 73
  - price categories, 78
  - price ranges, 27, 72–73
  - rack rate, 70–71
  - value-added tax (VAT), 73
- Covent Garden, 63
- for disabled travelers, 92
- Earl's Court, 69–70, 86, 103
- gay or gay-friendly, 101
- Holland Park, 69
- Hotel Preferences Worksheet, 108–9
- index of hotels
  - by location, 78
  - by price, 79, 82
- Kensington, 69, 86, 91, 106
- kid-friendly, 11, 75
- Knightsbridge, 68
- Leicester Square, 66
- Marylebone, 68
- Mayfair, 67
- most romantic, 103
- Notting Hill, 70, 86, 97
- Paddington, 70
- Piccadilly Circus, 66
- reservations, 62
  - arriving without, 76
  - cancellation policy, 73
  - Web site, 75
- St. James's, 67, 82, 86
- self-catering units, 30
- for seniors, 75
- service charges and tipping at, 333
- Soho, 66
- South Kensington, 69
- splurges, 90
- The Strand, 63
- Stratford-upon-Avon, 323–24
- types of, 73–74
- types of rooms, 74–75
- Victoria area, 67
- with a view, 97
- Web site, 75
- West End, 63, 66–68
- Westminster, 66
- wheelchair-accessible, 18

Adam, Robert, 229
Adapter, 59
Adare House, 87
Addresses, 118
Admiralty Arch, 210, 254
Afternoon tea, 180–81
AIDS 24-hour hotline, 330
Ain't Nothing But Blues Bar, 304–5

Airbus, 17–18, 39, 115–16
Air/hotel packages. *See also* Package tours
  accommodations rates and, 71
Airlines and airfares
  cost-cutting strategies, 30
  discounts for senior travelers, 14
  finding the best, 37–39
  full fare, 37
  off-season, 5
  package tours. *See* Air/hotel packages; Fly/drive packages; Package tours; Theatre packages
  worksheets, 38
Air New Zealand, 334
Airports, 39–40
  duty-free shopping at, 237–38
Air Transportation of Handicapped Persons, 16
Air travel. *See also* Airlines and airfares; *and specific airlines*
  bulkhead seats, 40
  clothes and, 40–41
  duration of flights, 12
  emergency exit row seats, 40
  jet lag and, 41
  with kids, 12
  special dietary needs, 40
  toiletries for, 41
  worksheets, 41–45
Albemarle Booking Agency, 55, 286
Albert Memorial, 199
Alcoholics Anonymous, 330
All England Lawn Tennis Club, 9
American Airlines, 334
  fly/drive packages, 52
  Web site, 39
American Airlines Vacations, 36
American Bar, 307
American English, 126
  restaurant menu items, 140
American Express, 23, 34, 328
  emergency number, 25
  foreign exchange bureau, 25
  traveler's checks, 22, 25
American Express Vacations, 36
American Foundation for the Blind, 16
American Trans Air, 334
Anne Hathaway's Cottage (Stratford-upon-Avon), 320, *321*
Antiquarius, 251
Antiques, 251, 252
  Chelsea Antiques Fair, 10
Apollo Hammersmith, 299
Apple Market, 248
Aquarium, London, *216,* 222
Arco Bars of Knightsbridge, 177
Arden, Mary, House & the Shakespeare Countryside Museum, *321,* 322–23
Area codes, 328
Aromatherapy products, 248
Art. *See also* Museums and galleries
  Royal Academy Summer Exhibition, 9
Art shops, 252
Artsline, 16, 295
Ashmoleon Museum (Oxford), *315,* 316, 318
Assembly Rooms (Bath), 314
Aster House Hotel, 87
Aston's Budget Studios & Aston's Designer Studios and Suites, 90–91
AT&T USA Direct, 332
Atlantic Bar & Grill, 307
ATMs, 22–23
Attractions. *See* Sights and Attractions
Aubergine, 150
Auckland (New Zealand), British Tourist Authority (BTA) office in, 3
Au Jardin des Gourmets, 150
Austen, Jane, 219
Australia
  British Tourist Authority (BTA) office in, 3
  high commission, 329
  long-distance access codes, 332
Australia House, 329
Auto Europe, 52
Avis, 17, 52
Avonmore Hotel, 91

B

Baby-Sitters Unlimited, 13
Baby-sitting services, 13
Baker Street, 123
B&Bs (bed and breakfast), 73–74
  families with children and, 11
  reservation and booking agencies, 76
  service charges and tipping at, 333

Bank holidays, 7
Bank of England Museum, *216,* 220
Banqueting House, 265
Barbers, tipping, 333
Barbican Art Gallery, 218
Barbican Centre, *216,* 218, 290
Barbican Hall, 218, 296, 298
Barbican Theatre, 218
Bar Italia, 307
Bar Rumba, 306
Barry, Charles, 198
Bars, 307. *See also* Pubs
Bateaux London, 188
Bath, 312–14
Bath Abbey, 312, 313
Bath and beauty products, 248
Bayswater, 125
  accommodations, 70, 93
  patisserie, 180
  restaurant, 173
BBC Henry Wood Promenade Concerts, 9
Beauchamp Place, 249
Bed & Breakfast (agency), 76
Beef, safety of eating, 54
Beefeater Cup, 8
Beer, 138, 304
Belfast, H.M.S., *216,* 226, 263
Belgravia, 123
  accommodations, 68, 95
Bellhops, tipping, 29
Bell tower, Magdalen College (Oxford), 317
Berk, 245
Berwick Street Market, 248
Bethnal Green Museum of Childhood, *216,* 222
Beverly Hills Bakery, 179
Big Ben, *193,* 198
Black Friar, 301
Blair House Hotel, 91
Bliss the Chemist, 329
Bloody Tower, 208
Bloomsbury, 122
  accommodations, 66, 87, 91, 94, 98, 100, 101
  patisserie, 180
  restaurants, 167, 168, 181
Blooms Hotel, 91–92
Bluebird, 151
Blue Cross/Blue Shield, 54
Blue Note, 301
Blues, 304–5
Boat trips
  to Hampton Court Palace, 230–31
  to Kew Gardens, 229
  to London Zoo, 201
Bodleian Library, *315,* 317
Body Shop, The, 245, 249
Boleyn, Ann, 208, 230
Bombay Brasserie, The, 151
Bond Street
  Christmas lights, 10
  shopping on, 246
Book of Deals, The, 14
Books, on London (guidebooks), 4, 33
Books Etc., 247
Bookstores, 241, 247, 251
Boots The Chemist, 237
Boston Court Hotel, 92
Botanical gardens. *See* Parks and gardens
Boutique hotels, 74
Boxing Day, 7
Box Tree Restaurant (Stratford-upon-Avon), 324
Bracewells Bar, 307
Braille maps, 17
Bramah Tea and Coffee Museum, *216,* 221
Brasserie at the National Gallery, 177, 254
Brasserie St. Quentin, 151
Brass Rubbing Centre (Salisbury Cathedral), 325
Breakfast, best restaurants for, 158
Britain for People with Disabilities, 15
Britain Visitor Centre, 76
British Airways, 334
  car rentals, 52
  fly/drive packages, 52
  package tours, 37
  Web site, 39
British Airways Holidays, 36
British Designer Knitwear Group, 244
British Hotel Reservation Centre, 76
British Library Exhibition Centre, *216,* 219–20
British Museum, *193,* 195, 260, *260*
British Museum Restaurant, 176–77, 260
British Music Information Centre, 295
British Rail, 18
British Tourist Authority (BTA), 2–3
  Britain for People with Disabilities, 15
  London Planner, 294–95
  Web site for, 3
British Travel Centre, 125
British Travel Shop, 15

BritRail passes, 310
Brixton Academy, 299
Brompton Road, 249
Brown's Hotel, 90
Bryanston Court Hotel, 92
Bucket shops (consolidators), 38
Buckingham Palace, 9, 123, *193,* 196, *255,* 256, *257*
  Changing of the Guard at, 186
Budgeting, 26–29
  attractions, 28
  basics of, 27
  cost-cutting strategies, 29–30
  cost of typical items, 27
  dining, 28
  lodging, 27
  shopping & entertainment, 28–29
  time, 271–72
  transportation, 28
  worksheet, 27, 31
Budget Rent-a-Car, 52
Bulkhead seats, 40
Burberry, 241
Bureau of Consular Affairs, U.S. Department of State's, 47, 50
Bureaux de Change, 24–25
Burghers of Calais, The, 263
Burlington Arcade, 244
Buses, 130–31
  from Heathrow, 115–16
  from London City Airport, 117
  night, 131
  to Stratford-upon-Avon, 319
Business hours, 328
Bus passes, 131
Bus stops, 130
Byron Hotel, The, 93

C

Cabaret, 308
Cabinet War Rooms, 215, *216,* 265, *266*
Cadogan Hotel, The, 93
Café Boheme, 307
Cafe-in-the-Crypt, 210, 254
Cafes, 139
  museum, 176–77
Café Spice Namaste, 154, 262
Cafe Uno, 181
Café Valerie, 179
Calendar of events, 8–10
Camden Palace, 306
Canada
  British Tourist Authority (BTA) office in, 3
  high commission, 329
Canada Direct, 332
Canadian Muffin Company, 179, 180
Canon Photography Gallery, 211
Capri Sandwich Bar, 177
Cardphones, 332
Carfax Tower, *315,* 317
Carlyle, Jane, 220
Carlyle, Thomas, 220
Carlyle's House, *216,* 220
Carnets, 130
Carnival
  Guy Fawkes, 10
  Notting Hill, 10
Carry-on luggage, 58
Cars and driving
  disability parking stickers, 17
  rentals, 50–52
    hand-controlled cars, 17
Carvery, The, 154
Cash advances, ATM or credit card, 23
Cassette players, personal, 58
Caswell Hotel, 93
Catamaran Cruisers, 187–88
Catherine, Queen, 205
CDs. *See* Music stores
CDW (collision-damage waiver), 51
Cecil Sharpe House, 306
Central London, 119
Ceremony of the Keys, 208
Changing of the Guard, 186, 196, 197
Chaplin, Charlie, 200
Charbonnel et Walker, 246
Charing Cross, 122
Charing Cross Road
  accommodations, 66
  shopping on, 247
Charles, Prince, 205, 206
Charles II, 205
Chaucer, Geoffrey, 211, 226
Chelsea, 124
  accommodations, 68–69, 91, 93, 106
  restaurants, 150, 151, 155, 160
  shopping in, 249, 251
Chelsea Antiques Fair, 10
Chelsea Antiques Market, 251
Chelsea Flower Show, 6, 8, 189, 228
Chelsea Kitchen, 155
Chelsea Physic Garden, *216,* 228
Chemist shops (drugstores), 329
Cherwell Boathouse Restaurant (Oxford), 318

Cherwell River, 316
Cheval Place, 249
Chez Nico at Ninety Park Lane, 155
Chiang Mai, 155
Chicago, British Tourist Authority (BTA) office in, 3
Chicago Rib Shack, 158
Childminders, 13
Children
  accommodations, 11, 75
  air travel and, 40, 41
  baby-sitting services, 13
  bus fares, 131
  information sources, 126
  legal drinking age, 138
  passports for, 49
  staying in same room with you, 30
  tips on traveling with, 11–13
  Underground fares, 129
Children's Book Centre, 251
Children's information line, 126
China, shopping for, 244, 249
Chinatown, 66
Christ Church College, *315,* 317
Christmas, 7
Christmas lights, 10
Christmas tree in Trafalgar Square, lighting ceremony of, 10
Churches, concerts at, 297
Churchill, Winston, 215
Church's, 246
Cigarettes, customs regulations on, 50
Cinema, 299
Cirrus ATM card network, 22
Citibank traveler's checks, 22
Citisights of London, 189
Citizenship, passports and proof of, 48
Cittie of Yorke, 300–301
City, The, 119
  pubs, 300–301
  restaurants, 154, 159, 162, 163, 169, 174
City codes, 7
City of London Festival, 9
Cityrama, 185–86
Clarence House, 205, 254
Claridge's, 90
Clarke's, 158
Classical music, 296–97. *See also* Concerts
Claverley Hotel, 93–94
Clink Prison Museum, *216,* 224–25
Clothing
  for air travel, 40–41
  packing tips, 56–58
  at restaurants, 139
  at theatres, 292
Clothing stores, 241, 245, 246, 249. *See also* Department stores
  vintage, 251
Clubs
  blues, 304–5
  comedy, 307–8
  dance, 305–6
  gay and lesbian, 308
  jazz, 301, 304
Cockneys, Pearly Harvest Festival, 10
Cocktail bars, tipping in, 333
Collectibles, 248
  royal, 240
Collision-damage waiver (CDW), 51
Comedy clubs, 307–8
Comedy Spot, 307–8
Comedy Store, The, 308
Complete Guide to London's West End Theatres, The, 290
Complex, The, 305
Computers, laptop, 59
Concerts
  Academy of St. Martin-in-the-Fields, 210
  at churches, 297
  classical music, 296–98
  Kenwood Lakeside, 9, 229
  The Proms, 9
  rock, 298–99
Concourse Gallery, 218
Connex South-Central train, 117
Conran, Sir Terence, 135–36
Consolidators (bucket shops), 38
Constable, 202
Continental Airlines, 334
  fly/drive packages, 52
  London City Stay package, 37
  Web site, 39
Continental Airlines Vacations, 36
Converter, currency, 59
Coronation Chair, 211
Costas Fish Restaurant, 178
Cost-cutting strategies. *See* Money-saving tips
Costume, Museum of (Bath), 314
Council Travel, 38
Country codes, 7, 332

Covent Garden, 122, *258,* 259
- accommodations, 63, 94, 96
- Christmas lights, 10
- restaurants, 161, 164, 170, 171, 178
- shopping in, 248–49
- tearooms and patisseries, 179

Covent Garden Hotel, 94
Covent Garden Market & Piazza, *193,* 197–98, 248
Crank's In London, 158
Cranley, The, 94
Credit cards, 23. *See also specific credit card companies*
- cash advances, 23
- flight insurance, 52
- for public pay phones, 332
- stolen, 25

Crescent Hotel, 94–95
Crime, 15
Crockford's, 308
Crown jewels, 208
Cruises. *See also* Boat trips
- Thames, 187–88

Culpeper the Herbalist, 248
Currency
- euro, 21
- exchange, 24, 115
- exchange rate, 21
  - traveler's checks and, 22
- exchange services (Bureaux de Change), 24–25
- units of, 20

Currency converter or transformer, 59
Curzon, 299
Customs regulations, 50, 238
Cutty Sark, 187, 231–32

D

Daily Guardian, Web site for, 3
Daily Telegraph, The, 55
Dance clubs and discos, 305–6
Dance performances, 298
- half-price ticket booth, 200

Davies Mews, 246
Davies Street, 246
Daylight saving time, 333
Day trips from London, 310–27
Dell Restaurant, 199, 261
Delta Air Lines, 334
- City Stay Vacations, 37
- fly/drive packages, 52
- Web site, 39

Delta Dream Vacations, 36
Dentists, 328
Department stores, 239–40
- restaurants at, 178–79

Departure tax, 331–32
Design Museum, *216,* 221
Devonshire Arms, 159
Diana, Princess, 68, 199, 202, 203, 206, 211, 227, 239, 240, 305
Dickens, Charles, 211, 220
Dickens' House Museum, *216,* 220
Dickens Inn by the Tower, 159
Diners Club, 23
Diplomat Hotel, 95
Directory assistance, 332
Disabilities, travelers with, 15–18
- accommodations, 92
- information and advice for, 15–16
- sightseeing, 191

Disabled Guide to London's Theatres, The, 16
Discos, 305–6
- gay, 308

Discounts, 30. *See also* Money-saving tips
- accommodations, 71, 72
- on car rentals, 51
- for disabled persons, 18
- half-price ticket booth for performing arts, 200
- sales, 237
- for senior citizens, 13–14
- sightseeing, 194

Disney Store, The, 244
Doctors, 53, 54, 328–29
Doctor's Call, 328
Doorpersons, tipping, 29
Dorchester, The, 90
Dorset Square Hotel, 95
Downing Street, 265
D'Oyly Carte Gilbert & Sullivan company, 298
Dr. Marten's Department Store, 249
Drake, Sir Francis, 226
Dress Circle, 246
Drinking age, legal, 138
Driver's license, 51
Drugstores (chemist shops), 237, 329
DSP-82, 49
Dukes (Stratford-upon-Avon), 323–24
Durrants Hotel, 95–96
Duty-free shopping at airports, 237–38

E

Earl's Court, 19, 124
accommodations, 69–70, 86, 103
Easter, 7
Eastman Dental Hospital, 328
Ebury Wine Bar, 159–60
Ed's Easy Diner, 160, 224
Edward Lear Hotel, 96
Edwards & Edwards Globaltickets, 285–86, 295
Edward the Confessor, 198
Egyptian mummies, 195
Eisenhower, Dwight D., 325
Elderhostel, 14
Electricity, 58–59, 329
Electronics, 58
Electronic Telegraph, 55
Elgin Marbles, 195
Elizabeth I, 211
Elizabeth II, 3, 9, 196, 230, 239
at State Opening of Parliament, 10
Embassies & high commissions, 329
Emergencies
legal, 330
number for, 53
police or medical, 330
Emergency hospital care, 53
English House, 160
English National Opera, 296
Entertainment. *See* Nightlife and entertainment
Epicurious Travel, 39
Equinox, 305
Eros, statue of, 204
Euro, 21
Eurocard, 23
Europa House Hotel, 96
Evan Evans, 187
Evening Standard, 56
Everything Left Handed, 244
Exchange rate, 21
Expo Garden Tours, 189
Extravaganza in Chelsea, 189

F

FA Cup Final, 8
Fall in London, 6
Families, 11–13
Family Travel Times, 11
Farlows, 241
Fashion. *See* Clothing stores
Fast-food restaurants, 11
FastTrain, 39, 116
Fawkes, Guy, 10
Fenwick of Bond Street, 240
Festivals and special events, 8–10
Fielding Hotel, 96–97
Fifth Floor at Harvey Nichols, 178–79
Film, London Film Festival, 10
Filofax Centre, The, 245
Financial Times, Web site for, 4
Fireworks, 10
First Call, 286, 295
First Option Hotel Reservations, 76
Fish-and-chips, 177–78
Five Sumner Place, 97
Flask Walk, 229
Fleet Street, 119
Flower Show, Chelsea, 8, 189, 228
Fly/drive packages, 52
Flying Wheels Travel, 16–17
Folk music, 306
Food For Thought, 161
Football Association FA Cup Final, 8
Form DSP-11, 47
Form DSP-82, 47
Forte and Le Meridien Hotels & Resorts, 36, 334
Fortnum & Mason, 239
restaurants at, 161, 178, 180, 259
Founders Arms, The, 161–62
Fountain, The, 259
Fountain Restaurant, The, 161, 180
Four Seasons Hotel, 90
Fox & Anchor, 162
Franzus Corporation, 59–60
Frommer's books on London, 4
Fryer's Delight, 178
Full fare, 37

G

G.A.Y., 308
Gallery, The, 97
Gardening Club, 308
Gate Hotel, The, 97–98
Gatwick Airport, 39
arriving at, 116, 117
Gatwick Express, 40
Gay Hussar, The, 162
Gay London Guide, 19
Gays and lesbians, 18–19
cafe-bars, 138
clubs and discos, 308
hotels and B&Bs, 69
Silver Moon Women's Bookshop, 247
Summer Rites, 10
walking tour, 189
Gay Times, 19
Gay Village, 19, 66, 122
Gay Walk, 189
Geales, 178
George, The, 162–63
George III, 228
George & Vulture, The, 163

Georgian Restaurant, The, 181
"Ghosts, Ghouls & Ancient Taverns" tour, 186
Gibbs, James, 210
Gieves & Hawkes, 245
Giovanni's Sandwich Bar, 177
Globe Cafe, The, 226
Globe Restaurant, The, 226
Globe Theatre & Exhibition, Shakespeare's, 225
Golden Hinde, 178, *216,* 226
Golden Nugget, 308
Golden Tours, 187
Goodge Street, 66
Gore, The, 98
Gourmet Pizza Company, 163, 259
Granary, The, 163–64
Grand Circle Travel, 14
Grand Tour, The, 185
Great Fire of London, 227
Green Park, 133, 205
  picnicking in, 182
Green Route, 186
Green Village Restaurant (Greenwich), 233
Greenwich, 231–33
Greenwich Mean Time, 333
Greenwich Park, 232
Greenwich Tourist Information Centre, 233
Grey, Lady Jane, 208
Grosvenor Square, 67
Guided Tour, The, 17
Guided tours, 184–87
Guide Friday Tourism Center (Stratford-upon-Avon), 320
Guildhall, *216,* 218
Guy Fawkes Night, 10

H

Häagen-Dazs, 181–82
Hairdressers, tipping, 29, 333
Hair dryer, 60
Halcyon Hotel, 90
Hall, John and Susanna, 322
Hall's Croft (Stratford-upon-Avon), *321,* 322
Hamleys, 244, 249
Hammersmith Mall, 8
Hampstead Heath, 229
Hampton Court Palace, 230
Hanover Grand, 306
Hanson, Duane, 219
Hard Rock Cafe, 164
Hardy, Thomas, 211, 219
Harlingford Hotel, 98
Harper's Restaurant (Salisbury), 327
Harrington Hall, 98–99
Harrods, 124, 261
  Georgian Restaurant, 181
  sales, 237
  shopping at, 239
Harrods Famous Deli Counter, 178
Harrods Ice Cream Parlour & Crêperie, 182
Hart House Hotel, 99
Harvey Nichols (Harvey Nicks), Fifth Floor at Harvey Nichols, 178–79, 239
Hatchards, 241
Hathaway, Anne Cottage (Stratford-upon-Avon), 320
Hawking, Stephen, 222
Hayward Gallery, *216,* 218–19
Hazlitt's 1718, 99
Health, 53–54
  disabled persons, 18
  mad-cow disease, 54
Health insurance, 53, 54
Heathrow Airport, 39
  arriving at, 114–16
Heaven, 308
Hempel, The, 90
Henry VII chapel, 211
Henry VIII, 205, 230
Hertz, 52
High commissions, 329
High tea, 180
Hilton International, 36, 334
Hippodrome, 305
Hirst, Damien, 219
Historical Walks of London, 189
Hogarth, William, 200, 221
Holborn, 122
Holiday Care Service, 16
Holidays, 7
  bank, 7
  school, 7
Holland Park, accommodations, 69
Holland Park Theatre, 296
Holmes, Sherlock, 123
Holy Trinity Church (Stratford-upon-Avon), *321,* 322
Horatio, Viscount Nelson, 210
Horse Guards, 265
Horse Guards Building, 197
Horse Guards Parade, 265
Hospitals, 53, 330
Hotel 167, 99–100
Hotelink, 116
Hotel La Place, 100
Hotel Russell, 100
Hotels. *See* Accommodations
Hot lines, 330

Household details, checklist of, 59
Household goods, 251
House of Commons, 198
House of Lords, 198
Houses of Parliament, *193,* 198, 263, *264, 266*
Howard, Catherine, 208
How To Travel (A Guidebook for Persons with a Disability), 15–16
Hunter, John, 200
Hyatt, 36
Hyatt Carlton Tower, 90
Hyatt Hotels and Resorts, 334
Hyde Park, 12, 133, 198–99, *260,* 261
  picnicking in, 182

I

IAMAT (International Association of Medical Assistance to Travelers), 54
Ice-cream parlors, 181–82
Icelandair, 334
  Web site, 39
Illnesses, 53–54
IMAX 3-D Cinema, 224
Imperial War Museum, *216,* 218
Indian restaurants, 136, 151, 154, 167
Information sources, 2–4, 125–26
  on weekly London events, 8
Insurance
  automobile, 51
  health, 52, 53, 54
  travel, 35, 52–53
Inter-Continental Hotels and Resorts, 36, 334
International Association of Medical Assistance to Travelers (IAMAT), 54
International Certificate of Vaccination, 50
Internet, the. *See* Web sites
Irish embassy, 329
Irish Linen Company, 245
Irish Shop, The, 249
Italian Gardens, 199
ITT Sheraton, 36
Ivanhoe Suites Hotel, 100
Ivy, The, 164

J

Jack the Ripper, 186, 201
James House/Cartref House, 101
Jazz Café, 304
Jazz clubs, 301, 304
Jellied eels, 181
Jenkins Hotel, 101
Jermyn Street, 241*, 258*
Jet lag, 41
Jewel House, 198
Jewelry, 251
Joe Allen, 164–65
Johnson, Samuel, 57
Jubilee Gardens, 264, *264*
Jubilee Market, 248
Jubilee Walkway, 125, 133

K

Katharine Hamnett, 249
Keith Prowse/Firstcall, 8, 55, 286
Kemwel Holiday Autos, 52
Ken Lo's Memories of China, 165
Kennard Hotel (Bath), 314
Kenning, 17
Kensington, 124
  accommodations, 69, 86, 91, 106
  restaurants, 159, 167
  shopping in, 251
Kensington Church Street, 251
Kensington Gardens, 12, 199, *267,* 267
  picnicking in, 182
Kensington High Street, 251
Kensington Palace, *193,* 199–200, 267, *267*
Kenwood, 229
Kenwood Lakeside Concerts, 9, 229, 297–98
Kew Gardens (Royal Botanic Gardens), 228–29
Kew Palace, 228
Kids. *See* Children
Kidsline, 126
Knightsbridge, 123–24
  accommodations, 68, 93–94, 101
  restaurants, 158, 168, 171, 173, 174, 181
  shopping in, 240, 249
  tearoom, 179
Knightsbridge Hotel, 101
Knitwear, shopping for, 244, 245, 249

L

Ladbroke Arms, 301
Landing card, 115
Landmark London, 102
Lanesborough, The, 181
Langan's Bistro, 165–66
Langham Hilton, The, 90
Laptop computers, 59
Lawleys, 244
Legal emergencies, 330

Leicester Square, 122, *193,* 200, 256, 259
  accommodations, 66
  restaurants, 154, 163, 166, 173, 181
  shopping in, 246–47
Leicester Square Gardens, 200
Le Pont de la Tour, 166
Lesbians, 18–19
Liberty PLC, 239–40
Liberty Travel, 36
Library, The, 307
Lilley & Skinners, 245
Lillian Baylis Theatre, 298
Lillie Langtry Bar, 307
Limelight, 306
Lime Tree Hotel, 102
Linens, shopping for, 245, 249, 251
Liquor laws, 330
L'Odeon, 166
Lodging. *See* Accommodations
London Aquarium, *216,* 222
London A to Z, 118
London Bed and Breakfast Agency Limited, The, 76
London Brass Rubbing Centre, 210
London City Airport, 40, 117
London Coliseum, 298
London Dungeon, *216,* 225
London Film Festival, 10
London *Financial Times,* Web site for, 4
London for Less discount card, 194
London Marathon, 8
London Parade, 8
London Planetarium, *216,* 222
London Planner, 8, 285, 294–95
London Pride Sightseeing, 185
London Pub Walks, 189
London Symphony Orchestra, 218, 296
London Tourist Board, Visitorcall, 8
London Transport Museum, *216,* 223
London Transport Unit for Disabled Passengers, 17
London Walks, 188
London Waterbus Co., 201
London Zoo, *193,* 200–201
Lord Mayor's Coach, 202
Lord Mayor's Show, 10
Lost luggage insurance, 52
Luggage. *See also* Packing
  carry-on, 58
  stolen or lost, 52
Lumiere, 299
Luton Airport, 40, 117

M

MacDonald House, 329
Madame Jo-Jo's, 308
Madame Tussaud's, 123, *193,* 201–2
Mad-cow disease, 54
Magazines, gay, 19
Magdalen College, *315,* 317
Maggie Jones, 167
Magna Carta, 195, 219, 325
Mail, 330
Main Post Office, 331
Mall, The, 205, 254
Manze's, 181
Map House, 249
Maps
  Braille, 17
  bus, 130
  London A to Z, 118
  shopping for, 247, 249
  Underground, 119, 128
Margaret, Princess, 69, 199
Marks & Spencer, 240
Mary Arden's House & the Shakespeare Countryside Museum, *321,* 322–23
Mary I, 211
Marylebone, 122–23
  accommodations, 68, 92, 95, 96, 99, 100, 102
  patisserie, 179
  restaurants, 168, 178, 181
Mary Queen of Scots, 211
MasterCard, 23
  emergency number, 25
  traveler's checks for, 22
Mature Traveler, The, 14
May Day, 7
Mayfair, 122
  accommodations, 67, 100, 103
  restaurants, 155, 164, 169
MDC Classic Music, 247
Meat pies, 181
Medic Alert identification tag, 53
Medical Express, 328–29
Medical insurance, 52, 53, 54
Medications, for disabled persons, 18
Merton College, *315,* 317
Microsoft Expedia Travel, 38
Millennium, 7
Millennium Dome, 232
Mobility International USA, 15

Modern British cuisine, 136
Money, 20–31. *See also* Budgeting; Currency
  ATMs, 22–23
  changing, 24–25
Money-saving tips. *See also* Discounts
  accommodations, 67
  off-season, 5
Monument, The, *216,* 227
Moonlight World, 200
More, Sir Thomas, 208
Mounted Guard Changing Ceremony, 197
Movies, 299
Murder One, 247
Museum of Costume (Bath), 314
Museum of London, *193,* 202
Museum of Mankind, *216,* 223
Museum of the Moving Image, *216,* 223
Museums and galleries
  Ashmoleon Museum (Oxford), *315,* 316, 318
  Bank of England Museum, *216,* 220
  Barbican Centre, *216,* 218
  Bethnal Green Museum of Childhood, *216,* 222
  Bramah Tea and Coffee Museum, *216,* 221
  British Museum, *193,* 195, *260*
  cafes and restaurants at, 176–77
  Clink Prison Museum, *216,* 224–25
  Design Museum, *216,* 221
  Dickens' House Museum, *216,* 220
  Hayward Gallery, *216,* 218–19
  Imperial War Museum, *216,* 218
  London Transport Museum, *216,* 223
  Madame Tussaud's, *193,* 201
  National Gallery, *193,* 202–3, *255, 257, 258*
  National Maritime Museum, 232
  National Portrait Gallery, *193,* 203, *258*
  Natural History Museum, *193,* 203, *267*
  Roman Baths Museum (Bath), 312
  Royal Academy of Arts, 219
  Saatchi Gallery, *216,* 219
  Science Museum, *193,* 204–5
  Sir John Soane's Museum, *216,* 221–22
  Tate Gallery of Modern Art, *193,* 207, *264*
  Theatre Museum, *216,* 222
  Victoria and Albert Museum, *193,* 211
  White Card, 194
Museum Street Café, 167, 260
Music
  blues, 304–5
  British Music Information Centre, 295
  classical, 296–97
  folk, 306
  jazz, 301, 304
  opera, 295–96
Music stores (records and CDs), 241, 246, 247
Mutual of Omaha, 53

N

Nanny Service, 13
Nash, John, 205
Nash's House (Stratford-upon-Avon), 320, *321,* 322
National Council of Senior Citizens, 13
National Film Theatre, 299
National Gallery, *193,* 202–3, 254, *255,* 256, *257*
  Brasserie at, 177
National Maritime Museum, 232
National Passport Information Center, 49
National Portrait Gallery, *193,* 203, *258,* 259
Natural History Museum, *193,* 203–4, 266, *267*
Neal's Yard Remedies, 248
Neighborhoods
  for accommodations, 118, 119–25
  for restaurants, 137
Nelson, Viscount (Lord) Horatio, 206, 210
Nelson's Column, 210
New College (Oxford), *315,* 318
New Inn & Old House, The (Salisbury), 327
New Place (Stratford-upon-Avon), 320, *321*
New Scotland Yard, 330

Newspapers, for current theatre listings, 285
Newspapers and magazines, 330
Newton, Sir Isaac, 200
New Year's Eve, 10
New York, British Tourist Authority (BTA) office in, 2–3
New Zealand
  British Tourist Authority (BTA) office in, 3
  high commission of, 329
  long-distance access codes, 332
Night buses, 131
Nightlife and entertainment
  bars, 307
  budgeting and, 28–29
  clubs
    blues, 304–5
    comedy, 307–8
    dance, 305–6
    gay and lesbian, 308
    jazz, 301, 304
  music
    blues, 304–5
    British Music Information Centre, 295
    classical, 296–97
    folk, 306
    jazz, 301, 304
    opera, 295–96
  performing arts, 294–99
    current listings, 55–56, 294
    tickets, 295
  planning, 281–82
  pubs, 300–301
    eating in, 138
    tipping in, 333
    walking tours of, 189
  theatre, 284–93
    booking seats, 285–87
    The Complete Guide to London's West End Theatres, 290
    current listings, 285
    curtain times, 292
    dinner before or after, 292–93
    dressing for, 292
    etiquette, 292
    on the fringe, 291
    half-price ticket booth, 200, 287
    package tours, 37, 288
    reservations, 54–55
    scalpers, 288
    stalls, 292
    standby seats, 286
    ticket agencies, 285–87
    Web sites, 285
    West End (Theatreland), 287–90
Nonsmoking rooms, 74–75
Noor Jahan, 167
North Sea Fish Restaurant, 168, 178
Northwest Airlines, 334
  Web site, 39
Northwest Airlines Vacations, 36
Notting Hill, 125
  accommodations, 70, 86, 97
  restaurants, 158, 178
  shopping in, 251–52
Notting Hill Carnival, 10
Number Sixteen, 102

O

Oak Room Lounge, 180
Odeon Marble Arch, 299
Odin's, 168
Office, The, 306
Official London Theatre Guide, The, 287
Off-season, 4, 5, 29, 36
Old Compton Street, 19
Olde Mitre, 301
Old Operating Theatre and Herb Garret, *216,* 220–21
Old Royal Observatory (Greenwich), 232
1-800-FLY-4-LESS, 38
1-800-FLY-CHEAP, 38
101 Tips for the Mature Traveler, 14
Opera, 295–96
  half-price ticket booth, 200
Opposition (Stratford-upon-Avon), 324
Orangery, The, 200, 267
Oratory, The, 168, 267
Orientation tours, 185–87
Original London Sightseeing Tours, 186
Oxford, 314–19
Oxford and Cambridge Boat Race, 8
Oxford Story, *315,* 318
Oxford Street, 241, *260,* 261
  Christmas lights, 10
  shopping on, 245–46
Oxford University, 314
Oxo Tower Brasserie, 169

P

Package tours, 26, 30
  peak season vs. off-season, 36
  pros and cons of, 35
  sample prices, 36–37

selecting, 35–36
theatre, 288
Packing, 56–58
Paddington, 125
accommodations, 70, 87, 96
PAI (personal accident insurance), 51
Palaces
Buckingham Palace, 9, 123, 186, *193,* 196, *255, 257*
Hampton Court Palace, 230
Kensington Palace, *193,* 199–200
Kew Palace, 228
St. James's Palace, 205
Pall Mall, 205, 256, *257*
Palm Court at the Waldorf Meridien, 181
Palm Court Lounge, 180
Parking, 50
disability parking stickers, 17
Park Lane Hotel, 103
Parks and gardens, 133
Chelsea Physic Garden, *216,* 228
Green Park, 205
Hyde Park, 198–99, *260*
Jubilee Gardens, 264, *264*
Kensington Gardens, 199
Magdalen College botanic garden (Oxford), 317
Regent's Park, 204
Royal Botanic Gardens (Kew Gardens), 228
St. James's Park, 205, 254, *255*
Parliament, State Opening of, 10
Parliament, Houses of, *193,* 198, 263, *264, 266*
Passport Control, 115
Passports, 46–50, 115
applying for or renewing, 47–49
for children 14 to 18 years of age, 49
lost, 50
Pasta restaurants, 163, 169, 181
Patio, The, 259, 161
Patisserie Cappucetto, 179
Patisserie Deux Amis, 180
Patisserie Française, 180
Patisseries, 179–80
Patisserie Valerie, 179, 180
Peak season, 4–5, 36
Pearly Harvest Festival, 10
Pence (p), 20
Penhaligon's, 248
Pepsi Trocadero, 204, *216,* 224
Performing arts, 294–99
current listings, 55–56, 294
tickets, 295
Perfumes, 248
Personal accident insurance (PAI), 51
Peter Jones, 251
Peter Pan, statue of, 199
Philbeach Hotel, 103–4
Phone calls
from hotel rooms, 73
from the U.S., 7, 63
Phonecards, 332
Piccadilly (street), shopping on, 241
Piccadilly Circus, 122, *193,* 204, *258,* 259
accommodations, 66, 104
restaurants, 154, 163, 166, 173
Picnics, 12, 182
Pierre Victoire (Bath), 314
Pimlico, 123
Pippa Pop-ins, 13
Pit, The, 290
Pizza Express, 304
Pizza on the Dock, 159
Pizza on the Park, 304
Pizza restaurants, 163, 169
Pizzeria Condotti, 169
Place, The, 298
Planetarium, London, 222–23
Planet Hollywood, 224
Ploughman's lunch, 138
PLUS ATM card network, 22
Poets' Corner, 211
Police, 330
reporting stolen credit cards to, 26
Poons in the City, 169–70, 262
Porters, tipping, 29
Porter's English Restaurant, 170
Portobello Market, 251–52
Portobello Road, 125
Postal areas, 118
Post offices, 331
Pound sterling (£), 20. *See also* Currency
Prime meridian line, 232
Proms, The, 9, 297
Pubs, 300–301
eating in, 138
tipping in, 333
walking tours of, 189
Pugin, A.W.N., 198
Pulteney Bridge (Bath), 314
Pump Room (Bath), 312, 313
Purcell Room, 296

Q

Quaglino's, 170
Queen. *See* Elizabeth II
Queen Charlotte's Cottage, 228
Queen Elizabeth Hall, 296, 298
Queen Mary's Rose Garden, 204
Queen's Gallery, 196, 197, 256
Queen's House (Greenwich), 232
Queens' Walk, 263
QX (magazine), 19

R

R. S. Hispaniola, 170–71
Rack rate, 70–71
RADAR (Royal Association for Disability and Rehabilitation), 16
Radcliffe Camera, *315,* 317
Radio, 331
Railair Coach Link, 118
Rail Travel for Disabled Passengers, 17
Rainfall, average, 6
Rainforest Cafe, 224
Raleigh, Sir Walter, 203, 208
Rape Crisis Line, 330
Raphael, 211
Red Lion Public House, 265
Regency Hotel, The, 104
Regent Milk Bar, 182
Regent Palace Hotel, 104
Regent's Park, 122, 204
Regent's Park Open Air Theatre, 291
Regent Street, 241
  Christmas lights, 10
  shopping on, 244–45
Reject China Shop, 249
Rembrandt, 202
Reservations
  hotel, 7, 62
  performing arts, 54–55
  restaurant, 54–55
Restaurants, 134–82
  Bayswater, 173
  Bloomsbury, 181
  British, 154, 159–65, 167, 170–74
  cafes, 139
  for celebrity spotting, 163
  Chelsea, 150, 151, 155, 160
  Chinese, 165, 169
  The City, 154, 159, 162, 163, 169, 174
  cost-cutting strategies, 30
  Covent Garden, 161, 164, 170, 171, 178
  department store, 178–79
  fast-food, 11
  fish-and-chips, 177–78
  French, 150, 151, 155, 164, 165, 166, 169, 170, 173
  gay cafe-bars, 138
  Hungarian, 162
  ice-cream parlors, 181–82
  index of
    by cuisine, 145, 148, 150
    by location, 142, 144
    by price, 144
  Indian, 136, 151, 154, 167
  International, 155, 159, 166, 168
  Italian, 171, 174
  Japanese, 174
  Kensington, 159, 167
  kid-friendly, 11–12, 154
  Knightsbridge, 158, 168, 171, 173, 174, 181
  Leicester Square, 181
  Marylebone, 168, 178, 181
  Mayfair, 155, 164, 169
  mealtimes, 139
  Modern British, 159, 161, 167, 168, 314
  Modern European, 151, 158, 170
  at museums and galleries, 176–77
  with music, 306
  neighborhoods for, 137
  North American, 160, 164
  with no-smoking sections, 137
  Notting Hill, 158, 178
  Oxford, 318
  pasta, 163, 169, 181
  Piccadilly Circus/Leicester Square, 154, 163, 166, 173
  pizza/pasta, 163, 169
  price ranges, 137, 142
  pubs, 138
  reservations, 54–55
  St. James's, 161, 163, 170
  sandwich bars, 177
  service charges and tipping at, 139, 333
  set-price menus, 137–38
  for soaking up "the scene," 173
  Soho, 150, 155, 158, 160, 162, 164, 174
  South Bank, 161, 166, 169

South Kensington, 151, 167
The Strand, 162, 170, 171–72
Stratford-upon-Avon, 324
Thai, 155, 173
before or after theatre, 292
unfamiliar terms on menus, 140
VAT (value-added tax), 139
vegetarian, 158, 161
with a view, 169
Westminster/Victoria, 159, 165, 172
wheelchair-accessible, 18
wine bars, 138
Rest rooms, 331
Revenue Canada, 238
Reynolds, Sir Joshua, 200, 202
Richard III, 208
Richoux tearooms, 179
Ritz Palm Court, afternoon tea, 180
River cruises, 187–88
Riverside Studios, 298
River Thames, 119
Rock Circus, *216,* 224
Rock clubs, 305
Rock concerts, 298–99
Rock Garden, 305
Rock & Sole Plaice, 178
Rodin, Auguste, 263
Roll Around Britain, 17
Roman Baths Museum (Bath), 312
Ronnie Scott's, 301
Rosetta Stone, 195
Rotten Row, 198
Royal Academy of Arts, *216,* 219
Royal Academy Summer Exhibition, 9
Royal Albert Hall, 297, 299
The Proms at, 9
Royal Arcade, The, 246
Royal Association for Disability and Rehabilitation (RADAR), 16
Royal Ballet, 298
Royal Botanic Gardens (Kew Gardens), 228–29
Royal Ceremonial Dress Collection, 199
Royal Chapels, 211
Royal Crescent (Bath), 314
Royal Festival Hall, 296
Royal Free Hospital, 330
Royal Mews, 196, 197, 256
Royal National Theatre, 290–91
Royal Naval College, 232
Royal Opera, Web site, 56
Royal Opera House, The, 295–96
Royal Philharmonic Orchestra, 296
Royal River Thames Cruise, 188
Royal Shakespeare Company, 218, 290
Royal Shakespeare Theatre (Stratford-upon-Avon), 319, *321,* 323
Royal Tournament, 9
Rules restaurant, 171
Russell Square, 66

S

Saatchi Gallery, *216,* 219
Sadler's Wells, 298
Safety, 15
SAGA International Holidays, 14
St. Giles in the Barbican, 297
St. James Garlickhythe, 297
St. James Restaurant, 161, 180
St. James's, 123
accommodations, 67, 82, 86
patisserie, 180
restaurants, 161, 163, 170
St. James's Palace, 205, 254
St. James's Park, 205, 254, *255*
picnicking in, 182
St. James's Square, 256
St. Margaret's Westminster, 264, *264,* 297
St. Martin-in-the-Fields, *193,* 210, 254, 298
St. Patrick's Day, 8
St. Paul's Cathedral, *193,* 205–7, *262,* 263
St. Peter's Eaton Square, 297
Sales, 5, 237
Salisbury, 324–27
accommodations and restaurants, 326–27
Salisbury Cathedral, 325
Salisbury Haunch of Venison, 327
Samaritans, 330
Sandwich bars, 177
San Lorenzo, 171
Savoy, The, 104–5
Savoy Grill, The, 171–72
Scalpers, 288
School holidays, 7
Science Museum, *193,* 204–5, 266, *267*
Scotch House, 244
Screen on Baker Street, 299
Seafresh Fish Restaurant, 178
Sea-Shell, 178
Seeing Eye dogs, 16
Segaworld, 224

Select Travel Service, 189
Self-catering units, 30
Selfridges department store, 126, 240
Senior citizens, 13–15
 accommodations, 75
SeniorsSearch—U.K., 75
Serpentine Gallery, 199
Serpentine lake, 198
Service charge, at restaurants, 139
Seven Stars, 301
Shakespeare, William, 200, 203, 208, 219, 226, 291
 Stratford-upon-Avon sights and attractions, 319–24, 322
  Anne Hathaway's Cottage, 320
  Birthplace, 319–20, *321*
  Hall's Croft, *321*, 322
  Holy Trinity Church, 322
  Mary Arden's House & the Shakespeare Countryside Museum, *321*, 322–23
  Nash's House, 320, *321*, 322
  New Place, 320, 322
  Shakespeare Centre, 320
Shakespeare Birthplace Trust, 322
Shakespeare Centre (Stratford-upon-Avon), 320, *321*
Shakespeare Countryside Museum, Mary Arden's House & the, *321*, 322–23
Shakespeare's Globe Theatre & Exhibition, *216*, 225, 291
Sheldonian Theatre, *315*, 317
Shepherd's, 172
Sheraton Hotels & Resorts, 334
Shipping goods from London, 235
Shopping, 234–52
 bargains, 235
 budgeting and, 28–29
 customs regulations and, 238
 department stores, 239–40
 drugstores, 237
 duty-free, at airports, 237–38
 hours, 235
 sales, 237
 shoes, 245, 246, 249
 VAT (value-added tax) refunds, 235–37
Short hop ticket, 131
Sights and attractions, 190–233
 for art lovers, 218–19
 disabled persons and, 18
 Greenwich, 231–32
 Hampstead, 229
 for history buffs, 215–18
 index of
  by location, 191
  by type of attraction, 194
 literary, 219–20
 palaces. *See* Palaces
 parks and gardens. *See* Parks and gardens
 Shakespeare, 225–26
 ships, 226, 231–32
 top sights, 195–213
 worksheet, 190–91, 213
Silver Moon Women's Bookshop, 247
Simpson's-in-the-Strand, 172
Sir John Soane's Museum, *216*, 221–22
606 Club, 304
Sloane Rangers, 68
Sloane Street, 249
 shopping on, 249, 251
Smoking, 331
Soane, Sir John, Museum, 221–22
Soaps and toiletries, 248
Sobell Pavilion for Apes and Monkeys, 200
Soccer, Football Association FA Cup Final, 8
Society for the Advancement of Travel for the Handicapped, 16
Society of London Theatres, 16, 287
Society of Ticket Agents and Retailers (STAR), 287
Soho, 122, 256, *257*
 accommodations, 66, 99
 restaurants, 150, 155, 158, 160, 162, 164, 174
 shopping in, 248
 tearooms and patisseries, 179
South Bank, 119, 125, 264
 picnicking in, 182
 restaurants, 161, 166, 169
South Bank Centre, 264, *264*, 290, 296
South Kensington, 124
 accommodations, 69, 87, 90, 94, 97, 98, 99, 102, 104, 105

Canadian Muffin Company, 180
museums, 266
restaurants, 151, 167
Southwark, *262,* 263
walking tour, 189
Southwark Cathedral, *216,* 225–26, 297
Souvenirs, 30
Spaghetti House, 181
Speaker's Corner, 199, 261
Special events and festivals, 8–10
Spencer House, *216,* 227
Sporting events, London Marathon, 8
Sportsman Club, 308
Spring in London, 5–6
Stanfords, 247
Stansted, 40
Stansted airport, 117
Stansted Express Train, 40
State Apartments, 199
State Opening of Parliament, 10
State Rooms of Buckingham Palace, 256
Stationery stores, 245
Stationlink, 17
Steinberg & Tolkien, 251
Stepping Out, 189
Stockpot, The, 173
Stonehenge, 326
Strand, The, 122
accommodations, 63, 104–5
restaurants, 162, 170, 171–72
Stranger's Gallery, 198
Stratford-upon-Avon, 319–24
accommodations, 323–24
guided tours, 320
restaurants, 324
Shakespeare sights, 319–24, 322
Anne Hathaway's Cottage, 320
Birthplace, 319–20, *321*
Hall's Croft, *321,* 322
Holy Trinity Church, 322
Mary Arden's House & the Shakespeare Countryside Museum, *321,* 322–23
Nash's House, 320, *321,* 322
New Place, 320, 322
Shakespeare Centre, 320
tourist information, 319
traveling to, 319
Summer, 6
Summer Rites, 10
Sunday Times, The, 56
Web site for, 4
Sutton Hoo Treasure, 195
Swiss House Hotel, 105
Sydney (Australia), British Tourist Authority (BTA) office in, 3

T

Tate Gallery, *193,* 207, 263, *264*
Tate Gallery of Modern Art, 207
Tate Gallery Restaurant, 177, 263
Taxes, 331–32. *See also* VAT (value-added tax)
Taxi and minicab drivers, tipping, 29, 333
Taxis, 132
from Gatwick, 117
from Heathrow, 116
Tea
afternoon, 180–81
high, 180
Tearooms, 179–81
Telephone, 332
Telephone calls, 332
from the U.S., 7, 63
Temperatures, average, 6
Tennis, Wimbledon Lawn Tennis Championships, 9
Thames, cruises, 187–88
Thames Festival, 10
Thameslink, 117
Theatre, 284–93
booking seats, 285–87
The Complete Guide to London's West End Theatres, 290
current listings, 285
curtain times, 292
dinner before or after, 292–93
dressing for, 292
etiquette, 292
on the fringe, 291
half-price ticket booth, 200, 287
package tours, 37, 288
reservations, 54–55
scalpers, 288
stalls, 292
standby seats, 286
ticket agencies, 285–87
Web sites, 285
West End (Theatreland), 287–90
Theatre Direct International (TDI), 287
Theatreland. *See* West End, theatres
Theatre Museum, *216,* 222
Theatre packages, 37, 288
Thistle Hotels Worldwide, 36, 334

Ticket agencies, 55
  theatre, 285–87
Ticketmaster, 286, 295
Tiddy Dols, 306
Time, 24-hour clock, 114
Time Out, 19, 55, 126, 294
  for theatre listings, 285
  Web site for, 3
Times, The, 56
  Web site for, 4
Time zones, 333
Tipping, 29, 333
  at restaurants, 139
Toiletries, for long flights, 41
Tophams Belgravia, 105
Toronto, British Tourist Authority (BTA) office in, 3
Tottenham Court Road, 66
Tour guides, tipping, 333
Tourist information, 125–26
Tourist Information Centres
  Bath, 312
  London, 76, 125–26
  Salisbury, 324
Tourist offices, 2–3
Tourist seasons, 4–5
Tours
  for disabled travelers, 16–17
  escorted, 34–35
  garden, 189
  guided, 184–87
    The Oxford Story, 318
    Stratford-upon-Avon, 320
  orientation, 185–87
  package, 26, 30
    peak season vs. off-season, 36
    pros and cons of, 35
    sample prices, 36–37
    selecting, 35–36
    theatre, 288
  for seniors, 14
  walking. *See* Walking tours
Tower Bridge Experience, *216,* 227, *262,* 263
Tower Green, 208
Tower Hill, 223–24
Tower Hill Pageant, *216,* 224
Tower of London, 119, *193,* 208–9, 262, *262*
Tower Records, 241
Toys
  Bethnal Green Museum of Childhood, 222
  shopping for, 244
Trafalgar Square, *193,* 210, 254, *255, 258,* 265, *266*
  Christmas tree lighting ceremony, 10
Train travel
  to Bath, 312
  to Oxford, 316
  passes, 310
  to Salisbury, 324
  Stansted Express Train, 117
  to Stratford-upon-Avon, 319
Transit information, 333
Transportation
  buses, 130–31
    from Heathrow, 115–16
    from London City Airport, 117
    night, 131
    to Stratford-upon-Avon, 319
  cost of, 28
  taxis, 132
    from Gatwick, 117
    from Heathrow, 116
  trains. *See* Train travel
  Underground. *See* Underground
Transport Museum, London, 223
Trans World Airlines, 334
Trans World Airlines (TWA) Getaway Vacations, 36
  London Theatre Week package, 37
  Web site, 39
Travel agencies
  for families with children, 11
  for seniors, 14
Travel agents, 32
  accommodations rates and, 71
Travelcards, 127, 129
Traveler's checks, 21–22, 24
  replacement, 25–26
Travel Guard International, 53
Travel Information Service, 15, 16
Travel insurance, 35, 52–53
Travel Insured International, 53
Travelocity, 38
Trip cancellation insurance, 52
Tripscope, 16
Trooping the Colour, 9
Turf Tavern, The (Oxford), 318–19
Turner, J. M. W., 202
Tussaud, Madame, 123
22 Jermyn Street, 82, 86, 103
TWYCH (Travel With Your Children), 11

U

Underground, 127–30
automated entry and exit gates, 129
to/from Heathrow, 114
maps and timetables, 119, 127, 128
tickets, 129
carnets, 130
Travelcards, 127, 129
Underworld, 305
United Airlines, 36, 334
fly/drive packages, 52
Web site, 39
United States embassy, 329
Universal Aunts, 13
University College Hospital, 330
U.S. Customs Service, 238
U.S. Passport & Citizenship Unit, 329

V

VAT (value-added tax), 29
for accommodations, 73
refund, 235–37
at restaurants, 139
Vecchia Milano, 181
Venom Club/The Zoo Bar, 306
Veronica's, 173
Vicarage Private Hotel, 106
Victoria, restaurants, 159, 165, 172
Victoria, Queen of England, 199
Victoria and Albert Museum, *193,* 211, 222, 266, *267*
Victoria Station, accommodations near, 67
Victoria Tower Gardens, 263
Virgin Atlantic Airways, 334
Web site, 39
Virgin Atlantic Vacations, 36
Virgin Megastore, 246
Visa, 23
emergency number, 25
traveler's checks, 22
Visas, 50
Visitorcall, 8, 126
Visitors Sightseeing Tours, 186
Vivienne Westwood, 246
Vong, 173–74

W

Wagamama Noodle Bar, 174
Wag Club, 305
Waiters, tipping, 29
Waldorf Meridien, Palm Court at the, 181
Walking, 30, 132–33
Walking tours, 185
Greenwich, 233
guided, 188–89
Bath, 312
self-guided, 253–67
British Museum to Harrods, 259
designing your own itinerary, 268–82
Green Park to Soho, 256
Piccadilly Circus to Covent Garden, 258–59
South Kensington Museums, Kensington Gardens and Kensington Palace, 266–67
Tate Gallery to the South Bank, 263–65
Tower of London to St. Paul's Cathedral, 261–63
Trafalgar Square to Buckingham Palace, 254, 256
Westminster Abbey to Trafalgar Square, 265
Wallace Collection, *216,* 227–28
Wareham Bears, The, 325
Warner West End, 299
Washroom attendants, tipping, 29
Waterstone's, 247
Weather, 5–6, 57
Weather information, 333
Weather report, 5
Web sites
accommodations, 75
air travel, 38–39
Blue Cross/Blue Shield, 54
Bureau of Consular Affairs, 47
for gays and lesbians, 19
monarchy, 3
performing arts events, 295
theatre, 285
theatre and other performing arts, 55–56
Time Out, 294
tourist information, 3–4
Welcombe Hotel (Stratford-upon-Avon), 323
Wellington, Duke of, 206
Wembley Arena, 298

Wembley Stadium, 298
West End, 119, 122–23
  accommodations, 63, 66–68
  shopping in, 240
  theatres, 284, 287–90
West London, 119
  pubs, 301
Westminster, 123
  accommodations, 66
  restaurants, 159, 165, 172
Westminster Abbey, *193,* 211–12, 264, *264,* 265, *266*
Westminster Passenger Service Association, 229, 231
Westminster/Victoria, accommodations, 93, 101, 102, 105
W & G Foyle, Ltd., 247
Wheelchair accessibility, 17–18
  to sights and attractions, 191, 215
Wheelchair Travel, 18
Wheeler's, 159
Where to Take Children, 126
Whispering Gallery, 206
White Card, 194
Whitehall, 265, *266*
White Hart (Salisbury), 326–27
Wigmore Hall, 297
Wilbraham Hotel, 106
Wilde, Oscar, 212
William III, 199
William the Conqueror, 230
Wilton House, 325
Wimbledon Lawn Tennis Championships, 9
Windsor, House of, 3
Windsor Castle, 230
Wine bars, 138
Winter, 6
Wintons Soda Fountain, 182
Wolsey, Cardinal, 230
Wood, John, the Younger, 314
Woolens, shopping for, 244
World of Options, A, 15
World War II, 215
Worldwide Bed & Breakfast Association, 76
Wren, Sir Christopher, 199, 205–6, 210, 227, 230, 232, 316, 317

Y

Yahoo! Travel, 38
Ye Olde Cheshire Cheese, 174

Z

Zafferano, 174–75
Zia Teresa, 181
Zoo, London, *193,* 200–201